Second Edition

EARTH SCIENCE

An Integrated Perspective

Second Edition
EARTH SCIENCE
An Integrated Perspective

Donald J. Conte
California University of Pennsylvania
Donald J. Thompson
California University of Pennsylvania
Lawrence L. Moses
California University of Pennsylvania

 **McGraw-Hill Primis
Custom Publishing**

New York St. Louis San Francisco Auckland Bogotá
Caracas Lisbon London Madrid Mexico Milan Montreal
New Delhi Paris San Juan Singapore Sydney Tokyo Toronto

McGraw-Hill Higher Education
A Division of The McGraw-Hill Companies

Earth Science: An Integrated Perspective

1 2 3 4 5 6 7 8 9 0 CPB CPB 0 9 8 7 6 5 4 3 2 1 0

ISBN 0-07-251048-X

Editor: Debbie Quigley
Cover Design: Maggie Lytle
Printer/Binder: Central Plains Book Manufacturing

Dedication

Just as we write about
interrelationships in
this holistic text,
we wish to dedicate
this book to those
whose relationships with us
have made our lives whole and
our planet truly
a home.

To Donna, and to
Michael, and Christian Conte and Melanie Conte Chase

To Ardith, and to
Laura, Michael, and Matthew Thompson
and Pamela Thompson Luketich

To Lisa and Leslie Moses and Kathy Lawrence

Contents

PART 4

Geological Composition and Processes   155

Preface

The study of Earth is the study of a home. This book is about the nature of our residence—its origin, composition, and processes. To explain this complex planet, we intend to integrate its many physical interrelationships in an approach called *holistic*, a term we explain in chapter 1.

A HOLISTIC APPROACH

Earth science is traditionally subdivided into astronomy, meteorology, geology, and oceanography, and we have not ignored this sound practice. What is different about our approach is the integration we achieve within the limitation of an easy-to-read, relatively short exposition.

The overall structure of this approach can be envisioned as a spiraling inward—from large, encompassing concepts to the specifics of the four earth science subdisciplines. Because many students are unfamiliar with the excitement of science, we begin with an overview that avoids describing a "scientific method" in sterile terms. Instead, we relate what scientists do to familiar experiences, and we present the scientific method as a diverse approach to the world. Then, we explain the four earth science subdisciplines with specific examples and anecdotes. We believe that many nonscientists can find meaning in the explanation of a real event, such as a hurricane or an earthquake, that affected real people. This text offers a very practical logic behind the scientific method and scientific inquiry because the book's focus is always on the planet as the personal home of its readers.

The intended audience of this book is the entry-level college student whose scientific background is limited and whose interest can be enhanced by a storylike, conversational style. We want our readers to be comfortable as we lead them toward and through the specifics of earth science. Consequently, we define many terms within the context of a subject, but we have included both in the text and in a glossary the strict, formal definitions many professors expect to see.

The holistic integration that we present changes the typical categorization of earth science topics. For example, instead of grouping our explanations of coastal processes with oceanographic topics exclusively (a practice of others), we place our coverage of coastal geomorphology in sequence with our discussions of the geologic surface processes. We also incorporate descriptions of atmospheres on other planets into a discussion of Earth's atmosphere, tying our planet to the Solar System.

We summarize our holistic approach in two diagrams found early in the book. Figures 1.2 and 1.5 exemplify the interrelationships that we strive to convey. Such illustrations and the many cross-references within this book enable readers unfamiliar with earth science to imagine the relationships among the universe, the Solar System, and our planet, and the ties among the diverse earth features and processes. A central thread is energy; thus, we define it early and refer to it often. It is, for example, a key component in our explanation of the surface processes.

After an introductory chapter that lays the intellectual foundation for the holistic study of Earth, we begin the text proper in chapter 2 with astronomy. We explain the origin and fundamental composition of our universe and then move into an explanation of the Solar System in chapter 3. Our intention in the astronomy coverage is to show the whole picture—helping our readers to see the forest before we examine individual trees. It is also our intention to relate the universe directly to our planet.

The treatment of weather and climate, chapters 4 through 6, begins with a familiar experience, as we narrate the passage of a hypothetical storm system. The story of this dynamic weather system unfolds in the context of the televised forecasts familiar to the general public. We then explain the nature of Earth's atmosphere against the background of this storm system, including the processes responsible for weather. The holistic science of climatology is thoroughly covered in chapter 6 with numerous examples, photographs, tables of characteristics, and climagraphs, all of which help to reveal to entry-level students the causes of climatic difference.

We explore the composition of the solid Earth by relating minerals and rocks in chapter 7 to discussions of matter in chapter 2. Our exposition of geology continues in chapter 8 as we turn our readers' attention to the processes that shape Earth's surface. By revealing the nature of earthquakes, we lay the groundwork for the holistic study of Earth systems in chapter 9, the study of plate tectonics. We treat this topic not only for the value of its integrative concepts, but also as a lesson in the scientific method. It is in chapter 9 that we explain the process of multiple working hypotheses, first introduced in chapter 1, by tracing the history of plate-tectonic theory in a storylike fashion. The six surface agents of change—streams, groundwater, glaciers, wind, waves, and currents—are the focus of chapters 10 through 13.

When we turn our readers more specifically toward oceanography in chapter 14, we adopt an apparently traditional approach, but chapter 15 extends the chemistry, geology and dynamic interrelationships of the oceans to the study of marine and near-shore environments in a way unique to this book. This approach enables us to show the complexity of ocean basins, while relating oceans to surface processes, tectonics, and life.

Our book ends with chapter 16, which ties the earth sciences together in the explanation of Earth's resources by integrating climate, tectonics, erosion, and sedimentation.

PEDAGOGICAL FEATURES AND ANCILLARIES

Almost every major point in this book is accompanied by a photograph, a line drawing, or a chart. We have also included two kinds of boxes on topics of interest. One variety of box, titled "Further Consideration," briefly explores interesting topics that are related, but not essential, to the understanding of principal chapter concepts. Often, these deal with new directions and initiatives in the earth sciences. The second type of box, called "Investigating the Environment," has an environmental flavor and shows how Earth's processes affect our lives.

To enhance the learning process, we include at the end of each chapter a list of significant points, a list of essential terms, review questions, and "challenges" to the students to explore some topics in greater depth. An *Instructor's Manual* with a *Test Item File* includes prose summaries of the chapters. Classroom Testing Software, available in Windows and Macintosh formats, facilitates the instructor's evaluation of student progress. Full-color 35 millimeter slides of photographs from the text are also available, as are full-color transparencies of key text diagrams. A *Student Study Guide* with questions on each of the almost 500 illustrations and with practical earth science exercises for each chapter will aid students in assimilating the details of earth science, provide a sound review of essential principles and terms, and give students laboratory-like experiences. The text also contains an extensive glossary and appendixes with matter germane to the study of earth science.

SECOND EDITION IMPROVEMENTS AND ADDITIONS

Use this book in the order of your preference; its individual parts are stand-alone units. Remember, however, that this is a holistic text that emphasizes the interconnectedness of Earth's features and processes. It is a story best read from front to back.

This book is fatter than the first edition. We believe, however, that the weight gained is all muscle. Earth science has progressed by design and by accident since the first edition. Significant Earth events, such as the tragedies in Kobe, Japan,

and Northridge, California, have revealed additional information about the mechanisms of earthquakes. Kobe, sitting on a sedimentary basin in the vicinity of a junction of four plates, suffered an enhancement of seismic energy because its nearby mountains reflected earthquake vibrations back through the city. Northridge showed us the dangers associated with blind thrust faults. By accident, a comet passing Jupiter had its path deflected sufficiently to send it into the atmosphere of the giant planet. When comet Shoemaker-Levy 9 struck Jupiter, the Hubble Space Telescope and the *Galileo* spacecraft observed the event. By a stroke of good fortune, both observing platforms were up and working well for Jupiter's encounter. Hubble's repair also has meant unexpected discoveries, including one that has stirred the controversy about the age of the universe.

To meet the needs of those who focus on geological earth science, we have reorganized and expanded our sections on minerals, rocks, earthquakes, tectonics, and the surface processes. Readers will find a description of the Kobe earthquake, an expanded discussion of terranes, and new chapters on the six surface processes. We have included a section on flooding, with special reference to the 1993 catastrophic floods of the Midwest, a subject that received only brief coverage in the first edition.

Additions to the text include a new chapter division in astronomy. We still begin our text with astronomy because we want readers to spiral in from the largest of concepts. We also believe that a discussion of matter and energy, so important for all the physical processes on our planet, belongs in astronomy. The Hubble Space Telescope has imaged newly forming star systems, colliding galaxies, and planets beyond our own Solar System. Because most earth science professors traditionally cover the sun with stellar theory, we have moved its coverage into its more familiar textbook position. We do this as a concession, however, because we believe it belongs just as logically in a discussion of the atmosphere in an earth science text. We separated our discussion of the planets from that on the universe and the stars. The additional chapter provides readers with an opportunity to view new images of the Venusian topography and the Jovian atmosphere.

We condensed four chapters on meteorology and climatology found in the first edition into three chapters. The second edition also contains a fuller explanation of upper-air winds and on the dangers associated with global warming. Global warming now appears to be a reality, and with it, citizens of temperate climates may find themselves jeopardized by tropical diseases and greater weather extremes, including more potent hurricanes. The numerous hurricanes of 1995 may be only an anomaly, but they occurred during a warmer-than-average year.

Our additional coverage of minerals and rocks should fill the needs of professors in earth science survey courses. Because users of the text have reported that they prefer coverage of earthquakes and tectonics to precede that of surface processes, we have rearranged those chapters. The expansion of topics on the surface processes makes the new chapters a virtual introductory course in geomorphology. Mass wasting and geologic work are the subjects of the first of the new chapters. These tie energy and gravity to the surface processes. Our new chapter on glaciers and wind enhances the climatic information on deserts found in chapter 6.

We have added more information about Earth's landforms, using them to distinguish continental and oceanic structures. The oceanography chapters are essentially the same, as is the chapter on Earth resources. To help the introductory student comprehend geologic time, we have included in appendix I an analogy for geologic time that compares it to running a 1-mile race, and we also have added the epochs to the Tertiary time period.

Acknowledgments & List of Reviewers

ACKNOWLEDGMENTS

From inception to publication, this project had many helpers and benefactors, whose work we acknowledged in the first edition. This second edition has been a complex project that owes much to the special help of one person in particular. Leigh De-Haven, a talented graduate assistant in earth science at California University of Pennsylvania, devoted many hours to researching additional topics, cutting and pasting, and proofreading. We cannot overemphasize the value of her assistance. She was an efficient facilitator without whose help this edition's completion would have been delayed. The editors and staff at Wm. C. Brown Publishers kept the project on track. Without their constant help, suggestions, and constructive criticism, this book could never have been completed. We especially want to acknowledge Lynne Meyers: She was the beacon who guided us through some foggy times. Finally, we wish to thank the many reviewers and users of the first edition.

SECOND EDITION REVIEWERS

W. Patrick Seward, Ph. D., *Oklahoma Panhandle State University*
Mark J. Camp, *University of Toledo*
Stan Celestian, *Glendale Community College*

Michael E. Lewis, *University of North Carolina at Greensboro*
Robert F. Champlin, Ph. D., *Fitchburg State College*
Steve LaDochy, *California State University–Los Angeles*
Paul D. Nelson, *St. Louis Community College at Meramec*
Mark J. Sutherland, *College of DuPage*
Dr. Morris L. Sotonoff, *Chicago State University*
Sabine F. Thomas, *University of Texas–San Antonio*
Jay P. Clymer III, Ph. D., *Marywood College*
James Albanese, *State University of New York–Oneonta*
Mark Finley, *Heartland Community College*
Tracy Jones, *University of North Alabama*

FIRST EDITION REVIEWERS

S. Roger Kirkpatrick, *Marietta College*
Alan L. Kafka, *Boston College*
Judy Ann Lowman, *Chaffey College*
John F. Looney, Jr., *University of Massachusetts-Boston*
John P. Szabo, *University of Akron*
Paul Nelson, *St. Louis Community College–Meramec*
Stephen Wareham, *Fullerton College*
Steve Leavitt, *Tree-Ring Lab, University of Arizona*

Second Edition

EARTH SCIENCE

An Integrated Perspective

PART **1** Introduction to a *Holistic* Science

*E*arth science is an encompassing discipline that incorporates astronomy, meteorology, geology, and oceanography into a holistic explanation of our planet. By clarifying the nature of Earth, this multidisciplinary approach provides us with information necessary for our well-being. We are earthbound beings, and this planet is our only home. After all, even astronauts must return from their space voyages. Learning about our home is a sensible practice.

At the *End* of *Part* 1, *You Will Be Able* to:

1. Illustrate the holistic philosophy of earth science.
2. Explain the nature of the scientific method and scientific modeling.
3. Distinguish between personal experience and scientific information.
4. Recognize variations of the scientific method.
5. Classify the disciplines of earth science.
6. Cite evidence for the practicality of earth science studies.

Earth Prayer

Attributed by many to Chief Seattle

This Earth we know.
The Earth does not belong to us;
we belong to the Earth.
This we know.
All things are connected
like the blood which unites one family.
All things are connected.

Chapter 1

Study Earth Science for Obvious Reasons

Mt. Rainier, Washington.
A volcanic peak in the Cascade Range.

INTRODUCTION

We do not have much of a choice when it comes to livable worlds: *Earth is all we have.* We can dream of future explorations and colonies on other planets, but the truth is that other worlds, even in our own Solar System, are either too far from Earth or too inhospitable for prolonged visits. So, our dependence upon this world is undeniably obvious, and understanding its composition, features, and processes makes good sense. Think of earth science as a way of learning about your home.

Pictures of Earth reveal a special world, one with vast liquid oceans surrounding landmasses and a sphere of life-supporting gases and abundant water clouds (fig. 1.1). Supplied by energy from the sun and by gravity, the waters and gases of this predominantly blue world are in constant motion, shaping and changing Earth's surfaces. Occasionally, catastrophic events caused by either earthquakes or volcanic eruptions hint that below the planet's surfaces other processes also generate change. Earth science is an ongoing attempt to understand not only the agents of planetary change but also the resultant features, such as mountains, plains, lakes, ocean basins, river systems, glaciers, and weather patterns.

MODELS, THEORIES, AND HYPOTHESES

Generally, earth scientists are in the business of creating **models,** or conceptual representations, of the real world. They constantly define our planet's processes, cycles, patterns, irregularities, composition, and structure to provide us with understandable representations. Ultimately, the work of earth scientists may lead to a holistic model of all that makes up our world. The encompassing nature of such a model would give a perspective from which humans could view all interrelationships among the world's component parts and functions. By tying together the origins, compositions, forms, and processes of our planet's features, earth scientists work to establish a unified theory of Earth, one that gives meaning to a complex planet and its universe.

In science, a **theory** is a model based on fact, *not* on idle speculation. To form a unified theory of Earth, scientists must take into account natural forces, such as gravity, which govern the formation of Earth's features and the changes these features undergo. They must also rely on other disciplines, such as mathematics, chemistry, and physics. The variety and complexity of our planet's features and processes make modeling difficult.

Figure 1.1 Our home as viewed from space.

Until their understanding of various natural processes and features is framed in a theory, earth scientists rely on a **hypothesis**, which is an explanation or speculation based on current knowledge. Hypotheses provide scientists with an early conceptual framework on which to organize their investigations. If scientists observe a change in weather after a volcanic eruption, for example, they may hypothesize that the volcanic activity is responsible for that change. Then they focus on demonstrating the truth of their speculation, possibly by making measurements of the amount of sunlight-blocking volcanic ash thrown into the atmosphere (fig. 1.2). If their hypothesis is correct, they can relate a cause (volcanic ash in the atmosphere) to an effect (weather change) and conceptualize a model that is applicable whenever and wherever they detect similar circumstances.

As figure 1.2 shows, just one earth feature may represent many interrelationships. Great volcanoes like Mount Saint Helens in southern Washington or Mount Pinatubo in the Philippines are complexes of ash, rock, ice, and water that cast their influence over wide areas. Active volcanoes can affect the weather, cause devastating floods and mudflows, and blanket a region in ash. In turn, volcanoes result from unseen processes acting beneath the planet's surface. The lesson is that none of our planet's features or processes exists in a vacuum. Each either influences or is influenced by other features and processes. Holistic models, therefore, are attempts at clarifying the many interrelationships among Earth's processes, composition, structure, and forces.

THE IMPORTANCE OF OBJECTIVITY IN SCIENCE

Each of us learns about the world through personal experiences, but the knowledge we attain is limited by our emotions, concentration, and previous experience. We know our surroundings through sense perceptions: We see, hear, feel, taste, and smell the world around us, and we rely on these perceptions to furnish us with information about our environment. What we perceive through our senses, however, can be misleading. For example, if you have suffered from a fever, you know that the temperature you sense with that illness is different from that sensed by a healthy person. Similarly, a dry day may not seem as "hot" as a day of equal temperature but with higher humidity. The difference lies not in the actual heat of the air but in our perceptions. Because we rely on a mechanism such as perspiring to regulate body temperature during excercise and hot weather, our personal comfort—and, thus, our sense of temperature—depends on the capacity of the air around us to absorb moisture through evaporation, which is a cooling process (discussed in chapter 5).

Because of human limitations, earth scientists cannot rely merely on the five senses to determine the physical nature of the world—

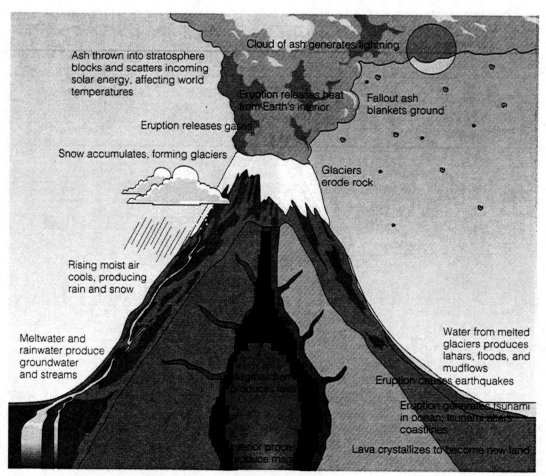

Figure 1.2 A volcano is a local complex of interrelated features and processes that may have a worldwide impact.

that is, to explain Earth's composition, processes, and features. They know that much of our planet is invisible to us, or beyond our reach, and is odorless, colorless, and tasteless. They also realize that misinterpreting the information garnered by the senses is a common way of missing the truth. Although the senses do not lie to us personally, we often err when we assume that what we sense is reality. To avoid the limitations of personal involvement in learning about Earth, scientists work to eliminate, or at least reduce, subjectivity in their investigations. Gathering information for science, therefore, is different from personal learning.

As they eliminate subjectivity, earth scientists try to recognize patterns in Earth's composition, processes, and features. Such patterns, revealed by the gathering of specimens and the use of instruments that record data without human variations, help scientists to create the models by which we understand Earth objectively.

The Traditional Scientific Method

Because objectivity is essential for a scientific explanation of natural processes and features, scientists pursue knowledge through a carefully arranged plan of investigation. Generally, before they present their conclusions to other scientists, they follow a traditional procedure known as the **scientific method.** The scientific method consists of a series of logical steps that attempt to eliminate subjectivity:

1. Through an accidental or purposeful observation, a scientist recognizes that there is a gap in our knowledge. This recognition leads to a statement of a defined problem.
2. The scientist researches how others may have explained or solved the problem or related problems.
3. After reviewing the possible explanations or solutions that stem from all the available information, the scientist forms a hypothesis.
4. The scientist then attempts to verify the hypothesis through some form of experimentation. In many instances, an experiment is an exercise to acquire additional information by subjecting a control group and an experimental group to a series of tests.
5. With the experimental results in hand, the scientist interprets the data and constructs a conceptual model.
6. The same scientist or other scientists attempt to validate the model through repeatable tests.
7. The scientist then explains the model in a publication read by the scientific community.

Variations of the Scientific Method

Because scientific knowledge is derived from a variety of intellectual pursuits, the traditional scientific method may not always strictly apply to an investigation of natural processes and features. Although many scientific investigations require some form of experimentation, scientists often do not perform experiments to discover a truth. In fact, they may employ methods that do not require any specimens or apparatus, but that instead rely solely upon observations of naturally occurring events or objects. Occasionally, they may even stumble upon something totally unexpected.

Science is an attempt to model diverse natural phenomena, and a long history of incidents reveals the varied character of scientific approaches. For example, after having visited some coral atolls of the Pacific Ocean in the nineteenth century, Charles Darwin reasoned that these ringlike islands formed as coral reefs on volcanic islands that sank beneath the sea's surface. His explanation remained a reasonable "guess" until twentieth-century explorations confirmed his speculation. Early in this century, Albert Einstein laid the foundation for determining the relationship between matter and energy without personally running experiments on atomic fission or fusion, although he did rely on some data from experiments that he and others had performed. Confirmation of his famous formula $E = mc^2$ can be found in the nuclear power plants that today supply many people with electrical energy. In some respect, the "sciences" of Einstein and Darwin were similar. Each recognized that a gap in our knowledge left us unable to explain something about our world. In addition, both men suggested a hypothesis that focused the investigations of other scientists.

One important scientific approach is the gathering of information on processes and features. Because many features in our world may initially appear to be too complex for investigation, scientists who organize their observations and information into a coherent framework of ideas called a **classification** provide an important scientific service. Classification lays the groundwork for further science by revealing processes and features that share common elements. For example, we all know that clouds seem to occur in a variety of shapes and sizes. After years of observation, weather scientists have classified clouds by their shapes, altitude, and associated weather and thus have made forecasting more reliable.

The Rate of Scientific Discovery

In many instances, scientists recognize a problem and then attempt to find a solution by carefully arranging, observing, and interpreting a repeatable process. Under such circumstances, scientific discovery can be slow because data collection and interpretation may be difficult or filled with trial and error. An example lies in the attempts to study Earth's interior, where overlying rocky layers prevent direct observation. Use of sensitive instruments that "see" into the planet by recording Earth's vibrations has led to the accumulation of vast amounts of data over the past several decades. Scientists, however, have interpreted this data in several ways. Adam Dziewonski and Wei-Jia Su of Harvard University believe that earthquake vibrations indicate that Earth's predominantly iron core acts like a single crystal to focus or channel energy in the same way a lens orients light. Using a type of diamond press that exerts tremendous pressure on a small sample of iron, Swedish scientists S. Saxena, G. Shen, and P. Lazor were able to make a new type of iron crystal that might be similar to the crystal that Dziewonski and Su think they discovered. Other scientists, however, believe that further investigation is necessary to determine the true nature of Earth's core. An indisputable interpretation still is probably years away, but the picture of Earth's deep interior is becoming clearer.

Sometimes, rather than a slow revelation of the truth, scientific knowledge comes quickly and unexpectedly, as when someone discovers something previously unknown. Such a find occurred on February 17, 1977, when oceanographers, including Tjeerd van Andel, explored a portion of the ocean floor in a deep-diving submersible called *Alvin* to examine a flow of hot water in a volcanically active area. Van Andel saw the previously unknown "vent communities" of clams, mussels, white crabs, and long tube worms (see fig. 15.30).

Van Andel's surprising discovery helps us to define how scientists obtain information without the stereotype of a single scientific method. His discovery stemmed from good reasoning and persistence in cooperation with other scientists. Three years before van Andel's deep dive to the vent community, Richard von Herzen and David Williams had detected some warm water on the ocean floor. Von Herzen and van Andel then hypothesized that hot springs should be associated with volcanic activity on the ocean floor, just as they are on Earth's land surfaces. Their attempt to demonstrate the validity of their hypothesis led to their discovery of the vent communities and presented them with a problem: What food supply supported the abundant life of the vent communities on the dark ocean floor?

At the ocean's surface—indeed, at the land's surface—the primary energy source for life is the sun, whose rays supply energy to plants that convert carbon dioxide and water to food through a process known as **photosynthesis.** Since sunlight does not reach the deep ocean floor, however, scientists had to hypothesize about the energy source for food production there. Van Andel and others almost immediately guessed that vent communities survive because of **chemosynthesis,** the conversion of chemicals into food. Later, by adopting a scientific approach that employed repeatable experimentation, John Baross and Holger Jannasch verified the presence of chemosynthetic organisms that serve as the basis of the vent community food chain. Bacteria living in the hot-water springs produce food from water and carbon dioxide, just as plants in sunlight do. Whereas sunlight provides energy for this food production at Earth's surface, sulfur-rich chemicals dissolved from ocean rocks provide the energy by combining with oxygen atoms in the volcanic vents on the deep ocean floor.

When van Andel dove to the sea bottom in the *Alvin,* he was really riding in a package of sophisticated instruments. In the twentieth century, technological advancement has increased our ability to observe features and processes that were once hidden. We send other sophisticated instrument packages into deep space, into our atmosphere, and even into the craters of volcanoes. These instruments, coupled with fast microprocessors, have given us even more refined data on natural phenomena. Because of technology, the rate of scientific discovery is increasing rapidly.

Multiple Working Hypotheses and Scientific Verification

The preceding material about finding evidence for crystalline iron in Earth's core or for chemosynthetically supported life is instructive about the earth sciences. Because Earth is a complex of interrelated objects and events, an analysis from a single perspective may not fully explain a feature or a process. In addition, because many features and processes are hidden from direct observation, earth scientists take different paths to arrive at similar conclusions. These "paths" are hypotheses that may merge as scientists follow lines of evidence.

A scientific approach that involves two or more types of investigation that may produce a rational explanation of a natural process or feature is known as the method of **multiple working**

hypotheses. Because most natural phenomena are complex, this method enables scientists to pursue all intellectual, experimental, and observational avenues that may lead to an explanation of the process or feature under investigation.

A good example of this method lies in the work by those scientists who now have evidence that Earth's iron core may be a single crystal of a new type of iron. For most of this century, scientists have known from studies of Earth's vibrations that Earth's innermost core is composed predominantly of iron. However, because the core is hidden from us by the surrounding solid planet, most descriptions or explanations of the core have been questionable. As discussed previously, the recent work of two groups of scientists now appears to support a new description. One group hypothesized about the way vibrational energy would move through the planet, and the other group experimented with pressures similar to those suspected in Earth's deep interior. Both arrived at an explanation involving crystalline iron. Apparently, Earth's inner core acts like a large crystal, and the manner in which a diamond crystal can concentrate light is an analogy for how the core focuses vibrations.

Although the history of science holds many examples of multiple working hypotheses, none appears to be more illustrative of the method than those that led to the theory of **plate tectonics,** probably the most holistic theory in the earth sciences. The subject of chapter 9, plate tectonics explains how mountains form, how continents and ocean floors move, how the outermost layer of Earth is related to interior layers, why most earthquakes and volcanic eruptions occur, and why ore deposits are localized in certain areas. The theory evolved from scientific investigations of fossils, minerals, rocks, mountains, oceans, earthquakes, volcanic eruptions, and magnetism.

With respect to scientific investigations, the method of multiple working hypotheses has a distinct advantage: It allows for the development of new understandings and keeps science from becoming a list of dogmatic statements and principles. Whenever scientists uncover new evidence, the evidence may negate some hypotheses, strengthen others, or suggest new hypotheses. The scientific method of multiple working hypotheses is, therefore, a mechanism for testing and retesting concepts and for refining knowledge.

Because the conclusions of true science are testable, scientists continuously subject their findings and hypotheses to verification. The kinds of tests, however, vary greatly. One kind of "test" for science lies in the repeatability of a process. An example of this lies in the formation of a horseshoe-shaped lake called an oxbow (see chapter 11). Oxbows develop in broad, flat areas where a river's channel meanders, or bends, laterally back and forth, sometimes isolating and abandoning part of the meander as the river changes course. Oxbows can be duplicated in a laboratory setting by running a channelized stream of water through sands and muds in a rectangular box called a stream table. Another kind of verification comes from repeated observations in natural settings, where, for example, oxbows have formed. Repeating an observation is also a way to advance our knowledge of natural conditions. Van Andel is not the only one to have found a vent community; others who read of his discovery have repeated the find elsewhere, including at sites with sulfur compounds not associated with volcanic activity.

Uniformitarianism and Actualism

Scientists do make some assumptions before they begin hypothesizing. Chief among these is that processes and features observed today are probably not different in kind from those of the past. If streams flow downhill because of gravity and if they erode their banks, then one can assume that the process of stream erosion is repeatable. It is not unreasonable to assume that past streams also flowed downhill and eroded their banks. This repetitiveness of a process or the similar construction of natural features like stream valleys is an expression of the principle of **uniformitarianism.** The concept of uniformitarianism has been essential to the development of the earth sciences because it relates what we observe today to a previous natural state: The present unlocks the door to the past and opens the window to the future.

Because the rates of natural processes fluctuate, scientists often refine their uniformitarian perspective with the concept of **actualism.** This concept allows scientists to account for differences in location, intensity, or frequency of natural processes. These differences, however, do not alter natural processes. Californians suffered from terrible flooding in January and March of 1995, and they suffered from deadly flooding in 1992 (fig. 4.1). People in the Midwest suffered from flooding in the summer of 1993. Stream flooding occurs in varying locations, intensities, and frequencies, but the process is fundamentally the same: A volume of water greater than can be accommodated by a stream channel flows onto surrounding areas.

SCIENTIFIC DATA GATHERING AND TECHNOLOGY

Because our senses have limited ranges and because we often misinterpret exterior reality by misreading our sensory data, scientists use instruments to observe natural phenomena. Specifically designed for registering what we cannot perceive (or sense precisely) through our five senses, instruments provide scientists with information both in and out of a laboratory setting. In some instances, scientists use instruments to enhance local observations; in others, they send packages of instruments to remote destinations to gather information and samples. These remote sensing devices extend our human senses, reliably observing an event, object, or environment in situations where danger or expense often prohibits direct human observation.

Detecting the Invisible

One of the most obvious examples of studying the world invisible to the human eye is research into the nonvisible portions of the **electromagnetic spectrum.** The spectrum is a range of energy forms known as **radiation. Electromagnetic radiation** is energy in wave form that originates from every vibrating body in the universe (which is *every* body in the universe) and that travels across the near vacuum of space at the speed of light. Included within this general category are the forms of radiation familiar to many of us, at least in name: gamma rays, X rays, ultraviolet rays, light, infrared rays, microwaves, and radio waves. All of these forms are alike, except for their wavelengths, which vary from extremely short lengths for gamma and X rays to very long lengths for radio waves

Figure 1.3 The electromagnetic spectrum. (Source: Alyn C. and Alison B. Duxbury, *An Introduction to the World's Oceans,* 4th ed. Copyright © 1994 Times Mirror Higher Education Group, Inc., Dubuque, Iowa.)

(fig. 1.3). Hotter bodies produce more short wavelengths than cooler bodies. Thus, the sun produces much more ultraviolet and visible light radiation than the much cooler Earth.

Since the mid-1970s, scientists have become aware that solar **ultraviolet (UV) radiation,** which causes sunburn and skin cancer, has intensified in various high-latitude regions, particularly over Antarctica and latitudes above 50°N. Further research into this invisible, but dangerous, radiation has revealed a link between its intensification and a "hole," or a decrease in abundance of **ozone** (O_3), a gas found at high altitudes in our atmosphere (fig. 1.4). Although ozone molecules form naturally in the stratosphere, they are also synthesized by humans at Earth's surface, primarily through the burning of fossil fuels and through reactions with nitrogen compounds. This surface ozone is largely responsible for the photochemically produced smog that often shrouds the Los Angeles area. At Earth's surface, this gas is a pollutant and a health hazard. Twenty-five kilometers (15.5 mi) above the surface, however, ozone acts like a protective filter. In a photochemical reaction with the incoming solar radiation, ozone separates into O and O_2, absorbing the ultraviolet end of the spectrum in the process and reducing the amount of UV radiation (wavelengths between 0.2 and 0.3 μm) that reaches Earth's surface.

The discovery of the ozone "hole" at altitudes between 14 and 25 kilometers (9 and 15.5 mi) required the combined work of chemists, meteorologists, aerospace engineers, climatologists, and physicists. This is typical of how earth scientists work to learn about Earth objectively and establish models that explain some of Earth's complex interrelationships, including those influenced by human activities. Now, many scientists have adopted a multidisciplinary approach to study the ozone hole. Such an approach may lead to a model that can adequately explain the hole as a conse-

Figure 1.4   Changing (decreasing) ozone levels over the south polar region from October 1979 to October 1994.

quence of both natural and human processes (see box 4.2, "Ozone-Depleting Compounds and Stratospheric Ice").

Observational Refinement and Holistic Modeling

In a time of rapidly changing technologies, scientists depend upon ever more sophisticated instruments to refine their observations. In scientific work, the level of refinement becomes an important consideration before conceptualizing a model. An observation of Earth from a spacecraft orbiting at an altitude of 100 kilometers (62 mi) may reveal a snow- and ice-capped volcanic mountain. Observations from an airplane at 10 kilometers (6.2 mi) would reveal valleys and individual ice streams (called valley glaciers). A mountain climber, however, would see individual blocks of ice and rock, small snow-bridges made by the wind, and loose rock debris. The level of refinement can be further enhanced through instruments. A magnifying glass would provide the climber with a closeup view of tiny components of the rocks, and a microscope would enable the climber to see small mineral crystals. With a

doctor's stethoscope, the climber might be able to listen to the mountain or its glacial ice groan under the strain, and with even more sensitive instruments that "feel" small vibrations, the climber might possibly detect movements of liquid rock in the volcanic mountain's deep interior.

At each of these levels of observation, a scientist could conceptualize a model of the mountain, but each model would encompass different information. The view from space, for example, reveals the volcanic mountain in a regional setting of landforms, whereas the view through a microscope shows the compositional nature of a region's rocks. The resulting models would be either broad or narrow, respectively, and their scientific usefulness would vary, or would combine to make a comprehensive, holistic model. A **holistic approach** to natural phenomena uses observational data in varying levels of refinement to relate objects, processes, events, and environments in a conceptual scheme that explains how our world works, why it has particular types of component parts, and why those parts have a particular distribution.

Earth Science and Natural Law

Processes that occur without human cause are called "natural," and for particular circumstances, these natural processes never vary, making them universal processes. An expression (or statement) of this universality is known as a **natural law.** Scientists have identified a number of natural laws that concisely state a framework for understanding Earth and its place in the universe. Thus, we know from a Law of Universal Gravitation that each particle of matter in the universe attracts other particles of matter. This law helps us to understand why the moon, for example, orbits our planet, and why Earth orbits the sun. On Earth's surface, the same law accounts for processes that are apparently unrelated: landslides, waterfalls, and tides.

Earth scientists must explain natural phenomena first in terms of the applicable natural laws. Weather scientists rely on the General Gas Law, which explains how temperature, pressure, and gas volume are interrelated. The General Gas Law enables scientists to state how a gas behaves in certain circumstances and helps them, for example, to forecast the weather. Geologists rely on the Law of Superposition to explain that younger sedimentary rocks always lie on the top of older undisturbed rock layers. Sometimes, an earth scientist's primary goal is to discover which natural law is applicable to a natural phenomenon.

This reliance on natural laws makes earth science holistic. Earth scientists commonly use physics, chemistry, and biology to explain Earth's processes and features in four contexts: the universe, the atmosphere, the solid Earth, and the oceans.

CLASSIFICATION OF THE EARTH SCIENCES

As earth scientists have acquired knowledge about our home, they have established four inclusive classes of information to explain Earth as a planet: astronomy, meteorology, geology, and oceanography. A unified theory relies on seeing the interrelationships among these four disciplines. Thus, in their study of our planet, earth scientists borrow information from each of the four (fig. 1.5).

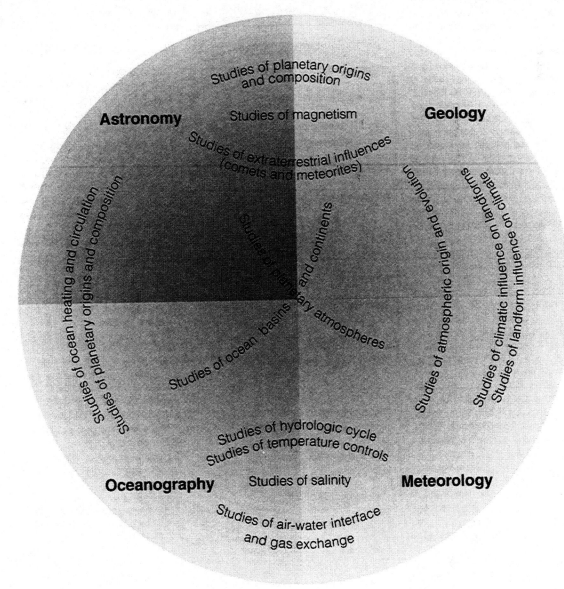

Figure 1.5 Earth scientists interrelate the four disciplines for a holistic modeling of our planet.

Box 1.1

Investigating the Environment

EARTH SCIENCE ON THE INTERNET

The Internet is a computer network system that evolved from ARPANET, which stands for *Advanced Research Projects Agency Network*. Originally a U.S. government communications system that protected Department of Defense information in the event of a nuclear attack, ARPANET deployed a connection called "packet switching" among four universities. Eventually, this network expanded to include other sites, such as military bases. During the 1960s, ARPANET served as a model for similar computer networks that have since joined to become the Internet. This large conglomeration of networks now includes universities, governmental departments and agencies, corporations and companies, and private and special interest groups. Hundreds of millions of computer users can now access more than 3 million computers that serve as sources or "hosts" of information. The network host computers provide almost unrestricted freedom in acquiring information from any Internet "address."

Internet addresses are filed with the Network Information Center (NIC) at "host-master@nic.ddn.mil." You can obtain access to different kinds of addresses (Internet protocol [IP] addresses) that end in a designation called a "domain." The domain for educational institutions, for example is "edu." The governmental domain is followed by "gov," as in "nasa.gov," or "mil.gov" (for military addresses). The designation "org" is used by private organizations. Once you get into the address, you may want to download information. To do this, you use a File Transfer Protocol (FTP). The address from which you download information or software is the FTP site.

To find information on the Internet, you can use published directories and "yellow pages," or you can forge your own paths, using a system like Gopher. Named after the University of Minnesota's Golden Gophers, Gopher is a "server" that has lists of topics that can be retrieved through a series of "double clicks" on a computer mouse. Some of these lists, or menus, open other lists

that lead to more specific files. Other systems that are similar to Gopher in that they allow you to scan through the topics available on Internet include Veronica and WAIS (Wide Area Information Service).

The Internet is an excellent source of information on the earth sciences. It can provide up-to-date information on weather, earthquakes, and research. Most of the addresses allow you free access to information that will not be readily available in print media. Table 1.A lists a selection of addresses and the information that can be obtained at each address.

Apply Your Knowledge

1. What current seismic activity has been listed by the U.S. Geological Survey?
2. What data sets are available from the National Oceanic and Atmospheric Administration?

TABLE 1.A	Selected Internet Addresses
Internet Address	**Type of Information**
ashpool.micro.umn.edu/weather	Weather forecasts, earthquake and storm information for the 50 states and Canada
aurelie.soest.hawaii.edu	Sea-surface temperature data (near-real-time)
climst@hstvma.bitnet	Climatology information and news
gopher info.er.usgs.gov	U.S. Geological Survey; geology, hydrology, cartography, and geographic information
gopher info.umd.edu/educational resources	Documents from the United Nations Conference on the Environment
gopher nywork1.undp.org	Text of United Nations press releases, Conference on Environment and Development reports
gopher somalia.earth.nwu.edu/seismology	U.S. Geological Survey weekly seismicity report for earthquake activity around the world
gopher stis.nsf.gov/otheru/s/government	Over a dozen U.S. government gopher systems
gopher wx.atmos.uiuc.edu	University of Illinois weather machine, current conditions, forecasts, severe storms, satellite images for 50 states, Canada, Mexico, and the Caribbean
gopher.stolaf.edu/internet resources	Frequently updated worldwide earthquake information, mission summaries, questions answered, online catalog of Environmental Protection Agency libraries
scilibx.ucsc.edu	U.S. Geological Survey information
telnet epaibm.rtpnc.epa.gov/public/ols	Environmental Protection Agency online library system
telnet esdim1.nodc.noaa.gov	National Oceanic and Atmospheric Administration, earth and space science data sets
telnet nssdca.gsfc.nasa.gov	National Aeronautics and Space Administration database, catalog of space science data from worldwide research centers
telnet spacelink.msfc.nasa.gov	National Aeronautics and Space Administration news releases, shuttle status reports with worldwide earth science data

In the study of the atmosphere, for example, earth scientists may draw on information about mountains and plains, ocean currents, and even solar events, such as increases in the number of sunspots (see box 1.1).

This text treats these interrelationships as the foundation of earth studies, beginning with astronomy and the origins of the universe and Solar System. Because Earth is just one of countless bodies in the universe, a definition of its position and nature in time and space is important. The other three disciplines—meteorology, geology, and oceanography—follow in a sequence that makes necessary and frequent references to the preceding information. In this text, for example, discussion of the composition of Earth's atmosphere appears in the context of planetary atmospheres; and changes along coastal zones, ordinarily covered in oceanography sections in the traditional approach, are discussed here in the context of other surface processes.

Astronomy

Earth scientists follow a strong tradition of incorporating observations of bodies other than Earth in their studies of our planet. This is the study of **astronomy.** Earth does not exist in a void. It is part of a large Solar System that includes the sun, Earth's moon, and other planets. In addition, the Solar System is part of an even larger system of suns called the Milky Way Galaxy, and it, in turn, belongs to a cluster of sun systems. The connection between Earth and these systems is unavoidable. Electromagnetic radiation from many sources, as well as uncountable and unseen small particles, continuously bombard our planet (see box 3.2, "Will an Asteroid Hit You on the Head?"). Whenever we see the flash of a meteor, we know that collisions with comets and rocky bodies that cross Earth's orbit are possible. The Barringer Crater near Winslow, Arizona, is a good example of the devastating nature of such collisions (fig. 1.6). During the 1980s, the possibility of such impacts led some scientists to speculate that a very large impact may have dealt the last species of dinosaurs a death blow about 65 million years ago and that periodic collisions may have influenced the evolution of life.

As large as our planet may seem to us when we traverse its continents and oceans, Earth is just a tiny part of the universe. This size relationship becomes apparent whenever we consider the distances to other bodies in the universe. For instance, after more than two decades of travel at 46,600 kilometers (28,900 mi) per hour, the *Pioneer 10* spacecraft is just a little more than 8 billion

Figure 1.6 Barringer Crater, also known as Meteor Crater, in central Arizona, photographed from an altitude at 1,350 meters (4,500 ft). The circular crater is approximately 1,220 meters (4,000 ft) in diameter and 180 meters (600 ft) deep. It is the impact site of a meteorite with a diameter estimated at less than the length of a football field.

Box 1.2

Investigating the Environment

RADIATIVE FORCING OF EARTH'S ATMOSPHERE

Scientists now know that a number of gases act like greenhouse glass, holding heat in an atmosphere the way glass in a greenhouse holds heat within a building. This process has been commonly called the greenhouse effect, but it is also known as *radiative forcing*. The latter term derives from the role of certain radiatively active gases. Although the greenhouse gases are transparent to incoming sunlight (shortwave radiation), they absorb outgoing longwave radiation (heat), forcing an additional heating of the atmosphere that would not occur in their absence. In fact, without the effect of these naturally emplaced gases, Earth's surface temperature would be 15.5° C (28° F) colder than its current average temperature.

Water vapor is both the most abundant and the most efficient of the naturally occurring greenhouse gases. Evaporation from many water sources produces a constant supply of the odorless, colorless water vapor in our atmosphere. The atmosphere gets its water vapor from oceans, lakes, rivers, volcanic eruptions, geysers, soils, and plants. Other greenhouse gases also occur naturally, but human industrial and technological activities have increased these gases and added unnatural gases to our envelope of air.

Carbon dioxide (CO_2) is chief among the naturally occurring greenhouse gases that have been increased in Earth's atmosphere as a result of human activities. Since the preindustrial era (1750–1800), the amount of carbon dioxide in our atmosphere has risen 25%. During the past two centuries, the amount of carbon in our atmosphere has increased by 160 billion tons through the addition of carbon dioxide and other carbon-containing gases. When scientists exclude the effects of water vapor, they find that carbon dioxide now accounts for 66% of the radiative forcing by gases in our atmosphere (table 1.B). The sources of carbon dioxide include the burning of fossil fuels, cement production, and deforestation.

Other greenhouse gases that have increased since the rise of industrialization are methane (CH_4), nitrous oxide (N_2O), and chlorofluorocarbons (CFCs). The concentration of methane has almost doubled during the past two centuries, and nitrous oxide has increased by 8%. Methane, the major component of natural gas, is produced by anaerobic decomposition in biological processes, by rice cultivation, by intestinal fermentation in animals, and by the decomposition of animal and municipal solid wastes. Methane is also released in coal mining.

Whenever deforestation strips the land of its plant cover, soils release additional nitrous oxide. Nitrate and ammonium fertilizers and the leaching of nitrogen fertilizers from soils into groundwater also increase this greenhouse gas.

CFCs, manufactured solely by humans, are currently increasing in the atmosphere at the rate of 4% per year. We use these gases as refrigerants, aerosols, foam-blowing agents, and solvents. The primary CFCs in use are compounds that contain chlorine but no hydrogen atoms. Called "fully halogenated CFCs" for their lack of hydrogen, two of these gases are more important than the other CFCs in radiative forcing. CFC–11 (CCl_3F) and CFC–12 (CCl_2F_2) were both used extensively as aerosol propellants until the United States banned their use by 1980, but both gases will remain in the atmosphere for many years (table 1.B). Currently, companies are searching for CFC substitutes because of the 1987 Montreal Protocol, an international agreement that limits CFC use. In the United States, the 1990 Clean Air Act amendments prohibit CFC production and use by the year 2000.

Nitrogen oxides, referred to as NO_x, include the two gases NO and NO_2, which are formed in lightning, by natural fires, in fossil-fuel combustion, and in the stratosphere from nitrous oxide. NO_x contributes to the greenhouse effect by increasing the formation of ozone, an effective greenhouse gas in the upper troposphere and lower stratosphere.

In addition, a gas such as carbon monoxide (CO), though not directly a greenhouse gas, indirectly affects the amount of methane and ozone in the atmosphere. By reacting with the hydroxyl radical (OH), carbon monoxide limits natural reactions between OH and both methane and ozone that would remove those two gases from the atmosphere.

The U.S. Environmental Protection Agency has adopted a unit of measure that expresses the quantities of gases in "carbon dioxide equivalents."

This convenient system enables scientists to quantify the contribution of the various greenhouse gases to radiative forcing. For example, on an equivalent scale, methane is 11 times more effective at radiative forcing than an equal quantity of carbon dioxide. Thus, even though there

TABLE 1.B	**Global Contributions to Radiative Forcing by Greenhouse Gases Other Than Water Vapor and Atmospheric Residence Times**	
Greenhouse Gas	**Percent of Radiative Forcing**	**Atmospheric Residence Time (Years)**
Carbon dioxide (CO_2)	66	120
Methane (CH_4)	18	10.5
CFCs	11	55(CFC–11); 116(CFC–12)
Nitrous oxide (N_2O)	5	132

Source: U.S. Environmental Protection Agency, *States Workbook*, November 1992.

is less CH_4 in the atmosphere than CO_2, the former has a disproportionate influence on global warming.

In April 1995, the world community met in Berlin to address for a third time (the subject was addressed at the meeting in Montreal in 1987 and at the Earth Summit in Rio de Janeiro in 1992) the issue of global warming and the reduction of greenhouse gas emissions. Some countries concede that reducing emissions is not currently economically feasible. China, for example, depends on the burning of coal for electricity, and it has no comprehensive plan to reduce that dependence or to reduce emissions. As the most populated country, China will increase, rather than decrease, its use of coal for energy. The United States also depends on the burning of large quantities of coal to produce electricity. About 1 billion tons of coal are mined annually in the United States, and most of it is burned in power plants. To understand the magnitude of this in terms of global warming, apply the ratio 44:12, which is the ratio of carbon to carbon dioxide. Carbon–12, the common type of carbon, combines with two atoms of oxygen–16 (16+16+12=44), making the weight of CO_2 produced by the burning of a ton of coal greater than the weight of the coal burned (for more on the "weight" of atoms, see chapter 2).

Scientists working on the problem of global warming have attempted to model the planet's atmosphere and its ability to cycle greenhouse gases through different Earth systems. For example, cold ocean surface waters can absorb CO_2 as a dissolved gas, whereas warm ocean surface waters release that gas to the atmosphere. Whenever an Earth process or feature absorbs a greenhouse gas, it is said to "sequester the gas." Sequestration is an important consideration for those who attempt to model the atmosphere's temperature fluctuations. The typical models now predict that a doubling of CO_2 in the atmosphere that may occur by the middle of the next century will increase global temperatues by 1.5 to 4.5° C (3 to 8° F). The temperature rise will depend on many interrelated processes and features, including the type and distribution of vegetation. One vegetation-based model that foreshadows changes in world climate is known as DOLY (but stands for Dynamic

Global Phytogeography Model), developed under the direction of Ian Woodward, a botanist at the University of Sheffield. The DOLY model ranks vegetation on its potential to absorb CO_2.

The complexity of interacting Earth processes and features (see fig. 1.2 for an example) makes the current generation of computer models appear to be simplifications. Increased CO_2 may on first consideration seem to increase plant growth and, therefore, CO_2 sequestration. But many plants close up their stomates when CO_2 levels increase; they do this to conserve water that would evaporate (transpire) through the leaves, leading to drying. The process increases the heat in plants. Thus, if plant growth increases in response to increasing CO_2, would the eventual heat generated in these plants add to the global warming potential? This question and others posed by those who doubt that human activities influence global temperature changes make a world consensus difficult to achieve and postpone any action on reducing emissions.

Taking time to decide, however, may compound the problem, since substantial time is required to remove the artificial greenhouse gases from the atmosphere. The residence time for some of these gases exceeds a century, suggesting long-term effects. Even if we were to stop emissions of carbon dioxides, for example, the gas already released to our atmosphere will affect radiative forcing for more than a century (table 1.B).

Will global warming jeopardize life or change its distribution on the planet? Just as palm trees cannot grow in Antarctica, and polar bears do not live in tropical rain forests, certain parasites and diseases appear to have distributions on the planet. Tropical diseases, one of the dangers of living in hot, humid climates, may spread to higher, formerly cooler latitudes. Increased atmospheric heat may provide environments for organisms that do not now plague the populations of Europe, northern Asia, and North America. In 1993, the hantavirus killed 16 people after a period of excessive heat and drought in the Four Corners area of the American Southwest. When the drought ended in heavy rainfalls, pinion nuts that grew in abundance provided food for a burgeoning rat population, whose droppings spread the disease.

Increased surface water temperatures along the coast of South America may have fostered an outbreak of cholera that killed 5,000, according to Rita Colwell of the Maryland Biotechnology Institute and Timothy Ford and Paul Epstein, two scientists associated with Harvard University. Some cases of malaria have now been reported in Houston, Texas, and after temperatures that exceeded 51° C (124° F) in India's Maharashtra state, more than 60 people died from an outbreak of the pneumonic plague. According to one study by Dutch scientists, malaria-carrying mosquitoes could reach Europe and the northern United States if the predicted global warming occurs by the middle of the next century, and according to Robert Shope of Yale University, yellow fever and dengue fever may spread to midlatitude populations. The Intergovernmental Panel on Climate Change sponsored by the United Nations predicts that up to 7,000 deaths from the heat alone might occur annually in 15 U.S. cities under global warming conditions. As with the general argument about global warming, scientists cannot agree on the extent to which global warming may affect the spread of disease. Most agree, however, that some warming has occurred. Apparently, average global temperatures have risen by 0.5° C/0.9° F during the past 100 years.

Apply Your Knowledge

1. Name the artificially produced greenhouse gases.
2. Which artificially produced greenhouse gases also occur naturally?
3. How does carbon monoxide indirectly affect radiative forcing?
4. How can the deforestation of Brazil's tropical rain forests contribute to radiative forcing?
5. How can global warming affect public health?
6. How can the oceans help to abate or exacerbate the suspected global warming trend?

kilometers (5 billion mi) from Earth. If it continues uninterrupted in its journey, it will pass within 29 trillion kilometers (18 trillion mi) of the star called Ross 248 in 32,600 years. If those numbers seem large, you should realize that many objects lie millions of times farther from Earth than Ross 248 (see box 2.1, "Red-Shifted Galaxies: New Measurements and Controversies").

The objects of the universe beyond Earth and the composition of the basic constituents of matter are the topics of chapters 2 and 3.

Meteorology

We usually take for granted the everyday work of weather scientists. They tell us in a word or phrase that we should dress for heat, or cold, or rain, and we question their skills when their forecast is faulty. But these earth scientists play more than a fashion consultant role.

Through one branch of atmospheric study, known as **meteorology,** we have learned about potential global catastrophes whose economic effects make the costs of individual violent storms seem like very small change. For example, the costs of the **greenhouse effect,** a worldwide warming trend caused by the addition of carbon dioxide and other heat-absorbing gases to the atmosphere, may exceed the resources of the collective world economies (see box 1.2). The warming may cause the expansion of the heated oceans by at least 1 meter (39.37 in) and a significant melting of polar and high-mountain ice, adding enough water to the oceans to drown the highly populated coastal cities. What will it cost to replace a drowned New York, London, Amsterdam, Copenhagen, and Sydney? Consider Houston, Texas, for example. The city lies 80 kilometers (50 mi) inland, but it stands only 15 to 30 meters (50 to 100 ft) above the current sea level. Or, consider the plight of Delaware. The highest elevation in the state is 18 meters (60 ft). The loss of Delaware, a rich farmland, would be tragic, of course, but add to that the loss of the Netherlands, Bangladesh, and much of Denmark. Their entire populations would be displaced by an inundation of seawater.

A global warming trend could also modify the climates and, therefore, the productivity of agricultural regions. Whenever excessively hot weather continues unaccompanied by rains, soils dry out. America suffered a terrible drought in the 1930s, known as the Dust Bowl years, which wreaked havoc on the country's economy and the lives of many farmers (see box 12.4, "The Great American Dust Bowl"). Similarly, the drought of 1988 severely burdened the farmers of the Midwest, and the lack of rain during the last two decades in Northeast Africa has inflicted hardship on millions of people in Ethiopia and Somalia. If the warming trend initiates a long-term drought, who will make up for the decrease in American food production, just when world population is increasing rapidly? (See box 4.3, "Greenhouse Cooling?" for a discussion of how the accumulation of greenhouse gases may affect the temperature of the upper atmosphere.)

Weather scientists constantly monitor the atmosphere's composition, structure, and movement. Acquiring such data requires the use of familiar and unfamiliar instruments, from thermometers to remote sensing satellites. It also requires meteorologists to understand the interrelationships among Earth's geography, incoming solar radiation, and atmospheric composition and process-

es. As a result of their continuing efforts, a specialized group of atmospheric scientists, called climatologists, have classified regional weather patterns. Chapter 6 discusses the holistic science of climatology. Since the formulation of this branch of earth science, climatologists have pointed out interrelationships among sun activity, latitude, altitude, temperature, precipitation, storms, soils, stream and groundwater levels, erosion, glaciation, vegetation, and agriculture.

Geology

Just as atmospheric scientists need instruments to "sense" the invisible air, scientists in the field of **geology** require tools for peering into those portions of Earth hidden by miles of unpenetrated hard rock. The practical importance of such "seeing" into Earth lies in scientific predictions of earthquakes and volcanic eruptions, based on models of geologic interrelationships. Since World War II, earth scientists have worked with sophisticated apparatuses to determine the causes of geologic activity and features. Instruments used in the detection of nuclear bomb detonations have been applied to the study of Earth's interior, revealing a complex of layered spheres, from a solid inner core to a relatively thin outer shell, called the crust.

The instrument that has provided the most knowledge of Earth's interior is the **seismograph,** which is sensitive to vibrations within the planet. The seismograph, discussed more fully in chapter 8, was one of the principal instruments used by U.S. intelligence to "listen" for violations of the nuclear test ban treaty signed in the 1960s. The network of seismographic stations soon recorded an abundance of earth movements beyond those generated by atomic explosions. These natural motions, which included major earthquakes, established a pattern for the planet's interior, based on how the seismic vibrations were distributed. The network of seismographs has been refined for specific research into the structure of Earth's crust and deep interior. Now called **seismic tomography,** the study of both crust and interior through seismic wave analysis incorporates a number of seismic stations, whose operators pool data to create a three-dimensional picture. Through this developing system of "seeing" Earth's interior, scientists are acquiring more detailed pictures of the structures and processes of the **lithosphere,** the planet's rocky outer layer, which includes the continents and the ocean floors.

Although geologists find seismic and other remotely sensed data valuable, to understand the lithosphere they rely heavily on the examination of tangible specimens. Fortunately, geologists have been able to explore and sample the continental rocks and a considerable area of the ocean floor. Their explorations have given us a great deal of information about the composition of the surfaces on which we live.

Thus, like the other earth science disciplines, geology has its own subclasses of information. Some geologists specialize in the study of minerals and rocks, others in the processes that shape the landscape, and still others in geologic hazards and the large forces at work within our planet (see box 8.2, "Earthquake Prediction: Where, When, and How Big?"). This text divides geology into the study of materials, processes, landforms, and resources.

Figure 1.7 Sea surface temperatures imaged from an altitude of 960 kilometers (600 mi). The Gulf Stream flows along the eastern coast of the United States as a warm water current (red and orange). Temperatures diminish (yellow and green) as the current mixes with surrounding water. The location indicated by the number 1 is the site of a cold-water eddy caused by a cutoff meander of the Gulf Stream.

Figure 1.8 A portion of the devastation caused by the 1906 San Francisco earthquake. Some buildings collapsed, and others were gutted by fire.

Oceanography

Figure 1.1 provides evidence that from the perspective of space, no earth feature is more apparent than the oceans, which cover 71% of our planet's surface and contain more than 1 billion cubic kilometers (240 million cu. mi) of water. The oceans are the source of water for the **hydrologic cycle,** which moves water as a liquid, solid, and gas; the oceans are efficient distributors of the sun's heat from low to high latitudes through surface currents; and they are the ultimate sinks for everything that runs off the continents. Keeping track of the movements of the oceans, their interactions with the atmosphere, their effects on the coastal environment, and their great varieties of plants and animals has required cooperation among oceanographers, meteorologists, and biologists. **Oceanography,** as you might have guessed, is a cooperative venture that aims to explain these interrelationships.

The surface waters of the oceans move in large currents driven by the general circulation of the atmosphere. In moving, they transport not only water but also heat from the equatorial regions. Tracing this flow of both water and heat has required observations at sea and from space, where satellites "image" the oceans in a variety of wavelengths. The satellite images, called "false color" *Landsat* and Thematic Mapper images, show oceanic boundaries invisible to the naked eye. Through such imaging, earth scientists have been able to delineate various **eddies,** or spinning bodies of water, within the oceans and to plot the locations and movements of marine life (fig. 1.7).

"Seeing" under the water has also added to the understanding of earth systems. Recent adaptations of the sonar technology developed during World War II to oceanographic studies have revealed details as small as 100 meters (330 ft) on the deep ocean floor. New views of an extensive volcanic mountain chain that is part of the ocean floor now provide marine geologists and geophysicists with corroborating evidence that the seafloor newly forms and spreads along breaks or rifts. The theory of seafloor spreading, first promulgated in 1959, is now part of a larger, more encompassing theory called plate tectonic theory, the subject of chapter 9. *This theory is the most complete perspective, or model, that earth scientists have to unify earth studies.* The formulation of plate tectonics was only possible because of instruments that extend human senses to the invisible and the hidden.

THE PRACTICALITY OF EARTH STUDIES

As our only home, Earth is analogous to the houses in which we live. There is much to learn about a house, which the house itself can teach. The materials used in its construction are clues to its origin; the layout is a clue to its structure; and the daily processes, such as the entering and exiting of water through pipes, the weathering of paint and mortar, and the heaving of sidewalks after a winter and spring of freezing and thawing, all provide clues about the house and its surroundings. The more a home owner knows about a dwelling, the better prepared that owner is to anticipate problems and seek remedies: *Ignorance is usually expensive and sometimes very dangerous.* Earth, like a house, reveals much about itself.

Costly Neighborhoods, Dangerous Circumstances

A good example of expensive ignorance is the location of San Francisco in an earthquake zone. The city's founders, unaware of the area's potential for violent tremors, established the community in what seemed to be an ideal setting. In the last century and in the first decade of the twentieth century, the city grew to more than 400,000 people. In 1906, the city was the "Gem of the Pacific," but on April 18 at 5:12 A.M., a powerful earthquake shook the region and started fires that eventually burned through more than 10 square kilometers (4 sq. mi) of the city. More than 2,000 died, and most of the businesses were destroyed (fig. 1.8).

Figure 1.9 Collapsed segment of the Nimitz Freeway (I–880) in Oakland, California.

Of course, the survivors rebuilt the city, and as the decades passed, San Franciscans learned from scientists that other earthquakes of similar strength were possible. The information led to architectural standards for "earthquake-proof" buildings. In October 1989, the city felt it was prepared for an earthquake, and its residents and others around the United States may have joked about the "big one," a predicted earthquake as powerful as the quake of 1906. As the third game of the World Series between the Oakland Athletics and the San Francisco Giants was about to begin at Candlestick Park, the ground shook again. Sixty-two people lost their lives, most on the lower level of a double-deck highway in nearby Oakland (fig. 1.9). During the earthquake, which originated in the vicinity of Loma Prieta, just south of the Bay area, 3,757 people suffered injuries, 12,000 lost their homes, 367 businesses were destroyed, and property damage exceeded $7 billion, according to government figures (see box 8.1, "Earthquake Engineering: 'Bracing' for the Big One").

Knowledge about Earth Saves Lives

Its extensive damage made the October 17, 1989, earthquake in San Francisco one of the costliest natural catastrophes in American history. That remarkably few lives were lost, however, was partly

Figure 1.10 Storm damage in coastal South Carolina from Hurricane Hugo in 1989.

the result of those architectural designs governed by geophysical and geological information that earth scientists had provided.

In fact, earth scientists had a hand in saving other lives on the East Coast just 6 weeks prior to the earthquake. When Hurricane Hugo powered its way over South Carolina, it damaged or destroyed more than 35,000 homes, toppled trees worth an estimated $1 billion, and ruined about $500 million in crops (fig. 1.10). The 24 counties hit hardest by Hugo suffered $5 billion in damages. As in the West Coast tragedy, the work of earth scientists significantly reduced the number of casualties (18 died). Meteorologists and oceanographers had broadcast warnings of the storm's strength and direction, giving government officials sufficient time to arrange evacuations of those coastal areas most susceptible to the high winds and waters of the approaching hurricane (see box 5.3, "Hurricane Andrew: America's Most Destructive Storm").

The warnings of earth scientists are not always heeded. When Mount Saint Helens showed signs of increased volcanic activity in 1980, the warnings of geologists were ignored by disbelieving and uncooperative people who did not understand the power such a volcano could generate. In particular, a longtime resident named Harry Truman refused to evacuate, claiming he would be there as long as the mountain was. Part of the mountain is gone now, obliterated in the May eruption. Harry Truman, unfortunately, is gone also. He did not seem to understand the nature of his home.

Incomplete Knowledge

Even earth scientists cannot predict the intensity of earthquakes, volcanic eruptions, and some storms. On November 15, 1989, for example, meteorologists watched the development of a storm system as it approached the southeastern United States. The National Weather Service issued a severe storm watch for several states, but no one knew that before this weather system moved over the Atlantic Ocean, its destructive winds would kill 29 people from Alabama to Canada. On that November day, the severe weather hit Huntsville, Alabama, at 4:37 P.M., as a tornado with winds estimated at 400 kilometers per hour (250 mph) destroyed 1,000 cars, 259 homes, 3 churches, 10 public buildings, and scores of electric power structures (fig. 1.11). In about 10 minutes, the storm fatally injured 17 people along its 26-kilometer (16-mi) path. Because weather systems move, they can devastate widely separated areas. While the people of Huntsville were assessing the damage on the following day, the same storm system generated unexpected high winds in Newburgh, New York, collapsing a cafeteria wall and killing seven children in an elementary school (see box 5.2, "Tornado: A Late Autumn Storm").

Our incomplete knowledge of Earth's processes is characterized by a statement a National Weather Service meteorologist made to reporters following the devastation of the Alabama storm. He described the Huntsville tornado as "a weatherman's nightmare. We couldn't see it on radar." In spite of many technological advances and scientific studies, we have much to learn before we fully understand our home planet. Earth scientists can enhance our knowledge of Earth.

Figure 1.11 A small part of the destruction in Huntsville, Alabama, caused by a tornado on November 15, 1989.

Questions for Earth Scientists

Through the efforts of earth scientists, we now have an elaborate catalog of knowledge about our planet. We also know about conditions and processes that can change Earth's ability to support life. This introductory chapter has hinted at possible disasters, leaving us with many unanswered questions: Will our planet collide with a large comet or meteorite? Can we change the warming trend? Can we predict destructive storms with greater accuracy? Can we predict earthquakes? Earth scientists are working to answer these and other questions about our planet. Although they have only partial answers, they do know, through years of observation and research, the major causes of these phenomena.

Common sense tells us that knowledge is better than ignorance. On the level of our ordinary, daily activities, earth science can teach us much with practical meaning: What is the origin of our drinking water? of our gasoline? of our gemstones and gold? of aluminum and iron? What—and this is a very large question indeed—is the origin of Earth?

Questions for You

Even more important for you is a series of questions about your community. What causes changes in your weather? How do the vast oceans affect your life? Why does your landscape take the forms you see? What is the composition of those forms, and what lies beneath their surfaces? What natural phenomena might threaten the stability and safety of your region?

Answers to these and other questions about your home come from the work of earth scientists: They explore, study, observe, and explain the processes, composition, features, history, and future of our house, the planet we call Earth. Study earth science for an obvious reason: A familiar home is not only a comfortable one; it may also be less costly and safer than an unfamiliar home.

FURTHER THOUGHTS: A HOLISTIC AND PRACTICAL SCIENCE

Because earth science is an eclectic mix of ways to look at and understand our planet, it is a holistic science. Although individual earth scientists may strive for knowledge about a single feature or process outside of, on, or in the planet, the overall tendency of earth science observations and research is toward integrative models of Earth that show the interconnectedness of its features, processes, and life.

Earth science also serves many practical purposes. By explaining how and why volcanoes erupt, the land quakes, and the atmosphere moves, for example, earth scientists lay the framework for safety. By exploring the planet with instruments that probe beyond the capabilities of human senses, they show us where we can mine the natural resources that support our technological societies. With this synthesis of knowledge about Earth, you should be able to understand many natural phenomena that affect your daily life.

SIGNIFICANT POINTS

1. Earth is a unique planet because it supports life.
2. Earth scientists attempt to model the processes and features of our planet.
3. In science, a theory is a model that explains natural phenomena on the basis of substantiated fact.
4. Scientists develop a hypothesis as an initial explanation for natural phenomena and as a focus for their investigations.
5. By adopting a scientific method, scientists attempt to eliminate subjectivity from their investigations.
6. Classification is a process by which scientists build a coherent framework of ideas, observations, and information.
7. The scientific approach to natural phenomena that incorporates the work of many scientists in different scientific disciplines is called the method of multiple working hypotheses.
8. The most significant earth science theory, called plate tectonics, was largely the product of multiple working hypotheses.
9. Scientists use instruments to detect whatever lies beyond human sensory perception. They can study, for example, the full extent of the electromagnetic spectrum, which lies beyond the wavelengths of visible light.

10. Four earth science disciplines—astronomy, meteorology, geology, and oceanography—are interrelated branches of knowledge.
11. Earth is subject to radiation from the sun and other sources, meteorite impacts, and other astronomical influences.
12. Our planet is relatively small in comparison to the great distances to other objects in our universe.
13. The study of the atmosphere has yielded clues about changes in worldwide weather patterns, given us warnings about violent storms, and led to predictions of future dangers.
14. Geologists have ascertained the nature of Earth's interior through the use of the seismograph, an instrument sensitive to ground vibrations.
15. Geologists rely on the analysis of specimens to ascertain the exact composition of the lithosphere.
16. Oceanographers study both the ocean basins and the waters they contain. Like the other earth scientists, they use instruments, such as satellites, to discern oceanic patterns and features.
17. Knowledge about Earth is very practical. Because we must rely on the planet to sustain our lives, we should understand the processes and features that affect us.

ESSENTIAL TERMS

model *5*
theory *5*
hypothesis *6*
scientific method *7*
classification *7*
photosynthesis *8*
chemosynthesis *8*

multiple working
   hypotheses *8*
plate tectonics *8*
uniformitarianism *9*
actualism *9*
electromagnetic
   spectrum *9*

radiation *9*
electromagnetic
   radiation *9*
ultraviolet (UV) radia-
   tion *9*
ozone *9*
holistic approach *10*

natural law *11*
astronomy *13*
meteorology *16*
greenhouse effect *16*
geology *16*
seismograph *16*
seismic tomography *16*

lithosphere *16*
hydrologic cycle *17*
oceanography *17*
eddies *17*

REVIEW QUESTIONS

1. How does scientific information gathering differ from sensory perception?
2. What is the ultimate goal of the earth sciences?
3. How does a scientific theory differ from speculation?
4. How does actualism differ from uniformitarianism?
5. What led to the detection of the hole in the ozone layer of the stratosphere?
6. Why are multidisciplinary approaches to the study of Earth essential to earth scientists?
7. What evidence do we have that objects from beyond Earth's boundaries influence the planet?
8. How can atmospheric warming affect civilization?
9. What enables geologists to see into Earth's interior?
10.. How can the oceans influence weather?
11. What recent natural disasters have produced fewer deaths than comparable past events because of earth scientists?

CHALLENGES

1. How would you categorize the natural surroundings of your home? If you have observed your area's weather and landscape for a number of years, you have at least a general idea about how hot, wet, flat, or hilly your neighborhood is. Would you make a comparison with some other area you have visited to establish your categorization?
2. What are your primary food sources? How would these sources be affected by changes in rainfall brought on by a global warming trend? Would your sources of meat be affected as much as your sources of grains, fruits, and vegetables?
3. What would happen to river mouths if global warming increased sea level? How would seaports be affected by such a change?
4. What characteristics or needs of life make living on other planets, even in artificially maintained Earth-like environments, difficult or impossible? Is there one characteristic or need you can identify as the most important?
5. What physical processes are at work to change your area?
6. How can the knowledge gained through earth studies help government officials protect citizens?

PART 2

The *Big Picture*

*A*lthough we are earthbound, we cannot avoid the relationship between our planet and all that lies beyond its boundaries. Earth did not form in a void, and it both influences and is influenced by other bodies. For thousands of years, humans have attempted to explain the composition, structure, and evolution of the universe and to understand the interrelationships among its many bodies. Today, our knowledge of bodies outside Earth is aided by sophisticated instruments, many of which have been launched into outer space.

At the *End* of *Part 2, You Will Be Able* to:

1. Identify the methods astronomers use to measure the universe.
2. Recognize the dual nature of light.
3. Recognize and cite evidence for the significance of gravity and energy.
4. Differentiate the components of matter.
5. Explain the origins of the universe and Solar System.
6. Compare the types and evolutionary stages of stars.
7. Explain the structure of the sun.
8. Explain the source of solar energy.
9. Generalize from data the nature of the planets and other celestial bodies.

The *Meditations of Abu-al-ala Maárri* (973–1057)

XVII

Two fates still hold us fast,
A future and a past;
Two vessels' vast embrace
Surrounds us—Time and Space.

Chapter 2

The Universe, Matter, and Energy

The Cat's Eye Nebula,
3,000 light-years from Earth.
Expanding shells of gases ejected from the
central star reveal a complete stae of stellar evolution called a
planetary nebula. The image was obtained with the Hubble
Space Telescope's Wide-Field and Planetary Camera 2 on
September 18, 1994.

Early on February 24, 1987, an infrequently observed event briefly changed a small portion of the sky over the Southern Hemisphere. A Canadian astronomer working in the Andes Mountains discovered an unexpectedly bright object in a nearby cluster of stars called the Large Magellanic Cloud. The bright spectacle was, in historical terms, unusual because very few such events have occurred relatively close to Earth. In fact, the last recorded object of similar brightness in Earth's vicinity appeared in 1604. To get some idea of just what is meant by "relatively close," you might consider the distance to the star cluster in which the bright object lay. The Large Magellanic Cloud is about 15,770,000,000,000,000 kilometers (9,780,000,000,000,000 mi) from our planet. As an astronomical event, the bright object was distant enough to appear small to the earthbound naked eye, but in its star cluster, it was probably very significant. Regardless of its apparent size, the event was of enormous importance to scientists. It gave them a chance to study the catastrophic death of a star in an explosion called a **supernova.** The star that blew up was Sanduleak, pictured in figure 2.1 in the center of its shell of gases expanding into the surrounding space.

Because the supernova of 1987 occurred during our technological age, it became the first nearby disruption of a star to be recorded on sensitive instruments and observed through powerful telescopes. Previously studied supernovae have been too distant for accurate data collection on the scale presented by Sanduleak. To the scientists who study outer space, the event was important in three ways. First, its proximity allowed telescope views with a high degree of resolution, or clarity. Second, the observation was accompanied by the detection of very small particles, called **neutrinos.** These virtually massless, high-speed particles pass through the planet all the time, rarely being detected because they do not interact with matter easily. Although hard to observe, neutrinos by the trillions probably passed through Earth at about the same time the astronomers first witnessed the light of the Sanduleak explosion. Third, the event was observed through a variety of instruments, such as radio-wave antennae and infrared sensors.

To a novice in the study of outer space, the data released by the scientists who studied the 1987 supernova may serve to introduce the great distances of the universe. The supernova may also serve as a lesson about stars: They are *not* indestructible. This is significant because *our own sun is also a star,* and as a star, it will also change its character and undergo a kind of death throe. Although our sun's change will not mimic the supernova, it will entail an alteration radical enough to destroy our planet. The destruction of Earth's sun is far off in the future, probably about 5 billion years hence, but a phase of the sun's development may jeopardize life in less than one-fifth that time.

Big Numbers, Long Times

Big numbers associated with time and distance are common in astronomy, which is the study of the universe beyond Earth's confines. The quadrillions of kilometers to the 1987 supernova Sanduleak, in the Large Magellanic Cloud, for example, comprise a short distance by astronomers' standards. Objects that are tens of thousands of times farther away than the Large Magellanic Cloud

are known to exist. Even sizes are astoundingly large. Our sun, for example, is a little under 1,394,000 kilometers (864,000 mi) in diameter. Sanduleak was an estimated eight times larger than our sun.

Comprehending the great distances and sizes in the universe is an exercise in imagination for the residents of Earth, an oblate spheroid only 12,785 kilometers (7,927 mi) in diameter at its equator. Despite our advances in technology, most of us are bound to our planet (astronauts are very few in number). Our robot spacecraft are also mostly earthbound. Of the many space vehicles we have launched, most have merely orbited our planet. A few have traveled throughout the sun's system of planets, and two, *Pioneer 10* (see chapter 1) and *Voyager I*, have left the Solar System.

Astronomical Questions

Sanduleak's abrupt end in a supernova is an indication that stars are not eternal. We live on a planet that is also destined to have an ending, which is tied to the fate of our sun. The idea of planets and stars having endings may seem like material for science fiction, but throughout the universe, many such objects explode, implode (burst inward), change shape, or break up.

Before you learn of our sun's fate—and the fate of our planet—you should ask a series of questions about astronomy as a science. The great distances and sizes discussed require measurements, but most of the objects astronomers study are too far away to visit for measurements or samples. How, then, do astronomers quantify the universe?

Once you have established how astronomers operate, you can begin to understand the great wealth of information they have gathered through centuries of observation. You can also learn about such objects as Sanduleak and our own sun and planets. Where and how, for example, did the universe, stars, and planets originate? Of what are they composed, and what is the origin of that material? How many are there? What is their behavior? Why are they located where we see them? And finally, what is their future?

Figure 2.1 Sanduleak (Supernova 1987A) appeared to observers in the Southern Hemisphere as a supernova in the Large Magellanic Cloud.

MEASURING THE UNIVERSE

Because the distances and sizes in the universe are so great that measurements on the scale of Earth are inadequate, astronomers use the terms *light-year* and *parsec* to quantify the distances to the stars. A **light-year (lt-yr)** is simply the distance light travels in a

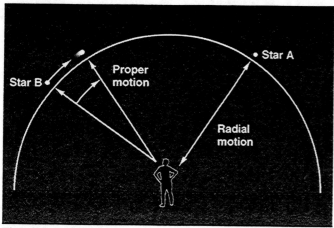

Figure 2.2 Star A exhibits radial motion, whereas Star B exhibits proper motion.

single year, which, at 299,792 kilometers (186,000 mi) per second, amounts to a little under 9.5 trillion kilometers (6 trillion mi). Astronomers also use a unit called a **parsec (pc),** which is 3.26 light-years. Such large numbers are staggering, especially when you consider that Sanduleak's supernova event was considered close, yet the Large Magellanic Cloud is more than 163,000 light-years (50,000 pc) away. In other words, Sanduleak exploded about 163,000 years ago, and its light and neutrinos just recently passed by Earth. Measuring the distance to distant stars requires techniques involving triangulation and brightness. You will learn about both of these techniques in this chapter.

Astronomers also use the **astronomical unit (AU)** to measure distances within our Solar System. One AU is 150 million kilometers (93 million mi), or the distance between Earth and the sun. Planets closer to the sun than Earth are less than 1 AU, whereas the farthest planet, Pluto, is 39 AU from the sun.

In your study of astronomy, you should consider two other aspects of measurement: direction and motion. To understand these aspects, imagine yourself at the center of a sphere. Motion within that sphere can be perceived in several ways (fig. 2.2). Objects that move away from or toward you move along the radius of the sphere. Astronomers call such a positional change the **radial motion** of an object. When they determine an object's speed along the radial line,

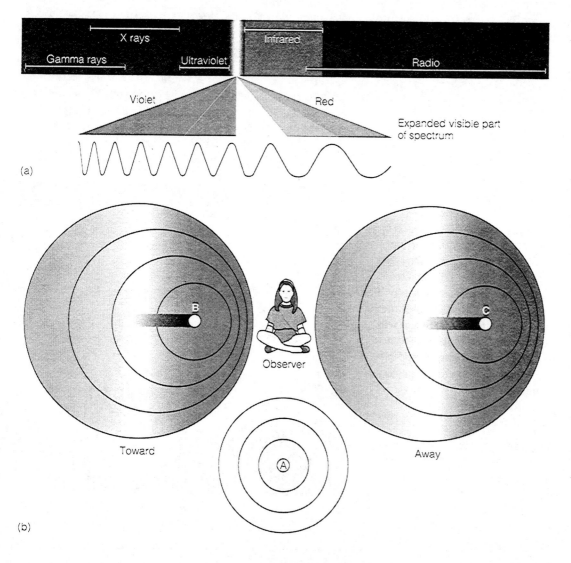

Figure 2.3 (*a*) Electromagnetic spectrum with the visible portion expanded to show longer wavelengths at red end and shorter wavelengths at violet end. (*b*) As a light source (A) remains at a fixed distance from the observer, no change in its wavelengths is perceived. As a light source (B) approaches an observer, the waves are compressed and the wavelengths shortened, emphasizing the violet end of the spectrum. As a light source (C) moves away from an observer, the waves spread out, or lengthen, emphasizing the red end of the spectrum. This latter phenomenon is known as the "red shift" and is evidence that a light source is receding.

astronomers calculate the object's *radial velocity.* Of course, not every object moves along a radial line, and movements other than those directly toward or away from you appear to run along the arc of the sphere. The movements that change the position of an object across the hemispherical sky are known as **proper motions.** The rate at which a proper motion occurs is the *tangential velocity* of an object. Proper motions can be given in degrees, or fractions of degrees, of arc. Degrees are subdivided into minutes and further subdivided into seconds. The smallest proper motion, therefore, can be a fraction of a second.

Recognizing Motion

Proper motion is easily recognizable whenever the motion occurs against a frame of reference or background, such as the horizon or some distant background of stars. Radial motion, however, occurs along the line of sight. If someone throws you a ball, you see it appear to increase in size as it approaches you. When you throw it back, you observe it decrease in size. Unfortunately, astronomers deal with objects that never get as close as a thrown ball and that lie at great distances, where a change in size is difficult to perceive. They need another method to determine radial motion and are fortunate to have one based on changes in the electromagnetic spectrum (see chapter 1).

The Doppler Effect

The wavelengths between 0.4 and 0.7 micrometers (visible light) are not the only electromagnetic frequencies studied and used by astronomers (fig. 2.3*a*). When they observe electromagnetic radiation from a distant object, astronomers can measure a change in frequency called the **Doppler effect.** To understand this effect, consider the changing pitch of a passing train, which not only sounds louder as it approaches but also musically higher. By comparison, figure 2.3*b* shows a light source shining in all directions. As long as the source remains stationary, the wavelengths will be equal for an observer, but movement of a source toward or away from an observer changes the wavelengths. Whenever a celestial object that emits light is approaching, its light shifts toward the shorter, violet end of the spectrum, just as the sound waves for an oncoming train shorten and increase in pitch. An object heading away from Earth has its light shifted toward the red end. The electromagnetic shift toward longer wavelengths, derived from the radial motion of an object away from an observer, is called the **red shift** (see box 2.1).

Parallax

One method astronomers use to measure the distance to stars involves measurements of **parallax,** which is the *apparent positional change of an object that results from a change of perspective* (fig. 2.4). To visualize this apparent change, hold up one finger steadily and look at it first with one eye, then the other. Your finger appears to move along a plane, even though it remains stationary.

(a)

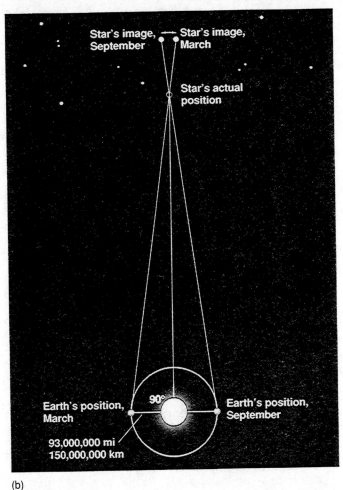

(b)

Figure 2.4 (*a*) Parallactic movements change shape with changing perpectives. (*b*) *Parallax* refers to the way in which the position of a nearby star seems to shift against its background as Earth orbits the sun. By simple trigonometry, that shift can be used to calculate the star's position in March and then six months later, in September. The star's apparent movement across the celestial background is measured on the photographs as an angle, greatly exaggerated here. Halving that measurement yields one angle of a right triangle that has the star, the sun, and Earth at its vertices. Because the sun-to-Earth distance is known, the leg of the triangle representing the star-to-Earth distance is easily determined. With ground-based instruments, the technique is reliable only out to about 600 light-years.

Box 2.1

Further Consideration

RED-SHIFTED GALAXIES: NEW MEASUREMENTS AND CONTROVERSIES

The relationship between distance from our galaxy and recessional speed of distant galaxies can be revealed by examining the spectra of distant galaxies. Nearby galaxies do not move away from the Milky Way as fast as galaxies farther out. Their movements can be seen in the shifts in the *H* and *K lines* resulting from calcium absorption (fig. 2.A).

The basis for understanding the relationship between the rate of recession and distance is known as *Hubble's law.** According to the law, the rate of recession equals distance multiplied by the quantity *H*, called *Hubble's constant*. Hubble's constant is a debated number, but many astronomers tentatively accept values around 15 kilometers per second per million light-years. Different values for Hubble's constant change the age and size of the universe. Figure 2.A shows distant galaxies and their rates of recession with respect to the Milky Way. Based on a constant of 15 kilometers per second per million light-years, the distant Hydra is receding from our galaxy at 61,000 kilometers per second (37,820 mi/sec).

Recent measurements based on observations through the Hubble Space Telescope have stirred up the controversy over the value of Hubble's constant. Michael Pierce and others at Indiana University have set the distance to the Virgo cluster of galaxies (fig. 2.A) at 45 to 50 million light-years. This distance is 28 to 33 million light-years shorter than the traditionally accepted measurement, and it implies a universe that is 9 to 12 billion years old. Using the Hubble Space Telescope, Wendy Freedman of the Carnegie Observatories has also challenged the accepted values of measurements to the Virgo cluster and to M100 (fig. 2.B).

Freedman's estimate of the age of the universe is based on a Hubble's constant of approximately 73 kilometers per second per megaparsec. Allan R. Sandage, another astronomer at Carnegie Observatories, derived a constant of 57 by using Cepheids to determine the distance to supernovae in distant galaxies. This smaller constant indicates a universe 11 to 16 billion years old.

These new measurements have presented astronomers with a difficult problem. If Pierce, Freedman, and others are correct in their measurements and in their assessment of the age of the universe, how can they account for the apparent discrepancy of a 9- to 12-billion-year-old universe that houses stars that appear to be 14 billion years old?

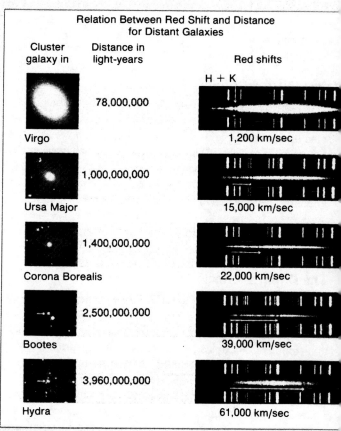

Relation Between Red Shift and Distance for Distant Galaxies

Cluster galaxy in	Distance in light-years	Red shifts
Virgo	78,000,000	1,200 km/sec
Ursa Major	1,000,000,000	15,000 km/sec
Corona Borealis	1,400,000,000	22,000 km/sec
Bootes	2,500,000,000	39,000 km/sec
Hydra	3,960,000,000	61,000 km/sec

Figure 2.A Spectra of galaxies. Photographs (*left*) and spectra (*right*) of galaxies in several rich clusters. The clusters range in distance from nearby (Virgo) to remote (Hydra). In the spectra, prominent absorption features are indicated by arrows; these lines, known as the H and K lines, are due to calcium absorption. The lines in cluster spectra are very broad, compared with lines in individual stellar spectra because the motions of the stars in each galaxy contribute to the spectrum. The absorption lines are progressively red shifted as the distance to the cluster increases. This red shift is due to the Doppler effect and can be expressed in terms of the relative velocity of recession of the cluster. The recession velocity is found to increase linearly with distance to these clusters.

Another interesting ramification of a younger universe is a solution to the "Why is the sky dark?" problem. If the universe is only 9 to 12 billion years old, then the light from many different stars and galaxies may not have reached us yet. The universe is not dark because of intervening clouds that absorb electromagnetic radiation (absorbing radiation would heat the clouds to glow) but because much of the universe's radiation has not permeated all its volume.

*Edwin Hubble (1889–1953) began his influential career in astronomy when he was asked to work with the 100-inch telescope on Mount Wilson in California. He demonstrated that the universe contains galaxies other than our own. Hubble also established that the electromagnetic shift in frequency associated with moving, luminous objects first observed by Christian Doppler in 1842 could be applied to the light from distant galaxies.

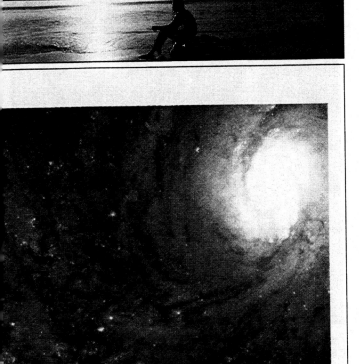

Figure 2.B M100 galaxy in the Virgo cluster. Using the Hubble Space Telescope, the Wendy Freedman team measured the distance to M100 by studying Cepheid variable stars.

Apply Your Knowledge

1. What is the relationship between distance and recessional speed?
2. What is the method used to determine the direction of motion for a distant galaxy?
3. What is Hubble's constant?
4. Why is the value of Hubble's constant important to an interpretation of the age of the universe?
5. How has the Hubble Space Telescope cast doubt on the value of Hubble's constant?

To measure stellar parallax, astronomers need a greater distance between observation points than that between two eyes. Stars are farther away than our fingers, and greater distances mean smaller changes in the parallax angle. To expand their perspective, therefore, astronomers use as their vantage points the opposite sides of Earth's orbit because it has a diameter of 2 AU. Unlike your looking at a finger, however, astronomers get a view of objects lying in different planes relative to Earth's orbit and shifting observation points. A distant star that lies in a plane perpendicular to our orbit would appear to move differently from one that lies on the same plane. At a perpendicular position, a star's movement would appear to be in a circle, while one in the same plane as our planet would appear to move back and forth in a straight line. Any star at an oblique angle to our orbit would describe an ellipse (fig. 2.4a).

For the great distances represented by star positions, parallax measurements are made in seconds of degree of arc equated to parsecs (fig. 2.4b). Identifying the parallax of close stars is equivalent to your recognizing with unaided eyes the thickness of this book if it were 3.2 kilometers (about 2 mi) away. Because most stars lie at very great distances, the triangle becomes a very thin geometric feature that is difficult to measure. In fact, based on observations at 2 AU, parallax measurements within a 10% margin of error only can be made for approximately 700 nearby stars. To measure distances to more distant stars, astronomers use a variety of methods, including stellar brightness.

Magnitude

The brightest object in our sky is the sun, but the scale of brightness astronomers use is based on the bright but distant stars Aldebaran and Altair. Norman R. Pogson devised this scale in 1856 to rank stellar **magnitude**, or brightness. On his scale, Aldebaran and Altair are magnitude 1 stars. Dimmer objects are represented by higher positive numbers. Since our sun *appears* to be brighter than either star, its magnitude must be expressed by a negative number, −26.5. This is the *apparent magnitude,* which results from the sun's proximity to Earth (table 2.1). Compared with Sirius, the brightest star visible from the Northern Hemisphere, our sun appears 10 billion times brighter. In reality, however, the sun is not as intrinsically bright as any magnitude 1 star. Its *absolute magnitude,* or its brightness based on what it would look like if it were 10 parsecs away from us, is 5. The stars have intrinsic magnitudes; they are hot objects that produce their own bright electromagnetic radiation.

TABLE 2.1	Selected Apparent Magnitudes	
Object	**Apparent Magnitude**	**Distance (lt-yr)**
Our Sun	−26.5	1/62,365
Sirius (Canis Majoris)	−1.58	8.7
Vega (Lyrae)	0.14	26.5
Aldebaran (Tauri)	1.06	68
Polaris (Ursae Minoris)	2.12	680

Variable Stars and the Doppler Effect

Some stars vary their magnitudes over short periods of 1 to 50 days. These **variable stars** have been classified according to their magnitude fluctuations, and one particular classification—the Cepheid Variables—has been used in distance measurements. The name *Cepheid Variables* derives from Delta Cephei, a giant star that contracts and expands at regular intervals. As Delta Cephei expands, it gives off more light, and as it contracts, less light. The process by which such an object produces its light will be discussed later, but its magnitude change is significant for measurements.

This shifting of frequencies can be used to interpret a Cepheid Variable's expansion and contraction—alternating radial motion that is, respectively, either toward or away from Earth. The Cepheids may change size by as much as 10% within a matter of days. For enormous stars like the Cepheid Variables, that translates into millions of kilometers and a shift in frequency. If astronomers know the apparent (m) and absolute (M) magnitudes of a variable, they can calculate its distance (d) based on a well-established formula: $M = m + 5 - 5 \log d$.

Measuring Light and Other Radiation

Light decreases proportionally to the square of the distance from its source. This is a matter of experience for all of us. A flashlight held close to your face appears much brighter than one held a city block away. You can think of this as a change in the light's intensity. A Cepheid Variable's visible, regularly changing magnitudes can be observed through a telescope or quantified through a process by which light striking an instrument called a **photomultiplier** yields a measurement of intensity by converting the light into a measurable electrical current. A device called a **spectrophotometer** acts like a prism to divide the light into colors (different wavelengths) before it enters the photomultiplier so that astronomers can look at a star's full spectrum. The total (all the wavelengths) magnitude of radiation is called the *bolometric magnitude*, a quantity measured by these astronomical instruments.

The Nature of Light

Throughout this chapter, you have read about "brightness" and "light," two words that occur frequently in our everyday language. We have already considered brightness, but light itself is essential to astronomy, for this science began in ancient times as a study of the "lights" in the sky. But just exactly what is light?

The electromagnetic spectrum shows light as a range of wavelengths: those falling between the shorter wave ultraviolet and longer wave infrared. Commonly, light is thought of as waves, allowing a comparison between light waves and water waves. Water waves can interfere with one another if they come from different directions. In water waves, the high points (crests) and low points (troughs) can cancel or reduce each other's vertical dimension whenever they meet (see chapter 13). Similarly, light waves can interfere with one another, and you can observe this interference as a set of parallel dark lines where the waves cancel each other.

To make your observation, just squint as you look at a light source through the very small space between two almost-touching

Figure 2.5   Wave interference can be seen as small, parallel, dark lines between two almost-touching fingers.

fingertips (fig. 2.5). Light observed in this fashion appears to be made of waves. A peculiar behavior of light, however, makes it appear more like flows of discrete particles. These particles of light, called **photons,** are energy packages that can make a photomultiplier active. As the photons strike the tube-shaped instrument, they release negatively charged particles called **electrons,** which a detector can count. Astronomers, therefore, can objectively determine light magnitude. They can also observe other wavelengths in the electromagnetic spectrum with the aid of the spectrophotometer.

Light, therefore, has two identities. How we choose to observe light determines its identity. Whenever we want to observe it as waves, we see it act like waves. If we want to observe it act like particles, we see it act like particles. These are important considerations because much of astronomy is based on the interpretation of the light from sources that lie at distances too great for other kinds of study. For earth scientists, however, the physics of light composition is less important than its speed. *Nothing goes faster* (see p. 26). Its speed in a vacuum is a constant that can be used as a measuring stick for distance and as a universal clock.

Traveling at the speed of light, the messages from *Pioneer 10* take more than 7 hours to reach Earth. This means that the information is about something that has already happened, just as the 1987 supernova Sanduleak occurred before *Homo sapiens* first walked on our planet. Light is our "time machine," and it gives us, along with the rest of the electromagnetic spectrum, a way of reaching into the distant past and the origin of the universe.

Revelations from the Time Machine

What do we see when we look through this "time machine"? First, we recognize that *the universe is, at the very least, indefinite.* No one has found an end, and similarly, no one has found a center.

Second, the universe appears to be very old, with some astronomers agreeing on an age greater than 12 billion years and other astronomers arguing for a younger universe (see box 2.1). Third, we see a visible universe that is apparently lumpy, with stars and groups of stars gathered in masses. Fourth, through the wavelengths of visible light, we view a universe whose objects appear to be composed of matter. Because of this apparent dominance of matter in the composition of the universe, and in preparation for the discussion of minerals in chapter 7, you should have a basic understanding of matter.

MATTER AND GRAVITY

The objects of our universe are composed of matter. In the simplest terms, **matter** is anything that occupies space and has mass. Matter also exerts an attractive force called gravity, as the mass of one substance pulls against the mass of another. Gravitational force increases with increasing mass and with decreasing distance. Thus, the pull of our planet's gravity is an attractive force that keeps you earthbound and prevents your drifting away into space. You recognize this force as your weight, and you would not weigh as much standing on the smaller mass of the moon. Your "moon weight," for example, would register only one-sixth of your "earth weight." Astronauts who have visited the moon have been able to move with relative ease, despite wearing spacesuits and backpacks that would add 35 kilograms (77 lb) to their earth weight.

The book you are holding has mass. You know the book's mass as its weight, which is the product of gravitational attraction between the book and Earth. The book also occupies space and has evident boundaries. It is a solid, visible form of matter. The air around you is also matter. It is not, of course, visible like the book and does not appear to have definite boundaries, but you can feel it just by blowing on your hand. As a gas, the air we breathe also occupies space and has weight. In fact, quintillions (10^{18}) of kilograms of air encompass our planet. Liquid water is also matter. Its boundaries are perceived as the container in which it lies, regardless of whether that container is a bucket, a river channel, a lake, or an ocean basin.

The Composition and Structure of Matter

Our understanding of matter has changed over the centuries, but a common thread has often wound its way through the changing theories of matter. The connection among theories is the belief that different forms of matter have a common underlying makeup. Even the alchemists of the Middle Ages held this belief, as evidenced by their attempts to transmute other metals into gold. Their intuition told them that all substances have an inherent uniformity and that they might be manipulated to change forms.

In a sense, this is true, because all matter is fundamentally composed of just three important types of particles: protons, electrons, and neutrons. Various combinations and arrangements of these three particles make up the solids, liquids, and gases of our universe.

Atoms

The three elementary particles join to make **atoms,** the smallest forms of matter that can maintain recognizable characteristics. The **proton** is a positively charged particle close to the mass of a **neutron,** a particle that carries no charge. Both protons and neutrons can be found in the corelike nucleus of an atom. Electrons are negatively charged particles that orbit the nucleus in energy "shells" or levels, so-called because energy is required to keep the electrons in their orbits. Within any given atom is a distinct segregation that keeps the protons and neutrons in the very dense central core and the electrons in their orbits. Because the electrons are moving in paths at velocities that enable them to make billions of orbits each second, there is a natural outward force—centrifugal force—that would normally cause them to fly away from the atom's nucleus. You can imitate this movement by whirling a key on a string and then releasing your hold, allowing both key and string to fly. This outward force is counteracted in the atom, however, by the naturally attractive force between the opposing charges of the protons and electrons. All but the most distant electrons remain firmly associated with the atom.

The nucleus of the atom is held together by the **strong nuclear force,** which overcomes the natural repulsion of the crowded, like charges of the protons. (A weak nuclear force exerts control on the subatomic particles that aggregate to form protons and neutrons and also on radioactive decay.) This dense nucleus accounts for more than 99.9% of the atom's mass. The number of protons and neutrons is the **mass number,** a close approximation to the weight of the entire atom. Scientists also categorize atoms on the basis of the number of protons in the nucleus, which is the **atomic number** of an atom. Hydrogen, for example, with one proton in the nucleus, has an atomic number of 1.

All three types of subatomic particles are unimaginably light and small. A proton, for example, has a mass of about 1.5 septillionths of a gram. The dimensions of atoms are just as unimaginable as their weights. The diameters of about 40 million atoms would be required to stretch over a centimeter (more than 100 million per in). In addition, the diameter of an entire atom is about 100,000 times greater than that of its nucleus.

The three subatomic particles can be combined in different numbers, resulting in various atoms (fig. 2.6). Ninety-two combinations of these particles occur naturally and are called **elements.** In addition, scientists have been able to synthesize other combinations yielding a total of 105 named elements and others yet to be named.

The differences among the atoms in figure 2.6 lie in the numbers of protons, neutrons, and electrons. Heavy atoms, such as gold, contain more protons and neutrons than lighter atoms. Regardless of their atomic number, however, atoms maintain an electrical equilibrium. The balanced numbers of protons and electrons within atoms make atoms electrically neutral.

The elements can be grouped according to similar characteristics. The *periodic table of the elements,* shown in figure 2.7, is organized so that elements in the vertical columns have similar properties. In the far right column are the elements helium, neon, argon, xenon, radon, and krypton. These elements have their outermost energy levels completely filled with electrons, and each

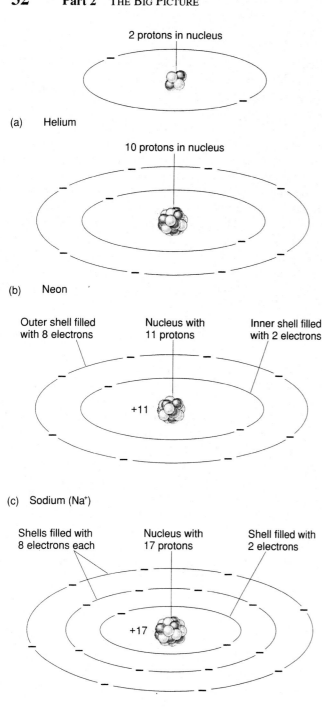

Figure 2.6   Simplified models of (a) helium atom, (b) neon atom, (c) sodium ion, and (d) chlorine ion.

one is nonreactive or inert. Because of their complete nature, these "noble gases" do not react with other elements. Having the outermost energy level full of electrons gives stability to atoms, and in nature, there is a mechanism for arranging this stability.

Combinations of Elements

All of the elements other than the noble gases have incomplete outer energy levels, which can result in either the loss or gain of electrons in reactions with other atoms. These reactions form combinations of atoms called **molecules.** Understanding these combinations is important because they dominate the composition of our world.

Molecules are the smallest units of **chemical compounds,** which are combinations of two or more atoms. The number of electrons in the outermost energy level is the control on molecular formation. For example, in figure 2.8, common table salt is shown as a combination of sodium (Na) and chlorine (Cl). The sodium atom contains a single orbital electron in its outermost energy level. The great distance between the nucleus and that single electron enables the latter to overcome the attractive force of the protons and escape. With one less electron, the atom loses its electrical balance and becomes positively charged. This new form of sodium is an **ion,** which is an atom with an electrical charge. By contrast, the chlorine atom has seven electrons in its outermost energy level. To complete its outer shell, the chlorine atom simply picks up the single electron that abandoned the sodium atom or any free electron. With the addition of the new electron, the chlorine becomes a negatively charged ion because it contains more electrons than protons.

The two oppositely charged ions can now attract one another and form a molecule. This welding together of oppositely charged ions is called *ionic bonding* and is an important mechanism by which chemical compounds are created. Bonding can occur in other ways as well, such as by the sharing of electrons in outer shells by adjacent ions, an arrangement known as *covalent bonding* (*co,* meaning "with"; *valentia,* meaning "capacity"). This, too, has the effect of forming filled outermost electron shells and, consequently, of giving stability to the atoms. As you will see in chapter 14, this is the mechanism by which the water molecule forms.

Isotopes

Atoms can also alter their atomic mass units by the addition of neutrons to the nucleus, which is the same process by which all but one of the elements formed. Common hydrogen has a single proton in its nucleus. A second form of hydrogen, called **deuterium,** has a proton and a neutron in the nucleus (fig. 2.9). Such an atom differs not in atomic number but in atomic mass. The different atomic weight makes deuterium an **isotope** of hydrogen. Hydrogen has another isotope called **tritium,** an atom with two neutrons and one proton in the nucleus. Isotopes, therefore, are variants of an element based on mass number. Because the atomic number is based solely upon the count of protons and because that number does not change for isotopes of an element, the atomic number becomes the most fundamental characteristic for categorizing the elements.

COLD DARK SPACE

We do not see light, but rather, light sources and whatever light illuminates. In space, light mostly travels through a vacuum, but it impinges on objects that allow it to pass on, that reflect it, or that absorb it. Between the widely scattered objects of the universe, however, light energy passes without illuminating anything. Thus, space is dark, not light, and we observe either that which emits light or that which reflects it (see box 2.1).

Figure 2.7 The periodic table of elements.

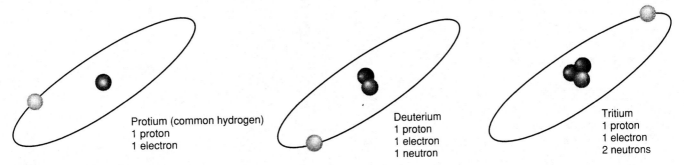

Figure 2.8 A molecular model for common table salt, halite.

Protium (common hydrogen)
1 proton
1 electron

Deuterium
1 proton
1 electron
1 neutron

Tritium
1 proton
1 electron
2 neutrons

Figure 2.9 The three isotopes of hydrogen.

Outer space is also cold. Our astronauts wear protective suits to provide a livable environment and to insulate them from the cold whenever they emerge from their spacecraft for space walks. But what does "cold" mean?

MOLECULES, TEMPERATURE, AND ENERGY

Of all the interrelationships we find on Earth and in the universe, the one between matter and energy is the most fundamental. Although it finds its expression in different forms, this relationship manifests itself in one commonly known way: **temperature.**

In a general way, everyone understands temperature. Weather forecasters tell us that the next day will be 21° C (70° F). We learn the scale they use by experience. We know that a day when the temperature reaches 35° C (95° F) is much hotter than one on which the temperature is only 0° C (32° F). The letters *F* or *C* are abbreviations for two scales. The **Fahrenheit** (F) scale uses 32° as the initial freezing temperature of water and 212° as water's initial boiling point. The **Celsius** (C), or centigrade, scale uses 0° and 100°, respectively, for freezing and boiling. Both scales meet at −40°. Scales are used as measuring devices because they quantify the observable. Just what do temperature scales measure?

Atoms are highly energetic entities. As you read earlier, electrons make high numbers of revolutions in their energy shells every second. Molecules possess similar motions. A water molecule, for example, written chemically as H_2O, breaks up and reforms hundreds of thousands of times every second. In addition to this internal molecular activity, molecules move and interact within their environment. This random motion is interpreted as **heat,** as molecules vibrate against one another. Faster motions among molecules generate greater heat.

Motion is a common form of energy release. In fact, **energy,** often defined as the ability to do work, usually means infusing some matter with motion. All forms of matter are associated with some motion. Earth orbits the sun, the wind blows, trees sway, people walk, and at the unseen level of atomic vibration, electrons move in their shells. Because energy provides the mechanism that drives all earth processes discussed in this text, we will review the forms energy takes.

Potential energy is "stored" energy, or the energy that any body possesses because of its position or location. Water behind a hydroelectric dam, before it is sent through the turbines under the force of gravity to produce electricity, possesses potential energy. A boulder on a hillside also possesses this form of energy, as does a child poised on a diving board.

The energy of motion is called **kinetic energy.** Thus, when the water rushes through the turbines, it releases kinetic energy. Similarly, as the boulder rolls downhill or the child dives into the water, they release kinetic energy. On the molecular level, the vibrational motion of the individual

ions releases kinetic energy. Thus, temperature is more specifically defined as the mean kinetic energy of molecules. In addition to the Fahrenheit and Celsius scales, the Kelvin (K) scale measures this kinetic energy from a hypothetical status of no molecular motion, called **absolute zero.** The relationships among these three scales are shown in figure 2.10.

How hot can matter get? This question is similar to asking how fast molecules and ions can vibrate. Although outer space is cold, the cold is interrupted by intense concentrations of kinetic energy. One such concentration was the supernova Sanduleak, discussed at the beginning of this chapter. Estimates of the energy inside the core of this exploding star put its temperature during a 10-second outburst at 100 billion K. Temperatures greater than these were once the norm for our universe. Sufficient evidence now suggests that *the universe had a very hot origin.*

THE ORIGIN OF THE UNIVERSE

Astronomers have determined that the farthest observable sources of electromagnetic radiation are billions of light-years away. That also means, of course, that they are billions of years old. The most distant objects are also among the most energetic, and their red shifts indicate radial motions that make them appear to be moving

$$°C = 5/9(°F - 32) = °K - 273$$
$$°F = 9/5°C + 32$$
$$°K = °C + 273$$

Figure 2.10 Relationship between the Fahrenheit (F), Celsius (C), and Kelvin (K) temperature scales.

away from us at a rate more than one-tenth that of light speed. *The universe appears to be expanding.*

Other evidence seems to support this expansion. In 1989, NASA launched *COBE* (*COsmic Background Explorer*), a satellite that has confirmed a background radiation that seems to be related to an expanding universe. The background radiation is a low-temperature phenomenon, colder than anything commonly experienced on Earth. Unlike the radiation in your microwave or in your fireplace, this radiation cannot be recorded on an ordinary household thermometer. It lies at a temperature of only 2.7 K. This radiation has no point source. Unlike a beam of light from a flashlight, which your eyes can follow back to its source, the background radiation seems to be originating almost equally from every direction. The most commonly accepted theory to explain both the apparent expansion of the universe and the background radiation is known as the **big bang theory,** the rapid expansion of superheated matter between 12 and 15 billion years ago (new evidence suggests that the big bang may have occurred between 9 and 12 billion years ago—see box 2.1).

The big bang theory is the temporal limit of science. The scientists who have worked on its description cannot be certain about the moment it occurred, but they can explain what happened in the first microseconds of the expansion. The explanation goes something like this: About 12 to 15 billion years ago, the universe was unformed. It existed as a superheated form of matter called **plasma,** occupying a significantly smaller volume than the present universe. A plasma is composed of the parts of atoms, but its high temperatures prohibit atom formation. The temperatures of the big bang plasma may have reached 10^{32} K. At that high temperature, gravity, the strong and weak nuclear forces, and electromagnetism were probably not separate, and not even the elementary particles (protons, neutrons, and electrons) could exist. This condition prevailed for about one billionth of a second. With the rapid expansion of the plasma during the big bang, electromagnetic wavelengths increased and

temperatures dropped (hotter, blue wavelengths, for example, stretched to become cooler, red wavelengths). By the end of the first full second, the temperature of the universe had fallen to tens of billions K, and this drop was accompanied by a rapid formation of elementary particles. Between 3 and 5 minutes after the big bang, protons and neutrons formed nuclei (nucleosynthesis) of hydrogen and helium. For about 300,000 years, however, the universe was still too hot for electrically neutral atoms to form because highly energetic photons knocked electrons away from protons. During, or shortly after, this time, the universe became cool enough for atoms of hydrogen, deuterium (hydrogen nucleus with a neutron), helium, and some lithium to form (fig. 2.11). *COBE* detected the radiation from this atomic synthesis, and the Hopkins Ultraviolet Telescope (HUT) carried by the space shuttle in March 1995 as part of the Astro 2 Observatory, confirmed the presence of primordial helium that was associated with the background radiation.

As already mentioned, the rapid expansion of the plasma following the big bang was accompanied by a rapid temperature

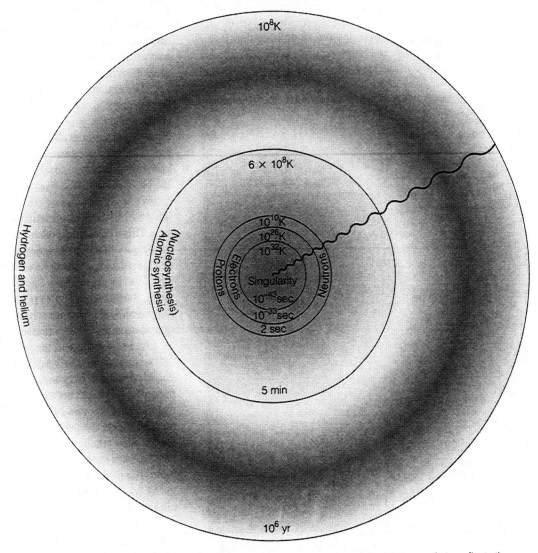

Figure 2.11   Model of the big bang. Units shown are time and temperature, not distance. Color reflects the stretching of the electromagnetic energy in an expanding universe. Shorter and hotter blue wavelengths give way to longer and cooler red wavelengths. Today the background radiation is about 2.7 K.

drop, allowing, in sequence, neutrinos, electrons, protons, and neutrons to form. An opposite kind of matter also formed. Called **antimatter,** it was composed of antineutrinos, positrons, and antiprotons. Whenever antimatter and matter collided, they annihilated each other, producing short-lived subatomic particles and releasing energy. The matter of our universe, therefore, suggests a mystery: Why did the universe not completely alter itself to these ephemeral particles just after the big bang? For some unexplained reason, matter dominated, and antimatter was generally annihilated. There might still be regions of antimatter today, but they would be virtually unrecognizable as such from Earth.

Eventually, the subatomic particles of matter formed atoms, and they, in turn, formed molecules (fig. 2.11). The expansion is generally perceived to be relatively uniform because of the 2.7 K universal background radiation, sometimes called the "echo of the big bang." If the expansion were not approximately uniform, then what could account for the near uniformity of temperature of the background radiation?

A Lumpy Universe

The big bang theory is adequate for explaining the origin of matter and the background radiation, and the slight irregularities in the nearly uniform background radiation detected by *COBE* can explain the distribution of visible matter in the universe. The pic-

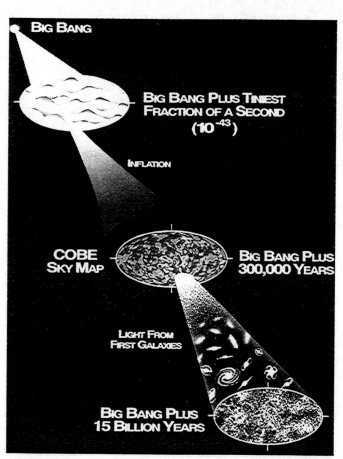

Figure 2.12 COBE DMR (Differential Microwave Radiometer) image of warmer (red) and cooler (blue) temperatures of 300,000-year-old universe. Temperature variations may be related to the lumpiness of the universe and the formation of galaxies.

ture of the universe now emerging is one in which matter has been lumped together into many objects, including stars, and aggregations of stars called **galaxies.** Earth, for example, is composed of matter, and it belongs to a group of loosely similar bodies called the planets. The planets, in turn, belong to a larger system held together by the gravity of the sun, which is a large concentration of gases and plasma. The sun, though apparently widely separated from other suns, belongs to an aggregation of an estimated 100 billion suns called the **Milky Way Galaxy.** The Milky Way is itself part of a group of galaxies. This lump of matter, covering millions of light-years, is just one of billions of similar lumps. When NASA astronomers announced in 1992 that the *COBE* satellite had detected minute variations in the temperature of the "echo" radiation of the big bang, they established the reason for the distribution of matter. These variations appear to explain the lumpiness; that is, *the big bang was not a perfectly uniform expansion.* The *COBE* "sky map" image of figure 2.12 reveals a universe that was already uneven just 300,000 years after the big bang.

Galaxy Lumps

Individual galaxies like the Milky Way contain not only billions of stars but also dust and gases as interstellar ("between the stars") matter. Some of the smaller star aggregations have been called **globular clusters.**

The explanations for galaxies that derive from the big bang model suggest that once matter began to mix out of the rapidly cooling plasma, gravity began to dominate its location. Smaller clusters of matter gradually pulled together to make larger clusters. This may not seem like a problem, but astronomers want to know why the matter of the universe is distributed in lumps. The big bang offers a solution to the problem of lumpiness. In this *cosmology,* or model of the universe, the lumpiness of matter results from the accumulation of increasingly larger galaxy clusters. This explanation of the universe relies on a very high initial density of electromagnetic radiation and plasma. At the great temperatures and densities of the big bang plasma, electromagnetic radiation could not have traveled through the opaque universe. With increasing expansion and declining temperatures, the universe became more transparent, and gravity became the dominating force that created the matter lumps (fig. 2.12).

A brief summary of the universe might read like this: The first 100 seconds of the big bang comprise the era of radiation. After this era, matter and energy separated, and an era of matter dominated the universe. Matter became associated with gravity, the chief control on the lumpiness of the universe. The current distribution of matter reflects the uneven nature of the big bang that *COBE* detected. As a result, the matter of the universe appears to be distributed very much like random cracks in a pane of glass, and the lumps lying along these "cracks" attract one another. For example, the Milky Way and its local group of associated galaxies are moving rapidly toward a lump of galaxies called the Great Attractor. Although we do not feel the motion, our galaxy is traveling about 600 kilometers per second (or over 1 million mph) toward this large, distant lump of matter.

The Hubble Space Telescope has enabled us to see lumps, or more precisely, clusters, of galaxies with greater clarity than was previously possible from ground-based observatories. The Coma Cluster, shown in figure 2.13 represents one such cluster. Containing at least 1,000 large galaxies like NGC 4881, seen on the left side of the image, the Coma Cluster comprises a group of thousands of galaxies that lie 300 million light-years from Earth. Within the image, but not within the Coma Cluster, is a pair of colliding galaxies, providing evidence that galaxies can interact as they move through the universe.

GALAXY STRUCTURE AND INTERACTION

Originally coalescing from lumps of hydrogen and helium, galaxies began to form under the influence of gravity about 1 billion years after the big bang. In visible light, some galaxies evolved as flattened disks of stars, gases, and dust, whereas others seem more spherical, and still others appear somewhat shapeless, or irregular (fig. 2.14). The strongest controls on these shapes are gravity,

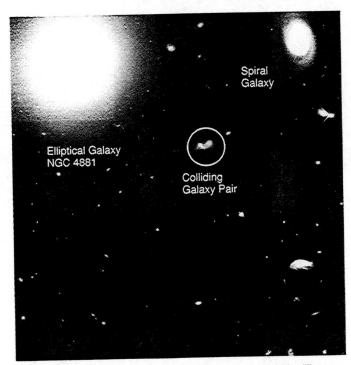

Figure 2.13   The Coma Cluster of galaxies lies about 300 million light-years from Earth. It contains about 1,000 large galaxies and thousands of smaller galaxies. An example of a large elliptical galaxy can be seen on the *left*, where NGC 4881, three times larger than our galaxy, spans 300,000 light-years. Mapping the entire cluster would require about 1,000 Hubble Space Telescope images similar to the one shown. The colliding galaxies seen in the image lie beyond the cluster.

Figure 2.14   Hubble classified galaxies by shape. (*a*) Spherical. (*b*) Elliptical. (*c*) Barred spiral. (*d*) Spiral.

Ring of
new stars

Re-emerging
spiral arm

Figure 2.15   Cartwheel Galaxy, 500 million light-years from Earth. Another galaxy passed through the Cartwheel, generating a shock wave that pushed gases outward at 322,744 kilometers per hour (200,000 mph). New stars are forming in the outer, compressed ring.

angular momentum, or "spin," and the rate of formation as lumps of matter contracted and rotated. Rapid star formation in an early, gassy stage of galaxy development, called the protogalaxy, may have produced the spherical shapes. Spiral galaxies may have resulted from slower formation and increased spin. Elliptical galaxies may reflect the randomness of their stars' movements. Apparently, galaxies may change their shapes, but the causes for change are debatable. The Cartwheel Galaxy of figure 2.15 and the colliding pair of galaxies of figure 2.13 reveal one possible mechanism for change: interaction among neighboring galaxies.

Attraction among galaxy clusters is a force that moves a galaxy like ours at high speed through the universe. Because countless galaxies are involved, some pass through each other during their wandering, though their individual stars may only rarely collide. In October 1994, the Wide Field and Planetary Camera 2 on the Hubble Space Telescope recorded an image of the Cartwheel Galaxy that lies 500 million light-years from us (fig. 2.15). This galaxy, about 1.5 times larger than the Milky Way, appears to have undergone a collision with one of the two galaxies shown on the right. The collision changed the shape of the Cartwheel Galaxy. As

the other galaxy passed through the Cartwheel Galaxy, it produced a wave of energy that moved gas and dust at more than 322,000 kilometers per hour (200,000 mph), compressing them into an expanding ring of billions of newly forming stars. The collision quickened the pace of star formation and reshaped the Cartwheel Galaxy, which is forming new spiral arms that are faintly visible between the outer ring and the core. Other collisions in the universe have distorted the original shapes of some galaxies and made others appear irregularly shaped.

Galaxies are large, and our own galaxy's great dimensions prevent us from knowing its exact shape. Astronomers estimate that the Milky Way has a diameter of 100,000 light-years and a core thickness of 10,000 light-years. Since we cannot get outside our own galaxy to look back—the distances are too great—we must look toward other galaxies to discern their general form and to surmise the shape of the Milky Way. The structure of galaxies can be generalized from the photo of the Andromeda Galaxy in figure 2.16. The structure includes a core, or bulge, where stars are most densely located. Even though they are relatively close, they are still billions to trillions of kilometers apart. Outside the core is

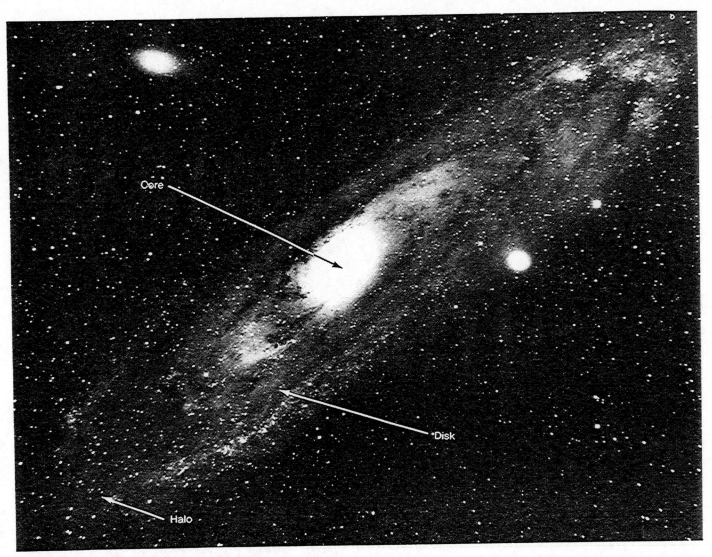

Core

Disk

Halo

Figure 2.16   The Andromeda Galaxy.

the disk, which contains relatively young stars and gases. These young stars are known as *population I* stars. A halo encompasses the disk and contains clusters of older, *population II* stars with little or no interspersed gases. Finally, a large region probably at least as large as the visible galaxy lies outside all that is seen. This is the featureless region suspected to contain **cold dark matter,** so-called because it is only indirectly detected.

The revolving disks of galaxies present a problem. They should rotate at varying speeds, with faster rates nearer the central core of each disk, but they do not. Instead, many disks show a uniform rotation speed throughout their visible mass. The only solution to this problem appears to lie in some missing mass, the assumed cold dark matter of the universe. Recent speculations about the cold dark matter suggest that it is the dominant form of matter, greater by far than the hydrogen and helium of the visible cosmos and making up as much as 95% of the universe. Its assumed low temperature may be near that of absolute zero, and it is not detected by any of our current astronomical instruments. Knowledge of the cold dark matter, therefore, is limited to what can be derived from the motions of the galaxies and from its possible absorption and refraction of electromagnetic radiation. Speculation

about the composition of cold dark matter varies widely. Some suspect that neutrinos may account for the missing mass; others suspect as yet unidentified clouds of hydrogen or some superdense material produced in the big bang.

THE FORMATION OF STARS

Each of the billions of galaxies contains millions to billions of stars. Our own galaxy, which is not unusual, has an estimated 100 billion stars. For certain, then, stars are common objects in the universe, and our own sun, whose structure is treated extensively later in this chapter, is such an object.

Our sun, which is similar to many stars, is composed chiefly of hydrogen and helium and is about 5 billion years old. Its large gravitational attraction holds in orbit nine planets and numerous smaller bodies that, together with the sun, make up the **Solar System.** The origin of this hydrogen ball and its attendant bodies lies in a contraction of matter within one of the "arms" of the Milky Way's disk.

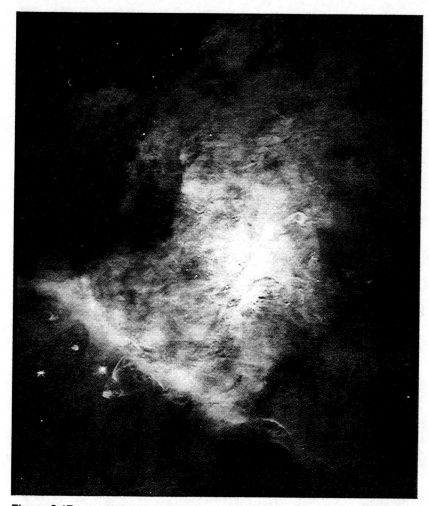

Figure 2.17 A stellar nursery in the Orion Nebula.

Figure 2.18 A newborn star illuminates a dusty disk, while the star itself remains cloaked behind a dense band of dust. The jet originates from either the innermost region of the disk or from the star itself. The bar in the lower *left* represents 1,000 times the Earth-sun distance.

Stages in Stellar Evolution

From its beginning to end, a star undergoes a series of changes dependent upon its initial mass. Generally, these changes fall into beginning, middle, and end stages in the life of a star.

The First Stage: Nebular Collapse The collapse of a cloud with the mass equivalent to our Solar System eventually makes a very dense, opaque nebula that begins to radiate and absorb infrared energy. This first stage of stellar development, which produces a *protostar,* takes place beneath a thick, energy-absorbing blanket of dust and gas, through which only radio waves easily pass. During its protostar stage, our sun probably covered thousands of astronomical units, but it continued to collapse.

Eventually, the protostar heats mechanically by kinetic energy through movements of gas and dust in the shrinking volume of the cloud. When its outer layers reach temperatures between 2,500 K and 3,500 K, the protostar begins to give off light that penetrates the surrounding gas and dust. Figure 2.19 shows the protostar and subsequent stages of stellar evolution.

The Second Stage: Turning on the Solar Furnace During the second stage of development, a young star produces a fluctuating release of energy that makes it variable in appearance. As it strives to reach an equilibrium between gravitational collapse and expansion from its energy output, it turns into an intermediate, cool, variable stellar object known as **T Tauri** (named after a particular star). In a vast nebula from which many stars can form, T Tauri stars often appear in groups called T associations.

The mechanical generation of heat and light is not the main source of a star's energy. Deep inside the mass of gas, which is mostly hydrogen, the protons of hydrogen atoms are driven so

Nebulae and Star Formation

Stars arise from giant "clouds" of gases and dust called **nebulae,** which may be more than 1 parsec thick. Gravitational contraction, enhanced either by a supernova's shock wave or by magnetic fields, compacts the cloud. Eventually, a large nebula divides into many smaller nebulae that may evolve into individual suns and solar systems. The Orion Nebula, a large, gassy cloud that lies 1,500 light-years from Earth, is an example of this type of stellar nursery, where young stars are forming from individual nebulae (fig. 2.17).

Each newly forming star appears to have its own cloud of gases and particles that may condense into planets. The individual nebulae are initially cold, but as they begin to rotate, their temperature rises. Because a nebula is vast, its rotational contraction to the size of our sun would spin parts of the cloud close to the speed of light if some force did not slow down its turning. Magnetic field lines of nearby gas clouds may direct some of the momentum (the "angular momentum") away from the cloud during its early stages of collapse. The Hubble Space Telescope revealed another mechanism that slows a cloud's rotation. Apparently, a young star can eject enormous volumes of gas perpendicular to the plane of its rotation. The ejection robs the disk of some of its angular momentum (fig. 2.18).

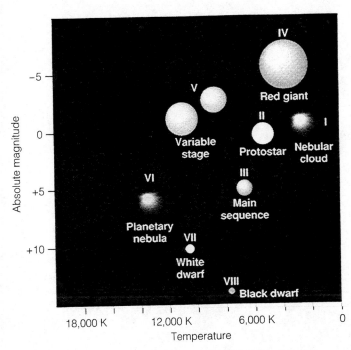

Figure 2.19 Stellar evolution based on the mass of Earth's sun.

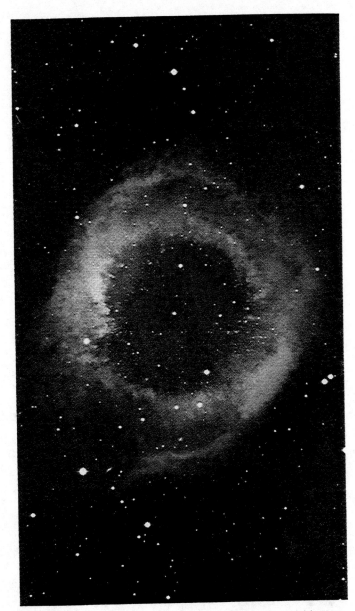

Figure 2.20 Ring nebula formed by the explosion of a variable star. The star's core, a white dwarf, is shown in the center.

closely together that they begin to join or fuse to form helium and release energy. This **fusion** of protons generates temperatures in excess of 15,000,000 K in the core of a *main-sequence* star like our sun and supplies enough outward energy to halt the star's further gravitational collapse.

The Third Stage: From Stability to Instability As long as a main-sequence star has an adequate supply of hydrogen for fusion, it remains relatively constant in size and energy output; thus, an equilibrium characterizes the third stage. The surface of our sun, for example, has not radically altered its radiation during recorded time, maintaining its approximate 6,000 K temperature.

Remember that Sanduleak is evidence that stars are not eternal. Even our sun will change from its current, main-sequence stage to a larger, different-colored star. Whenever our sun has used about 60% of its hydrogen in fusion reactions, it will resume its initial collapse. As a result, its interior will become tens of millions of degrees hotter by compaction, possibly reaching 100,000,000 K, and it will turn helium into carbon during a stage known as the **helium flash.** The release of energy from helium fusion will do two things. First, it will halt the collapse. Second, it will make the outside layers of the sun expand into a **red giant,** an enormous star with a relatively cool exterior. Some red giants have diameters approaching 10 AU, but our sun will probably swell to no more than 2 or 3 AU. Eventually, the outer part of a red giant, comprising at least 10% of the star's mass, will detach itself from the core, making a *planetary nebula* like the ring nebula pictured in figure 2.20 and the Cat's Eye Nebula shown in the opening photo of this chapter.

During this last stage of development, the star's interior shrinks further, becoming a **white dwarf** only a few times larger than Earth. The small size of a white dwarf is not an indication of its mass, however. Except for the expulsion of a planetary nebula, the remnant core of a white dwarf may contain as much mass as our sun. The extraordinary gravitational compaction of matter into the stellar interior results in a star that has a density greater than anything in our Solar System. So much matter is packed into so little space in a white dwarf that a cubic centimeter of its matter would weigh at least a metric ton on Earth. Within this compact, hot white dwarf, ordinary gases like those found in our atmosphere cannot exist. At the very high temperatures found in the dwarf, electrons separate from atomic nuclei, producing a **degenerate gas.**

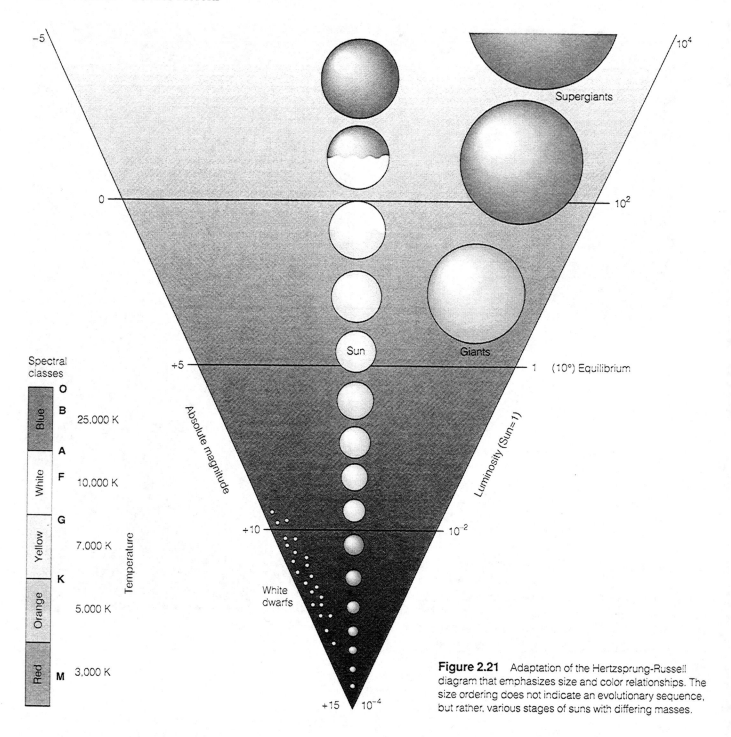

Figure 2.21 Adaptation of the Hertzsprung-Russell diagram that emphasizes size and color relationships. The size ordering does not indicate an evolutionary sequence, but rather, various stages of suns with differing masses.

The Hertzsprung-Russell Diagram

Astronomers categorize stars on the bases of their mass, size, color, and surface temperatures. Stars exhibit wide ranges of these properties. Our sun, for example, is an average star, though it is large enough to encompass 1 million Earths. As large as that may seem, it is small by comparison with giant and supergiant stars, which may be larger than thousands of our suns. Other stars are more massive or brighter, and some are much hotter than our sun. A white dwarf, for example, may have a surface temperature in excess of 12,000 K.

These properties can be visualized on the **Hertzsprung-Russell diagram,** usually shown as a graph similar to figure 2.19, but altered in figure 2.21 to emphasize stellar size and color. The diagram shows the relationship between star luminosities and surface temperatures. As a classification based on size, figure 2.21 begins at the bottom with the ultimate gravitational collapse of a massive star, which cannot be halted by any energy output. Such a point is called a **black hole,** and it represents the end of a star about ten times more massive than our sun. When such a star begins its final gravitational contraction, it crushes itself into a gravitational point. Its gravity is evident, but nothing of the former

1. Two hydrogen nuclei (protons) are driven close together in the sun's core. One proton decays to a neutron and a nucleus of deuterium is formed.

2. The deuterium nucleus and a single proton fuse to form helium ($_2He^3$).

3. Two helium ($_2He^3$) atoms combine to form an atom of common helium ($_2He^4$). Two protons are lost in this process and a significant amount of energy is released.

positron

neutrino

Figure 2.22 The proton-proton fusion reaction is a three-step process that occurs under great pressure and high temperature.

star remains to be seen. Unlike objects that are visible because light can escape from them, the black hole has no escape velocity. In contrast, Earth's escape velocity is 40,000 kilometers (24,800 mi) per hour, the speed the astronauts aboard the *Saturn V* rocket had to attain to travel to the moon. With a gravitational attraction billions of times greater than we experience on Earth, a black hole is too powerful for light to escape; thus, it is black.

Farther up the scale are the main-sequence stars. Their color and absolute magnitudes are close to that of our yellow sun, which is marked on the vertical line. With the red giants, however, both the color and the magnitude change, and the hot blue giants have magnitudes in negative numbers. Although the red giants have cooler surface temperatures than our sun, they are so much larger that their extensive surface area radiates more total energy.

In addition to the numerical designation given to each star on the basis of its luminosity and temperature, the key in figure 2.21 also marks the spectral classes, specified by capital letters for a star's characteristic spectrum. Our sun, for example, falls into the spectral class G, giving it a surface temperature between 5,000 K and 6,000 K and a yellow color. The spectral type O stars can be a million times more luminous than our sun.

THE SUN

The most influential body in the Solar System is the sun. Its gravity holds the system together, and its energy illuminates the planets. To comprehend the full story of Earth's atmosphere, as presented in chapters 4, 5, and 6, you should understand the source and nature of the energy that drives the various gases in the process we call weather.

Fusion and Electromagnetic Radiation

The reactions generating the energy that eventually drives Earth's atmosphere occur in a process known as proton-proton fusion

(fig. 2.22). Although other fusion reactions are possible, the proton-proton reaction is the dominant process of the sun's interior. When two protons are driven very closely together under the intense heat of the sun's core, the strong nuclear force binds them. As figure 2.22 shows, one of the protons decays into a neutron, a positron, and a neutrino, and the departure of the latter two transfers kinetic energy away from the reaction site. Now, the remaining proton and the newly formed neutron are free to combine with another proton, making an isotope of helium. Under the same intense heat and pressure that initially drove the protons together, helium isotopes then combine, releasing two protons with about half the energy obtained in the fusion reaction.

One of the problems most of us have in visualizing this reaction lies in our considering protons and other subatomic particles as separate entities with well-defined boundaries, something like baseballs. The protons that combine do so when they overcome the repulsion they mutually offer because of their positive charges. The analogy most often used to describe this fusion is one given by the German-born American scientist Hans Albrecht Bethe, who envisioned a "tunneling" by one proton into the vicinity of another. With enough protons attempting this joining under the great pressures of the sun's interior, some accomplish it. The production of kinetic energy in the sun's core is just the first step in driving Earth's atmosphere through electromagnetic energy. The energy changes form as it travels from the sun's interior to our planet.

Structure of the Sun and Transposition of Energy

The energy produced by the sun must travel through the sun's layered structure and across the approximate 150-million-kilometer (93-million-mi) vacuum of space to reach our planet. Traversing those obstacles of sun and space changes the form in which the energy is transferred.

Fusion generates energy in the form of shortwave electromagnetic radiation, and it begins a sequence of atomic-scale events that produces a spectrum of energy, including gamma rays, X rays, radio waves, ultraviolet and infrared radiation, and visible light. It is this radiation that eventually makes its way throughout the Solar System and that, today, strikes the planetary surfaces and atmospheres. In addition to electromagnetic radiation, the sun also produces *corpuscular* (from the Latin for "little body") *radiation,* or charged atomic particles, which make up the **solar wind.** The solar wind eventually interacts with Earth's upper atmosphere and its magnetic field, which directs the corpuscular radiation toward our planet's magnetic North Pole.

The Core and Radiative Zone

The sun's energy is generated deep inside its 1.38 million kilometer (863,000 mi) diameter. The central portion of the sun, about one-half the solar diameter, is occupied by a *core,* or solar furnace, in which the fusion reaction converts 400 to 600 million tons of hydrogen into helium and 4 million tons of matter into kinetic energy each second. The reaction occurs inside a plasma that exceeds 15,000,000 K. The core is also under tremendous pressure, probably more than 200 billion times that which we experience under our planet's atmosphere (fig. 2.23). At the diffuse boundary of the core, temperatures drop several millions of degrees, and no fusion occurs. The radiation from the sun's interior then continues outward through a zone that has the density of water. This zone, called the **radiative zone,** extends from the core to about seven-tenths of the way to the sun's surface.

Within the zones of the sun, neutrons make their way to the surface, but positrons collide with electrons, producing short-wave electromagnetic radiation in the form of gamma rays. The gamma rays move to the radiative zone, where they are converted to the less energetic X rays and ultraviolet rays. As this energy passes to the surface, or **photosphere,** energy is transformed to longer wavelengths, producing visible light.

The Convective Zone

Within the upper 30% of the sun's radius is a highly opaque zone, and the radiation initiates a convective activity, where masses of the sun's matter rise and fall as they carry and lose the heat generated by fusion. In this **convective zone,** continuous plumes of gas rise toward the sun's surface to release energy. The time taken by the energy of fusion to pass through the various solar zones may exceed 10 million years.

The Sun's Surface Zone and Atmosphere

Above the sun's surface lies its atmosphere, the only visible part of the sun. The surface zone and atmosphere have three identifiable regions: the *photosphere, chromosphere,* and *corona.*

The Photosphere and Sunspots   The 6,000 K photosphere is the brilliant surface we see. It is this surface that houses **sunspots,** dark depressions in the photosphere with temperatures below 4,000 K (fig. 2.24). A typical sunspot is dark only because it does not emit as much light as the surrounding photosphere. Actually, if we were to see one by itself at night, we would observe an object ten times brighter than a full moon. Sunspots are also associated with strong magnetic fields, and scientists suspect that the magnetism is somehow responsible for the cooler nature of the spots. Additionally, their relationship to the sun's magnetic field is tied to a cycle between maximum and minimum periods of sunspot activity. Periods of greatest sunspot numbers occur on an average of every 11.1 years. Researchers have now identified reversals in the polarity of the sun's magnetic fields. For that reason, scientists also speak of a 22-year cycle linked to those shifts in polarity. Because sunspots can be tracked in their journey across the sun's surface, scientists now know that our star rotates. The rotation is a differential movement, with low

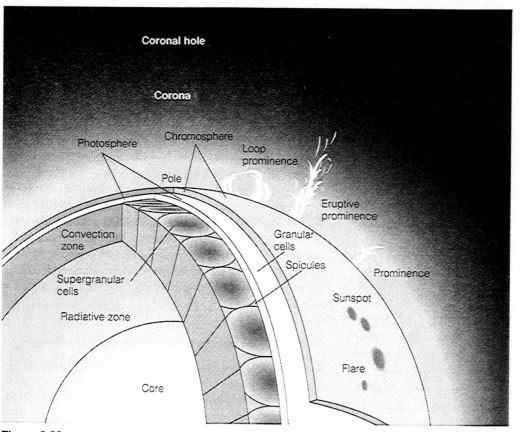

Figure 2.23   Structure of the sun. Energy generated in the core through the proton-proton chain reaction must first pass through the radiative zone, which is the thickest of the sun's spheres. Within the radiative zone, the electromagnetic wavelengths increase toward visible light. Turbulent cells of hot gas then carry energy through the convection zone toward the photosphere, which releases energy to the Solar System.

latitudes moving faster than higher ones. From 10°N of the solar equator to 10°S, the sun rotates once every 27 days.

The Chromosphere and Spicules   The **chromosphere** is a thin, reddish rim from which **spicules, solar flares,** and **prominences** appear to erupt (see fig. 2.23). The eruptions vary in size. Spicules are the smallest and most common of these outward movements of solar gas. Prominences are the largest (fig. 2.25).

The Corona   The outermost part of the sun is a very-low-density, uneven shell called the solar **corona.** The corona is observed when the sun is blocked by the much closer and smaller (but intervening) moon during an eclipse. The corona has a density only a hundred-billionth that of Earth's atmosphere, but it is very hot, reaching temperatures above 2,000,000 K. Both the great temperature of the corona and its shape appear to be the product of magnetism. Observations made by astronauts aboard *Skylab* revealed that the corona is also punctured by "holes," through which charged particles, called the *solar wind,* stream.

Corpuscular Radiation: The Solar Wind

The production of charged particles in the fusion reactions of the sun leads to a "wind" of plasma, composed of highly energetic pro-tons and electrons. This solar wind moves out from the sun at high speed, encountering the planets as it moves through the Solar System. On Earth, the solar wind collides with molecules and atoms in the atmosphere, generating a light called the **aurora borealis,** or the northern lights. In high latitudes, the aurora borealis is a colorful display of wavelike movements. People in Canada and Alaska are fortunate to see these colors frequently. Farther to the south, the aurora loses its colors, and at the latitude of New York City, it is rarely seen. Occasionally, however, a particularly brilliant aurora occurs. In 1991, observers saw a color display in New York State. Ordinarily, when the aurora is visible in the lower 48 states, it is white.

In March 1989, the solar wind produced a geomagnetic storm powerful enough to cause a failure in Quebec's chief electrical grid. The blackout resulted from a surge of direct current in lines that ordinarily carry an alternating electrical current. The mass of plasma in this surge from the sun probably exceeded billions of tons and held enough energy to boil a million cubic kilometers of water.

According to studies made aboard *Skylab,* the solar wind is associated with the *coronal holes.* Coronal holes are 500,000 K cooler than the rest of the corona, and the cooler temperatures seem to be related to the generation of the solar wind.

Figure 2.24 Sunspots appear dark because they are cooler than the background of the photosphere against which they are seen.

Figure 2.25 Solar prominences follow paths dictated by magnetic fields. Often, these paths form arcs of brilliant plasma.

Further Thoughts: Some Say Fire; Some Say Ice

In a clever poem entitled "Fire and Ice," Robert Frost speculates on the end of the "world." Although his poem focuses on destruction by desire or hate, the metaphors of fire and ice aptly pertain to the current argument about the end of the universe.

We have learned about the beginning of the universe in the big bang and about the ensuing rapid expansion. An often-asked question centers on whether or not the expansion will continue indefinitely. If the universe has sufficient matter to exert a gravitational attraction that will slow and stop the expansion, then the universe will begin to contract. If contraction occurs, then a hot plasma will once again be generated in a big crunch. If insufficient matter exists to slow and reverse the expansion, then the ultimate destiny of the universe is to expand and cool even below the background radiation detected by *COBE*.

The importance of the answer lies in its revelations about the kinds and quantities of matter that exist. The search for dark matter (or cold dark matter) has led scientists from particle accelerators to telescopes. Suspect observations point to a variety of potential types of matter, including primordial helium, heavy neutrinos, and dwarf stars. There may even be an abundance of primordial, and very tiny, black holes left over from the big bang.

If the world ends in ice, then a new kind of matter may form. Called a Bose-Einstein condensate, this type of matter forms whenever atoms are cooled close to absolute zero (0 K or $-273°$ C). In 1995, scientist Eric A. Cornell and others at the National Institute of Standards and Technology and at the University of Colorado cooled rubidium atoms to 10 billionths of a degree above absolute zero. At that temperature, the atoms did something that we cannot experience at higher temperatures: They joined, not just as atoms join to make a molecule, but in a way that allowed them essentially to occupy the same state.

If the world ends in fire, then a plasma similar to that just prior to the big bang would form, and temperatures would once again climb to 10^{32} K. Not even protons could survive such temperatures. Such a hot ending might turn immediately into a beginning for a new universe in another rapid expansion. At this point, we may not know whether or not the world will end in fire or in ice, but speculation will drive physicists and astronomers to further discoveries.

Significant Points

1. In addition to other changes, the supernova Sanduleak demonstrates that stars change their shapes. Since our sun is also a star, it, too, will change, ultimately undergoing a kind of death in about 5 billion years.

2. By comparison with the rest of the universe, Earth is a very small object. In their study of objects beyond our planet, astronomers use large measuring units, such as the light-year, parsec, and astronomical unit.

3. Radial and proper motions help astronomers to understand the relationships among the objects beyond Earth. Parallax measurements yield the distances to about 700 stars.

4. Brightness, called magnitude, provides clues to the distance of very distant stars.

5. Light acts like both waves and particles. The unmatchable velocity of light is 299,792 kilometers (186,000 mi) per second.

6. Matter is anything that has mass and occupies space. The fundamental building blocks of matter are protons, neutrons, and electrons.

7. Ninety-two types of naturally occurring atoms, called elements, are arranged by atomic number in the periodic table. Humans have synthesized other elements.

8. Elements can combine to make chemical compounds.

9. The kinetic energy of molecules is expressed as temperature.

10. New evidence suggests that the big bang may have occurred between 8 and 12 billion years ago, but its age is a controversial subject because evidence for an older universe is substantial.

11. A lumpy universe is filled with matter aggregations called galaxies and globular clusters. These are collections of stars, gases, and dust, plus suspected cold dark matter. Many galaxies have older, population II stars in their cores and a halo of stellar clusters. The spiral arms of the galaxy's disk house younger, population I stars and abundant gases.

12. Within galaxies and clusters, large nebulae collapse and divide to become stars and solar systems.

13. A star begins in a nebular cloud, and it evolves through a series of stages. A star can take various forms, including the initial protostar and variable T Tauri forms. The main-sequence star is a form like our sun. After a star such as our sun uses up its fusion fuel, it changes into a red giant, then a planetary nebula, and finally, a white dwarf. Larger stars can become black holes.

14. The sun is the ultimate source of energy for atmospheric movements. Its energy arrives at our planet in two forms: electromagnetic radiation and corpuscular radiation (solar wind).

15. The sun derives its power from the proton-proton fusion reaction in its core, where hydrogen forms helium under temperatures in excess of 15,000,000 K. The fusion releases kinetic energy when subatomic particles leave the reaction site.

16. The sun has a layered structure. Outside the core is a radiative zone, where shortwave gamma rays are produced. This energy migrates to the next zone, called the convective zone, where plumes of gases continuously rise to release energy at the sun's surface.

17. The sun's atmosphere has three regions. The photosphere is the part of the sun we see. It contains cooler regions called sunspots. These sunspots are related to magnetic fields. The chromosphere is the source of spicules, solar flares, and prominences. The corona, visible only during an eclipse, is an uneven plasma of 2,000,000 K with cooler "holes," through which the solar wind "blows."

ESSENTIAL TERMS

supernova *25*
neutrino *25*
light-year (lt-yr) *26*
parsec (pc) *26*
astronomical unit
   (AU) *26*
radial motion *26*
proper motion *27*
Doppler effect *27*
red shift *27*
parallax *27*
magnitude *29*
variable star *30*
photomultiplier *30*

spectrophotometer *30*
photon *30*
electron *30*
matter *31*
atom *31*
proton *31*
neutron *31*
strong nuclear
   force *32*
mass number *32*
atomic number *32*
element *32*
molecule *33*
chemical compound *33*

ion *33*
deuterium *33*
isotope *33*
tritium *33*
temperature *34*
Fahrenheit *34*
Celsius *34*
heat *34*
energy *34*
potential energy *34*
kinetic energy *34*
absolute zero *34*
big bang theory *35*
plasma *35*

antimatter *36*
galaxy *36*
Milky Way Galaxy
   36
globular cluster *36*
cold dark matter *39*
Solar System *39*
nebula *40*
T Tauri *40*
fusion *41*
helium flash *41*
red giant *41*
white dwarf *41*
degenerate gas *41*

Hertzsprung-Russell
   diagram *42*
black hole *42*
solar wind *44*
radiative zone *44*
photosphere *44*
convective zone *44*
sunspot *44*
chromosphere *45*
spicule *45*
solar flare *45*
prominence *45*
corona *45*
aurora borealis *45*

REVIEW QUESTIONS

1. What is parallax? How do astronomers use it?
2. What is the speed of light, and how is it used to establish a measuring scale?
3. What is the difference between radial and proper motion?
4. How does a shift in wavelength reveal the direction of movement for a distant star or galaxy?
5. Why do some stars appear to vary in magnitude?
6. What are the fundamental components of matter?
7. How does atomic number differ from atomic mass number?
8. What are chemical compounds? What is covalent bonding?
9. What discovery led to the big bang theory?
10. What is the echo of the big bang? How did the *COBE* satellite confirm the big bang?
11. What is a galaxy? What forms do galaxies take? How do the star populations vary within galaxies?
12. What are the dominant forms of matter in the visible universe? What kind of matter may actually dominate the composition of the universe?
13. How do stars evolve? What is their primary source of energy in the main-sequence stage?
14. What is the primary source of energy for Earth's atmosphere?
15. What is the source of the sun's energy?
16. What is corpuscular radiation?
17. How is the sun layered? (Draw and label a diagram, showing zonation in the sun.)
18. What is the aurora borealis?

CHALLENGES

1. How far in kilometers (or miles) is an object that lies 2 parsecs from Earth?
2. What obstacles would hamper us from communicating with life outside our Solar System?
3. How are we solar-powered beings?
4. What might cause an increase in intensity in the aurora borealis?

Chapter 3

The Solar System

Chapter Outline

Earth as viewed from the surface of the Moon.

INTRODUCTION

Ancient astronomers were the first to notice that the proper motions of some heavenly lights appear to be very rapid. Unlike the stars, which seem to be stationary, these "wanderers" change positions over the seasons. With the invention of the telescope, observers realized that these bodies are not the same as the stars. They do not lie at great stellar distances, and they follow nearby, somewhat elliptical paths. We call these wanderers the planets.

In this text, some information on the planets is integrated with the discussion of Earth features and processes. The planets that have atmospheres, for example, differ from Earth in the composition, thickness, and structure of their envelopes of gas and clouds. Their atmospheres, however, obey the same physical laws to which Earth's atmosphere is subject. A comparison of planetary atmospheres, therefore, is included in the discussion of atmospheric composition in chapter 4. Similarly, the volcanism with which we are familiar on Earth has its parallel in the history and current geologic activity of some of the other bodies in the Solar System. Thus, planetary geology is included in the discussion on volcanism in chapter 7.

Astronomers eventually catalogued eight planets, in addition to Earth, that orbit the sun. Two are closer than 1 AU, and the other six are farther away. The most distant planet, Pluto, remains an average distance 39 times farther from the sun than we are. Table 3.1 summarizes the characteristics of the planets. The presence of the planets begs a question similar to the one about the universe: What is their origin?

TABLE 3.1 The Planets

Property	Mercury	Venus	Earth	Mars	Jupiter	Saturn	Uranus	Neptune	Pluto
Mean distance from sun (10^6 km)	57.9	108.2	149.6	227.9	778.3	1,427	2,873	4,498	5,914
Mean distance from sun (10^6 mi)	36	67.2	93	141.5	483.3	886.1	1,783	2,793	3,666
Mean distance from sun (AU)	0.387	0.723	1.0	1.524	5.203	9.539	19.18	30.06	39.44
Equatorial diameter (km)	4,880	12,104	12,756	6,787	142,800	120,600	51,300	49,100	2,300(?)
Equatorial diameter (mi)	3,033	7,523	7,928	4,222	89,424	74,914	31,770	31,410	1,519(?)
Mass (g)	3.3×10^{26}	4.9×10^{27}	6.0×10^{27}	6.4×10^{26}	1.9×10^{30}	5.7×10^{29}	8.7×10^{28}	1.0×10^{29}	1.5×10^{25}
Mass (Earth=1)	0.055	0.815	1.0	0.1	317.9	95.2	14.4	17.2	0.1(?)
Volume (Earth=1)	0.06	0.88	1.0	0.15	1,316	755	67	57	0.1(?)
Specific gravity	5.4	5.2	5.5	3.9	1.3	0.7	1.3	1.6	2.0
Period of revolution	88 days	224.7 days	365.26 days	687 days	11.86 years	29.46 years	84.01 years	164.8 years	247.7 years
Period of rotation	59 days	243 days*	23 hr, 56+ min	24 hr, 37+ min	9 hr, 50+min	10 hr, 14 min	17 hr, 12 min*	22 hr	6 days, 9 hr
Inclination of axis	0°	178°	23°27'	23°59'	3°5'	26°44'	82°5'	28°48'	?
Inclination of orbit to Earth's orbital plane	7°	3°24'	0°	1°51'	1°18'	2°29'	0°46'	1°45'	17°12'
Orbital eccentricity	0.206	0.007	0.017	0.093	0.048	0.056	0.047	0.009	0.25
Orbital speed (km/sec)	47.9	35.0	29.8	24.1	13.1	9.6	6.8	5.4	4.7
Number of satellites	0	0	1	2	16	23	15	8	1
Surface temperature (°C)	467(days); −183(nights)	457	25	-50	-130	-185	-200	-200	-230
Ring structure	no	no	no	no	yes	yes	yes	yes	?
Gravity (Earth=1)	0.38	0.90	1.00	0.38	2.54	1.07	1.17	1.2	low
Escape velocity (km/sec)	4.3	10.4	11.2	5.0	60.2	37.0	22.5	23.9	low
Atmosphere (%)	He(98), H_2	CO_2(96), N_2	N_2(77), O_2(21)	CO_2(95), N_2	H_2(89), He	H_2(87), He	H_2, He, CH_4, NH_3	H_2, He, CH_4	CH_4
Surface atmospheric pressure (bars)	10^{-6}	90	1	6×10^{-3}	>>100	>>100	>>100	>>100	?
Magnetic field	Weak	Yes	Strong	Weak	Strong	Strong	Strong	?	?
Internal composition (estimated)	Fe core silicates	Fe-Ni core silicates	Fe-Ni core silicate mantle and crust	Solid Fe-FeS core, silicates	Ice-silicate core, liquid H_2 mantle	Ice-silicate core, liquid H_2 mantle	Rocky core, liquid H_2O mantle	Rocky core, ice mantle, H + He crust	CH_4

*Indicates retrograde rotation

Figure 3.1 The nebular hypothesis for the origin of the Solar System. (*1*) The solar nebula takes form. (*2*) It begins to rotate, then flattens and contracts. (*3*) The nebula is now distinctly discoidal and has a central concentration of matter that will become the sun. (*4*) Thermonuclear reactions begin in the primordial sun as material in the thinner area of the disk condenses and accretes to form protoplanets. (*5*) In this late stage in the evolution of the Solar System, planets are fully formed, and materials not incorporated into planets are largely swept away by solar wind and radiation.

THE NEBULAR HYPOTHESIS

As the sun was contracting from the nebular cloud, the flattened plane of the cloud began to dissociate itself into its own matter lumps (fig. 3.1). Small bodies moving through the dust and gas of the cloud began to collide and accumulate. The largest of these bodies probably had diameters no greater than a few tens of kilometers, and they have been appropriately called **planetesimals** ("little planets").

Even though the orbiting planetesimals traveled swiftly about the newly forming sun, their speed relative to one another was not great, and they were attracted by gravity into larger and larger masses. These larger bodies, called **protoplanets,** were bombarded by planetesimals as they swept through their orbital paths. Earth grew, therefore, from the *accretion of planetesi-*

mals. This accretion began about 4.6 billion years ago, and it most likely ended with a completed Earth by 3.8 billion years ago. The end of the planetesimal bombardment can be surmised from the 3.9-billion-year age for the oldest rocks found on our planet. Any older rock material was probably destroyed by the high-speed impacts of these gravitationally attracted bodies. Because the planetesimals accreted in the nebular cloud from which the sun also formed, this explanation for planetary formation is known as the **nebular hypothesis.**

Our sun's system of planets and other bodies does not appear to be unique. With the help of the Hubble Space Telescope, some satellites, and ground-based radio and optical telescopes, astronomers have now identified increasing numbers of suns enveloped in nebular clouds. The picture of the Orion Nebula, a stellar nursery, in figure 2.17 reveals the common occurrence of disks from which planets can form. Typically, the disks have larger diameters than our Solar System, with the largest observed disk having a diameter of almost 84 billion kilometers (53 billion mi). One of the young Orion stars and its attendant disk are shown in figure 3.2*a.* In figure 3.2*b,* another view of the Orion Nebula shows a disk heated by the star Theta C Orionis, revealing lumps of matter that may be evolving into protoplanets.

As the protoplanets of our Solar System accreted from the nebular cloud, the four closest to the sun formed from an abundance of silicon and iron, becoming largely rocky bodies. These planets— Mercury, Venus, Earth, and Mars—are very dense spheres, and because they are relatively small and Earth-like, are known as the **terrestrial planets** (from *terra,* Latin for "earth"). By contrast, four of the five outer planets are very large. Called the **Jovian planets** (after the Roman god Jove, or Jupiter), Saturn, Uranus, Neptune, and Jupiter are large, gaseous spheres with unknown interiors. The cloud covers on these planets are too thick for cameras and telescopes to penetrate.

Regardless of their clouds and their distance from us, we know much about the planets and other celestial bodies, such as comets and Earth's moon, because of observations made with the aid of telescopes and spacecraft (see box 3.1). We have sent spacecraft to land on both Mars and Venus, and all but Pluto have been visited by instrument packages, such as the *Voyager* craft. In December 1995, the *Galileo* spacecraft sent a probe into the upper atmosphere of Jupiter. What follows is a brief summary of what we have learned.

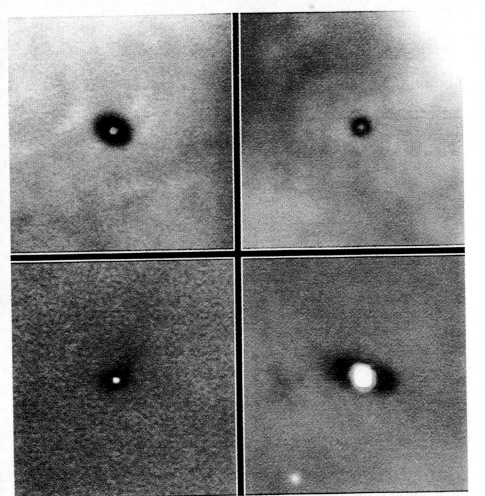

Figure 3.2 (*a*) HST images of newly discovered protoplanetary disks around young stars in the Orion nebula, 1,500 light-years away. These circumstellar disks appear dark against a background of hotter gases. The central red glow of each is a newly formed (1 million-year-old) star with masses ranging from 30% to 150% of our sun. Each image is 257 billion kilometers (167 billion mi) across, or 30 times our Solar System's diameter. (Oxygen appears blue; hydrogen, green; and nitrogen, red.)

Figure 3.2 (*b*) An infrared image of the central Orion Nebula showing thermal emission from dust grains at about room temperature. Several knots of emission (arrowed) appear to be disks of gas and dust which may be precursors of future planetary systems. The cross indicates θ^1 Orionis C, a massive start that in visible light would be the brightest in the field.

THE PLANETS

The nebular cloud from which our sun condensed also produced nine planets. These bodies exhibit quantifiable characteristics, such as their motions, composition, and structure (see table 3.1). We may think that living on a planet makes us all authorities on the nature of planets. In reality, the planets seem to have as many differences as they have similarities.

Planetary Motions

Planets exhibit two types of motion. The first, **rotation,** is a spinning motion centered on an axis. The ends of the axis are the poles, labeled north and south. As planets rotate, they turn their spheroid shapes simultaneously toward and away from the sun. The side opposite the sun experiences night, with little incoming radiation (none from the sun). The side oriented toward the sun experiences day, and the sun's electromagnetic radiation warms the surface. One rotation is a *day,* but each planet's period of rotation (thus, its day) is different.

Earth's rotation has been divided into 24 units, or hours, that represent 15° of rotation (see box 4.1, "Time Zones"). Based on Earth's rotation, other planets have either longer or shorter days. Mercury, for example, requires 59 Earth days for a single rotation; Neptune, by contrast, rotates in only 22 hours (see table 3.1). Because the planets differ in size, each spins about its axis at a different rate. Although Neptune's day is only 2 hours shorter than Earth's, its spinning must be much faster to turn a spheroid about four times larger. Jupiter, the largest planet, turns its 448,620-kilometer (280,934-mi) equatorial circumference in just 9 hours and 50 minutes.

The second type of planetary motion is **revolution,** an almost circular motion around the sun in a path called an *orbit* (see table 3.1). Astronomers designate Earth's revolution as a *year.* Because a period of revolution is dependent on distance from the sun, planets farther than 1 AU have longer years than Earth: Saturn's year is equivalent to 29.46 Earth years; Pluto requires 247.7 Earth years for one revolution. The orbital speed of the planets slows with increasing distance from the sun. Earth travels around the sun at 24.1 kilometers

Box 3.1

EARTH'S MOON

One celestial object we now know very well is the moon. Its diameter of 3,484 kilometers (2,160 mi) makes it smaller than Earth, and its mass is only 1/81 that of our planet. Because gravitational pull is related not only to mass but also to diameter, the moon exerts a pull 1/6 that of Earth's gravitational field. Thus, a 68-kilogram (150-lb) person would weigh 11.4 kilograms (25 lb) on the moon.

The moon's gravitational field is insufficient to hold an Earth-like atmosphere, but the moon does appear to have a thin, asymmetrical veil of sodium atoms that extends almost 14,000 kilometers (8,694 mi). The confirmation of this atmosphere came in 1995, when Michael Mendillo and Jeffrey Baumgardner of Boston University reported their observations during a total lunar eclipse. Produced mostly by sunlight striking the moon's surface, this atmosphere may also be caused by the solar wind and by the impacts of micrometeorites.

As Earth's only natural satellite, the moon revolves around our planet in an elliptical orbit from **perigee,** or its closest position, to **apogee** or its farthest. If we consider the moon's orbit against the reference point of the sun, then one revolution, called the **synodic month** takes 29.53 solar days. Against the background of distant stars, the moon's revolution takes 27.32 solar days, giving us the **sidereal month** (fig. 3.A). Because the moon rotates on its axis only once during a synodic month, observers on Earth see only one side.

One way we characterize the moon is by its so-called phases, or appearances. Throughout a synodic month, the moon appears to undergo a series of shape changes. These result from our view and from the revolution of the moon, which do not always allow us to see the complete sunlit side (fig. 3.B). During the new-moon phase, the side opposite that which faces Earth is lit, but the side facing Earth is in shadow. During the full-moon phase, just the opposite occurs, as the side facing Earth is fully lit. Between these darkened and lightened phases, the moon appears crescent and gibbous. A phase change

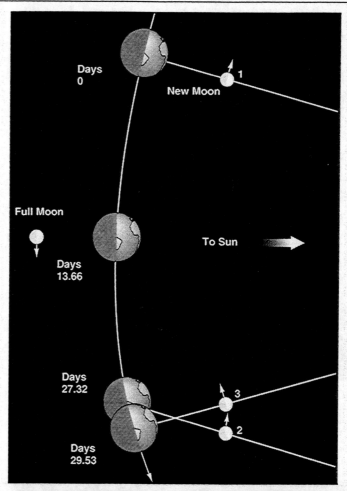

Figure 3.A Difference between a sidereal month and a synodic month. The interval between two successive conjunctions the moon with a given star is 27.32 mean solar days one sidereal month (1–2). The interval between two successive conjunctions of the moon with the sun, however, is 29.53 mean s days, or one synodic mo (1–3). All angular relationships and relative sizes of Earth and the m are to scale.

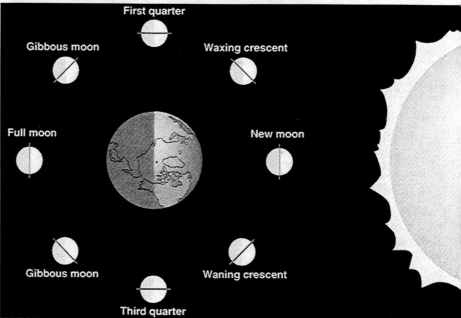

Figure 3.B Phases of the moon.

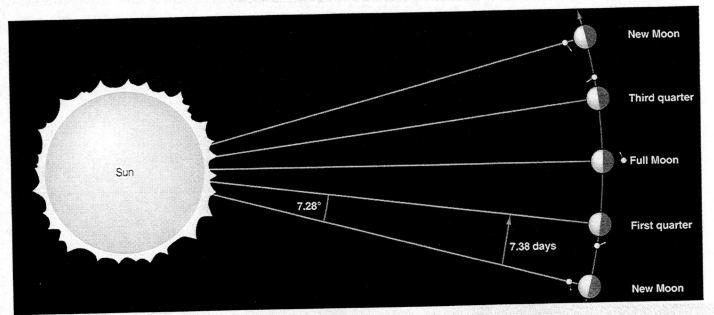

Figure 3.C   One synodic month is the elapsed time between one new moon and the next. At the new moon (*bottom*), Earth, the moon and the sun are all aligned; 29.53 days later (*top*), they are again aligned. The intervening phases of the moon are separated from one another by one-quarter of this interval; 7.38 days, or approximately 1 week, during which time Earth moves through an angle of 7.28° along its orbit. Angles are not exaggerated.

from new moon toward full moon is called waxing, whereas a change from full moon to new moon is called *waning*. The moon appears in a new phase whenever it completes one-fourth of its orbit: Thus, the phases change once every 7.38 solar days (fig. 3.C). During the quarter-moon phases, an interesting visual phenomenon occurs as the light reflected from Earth partially lights the nighttime portion of the moon's disk.

Sometimes, the moon's shadow falls on Earth to make a **solar eclipse.** On other occasions, Earth's shadow falls on the moon to make a **lunar eclipse.** Both lunar and solar eclipses block out some or all of the sun's light. On rare occasions, either Earth or the moon block out the full disk of the sun in a total eclipse (fig. 3.D).

The moon is the only body beyond Earth that human beings have visited, and its proximity (average distance 381,555 km or 236,564 mi) makes some of the moon's features visible to the unaided eye. What is this bright body that, though it gives off no light of its own, can be visible both day and night?

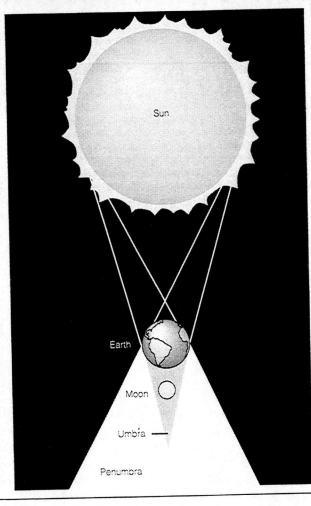

Figure 3.D   Earth's shadow is broad enough to immerse the moon if the moon is aligned with Earth and the sun during opposition. The umbra is the region in full shadow. The penumbra is the partially lit region.

Continued

EARTH'S MOON (CONTINUED)

Because the moon is close to Earth, optical studies of the moon are as old as the human eye, and telescopes provided close-up views of its rugged surfaces long before Neil Armstrong and Edwin Aldrin landed the *Apollo 11* module on July 20, 1969. From the perspective of the unaided, earthbound eye, the moon is a body of contrasting dark and light areas. The reason for the contrasts lies in the **albedo,** or reflectivity, of the moon's surfaces. For example, its plains, called **maria** because they looked like seas to Galileo, do not reflect light as efficiently as its highlands. From the perspective of two astronauts standing on the moon's surface, however, the body is planet-like, wet sand or ash colored, and not nearly as rugged as more distant perspectives from Earth indicate (fig. 3.E).

When the Apollo astronauts returned with moon rocks, they added a new dimension to our knowledge. We now have samples that tell us not only something of the moon's composition but also something of the Solar System's history. Scientists dated the moon rocks through a method known as **radiometric dating.** The rocks yielded various dates, with the oldest sample registering 4.4 billion years. Interestingly, this age agrees favorably with the estimated 4.6-billion-year age of the Solar System, but some moon rocks yield younger ages. Unlike Earth's rocks, those on the moon lie under airless and waterless conditions that prevent erosion on the scale present on Earth. Except for the changes caused by impacts from incoming micrometeorites, meteorites, and high-speed

Figure 3.E *Apollo 17* astronaut Harrison Schmitt collects a lunar sample.

atomic particles, the moon's rocks have undergone comparatively little change over several billion years.

The impacts have been significant, however. Some of the rocks and lunar dust brought back had glassy beads on them, indicating that the rocks had been subjected to heat sufficient for melting and rapid cooling. Heat of this nature is associated with volcanic activity and impacts. Apparently, the two processes are related. Impacts of explosive force have cracked the moon's surface, dug craters, thrown ejecta hundreds of kilometers, and generated enough heat for **lavas** to form. The dark lavas, generally called *basalt,* contrast with the lighter-colored *anorthosite* of the highlands. Both basalt and

anorthosite are **igneous rocks,** which means that they were once molten. Both types of rocks also occur on Earth. Because the basaltic lavas of the moon did not have the same **viscosity** as those of Earth, moon lavas flowed widely after extruding through the **fissures** (or cracks) caused by impact.

Apply Your Knowledge

1. How many solar days are required for the moon to change from new moon to full moon?
2. During which phases do the moon, sun, and Earth lie in a straight line?

per second (14.94 mph), whereas in its orbit, Pluto orbits the sun at 4.7 kilometers per second (2.96 mph).

Planetary Compositions and Structures

The planets differ in composition because they formed in different parts of the nebular cloud. The terrestrial planets seem to be dominantly formed from oxygen, silicon, iron and aluminum, whereas the Jovian planets are gaseous balls of hydrogen and helium. Other elements and many compounds, including those that make up rocks, are also present in the Jovian realm. Water (and thus, oxygen) is an important component, but it exists mostly as ice, such as the particles that make up the

rings of Saturn or its ice-ball moon Enceladus. At least five of Uranus's moons are ice.

The inner planets all appear to have dense cores dominated by iron. These cores vary in size, and each seems to be overlain by a sphere of rocky material called a **mantle.** The outermost structure, the surface, is a crust that has been shaped by volcanic activity, chemical reactions, physical processes, planetesimal or meteorite bombardment, and internal forces. The structure of the outer planets is difficult to determine. The Jovian planets' thick veils of gas prevent observation of their interiors. An attempt to penetrate the atmosphere of Jupiter was part of the *Galileo* spacecraft's mission, and its probe entered the planet's atmosphere in July 1995 (see chapter 4).

Figure 3.3 The highly cratered surface of Mercury.

Mercury

Mercury, the smallest of the terrestrial planets and the closest to the sun, was named for the fleet-footed Roman messenger to the gods. Because of its proximity to the sun, it has the shortest and fastest orbit around the sun (88 Earth days). Its period of rotation, however, is relatively long (58.65 Earth days), which leads to temperature extremes of 467° C on the day side to −183° C on the night side.

The airless surface of Mercury is heavily cratered, with one crater, the Caloris Basin, approximately 1,300 kilometers (806 mi) in diameter (fig. 3.3). Craters are more dominant on highland areas, which are thought to represent older terrain. Basinal areas appear to be filled with lava (although no other volcanic features are apparent) and contain few craters, indicating a decreasing rate of meteorite bombardment and a more recent origin for this terrain. Experts suggest that the volcanic activity occurred early in the planet's history and probably ended some 3 billion years ago. Other surface features include landsliding and cliffs, called scarps, some as much as 3.2 kilometers (2 mi) high and hundreds of kilometers long.

Mercury possesses a magnetic field that is only 1% of the strength of Earth's. Its presence, however, suggests that the planet has or had a liquid core because such fields are attributed to convective currents flowing within a liquid core.

Venus

Venus, named for the Roman goddess of love and beauty because of its brightness in the night sky, is Earth's nearest planetary neighbor. Because of its almost identical size and density, it is often referred to as Earth's twin. Venus is perhaps best known for the 90-kilometer (56-mi) thick layer of clouds composed primarily of carbon dioxide (CO_2) (96%) and Nitrogen (N_2) (3.5%), with small amounts of sulfuric acid droplets. The greenhouse effect (see chapter 1) caused by the thick cloud cover, as well as its nearness to the sun and the atmosphere's composition, imparts to Venus the highest planetary surface temperatures known in the Solar System (about 500° C). The thick cloud cover also gives rise to an enormous atmospheric surface pressure up to 90 times that of Earth's.

The *Magellan* spacecraft, placed into orbit around Venus in August 1990 after a 15-month journey from Earth, mapped as much as 90% of the Venusian terrain. Surveys from the *Magellan* and the earlier U.S. *Mariner* and Soviet *Venera* spacecrafts indicate a subdivision of surface terrain into lowlands and extensive, gently rolling to rugged highlands. The massive Maxwell Montes (mountains) rise some 11,000 meters (36,000 ft) above the adjacent lowland terrain. The identification of volcanic terrain is still tentative, but the *Magellan* probe appears to have detected a lava

Figure 3.4 An enhanced *Magellan* image that shows an apparent lava flow associated with Maat Mons on Venus.

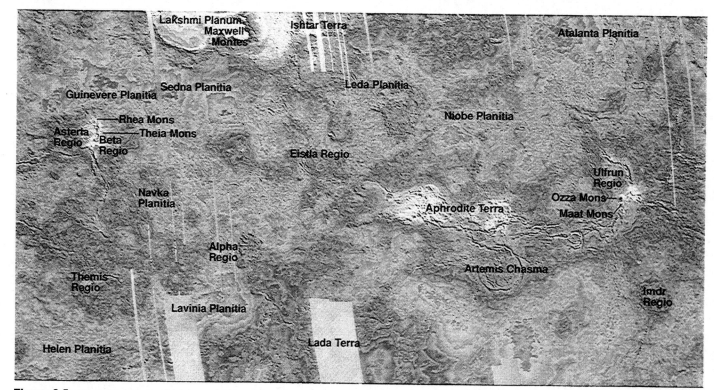

Figure 3.5 Venusian topography from radar imagery.

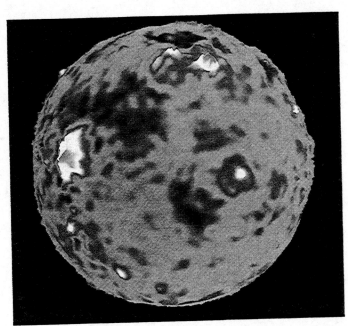

Figure 3.6 Gravity map of Venus. Maxwell Montes is the bright area on the *left* side of the image.

(a)

(b)

Figure 3.7 (*a*) Concentric cracks around Aine Corona. (*b*) Mead Crater, an impact site on Venus.

flow from Maat Mons, the second tallest mountain on Venus (fig. 3.4). Additional data point to large impact craters and rift valleys. This varied surface is hot, dry, and almost certainly lifeless.

The *Magellan* mission to Venus has increased our knowledge of the planet's surface features through radar images and gravity measurements. The former were obtained by bouncing pulses of radio waves off the planet from the elliptical orbit of the spacecraft. The radar penetrated the thick Venusian atmosphere, and the return signal was timed to measure the altitude of the reflecting surfaces (fig. 3.5). Small changes in the orbit of *Magellan,* caused by a stronger or weaker tug of gravitational attraction, enabled scientists to map high-standing features like Maxwell Montes, where the spacecraft eventually crash-landed (fig. 3.6).

Because radar reflects with greater or lesser intensity from varying surfaces, *Magellan* not only mapped the topography of the planet but also gave us clues to its surface composition. Robert Brackett, Raymond E. Arvidson, and Bruce Fegley suggest that the bright reflectance off highlands like Aphrodite Terra and Maat Mons indicates a metallic frost that formed from volcanic gases. Gordon Pettingil, *Magellan's* principal radar investigator, suggests that an iron-sulfur mineral called pyrite (known as "fool's gold") may lie in a thin veneer on the highlands. Most investigators now believe that the outermost rocky layer is a crust of basalt, a volcanic rock commonly found on Earth's ocean floor.

Magellan also revealed the details of interesting surface features. Figure 3.7*a* shows concentric cracks hundreds of kilometers in diameter around Aine Corona. These cracks resulted from an uplift and subsidence when a plume of magma rose beneath the surface and then withdrew to greater depths. In figure 3.7*b*, the circular Mead Crater is Venus's largest impact site and one of 900 such sites on the planet. Apparently, many other impact sites have been buried or destroyed by volcanic resurfacing events estimated to have occurred about 500 million years ago.

Mars

Named for the Roman god of war, Mars is the outermost of the terrestrial planets and is probably the best known and most written about of our sister planets. Although often referred to as the red planet, it varies in color from blue-green during the spring to brown in the fall. The seasonal differences result from an axis of rotation that is tilted to its plane of revolution. With a period of revolution approximately twice that of Earth, Martian seasons are ·longer than Earth's. The Martian day, however, is approximately equal to ours because its period of rotation is only slightly longer. Its distance from the sun makes Martian temperatures relatively low, ranging from a high of 0° C at the equator during the daytime to −130° C at night.

Figure 3.8 View of a rock-littered Martian landscape taken from the *Viking 2* lander.

The surface of Mars is known for a number of interesting features, some of which may be analogous to those on Earth. The *Mariner* orbiters and *Viking* landers sent back photos of a cratered, moonlike surface as well as data on Martian "soil" and rocks (fig. 3.8). When tested by *Viking,* the soils were found to be free of organic compounds and, thus, of any indication of life.

The Martian atmosphere is thin (less than 1% of that of Earth) and consists primarily of carbon dioxide. As thin as the atmosphere is, however, wind is an important surface activity and

gives rise to spectacular dust storms and gigantic dune fields. Mars, in fact, possesses the largest sandy desert in the Solar System. The carbon dioxide atmosphere is also related to the famous polar caps, which expand and contract with the seasons.

Running water apparently played a major role in the early shaping of the Martian surface. Massive canyons, such as Valles Marineris, stretch for hundreds and even thousands of kilometers. Tributary dendritic (branchlike) canyons, meandering channels, and even braided channels are evident. Such features may indicate a time of milder climate during which rainfall occurred or large quantities of ground ice melted (see box 11.2).

The interpreted history of Mars is one of early heavy meteorite bombardment (particularly of the uplands), followed by extensive volcanism. The Solar System's largest volcano, the shield volcano Olympus Mons, is 550 kilometers (341 mi) in diameter and 27 kilometers (16.75 mi) high and dwarfs any similar feature found on Earth (fig. 3.9). Olympus Mons stands on a topographic swell, which may be the upwarping of a "hot spot." Fractures and faults are found around the base of this uplift.

Jupiter

Jupiter, named for the son of Saturn and the king of all the gods in Roman lore, is the largest of the giant outer planets.

Recently, the planet twice attracted worldwide attention: during the week of July 16–22, 1994, when comet Shoemaker-Levy 9 collided in a series of impacts, and during the following July, when the spacecraft *Galileo* sent a probe into the Jovian atmosphere. Jupiter's colorful clouds shot plumes of gases as much as 3,000 kilometers (1,863 mi) upward at the Shoemaker-Levy 9 impact sites (see box 3.2).

Best estimates of the structure and composition of Jupiter attribute to it a core of iron-rich rock, covered by a thick layer of liquid hydrogen, and surrounded, in turn, by dense layers of clouds of hydrogen (mostly) and helium (fig. 3.10). It is not unlike the sun in composition but would have to be some ten times larger to attain temperatures at which it would become self-radiating (i.e., a star).

The thick atmosphere of Jupiter is subject to a complex circulation and storms. The most notable storm is the Great Red Spot, an oval storm that is 40,300 kilometers (25,000 mi) long and 14,500 kilometers (9,000 mi) wide. Smaller storms traverse the planetary atmosphere at speeds of up to 360 kilometers (225 mi) per hour.

Associated with Jupiter are 16 satellites, 4 of which exceed 3,000 kilometers (1,860 mi) in diameter. Analyses made during the passages of *Voyagers 1* and *2* indicate that all of the larger moons have ice-rock crusts and that each also has its own peculiar features. Io, for example, has sulfur-burning volcanoes (fig. 3.11). Europa has a geologically young surface crisscrossed with an intricate system of intersecting lines that may represent faults or fractures in the icy surface. Ganymede has a cratered surface, a "grooved" terrain, and a system of fractured mountains.

Saturn

Saturn, the ringed planet, was studied during the flybys of *Pioneer 11* and *Voyagers 1* and *2*. It was named for the Roman god of time because the planet had the longest period of change in the sky that ancient astronomers could recognize.

Figure 3.9 The Martian volcano Olympus Mons, one of the three largest volcanoes in the Solar System, is shown here with the outline of Missouri for scale. The volcano is about 550 kilometers (342 mi) in diameter and 27 kilometers (17 mi) higher than the surrounding Martian surface.

Figure 3.10 This photomontage of the Jovian System shows Jupiter and its four natural Galilean moons. Cloud bands parallel Jupiter's equator, each flowing in the opposite direction to the adjacent one. Io (*far left*) is closest to Jupiter, followed by Europa (*center*), Ganymede (*lower left*), and Callisto (*lower right*).

Figure 3.11 Sulfur eruption from a volcano on Io, one of Jupiter's 16 moons. Photo was taken from *Voyager II* on March 4, 1979, at a distance of 500,000 kilometers (310,750 mi). Jupiter's gravitational pull on Io may be responsible for a tidal influence.

Box 3.2

*Investigating the
Environment*

WILL AN ASTEROID HIT YOU ON THE HEAD?

In December 1992, a dual asteroid called Toutatis missed Earth by a mere 3.54 million kilometers (2.2 million mi). Toutatis is composed of two, rough edged objects that are 2.6 and 4 kilometers (1.6 and 2.5 mi) in diameter (fig. 3.F).

A smaller asteroid, about 13 meters (43 ft) in diameter and designated 1994 XM₁, missed Earth by about 100,000 kilometers (62,000 mi) 2 years after the flyby of Toutatis.

These asteroids belong to a group of thousands of objects that pass through Earth's orbit and threaten to strike our planet (fig. 3.G). These objects, called **near-Earth-objects (NEOs),** can be as large or larger than Toutatis, and they may be either former asteroids, bumped from the asteroid belt, or the cores of comets.

One NEO that may collide with Earth is the comet Swift-Tuttle (fig. 3.H). Particles strewn throughout its orbit give us an annual August meteor shower. The comet itself will pass close to our planet on August 14, 2126, and recent calculations predict a likely collision in August 3044.

The extinction of the dinosaurs 65 million years ago has been tentatively linked to the impact of a large NEO. If such an object hit the planet today, human existence would be threatened. On impact, an object the size of a football field would release the energy equivalent to a 10-megaton nuclear bomb. The energy released by the collision of an object the size of Toutatis or larger would be devastating.

A telling example of the energy associated with impacts was observed from July 16–22, 1994, when comet Shoemaker-Levy 9 collided with Jupiter in a series of impacts that made Earth-size holes in the planet's atmosphere (fig. 3.I). Broken up by a previous encounter with Jupiter's gravity, Shoemaker-Levy 9 punched holes in the rotating planet's atmosphere, sending plumes of gases 3,000 kilometers (1,863 mi) above the Jovian stratosphere.

Figure 3.F   The near-Earth-object known as Toutatis is composed of two companion asteroids.

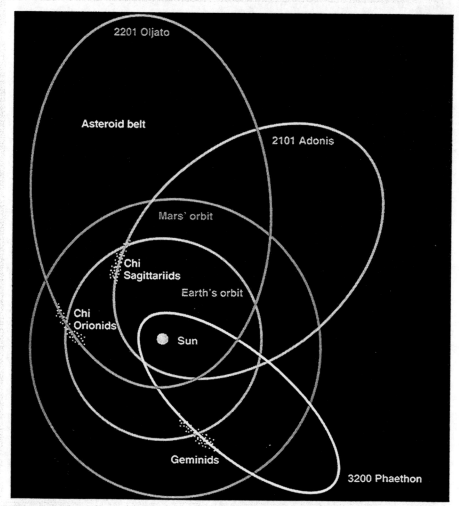

Figure 3.G   The highly elliptical orbits of near-Earth-objects take them on possible collision courses with the inner planets. The orbits shown here are noteworthy because of their associated meteor showers.

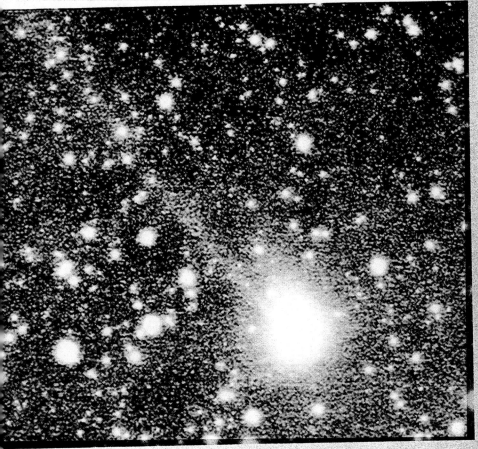

Apply Your Knowledge

1. What is the name of the asteroid that almost struck Earth in 1992?
2. What comet may strike the planet?
3. Why is it difficult to detect many of the potential NEOs?

e 3.H   Comet Swift-Tuttle may strike Earth in August 3044. Here, the comet's tail can be seen.

Figure 3.I   This image of Jupiter reveals the sites of fragments "D" and "G" from Comet Shoemaker-Levy-9. The larger feature occurred when fragment "G" entered the planet's atmosphere from the south at an angle of 45° and struck Jupiter's southern hemisphere at 44° S. The central dark spot of the impact site is 2,500 kilometers (1,550 mi) in diameter. The thin dark ring is 7,500 kilometers (4,660 mi) in diameter, and the outermost ring's inner edge is 12,000 kilometers (7,460 mi) in diameter. By comparison Earth is 12,756 kilometers (7,928 mi) in diameter.

Figure 3.12 Saturn and its rings.

Saturn moves through a 29-year orbit around the sun. Because of its great mass and distance from the sun, Saturn actually generates more heat than it receives. As best as can be determined, Saturn possesses a thick, turbulent atmosphere that is 1,000 kilometers (621 mi) thick and consists primarily of hydrogen. Wind speeds within this atmosphere are estimated to be in excess of 1,775 kilometers (1,100 mi) per hour.

The most notable feature of Saturn has always been its rings (fig. 3.12). Three major rings are easily visible, but close-up photos reveal that these are each composed of 500 to 1,000 smaller rings, which, in turn, consist of billions of particles from the size of icy dust to the size of boulders. The rings are very thin in proportion to their width.

Saturn has more than 20 moons. The largest, Titan, is comparable in size to the inner planets, and its atmosphere will be discussed in chapter 4. Most of Saturn's moons are small, irregularly shaped, and cratered, and consist of ice-rock mixtures.

Uranus

Uranus, named for the Greek god of the heavens, is one of the gas giants, about four times larger than Earth. Much of what we know about Uranus comes from the *Voyager 11* flyby in 1986. Uranus apparently consists of a rocky core; a zone of liquid water, methane,

and ammonia; and a thick cloud layer of hydrogen (87%) and helium (13%). The atmosphere, blue-green in color from methane, shows only a faint banding of its clouds (see fig. 4.7a). While wind speeds of 360 kilometers (225 mi) per hour are estimated, Uranus is the only giant planet without oval storm systems. The planet possesses a magnetic field almost as strong as Earth's, and it is orbited by 15 moons, which show impact craters and fault scarps bounding rift basins. Uranus also possesses a set of 11 rings, which was detected during the *Voyager* flyby.

Uranus differs from the other planets in that its axis of rotation is inclined 98° from the vertical, thus giving it a retrograde (or backward) rotation. As expected at this distance from the sun, its period of revolution is long, some 84 years.

Neptune

Neptune, the fourth largest planet in the Solar System, is the densest of the giant planets. Long before it was actually observed, the presence of Neptune was predicted from perturbations it caused in the orbit of Uranus. Based on data from the 1989 flyby of *Voyager 11*, Neptune appears to be similar in composition and structure to Uranus, including an atmosphere rich in hydrogen and helium (fig. 4.7b). This atmosphere also contains a small amount of methane, which gives the planet a distinct bluish color. Consequently, Neptune is often referred to as the Blue Planet and is named for the god of the sea.

Whereas the atmosphere of Neptune is similar in composition and structure to that of Uranus, it differs in that it is characterized by clouds and numerous oval storm systems. A dark, turbulent zone near the equator and called the Great Dark Spot appeared in our first close-up images, but it has since disappeared. That Neptune is approximately the same temperature as Uranus, but much farther from the sun, suggests that it has an internal heat source.

Neptune has eight moons. Two of these, Triton and Nereid, have very eccentric orbits. The larger, Triton, is similar in size to the inner planets. It has an atmosphere of methane (probably) and an icy crust of nitrogen and methane. The surface is characterized by a series of dark streaks that are thought to have been formed by ice volcanoes driven by liquid nitrogen. In addition to its moons, Neptune also possesses several rings.

Pluto

Pluto, the outermost of the known planets, differs significantly from other planets in that its orbit lies some 17° outside of the plane of the ecliptic. The orbit is so highly eccentric that at times it actually brings Pluto inside Neptune's orbit during Pluto's 248-year journey around the sun. Pluto resembles the outer planets in composition and location but is most akin to the inner planets in size. The idea is widely held that Pluto may not have been a planet originally but rather was a large asteroid or a moon of Neptune that escaped that planet's gravitational pull.

Pluto probably consists largely of ice, with a surface of frozen methane at a maximum temperature of −230° C (−350° F). Its atmosphere is thin and composed of methane and some heavier gases. Pluto has one moon, Charon, which is very close to the planet and has a diameter 40% as large as that of Pluto.

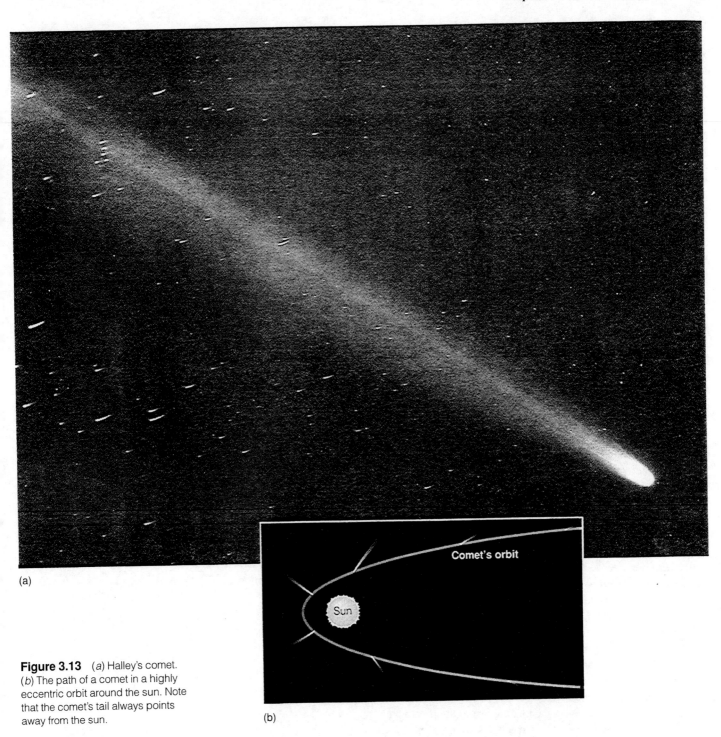

(a)

Figure 3.13 (*a*) Halley's comet. (*b*) The path of a comet in a highly eccentric orbit around the sun. Note that the comet's tail always points away from the sun.

(b)

Speculation regarding the existence of a tenth planet, planet X, is the result of studies of the movements of Charon, which are too large and/or different to be accounted for by the gravitational attraction of Pluto. In addition, Pluto alone has too little mass to account for minor discrepancies in the orbits of the planets from Jupiter outward. In fact, its small mass makes some scientists challenge its status as a planet. Planet X, if it exists, must have a mass two to five times that of Earth and an orbit between 50 and 100 AU from the sun, with a highly inclined plane of revolution similar to that of Pluto.

OTHER BODIES IN THE SOLAR SYSTEM

Three other types of bodies exist in the Solar System: comets, asteroids, and meteoroids. **Comets,** like Halley's comet shown in figure 3.13*a*, are mixtures of ice and rock material that make brief visits to the inner Solar System on their highly eccentric orbits (fig. 3.13*b*). They are characterized by a "tail" of gases

Figure 3.14   The 52-kilometer-(32-mi) long asteroid Ida and its moon Dactyl. Dactyl is 1.6 by 1.4 kilometers (1.0 by 0.9 mi), and it orbits Ida at a distance of 100 kilometers (62 mi).

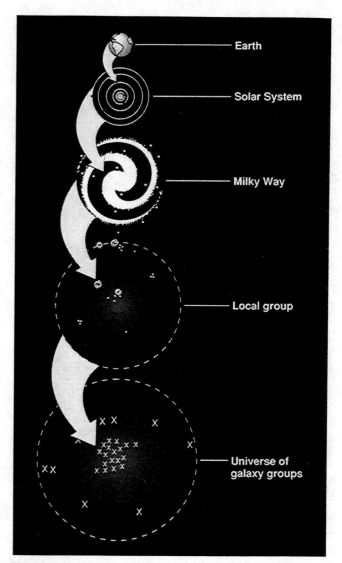

Figure 3.15   Earth's place in the universe.

that streams out from the solid "head" of the comet as it encounters high-speed particles emanating from the sun. The tail, therefore, always points away from the sun, regardless of the direction of the comet's motion. Matter in a comet's tail will be sampled early in the twenty-first century. The *Stardust* spacecraft that will be launched in 1999 will pass within 100 kilometers (62 mi) of comet Wild-2. Then, it will send a return capsule with the comet's "dust" for direct examination in 2006.

Asteroids are solid, rocky bodies that occupy an orbit between Mars and Jupiter. They range in size from dust particles to more than 700 kilometers (434 mi) in diameter, and they number in the thousands. Because of their orbital position, scientists believe that asteroids are fragments that never accreted to form a true planet or that they represent the remains of a disintegrated planet. In August 1993, the *Galileo* spacecraft passed close to 52-kilometer- (32-mi) long asteroid Ida and discovered a small moon named Dactyl (fig. 3.14). Dactyl, about 1.6 kilometers (0.9 mi) long, orbits Ida at a distance of 100 kilometers (62 mi).

Meteoroids are rocky or metallic bodies traversing the Solar System by the millions and intersecting the orbits of Earth and the other planets, where they are influenced by gravity. As they come under the gravitational pull of Earth, for example, meteoroids fall through the atmosphere. Frictional heating makes them burn and glow, causing the streaks of light, or **meteors,** in the night skies. If a meteoroid is so large that it does not burn up completely, its remnant becomes a *meteorite* as it strikes the surface. Some meteorites contain carbon, which has led to the speculation that life is not indigenous to Earth.

FURTHER THOUGHTS: EARTH IS A SPECIAL PLACE

A study of the universe beyond Earth puts into perspective the special character of our planet. Although other suns, such as the star Vega, appear to have systems of associated matter, no one has yet found evidence of other planets with life. We do, however, have a good idea about our place in the universe (fig. 3.15). The great distances between us and other solar systems preclude our traveling to the stars, leaving us with radio-wave receivers and other sensors as our only means of detecting any signs of intelligence beyond our solitary home.

As a small planet that revolves around an average star, Earth's special character is largely determined by its relationship to the sun. In the next chapter, you will read about the sun as the primary influence on the movement of our atmosphere. In the form of electromagnetic radiation, energy produced in the sun's interior strikes our planet's surfaces, warming them and the air that overlies them. Increased warming means increased molecular motion, expansion of the atmospheric gases and surface waters, and decreased density. The lighter, warmed air rises, often carrying with it great quantities of evaporated water, transferring the sun's energy into atmospheric movements that drive the weather systems.

SIGNIFICANT POINTS

1. Their proper motions make the planets "wanderers" across our sky.

2. The Solar System condensed from a collapsing nebular cloud. Planets grew from the accretion of smaller bodies called planetesimals. Nine planets are known to orbit our sun.

3. The innermost four planets are terrestrial, or Earth-like. They are relatively small and dense, when compared to the Jovian, or Jupiter-like, planets, which are gas giants.

4. Planets exhibit two types of motion. Rotation is a spinning motion on an axis that causes day and night. Revolution is a movement in an orbit around the sun. One Earth revolution is a year.

5. The composition of the terrestrial planets is dominated by iron, oxygen, silicon, and aluminum. The Jovian planets are rich in hydrogen, helium, methane, ammonia, and water (mostly in the form of ice). Some of the Jovian planets' moons are chiefly composed of ice.

6. Mercury has an airless, cratered surface. Venus has a greenhouse effect that keeps its surface temperature at about 500° C. Mars exhibits signs of ancient river erosion but has no flowing water today.

7. Jupiter, Saturn, Uranus, and Neptune have high-speed winds, indicated by the movements of their clouds. Jupiter's Great Red Spot is a storm about three times Earth's diameter. A similar storm observed by *Voyager 11* in Neptune's atmosphere has since disappeared.

8. The plane of Pluto's orbit is highly eccentric. It lies about 17° outside the plane of the ecliptic.

9. A number of smaller bodies orbit the sun, including comets, asteroids, and meteoroids. Comets are dominated by ice and have highly eccentric orbits. Asteroids are solid, rocky bodies, most often found in a belt between Mars and Jupiter. Meteoroids are rocky or metallic bodies that traverse the Solar System.

ESSENTIAL TERMS

planetesimal *50*	revolution *51*	lunar eclipse *53*	igneous rock *54*	comets *63*
protoplanet *50*	perigee *52*	albedo *54*	viscosity *54*	asteroids *64*
nebular hypothesis *50*	apogee *52*	maria *54*	fissures *54*	meteoroids *64*
terrestrial planets *50*	synodic month *52*	radiometric dating *54*	mantle *54*	meteors *64*
Jovian planets *50*	sidereal month *52*	lava *54*	near-Earth-object (NEO)	
rotation *51*	solar eclipse *53*	anorthosite *54*	*60*	

REVIEW QUESTIONS

1. What evidence is turning the nebular hypothesis into a theory?

2. What are the four terrestrial planets?

3. What are the four Jovian planets?

4. What are the common characteristics of the terrestrial planets?

5. What are the common characteristics of the Jovian planets?

6. What is the relationship between distance from the sun and revolution?

7. Why is the surface temperature of Venus about 500° C?

8. What spacecraft imaged the surface of Venus? How did it obtain images?

9. What is the largest volcano in the Solar System?

10. What is the Great Red Spot?

11. What is a near-Earth object?

12. What determines the orientation of a comet's tail?

13. How do asteroids differ from comets?

CHALLENGES

1. What benefits might be derived from a manned mission to Mars? Would the benefits be worth the possible risks?

2. What can we learn from the impacts that comet Shoemaker-Levy 9 made on Jupiter that might be useful on Earth?

3. How is the status of life on Earth a delicate balance between catastrophe and preservation?

4. Should you expect outer-space aliens to land on Earth?

PART 3

The Invisible Envelope

*E*arth has a dynamic atmosphere that transposes solar energy into the changes we call weather. Our daily activities and fashions reflect the influence of those changes. At times, the influence is minor, requiring us to add or subtract an article of clothing for comfort. But on occasions, the influence is substantial, as it is, for example, during violent storms.

At the *End* of Part 3, *You Will Be Able* to:

1. Describe the source of energy that drives atmospheres.
2. Identify and cite evidence for Earth's seasons.
3. Identify the variable compositions of different planetary atmospheres.
4. Distinguish the structure of Earth's atmosphere.
5. Integrate the quantifiable elements of weather.
6. Classify weather patterns.
7. Discuss the influence of weather on life.

From Ode to the West Wind

by Percy Bysshe Shelley (1792–1822)

Drive my dead thoughts over the universe
Like withered leaves to quicken a new birth!
And, by the incantation of this verse,
Scatter, as from an unextinguished hearth
Ashes and sparks, my words among mankind!
Be through my lips to unawakened earth
    The trumpet of a prophecy! O, Wind,
If Winter comes, can Spring be far behind?

Chapter

4

Prelude to Weather

Dew forms from condensed
water vapor, one of the components of our
atmosphere.

INTRODUCTION

The effects of weather are direct and significant. We dress for it, plan picnics around it, suffer from its extremes, and construct our buildings for protection from it. We alternately engage in indoor or outdoor activities as the weather allows, and we attempt to predict atmospheric conditions for days, weeks, and even seasons. In spite of our efforts, many predictions, regardless of the methods we use to obtain them, often yield inadequate warnings of rapid atmospheric change. On June 14, 1990, such an unpredictable change deluged the eastern Ohio town of Shadyside, filling a local stream called Wegee Creek to flood stage and devastating the small community. The individual storm that caused that flooding had its origin in a series of storms that moved across the Midwest and gathered strength as they approached eastern Ohio. Although forecasters knew that storms were on their way through the area, they did not know that one particular cell of the storm system would produce the localized downpour that filled Wegee Creek with 4 to 7 meters (15 to 25 ft) of water and killed dozens of Shadyside's inhabitants.

Storms are inseparable from water in some form. While still suffering from a long-term drought in February 1992, California's Los Angeles and Ventura Counties suffered from flash flooding when heavy rains fell along the Malibu coast and in the Santa Monica Mountains (fig. 4.1). In some areas, such as Woodland Hills, the floodwaters raced along at 56 kilometers (35 mi) per hour. By the time the water receded, it had caused damages estimated at $23 million and killed nine people.

Liquid water, however, is not the only devastating product of storms. Communities throughout Canada, the northern United States, and many mountainous regions are sometimes buried by heavy snowfalls. In the American Midwest, large hailstones have damaged property and crops.

The worst storms, however, are associated with coastal and island populations, where seawater rises to inundate the land. In 1970, a powerful storm not only flooded the Ganges River but also drove water from the Bay of Bengal over low-lying Bangladesh (then called East Pakistan), killing more than 300,000 people. Giant storms also occur in the

Pacific Ocean, where they are called typhoons, and in the Atlantic Ocean, where they are known as hurricanes. To their victims, these storms are terrible events. For earth scientists, these occasional storms, however severe and tragic, punctuate the processes that continuously operate on our planet.

The Study of Weather

The condition, or state, of an atmosphere's gases and other components is called **weather.** Because of a continuous, planetwide movement of the **atmosphere,** which is the sphere of gases that envelops our planet, and because of fluctuations in

Figure 4.1 After six years of drought, Los Angeles and Ventura Counties in California were subjected in 1992 to their worst flooding since the 1930s. These winter rains caused more than $20 million in damages and killed nine people. Although the 1992 storms produced abundant rainfall, they did not relieve the drought conditions.

Figure 4.2   A storm system that enters the continent from the Pacific Ocean appears as a large comma-shaped cloud band. The movement of the system is west to east, or left to right in this space photo.

such characteristics as the temperature, pressure, and moisture content of those gases, the weather constantly changes. No place on Earth's surface is exempt from such change. Even the daily heat of deserts, such as those in New Mexico, Arizona, and California, is followed by cool, and sometimes cold, nights. The deserts also get infrequent but often torrential rains that scour the land. Keeping track of the ubiquitous changes in weather requires a worldwide network of observers, as well as observation platforms that house sophisticated instruments. The invisible atmosphere, however, still surprises us with unpredicted storms and droughts.

The study of weather is **meteorology,** and those who study weather are **meteorologists.** As they strive to model our atmosphere's composition and processes, meteorologists provide the bases for accurate weather forecasting. Their efforts to understand the invisible envelope of air surrounding the planet have saved lives and informed most of us about the causes and aspects of daily weather.

If you live in the United States or Canada, then you are well advised to learn the natural mechanisms that drive a storm system from the northern Pacific Ocean across the 48 contiguous states and Canadian provinces and out into the Atlantic. The weather in Seattle on Monday may well be a clue to weekend conditions in New York, and a hurricane over Brownsville, Texas, may be the cause of rainy weather in Brownsville, Pennsylvania, within a week. The snowstorm that whitens the streets of Buffalo, New York, may also cover the roads in Montreal.

Televised Weather Lessons

One reason why local television meteorologists show more than the area's weather is that they are aware of the interrelationship between the geography of a country and the movements and changes of the air over the country. A well-informed viewer can learn much about the local forecast by looking at the big picture of an entire country's weather. In the usual format, the forecaster shows a view of a large landmass or an entire country from space and then a series of regional and local radar images, which define rainfall and snowfall patterns. Typically, we also receive information of little interest to many, such as barometric pressure and tendency, upper air conditions and patterns, and wind direction. Although this information may seem irrelevant, it is actually the basis of the forecast. By studying this and the next chapter, you will become familiar with the terms meteorologists use. You will also understand why forecasters give information about the weather conditions at great distances from the local area and at considerable altitude above the local surface.

The Weather Story

Weather observers and forecasters are coauthors of a daily or hourly story. Observers collect details on atmospheric conditions and funnel their information into a network of the National Weather Service, which in the United States is centralized in Suitland, Maryland. The National Weather Service then tracks air movements on a series of maps, which act as a story line for the nation's weather. This story line can provide clues to the science of weather, but it does not give the entire saga of Earth's atmosphere and atmospheric processes. The details in the short story of daily or weekly weather are covered in this chapter and in chapter 5. With these details in hand, you can understand the global patterns of weather discussed in chapter 6.

THE BIG PICTURE: A HYPOTHETICAL STORM CROSSES THE CONTINENT

Although Earth receives only two-billionths of the sun's energy output, enough insolation arrives at the planet's surface to power the atmosphere into a series of changes that we call weather. The many observers and observation platforms that gather information on these changes help forecasters tell an important story about atmospheric conditions. Each day's weather is only a subplot of a larger tale, and your local weather may originate thousands of kilometers away. Although we have not yet covered the details of meteorology, you may find it instructive to follow a hypothetical storm system as it crosses the North American continent. You are already familiar with much of this story because forecasters have given you bits and pieces of similar tales and shown you similar maps during the daily television news. Once you have followed the hypothetical storm, you will read about meteorology in the context of typical atmospheric changes.

AN AUTUMN STORM SYSTEM IS BORN ALONG THE NORTHWEST COAST

Somewhere over the North Pacific Ocean during November, a great mass of water vapor and air rotates counterclockwise around a relatively warm center of rising air. The rotation continues to pick up speed as the entire mass migrates southeastward, like a giant top spinning across a floor. The growing storm, as viewed from space, takes on the appearance of a large comma. It approaches British Columbia, Washington, and Oregon with steadily increasing wind speeds, some close to 120 kilometers (75 mi) per hour near the center of the system. Such a system would appear as a swirling band of clouds similar to that shown in figure 4.2.

With the approach of the storm, meteorologists in the Northwest predict rain. These rains come as forecasted when the storm initially enters the continent by rising over the coastal mountain ranges of western Oregon and Washington. A heavy rainfall accompanies the movement over the steep increase in elevations, with the Olympia Mountains, the highest elevations along Washington's coast, receiving the heaviest downpours. The rains also drench the valleys from Puget Sound southward through the Willamette Valley, and both Portland and Seattle forecasters track the same storm system.

East of the valleys lie the high Cascades, a line of north/south-trending volcanoes that includes Mount Saint Helens and Mount Hood. With elevations in excess of 3,000 meters (10,000 ft), the Cascades present a formidable obstacle to the southeastward-moving air. In the vicinity of the volcanoes, the air rises rapidly, drops in temperature, and loses more of its supply of water vapor as rain. As the air continues to rise, it precipitates snow instead of rain on the higher elevations, those

Figure 4.3 Map expression of the northwest coast of the United States as a storm system enters the continent. All the terms used in the map and in the description of the hypothetical storm are explained in chapters 4 and 5.

above 2,100 meters (7,000 ft), where the temperatures on this cold November day fall below freezing. High winds whip the snow into a low-visibility blizzard that sweeps over the high plateau country of eastern Washington and Oregon and nearby sections of southern Idaho, southwestern Montana, and western Wyoming. Countrywide, American meteorologists report, "It is a bleak November day in the Northwest." At the same time, Canadian meteorologists note that this mass of airborne moisture will soon move southeastward and exit British Columbia.

Eventually, the storm picks up more cold air, which moves southward from Canada and joins the swirling system like flotsam drawn into a whirlpool. The Canadian air is drier than the Pacific air and, coupled with the storm's movement away from the ocean as it crosses the rough surfaces of the western states, weakens the system (fig. 4.3). The storm wends its way toward New Mexico, where newscasters announce the coming of a weak, winterlike storm. By the time the storm reaches the state, it is almost devoid of the precipitation and strong, circular winds that plagued the Northwest.

The System Enters the American Southwest

Now in the region where Native Americans of the Southwest tell legends of the firebird Phoenix, the storm begins to revitalize like the mythical bird. The infusion of life into the dying storm comes in the form of a group of high-altitude, high-velocity winds collectively called the **jet stream.** The jet stream provides the storm with new circulation, moisture, and a driving energy that guides it into an eastward track.

The initial support of the jet stream drives the rejuvenated storm to the east and results in increased snowfall over the higher elevations of northern New Mexico and southern Colorado. The storm then moves farther eastward with greater strength and speed. Snow begins to spill onto the hill country of western Texas and onto the panhandles of both Texas and Oklahoma. Now the storm center lies over the Great Plains, where it generates a merger of two radically different air masses: the cold, dry air of the northern American Midwest and the warm, moist air of the Gulf of Mexico. Eastern and midwestern forecasters now begin to issue warnings that violent storms are probable. This hypothetical weather system now appears to be very similar to the 1989 and 1990 systems that caused death and destruction in Huntsville, Alabama (chapter 1), and Shadyside, Ohio.

The merger of the two types of air—warm, moist and cold, dry—creates a series of thunderstorms as the cold air wedges itself beneath the warm air. Some of these thunderstorms develop into severe storms with high winds, large hail, and in some areas, tornadoes. Emergency warnings flash across television screens of the lower Midwest, which is south of the storm center, where the intensity of the system is greatest. The U.S. National Weather Service issues two different sets of watches: South of the storm center, it announces a severe thunderstorm and tornado watch, while north of the center, it issues a winter storm watch. Forecasters along the storm track base their predictions on their area's position north or south of the jet stream, the boundary between winter- and summerlike storms. Residents of Kansas and southern Nebraska brace themselves for snow, sleet, and freezing rain.

The storm center continues to move through Oklahoma and into central Arkansas. Just north of the storm center, residents encounter narrow bands of freezing rain. About 160 to 240 kilometers (100 to 150 mi), north of the center is a zone of sleet. In Kansas and southern Nebraska, snowfall ranges between 15 and 30 centimeters (6 and 12 in). The strengthened storm now drives the snow into near-blizzard conditions. Farther to the north, the snow diminishes, and forecasters predict cold but relatively dry conditions from southeastern Saskatchewan to northern Wisconsin.

The System Influences the South and the East

Hourly forecasts warn of a winter storm headed toward the Northeast as the jet stream changes the storm center's direction (fig. 4.4). Additional moisture from the Gulf of Mexico reenergizes the storm system, which now heads along the western slopes of the Appalachians toward Ohio. On the southern and eastern sides of the storm center, thunderstorms and showers move toward the Northeast, but on the northern side of the center and the jet stream, winter storms begin to drop heavy snows from southern Illinois to southwestern Pennsylvania. All across the country, forecasters point out the relationship between the elevations and nature of the continent's surfaces, or its **topography,** and the moving storm. Now, they note the storm's encounter with the highlands of the Appalachians, where the air must once again rise to pass over the higher elevations.

As the storm center reaches Kentucky, it has distanced itself from the source of moisture, and it begins to weaken again. Almost simultaneously, however, another storm system forms

Figure 4.4   Map expression of the hypothetical storm as it passes over the American Midwest. (See Symbol Key with figure 4.3.)

Figure 4.5   Map expression of the hypothetical storm as it exits the continent and moves over the Atlantic Ocean. (See Symbol Key with figure 4.3.)

along the coast of North Carolina near Cape Hatteras. Supported by the northeastward-trending jet stream, the new storm increases in strength almost in inverse proportion to the old storm's decrease in intensity. Forecasters along the eastern seaboard note a transfer of energy from the old to the new storm system, and the heaviest snowfall shifts to the east (fig. 4.5). North Carolina, Virginia, and Maryland are successively buried under heavy snows. As much as 45 centimeters (18 in) fall on Washington, D.C., and Baltimore, Philadelphia, New York, and Boston all feel the effects of blizzard and near-blizzard conditions.

Having worked its way across the continent, the system brushes by Nova Scotia and Newfoundland on its way over the Atlantic Ocean. In its passage, this system would have affected the daily activities of millions of people.

METEOROLOGY AND CLIMATOLOGY

The hypothetical storm just described contains all the characteristics of a composite system, one that could occur but seldom does. The path and characteristics of this storm system show that the study of weather requires knowledge of the kind of surface over which the air passes, in addition to information about the atmospheric conditions from the surface to high altitudes. The weather is a product of short-term atmospheric processes in specific geographic areas, and forecasters usually limit their predictions to 12- to 48-hour periods in typical "today-tonight-tomorrow" forecasts.

Rapid changes in our fluid and invisible atmosphere require constant vigilance by weather observers. The weather is essentially the current conditions of the atmosphere at a given locality, and only by understanding how those conditions arise can a forecaster predict the impending weather.

When earth scientists look at the history of weather for a specific place, they derive its **climate,** or the aggregate weather for a geographic locale. Climatologists study regional and global weather patterns to discern their causes and effects over long periods, such as months, seasons, years, or even centuries and millennia.

Aggregate weather or climate should not be confused with average weather. To limit the study of climate to average temperatures and precipitation for a place is to miss the extremes that climatologists take into account. For example, to the casual observer, Des Moines, Iowa, and San Francisco, California, may have apparently similar average annual temperatures—in the 10° to 16° C (50° to 60° F) range—but they do not have the same type of climate. In fact, even slight differences in average temperatures indicate significant variations between the two locales. The San Francisco climate is influenced by the Pacific Ocean. Its relatively warm winters and cool summers give it a yearly average temperature of 13.6° C (56.5° F). Des Moines, landlocked in the central part of the country, undergoes greater extremes of temperature than San Francisco and has hot summers and cold winters.

INTERRELATIONSHIP: GEOGRAPHY AND WEATHER

Knowledge of the kinds of surfaces over which air moves is essential to an understanding of both weather and climate. The geography of the North American continent includes a variety of landforms that influence conditions in the lower atmosphere. Good weather forecasters, in fact, are reliable because they know the influence Earth's surfaces have on the moving air.

The landform map of North America shown in figure 4.6 reveals its eastern and western mountain systems, its broad central plains and lowlands, and its coastal plains. Each of these landforms governs, in part, the type of weather experienced in that area and passed on to neighboring landforms in a general west-to-east pattern. For example, in mountain ranges, moving and rising air masses lose moisture as either rain or snow, making the air drier on eastern slopes than on western slopes. Bodies of water, like the Great Lakes, add moisture to the passing air. Thus, the Buffalo, New York, region is known for its heavy snowfalls, with snowfall amounts diminishing to the southeast of Lakes Erie and Ontario.

Figure 4.6 Raisz physiographic map of the 48 contiguous states and southernmost Canada. (Copyright by Erwin Raisz 1957, reprinted with permission of Geoplus, Danvers, MA.)

Within the image:

CANADIAN SHIELD

Laurentian upland of low hills and many lakes

LANDFORMS OF THE UNITED STATES

by ERWIN RAISZ   Sixth revised edition, 1957

Scale

75

PLANETARY ATMOSPHERES

Earth's atmosphere may appear to be unique in its composition and structure, but in some ways, it is similar to the other atmospheres in the Solar System. Although the amount and proportion of gases may differ from planet to planet, *atmospheric gases everywhere obey the same fundamental physical and chemical laws.* The thick, blue atmospheres of Uranus and Neptune contain methane (fig. 4.7), and that gas is no different from the methane found on Earth, where it is subject to heating, cooling, and the planet's gravitational pull. The different temperatures and abundances of methane found on all three planets reflect only a difference in degree, not in kind. Similarly, carbon dioxide, which is the primary constituent in the atmosphere of Venus but comprises less than 1% of Earth's gases, acts like a greenhouse gas, regardless of its place in the Solar System. The proportion of this gas in the respective atmospheres of the two planets makes a significant difference in extent of the greenhouse effect (chapter 1). If Earth incorporated Venus-like quantities of carbon dioxide in its atmosphere, our planet's surface would be too hot to support life.

Before you proceed in your study of Earth's weather, you should have a general idea about the nature of atmospheres. Are the gases of the other planets similar to those of Earth? Are those atmospheres thicker or thinner than Earth's? Do other planets have weather? Is that weather similar in any way to Earth's? With a background in planetary atmospheres, you can then delve into the workings of our own gaseous covering. To answer these questions, we must rely on studies of the other planets, which have provided data on the probable origin, composition, and motions of their atmospheres.

Atmospheric Compositions

Earth's envelope of air, which allows jet airplanes like the Concorde to fly at altitudes approaching 16 kilometers (10 mi), is actually a relatively thin sphere of gases. The Jovian planets, by contrast, have very thick atmospheres. Jupiter's multicolored clouds conceal a planet dominated by an atmosphere of mostly hydrogen and helium, possibly hundreds of times thicker than Earth's atmosphere. Thick, rapidly moving clouds lying throughout Jupiter's upper atmosphere prevent us from knowing just how thick its gaseous layer really is. We do know that the great mass of this largest planet in the Solar System allows it to hold the lighter gases more effectively than the smaller Earth and the other three inner planets. The gravitational pull of Jupiter's mass creates an increasingly more dense atmosphere toward its interior, and liquid molecular hydrogen (H_2) may lie under tremendously high pressures only 965 kilometers (600 mi) below the outer gases. A probe sent by the *Galileo* spacecraft into the Jovian atmosphere in July 1995 found less helium and water than expected and an abundance of methane (CH_4) and hydrogen sulfide (H_2S). In contrast, the terrestrial planets are quite different simply because they are smaller, mostly solid bodies closer to the sun. The lightest gas, hydrogen, is easily lost to space in the uppermost regions of Earth's atmosphere, and water vapor, a constituent of

(a)

(b)

Figure 4.7 The "blue" planets. (*a*) Uranus. (*b*) Neptune. The Great Dark Spot of Neptune, imaged by *Voyager,* was not seen in a later image made by the Hubble Space Telescope.

our planet, appears to have escaped the confines of Mars billions of years ago.

Three of the four relatively small, inner planets may have had initial atmospheres of comparable size and composition, while Mercury, which is virtually airless today, probably lost its envelope of gases when it was formed. Gaps in our knowledge about the other planets have led to numerous speculations about their atmospheres, and until the 1970s, Mercury was thought to have a thin veil of sodium and helium. Interestingly, this innermost planet looks much like our cratered moon, which we now know leaves a trail of sodium atoms as it orbits Earth.

TABLE 4.1   Characteristics and Makeup of the Planetary Atmospheres

Planet or Moon	Color	Thickness	Main Constituents	Storms	Winds
Venus	White with dark lines	Thick	CO_2 (96%), N_2 (3.5%), H_2SO_4	?	Probable
Earth	Blue, rainbow colors	Thin	N_2(78%), O_2(21%), Ar, CO_2	Yes	Yes
Mars	Red	Thin	CO_2	Dust storms	High speed
Jupiter	Yellow, brown, red	Thick	H_2, He, H_2S, CH_4	Great Red Spot	High speed
Saturn	Yellow, tan, blue, green	Thick	H_2	Yes	High speed
Titan	Reddish	Thick	N_2, Ar, CH_4	No	Light
Uranus	Blue-green	Thick	H_2(87%), He(13%), CH_4	?	?
Neptune	Blue	Thick	H_2, He, CH_4	Yes	Yes
Triton	?	Thin	CH_4	?	?
Pluto	?	Thin	CH_4	?	?

Venus and Mars have atmospheres that now differ radically in structure and composition from Earth's. Both, however, may hold clues to Earth's initial atmospheric composition. The dominant gas of Earth's current atmosphere is nitrogen, which makes up 78% of the air we breathe (table 4.1). The dominance of this gas is surprising when you consider the atmospheres on Venus and Mars which are dominated by carbon dioxide. Many scientists believe that the early atmosphere of Earth was also rich in carbon dioxide.

The atmosphere of Venus is considerably denser than Earth's, as evidenced by the pressure it exerts on the Venusian surfaces. On Earth, you experience a sea-level average pressure of 1.04 kilograms per square centimeter (14.7 lb per sq. in), as the overlying atmosphere compacts itself under gravity. If you were to stand on Venus, you would literally be crushed by a pressure 90 times greater than that to which you are accustomed, or nearly 3/4 ton per square inch. The heavy atmosphere of Venus is 96% carbon dioxide. Mars also has a carbon-dioxide-dominated atmosphere, but unlike the air of Venus, it is not very dense, about 100 times less dense than Earth's.

Typically, a planetary atmosphere is densest near the planet's surface. *The proportion of individual gases found in the lower part of an atmosphere is relatively uniform horizontally because of mixing.* Near the solid or liquid surfaces of the planets, all atmospheres lie under the weight of overlying gases. Compressed by the great weight above them, the gaseous molecules of the lower atmosphere interact, exchanging whatever energy they absorb from their environment. The mechanisms of energy exchange will be discussed later, but it is important to realize that the energy exchange among molecules imparts a mixing that is characteristic of the homogeneous, or compositionally uniform, lower atmosphere.

Table 4.1 presents the main components of the planetary atmospheres. Whereas instruments on automated spacecraft have sampled atmospheres on Mars, Venus, and Jupiter, scientists have determined the gases of the other planets mostly by deduction. Astronomers, for example, can deduce that neither Uranus nor Neptune houses abundant free oxygen in its atmosphere. Because methane reacts with oxygen to produce water and carbon dioxide, any free oxygen would be bound by the following reaction:

$$CH_4 + 2\,O_2 \rightarrow 2\,H_2O + CO_2$$

Atmospheric Origins

How did the planets obtain the components of their atmospheres? The composition of each planet's atmosphere is the product of several influences, including the planet's point of origin in the nebular cloud from which the Solar System formed. The distribution of elements in the nebular cloud was an important control on the planetary components. Iron, for example, is a prominent component in the makeup of the terrestrial planets, but it does not exist as a gas in their atmospheres. Hydrogen and helium are important constituents of the Jovian bodies.

Another influence on the evolution of atmospheres was planetary size because mass determines the strength of the gravitational field that holds an atmosphere. Gravity coupled with surface temperatures may give even a relatively small body the ability to hold an atmosphere of moderately heavy gases. With its cold temperature of $-179°$ C ($-290°$ F), Saturn's moon Titan, the second largest moon in the Solar System, has a gravity strong enough to hold nitrogen, argon, and methane. Chemical reactions among the elements that produce compound gases like methane further sorted the gases that were gravitationally bound to each planet. For some of the planets, geological processes, such as volcanism, added gases from the interior, and on Earth, biological processes served to redistribute, cycle, and alter some elements and compounds.

Just how the proportions of gases on Earth developed is partly veiled in a hidden past, but the proliferation of life over the planet's surface has had a profound effect on the atmosphere's composition. Through **photosynthesis,** plants convert carbon dioxide, water, and sunlight into carbohydrates. Through **respiration,** animals assimilate oxygen. Whereas the former process gives off oxygen, the latter releases carbon dioxide, and both processes have altered radically the nature of Earth's initial atmosphere. The preponderance of carbon dioxide on Venus and Mars might be taken, therefore, as indirect evidence that no photosynthesis takes place on either planet.

Through a variety of experimental and exploratory methods, earth scientists have repeatedly attempted to discern the composition of Earth's atmosphere prior to the influence of life. Air from the relatively recent past, about 12,000 years ago, has been found trapped inside glacial ice. Much older air, captured in a bubble inside a sample of amber (hardened sap) from the age of the dinosaurs, has given some clues to the atmosphere's long-term composition. Surprisingly, the sample held air that was 9% richer in oxygen than the air we breathe.

The flyby of Titan by *Voyager I* in November 1980 resulted in sufficient data collection for speculation that Saturn's largest moon has an atmosphere somewhat like that in which life began on a young Earth. Titan's atmosphere contains acetylene (C_2H_2) and hydrogen cyanide, two gases that may have played a key role in the generation of organic molecules. The red moon also lacks molecular oxygen (O_2), making it a reducing, rather than an oxidizing, environment. Such an *anoxic* (oxygenless) atmosphere seems to have been necessary for life's compounds to form. After the rise of life on our planet, the balance of early component gases began to tip as plants absorbed and converted carbon dioxide into food and released molecular oxygen.

Atmospheric Motions

A significant aspect of Earth's atmosphere is motion. The air of the lower atmosphere constantly moves and mixes. This motion is the product of energy transfer as the sun's energy is converted into heat differentially along Earth's surfaces and is transferred to the atmosphere. Heat energy drives an atmosphere, but only when that heat is unevenly distributed. Thermodynamic studies tell us that heat flows from hotter to colder areas or from hotter to colder substances. A common experience, such as touching the handle of a hot pan, proves this. The energy flow from pot to hand is called **conduction**, which is a transfer of heat energy from one substance to another in contact with it.

Energy transfer in gases involves a different method. Heated gases rise. Whenever gases incorporate more energy, they do so through more rapid molecular motion. This motion results in an expansion of a heated gas; the gas occupies a larger volume and, as a consequence, becomes lighter. Less dense than the surrounding gases, the heated gas rises and takes its energy to a higher altitude, losing energy to the environment during its climb. This vertical heat transfer by a moving fluid is called **convection** (fig. 4.8).

Just about all atmospheres undergo uneven heating, which manifests itself in air movements, including some 548-kilometer-

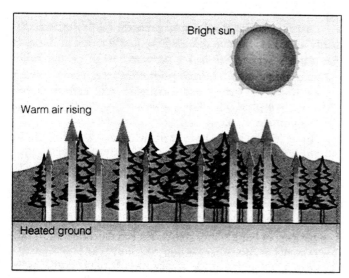

Figure 4.8 Convectional transfer of heat.

Figure 4.9 The Great Red Spot, more than 25,000 kilometers (15,500 mi) long, is the largest of Jupiter's storm systems.

Figure 4.10 Images taken by *Voyager I* at approximately 40-hour intervals show the counterclockwise rotation of the Great Red Spot of Jupiter. Small clouds approach the spot from the east and circle it in 6 to 10 days.

(340-mi) per-hour winds on Saturn. One atmosphere that appears to be rather even in its temperature, however, is that of Titan, where a relatively uniform, very cold temperature predominates at the moon's surface. As a result of the evenness of temperature, Titan probably has little atmospheric movement. On Earth, these atmospheric movements are well documented, and they contribute to our weather.

Although uneven atmospheric heating is the key to air motion, not all planets receive their heat energy from a single source. For example, Saturn has a suspected heat source in a helium rain that may have fallen more than a billion years ago. Also, Jupiter gives off more energy than it receives from the sun. Solar radiation that strikes Jupiter's upper atmosphere impinges upon a very thin layer of molecules, where little energy transfer can occur. Remember that closely packed or compressed gas molecules are more efficient at distributing energy than are widely separated molecules.

The motions of atmospheric gases depend on the energy influx derived from five possible sources:

1. Solar radiation
2. Planetary radiation (infrared radiation)
3. Fluid convection (the rising of a heated gas)
4. Friction (by compression of descending gases)
5. Condensation (changing from a gaseous to a liquid state)

Each of these sources of atmospheric energy is discussed in this and the next chapter. The movements generated by each source operating alone or in conjunction with the others can be quite spectacular. As terrible as hurricanes and typhoons are for residents of our planet, each of Earth's big storms, which serve to move atmospheric gases and redistribute heat, is tiny by comparison with stormlike movements in the upper atmospheres of the Jovian planets.

Jupiter and its neighbor Saturn have stormlike activity as swirling clouds called *eddies* move rapidly against the background of other clouds. The scale of these eddies is so large that the most famous Jovian storm, the long-lived Great Red Spot, rivals the size of our planet (fig. 4.9). A sequence of still photos taken once every 2 days on *Voyager I*'s approach to the planet reveals an animated vortex of reddish gases so dense that neighboring bands of clouds are deflected around the oval, counterclockwise rotation of the storm (fig. 4.10). Similar, though smaller, swirling cloud systems have been observed elsewhere on Jupiter, on Saturn, and on Neptune.

EARTH-SUN RELATIONSHIPS

The sun's electromagnetic radiation takes about 8 minutes to reach Earth. When it arrives, it meets a round planet whose rotational axis is tilted to the plane of the planet's orbit (fig. 4.11). Both the roundness and the tilt play important roles in the transfer of energy from the sun to our planet. To understand fully how that transfer works, you should learn about the relationship between the shape and orientation of Earth and the incoming electromagnetic radiation.

Earth is not a stationary planet, and its constant motion is an important control on incoming solar radiation. Because we are bound by gravity to our planet, we do not feel its motion, but our planet is traveling very fast in its journey around the sun. It also turns like a spinning top.

Rotation

The days result from Earth's **rotation,** which is a turning on its axis (fig. 4.11). This turning occurs at variable speeds, depending on your position on the planet's surface. Quito, Ecuador, located on the equator, makes a bigger circle during a single turn than does Chicago, Illinois. Thus, Quito must move faster than Chicago to make one rotation. In one day, Quito must travel the full circumference of our planet, or more than 38,700 kilometers (24,000 mi).

The importance of Earth's turning is dual. First, the sun does not light just one "side" of the sphere: The rotation distributes the energy *every 24 hours*. The "side" turned away from the sun loses energy, effectively preventing an out-of-control buildup of heat.

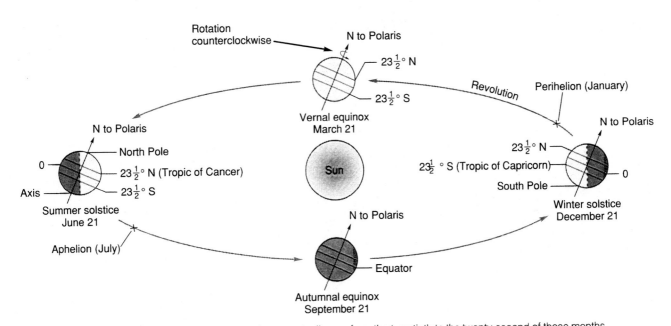

Figure 4.11 Earth-sun relationships. Solstices and equinoxes actually vary from the twentieth to the twenty-second of those months.

Box 4.1

TIME ZONES

Whenever Earth completes a single, complete turn about its axis, one Earth day has passed. Since ancient times, humans have attempted to divide this turning into convenient, trackable units. Today, we divide one rotation into 24 time zones, giving us a 24-hour day (fig. 4.A).

Because a circle—and, thus, a sphere—is divided into 360°, each of the time zones corresponds to 15° of rotation (360 ÷ 24 = 15). With an arbitrary starting point on Earth's surface, each 15° segment makes a 7.5° spread on either side of the center of a time zone. Since Earth turns from west to east, the 15° time zones equate to 15° of longitude, and the time of each zone is 1 hour later in an eastward direction.

If the 0° longitude (a meridian that runs through Greenwich, England) is a starting point, and it is 5 P.M. along that meridian, then at 7.6°W of the Greenwich meridian, the time is 4 P.M. Along the length of the longitudinal line that runs 7.6°E of the Greenwich meridian, the time is 6 P.M. The center of the time zone that includes the 7.6°W meridian is along the 15°W meridian. If Philadelphia

lies at 75°W of Greenwich, it lies in the middle of the fifth time zone west of Greenwich. If the 0° meridian's time is 5 P.M., Philadelphia's time is 12:00 P.M. Philadelphia will require five more hours to reach the position of Greenwich, relative to one rotation.

The time zones marked on maps do not, however, reflect a pure 15° division. Population densities and political boundaries, such as the borders of territories, states, and countries, are used as time-zone variants to allow citizens a common time reference. Thus, the time zones are not always straight north-south lines (fig. 4.B).

The solar day—the passage of the sun during the daylight hours—is divided into

Figure 4.A   Standard time zones of the world.

The rotation gives us day and night and the basis for our hours (see box 4.1 and table 6.2). Second, the differences in rotational speed over Earth's surface cause a deflection of objects moving over the spinning planet. This deflection is discussed later.

Revolution

Earth also revolves around the sun in an elliptical *orbit*. The time for this orbit is 1 year, or 365.25 days. This **revolution** takes our (fig. 4.11). As Earth now moves in its orbit, aphelion occurs during the Northern Hemisphere's summer; perihelion, during its winter.

Tilt and the Seasons

Earth's axis of rotation tilts 23.5° to the plane of its orbit. The direction of tilt does not vary as the position of the planet changes during its revolution, making the North Pole alternatively lean toward and away from the sun (fig. 4.11).

Earth's greater proximity to the sun in winter rather than in summer may seem surprising. You would expect temperatures to be warmer when Earth is closer to the source of its atmospheric heat. The reason for the apparent discrepancy lies in the tilt of Earth's axis. This tilt, or inclination, plus Earth's spherical shape, determine the intensity of the solar radiation at the surface. The explanation may seem complex, but it is, in fact, relatively simple. Just imagine shining a flashlight held perpendicular to a surface, as you see in figure 4.12a. The beam of light, which makes a right angle with the surface, concentrates its energy in a small circle. If you incline the flashlight, the circle of light becomes first an oval and then a parabola, as figure 4.12b and c show. The same effect occurs over the curved surfaces of a tilted Earth. Figure 4.12d shows the light from the sun as parallel arrows. Those arrows strike the tangents of the curved surface at different angles. As the angle approaches 90°, the energy is more concentrated per unit area.

During the year, the angles of the sun's rays change over the surface of the Earth (fig. 4.11). Tangents to Earth would reveal a shifting angle and either increasing or diminishing energy per unit of area. During the Northern Hemisphere's summer, the North Pole "leans" toward the sun, while the South Pole "leans" away. The result is a greater concentration of the sun's energy in the Northern Hemisphere than in the Southern Hemisphere. The circumstance reverses during the Northern Hemisphere's winter. The two hemispheres always lie in opposing seasons: fall-spring and summer-winter. The cause of the seasons, therefore, is not the distance of the Earth from the sun but rather *the tilt of the planet to the plane of its orbit,* an imaginary elliptic sheet that would run from the center of the Earth through the center of the sun.

A further examination of figure 4.12 reveals that the tropics, lying between 23.5°N latitude and 23.5°S latitude, would receive more energy during the year than would higher latitudes. The concentration of energy in low latitudes results in higher heat values for these latitudes than for the high latitudes, where the sun angle is greater.

Latitude, therefore, or distance from the equator, is the most significant control on the amount of heat available for the atmosphere. Between the tropic of Cancer (23.5°N) and the tropic of Capricorn (23.5°S) the *noon* sun angle never varies more than 47° from directly overhead. At higher latitudes, 23.6° to 90°, the angle varies to a greater extent. During the two hemispheres' respective winters, the latitudes greater than 66.5° are not lit by the sun for 2 to 6 months. The absence of incoming solar radiation, or *insolation,* results in a net loss of heat from the planet's dark (or nighttime) surfaces.

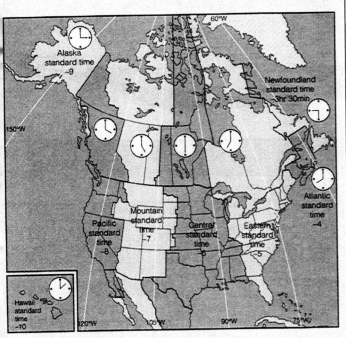

Figure 4.B Standard time zones of Anglo-America.

two units. Before the sun is halfway in its journey across the sky of the central time meridian of a zone, the time is *ante* (before) *meridian* (A.M.). After the sun reaches the midpoint of its journey across the central meridian's sky, the time is *post* (after) *meridian* (P.M.). The western portion of a time zone does not have the same sun-time as the eastern portion because the sun rises in the east. The standard time for the zone, however, ignores the actual relationship of the zone's east and west boundaries to the sun.

Apply Your Knowledge

1. What time is it in Los Angeles when it is 12:00 P.M. in New York City?
2. What time is it in Miami, Florida, when it is 12:00 P.M. in Perth, Australia?

planet as close as 147.25 million kilometers (91.5 million mi) and as far away as 152 million kilometers (94.5 million mi) from the sun. At its closest approach to the sun, Earth is said to be at **perihelion.** When it is farthest from the sun, Earth is at **aphelion**

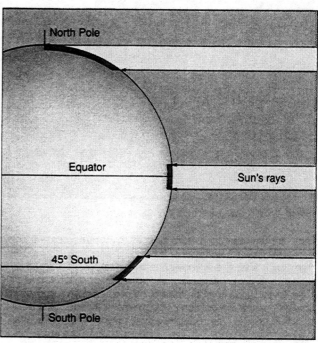

(d)

Figure 4.12 Diagrams (*a*) through (*c*) show an increasing areal coverage by the same amount of energy, lessening the intensity per unit area. Diagram (*d*) shows this same effect on the surface of Earth for the equinox.

STRUCTURE OF EARTH'S ATMOSPHERE

The pull of gravity concentrates the atmosphere over Earth's surface, making the lower part of the atmosphere more dense than the upper part. In fact, about one-half of the atmospheric mass lies in the lowest 6.5 kilometers (4 mi). Weather scientists recognize this gravity-generated distribution as one basis for a classification scheme that divides Earth's air into two spheres whose mutual boundary lies at about 80 kilometers (50 mi) above the ground. The lower of these two is the dense **homosphere,** so named because its composition is relatively uniform. The uniformity results from the vertical and horizontal mixing of crowded gases, which, even on a molecular level, frequently collide. The outer, less-dense layer is the relatively unmixed **heterosphere,** a zone where widely spaced, and generally lighter, molecules rarely collide and where mixing is infrequent. The lighter gases of the heterosphere, then, extend from 80 kilometers (50 mi) to the top of the atmosphere and do not exhibit the movements characteristic of the lower, heavier gases of the homosphere.

Figure 4.13 shows the extent of both segments of the atmosphere. It also presents another classification of atmospheric zones not based on gravity separation and mixing but rather on temperature. The four spheres that comprise this classification are the **troposphere, stratosphere, mesosphere,** and **thermosphere.** The temperatures throughout the spheres vary widely and follow different trends (see box 4.3). In two of the spheres (the stratosphere and thermosphere), temperatures generally rise with increasing altitude, whereas in the other two spheres (the troposphere and mesosphere), temperatures decrease with increasing altitude. Meteorologists call the drop in temperature with increasing altitude a **lapse,** and they refer to a rise in temperature with increasing altitude as an **inversion.** The fluctuating upper-boundary layer of each sphere is characterized by a steady temperature, where no change occurs with increasing altitude, giving rise to the term **pause.** Thus, the stratosphere ends at the **stratopause;** the troposphere ends at the **tropopause.**

Another basis for classifying the spheres is **air pressure,** which is dependent on the amount of air above any level, since pressure is a function of weight. Death Valley, the lowest point on

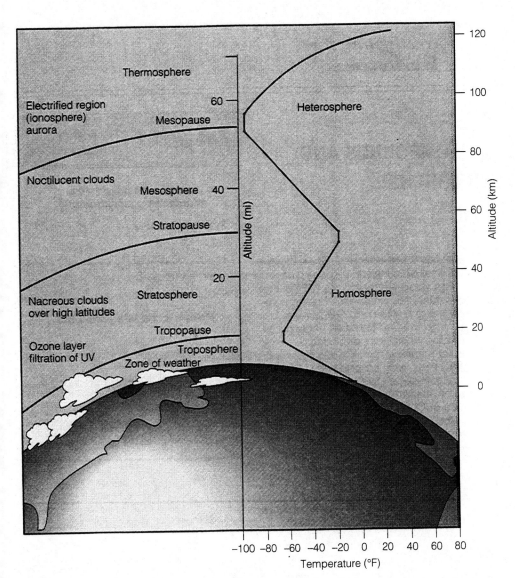

Figure 4.13   Layered structure of the atmosphere.

learned earlier in the chapter, the spread of this radiation is unequal over the planet's surface for two reasons: Earth is tilted to the plane of its orbit, and its surface is curved.

Differential Heating

The differential heating that results from these two controls on the concentration of solar energy is reflected in the uneven heating of the molecules in the troposphere. Electromagnetic radiation from the sun strikes Earth's surfaces, where it is reradiated into the surrounding envelope of gases, heating them by transferring solar energy. Wherever air molecules receive more heat energy, they vibrate faster. Faster molecular motion is synonymous with higher temperatures. On a hot summer day, the concentration of solar radiation and subsequent reradiation produce molecular collisions at a greater rate than that produced on a cold winter day, when solar rays are less concentrated.

Pressure

Another influence on the proximity and motions of air molecules is the sheer mass of the atmosphere. The tremendous weight exerted by the quadrillions of kilograms of overlying air makes the molecular collisions in the tropospheric gases frequent and violent. Each second, molecular collisions impinge on gases and planetary surfaces, and these motions can be recorded as air pressure. Density, pressure, and temperature are, therefore, interrelated in Earth's troposphere. Close to the surface, pressures are relatively high, molecules are crowded, and reradiation transposes solar energy. Farther up in the troposphere, pressures are lower, molecules are less crowded, and the source of reradiation is farther away.

The interrelationships among pressure, heat source, and temperature are even more evident when you consider atmospheric movements. Heated molecules move rapidly, collide frequently, occupy a greater volume, and become lighter. As the heated air rises, pressures are not as great as they were below. Under lower pressures, air collisions diminish, and temperatures fall. Falling temperatures mean more compact, more slowly vibrating molecules with increasing weight per unit volume. The product is a heavy, cold air mass that descends toward the surface, displacing the air below. In this way, the gases of the troposphere constantly intermix through a vertical exchange. Winds also mix the troposphere, and, like vertical movements, they result from pressure differences. Wind and pressure are discussed later in this chapter.

the North American continent, experiences greater air pressures than the summit of Mount McKinley, simply because it has more overlying air. At the approximate altitude of 5.5 kilometers (18,000 ft), the pressure is about half that at Earth's sea-level surface.

The dense, lowest 16 to 24 kilometers (10 to 15 mi) of atmosphere, known as the troposphere or **zone of weather,** is the region of greatest importance to humans and the focus of this text. It is the region directly responsible for maintaining life on Earth's surface, and it affects life-forms with its daily and seasonal changes. The stratosphere, however, has recently drawn the close attention of scientists because its boundaries encompass the ozone layer, which appears to be under attack by industrially produced gases, such as the CFCs (see chapter 1 and also box 4.2).

ZONE OF WEATHER

As you can see in figure 4.13, the troposphere is part of the homosphere. In this dense, lower layer of the atmosphere, overcrowded molecules vibrate and collide at great velocities in random motions. The energy for this movement derives chiefly from the sun. As you

BOX 4.2   *Investigating the Environment*

OZONE-DEPLETING COMPOUNDS AND STRATOSPHERIC ICE

TABLE 4.A	Artificially Produced ODCs

Fully-Halogenated CFCs (containing no hydrogen)

CFC-11 (CCl_3F)
CFC-12 (CCl_2F_2)
CFC-113 (CCl_2CClF_2)
CFC-114 ($CClF_2CClF_2$)
CFC-115 ($CClF_2CF_3$)

Halons (containing bromine)

Halon 1211 ($CBrClF_2$)
Halon 1301 ($CBrF_3$)

Other ODCs

HCFC-22 ($CHClF_2$)
Methyl chloroform (CH_3CCl_3)
Carbon tetrachloride (CCl_4)

Earth's stratosphere houses the important ultraviolet-absorbing gas ozone. The relatively recent (1980s) discovery of a "hole"—actually, a lessening—in the ozone layer over Antarctica has increased speculation that some mechanism speeds up the process of depleting the ozone layer.

Ozone-depleting compounds (ODCs) are trace gases that release chlorine and bromine into the stratosphere. ODCs effectively deplete stratospheric ozone because they are capable of surviving the journey through the troposphere until they encounter the stratosphere, where they release their chlorine and bromine atoms.

The chlorofluorocarbons (CFCs) that are partially responsible for the ozone depletion are not the only ODCs manufactured by humans (table 4.A). Other gases, including the halons (compounds with one or more bromine atoms) and compounds containing hydrogen, also act as ODCs.

According to Owen P. Toon of NASA's Ames Research Center and Richard P. Turco of UCLA, the CFCs that reach the stratosphere are broken apart by ultraviolet light, releasing chlorine that exists in a

Figure 4.C   Unless they are effectively removed from the cycle, chlorine atoms can repeatedly destroy ozone molecules.

Water and Heat Transfer

The bottom of the troposphere comes in contact with the planet's surface, almost three-quarters of which is water. The interrelationship between the air and water effectively moves most of the heat energy that the atmosphere indirectly derives from the sun.

The significance of water vapor in the atmosphere can be experienced on several levels. On a personal level, hot, humid days make us more uncomfortable than hot, dry days. On a larger scale, the introduction of water vapor into the air can turn a pleasant day into a stormy one. In the hypothetical

storm system described earlier in this chapter, for example, water vapor from the Gulf of Mexico reenergized the storm.

Water vapor absorbs, holds, and transfers heat energy in measurable units known as calories. A calorie is 1/100 of the amount of heat energy needed under Earth's standard sea-level atmospheric pressure to raise the temperature of 1 gram of water 1° C. The mechanisms through which these quantifiable heat absorption and transfer processes occur are:

1. **evaporation,** the heat-absorption process that turns liquid water into water vapor

Figure 4.D Stratospheric clouds can form over the polar regions if the air cools sufficiently during the winter. Nitric acid trihydrate clouds are visible as thin, dark orange layers lit by a setting sun. The water-ice clouds appear whitish. The clouds, such as these over Stavanger, Norway, help to initiate the chemical reactions that destroy ozone.

areas. An atypical formation of the clouds, however, appears to occur at higher temperatures (278°C), particularly over Antarctica. The clouds, composed of ice crystals of varying size, have been called polar stratospheric clouds (PSCs), (fig. 4.D). Within these clouds, the reservoirs of chlorine are prevented from forming, as nitric acid (HNO$_3$) is precipitated.

The chief contribution of the clouds to ozone depletion lies in the removal of nitrogen, an element that reacts with chlorine to make a molecule that does not react with ozone. The process of freeing chlorine to react with ozone begins in the Antarctic spring, as sunlight dissociates molecular chlorine into atomic chlorine. The chlorine atom destroys ozone by taking on one of the oxygen atoms, leaving an oxygen molecule behind. Chlorine monoxide (CIO) then reacts with atomic chlorine to make Cl$_2$O$_2$, which sunlight breaks apart, freeing the chlorine to destroy additional ozone. Bromine in the stratosphere also removes an oxygen atom from the ozone molecule to form bromine monoxide (BrO) and molecular oxygen. When the bromine monoxide encounters chlorine monoxide, a reaction frees the bromine and chlorine atoms and produces molecular oxygen. The bromine and chlorine are then free to react with additional ozone molecules.

Apply Your Knowledge

1. What ODCs are CFCs?
2. What are the chlorine reservoir molecules?
3. How do chlorine and bromine destroy ozone?

free state or that reacts with ozone to form chlorine monoxide (CIO) (fig. 4.C). The chlorine eventually reacts with other gases, and the new compounds have no effect on the ozone. In a reaction with atmospheric methane, chlorine forms gaseous hydrochloric acid (HCl), and in a reaction with nitrogen dioxide (NO$_2$), it forms chlorine nitrate (CIONO$_2$). Both of these compounds become reservoirs for chlorine atoms. Some process, however, appears to release the chlorine from the reservoirs, enabling it to destroy more ozone.

The process appears to take place in large (10–100 km, or 6–60 mi, long) lens-shaped, iridescent clouds. These "nacreous" (mother-of-pearl) clouds remain stationary, even though high winds can move through them. Typically associated with very cold temperatures (283° C), nacreous clouds often form as high winds that reach into the stratosphere form waves over mountainous

2. **condensation,** the heat-release process that turns water vapor into liquid water
3. **sublimation,** the process by which ice turns into water vapor

In evaporation, liquid water with an initial temperature of 0° C must absorb 600 calories per gram to turn into gaseous water. That heat energy is stored as the **latent heat of vaporization** by the more rapidly moving gas molecules. Those molecules remain a gas as long as they hold that energy, but a loss of that energy returns the water vapor to the more slowly vibrating liquid state. To acquire the energy necessary for vaporization, water

molecules rob energy from neighboring molecules. The surrounding environment cools as a result. This process accounts for your being chilled after stepping out of a shower, bath, or swimming pool. Evaporation from the surfaces of your body robs the skin of heat energy. Thus, evaporation is a cooling process.

By contrast, condensation is a heating process. As the gaseous water turns once again into liquid water, it releases its latent heat into the surrounding environment. When evaporated water migrates in air currents and then condenses, it transfers heat from one place to another.

Box 4.3

GREENHOUSE COOLING?

In chapter 1, you learned that the atmosphere is subject to radiative forcing because of the accumulation of greenhouse gases. Ironically, the artificial production of greenhouse gases, particularly carbon dioxide, may cool both the mesosphere and the thermosphere. If carbon dioxide doubles, according to George L. Siscoe of the U.S. Air Force Geophysics Laboratory and Timothy L. Killeen of the University of Michigan, the mesosphere (80–100 km, or 50–62 mi) will cool nearly 10° C (18° F), and the thermosphere (above 100 km, or 62 mi) will cool almost 50° C (90° F).

If the gases of the heterosphere continue to cool, their density will increase (fig. 4.E). Within as little time as a century, the heterosphere may shrink by compressing itself against the upper reaches of the homosphere. The ramifications of this compressed heterosphere are not fully understood, but scientists are attempting to explain the possible effects through sophisticated computer models. R.G. Roble of the High Altitude Observatory of the National Center for Atmospheric Research in Boulder, Colorado, suggests that these models predict a considerable change in the vertical structure of the atmosphere by the end of the twenty-first century. Roble notes that the temperature near 50 kilometers (31 mi) has already decreased by 3 to 4° C (5.4 to 7.2° F) during the past 10 years. As the temperature of the upper atmosphere continues to drop, chemical and physical processes throughout the entire atmosphere may undergo changes.

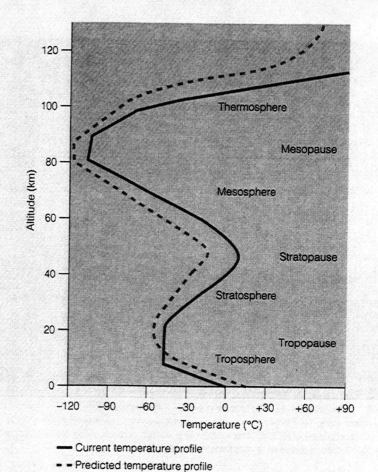

Figure 4.E The present vertical temperature structure of the atmosphere (solid curve) and the predicted temperature structure at the end of the twenty-first century, when the concentrations of various trace gases are expected to double.

These changes may affect climate in ways that are adverse to human life.

Apply Your Knowledge

1. Using figure 4.E, determine where the temperature structure of the atmosphere will change the most.

2. If the atmosphere contracts when it cools, what happens to it when it is heated?

3. What would be the effect of a shrinking atmosphere on Earth-orbiting satellites?

Sublimation, which is the process by which ice turns into water vapor, also serves to transfer heat. Sublimation usually occurs at high altitudes, at high elevations, and on cold winter days.

With almost three-fourths of the planet's surface covered by oceans, water vapor is readily available to the troposphere and plays an important role in the **heat budget,** or heat transfer, over the planet. Its presence in the air is, however, variable, amounting to as much as 4% of the volume of a given air mass. Obviously, air over water has a better opportunity to acquire moisture than air over land, and therefore, masses of air can be thought of as being either moist or dry.

AIR MASSES

If you think of the troposphere as a three-dimensional model, you can appreciate not only its horizontal and vertical components but also its depth. The troposphere contains an ever-changing series of **air masses,** each with its own short-lived characteristics. Air masses of different sizes rise to different heights, move at different rates, maintain their own patterns of temperature and pressure, and contain different amounts of moisture, depending on their origin over either land or water.

Figure 4.14 Source regions for North American air masses.

Except for their clouds, they are invisible; nevertheless, meteorologists can describe and classify them.

The hypothetical storm system discussed earlier in this chapter, for example, evolved in the northern Pacific, where it emerged from a cool but moist region. It carried the moisture it picked up from the surface waters of the Pacific into southern British Columbia and the northwestern United States, where rains fell over Washington and Oregon. The system's point of origin is a **source region** for the development of cool, moist air masses called **maritime polar (mP) air** (fig. 4.14).

Other source regions provide the troposphere with air masses with different characteristics. Air masses that develop over land are generally drier than those that originate over water. Therefore, during summers, a region such as the American Southwest is a source for **continental tropical (cT) air.** Temperatures are relatively high over such states as Arizona and New Mexico. Both states are landlocked and unable to provide an extensive source of water, so the air becomes dry (continental) and warm (tropical).

Once air masses become homogeneous units, they leave their source regions at varying rates. They alter their characteristics as they encounter other air masses, and they eventually mix with the **ambient air** (surrounding air) and with new air masses. Thus, the hypothetical storm system, which developed from maritime polar air, lost most of its moisture by the time it crossed a great expanse of land and moved into New Mexico.

An air mass is either cooler or warmer or drier or wetter than the ambient air and any neighboring air masses. This is an important aspect of the weather. *Relative temperatures and pressures are the characteristics that determine how air masses interact.* Since cold air is denser than warm air, for example, a colder air mass will wedge itself under a lighter warm air mass. Although weather forecasters may announce the absolute or quantitative values for temperatures and pressures in a given air mass, they make their predictions largely on the relative differences among air masses.

FRONTS

The leading edge of a moving air mass is called a **front.** Fronts are the troposphere's lines of battle in the shifting wars among air masses. The leading edge of a relatively cool, dry air mass will force its way beneath warmer air and drive the warmer air upward. Additionally, cold air masses generally move faster than the less-dense warm air masses, and often, the front of the former overtakes the front of the latter and lifts it.

Because the size and density of air masses differ, these units of the troposphere are in constant conflict throughout their short lives. Conflicts among air masses produce one of three results:

1. A denser air mass plows beneath a less-dense air mass
2. A lighter air mass overrides a denser one.
3. Two air masses temporarily ward off each other's advance until the two mix.

These results, in turn, produce four kinds of fronts, which meteorologists classify on a relative basis (fig. 4.15):

1. A cold front, the leading edge of a cold air mass
2. A warm front, the leading edge of a warm air mass
3. A stationary front, the boundary between two relatively motionless air masses
4. An occluded front, a front that has been lifted, leaving a gap, or occlusion, between it and the ground.

QUANTIFIABLE CHARACTERISTICS OF AIR MASSES

Because scientific endeavors require objective analyses, meteorologists look for ways to measure characteristics of the atmosphere. The daily movements of air masses in the troposphere keep weather observers busy identifying the changing characteristics of the air. To define any one air mass as maritime polar or continental tropical, scientists constantly measure a specific set of **weather elements,** or quantifiable characteristics (table 4.2). These elements are the measurable properties of the atmosphere. A number of reliable instruments serve as the tools of weather observers. In chapter 5, you will read about the weather elements as they relate to weather mapping and forecasting.

Surface Temperature and Its Measurement

What are the hottest and coldest surface temperatures ever recorded on our planet? On September 13, 1922, Azizayah (or Azizia), Libya, experienced the highest atmospheric temperature officially recorded at Earth's surface. On that day, the temperature reached 57.7° C (136° F). Just 9 years earlier, Death Valley, California, had experienced the hottest day ever recorded in North America: 56.6° C (134° F). At the other end of the troposphere's heat spectrum are the cold temperatures of Antarctica, where in August 1960, scientists felt the sting of −89.44° C (−129° F). The February 3, 1947, temperature of −62.77° C (−81° F) at Snag, Yukon Territory in Canada, makes that date the coldest day on record in North America.

For meteorologists, record keeping is the key to understanding the weather. Daily observations, therefore, are part of the regimen of meteorology, giving us temperature ranges. Ordinarily, the range of temperatures over 24 hours is relatively moderate. On some days, the high in a particular area may not vary more than a few degrees from the daily low. In other areas,

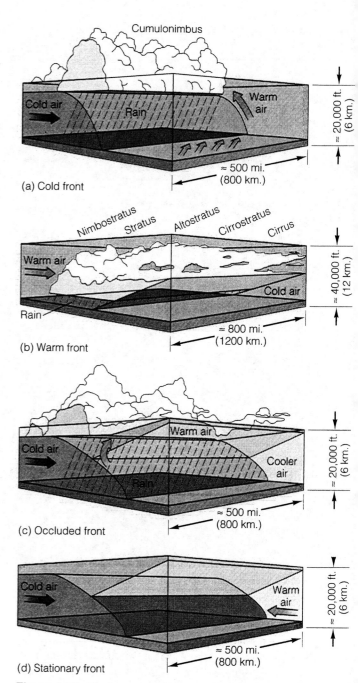

Figure 4.15 The four types of fronts and their map symbols. (*a* and *b*) Cold and warm fronts. (*c*) Occluded front. (*d*) Stationary front.

humans must adjust to a wide range of temperatures during a single day. Residents of Browning, Montana, experienced an extreme temperature range on January 23, 1916, when people arose to a very brisk −48° C (−54° F), but by late afternoon experienced a temperature of 6.7° C (44° F).

To measure temperature, scientists use a very common instrument, the **thermometer.** Thermometers are filled with either mercury or alcohol and measure temperatures by expansion and contraction of their liquid in a sealed tube. Heated, the liquid expands and rises in the tube, with calibrated markings representing degrees. Cooled, the liquid contracts, falling into a reservoir well or bulb at one end. A *maximum thermometer,* used by weather observers to record the highest temperature on a given day, has a constriction in the glass tube to prevent the mercury from returning to the reservoir when the temperature falls and the liquid contracts. A *minimum thermometer,* used to record the daytime low, has a thin, plastic pin inside the alcohol-filled tube that prevents the liquid from rising if the temperature subsequently rises. The minimum thermometer uses alcohol because its freezing point of −130° C (−202° F) is lower than mercury's freezing point of −39° C (−38.2° F).

A **thermograph** uses an ink-filled needle connected by a rod to two dissimilar metals curved into a spring. As the metals contract or expand, the rod rises or falls, allowing the ink to draw a line on graph paper attached to a rotating drum. Thermographs keep continuous records of temperature fluctuations electrically or mechanically, allowing observers to check the inked graph paper at their convenience.

TABLE 4.2 Quantifiable Weather Elements and the Instruments to Measure Them		
Weather Element	**Selected Instruments**	**Unit of Measurement**
Temperature	Thermometer Thermograph	Degrees Celsius or degrees Fahrenheit
Pressure	Aneroid barometer Mercurial barometer Barograph	Inches of mercury or millibars
Humidity	Hygrometer Sling psychrometer Psychrometer Hydrograph	Percent or grains or grams
Wind	Weather vane Anemometer	Compass direction, knots, miles per hour, meters per second
Precipitation	Rain gauge Tipping bucket	Millimeters or centimeters or inches

Surface Pressure and Its Measurement

Atmospheric air pressure is exerted by the random movements of the compressed fluids we call gases. The great weight of air that lies on Earth's surfaces provides more, however, than a simple crushing action. The force that compressed gases exert is as much a sideways action as a downward one. Rapidly moving gas molecules strike any surrounding molecules they encounter, including other air molecules. For this reason, a balloon expands with the increasing pressure of added, and therefore, compressed air. If the pressure inside the balloon were not equal in all directions, the balloon would collapse at the site of diminished pressure. An analogy that may make this clear is a punctured bucket of water (fig. 4.16). The water squirts out the sides of the bucket because the pressure from the weight of the water forces it against the insides of the bucket.

As you learned earlier in the chapter, the pressure at Earth's surface is approximately 1.04 kilograms per square centimeter (14.7 lb per sq. in). At this pressure, every 0.09 square meter (1 sq. ft) of surface holds 969.2 kilograms (2,116.8 lb), regardless of its orientation: horizontal, inclined, or vertical. That force of about a ton would seemingly crush each of us, except that the pressure is evenly distributed over and around all surfaces. The air inside your mouth, therefore, maintains a pressure that balances the air outside your cheeks.

Measuring air pressure in kilograms per square centimeter (or pounds per square inch) gives us a good sense of the amount of force the atmosphere exerts on surfaces. Meteorologists, however, prefer to use another method to quantify pressure. Because the pressure of our atmosphere can push a confined fluid up a pipe, meteorologists use a glass tube that looks very much like a large thermometer. It is called a **mercurial barometer** and is calibrated in both inches and millibars. The standard sea-level atmospheric pressure on our planet equals 29.92 inches of mercury in the tube, and this, in turn, equals 1,013.2 millibars (thousandths of a bar). The mercurial barometer shown in figure 4.17 is easy to read: Whenever air pressure decreases, the mercury falls in the tube; whenever air pressure increases, the mercury rises.

Although 1,013.2 millibars (29.92 in) is the standard pressure at Earth's sea-level surfaces, it represents an average only. Higher and lower pressures have been recorded. The lowest pressure on record was measured at sea just northwest of Guam in 1958, when the mercury fell to 877 millibars (25.9 in). By contrast, observers in Barnaul, Russia, registered a pressure of 1,079 millibars (31.89 in) on January 23, 1900; it was the highest surface pressure ever recorded.

Because the mercurial barometer is long, heavy, and cumbersome, many commonly used barometers measure pressure by another method. The **aneroid barometer** employs a corrugated, airless

Figure 4.16 Fluids (air and water) flow from areas of high pressure to areas of low pressure. (psi = pounds per square inch.)

Atmospheric pressure

Atmospheric pressure

High internal pressure (36 psi)

Figure 4.17 Meteorological instruments for measuring air pressure. (*a*) Barograph. (*b*) Aneroid barometer. (*c*) Mercurial barometer.

metal can that contracts and expands with changes in pressure. Whenever the can alters its shape, a needle connected to the center moves along a gauge calibrated in both inches and millibars. Often, the face of the gauge is marked "fair" or "stormy," as is the aneroid barometer in figure 4.17. A **barograph** uses an aneroid barometer to keep a running record of pressure changes.

Humidity and Its Measurement

Meteorologists use a variety of instruments to measure the amount of water vapor (gaseous water) in Earth's atmosphere. They also categorize their measurements to emphasize different relationships between the atmosphere and the water vapor it holds. Most weather forecasters quantify the moisture in an air mass by referring to the **relative humidity.** The term gives us a percent ratio between the actual amount of water vapor present and the vapor-carrying capacity of the air mass.

For most of us, the relative humidity is only of significance on a hot, very humid day. We feel discomfort on such a day because little water evaporates from our skin. In winter, a high relative humidity may have the opposite effect. On cold days, we need to conserve body heat, and a lack of evaporation from our skin keeps heat loss down. The body recognizes by its comfort or discomfort the importance of temperature to relative humid-

ity. On a more objective scale, the temperature of an air mass controls the mass's relative humidity: Warmer air has a greater carrying capacity than cooler air. Thus, more water vapor must be present in a warm air mass for it to have the same relative humidity as in a similar quantity of cool air. Because the U.S. National Weather Service recognized our need to know the apparent weather, or how we will feel, it implemented in 1984 a heat index scale that relates humidity to human perception.

Meteorologists also measure the **absolute humidity** of an air mass by determining the density of water vapor. Just as census takers can tabulate the number of people living in a given square mile, so meteorologists can determine the amount of water vapor in a parcel of air. Typically, absolute humidity is given as grams of water per cubic meter of air. Both relative and absolute humidity ratios change with alterations in the air parcel. If the air parcel's temperature rises, then the air expands, occupies a larger volume, and reduces the absolute humidity. Similarly, with a rise in temperature, the carrying capacity of the air parcel increases, and the relative humidity declines.

Because both measurements can change with the addition of heat and the subsequent expansion, another measurement gives a direct ratio dependent only on the amount of water put into or taken out of an air parcel. That quantity is the **specific humidity,** which reflects the ratio between the weight of the water vapor and the weight of the air parcel. It is a weight-to-weight, or a mass-to-mass, ratio expressed in either grams of water vapor per kilograms of air (g/kg) or in grains (0.065 g).

The instruments used to measure humidity depend on the absorption or loss of water and on evaporation. **Hygrometers** use water absorption or accumulation to register humidity. Each of us is equipped with a personal hygrometer in the form of hair. As our hair absorbs water, it expands and lengthens. Attached to a graduated scale, the hair, once calibrated to a standard, yields a reading of humidity. More accurate than the **hair hygrometer** and requiring less attention to calibration is the **electrical absorption hygrometer,** which uses a thin electrolytic film containing a water-absorbing salt. As the salt absorbs water, electrical resistance across the film changes, resulting in a reading of humidity. A **psychrometer,** an instrument composed of two thermometers, one with a cloth sock around the mercury bulb, uses evaporation to measure humidity. Once the cloth is soaked with water, evaporation cools the bulb, and the mercury in the tube falls to reflect the loss of heat. The wet-bulb temperature can then be compared to that of the dry-bulb thermometer. Greater differences between the wet-bulb and dry-bulb temperatures reflect greater evaporation and drier air. To speed up the evaporation process, some meteorologists employ a **sling psychrometer.** Spinning the two thermometers forces more air past the wet bulb, shortening the time required for evaporation (fig. 4.18).

Figure 4.18 A sling psychrometer.

Precipitation and Its Measurement

Measurements of snow and rain are usually given in inches, millimeters, and centimeters. A *rain gauge* is simply a calibrated tube opened on one end. Placed vertically, it catches falling rain. Some rain gauges work by mechanical or electrical recording devices connected to a *tipping bucket*. The bucket contains two funnel-shaped buckets that pivot and spill when they fill. Each overturn of the buckets sets off an electrical signal that records both the amount and the time of the precipitation. Still other gauges use floats connected to recording instruments. In addition to amount of rainfall, its intensity is also important. A 2.5-centimeter (1-in) rainfall covers an acre with more than 75,700 liters (20,000 gal) of water. If those gallons fall over 24 hours, their erosional impact on the soil is considerably less than that of a similar quantity falling in 1 hour.

Measurements of snowfall require a measuring stick, but weather observers usually translate inches of snow into their liquid water equivalent. Because of the space between snow crystals, an inch of snow does not equate to an inch of water. Melting the snow caught in a funnel yields the liquid water equivalent.

Precipitation amounts vary greatly around the world. At some sites in the Atacama Desert in Chile, precipitation has never been recorded. In contrast, Henderson Lake, Canada, holds the North American total annual rainfall record of 665 centimeters (262 in). The highest total annual rainfall on Earth occurred at Cherrapungi, India, where observers measured 2,646 centimeters (1,041.8 in). Reunion Island in the Indian

(a) No pressure difference

(b) Slight pressure

(c) Strong pressure

Figure 4.19 Differences in pressure result in varying movements of gelatin. (*a*) Gelatin bulges outward under its own weight. (*b*) Slight pressure causes oozing flow. (*c*) Strong pressure causes rapid movement.

Ocean experienced the heaviest daily total rain on March 15, 1962, when 187 centimeters (73.6 in) fell. The wettest place in the United States is Mount Waialeale, Hawaii, where an average 1,199 centimeters (472 in) fall each year.

Snowfalls vary as much as rains, and those who live in equatorial regions see snow only at higher elevations. The greatest yearly snowfall occurred at Paradise Station, Washington, during the 1955–56 winter, when 2,850 centimeters (1,122 in) fell. A 1-day snowfall of 193 centimeters (76 in) on April 14, 1921, gives Silver Lake, Colorado, the world record.

Wind and Its Measurement

Wind results from pressure differences because air—and any other fluid—flows from areas of higher pressure to areas of lower pressure. As the difference between pressures increases, wind speeds increase. You might visualize the movement of air by a thought experiment. If you were to press on the top of a gelatin dessert, it would ooze away from the pressure of your hand. A slow application of light pressure results in a slow oozing. If you punched the top of the gelatin mold, the dessert would fly outward at high speed. The difference between the slow outward oozing and the rapid flying of the dessert lies in the relative difference between the force exerted by your hand and the surrounding force of the air pressure (fig. 4.19).

Meteorologists measure both wind speed and wind direction. Wind speed can be measured by an **anemometer,** an instrument that uses three cups attached to a rotating axle. The cups capture the wind, spin, and turn the axle. The rotations of the axle can then be transferred to a counter or a dial, giving the wind speed in knots,

miles per hour, or meters per second. As you learned earlier, wind speeds in excess of 484 kilometers (300 mi) per hour have been observed on Saturn. Earth's highest recorded winds reached 363 kilometers (225 mi) per hour on New Hampshire's Mount Washington in April 1939. Tornado winds probably meet or exceed this figure, but the danger presented by these violent storms makes accurate measurements difficult, and estimates must suffice. Wind direction can be read from a **wind vane,** a device that uses a swiveling pointer that aligns with the wind.

FURTHER THOUGHTS: A COMPLEX AND DYNAMIC ATMOSPHERE

All atmospheres undergo some dynamic changes as energy is transferred from a planet's surface or as it arrives from the sun. If we judge by wind speed alone, we find that some planets have atmospheres far more dynamic than Earth's. The Giant Red Spot on Jupiter and the high-speed winds of Saturn and Mars, for example, would be devastating to life on our planet. Nevertheless, incidents of violent weather on Earth demonstrate that its atmosphere is in a state of constant flux.

Armed with knowledge of the atmospheric components and the physical laws that govern them, meteorologists have established practical atmospheric models that serve as the bases for everyday and long-term predictions. Keeping track of the atmosphere's dynamic complexity requires constant vigilance because humans cannot escape the effects of turbulence, heat, and precipitation. The next chapter establishes the meteorologic use of this knowledge and the model that represents Earth's weather.

SIGNIFICANT POINTS

1. Weather is the real-time condition of the atmosphere at a given locality.

2. Meteorologists, are atmospheric scientists who collect data on the daily movements among the gases of the atmosphere and centralize their information to establish a model of recognizable atmospheric phenomena. In the United States, the National Weather Service uses this information to make predictions.

3. The jet stream is a changing group of high-altitude, high-speed winds. It influences the movements of surface weather systems.

4. Weather is influenced by topography and surface composition. In part, air derives its weather characteristics from the surfaces over which it passes. Water bodies can add moisture to a weather system.

5. Aggregate weather trends for a locale or region over a period measured in decades are called climate.

6. Most of the planets have atmospheres, but each planet's envelope of gases evolved under different circumstances. On Earth, photosynthesis changed the composition of the early atmosphere by removing carbon dioxide and adding free oxygen.

7. Dominated by nitrogen, Earth's atmosphere contains, in addition to oxygen, significant amounts of carbon dioxide, water vapor, argon, and other gases. This collection of gases is both stratified and dynamic.

8. When its orbit takes our planet closest to the sun in January, Earth is at perihelion. Our elliptical orbit's farthest point from the sun is called aphelion. Aphelion occurs during July.

9. The rotation of Earth about its axis distributes the incoming solar energy over the planet's surfaces, gives day and night, serves as the basis for our time measurements, and causes a deflection of objects moving over the spinning planet.

10. The tilt of Earth to the plane of its orbit is the cause of seasons.

11. The dense, lowest part of the atmosphere is the troposphere, or zone of weather. Above the troposphere lies the ozone-rich stratosphere, which filters incoming ultraviolet light. Two more atmospheric zones, identifiable by temperature and pressure characteristics, lie above the stratosphere: the mesosphere and the thermosphere.

12. The fluctuating upper-boundary layer of each sphere ends in a "pause," a transition zone marked by a steady temperature.

13. The atmospheric component most influential in the formation of weather is water vapor. Its introduction into a mass of air can turn a nice day into a stormy one, and it is largely responsible for the transfer of heat.

14. The troposphere is the site of moving air masses that acquire identifiable characteristics. Air masses of varying sizes rise to different heights, move at different rates, maintain their own temperature and pressure patterns, and contain different amounts of moisture. Each of these masses originates in a source region from which it obtains its initial characteristic temperatures and moisture. Some are maritime, or moist, masses because they develop over water; others are continental because they evolve over land. Air masses can also be polar or tropical, depending on their latitude of formation.

15. Air masses undergo changes wrought by various influences, including the movement of high-altitude winds called the jet stream. As these masses move, their leading edges, called fronts, collide, causing various weather conditions.

16. Fluctuating heat, measured in degrees Fahrenheit or Celsius as temperature, is one of the dynamic weather elements, which also include pressure, wind, humidity, and precipitation.

ESSENTIAL TERMS

weather *69*
atmosphere *69*
meteorology *71*
meteorologist *71*
jet stream *72*
topography *72*
climate *73*
photosynthesis *77*
respiration *77*
conduction *78*
convection *78*
rotation *79*

revolution *80*
perihelion *81*
aphelion *81*
homosphere *82*
heterosphere *82*
troposphere *82*
stratosphere *82*
mesosphere *82*
thermosphere *82*
lapse *82*
inversion *82*
pause *82*

stratopause *82*
tropopause *82*
air pressure *82*
zone of weather *83*
evaporation *84*
condensation *85*
sublimation *85*
latent heat of
   vaporization *85*
heat budget *86*
air mass *86*
source region *87*

maritime polar
   (mP) air *87*
continental tropical (cT)
   air *87*
ambient air *87*
front *87*
weather elements *88*
thermometer *88*
thermograph *89*
mercurial
   barometer *89*
aneroid barometer *89*

barograph *90*
relative humidity *90*
absolute humidity *90*
specific humidity *90*
hygrometer *90*
hair hygrometer *90*
electrical absorption
   hygrometer *91*
psychrometer *91*
sling psychrometer *91*
anemometer *92*
wind vane *92*

REVIEW QUESTIONS

1. How does weather alter the human environment?
2. In what general direction do weather systems move across North America?
3. What is the primary source of energy for Earth's atmosphere?
4. How does the jet stream affect surface weather?
5. What were the major changes that occurred as the hypothetical storm crossed the continent?
6. What is the dominant gas of Earth's current atmosphere? Were the constituent gases of Earth's atmosphere ever different from those we breathe today?
7. What is the standard sea-level pressure?
8. How has photosynthesis affected the composition of the atmosphere?
9. How does Earth's tilt affect the heating of its surface?
10. What are the main influences on seasonal temperature variations?
11. Why is the lower atmosphere called the homosphere?
12. What characterizes the upper boundary of each atmospheric zone?
13. What is the significance of relative air temperatures?
14. How does water control Earth's heat budget?
15. What characteristics help define the boundaries of air masses?
16. What is a source region?
17. What are the four kinds of fronts?
18. How do air masses interact?
19. What are the quantifiable weather elements?

CHALLENGES

1. Why are weather predictions important to farmers?
2. How does weather affect the flow of goods and services in your area?
3. What area's weather is a precursor of the weather in your area?
4. What landform boundaries define the region for which your local forecasters predict weather?
5. How would your life change if no weather predictions were available?
6. Why are the North and South Poles shrouded in darkness during the winter months?
7. Why does the Northern Hemisphere have summer when the Southern Hemisphere has winter?
8. How would the intensity of radiation from the sun change between aphelion and perihelion?
9. How would a change in Earth's tilt affect the seasons?
10. What might happen to the distribution of agricultural regions like America's wheat or corn belts if Earth's atmospheric temperatures rise?
11. What photochemical reactions take place in our atmosphere?
12. What difficulties would space vehicles or space travelers have in acquiring information about a hard surface on the Jovian planets?
13. Would a piece of paper ignite in the high temperatures of the thermosphere?
14. Why would the tropopause lie at higher altitudes over the equator than over the North Pole?

Chapter 5

Understanding the Troposphere

Chapter Outline

Tornado at Binger, Oklahoma, on May 22, 1981.

INTRODUCTION

You now know that solar energy is the ultimate driving force behind air movements of the troposphere. The ways the sun's energy is converted to atmospheric motion all depend on the *transparency of the atmosphere to electromagnetic radiation.* After crossing the near-vacuum of space, the sun's predominantly short-wave radiation encounters a number of atmospheric obstacles on its way to our planet's surface. For some wavelengths, our atmosphere is almost opaque; thus, life on the surface is protected from the harmful, very short wavelengths of X rays and gamma rays. The envelope of gases blanketing Earth also selectively filters out other frequencies, including most short ultraviolet rays. In varying amounts, other frequencies, such as visible light and the longer wavelengths of the radio waves, pass through the gas molecules, dust particles, water vapor, and water droplets of our atmosphere to reach the surface, energizing both life and weather systems.

SOURCES OF ATMOSPHERIC HEAT ENERGY

Our planet is large enough to intercept only one two-billionths of the sun's total energy output, and of that fraction, less than half reaches the surface to be redistributed as heat by infrared radiation and by Earth's two moving surface fluids: air and water. As figure 5.1 shows, 34% of the incoming solar radiation is reflected to space by atmospheric dust, gases, and clouds and directly from Earth's surfaces. The dust, gases, and clouds of the atmosphere also absorb 19% of the incoming solar energy.

Figure 5.1 Distribution of incoming solar energy.

Another 28% of the radiation is diffused, scattered, and reflected toward Earth's surface, where, with the 19% that directly penetrates the atmosphere, it heats the land and waters. The 47% (19% + 28%) of the radiation that reaches the surface through reflection and absorption is transformed from shortwave to longwave, or heat, radiation and eventually warms the atmosphere. Remember that Earth radiates in longer wavelengths because it is a cooler body than the sun. This earth radiation is doubly significant: First, Earth, rather than the sun, directly heats our air; and second, weather is, ultimately, the mechanism by which the atmosphere moves this heat derived from the surface. Atmospheric warming is primarily a result of familiar processes: radiation, conduction, convection, and advection (wind).

Radiation and Atmospheric Opacity

Our atmosphere is almost opaque to thermal infrared energy coming from the surface, but about 20% of the terrestrial radiation escapes to space. Both water vapor and carbon dioxide absorb infrared radiation, and other gases, such as chlorofluorocarbons (CFCs) and methane, also intercept infrared energy from the surface. Among the gases that retard the loss of heat from Earth's surface, water vapor plays the dominant role, but its influence is mostly limited to the lower atmosphere, where contact with the oceans increases specific humidity.

The Role of Conduction in Moving Heat

Although gas is a poor conductor of heat, the atmosphere does come into contact with Earth's surfaces, where heat is transferred between molecules. Essentially a daytime and warm season process, conduction between surface and air does not play a major role in the redistribution of heat energy throughout the atmosphere.

The Roles of Convection and Advection in Moving Heat

As a mechanism for transferring heat, convection plays a role greater than conduction in the heating of the troposphere's upper layers and in moving heat over large areas of Earth's surface.

The vertical redistribution of heat energy through convection is related to other air movements. When heated air rises, carrying its heat energy aloft, it displaces cooler air, which sinks. Convection also allows replacement air to flow horizontally along Earth's surface in a movement called **advection,** which we commonly call **wind.** A complex set of interrelated movements between convection and advection currents is responsible for the day-to-day changes in weather and for the redistribution of heat around the planet. Vertical and horizontal airflow combine to move the atmosphere locally and regionally in wheel-like cells. These cells, sometimes referred to as **convection cells,** are unevenly distributed across Earth's surface, and the imbalances between rising and sinking air masses generate winds on both large and small scales. The largest cells power the general circulation of the atmosphere, creating advection currents that sweep across the planet's surface, redistributing heat.

THE GENERAL CIRCULATION OF THE ATMOSPHERE

The uneven heating of Earth's surface creates pressure imbalances that result in winds. On the largest scale, these winds circulate the gases of the troposphere.

Pressure Gradients

Figure 5.2 reveals how a pressure change can produce advection of different intensities. Mercurial barometers show the pressure readings for sites A and B on the surface. The mercury at site A stands at 1,024 millibars (30.2 in), while that at site B fills the barometer to 1,012 millibars (29.8 in). Because the distance between the two sites is relatively great, the slope between the tops of the two mercury columns is slight. That slope represents a **pressure gradient.** The difference between the barometric readings at sites C and D is greater than that at sites A and B; and, consequently, the slope, or gradient, is also greater. Because air flows from areas of higher pressure to areas of lower pressure, advection would occur in both instances. However, because C and D register a larger difference and a steeper pressure gradient, the wind between these two sites would be greater.

In an extension of the image of a pressure gradient, meteorologists think of high pressure as *ridges* and of low pressure as *troughs.* Thus, advection is an air movement comparable to water flowing off a hill and into a valley.

Over Earth's surface, very large ridges of high pressure feed air into neighboring low-pressure valleys. Chief among these ridges are the high-pressure systems of the subtropics, which form as air descends from altitudes near the tropopause, as figure 5.3 illustrates. These ridges lie between two low-pressure areas, one in the equatorial region, called the **equatorial low,** and another in the subpolar zone. The **subtropical highs** feed replacement air along the surface, generating very large, persistent wind systems. Smaller pressure gradients lie between the **subpolar lows** and the **polar highs,** but enough of a ridge exists to establish another wind system at high latitudes in both hemispheres.

Figure 5.2 Steeper pressure gradients produce faster-flowing winds. Winds move from higher to lower pressure. Site A: Chicago, Illinois. Site B: Buffalo, New York. Site C: Mobile, Alabama. Site D: New Orleans, Louisiana.

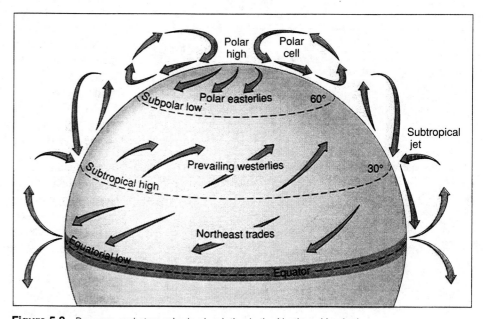

Figure 5.3 Pressure and atmospheric circulation in the Northern Hemisphere.

The Coriolis Force

A rotating Earth influences the direction of moving fluids across its surface. The influence stems from the various speeds different parts of the planet travel in a daily journey around the axis of rotation. By analogy, the rate of spinning is like the car tire rotation shown in figure 5.4. The outside of the tire has a greater distance

Figure 5.4 The outside of a car tire must travel a greater distance than the inside near the hubcap to make one rotation.

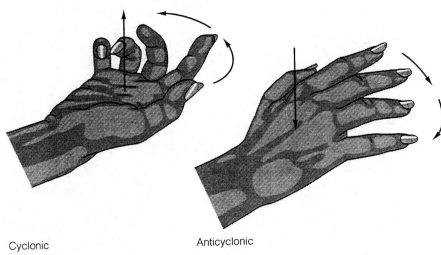

Cyclonic   Anticyclonic

Figure 5.5 Analogs of Northern Hemisphere cyclonic and anticyclonic rotation.

to travel than does the edge of the hubcap; yet, both make their respective turns in the same time. Similarly, during every 24 hours, a point on the equator must travel a greater distance than a point at 40°N. The rotational rate for the former is more than 1,609 kilometers (1,000 mi) per hour, while that of the latter is closer to 1,126 kilometers (700 mi) per hour. Any object "at rest" on the equator is thus traveling at a higher rate toward the east than a similar object "at rest" at higher latitude. A latitudinal motion between locations with different rotational speeds induces a deflection, or bending, called the **Coriolis force,** either to the right or to the left. The Northern Hemisphere experiences a right-hand deflection, whereas the opposite occurs in the Southern Hemisphere. The strength of the Coriolis force is great enough that a moving car, if not for the friction with the road and the driver's compensatory adjustments of the steering wheel, would also veer from a straight path.

Cyclonic and Anticyclonic Circulation

The large convection cells that produce surface high and low pressures and their resulting winds are subject to the Coriolis force. In the Northern Hemisphere, the ascending air of the equatorial and subpolar lows rotates in a **cyclonic** (counterclockwise) fashion, and the descending air of the subtropical highs rotates in an **anticyclonic** (clockwise) fashion as seen from space. You can use your right hand to demonstrate the direction of this advection in the Northern Hemisphere. Figure 5.5 shows a hand descending toward the ground and turning clockwise. The fingers, representing the flow of air, point outward and encounter the ground as an obstacle to further descent. Similarly, a mass of cold, descending air spreads outward whenever it encounters Earth's surface. By contrast, the palm-up right hand of the figure represents the rising, deflected air of a low-pressure system in the Northern Hemisphere. As the hand (air) ascends, it turns to the right, from the perspective of Earth's surface, or counterclockwise, from the perspective of space. The fingers (winds) flow inward, to fill the low-pressure area with replacement air.

Lower pressure

PGF — Pressure gradient force
CF — Coriolis force

Figure 5.6 Geostrophic wind.

The result of deflection is a system of winds trending out of either the east or the west. Along the equator, the *northeast and southeast trade winds* (or *trades*) blow from the east. At higher latitudes, the other sides of the subtropical highs produce winds that blow from the west called the *prevailing westerlies,* which in the Northern Hemisphere, pass over the bulk of the world's population. In the high latitudes, the weakest of the surface systems, the *polar easterlies,* spin out of the polar highs (see fig. 5.3).

Other Influences on Winds

When both the Coriolis force and the pressure gradient are equal, a state of **strophic balance** occurs, producing an *ideal* horizontal air movement called a **geostrophic wind.** Such a wind flows perpendicularly to the pressure gradient (fig. 5.6). With balanced forces around high- and low-pressure systems, the resultant airflow is called a **gradient wind,** which flows along either a curved clockwise or counterclockwise path (fig. 5.7). Another force acting on air closest to Earth's surface is **friction.** The landscapes and surface waters impede the free flow of air, producing a drag that influences wind direction and velocity (fig. 5.8). Under the influ-

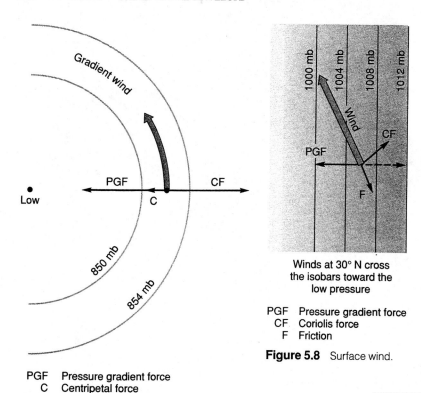

PGF Pressure gradient force
C   Centripetal force
CF   Coriolis force

Figure 5.7 Gradient wind.

Winds at 30° N cross
the isobars toward the
low pressure

PGF Pressure gradient force
CF   Coriolis force
F   Friction

Figure 5.8 Surface wind.

and warms itself as it approaches elevations of greater pressure. The result is the **chinook winds** of late winter and early spring. Because the warmth of these winds increases evaporation and melts snow, Native Americans called them "chinook" winds, which means "the snow eater." A similar wind occurs in the Alps, where it is called the **foehn.**

Generally, in regions where local elevations vary greatly, air drainage downslope sometimes creates weak winds. These are responsible for low night temperatures in the adjacent valleys. Whenever these downslope winds cover large areas for relatively long periods, they are called **katabatic winds.** In Alaska and northern Europe, where glaciers lie high in the mountains and higher plateaus, these winds can be stiff breezes, blowing steadily for days and weeks at a time. Similarly, the Adriatic Sea is the recipient of katabatic winds called **bora.** The same process produces the *mistrals* of the French Mediterranean. Note that with all these local and regional winds, special conditions take precedence over the general circulation of the atmosphere.

ence of *gravity,* denser air falls downslope (see katabatic winds in the next section).

REGIONAL AND LOCAL WINDS

Both the continents and the oceans affect the direction of Earth's surface winds. Mountains, lowlands, and ice caps on land are, more or less, dry, frictional barriers that impede the free flow of air along the surface. With less frictional resistance, oceans present broad, largely uninterrupted surfaces over which the air flows.

One of the most predictable winds influenced by the distribution of land and water and their resultant pressure systems is the **sea breeze.** Sea breezes develop whenever air pressure is low over the neighboring land and high over the water (fig. 5.9). Primarily an afternoon and early evening wind, the sea breeze is the movement of air from the cooler, descending air over the water toward the warmer, ascending air over the land. Because the heating of the land's surface is a daylight phenomenon, nighttime produces an opposite, seaward-flowing wind called a **land breeze.** This wind develops as the land rapidly loses its heat, while the adjacent water maintains its accumulated heat. Whereas the relatively cooler land produces a local high pressure, the warmer water heats the overlying air, causing it to rise and produce a relative low pressure.

Many areas of the world experience local winds that affect the local landscape. These winds generally form in mountainous or hilly regions, where uneven heating and cooling during certain seasons create a warming condition. On the **lee side** (side opposite that hit by the prevailing wind) of the Rocky Mountains in the United States, a downslope wind compresses

MOISTURE AND PRECIPITATION

In chapter 4, you learned that the kinds of surfaces over which air moves largely determine its moisture content. Air that moves over water is more likely to be moist than air that moves over land. *It is*

(a)

(b)

Figure 5.9 (*a*) Land breeze and (*b*) sea breeze.

important to understand that advection is just as responsible for moving moisture into the atmosphere as it is for redistributing heat. Moisture moves, however, on a two-way street. Moisture that becomes incorporated into the atmosphere eventually finds its way back to Earth's surfaces as some form of precipitation.

Sources of Moisture

Almost three-quarters of Earth's surface is covered with water. The air that comes into contact with the great expanses of oceans, large lakes, and extensive river systems picks up moisture along the air-water interfaces. Even plants, which pull water from soils, and the soils themselves supply water to the atmosphere. The process by which plants give off water is called **transpiration.** On a hot summer day, for example, the leaves of a large oak tree might transpire more than 300 liters (80 gal) into the atmosphere.

Evaporation

In chapter 4, you learned that evaporation is a cooling process. The energy required to evaporate water is stored as the **latent heat of vaporization,** which can be returned to the environment through condensation. Significantly, the amount of moisture already present in an air mass determines, with the air temperature, the rate at which evaporation—and transpiration—takes place. Motionless air, however, regardless of the presence of these two quantifiable elements, is not as efficient an evaporator as is moving air. This is

why advection is so important in the transfer of moisture from Earth's surfaces to the atmosphere. The principle behind this is as simple as what makes a hair dryer work. Moving air interchanges more molecules and, through more numerous molecular collisions, transfers more heat energy than does stationary air.

Although evaporation data are sketchy for the world's many surfaces, scientists have arrived at a few general statements about evaporation. Oceans are, obviously, more important than lands in adding moisture to the atmosphere. The zone of maximum evaporation from ocean surfaces occurs between latitudes 10° to 20°N and S of the equator. Over the continents, the maximum evaporation zone lies between the equator and 10° both north and south, especially because of the transpiration from the dense foliage of the tropical rain forests.

The Hydrologic Cycle

The **hydrologic cycle** is a recurrent process that moves moisture into and out of the atmosphere and through the life-forms, land-forms, rocks, soils, and standing water bodies of Earth's surface. Figure 5.10 shows the interrelationships required for the hydrologic cycle to be complete.

The bulk of the moisture that precipitates onto the continents derives from the oceans. Although local **evapotranspiration** (from evaporation + transpiration) does supply moisture, it does not compare in quantity with that produced by evaporation from the seas.

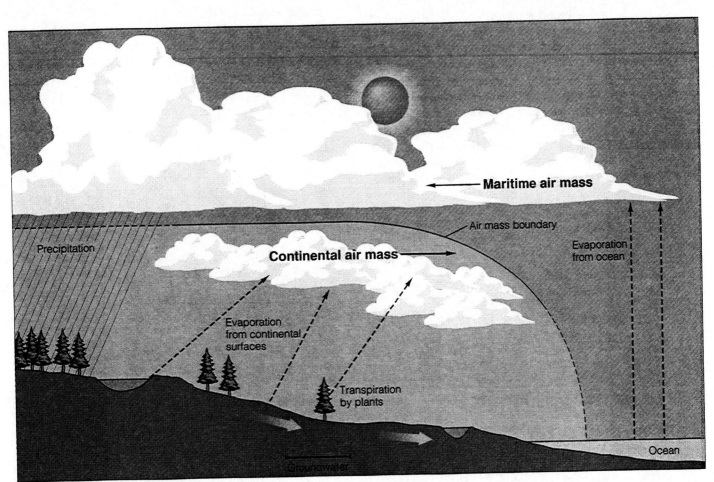

Figure 5.10   Hydrologic cycle correlated with the air-mass cycle.

Moisture in Air Masses

Air masses can be thought of as great invisible rivers that transport vast amounts of water vapor between sea and land or vice versa. Because of the general circulation of the atmosphere, humid, tropical, maritime air masses travel poleward, where they become cooler, lose most of their moisture through precipitation in one form or another, and ultimately transform themselves into polar continental air masses. In the reverse direction and process, continental polar air masses move toward the equator, warming as they travel to lower latitudes, and picking up moisture from soils, lakes, rivers, and vegetation. A continental air mass that migrates from Canada over the breadth and length of the Mississippi River's drainage area evaporates more water than the great river discharges in a comparable time. Eventually, **continental polar** (cP) air acquires enough moisture and heat to become **maritime tropical** (mT) air, precipitating moisture over the oceans.

The Dew Point

Warm air can hold more moisture than can an equal amount of cold air. To demonstrate this, visualize two sponges with different capacities. Cold air is like a somewhat compressed sponge; it has a reduced capacity for moisture. Warm air is an uncompressed sponge. Both sponges can hold moisture, but the uncompressed sponge has a greater capacity than the compressed sponge (fig. 5.11).

Note that both sponges can have their capacities diminished by further compression. The process that initiates condensation and the return of moisture to the surface is similar. Whenever an air mass is cooled, it acts like a squeezed sponge. The air, its volume decreased by lowered temperatures, begins to lose its moisture, first through condensation and then through precipitation.

The temperature at which an air mass becomes saturated, like a squeezed sponge at the limit of its capacity, is called the **dew point**. The relative humidity of an air mass at its dew point is 100%. If an air mass is cooled to its dew point above the initial freezing temperature (32° F, or 0° C), *dew* forms. You can make dew simply by removing a cold can from the refrigerator and placing it in a warm, humid room. As the air of the room comes in contact with the sides of the can, it cools and loses moisture, which condenses

as liquid drops on the sides of the can. Dew points reached below freezing produce water in the solid state and thin ice layers called **frost**.

Air masses with high relative humidity require only slight cooling to reach their dew points, while those with low relative humidity require significant cooling to reach their dew points. Condensation within and subsequent precipitation from an air mass is, therefore, dependent on the mechanisms that lower air-mass temperatures.

ATMOSPHERIC COOLING

Several mechanisms cool tropospheric air. Air that lies close to the surface can lose heat energy by conduction wherever the land or water is colder than the overlying air. Ordinarily, such cooling results in small-scale condensation. Another possible mechanism for cooling air is atmospheric mixing. As two dissimilar air masses merge, they lose their original temperatures and relative humidities, and the warmer of the two cools. This, too, is a relatively inconsequential mechanism. The dominant mechanism of air-mass cooling and condensation is **lifting**. As air masses either rise or are raised, they lose heat to the surrounding environment in a process called **adiabatic cooling**.

Rising air encounters lower pressures, and it expands. This leads to cooling. Air released from a car tire provides an analogy. The air pressure inside the tire exceeds that outside the tire. When released through the valve, the air expands and feels cool, even if the tire is heated by travel.

As unsaturated air rises through the atmosphere, it cools at the relatively rapid rate of 10° C per 1,000 meters (5.5° F per 1,000 ft) until it reaches its dew point. Such a rate is called the **dry adiabatic rate,** and it is a simple manifestation of cooling by expansion (fig. 5.12). Upon reaching its dew point, lifted air loses both heat

Figure 5.11 Squeezed sponge analog to cooled air. As the sponge is squeezed, it loses its capacity to hold moisture. Air that is cooled undergoes a similar reduction in capacity.

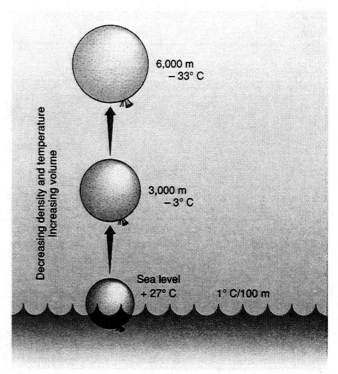

Figure 5.12 Dry adiabatic expansion.

and moisture through condensation. Since condensation is a heating process, the cooling rate decreases with further lifting. After it reaches its dew point, lifted air cools at the **saturated, or wet, adiabatic rate,** which varies with temperature but is about 6° C per 1,000 meters (3° F per 1,000 ft).

A parcel of air that rises is not in equilibrium with the ambient air because it is warmer and less dense. Such rising air is said to be **unstable air.** An unstable air mass continues to rise and move away from its original position until it matches the temperature of the ambient air. Whenever the ambient and air-mass temperatures match, a **stable equilibrium** exists with little or no vertical movement. If a parcel of air is colder (denser) than the surrounding air, it is **stable air** and has a tendency to return to its original position. Throughout the troposphere, as you learned in chapter 4, the ambient air undergoes a lapse, and instability in the atmosphere arises only when an air parcel is warmer at any altitude than the surrounding air.

CONDENSATION NUCLEI

Condensation takes place only on surfaces, such as on the cold can removed from the refrigerator. In the atmosphere, abundant microscopic particles, generally called dust and composed of industrial pollutants (particularly sulfurous compounds derived from the combustion of fossil fuels), volcanic ash, windblown soil and organic particles, pollen, and especially sea salts, provide condensation surfaces. Some of these surfaces attract water vapor. These tiny particles, called **hygroscopic, or condensation, nuclei,** must be present for condensation to occur.

FOG

Condensation in the air close to Earth's surface occurs as dew, frost, or **fog.** Fog is basically a cloud at ground level. Different kinds of fog have varied origins. In North America, a **radiation fog** occurs mostly during the fall and winter, when the air is cooled because of loss of heat through radiation. The ideal circumstance for a radiation fog is a clear night with no wind; clear skies allow radiation to escape without encountering a cover of clouds. Ordinarily, a radiation fog forms in inland areas, in river valleys, and over low-lying areas with moist ground. The fog is dispersed by an increase in wind intensity or the warming of the ground by the sun.

An **advection fog** can develop over either land or sea. Usually associated with winter and spring, this type of fog forms whenever warm air cools as it passes over cold land. The fog dissipates with a change of airflow and the heating of the land. Advection fogs are common over the seas during spring and early summer. At sea, and particularly along coastal areas, warm air cools as it moves over the cool sea surface. Whenever the wind shifts or the air warms, advection fogs dissipate.

Frontal fogs are associated with air-mass fronts, where warm air masses come into contact with colder air. There is no season during which such fogs are frequent. The fog disappears as soon as the front passes. **Upslope fogs** occur at higher elevations with the adiabatic cooling of rising air.

CLOUDS

Clouds are composed of water droplets and, at great heights, ice crystals. Clouds reflect the physical processes taking place in the atmosphere and thus are indicators of weather conditions. They also serve as building blocks of weather systems.

Lifting Mechanisms

Three kinds of lifting produce clouds (fig. 5.13). The first type is **convectional lifting.** Thermally induced, convection means un-

(a)

(b)

(c)

Figure 5.13 Three types of lifting mechanisms. (*a*) Convectional lifting. (*b*) Orographic lifting. (*c*) Frontal lifting.

stable air must rise to greater altitudes, where it cools, loses its ability to hold its moisture as it reaches the dew point, and forms clouds. Another type is **orographic lifting,** which occurs as air rises to pass over such topographic highs as plateaus and mountains. Orographic lifting is a mechanically induced process that moves air to higher altitudes, where cooling takes place. A third type of lifting is dynamically induced, requiring the leading edge of cold, denser air to plow under and lift warmer, lighter air. This type is **frontal lifting.**

Because air stability controls thermally induced lifting, the vertical development of clouds is dependent on the degree of instability in a given parcel of air. Stable air tends to produce **stratiform** (layered) **clouds,** but unstable air produces **cumuliform** (accumulated and vertically developed) **clouds** (table 5.1). Above stratiform clouds, a layer of warmer air caps the vertical extent of cloud formation (fig. 5.14).

Meteorologists categorize clouds according to their shapes. Those with layered structures are called stratus, whereas those with

(a)

(b)

Figure 5.14   (*a*) Cumuliform clouds with flat bottoms and dome-shaped tops indicate vertical air movement. (*b*) Stratiform clouds.

TABLE 5.1 Cloud Types

Altitude (in feet)	Type	Description
High, 20,000+ (cirro)	Cirrus (Ci)	Wispy clouds of ice crystals
	Cirrostratus (Cs)	Thin, whitish sheet; milky sky; sometimes, a halo forms
	Cirrocumulus (Cc)	Mackerel sky
Middle, 6,500–20,000 (alto)	Altostratus (As)	Uniform, sheet cloud
	Altocumulus (Ac)	Flattened globular masses
Low, surface–6,500	Stratocumulus (Sc)	Large globular mass with flattened section
	Stratus (St)	Low uniform layer of clouds
	Nimbostratus (Ns)	Rain-bearing, layered clouds
	Mammatus	Globular masses on the underside of a cumulonimbus that indicate a strong downdraft
Vertically developed, 1,000 to the top of the troposphere	Cumulus (Cu)	Thick, dense cloud with vertical development
	Cumulonimbus (Cb)	Heavy mass of cloud with great vertical development

ball-like accumulations are called cumulus. Both terms can serve either as prefixes or suffixes (fig. 5.15). The terminology for cloud types derives from a scheme devised in 1803 by British naturalist Luke Howard. In Howard's classification, a puffy cloud is *cumulus* (heaped); a sheetlike cloud is *stratus* (layered); a wispy cloud is *cirrus* (curly); and a rain-bearing cloud is *nimbus* (dark and rainy). Four cloud divisions based on height include high clouds (*cirro*), middle clouds (*alto*), low clouds, and finally, vertically developed clouds. A cumulonimbus cloud is a vertically developed, billowy, rain-producing cloud, whereas a nimbostratus is a layered, rain-bearing low cloud.

Cloud Mechanisms Responsible for Rain and Snow

Rain and snow originate in clouds of different temperature characteristics. In *warm cloud* formation, condensed water forms droplets that collide and coalesce as they fall through the cloud. Because of a slight buoyancy, the smaller droplets fall as fast as the larger droplets, ensuring collisions and droplet growth. Other influences on the formation of raindrops are *updrafts* (upward-moving air) and *electrical charges*. This last influence manifests itself after a flash of lightning, with which large droplets appear to be associated. Even without lightning, clouds establish electrical fields that appear to strongly influence droplet formation.

Condensation in cold clouds results in the formation of ice particles. As additional water condenses preferentially on the ice particles, they become the hexagonally shaped stars familiar to us as snowflakes. When they grow large enough, the snowflakes begin to fall. On their way through the cloud and the air below the cloud, they may encounter warmer temperatures, melt, and fall as

Figure 5.15 Cloud types.

rain. If the temperature is below freezing along the snowflakes' paths of descent, they maintain their form and fall as snow. Both types of precipitation are shown in figure 5.16.

MIDDLE-LATITUDE CYCLONES

Middle-latitude (between 35° and 65°) weather is characterized by a succession of pervasive, alternating, low- and high-pressure systems that move from west to east along the path of the prevailing westerlies. The movement of these pressure systems is responsible for the great variability of weather in the United States and Canada because they occur along zones of convergence and conflict between polar and tropical air masses. Thus, understanding these systems of counterclockwise and clockwise air movements, which direct air masses into and out of a region, is the key to interpreting most of North America's weather.

The daily mapping of those movements requires forecasters to identify the boundaries and internal structure of pressure centers. On weather maps, the National Weather Service uses millibar measurements to mark the air pressures that define cyclones and anticyclones. An important mapping symbol is the **isobar** (*iso*, meaning "equal," and *bar*, meaning "pressure"), which is a line that connects sites with identical pressure readings. *Isobars never touch* because they represent different pressure readings, and these readings are marked in arbitrary intervals, such as the 3-millibar units shown in figure 5.17.

Size, shape, speed, and direction vary for each cyclone, but some average characteristics are well known. Typically, the long axis of a low is about 100 times greater than its vertical thickness. Some cyclones are known to reach altitudes of about 10 to 11 kilometers (6 or 7 mi). Over North America, a winter cyclone might have dimensions of 1,048 by 1,935 kilometers (650 by 1,200 mi). Usually, cyclones move relatively fast, with summertime velocities reaching a little over 30 kilometers (20 mi) per hour and wintertime cyclones racing over the surface at speeds approaching 50 kilometers (30 mi) per hour. As they trend generally eastward, cyclones follow any one of nine different paths across southern Canada and the United States (fig. 5.18). The tracks largely determine how much moisture is associated with each cyclone. One that moves along the Alberta track passes over broad expanses of land until it reaches the Great Lakes, where it can pick up moisture. Because air in motion around a cyclone comes from different directions, air masses meet along the various kinds of frontal boundaries, which were introduced in chapter 4. The air masses then interact along their mutual and changing boundaries, producing by frontal lifting most of the inclement weather experienced in North America.

By the early twentieth century, some patterns of inclement weather were apparent. For a long time, scientists had known that precipitation was related to decreases in barometric pressure. Based on this information and on their surface observations, some Scandinavian scientists developed a model of middle-latitude cyclones. The stages in this model trace a cyclone from formation to dissipation.

In the initial stage of the model, two dissimilar air masses meet along a straight-line boundary (fig. 5.19). As the cyclone develops, this boundary bows and twists into two, then three, kinds of fronts. The energy for this process comes from converging air and from the heat released during condensation. In the final stage, a loss of this energy leads to the cyclone's dissipation.

If cyclones, in general, go through this process, why do some cyclones, in particular, generate more severe storms than others? The answer to this question lies in the relationship between the upper and lower portions of the weather sphere. At the surface, this relationship expresses itself in the development

(a)

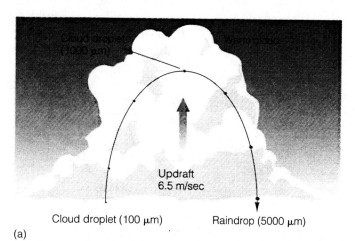

(b)

Figure 5.16   (*a*) Warm cloud precipitation. (*b*) Cold cloud precipitation.

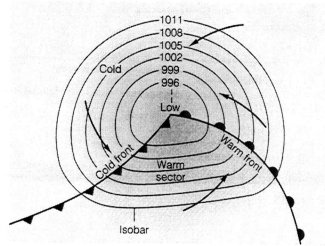

Figure 5.17   Isobar map indicating a low-pressure center. Interval is 3 millibars.

of fronts. Meteorologists represent fronts associated with cyclones and anticyclones by lines with attached symbols. The symbols lie on the leading side of the front. Although the air is invisible, its frontal shapes reveal themselves in certain types of clouds and patterns as seen from space. The constantly shifting air around the cyclone molds the accompanying cloud system into the shape of a large comma as seen from above. Precipitation can accompany the clouds, depending on the type and the instability of the air lifted along the fronts.

PRESSURE PATTERNS ALOFT AND VERTICAL AIRFLOW

In chapter 4, you learned that a high-speed wind called the jet stream flows in a general west-to-east trend across North America (see box 5.1). The position of this air stream and the atmospheric pressures associated with it influence cyclone development (cyclogenesis) by directing air vertically toward or away from the center of a surface pressure system.

By sending aloft an aneroid barometer, weather observers can map the pressure patterns of the upper air and trace the winds driven by the pressure gradient. Atmospheric pressure can change at any given altitude, just as it changes along the surface, and the upper-level air may flow where the barometer reads only 500 millibars. Because half of the atmosphere's mass lies below an altitude of approximately 6 kilometers (3.7 mi), the pressures associated with the jet stream are about half that of surface values. In this high-altitude, lower-pressure environment, winds move faster, on average, than surface winds, partly because they encounter no hard rock or water to rob them of energy through friction. The *upper-level winds* trend along a path parallel to the isobars, converging and diverging (flowing together or apart) in shifting locations.

Although the winds associated with a cyclone converge on the low at the surface, they begin to diverge as they rise (fig. 5.20). Whenever the winds aloft are directed away from Earth's surface by the pressure gradient, the surface pressure decreases as upward

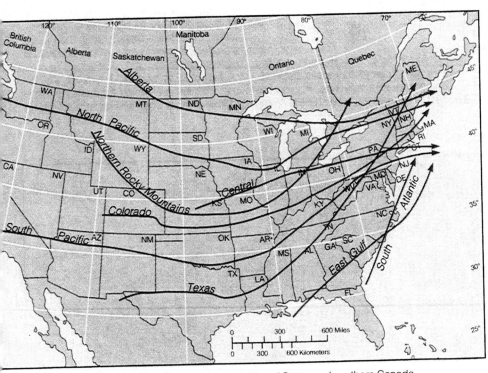

Figure 5.18 Typical cyclonic paths across the United States and southern Canada.

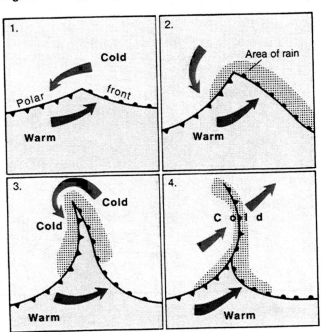

Figure 5.19 Formation of waves and fronts between two dissimilar air masses.

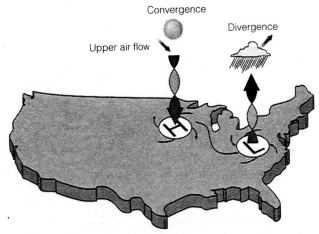

Figure 5.20 Convergence and divergence can intensify a cyclone or anticyclone. Whenever divergence aloft is greater than convergence at the surface, a low intensifies. Its cartographic expression yields closer spacing between isobars.

Box 5.1

Further Consideration

UPPER-LEVEL WINDS OF THE TROPOSPHERE

Narrow bands of fast-flowing winds, called jets, in the upper levels (10 to 14 km, or 6.2 to 8.7 mi) of the troposphere occur in zones of straight or meandering streamlines that develop because of steep pressure gradients. The gradients result from sharp temperature contrasts along boundaries or fronts that separate cold, polar air and warm, subtropical air. The gradients and the absence of friction (with the ground) intensify the speed of the jets. In the core of the jets, or the zone of maximum flow, wind speeds can exceed 100 knots (119 mph).

The jet stream's flow was first associated with fast-moving high clouds. These high-speed winds were encountered by pilots of high-flying military aircraft during World War II and are experienced today by pilots of commercial jets. Meteorologists monitor the circulation pattern of upper-level winds because these high-altitude winds are significant in the global transfer of energy and in the control of surface systems.

Figure 5.A shows a typical set of streamlines over North America, where a strong flow of cold, dry air moves equa-

951101/1200F000 250 MB STREAMLINES

Figure 5.A Streamlines for the 250-millibar level on Nov. 1, 1995.

torward along the western side of the jets, and a flow of warm, moist air moves poleward along the eastern side. The streamlines depicted here for November 1, 1995, are located at 10.3 kilometers (6.4 mi). On that date, the pressure at this level was 250 millibars, and the highest speeds were 55 knots, found in an area just north of the Great Lakes and depicted in figure 5.B. Over the United States, temperatures at this altitude ranged from 243° F above the Florida Keys to 257° F above Minnesota. At the surface, the western states experienced cold, and even snowy, weather, while the eastern states basked under relatively warm fall temperatures.

Apply Your Knowledge

1. Why do the winds in the upper levels of the troposphere move parallel to the isobars?

2. Where in figure 5.B are the highest wind speeds?

3. Why did the Southeast experience warm temperatures on November 1st?

4. What type of air mass was driven into the Southeast on November 1st?

5. Would rain be a likely weather condition in the Southeast according to figure 5.B?

951101/1200F000 250 MB WIND SPEED (KNOTS) - OBSERVED WIND BARBS

Figure 5.B   Wind speeds in knots for the 250-millibar level on Nov.1, 1995. Selected high wind speeds are shown.

flow increases. The ultimate effect of divergence aloft is to intensify the low at the surface. Such an intensification depends on a neighboring anticyclone. The replacement of air that exits the bottom of the anticyclone must come from above; thus, the strengthening of both systems is an interdependent process. Figure 5.20 also shows air converging aloft to replace that lost by advection at the surface of the high. For systems in the Northern Hemisphere, cyclone intensity increases the most when the surface storm has the proper upper air support, which is an upper-level trough of low pressure west of the surface low. Without this upper-level support, fully developed storms weaken.

FULLY DEVELOPED CYCLONES

Over many years of observations, meteorologists have framed the nature of a typical cyclone. Figure 5.21 shows the pattern most often seen in a fully developed, middle-latitude cyclone. The cold front generates a narrow band of showers. This band can develop as a zone of intense precipitation and storm activity called a **squall line.** Behind the cold front, cP air moves counterclockwise, catching the warm front to the east and lifting it to make an occluded front. Maritime tropical air moves north or northeastward ahead of the cold front. As this warm, moist air encounters cooler air, it rises to make a warm front. The air north of the warm front is composed of modified air that cooled as it moved northward.

Warm-Front Weather Patterns

A warm front is a long, gently sloping boundary between overlying warm, mT air and underlying cooler air (fig. 5.22). The gentle incline of this boundary has an average slope ratio of 1:150. Well ahead of the surface contact, the warm air rises to form cirrus clouds. Altostratus clouds or low stratocumulus clouds lie farther back, followed by lower, nimbostratus clouds, which bring prolonged light precipitation under stable air conditions. Some warm fronts are accompanied by relatively unstable conditions, producing storms intermixed with light precipitation. Figure 5.22 shows both stable and unstable conditions along a warm front.

Cold-Front Weather Patterns

Cold fronts are relatively steep slopes (1:50), where rapidly advancing cold air forces warm air upward. The gradient of a cold front can be four times steeper than that of a warm front. This abrupt boundary is the site of cumulonimbus formation and violent weather, often in the form of squalls, thunderstorms, or even tornadoes. Although the precipitation is heavy, it is usually

Figure 5.22 A warm front is a long, gentle slope with a leading edge of high cirrus clouds and a lower, trailing edge associated with periods of prolonged precipitation, which is usually light, as in (a), or with heavy precipitation where the air is unstable, as in (b).

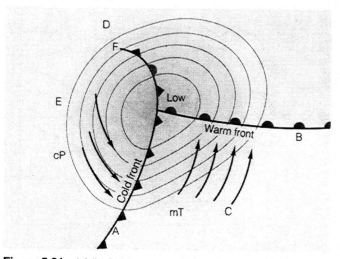

Figure 5.21 A fully developed cyclone in a map view: A marks the cold front; B is the warm front; C is mT air; D is the original center of the low; E is cP air; and F is the occluded front.

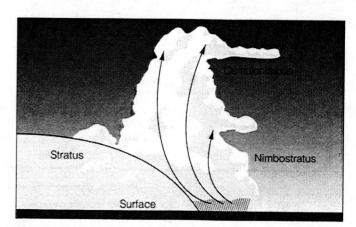

Figure 5.23 Structure of a cold front.

of shorter duration than that of the warm front. Behind the cold front, stratus, stratocumulus, and cumulus clouds are frequently followed by clear skies and fair weather (fig. 5.23).

THUNDERSTORMS

Severe thunderstorms form in unstable air where the wind speed increases rapidly with increasing altitude, often in the vicinity of the jet stream. As a thermodynamic machine, a thunderstorm converts the potential energy of the latent heat of vaporization into the kinetic energy released through condensation. Moist air, which is unstable, rises rapidly as violent vertical currents within the storm. Thunderstorms are capable of releasing torrential downpours of rain or heavy snows. Gusty winds, lightning, and, of course, thunder are all typical of these storms.

Thunderstorms evolve through three stages (fig. 5.24). In the first stage, converging surface winds center on a low, then rise to carry moisture through condensation levels. In the second stage, rain, snow, or hail begins to fall within the well-developed vertical cloud, while higher up, in the cloud "towers," ice begins to form. This mature stage of thunderstorm development brings a downdraft and lightning. In the third stage, the downdraft destroys the parent cyclonic cell. Along the surface, convergent winds shift to become divergent winds, cutting off the updraft and effectively blocking the system's energy source. Without further updrafts, the storm dies, and precipitation stops.

Thunderstorms may reach the tropopause in their mature stage. The great vertical development is generated by lifting. Ordinarily, more thunderstorms occur in low latitudes than in high latitudes, making convection the most important lifting mechanism. Figure 5.25 shows thunderstorm distribution by frequency of occurrence for various latitudes.

Lightning and Thunder

For some as yet unexplained reason, electrical charges in a thunderstorm separate during the second stage of development, making the upper cloud layers positively charged and the lower layers negatively charged. Precipitation may, however, play a key role in this polarization of charges. Whenever the electrical potential gradient becomes sufficiently imbalanced, a lightning flash occurs. The temperature of the lightning may reach $10,000°$ C ($18,032°$ F), causing rapid heating and expansion of the neighboring air. This expansion results in thunder, the noise of lightning. Because the speed of light is so much greater than the speed of sound, thunder is heard after the lightning flash. A rule of thumb that tells the observer how far away a lightning strike was relies on this temporal difference. Every 3 seconds between the appearance of the lightning and the sound of thunder represents 1 kilometer between the observer and the lightning (or 5 seconds for every mile of distance between the observer and the lightning).

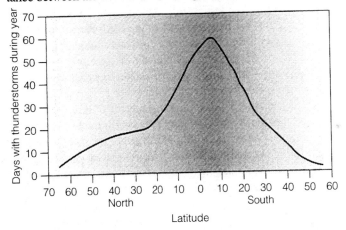

Figure 5.25 Latitudinal frequency of thunderstorms.

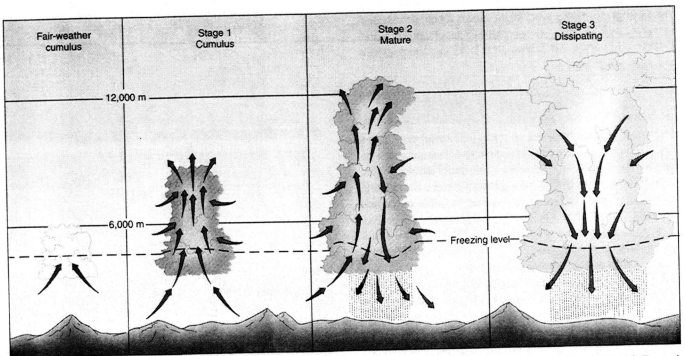

Figure 5.24 Stages in the development of a thunderstorm. (Source: Schroeder and Buck, *Fire Weather Agricultural Handbook 360*, U.S. Dept. of Agriculture, U.S. Forest Service.

Tornadoes

The most violent storms on this planet are **tornadoes,** which are funnel-shaped clouds accompanied by winds in excess of 322 kilometers (200 mi) per hour. This storm activity is centered on an intense low-pressure cell, which is related to a squall line of severe thunderstorms associated with a middle-latitude cyclone. Generally, a rapidly rotating updraft within a very unstable air mass creates a vortex of air that descends to the surface. Figure 5.26 shows this vortex within a cumulonimbus cloud. Once the funnel reaches the ground, a true tornado forms and moves rapidly, between 40 and 60 kilometers (25 and 35 mi) per hour. Tornadoes sometimes skip or jump over the surface, rather than moving smoothly in contact with the ground. The general trend of movement for these violent storms is southwest to northeast.

Because tornadoes are dangerous, our knowledge of them is still incomplete. Observations of tornadoes are often limited to chance sightings, although some weather scientists have made a career out of "chasing" tornadoes. Through their work and that of other scientists, we now know that the energy for tornadoes derives from a collision between two distinctly different air masses.

In North America, the colliding air masses are the cold, dry, and stable Canadian air designated as continental polar and the warm, moist, and unstable Gulf of Mexico air called maritime tropical. Because these air masses are capable of colliding throughout the year, tornadoes can occur in any season from southern Canada to the Gulf of Mexico. Within North America, most tornadoes occur in the interior plains, over which there are many air-mass collisions. In particular, the United States experiences 75% of its tornadoes between March and July (see box 5.2).

The violence of tornadoes is often tragic. During a 16-hour period on April 3, 1974, more than 100 tornadoes crossed the American Southeast, leaving a path of destruction, injuring more than 600 people, and taking 350 lives. The damage left behind by a passing tornado results from high winds, flying debris, and the great pressure differences between the center of the vortex and the interior of buildings. Buildings literally fly apart in response to the pressure gradient.

Occluded Fronts

Cold fronts move faster than warm fronts. In the proximity of the cyclonic center, they often catch and undermine warmer air, separating a warm front from the surface by a layer of denser, colder air. The result is an occlusion, or a gap between the warm front and Earth's surface. This type of air boundary is called a **cold occlusion** (fig. 5.27a). The air behind the cold front can also be less dense than the air preceding it. In figure 5.27b, the warm-front boundary stays in contact with the surface, while the cold front overrides it. This produces a **warm occlusion.**

Both types of occluded fronts are accompanied by precipitation. The amount and type of precipitation depend on the air temperature and the rate of lifting. If a cold occlusion passed over your location, you would experience a drop in temperature. A warm occlusion's passing would have the opposite effect. Often, the precipitation associated with an occluded front, regardless of type, is prolonged and heavy.

Figure 5.26   The vortex in a cumulonimbus cloud results in a tornado.

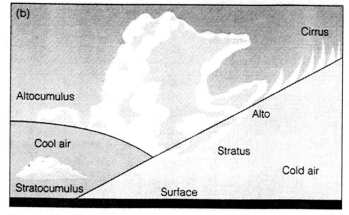

Figure 5.27   In a cold occlusion (a), the warm front is occluded, while in a warm occlusion (b), the cold front is occluded.

Box 5.2

TORNADO: A LATE-AUTUMN STORM

Tornadoes are the most destructive storm systems to move across the face of Earth. Although such systems can occur at any time of the year, most people do not associate tornadoes with late autumn, when many air masses show stability over the United States.

During a 3-day period from Saturday, November 21, to Monday, November 23, 1992, an unusual late-autumn thunderstorm system ripped a destructive path across nine southeastern states. According to the National Weather Service, 80 tornadoes were sighted, with at least 45 twisters touching down in a 24-hour period ending at 7:00 A.M. Eastern Standard Time on Monday.

The unseasonable weather was caused by a collision between moist air from the Gulf of Mexico and drier, cooler continental air. The maritime air first moved over Texas and Louisiana in association with a low-pressure system on Saturday; then it moved on to Mississippi, Alabama, and Georgia. By early Monday, the storm system had passed over North Carolina, before moving out to sea.

In the wake of the storm, tornadoes were responsible for 25 deaths, including 15 in Mississippi, 5 in Georgia, and 1 in each of the other states touched by the system. The destructive force injured over 300 persons, caused power outages, snapped trees, and destroyed property.

The tornadoes terrorized the region's population. One eyewitness said, "The sky turned black and there was a thunderous roar lasting for 30 minutes. The tornado then appeared, hugging the ground for miles, sweeping away everything in its path." A government official touring the storm's aftermath stated, "The area looks like a war zone."

Apply Your Knowledge

1. Where did the low-pressure system originate? Why?
2. Why is the appearance of mammatus clouds (see table 5.1) at the base of a severe thunderstorm a good initial indicator of the potential for tornado formation?
3. The weather maps in figures 5.C, 5.D, and 5.E are summaries of observations. Why is the southeastern part of the United States susceptible to tornado activity at any time of the year?

Figure 5.D Sunday, November 22, 1992. (NOAA Daily Weather Maps.)

Figure 5.C Saturday, November 21, 1992. (NOAA Daily Weather Maps.)

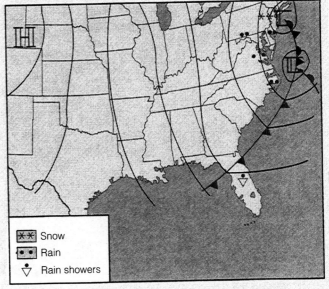

Figure 5.E Monday, November 23, 1992. (NOAA Daily Weather Maps.)

Box 5.3

Investigating the Environment

HURRICANE ANDREW: AMERICA'S MOST DESTRUCTIVE STORM

No natural disaster in American history has been more devastating than the August 1992 storm designated Hurricane Andrew. The total costs of Andrew's destruction have now exceeded $20 billion, mostly to Dade County, Florida. The storm severely damaged more than 60,000 residences in a path 48 to 80 kilometers (30 to 50 mi) wide (fig. 5.F). Some communities lost more than 90% of their buildings. In all, the storm displaced 250,000 people, ruined businesses and public facilities, and killed more than 20 people. Florida was just a brief passage for Andrew as the storm continued to move to the west and northwest, eventually striking Louisiana west of New Orleans (fig. 5.G).

Evacuations of both southern Florida, including the Florida Keys, and southern Louisiana saved lives, but Andrew's unexpected strength caught many by surprise. After witnessing the August 23rd devastation of southern Florida, the people of the Mississippi Delta knew that evacuation was the only short-term protection they could rely on for safety.

In the coastal waters of the Gulf of Mexico, where oil-drilling platforms stood in the storm's path, oil companies suffered damages estimated at $1.5 billion. Hurricane Andrew had an accompanying storm surge that probably reached 6 meters (18 ft) around some of the platforms. About 200 of these costly rigs were put out of commission with major damage.

Andrew's path was watched closely by the National Hurricane Center, which ranks storms according to their power. Although Andrew was not officially ranked as a category 5 hurricane, its path of destruction has led some scientists to conclude that it was, indeed, a rare example of Earth's most powerful storm.

When Andrew struck Florida, it stayed over land for only a short period (fig. 5.G). Ordinarily, hurricanes lose strength as they pass over land. However, because Florida is not very wide, Andrew passed from the warm Atlantic waters into those of the Gulf of Mexico and gathered renewed strength as it approached Louisiana.

You can see in figure 5.G that Hurricane Andrew lay east of the Bahamas on Sunday, August 23, 1992. The storm hit Homestead and surrounding communities in southern Florida on Monday and then quickly moved into the Gulf of Mexico. Pressure readings for the hurricane were not exceptional, and in fact, were relatively high, as the marked isobars reveal. Monday's pressure for the center of the storm registered 945 millibars. By Wednesday, Andrew's lowest reading was 975 millibars.

In the aftermath of the storm, weather scientists discovered that Andrew's winds reached strengths powerful enough to move cars and trucks. Most of the anemometers in the storm's path were broken, so accurate wind speeds are unavailable, but some scientists believe that the narrow paths of destruction seen in some communities (in particular, Homestead, Florida, and areas west of New Orleans in Louisiana) indicate that Andrew spawned a number of small tornadoes. The devastation in Florida, however, was in most cases so widespread that hurricane winds, not tornadoes, must have been responsible.

Apply Your Knowledge

1. Where did Hurricane Andrew originate? Why?
2. The weather maps are summaries of observations. What is the role of the National Hurricane Center, and how effective is its warning system?

Figure 5.F Typical scene of the devastation caused by Hurricane Andrew, August 1992.

(a) Sunday, August 23, 1992

(b) Monday, August 24, 1992

(c) Tuesday, August 25, 1992

(d) Wednesday, August 26, 1992

Figure 5.G The sequence of weather maps shows the movement of Hurricane Andrew from just east of the Bahamas to landfall in southern Louisiana. All are as of 7 A.M. Eastern Standard Time of the day indicated. (*a*) Sunday, August 23, 1992. (*b*) Monday, August 24, 1992. (*c*) Tuesday, August 25, 1992. (*d*) Wednesday, August 26, 1992. (NOAA Daily Weather Maps.)

TROPICAL CYCLONES

The most familiar classification of tropical cyclones is based on wind speed. A *tropical disturbance* is characterized by poor circulation and mild breezes. Its isobaric expression is open (fig. 5.28). A *tropical depression* produces higher wind speeds, usually about 56 kilometers (35 mi) per hour, and it turns under one or two closed isobars, showing increased intensity. A **tropical storm** is a more violent cyclonic movement, with wind speeds between those of a depression and 119 kilometers (74 mi) per hour. On a weather map, a tropical storm exhibits closed isobars.

Earth's biggest atmospheric storms are **hurricanes** (also called *typhoons*). You read in chapter 1 about how Hurricane Hugo devastated the Carolinas in 1989. These atmospheric events are so large that the National Weather Service assigns them identifying names. Wind speeds associated with hurricanes are usually well over 120 kilometers (75 mi) per hour, with some hurricanes accompanied for brief periods by winds as high as 290 kilometers (180 mi) per hour (see box 5.3 on pages 112–113).

Observations of many hurricanes have enabled meteorologists to label the main characteristics of these storms. Usually, they occur in late summer and early fall in the Northern Hemisphere because of the heat accumulated in warm-water areas during the high-sun period. The excessive latent heat of vaporization eventually becomes the enormous kinetic energy of these storms. Unlike the smaller cyclonic systems to their north, hurricanes ordinarily have no anticyclonic companion, and hurricanes also yield lower barometric readings. A low between 914 millibars (26.9 in) and 931 millibars (27.5 in) is not uncommon.

The tracks of hurricanes pass over and by some highly populated areas in the Western Hemisphere. The Windward Islands of the Antilles are extremely vulnerable, as are the large islands of the Greater Antilles. Texas is frequently hit, and a 6.2-kilometer (10-mi) seawall at Galveston is testimony to that community's resolve not to be inundated by the storm surge of seawater that rises in response to the lower barometric pressure associated

TABLE 5.2	A Comparison of Middle-Latitude Cyclones, Tornadoes, and Hurricanes		
	Cyclone	**Tornado**	**Hurricane**
Shape	Egg	Funnel	Disc
Pressure Gradient	Moderate	Very steep	Steep
Dimension	Large area (1,000+ km)	Small area (10+ m)	Intermediate area (300+ km)
Origin	cP–mT conflict	cP–mT conflict	Latent heat
Season	Winter	Spring	Late summer, fall

with hurricanes. The common tracks of hurricanes and typhoons are shown in figure 5.29. Table 5.2 compares the characteristics of cyclones, tornadoes, and hurricanes.

ANTICYCLONES AND FAIR WEATHER

Cells of high pressure with roughly concentric isobars and, in the Northern Hemisphere, clockwise circulation are often accompanied by fair weather. Anticyclones are generally larger than middle-latitude cyclones; they also move across the surface more slowly and have smaller pressure gradients. They are common to the middle latitudes both north and south of the equator, particularly during the warm season.

Beside light winds or even calm conditions, summer anticyclones produce clear skies and fair-weather cumulus clouds. With little cloud cover, these systems allow radiational cooling during the night. Winter anticyclones are usually continental in origin. Characteristically stable, dry air is sometimes stagnant, allowing pollutants to accumulate. Like the summer anticyclones, they produce clear night skies, but the temperatures are usually much colder.

Two summer anticyclones are of climatic significance for the United States. One, located in the western Atlantic and called the Bermuda High, funnels air into the country from the Gulf of Mexico and the region of warm water around eastern Florida. The other summer anticyclone is located along the coast of California, where it blocks the eastward movement of cyclones and diminishes precipitation over southern California. Both of these high-pressure systems ordinarily fade with the changing sun angle. In California, the result is winter rains in the vicinity of Los Angeles. The influence of these and other anticyclones on climate is discussed more fully in chapter 6.

A CYCLONE

A cyclone that moves into the north central United States is typified in figure 5.30. Table 5.3 shows what weather can be expected along several lines passed by the system. Unlike the hypothetical storm you read about in chapter 4, this is a real storm system. You should be able to pick out the regions of cP and mT air and the fronts associated with the cyclonic movement. Above this surface system lies a divergent wind system that intensifies the cyclone.

Figure 5.28 The isobaric expression of a tropical disturbance looks like a wave.

Figure 5.29   Common tracks of hurricanes (Atlantic Ocean) and typhoons (Pacific and Indian Oceans).

Figure 5.30
Movement of a typical cyclone through the central United States. (NOAA Daily Weather Maps.)

TABLE 5.3 Atmospheric Changes Resulting from Frontal Passage

Weather Element	Before Passing	While Passing	After Passing
Typical Weather Associated with a Cold Front			
Winds	South-southwest	Gusty, shifting	West-northwest
Temperature	Warm	Sudden drop	Colder
Pressure	Falling steadily	Sharp rise	Rising steadily
Clouds	Increasing Ci, Cs, then either Cu or Cb	Cu or Cb	Often Cu
Precipitation	Short period of showers	Heavy showers of rain or snow, sometimes with hail, thunder, and lightning	Decreasing intensity of showers, then clearing
Visibility	Fair to poor in haze	Poor, followed by improving	Good except in showers
Dew Point	High; remains steady	Sharp drop	Lowering
Typical Weather Associated with a Warm Front			
Winds	South-southeast	Variable	South-southwest
Temperature	Cool-cold	Steady rise	Warmer
Pressure	Usually falling	Leveling off	Slight rise, followed by fall
Clouds	In this order: Ci, Cs, As, Ns, St and fog; occasionally, Cb in summer	Stratus-type	Clearing with scattered Sc; occasionally, Cb in summer
Precipitation	Light to moderate rain, snow, sleet, or drizzle	Drizzle	Usually none; sometimes light rain or showers
Visibility	Poor	Poor, but improving	Fair in haze
Dew Point	Steady	Slow rise	Rise, then steady

FURTHER THOUGHTS: METEOROLOGY AND SAFETY

As this chapter illustrates, Earth's dynamic atmosphere constantly distributes energy over the planet's surface. The expression of this distribution is the daily weather. At times, this expression is an exhibition of great power, as it is in thunderstorms, tornadoes, and hurricanes. Because we now understand most of the mechanisms that drive the atmosphere and their quantifiable components, we can recognize tropospheric patterns on the bases of many observations.

Meteorologists can now predict violent or otherwise dangerous weather with greater accuracy and more lead time than was once possible. The practical consequence of knowledge about fronts, storms, and icy and foggy conditions is a safer world. As they did during Hurricanes Hugo and Andrew, weather predictions save lives. In conjunction with technicians and government agencies, scientists have invented elaborate warning systems that make our lives safer. Some airports now have weather detecting systems that warn pilots of powerful downdrafts that produce the wind shear that has been known to cause crashes. Along coasts, meteorologists issue small-craft warnings whenever storms produce dangerous wave conditions. In winter, meteorologists issue warnings about hazardous driving conditions caused by snows and icy rains. When we heed these warnings, we reduce the level of risk to property and life.

SIGNIFICANT POINTS

1. Solar energy is the ultimate driving force behind the atmosphere, but radiation from Earth's surface is the immediate source of atmospheric heat.
2. Atmospheric warming is primarily attributed to radiation, conduction, convection, and advection. Of these processes, the last two are the most significant.
3. The planet's surface is unevenly heated. Warmer surfaces heat the overlying air, causing it to rise in convection currents.
4. The atmosphere circulates through large convection cells, which are governed in their movement by friction, by the pressure gradient, and by the Coriolis force. Moving fluids trend to the right in the Northern Hemisphere and to the left in the Southern Hemisphere.
5. Steeper pressure gradients mean winds with greater velocities.
6. In the Northern Hemisphere, cyclonic action is a counterclockwise movement; anticyclonic action is a clockwise movement.

7. The atmosphere circulates through the trade winds, the prevailing westerlies, and the polar easterlies.

8. Sea breezes prevail during the day, and land breezes prevail during the night.

9. Local winds, such as the chinook of the lee side of the Rockies, prevail over the general circulation. Katabatic winds are downslope winds.

10. Evapotranspiration from the continents provides air masses with some moisture, but the chief source of moisture for the atmosphere is the oceans.

11. Air lifted by convection, by orographic barriers, and by fronts can cool adiabatically to reach the dew point. The dew point is the temperature at which a parcel of air becomes saturated. Condensation takes place on microscopic surfaces in the atmosphere called condensation, or hygroscopic, nuclei.

12. Clouds can be classified by their altitude and their shape. Layered clouds are called stratiform, while nonlayered clouds are called cumuliform.

13. Middle-latitude cyclones are associated with stormy weather; middle-latitude anticyclones are associated with fair weather.

14. Three types of fronts can produce precipitation. A cold front is associated with squall lines, including thunderstorms and tornadoes, when the air is very unstable. A warm front is often the moving site of prolonged precipitation. An occluded front can combine the effects of both kinds of fronts.

15. Lightning occurs when opposing electrical charges accumulate on opposite ends of a cloud. Most lightning is cloud to cloud.

16. Tornadoes are violent vortices with funnel shapes and high winds.

17. Hurricanes are enormous storms that develop in late summer and fall over tropical waters and then move, in the path of the trade winds, across the ocean, sometimes encountering land.

18. Hurricanes derive their energy from the latent heat of vaporization, which becomes kinetic energy during condensation.

ESSENTIAL TERMS

advection 95
pressure gradient 96
cyclonic 97
anticyclonic 97
strophic balance 97
geostrophic wind 97
sea breeze 98

land breeze 98
katabatic wind 98
transpiration 99
latent heat of vaporization 99
hydrologic cycle 99
evapotranspiration 100

dew point 100
dry adiabatic rate 101
saturated, or wet, adiabatic rate 101
hygroscopic, or condensation, nuclei 101

advection fog 101
frontal fog 101
upslope fog 101
convectional lifting 102
orographic lifting 102
frontal lifting 102

stratiform clouds 102
cumuliform clouds 102
isobar 104
squall line 108
tropical storm 112
hurricane 112

REVIEW QUESTIONS

1. Illustrate the distribution of solar radiation. Indicate the average percentage for radiation:
   a. Absorbed directly by the atmosphere
   b. Reflected or scattered
   c. Absorbed by Earth's surface
   d. Absorbed by the atmosphere after being reflected or reradiated from Earth

2. Explain how heat is transferred by conduction, convection, and radiation.

3. How does advection differ from convection?

4. What is a pressure gradient, and how does it influence air motion?

5. Identify the locations of Earth's pressure belts.

6. Explain the cause of the Coriolis force.

7. Illustrate the general circulation of planetary winds as they would appear on a rotating Earth.

8. Describe the various types of atmospheric motion, and give an example of each.

9. Sketch the pertinent aspects of the hydrologic cycle.

10. What role do hygroscopic nuclei play in the precipitation process?

11. Describe the physical properties of clouds.

12. Distinguish between warm-cloud and cold-cloud precipitation.

13. Illustrate the life cycle of a typical tropical cyclone.

14. Identify the weather pattern associated with a warm front.

CHALLENGES

1. Follow your local weather forecasts for 1 week, and compare them with your actual weather observations.

2. What landforms influence your local winds?

3. Compare barometric readings with local weather patterns.

Chapter

Climate

Chapter Outline

Mesquite Flats, Death Valley National Monument, California.

INTRODUCTION

Earth's troposphere envelops and supports life. Two of its gases, oxygen and carbon dioxide, are essential for life's primary processes: respiration and photosynthesis. Even sea animals and plants benefit from the ocean-air exchange of these gases. Because the interface of air, land, and ocean is also a dynamic zone, we experience frequent events that characterize the ephemeral nature of atmospheric conditions. The zone of weather also subjects life to both small and large stresses, such as hurricanes and droughts. With its changes in temperature, moisture, and pressure, the lower atmosphere undergoes the hourly changes called weather. These continuous changes significantly influence Earth's surface.

The atmosphere is a major influence on the natural landscapes of Earth's surface and on the life that inhabits those landscapes. If you have traveled beyond your local area, you may have noticed how Earth's atmosphere affects landscapes and vegetation. One common observation is that plant species are not universal. Their growth is limited by specific needs for water, temperature, and sunlight, three constituents of the weather. No one expects a palm tree, which is not a plant indigenous to the East Coast of North America, to grow and flourish in New York's Central Park or in the environs of Montreal. Palms require relatively warm weather year-round. Thus, when the residents of Florida planted their first imported palms, they had a good idea that the weather was conducive to these plants. Similarly, no one expects a California redwood tree to grow in Las Vegas. The dry, hot conditions in Nevada's desert are unfavorable to the growth of redwoods, which require cool, moist weather.

Differences in plant species are not the only changes you might notice from one landscape to the next. The colors of soils also change. If you travel from southern Florida to south-central Canada, you see soil color change from a very light tan (or even a dirty white) in Florida to a red in the South, and then to a brown and even black in Indiana, only to lighten somewhat at the border of the two countries. These color changes are indicative of varying soil types, and all soils are largely dependent on the regional, predominant atmospheric conditions.

Animal behavioral patterns also reflect the influences of weather elements. Polar bears, for example, live in cold areas, unlike the environments of their more southerly cousins, the black bears. Polar bears roam the pack ice of the Arctic and do not look for honey in beehives, as black bears do. Bees, because they rely on flowering plants, do not live in the same area as polar bears. The weather of a region apparently influences the evolution of variations within species.

Unlike other animals, humans can adapt to virtually every weather condition on Earth through technology. Our ability to control our environment through clothing, housing, and air conditioning makes us an exception to the controls that limit other animals' distribution. Yet, as the examples of storm damage given in the preceding chapters indicate, humans are also often at the mercy of atmospheric conditions. The human experience suggests that the elements of weather influence not only the natural landscape but also the character of human life.

CLIMATOLOGY

The composite weather, or the generalization of weather patterns, is **climate.** As an *average* of weather conditions, climate is, specifically, the historically collective states of the troposphere for a given area over a particular interval. The area could be as small as a farm, where the *microclimate* could be studied. It could also encompass a large metropolitan area, yielding the *local climate.* Or, it could cover several states or provinces, in which case, the composite of weather would be the *macroclimate.* Over long periods, weather observers gather detailed information on the temperature, humidity, precipitation, prevailing wind conditions, air pressure, and storms. Observers collate their data into daily, monthly, and annual averages. The averages and the extremes of individual weather conditions with their associated causes portray a climate. This portrayal is the work of climatologists, and their study of climatic conditions is **climatology.**

Climatologists have adopted several ways to study long-term weather. *Physical climatologists* study physical laws as they relate to such weather elements as the average energy input and the subsequent conversions of energy to temperature, precipitation, and atmospheric motion. *Regional climatologists* apply physical principles to geographical units to reach an understanding of the variations or patterns of climate over an area. A few specialized branches of climatology deal with time, scale, and place. For example, *paleoclimatology* is the study of ancient climatic conditions by such methods as examining the thickness of tree rings for signs of wetter or drier years and analyzing the oxygen isotope ratios in sea shells as temperature indicators and clues to glacial epochs.

CLIMATIC ELEMENTS

This chapter presents a survey of climatic elements and their effects. Climatologists such as Wladimir Köppen have given us ways of making sense of the varying weather patterns around the world. Köppen, in 1918, and his successors examined the quantifiable weather elements, particularly *temperature* and *moisture,* to determine a means of classifying and explaining the atmospheric conditions that prevail in different areas. As a result of their efforts, we now know why we can expect changes in vegetation as we travel through various regions. We know, also, how to classify rain forests, deserts, savannas, and tundras. Because of their work, climatologists can explain the associations among soils, vegetation, and weather patterns.

CLIMATIC CONTROLS

Through meticulous observation, climatologists have defined a set of climatic controls that govern soil, vegetation, and weather patterns. The cause-and-effect relationships between the weather elements and the various climatic controls *determine the range of temperature and the amount and type of precipitation in a given area.* Table 6.1 summarizes seven climatic controls and their simplified effects on climate.

The world's climates appear to be very diverse. Cool weather dominates the high latitudes; warm weather, the low

TABLE 6.1	Climatic Controls and Their Effects	
Control	**Effect**	
1. Latitude and sun angle	Influences the amount of energy available for the troposphere	
2. Distribution of land and water	Influences the rapidity of heat gain or loss from Earth's surfaces and the availability of moisture	
3. Altitude	Influences temperature and adiabatic changes	
4. Orographic barriers	Lessen moisture content	
5. Semipermanent highs and lows	Influence wind direction and air-mass development and movement	
6. Ocean currents	Influence pressure systems plus the amount of moisture available to an area	
7. Storms	Transfer energy and moisture between and across latitudes and longitudes	

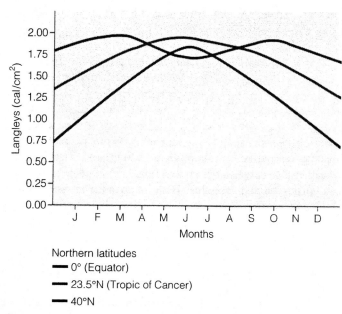

Northern latitudes
— 0° (Equator)
— 23.5°N (Tropic of Cancer)
— 40°N

Figure 6.1 Annual distribution of insolation.

latitudes. While most of the eastern half of North America is relatively humid, much of the western half has relatively dry weather. Some sections of the continent, like the Montreal region, have severe winters; others, like the islands near Charleston, South Carolina, have mild winters. At high elevations, the weather is usually very cool or even cold, regardless of the season. This regional variability results from one or more of the climatic controls. Understanding climate, therefore, requires knowledge of the seven controls listed in table 6.1 and explained in the sections that follow.

Latitude and Sun Angle

The chief influence on climate is **latitude,** or the position in degrees north or south of the equator (0°). The sun's energy arrives at the planet's curved surface, where, because of Earth's tilt to the plane of its orbit, it is mostly concentrated in the low latitudes. The incoming solar radiation (insolation) that falls on the surfaces of our world amounts to 6 months of daylight each year. As you learned in chapter 4, the intensity of that daylight is dependent on the **angle of incidence** for the insolation at any latitude (see fig. 4.11). This angle is the number of degrees from overhead where the sun appears at any time of day. As the sun appears higher in the sky, its electromagnetic radiation is more concentrated on the surface of any locale. Because the tropics experience a higher sun, on average, than do locations in the higher latitudes, more solar energy is available to warm low-latitude surfaces. These surfaces warm the air above them. As figure 6.1 shows, the insolation for three widely separated latitudes in the Northern Hemisphere varies in both intensity and yearly distribution. Thus, locations at 40°N experience a concentration of insolation during June and early July, while location on the equator experience two peak insolation periods, the equinoxes.

TABLE 6.2	Duration of Daylight for Selected Dates and Latitudes in the Northern Hemisphere		
Latitude	**March 21 and September 22**	**June 22**	**December 22**
0°	12 hr	12 hr	12 hr
10°	12 hr	12 hr, 35 min	11 hr, 25 min
20°	12 hr	13 hr, 12 min	10 hr, 48 min
30°	12 hr	13 hr, 56 min	10 hr, 04 min
40°	12 hr	14 hr, 52 min	9 hr, 08 min
50°	12 hr	16 hr, 18 min	7 hr, 42 min
60°	12 hr	18 hr, 27 min	5 hr, 33 min
70°	12 hr	2 months	0
80°	12 hr	4 months	0
90°	12 hr	6 months	0

In table 6.2, you can see what the difference in angle of incidence means for the daylight available at each of several locations during the cold and warm seasons. The tilt of Earth to the plane of its orbit prolongs summer daylight for both poles (90°N and S), but during this continued daytime, the poles still experience cold weather. In high latitudes, the angle of the sun is low even during summer, and insolation is not as intense as it is at lower latitudes, which undergo a daily period of night. Whereas the duration of daylight is relatively constant in the tropics, it fluctuates greatly in the middle and high latitudes.

Latitude controls both the daily and the seasonal influx of solar energy at Earth's surface. Since the dynamism of the troposphere is primarily the result of insolation transferring solar energy to the surface and atmospheric gases, latitude is the most important climatic control.

Figure 6.2 Clouds veil Mount McKinley, the highest peak in North America.

Distribution of Land and Water

Water is an efficient holder of heat, but a great amount of energy is required to change water's temperature. In our practical, everyday experiences, we encounter this phenomenon whenever we try to boil water. The old saying, "A watched pot never boils," refers to the apparently slow process of boiling water, which requires extended contact between the pot and a heating element or flame. Land, by contrast, heats up and cools off relatively quickly. The difference between the two substances becomes evident when you consider the flow of heat through them.

When the sun shines on the ocean, much of its energy is used in the evaporation of the water, a process that leaves surrounding water cooler. The transfer of energy that turns a liquid water molecule into a gaseous one is reversed whenever the gas returns to a liquid state through condensation. In the hydrologic cycle, that reversal occurs in the atmosphere every time water droplets form. The removal of heat energy through evaporation keeps the sea relatively cool compared to drier land areas, where much less water is available for evaporation. Because water molecules are tightly bound to one another through electrical attraction, they require a large input of energy to break their bonds (see chapter 14). Water, therefore, can store a greater amount of energy than can land. In addition, water is free to move convectively, allowing it to heat to greater depths than land. Land may be heated to depths counted in centimeters, while water, which allows more penetration by electromagnetic radiation, may be heated to depths counted in meters. The effect of this is that inland locations experience greater temperature ranges than do coastal areas.

Altitude

A May blizzard would not be unusual on the top of New Hampshire's Mount Washington, which stands over 1,800 meters (more than 6,000 ft) above sea level. At 6,194 meters (20,320 ft) above sea level, the peak of Mount McKinley has a constant covering of snow and ice (fig. 6.2). Quito, Ecuador, lies on the equator, but its average annual temperature is 12.8° C (55° F), reflecting its more than 2,743-meter (9,000-ft) altitude. As you learned from the graph of the atmosphere's structure in chapter 4, temperatures generally decrease through the troposphere (see fig. 4.13). The temperature changes you experience while hiking up a tall mountain are similar to the temperature changes that occur from the equator toward the poles.

Orographic Barriers

The troposphere is influenced by the topography. Whenever a highland interrupts the surface, air must rise to bypass the barrier. The subsequent windward rise and leeward fall cools, then heats, the air. Those mountains that lie along coasts, such as the Coast Range of western North America, can modify maritime air masses before they reach the continental interior. Collectively called **orographic barriers,** highlands strongly influence the leeward climate in their immediate vicinity, as katabatic, evaporating, and drier winds descend to make desert conditions.

One of the more telling instances of orographic influence occurs in the western United States. There, more than 125 cen-timeters (60 in) of precipitation fall annually on the windward sides of the Sierra Nevada. The shielded leeward lowlands to the east of the mountains have a desertlike climate (fig. 6.3).

Semipermanent Highs and Lows

Seasonal high- and low-pressure systems influence the flow of air across large regions. Called **semipermanent highs and lows,** these systems migrate, strengthen, and fade seasonally because of the changing sun angle. Under the dictates of the Coriolis force, winds swirl in clockwise and counterclockwise patterns around the pressure centers, like the Bermuda High, a warm-weather control off eastern North America (fig. 6.4*a*).

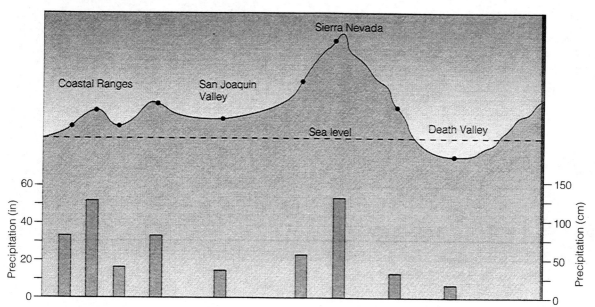

Figure 6.3 Influence of topography on precipitation. The vertical bars show average annual precipitation values at selected localities.

(a)

(b)

Figure 6.4 The (*a*) winter position and (*b*) summer position of semipermanent high-pressure systems that influence North America.

Along the coast of southern California, a summertime high-pressure system usually blocks maritime air from Los Angeles (fig. 6.4*b*), then moves southward during winter to allow rain to enter the country.

The positions of the semipermanent high- and low-pressure systems govern the surface winds. Thus, the prevailing westerlies and the polar easterlies migrate with the pressure changes. These two belts of opposing winds meet in the middle latitudes, where a kind of atmospheric conflict rages at their boundaries. Their changing positions cause a fluctuation in air temperatures over the North American continent. When the polar winds are stronger, a mass of cold air pushes toward the equator. The northward movement of warmer air signals the victory of the prevailing westerlies in their flow toward the poles. The alternating victories of one air system over another largely determine the weather for the central and eastern sections of the United States and southern Canada. These changes have been averaged into the classification of climates so that, for example, we can expect the Bermuda High to move maritime tropical air into the eastern half of the United States during summer. Residents of the southeastern seaboard and of the interiors of Alabama, Tennessee, Georgia, and the Carolinas know they must dress for warm, humid summer weather. When the Bermuda High weakens and shifts eastward toward the Azores, the flow pattern shifts. Figure 6.5 shows two maps, one with typical cP air migrating southward and the other with mT air moving northward under the influence of the Bermuda High.

Another influence of the semipermanent highs and lows is the monsoonal event that occurs yearly in the Indian Ocean and on the Indian subcontinent. A semipermanent high develops over Asia during the cold winter of the continental interior. During the subsequent warming of summer, the high fades, and a low-pressure system develops west of India. The low funnels air off the Arabian Sea to the east, where it encounters the mainland of India and the orographic barrier of the Deccan Plateau. Within the region, other areas, particularly Bangladesh off the Bay of Bengal, suffer the consequences of a season of abundant rainfall. In Bangladesh, the waters often inundate much of the lowland. In recent years, extensive monsoonal floods have temporarily displaced millions of that country's citizens, isolating them on a few dry places, such as elevated railroad tracks. Monsoonal rains are actually important in bringing many lands the moisture necessary for agriculture. South Floridians would be short of fresh water if it were not for the seasonal rains.

Semipermanent highs can be associated with either polar or tropical air masses and, in turn, with either cold or warm weather. Vigorously moving cold highs originating in Canada are likely to bring lower-than-normal temperatures, especially in winter, to the United States. Tropical highs, such as the Bermuda High of summer, are associated in the United States with above-normal temperatures and increased humidity. Fair weather and diminished or even absent cloud development are prevalent characteristics of both cold and warm highs.

By contrast, low-pressure systems are likely to bring higher-than-average temperatures in winter and lower temperatures in summer. As a general rule, the convergent air movements typical of a low-pressure center produce condensation, cloud cover, and precipitation.

Near 30°N and S of the equator is a series of anticyclonic systems usually called the subtropical highs. Because of the unequal heating of land and water, distribution of these anticyclones is modified considerably over a year. These deviations are most apparent in January and July, when one hemisphere experiences summer and the other winter. A close examination reveals that the highs are well developed and exist separately over the oceans during summer in each hemisphere. In addition to the

(a)

(b)

Figure 6.5 (*a*) Typical cP air mass moving southward. (*b*) Typical mT air mass moving northward under the influence of the Bermuda High.

(a)

Low pressures
- 990 mb
- 996
- 1002
- 1008
- 1014

High pressures
- 1014
- 1020
- 1026
- 1032
- 1038

→ Dominant wind forces

Isobars on map at intervals of 3 mb

(b)

Figure 6.6   (a) January distribution of pressure. (b) July distribution of pressure.

Figure 6.7 The Alaska Current, part of the North Pacific Drift, is a high-latitude current that flows toward Alaska and western Canada.

seasonal changes in intensity, the pressure belts shift their latitudes. A subtropical anticyclone of the Northern Hemisphere might shift about 10° between summer and winter. This seasonal shift corresponds to the direction of migration of the sun's vertical rays. The maps in figure 6.6 show Earth's distribution of surface pressure systems for both January and July. Note the shift of the land-based high between the Northern and Southern Hemispheres. The cold air that develops over the continents during winter sinks to make semipermanent highs that fade when summer returns and a prolonged and higher sun heats the land.

The dominant subtropical highs that influence North America are the Bermuda High and the California High. On either longitudinal side of these highs, the air acquires differing characteristics. As a rule, the eastern side of the high is characterized by stable, dry air, whereas the western side is usually the site of unstable, wet air. Along the two coasts of the continent, this relationship is evident as California experiences a seasonal dry period and the southeastern United States undergoes a wet period.

Although the seasonal shifts of the semipermanent pressure systems are documented, their cycle can be interrupted. A sporadic shift of these systems sometimes alters the cycle and changes regional weather patterns. One particular interruption, called El Niño, can cause excessive precipitation in some regions, while simultaneously causing drought in others (see box 6.2).

Ocean Currents

The surfaces of the oceans are waters in flux. Large clockwise and counterclockwise *gyres,* or whirlpool-like movements, circle the oceans. Because water holds heat well, those currents that flow away from the equatorial regions transfer heat to higher latitudes. The return flows, from high latitude to low latitude, serve as cold surfaces from which the air obtains its characteristics.

Ocean currents generally follow the prevailing winds, and they are influenced by the Coriolis force, turning right in the Northern Hemisphere and left in the Southern. This movement sets up a dominant pattern of cold currents along the western coastlines of major landmasses and warm currents along the eastern coasts. Like rivers of water within the oceans, these currents can be distinguished by flow rate, width, depth, and chemistry (chapter 14). Because they are surfaces over which air must pass, they also can be distinguished by the characteristics they imbue to the troposphere. Generally, *cold ocean currents make coastal weather cool and dry. Warm currents generate warm, moist coastal climates.* For example, part of the North Pacific Drift, a high-latitude current that wends toward Alaska and Canada, becomes the Alaska Current, a warm current that moderates the climate of North America's northwest coast (fig. 6.7). The water that does not spiral northward as the Alaska Current turns to the south, eventually becoming the

Figure 6.8 The Peru Current.

cold California Current and influencing the weather of Oregon, California, and Baja California.

You learned earlier that air masses obtain their characteristics from the surfaces over which they develop and that cold surfaces are associated with high pressure and little precipitation. In the Southern Hemisphere, a significant flow of cold surface water passes the western coast of Peru and Chile, producing one of the driest of coastal desert regions, including the high Atacama Desert, portions of which may not receive any rainfall for several decades at a time. The Peru, or Humboldt, Current often extends from 4 to 30°S (fig. 6.8).

Storms

Storms have relatively set patterns and are regular occurrences in many areas. From late summer to late fall, the Caribbean and the Gulf of Mexico are often in the paths of hurricanes. In Japan and the Philippines, yearly typhoons lash the coasts with torrential downpours. Storms also occur regularly around Cape Horn. In each area, storms provide moisture and transfer heat. In fact, the peoples of the Pacific Orient largely depend on typhoons to bring large quantities of fresh water to the islands. In most equatorial land regions, the climate is characterized by almost daily thunderstorms, usually occurring in the afternoon and evening. These storms support a lush growth called the *rain forest*, which is discussed later in this chapter.

GLOBAL PATTERNS OF TEMPERATURE

The distribution of Earth's mean annual temperatures for January and July appears in figure 6.9. These temperatures are informative because they represent the extremes of opposite seasons. In the discussion that follows, you will learn some of the more important tendencies of this temperature distribution.

Figure 6.9 shows a marked latitudinal shift of temperature between January and July. This reflects the migration of the noon overhead sun. Meteorologists map temperatures by plotting and then connecting equal temperatures with lines called **isotherms** (*iso,* meaning "equal"; *therm,* meaning "heat"). With changing values in insolation, the isotherms migrate. That migration is greater, as you may expect, over land than it is over water. Land, of course, heats up and cools off to greater extremes than does water, and the lowest temperatures occur over the large land areas of Asia and North America in January. The change in isotherms is manifest in another pattern. In the Northern Hemisphere, the July isotherms bend poleward over the continents, whereas they bend equatorward in January. The January isotherms for the oceans, which do not cool as much as the land, bend poleward. Why do the isotherms adopt this bend?

The cold weather of North America during winter extends far into the south central portions of the continent. Even Texas experiences cold temperatures as rapidly cooling land surfaces

Figure 6.9 Global (*a*) January and (*b*) July temperature patterns.

Figure 6.10 Annual range of surface temperatures (in degrees Fahrenheit).

lose heat in the absence of a high sun and in the presence of cP air masses. The cold temperatures of southward moving air masses, coupled with radiational cooling during a season of longer nights and shorter days, make the southern interior of the continent as cool as its more northern coastal areas. By contrast, Montana, another interior region far from the temperature-moderating influence of large water bodies, heats rapidly in summer, with the overlying air reaching temperatures more common to the lower latitudes. If you follow the isotherms for both seasons from the coasts to the interior, you will, in effect, trace a cold air bulge southward during winter and a warm air bulge northward during summer. You will also trace the extremes of surface cooling and heating in the heart of the continent.

In the Southern Hemisphere, the isotherms follow the parallels of latitude more closely than they do in the Northern Hemisphere. The principal reason for this lies in the land-water distribution. The Southern Hemisphere is chiefly an ocean hemisphere, and the uniformity of surfaces is mirrored by the latitudinal distribution of temperatures.

As noted earlier, temperature ranges are also affected by the distribution of land and water. In general, the annual *range of temperature,* which is the difference between the mean temperatures of the warmest and coldest months, is greater at higher latitudes (fig. 6.10). The range is also greater over land than over water, as you might expect. The smallest ranges occur at both low and high latitudes. The largest ranges are mostly confined to the Northern Hemisphere's continents, whose January–July temperature fluctuations reflect the rapid and extensive heating and cooling of land surfaces.

GLOBAL PATTERNS OF PRECIPITATION

Precipitation is the other important climatic element. Its significance is evident in the kinds of studies necessary for climatic groupings. In their attempt to classify weather patterns, for instance, climatologists collect various data about moisture, such as the average total amount of precipitation at a locale, the regularity of its occurrences, and the seasonal variability of rain and snowfall. Their interest in the data is more than scientific because all life is dependent on water. The surface ecologies of Earth are directly tied to the amount of precipitation and the moisture that is subsequently available to support life. Determining why certain areas have more abundant precipitation than others has meant identifying patterns and their causes.

Figure 6.11 shows a simplified distribution of precipitation in annual amounts for every 20° of latitude. The precipitation occurs as zonal or latitudinal patterns strongly bound to the general circulation of the troposphere. Practically all precipitation is the result of cooled ascending air masses. Therefore, precipitation is most abundant wherever air rises and least abundant wherever it sinks.

Keep in mind that global precipitation patterns depend on ascending and descending air. Ascending air carries moisture aloft, where lower air pressure causes the air to cool. The lower air temperatures cause the moisture to condense and become available for cloud formation and precipitation. Descending air warms as it reaches lower altitudes, and the heating inhibits cloud formation and limits precipitation by giving the air a greater capacity to hold its moisture. The four zones depicted in

Figure 6.11 A simplified distribution of annual precipitation. Zones I and II are relatively wetter zones, whereas zones III and IV are relatively drier zones.

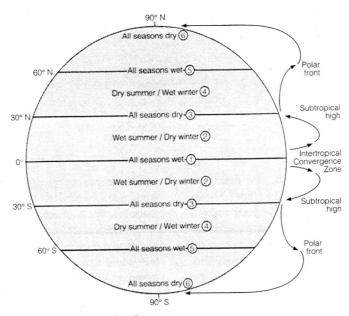

Figure 6.12 Seasonal distribution of precipitation (generalized).

figure 6.11 can be divided into two relatively wet (I and II) and two relatively dry (III and IV) patterns.

Zone I represents the wettest areas of the world, the equatorial to tropical regions that cover 20°N to 20°S latitude. Air rising in broad belts along the equator contains large amounts of water vapor because of high temperatures, warm surface waters, and high rates of evaporation. The rising warm air has a great capacity for moisture, but the ascent to higher altitudes decreases its holding power by lowering its temperature, and condensation inevitably follows the rise.

The other wet pattern falls in zone II. Poleward beyond 30°N and S lie the prevailing westerlies and accompanying frequent precipitation. With numerous cyclonic systems, air rises throughout the westerlies because of frontal lifting.

Zone III encompasses one of two dry patterns. At the polar limit of the equatorial region is the zone of subtropical high pressure. The predominantly descending air throughout this zone dictates an anticyclonic pressure distribution. The result is a rather dry region with little cloudiness, favoring the development of desert and semidesert climates.

The second dry pattern falls within zone IV, a region in very high latitude with abundant descending air. The sinking cold air at the poles contains little water vapor, and the mechanisms by which the low humidity might be condensed and eventually precipitated are generally lacking.

Seasonal Distribution of Precipitation

The precipitation of summer falls into warmer air than that of winter. Because warm air has a greater capacity to hold moisture than cold air, the moisture that falls in winter is not as easily evaporated as that which falls in summer. Cold winter air does not have the heat energy available for the efficient evaporation of water molecules. Therefore, the seasonal distribution of precipitation is a second important consideration of climatologists when they study the effect of moisture. Within most of the four zones of figure 6.11, there is a seasonal regularity, an important aspect of precipitation. In some of the zones, precipitation occurs evenly, with a seasonal balance (fig. 6.12).

Figure 6.13 Modifications to zonal precipitation patterns. Numbers correlate to those in text.

In general, humid conditions prevail all year under the equatorial low, in the westerly winds, and in the subpolar lows. By contrast, dry conditions are prevalent in the polar regions and the subtropical highs throughout the year. Seasonal precipitation occurs outside these zones, particularly in the tropical regions north and south of the equator because of the shifting trade winds at the so-called **Intertropical Convergence Zone (ITCZ).**

Modifications to the Latitudinal Precipitation Zones

The actual distribution of climates is the product of temperature and precipitation modified by the seven climatic controls. Figure 6.13 shows a *longitudinal modification* of the zonal precipitation patterns, largely based on the following:

1. Dry coastal areas adjacent to cold ocean currents
2. Humid coastal areas adjacent to warm currents
3. Humid windward sides of highlands
4. Dry lee sides of highlands
5. Dry continental interiors
6. Coastal areas not chiefly influenced by either cold or warm currents

THE CLASSIFICATION OF CLIMATES

The word *climatology* derives from the Greek *klima* ("region"), a related word of *klinein* ("to slope"). The significance of this origin may already be obvious to you. The composite weather patterns occur *regionally,* and they are primarily controlled by sun angle, a product of the curvature of a planet that is tilted, or sloped, to the plane of its orbit.

The ancient Greeks were, in fact, influential in establishing a common way of classifying weather patterns. In figure 6.14, the world is marked according to the Greeks' designations based on temperature and the astronomical phenomena of sun angle and planet orientation. Because they believed their own climate to be ideal, they called it "temperate." They deduced that, beyond the hot deserts across the Mediterranean, even hotter regions made human habitation impossible. These hot areas they called "torrid." From the experiences of travelers and their own wintertime experiences with occasional cooler winds blowing out of the north, they believed in a northern "frigid" zone.

The Greeks did well in recognizing that climate varies and that its variety has an apparent cause—sun angle. Their climatic system failed, however, to account for longitudinal variations and the different controls identified by scientific observers and thus is relatively useless. By contrast, modern classifications of climates have evolved from scientific observation and data collection and have resulted in quantitative approaches to weather—and climate—studies.

As mentioned earlier in the chapter, in 1918, Wladimir Köppen and other climatologists were examining quantifiable weather elements to determine a system for classifying atmospheric conditions that prevail in different areas. The purpose behind Köppen's classification was a practical one: He wanted to devise an objective classification scheme that would be applicable to climatic variability. For Köppen and other climatologists, there are differences in the way one region or another is

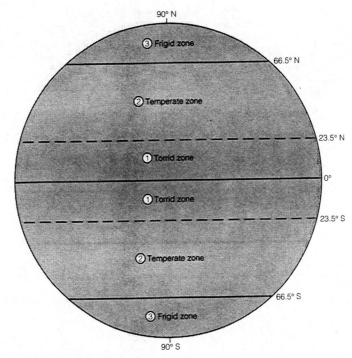

Figure 6.14 Ancient Greek climate system adapted to a round Earth.

TABLE 6.3 Letters Used by Köppen and Trewartha and Their Designations

Capital Letters	Designation	Lowercase Letters	Designation
A	Tropical climates	a	Long, hot summers
B	Dry climates	b	Short, warm summers
C	Low middle-latitude climates	c	Short, cool summers
D	High middle-latitude climates	d	Cold summers, cold winters
E	Polar climates	f	Precipitation in every month
S	Semiarid	w	Dry winter
W	Arid	s	Dry summer
T	Tundra	m	Monsoonal precipitation
F	Ice cap		
H	Highland		

"torrid." Some hot areas are dry; others, wet. The significance of these differences becomes apparent when climatologists look at vegetation, since plants reflect the character of the local, and regional, weather. Another climatologist, C. W. Thornthwaite, advantageously used vegetation types and distribution to define climates further and eliminate deficiencies in the Köppen system. Thornthwaite perceived a need for relating precipitation and evaporation to plant growth, a need not met by Köppen. Yet, what Köppen did is worth studying because no special knowledge is required to understand his classification.

To simplify the great variety of weather patterns, Köppen based his classification on *the monthly and annual temperature means and the total monthly and yearly amounts of precipitation for a locale.* Because he worked with such easily understood data, he made climate relatively easy to comprehend. In his attempt to make order from the apparent chaos called weather, Köppen employed five major climatic types, each represented by a capital letter. Generally, these letter symbols mimic the global pattern perceived by the Greeks in that they exhibit a latitudinal trend (fig. 6.15 on pages 132–133). After refinements by Köppen and G. T. Trewartha, these lettered climates now stand for more than simple latitudinal designations (table 6.3).

Köppen and Trewartha also qualified these major designations to account for both temperature and precipitation, using lowercase letters to complement the capital letters. Armed with

CLIMATIC REGIONS

Glenn T. Trewartha
The scheme of classification is modified and simplified from Köppen.

Scale 1:75 000 000 (approximate)
One inch to 1 200 miles

A. TROPICAL RAINY CLIMATES
- Tropical Rainforest (**Af. Am**)
- Tropical Savanna (**Aw**) Cooler uplands stippled

B. DRY CLIMATES
- Steppe (**BS**) Tropical and Subtropical Steppe (**BSh**) Middle latitude Steppe (**BSk**)
- Desert (**BW**) Tropical and Subtropical Desert (**BWh**) Middle latitude Desert (**BWk**)

C. HUMID MESO-THERMAL CLIMATES
- Mediterranean or Dry Summer Subtropical (**Cs**)
- Humid Subtropical (**Ca,** warm summer)
- Marine West Coast (**Cb, Cc,** cool summer)

D. HUMID MICRO-THERMAL CLIMATES
- Humid Continental, Warm Summer (**Da**)
- Humid Continental, Cool Summer (**Db**)
- Subarctic (**Dc, Dd**)

E. POLAR CLIMATES
- Tundra (**ET**)
- Ice Cap (**EF**)

H. UNDIFFERENTIATED HIGHLANDS

EXTENSIVE UPLANDS

The various alphabetical formulas designating climates on the map are explained on the opposite page. Each formula constitutes a short description of the chief characteristics of a climate.

Reprinted by permission:
"Elements of Physical Geography"
Copyrighted 1957 by Glenn T. Trewartha.
Published by the McGraw-Hill Book Company, Inc.

CURVES SHOW FAHRENHEIT TEMPERATURE
VERTICAL BARS SHOW RAINFALL IN INCHES

Af	Aw	BShs	BSk	BWh	BWk	Csa	Caw
Tropical rain-forest climate	Tropical savanna climate; with wet and dry seasons	Tropical and sub-tropical steppe climate	Middle latitude steppe climate	Tropical and sub-tropical desert climate	Middle latitude desert climate	Mild climate; summer drouth and winter rain	Subtropical climate; winter drouth and summer rain

Figure 6.15 The Köppen classification as modified by Glenn T. Trewartha. (Modification of Köppen classification from Glenn T. Trewartha, *Elements of Physical Geography*. Copyright © 1957, Glenn T. Trewartha. Reprinted by permission of McGraw-Hill Book Company, Inc.)

COMPARATIVE TEMPERATURE SCALE
Fahrenheit Celsius

COMPARATIVE RAINFALL

Type Regions and Subtypes

A – Tropical forest climates: coolest month above 64.4°F. (18°C.).

B – Dry climates (for limits see graph at right)

BS – Steppe or semiarid climate.

BW – Desert or arid climate.

*C – Mesothermal forest climates: coldest month above 32°F. (0°C.), but below 64.4°F. (18°C.); warmest month above 50°F. (10°C.).

*D – Microthermal, snow-forest climates: coldest month below 32°F. (0°C.); warmest month above 50°F. (10°C.).

E – Polar climates: warmest month below 50°F. (10°C.).

ET – Tundra climate: warmest month below 50°F. (10°C.) but above 32°F. (0°C.).

EF – Perpetual frost: all months below 32°F. (0°C.).

* Modification of Köppen definition

a – Warmest month above 71.6°F. (22°C.).

b – Warmest month below 71.6°F. (22°C.).

c – Less than four months over 50°F. (10°C.).

d – Same as "**c**," but coldest month below –36.4°F. (–38°C.).

f – Constantly moist; rainfall all through the year.

*h – Hot and dry; all months above 32°F. (0°C.).

*k – Cold and dry; at least one month below 32°F. (0°C.).

m – Monsoon rain; short dry season, but total rainfall sufficient to support rainforest.

n – Frequent fog.

n' – Infrequent fog, but high humidity and low rainfall.

s – Dry season in summer.

w – Dry season in winter.

Goode's Homolosine Equal Area Projection (Condensed)

Limits of the Regions of Dry Climate

BW   BS   BS/HUMID
BSh

Winter concentration of precipitation
Precipitation evenly distributed throughout the year
Summer concentration of precipitation

Caf — CHARLESTON — Moderate continental forest climate; mild winters

Cbf — DUBLIN — Moderate marine forest climate; mild winters

Daf — PEORIA — Continental forest climate; warm summer

Dbf — MOSCOW — Continental forest climate; cool summer

Dcf — MOOSE FACTORY — Continental taiga climate; very severe winters

ET — BARROW — Tundra climate

EF — EISMITTE — Glacial climate (Data incomplete)

CURVES SHOW FAHRENHEIT TEMPERATURE
VERTICAL BARS SHOW RAINFALL IN INCHES

Box 6.1

CLASSIFICATION OF CLIMATES

Köppen recognized five major climatic groups, which correspond to five principal vegetation groups. He designated a capital letter for each of the five. Further subdivisions of the major climates are represented by other, mostly lowercase, letters. The climatic formula modified by Trewartha is descriptive, giving the characteristics of the average monthly and annual temperatures and the total monthly and yearly precipitation. It also includes the seasonal trend of these two elements. The five groups are as follows:

A: Tropical rainy climates with no cool season; the average temperature of the coolest month is above 18° C (64.4° F).
Af: Tropical rain forest climate; f = rainfall of the driest month is at least 6 centimeters (2.4 in).
Aw: Tropical savanna climate; w = distinct dry season in winter or low sun period. At least 1 month has rainfall of less than 6 centimeters (2.4 in).
Am: Tropical monsoon climate;
m = monsoon-type climate that is intermediate between Af and Aw, resembling Af in the amount of

rainfall and Aw in the seasonal distribution. Precipitation of the driest month is less than 6 centimeters (2.4 in), but it is more than the amount computed from the following formula:

$$a = 3.94 - r/25$$

where a is the rainfall of the driest month and r is the annual rainfall.

TABLE 6.A	Methods for Delineating the B Climates	
	Boundary Between BS and Humid Climates	**Boundary Between BW and BS Climates**
Rainfall evenly distributed throughout year	$r = 0.44t - 8.5$	$\dfrac{r = 0.44t - 8.5}{2}$
Rainfall maximum in summer (70% or more of yearly total falls in warmest 6-month period)	$r = 0.44t - 3$	$\dfrac{r = 0.44t - 3}{2}$
Rainfall maximum in winter (70% or more of yearly total falls in coolest 6-month period)	$r = 0.44t - 14$	$\dfrac{r = 0.44t - 14}{2}$

these additional letters, you can now read the Köppen labels. A Cfb climate would be a middle-latitude climate with precipitation all year and a short, warm summer. Box 6.1 gives a more complete listing of the Köppen terminology.

CLIMATE DESCRIPTIONS

By plotting monthly average temperatures and total precipitation on a **climograph,** climatologists model a climatic type. In addition to their graphs, climatologists write prose descriptions that frame the characteristics of individual climates. The remainder of this chapter presents specific information about climates through maps of representative regions, lists of characteristics for the climatic subdivisions, and climagraphs of representative stations.

TROPICAL (A) CLIMATES

Throughout the year, hot and humid climates prevail in a belt that extends from about 15 to 25°N and S of the equator (fig. 6.16). These type A climates can be distinguished from all other types by their year-round high temperatures and abundant rainfall.

The yearly mean temperature in the tropical moist climate is generally between 21 and 27° C (70 and 80° F). The annual range of temperature is small and considerably less than the

daily variation. Slight seasonal variations in the angle of the sun's rays and the length of day are the primary controls on temperature, resulting in a yearly temperature range that is less than the daily range.

The amount of precipitation in the tropical climates is quite significant because it rarely falls below 88.9 centimeters (35 in) annually. Instability in the tropical air masses usually peaks during the late afternoon and evening, resulting in the numerous convectional thunderstorms that supply the A climates with abundant precipitation. In some A climates, hurricanes also produce considerable precipitation.

Because rainfall varies in amount and distribution with the time of year, with the locale, and from year to year, precipitation patterns are the basis for subdividing the tropical climates. All of the A-climate subdivisions receive sufficient moisture to be classified as humid. Some of these are represented by excessively wet weather patterns.

The relationship between the total precipitation for the year and the amount that falls during the driest month determines the different varieties of A climates. When there is no drought period, the climate is tropical rain forest (Af). If an area displays a definite drought during one season and rainfall during another, the climate is tropical savanna (Aw). In some locations, a brief drought and significant rainfall throughout the remainder of the year produces a tropical monsoonal climate (Am).

B: Dry climates; the common characteristic of the B climates is their aridity. The potential evaporation is greater than the rainfall. Köppen's formulas for identifying dry climates involve not only the annual average temperature and the total annual rainfall but also the season of maximum precipitation.

BW: Arid climate or desert.

BS: Semiarid climate or steppe.

Other letters used with the B designation are:

h = Average annual temperature over 18° C (64.4° F).

k = Average annual temperature under 18° C (64.4° F)

In Köppen's formulas for identifying a steppe (BS) and a desert (BW) margin, r is the annual rainfall in inches and t is the average annual temperature in degrees Fahrenheit (table 6.A).

C: Mesothermal climates; the average temperature of the coldest month is below 18° C (64.4° F).

Cf: No distinct dry season; the driest month of summer receives more than 3 centimeters (1.2 in).

Cw: Dry winter; at least ten times as much precipitation in the wettest month of summer as in the driest month of winter.

Cs: Dry summer; at least three times as much precipitation in the wettest month of winter as in the driest month of summer, and the driest month of summer receives less than 3 centimeters (1.2 in).

Letters used with *both* C and D climates are:

a = Hot summer; average temperature of the warmest month over 22° C (71.6° F).

b = Short, warm summer; average temperature of the warmest month under 22° C (71.6° F).

c = Cool, short summer; fewer than 4 months over 10° C (50° F).

d = Cool, short summer, with coldest winter month averaging below –38° C (–36.4° F).

D: Microthermal climates; the average temperature of the coldest month is below 0° C (32° F), and the average temperature of the warmest month is above 10° C (50° F).

Df: Cold climate with humid winter.

Dw: Cold climate with dry winter.

E: Polar climates; the average temperature of the warmest month is below 10° C (50° F).

ET: Tundra climate; average temperature of the warmest month is below 10° C (50° F) but above 0° C (32° F).

EF: Perpetual frost; average temperature of all months is below 0° C (32° F).

Apply Your Knowledge

1. What would a Csa climate represent?
2. What would a BSk climate represent?
3. Can a desert be cold?
4. What differentiates the C and D climates?

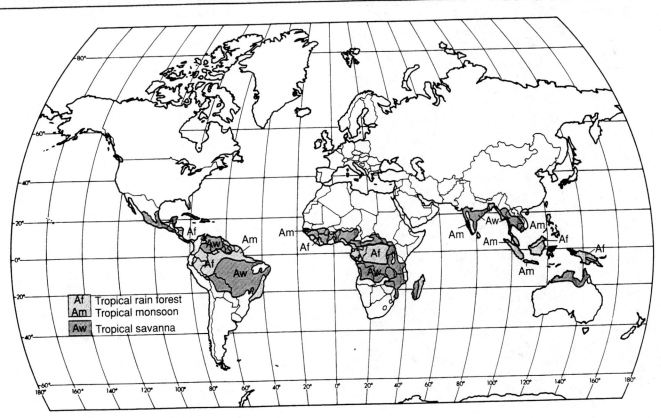

Figure 6.16 Distribution of type A climates.

TABLE 6.4	Characteristics of the Tropical Rain Forest (Af) Climate
Locations	Central Africa Central America Central South America East Indies (Asia)
Characteristics	Temperatures are uniformly high, with a very small annual range; the largest range occurs between day and night temperatures. Heavy precipitation is distributed throughout the year; there is no distinct dry season; storms are predominantly convectional.
Controls	Temperature is controlled by low latitude, high sun angle, and length of daylight. Precipitation is controlled by rising air between trade-wind belts and onshore trade winds.
Vegetation	Megatherms: a dense, broadleaf, evergreen rain forest; epiphytes.

Tropical Rain Forest (Af)

Tropical **rain forests** lie in the region of the equatorial low and the windward slopes of the trade winds (fig. 6.16). Table 6.4 summarizes the characteristics of the tropical rain forest climatic type. The trees in tropical rain forests may reach 45 meters (150 ft), forming a high canopy that contains the additional foliage of *epiphytes*, plants that grow on other plants (fig. 6.17).

Iauarete, Brazil, is encompassed by a tropical rain forest. Its equatorial location yields a heavy, evenly distributed pattern of rainfall (fig. 6.18). Typical of Af climates, the station exhibits a very small annual temperature range.

Tropical Savanna (Aw)

Located poleward of tropical rain forests, tropical savannas are transition zones between humid and dry conditions (fig. 6.16). Table 6.5 presents the major characteristics of an Aw climate, and figure 6.19 shows the type of grasslands called **savanna** commonly found under these climatic conditions.

A tropical savanna can be found at Cuiabá, Brazil, located 15°S of the equator (fig. 6.20). The station displays a seasonal rainfall pattern and three temperature periods: the hot, wet season during the rains (December through March); the cool, dry season at the time of low sun (April through August); and the hotter dry season just preceding the rains (September through November).

Tropical Monsoon (Am)

The tropical **monsoon** climate is a modification of the tropical rain forest. Located in the equatorial precipitation belt, this

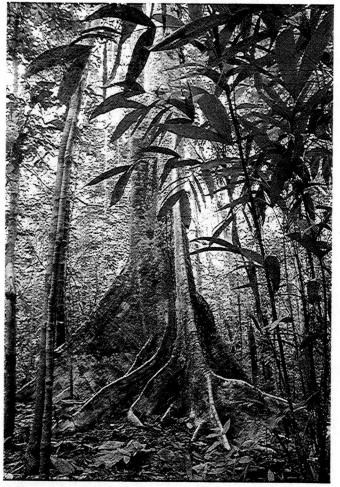

Figure 6.17 A tropical rain forest.

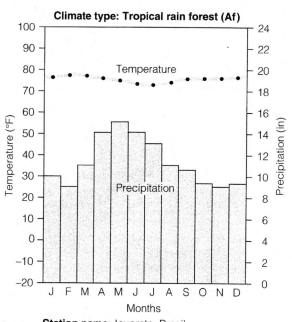

Station name: Iauarete, Brazil
Total precipitation: 138.03 in (350.6 cm)
Annual temperature: 77° F (25° C)
Range: 2.5° F (1.4° C)

Figure 6.18 Climograph of Iauarete, Brazil.

Figure 6.19   A tropical savanna.

TABLE 6.5	Characteristics of the Tropical Savanna (Aw) Climate
Locations	Northern Australia South and Southeast Asia Central America Coastal South America
Characteristics	Temperatures show seasonal variations, with highest temperatures coinciding with time of highest sun; annual temperature range is small. Precipitation shows a seasonal distribution with moderate annual amounts; precipitation amounts peak during high sun and diminish with the low-sun drought.
Controls	Temperature is controlled by tropical location, sun angle, and length of day. Precipitation is controlled by the migration of the ITCZ; the wet season is associated with mT air and convectional showers; the dry season is dominated by a subtropical high.
Vegetation	Savanna grasslands: growth of tall grasses with widely spaced trees.

Climate type: Tropical savanna (Aw)

Station name: Cuiabá, Brazil
Total precipitation: 54.5 in (138.4 cm)
Annual temperature: 79.7° F (26.5° C)
Range: 7.8° F (4.3° C)

Figure 6.20   Climograph of Cuiabá, Brazil.

variation occurs mainly near coastal regions where monsoonal winds flow onshore (see fig. 6.16). These seasonal winds govern the yearly distribution of precipitation. Table 6.6 gives the major characteristics of the Am climate, and figure 6.21 shows an environment associated with a tropical monsoonal climate.

Colombo, Sri Lanka, lies in a tropical monsoonal climate. The station is located in an area where the monsoonal wind system is particularly well developed (fig. 6.22). Colombo's heaviest rainfall occurs during the warm season. The dry season is neither as dry as nor as long as that of the tropical savanna.

TABLE 6.6 Characteristics of the Tropical Monsoonal (Am) Climate			
Locations	Coastal India Coastal South America Coastal Southeast Asia	**Controls**	Temperature is controlled by the tropical location and the high-sun angle. Precipitation is controlled by a coastal location, land-water distribution, monsoonal winds, and topography.
Characteristics	Temperatures are cool during the dry season and hot in the rainy season; the annual temperature range is somewhat greater than that of a tropical rain forest. Precipitation is heavy during the high sun; drought prevails during the low sun.	**Vegetation**	Jungle, a secondary tropical forest type that is a dense, relatively low-growing tangle of trees, shrubs, and lesser plants.

Figure 6.21   Environment associated with a tropical monsoon climate.

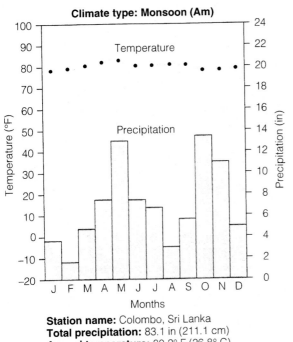

Station name: Colombo, Sri Lanka
Total precipitation: 83.1 in (211.1 cm)
Annual temperature: 80.2° F (26.8° C)
Range: 3.1° F (1.7° C)

Figure 6.22 Climograph of Colombo, Sri Lanka.

DRY (B) CLIMATES

Aridity is the common characteristic of B climate types, in which a meager precipitation falls in a region with a potential for excessive evaporation. Simply put, evaporation exceeds precipitation.

B climates are widely distributed (fig. 6.23). They are especially concentrated, however, in the vicinity of the subtropical high-pressure belts centered on 30°N and S latitudes. Other locations include regions adjacent to cold currents, the lee sides of mountain ranges, and continental interiors. Dry climates stretch over a wide latitudinal range and occupy a variety of continental positions. Compared to other climates in the same latitude, B climates usually show a wide annual temperature range. Some B climates are cold, whereas others are hot. In either instance, the heat is adequate to provide sufficient energy for extensive evaporation.

Based on precipitation, B climates fall into two patterns. In some areas, B climates are almost devoid of precipitation, and what does fall is insufficient to resupply that lost to evaporation. Such an arid climate is called a desert. Wherever precipitation falls in amounts abundant enough to support a sparse vegetative cover, a variety of B climate known as a **steppe** occurs.

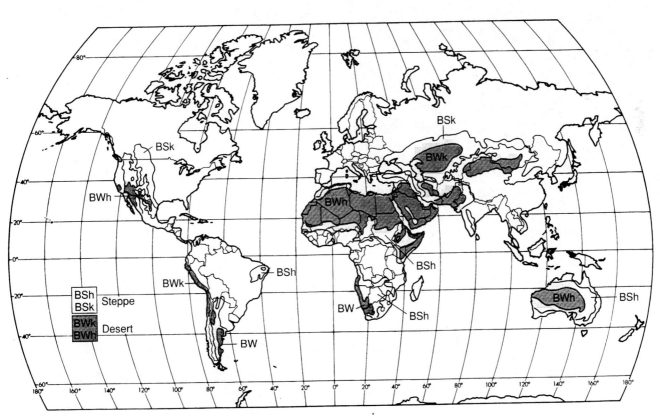

Figure 6.23 Distribution of type B climates.

TABLE 6.7	Characteristics of the Steppe (BS) Climate
Locations	Low latitudes (0 to 30°N and S): Africa, South America, Australia Middle latitudes (30 to 50°N and S): Asia, North America
Characteristics	Temperature is usually severe for the latitude; seasonal temperatures are extreme, with a large annual temperature range. Precipitation is meager, irregular, and seasonal.
Controls	Temperature is controlled by interior location and by the lee side of orographic barriers. Precipitation depends on distance from source of moisture, orographic barriers, subtropical high pressure, and cold ocean currents.
Vegetation	Steppe: a middle-latitude grassland with short grasses, scattered shrubs, and stunted trees.

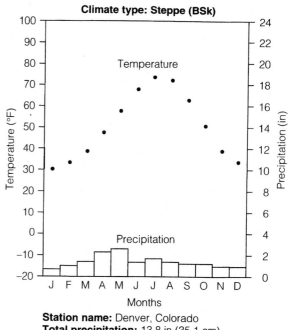

Station name: Denver, Colorado
Total precipitation: 13.8 in (35.1 cm)
Annual temperature: 50.7° F (10.4° C)
Range: 41.7° F (23.2° C)

Figure 6.25 Climograph of Denver, Colorado.

Figure 6.24 Native grasses of the Great Plains, typically found in steppe climates.

TABLE 6.8	Characteristics of the Desert (BW) Climate
Locations	Low latitudes (0 to 30°N and S): Africa, South America, Australia Middle latitudes (30 to 50°N and S): Asia, North America
Characteristics	Temperature is usually severe for the latitude; the daily and annual temperature ranges are exceptionally great. Precipitation is insignificant, irregular, and unevenly distributed during the year.
Controls	Temperature is controlled by latitude, dry air, and radiational cooling. Precipitation is controlled by interior locations, cold ocean currents, orographic barriers, and subtropical high-pressure belts.
Vegetation	Xerophytic: plants have structures and textures that inhibit evapotranspiration.

Steppe (BS) or Semiarid Climate

A transitional, semiarid climate that borders the true desert and the humid climates is a steppe (fig. 6.23). Table 6.7 outlines the characteristics of the BS climate. Semiarid climates do support plant growth, but the vegetation is sparse by comparison with that in humid climates (fig. 6.24).

At 39°N, Denver, Colorado, sits within a middle-latitude steppe. The summers are hot (22.2° C, or 72° F), whereas the winter is cold (0° C, or 32° F). The result is a large temperature range (22.2° C, or 41.7° F). The total annual precipitation is 35.1 centimeters (13.8 in). The yearly precipitation is usually lower than that of a tropical savanna, with the rainfall maxima falling in spring and summer (fig. 6.25).

Desert (BW) Climate

The **desert,** or arid, climate is distributed widely in both the tropical and middle latitudes. Nearly all continents have deserts (see fig. 6.23). The characteristics of deserts appear in table 6.8. Arid climates are home to *xerophytic* plants, which store water efficiently by inhibiting evapotranspiration (fig. 6.26).

Yuma, Arizona, is situated in a low, middle-latitude desert. Its warmest month is July, and its coolest is January. Precipitation is meager (fig. 6.27).

Figure 6.26 Xerophytes—plants designed to survive within zones of low precipitation and high evaporation—can be classified as annuals or perennials. Annuals have a short life cycle—growing, reproducing seed, and dying in one season. Perennials survive over longer periods of time by conserving water until the rains come. Water is stored in the structure of these Joshua trees on the Mojave Desert of California.

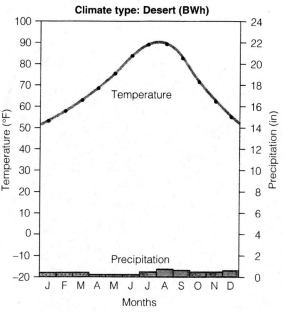

Station name: Yuma, Arizona
Total precipitation: 3.27 in (8.3 cm)
Annual temperature: 71.8° F (22.1° C)
Range: 37.6° F (20.9° C)

Figure 6.27 Climograph of Yuma, Arizona.

HUMID MESOTHERMAL (C) CLIMATES

The humid **mesothermal (C) climates** occupy the subtropical latitudes and some higher, middle-latitudinal positions under the influence of the prevailing westerlies, particularly on the western sides of continents (fig. 6.28). Because of the prevailing winds, marine influence is stronger on the western sides of continents than on the eastern sides. Poleward of the tropical climates, the mesothermal climates lack the constant heat of the tropics and the arid conditions of the B climates. Seasonal changes are the most evident characteristic of these climates.

Winter temperatures of the mesothermal climate group are relatively mild. The average monthly winter temperature is above 0° C (32° F). Latitude is an important temperature control. Marine influences are weaker on eastern coasts and stronger on western coasts.

Precipitation patterns vary among mesothermal climates. The humid mesothermal always has sufficient annual precipitation to distinguish it from the dry climates. Precipitation joins temperature as quantifiable characteristics that determine the subtypes of these climates. These subtypes include the humid subtropical (Cfa); the dry summer, subtropical (Cs); and the marine west coast (Cfb).

Humid Subtropical (Cfa) Climate

The humid subtropical climate is located at the equatorward margins of the middle latitudes between 25 and 35°N and S (fig. 6.28). Typically, this subtype of mesothermal climate is situated on the eastern side of landmasses. Table 6.9 gives the characteristics of the Cfa climate. A broadleaf forest is typical of this mesothermal climate.

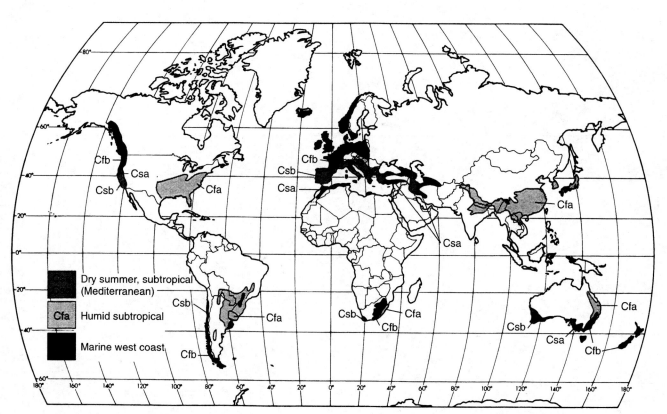

Figure 6.28 Distribution of type C climates.

St. Petersburg, Florida, has mild winters and long, hot, and humid summers (fig. 6.29). The precipitation pattern displays a maximum in summer (June through August).

Dry Summer, Subtropical (Mediterranean) (Cs) Climate

The dry summer, subtropical climate is modeled on a significant distribution of its features on lands surrounding the Mediterranean Sea. For this reason, this climatic type is also known as a Mediterranean climate. The Cs climates occur in the subtropical latitudes along the western sides of continents adjacent to cold ocean currents (fig. 6.28). The characteristics of this climatic type appear in table 6.10. The typical vegetation of a Cs climate is called Mediterranean scrubland (fig. 6.30).

TABLE 6.9	Characteristics of the Humid Subtropical (Cfa) Climate
Locations	Southeast South America Southeast United States East Australia Southeast China
Characteristics	Temperature is hot during long summers; winters are mild, and mesothermal climates have a moderate temperature range. Precipitation is evenly distributed, and the relative humidity is high.
Controls	Temperature is controlled by the subtropical sun angle; warm, moist air masses; and warm ocean currents. Precipitation is controlled by unstable, maritime air masses, the backside of subtropical highs, warm ocean currents, cyclonic activity in winter, and convectional storms in summer.
Vegetation	Mesothermal: broadleaf and mixed broadleaf-coniferous forest.

TABLE 6.10	Characteristics of the Dry Summer, Subtropical (Cs) Climate (Mediterranean)
Locations	Mediterranean Basin Coastal California Southern Australia South Africa Southwestern South America
Characteristics	Temperatures along coastal locations show a small temperature range; summers are usually warm, but short; interior locations have longer, hotter summers and a large temperature range. Precipitation is concentrated in winter, with a summer drought.
Controls	Temperature is controlled by subtropical latitude, cold currents, and coastal and interior locations. Precipitation is controlled by subtropical high pressure, seasonal shift of westerly winds, cyclonic storms, and cold currents.
Vegetation	Mediterranean scrublands: nearly dense cover of medium-size vegetation in the uplands; moderate-size trees in the lowlands.

Climate type: Humid subtropical (Cfa)

Station name: St. Petersburg, Florida
Total precipitation: 53.67 in (136.3 cm)
Annual temperature: 73.8° F (23.2° C)
Range: 19.7° F (10.9° C)

Figure 6.29 Climograph of St. Petersburg, Florida.

Figure 6.30 Mediterranean scrubland, typical of dry summer, subtropical climates.

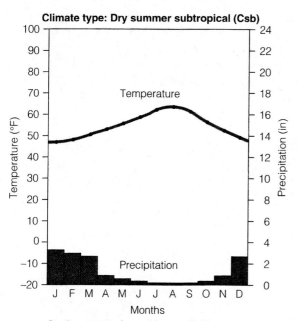

Climate type: Dry summer subtropical (Csb)

Station name: Santa Monica, California
Total precipitation: 14.67 in (37.3 cm)
Annual temperature: 61.5° F (16.4° C)
Range: 12.3° F (6.8° C)

Figure 6.31   Climograph of Santa Monica, California.

Santa Monica, California, is a community with a cool, mild, rainy winter. Its summer is warm and dry (fig. 6.31). Nearby ocean waters moderate temperatures and maintain a small annual temperature range.

Marine West Coast (Cfb) Climate

Marine west coast climates are characteristically mild. They occupy positions on the western or windward sides of middle-latitude continents, poleward of 40°N and S, where the onshore westerly winds bring predominantly marine conditions to the land (fig. 6.28). Table 6.11 lists the characteristics of the Cfb climate. Stands of Douglas fir are typical of Cfb vegetation (fig. 6.32).

With its elevation of 335 meters (1,100 ft), Valsetz, Oregon, is located in the coastal ranges of Oregon. The city receives a heavy winter precipitation that reflects orographic uplift and cyclonic activity. This station has a contrasting summer precipitation minimum (fig. 6.33). The shift of the subtropical high northward affects rainfall. The marine influence causes abnormally mild winters and cool summers.

TABLE 6.11	Characteristics of the Marine West Coast (Cfb) Climate
Locations	Northwestern Europe Pacific Northwest of United States British Columbia Australia South Africa
Characteristics	Temperatures are cool during summer and mild during winter; the temperature range is moderate. Precipitation shows an even distribution, but frontal storms can be heavy with orographic uplifting; cloudiness is common.
Controls	Temperature is controlled by latitude and the marine influence. Precipitation is controlled by marine influence of onshore westerly winds that blow over cold currents.
Vegetation	Mesothermal: middle-latitude forest; the North American Cfb is a principal source of high-grade softwoods, such as Douglas fir, California redwoods, and hemlock.

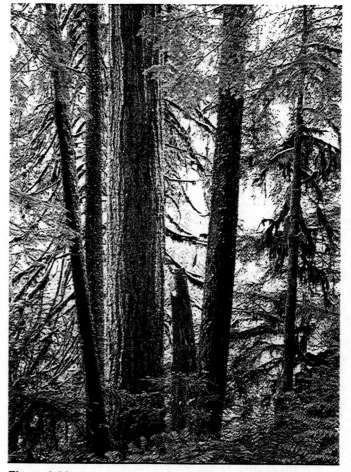

Figure 6.32   Stands of Douglas fir typical of marine west coast (Cfb) climates.

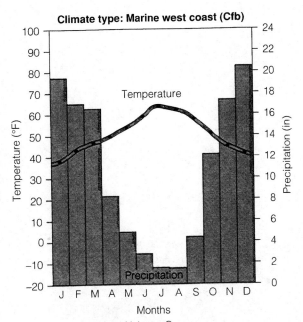

Station name: Valsetz, Oregon
Total precipitation: 126 in (320.6 cm)
Annual temperature: 49.9° F (9.9° C)
Range: 24.5° F (13.5° C)

Figure 6.33 Climograph of Valsetz, Oregon.

HUMID MICROTHERMAL (D) CLIMATES

Humid, **microthermal climates** are located in continental interiors and along eastern coasts poleward of the C climates in the Northern Hemisphere (fig. 6.34). Colder, longer winters and greater seasonal temperature ranges characterize these severe winter climates. Because the D climates result from extensive interior areas and from coasts without strong maritime air influences between 40 and 65°N, they do not occur in the Southern Hemisphere.

Close similarities among the subtypes of D climates produce classifications with subtle variations. Generally, precipitation varies by increasing from west to east and from north to south. The subtypes include those identified by long summers (Dfa), short summers (Dfb), and two subarctic environments (Dfc and Dfd).

Humid, Continental, Long-Summer (Dfa) Climate

Eastern Europe, central United States, and central China are extensive, middle-latitude, continental areas with long, hot summers and severe winters. Precipitation in these areas is either evenly distributed throughout the year or concentrated in

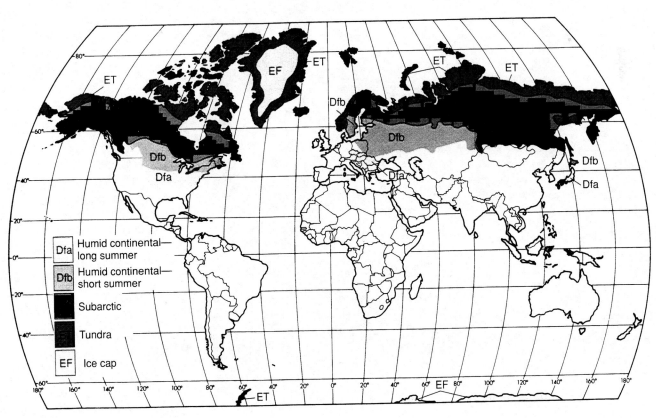

Figure 6.34 Distribution of type D and E climates.

Figure 6.35 An autumn mixed forest typical of humid, continental, long-summer (Dfa) climates.

Figure 6.36 Conifer forest typical of humid, continental, short-summer (Dfb) climates.

warmer months. The temperatures of Dfa regions result from length of day, sun angle, and the absence of maritime air masses. Precipitation occurs during cyclonic activity. The Dfa climate supports a mixed forest (fig. 6.35).

Humid, Continental, Short-Summer (Dfb) Climate

The humid, continental, short-summer climate of the high middle latitudes occurs in both North America and Europe. Although its seasonal temperature range is great, the Dfb climate has a warm, not hot, summer. The winter cooling of the continent is a strong temperature control. Precipitation patterns mimic those of the Dfa, but the forests are dominated by conifers (fig. 6.36).

Subarctic (Dfc and Dfd) Climates

Two variations of high middle-latitude climates occur in northern Canada, Alaska, northern Asia, and northern Europe. Both are typified by larger temper-

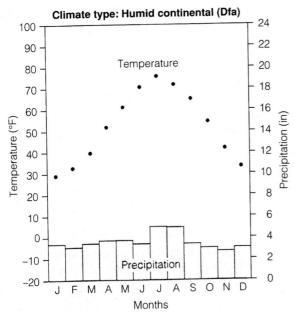

Figure 6.37 Climograph of Allentown, Pennsylvania.

Station name: Allentown, Pennsylvania
Total precipitation: 43.84 in (111.4 cm)
Annual temperature: 51.3° F (10.7° C)
Range: 44.9° F (24.9° C)

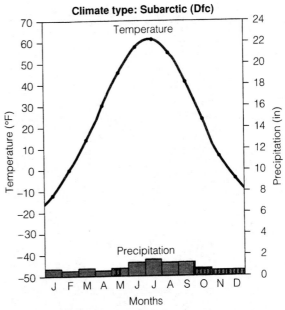

Figure 6.39 Climograph of Fairbanks, Alaska.

Station name: Fairbanks, Alaska
Total precipitation: 11.6 in (29.5 cm)
Annual temperature: 26.2° F (−3.2° C)
Range: 72.9° F (40.5° C)

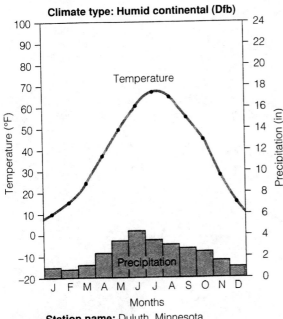

Figure 6.38 Climograph of Duluth, Minnesota.

Station name: Duluth, Minnesota
Total precipitation: 28.6 in (72.6 cm)
Annual temperature: 38.9° F (3.8° C)
Range: 56° F (31.1° C)

Figure 6.40 Climograph of Vilyuisk, Siberia.

Station name: Vilyuisk, Siberia
Total precipitation: 9.0 in (22.9 cm)
Annual temperature: 14.9° F (−9.5° C)
Range: 104° F (57.8° C)

ature ranges and short, cool summers, and both are influenced by high-pressure systems and cold, continental air masses. The vegetation of these D climates is called the **taiga,** a moist coniferous forest.

Allentown, Pennsylvania, has a typical Dfa climate (fig. 6.37). Duluth, Minnesota, which lies farther north and west of Allentown, has a Dfb climate (fig. 6.38). Its interior location prevents maritime air from moderating its temperatures. Fairbanks, Alaska, has the short and cool summers of a Dfc climate (fig. 6.39). Located beneath a great winter high-pressure system is Vilyuisk, Siberia, the site of a Dfd climate (fig. 6.40).

Polar (E) Climates

Some areas on Earth's surface have continuously cold and dry weather (fig. 6.34). Bitter winter temperatures and the lowest mean annual temperatures mark the E climates as the most severe on our planet. Even during summer, all sites within E climates experience low temperatures controlled by low sun angles and the energy absorption required to melt ice and snow. E climates have a low specific humidity that produces only meager precipitation. The Köppen system divides these climates on the basis of temperature. Where the warmest summer temperatures average 0° C (32° F), the climate supports the arctic tundra. Colder areas are covered by an ice cap.

Tundra (ET) Climate

The **tundra** lies in a region with no true summer (table 6.12). Temperatures briefly remain above freezing during the warm season, permitting a ground cover of mosses, lichens, and grasses (fig. 6.41). During most of the year, these plants lie under a covering of snow.

Cape Pembroke in the Falkland Islands has an E climate influenced by maritime conditions. The seasonal temperatures differ from those under continental influences. Cool summers and cold winters produce a small temperature range. Precipitation is enhanced by the maritime air (fig. 6.42). Sagastyr, Siberia, is a tundra under continental influence. Annual temperature ranges are large because of bitterly cold winters. Precipitation is meager (fig. 6.43).

Ice Cap (EF) Climate

Ice cap environments have small temperature ranges and very cold temperatures (table 6.13, fig. 6.44). A meager precipitation

TABLE 6.12	Characteristics of the Tundra (ET) Climate
Location	Arctic fringe
Characteristics	Temperatures are cool during high sun months; under maritime influences, temperature ranges are small; under continental influences, temperature ranges are large. Precipitation is meager, with a warm season concentration.
Controls	Temperature is controlled by latitude, low sun angle, length of daylight, and continental or maritime location. Precipitation is controlled by high pressure, low evaporation, and cool to cold air with little capacity for moisture.
Vegetation	Tundra

Figure 6.41 Tundra vegetation.

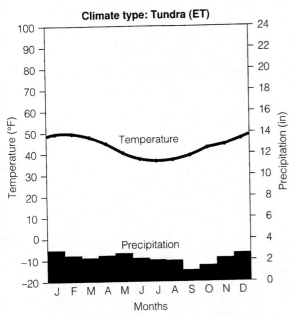

Climate type: Tundra (ET)

Temperature

Precipitation

Station name: Cape Pembroke, Falkland Islands
Total precipitation: 26.3 in (66.8 cm)
Annual temperature: 42.7° F (5.9° C)
Range: 12.6° F (7.0° C)

Figure 6.42   Climagroph of Cape Pembroke, Falkland Islands.

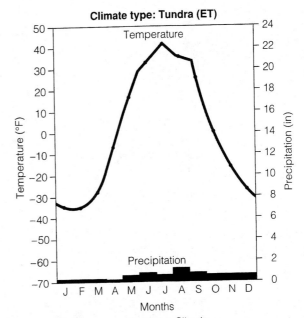

Climate type: Tundra (ET)

Temperature

Precipitation

Station name: Sagastyr, Siberia
Total precipitation: 3.3 in (8.4 cm)
Annual temperature: 1° F (−17.2° C)
Range: 77° F (42.8° C)

Figure 6.43   Climograph of Sagastyr, Siberia.

TABLE 6.13	Characteristics of the Ice Cap (EF) Climate
Locations	Central Greenland Antarctica
Characteristics	Temperatures are the lowest on Earth; coldest temperature ever recorded on Earth's surface was −59.7° C (−107° F) near South Pole. Precipitation is meager and nearly always falls as snow during the warmer months; cyclonic activity generates most of the snowfall.
Controls	Temperature is controlled by the high albedo of snow and ice, low sun angle, dry air, clear skies (radiational cooling), semipermanent high pressure, and long dark period. Precipitation is controlled by high pressure, low evaporation, and cold air moisture capacity.

Figure 6.44   Polar ice cap.

Box 6.2

Investigating the Environment

EL NIÑO AND THE SOUTHERN OSCILLATION

El Niño is a warming of the surface waters of the southeastern Pacific Ocean. A 2 to 3° C (3.6 to 5.4° F) warming off the coasts of Peru and Ecuador usually occurs at Christmastime, which explains the name El Niño ("The Child"). As an event, El Niño occurs irregularly every 2 to 7 years, but when it is accompanied by a warming of more than 6° C (10.8° F), it significantly influences weather throughout the world, overriding the climatic stability that underlies the Köppen system.

The **Southern Oscillation** is a fluctuation in the pressure systems of the western Pacific, where southern Asia is dominated by alternate high and low pressure. Because the Southern Oscillation cycles over approximately 30-month periods, it has been quantified in an index by Sir Gilbert Walker, who observed the changes in pressure as early as 1924. Walker developed an index for the Southern Oscillation that is calcu-

lated by subtracting atmospheric pressure in the western Pacific from the pressure of the eastern Pacific. Whenever the index value is positive, the difference between east and west is higher than normal (fig. 6.A).

Both El Niño and the Southern Oscillation (usually referred to as ENSO) affect climate and human activities. Successful farming in India has been linked to the Southern Oscillation, and fishing success can be interrupted in the Pacific with the occurrence of El Niño.

The warm water associated with El Niño appears to impact on global weather patterns. El Niño has been associated with drier weather in southeastern Africa, India, the western Pacific, and northern South America. During an El Niño event, the central Pacific and southeastern United States experience wetter than normal conditions. The 1982–83 El Niño was responsible for floods in California and an intensification

of the African drought. An El Niño event during the winter of 1991–92 appeared to be responsible for drenching Los Angeles, particularly during three storms spanning a 10-day period in February, when more than 20 centimeters (8 in) of rain generated floods and mudslides that killed several people. In some mountainous areas of southern California, more than 38 centimeters (15 in) of rain fell.

Apply Your Knowledge

1. What is El Niño?
2. What is the Southern Oscillation?
3. During what time of year does El Niño occur?
4. How frequently does El Niño occur?

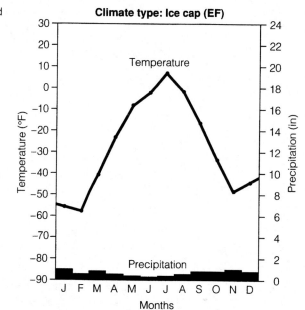

Station name: Eismitte, Interior Greenland
Total precipitation: 4.3 in (11 cm)
Annual temperature: −22° F (−30° C)
Range: 65° F (36.1° C)

Figure 6.45   Climograph of Eismitte, Greenland.

Figure 6.A Historical records of the Southern Oscillation index (*top*) and of the sea-surface temperature off the Peruvian coast (*bottom*) show that the two variables are linked, although the association is not perfect. The Southern Oscillation index is calculated by subtracting the atmospheric surface pressure at Darwin, Australia, from the pressure at Easter Island. When the index is positive, the east-west pressure gradient is greater than normal and the trade winds are stronger; conversely, a negative index indicates weak trade winds. The graph shown here is based on monthly averages of the surface pressure and has been statistically "smoothed." The graph of the sea-surface temperature at Puerto Chicama, Peru (7.7°S), shows the departure from normal monthly average temperatures. According to an analysis of these two and other variables by William H. Quinn of Oregon State University, strong El Niños occurred in 1957–58, 1972–73, and 1982–83. Moderate El Niños occurred in 1953, 1965, and 1976–77. Except for the late-starting 1982 event, the anomalous temperatures of the sea surface off Peru have tended to begin around March, after the Southern Oscillation index has fallen from positive values and the trade winds have slackened. Late in the year, the sea surface cools; then the warming resumes, climaxing early the following year. Some El Niños, such as that of 1972–73, were preceded by an intensification of the trade winds. A wind buildup in 1974, however, was not followed by El Niño, and the 1982 event began without a buildup. (Adapted from "El Niño" by Collin S. Ramage. Copyright © June 1986 by Scientific American, Inc. All rights reserved.)

falls as snow and turns to ice. Continental ice sheets, such as those on Greenland and Antarctica, reach thicknesses in excess of 3.2 kilometers (2 mi).

Eismitte, Greenland, is located at 3,030 meters (9,941 ft) on top of a thick ice sheet (fig. 6.45). Its interior location and high altitude prevent temperatures from rising above freezing. Eismitte experiences a large annual temperature range (36° C or 65° F) and meager annual precipitation (11 cm, or 4.3 in).

Highland (H) Climates

Highland climates, represented by an H on climate maps, have highly varying temperature and moisture characteristics. As you learned in the section on altitude earlier in this chapter, the vertical component of climate is in many ways a mirror of the latitudinal climate zones. At higher elevations, more polelike conditions are experienced. Highland climates are influenced by latitude, land-water distribution, orographic lifting and adiabatic changes, and, of course, altitude.

FURTHER THOUGHTS: CLIMATOLOGY IS HOLISTIC

Climatology is a model of interconnected systems. It binds sun, air, ocean, and land in an encompassing explanation of ongoing processes, and it simplifies the complexity of weather variability over Earth's surfaces. Because many weather observers have kept accurate records of local weather conditions for decades, climatologists have been able to classify weather patterns on the basis of temperature and precipitation.

Each of the four earth science disciplines offers a unification of principles, processes, and features. In astronomy, the ultimate unification lies in identifying the nature of distant and nearby celestial objects and in explaining the initial formation of the universe in the big bang. In meteorology, the unification lies in climatological classifications. But what about the solid Earth? Does it lend itself to a similar classification scheme? Can the mountains and valleys and their rocks also fit into a unifying model? In end of part 4, you will encounter a geological analog of climatology in your study of plate tectonics.

SIGNIFICANT POINTS

1. The atmosphere is a major influence on natural landscapes and life.
2. The composite of weather, or the generalization of weather patterns, is climate, which is based on data collected over a number of years.
3. Temperature and moisture are the primary weather elements that climatologists use to classify tropospheric patterns.
4. Cool weather predominates in high latitudes and warm weather in the low latitudes because distance from the equator is the most important climatic control. The angle of incidence for insolation changes with latitude; therefore, the sun shines with less intensity on areas at higher latitudes than those at lower latitudes.
5. Temperature ranges and extremes are affected by the distribution of land and water surfaces.
6. Altitude offsets the effects of latitude.
7. Orographic barriers rob the air of its moisture on their windward sides.
8. Semipermanent high- and low-pressure systems influence the longitudinal distribution of climatic patterns.
9. Warm ocean currents transfer heat from low latitudes to higher latitudes. Where cold currents lie off the western sides of continents, dry conditions prevail.
10. The distribution of land and water surfaces determines whether or not air masses are moist or dry.
11. Storms transfer energy and moisture latitudinally and longitudinally.
12. On an isothermal map of North America, the isotherms bend poleward in summer and equatorward in winter. These trends reflect the greater seasonal temperature variation that occurs in the continent's interior.
13. Zonal or latitudinal precipitation patterns are strongly bound to the general circulation of the atmosphere.
14. The classification of climates evolved from scientific observation of the atmosphere and atmospheric data collection, resulting in the quantitative approach to the study of climate.
15. The A climates are tropical, rainy climates with no cool season.
16. B climates are arid or semiarid.
17. The mesothermal, or C, climates have an average temperature below 18° C (64.4° F) during their coldest month.
18. D climates, called microthermal, have at least one month with an average temperature below 0°C (32° F).
19. E climates occur in polar regions, where the average temperature for the warmest month is below 10° C (50° F).
20. The A, C, and D climates are relatively wet, whereas the B and E climates are relatively dry.

ESSENTIAL TERMS

climate *119*	semipermanent highs	rain forest *136*	mesothermal	ice cap *148*
climatology *119*	and lows *122*	savanna *136*	climate *142*	El Niño *150*
latitude *120*	isotherm *126*	monsoon *136*	microthermal	Southern
angle of incidence *120*	Intertropical Conver-	steppe *139*	climate *145*	Oscillation *150*
orographic barrier *122*	gence Zone *130*	desert *140*	taiga *147*	highland climate *151*
	climograph *134*		tundra *148*	

REVIEW QUESTIONS

1. How does the atmosphere influence life?
2. What is climate?
3. What are the two weather elements upon which climate is determined?
4. What are the climatic controls?
5. What is the difference between temperature ranges over land and water?
6. How is sun angle related to the positions and strengths of semipermanent high-pressure systems?
7. How does the Alaska Current influence climate?
8. What do the capital letters A, B, C, D, and E stand for in the Köppen-Trewartha climatic system?
9. What type of climate supports the growth of epiphytes?
10. Why are Mediterranean-like conditions found along western North America?

CHALLENGES

1. Identify three factors that could change future global precipitation patterns.
2. What are some of the reasons that make it difficult to predict whether Earth's climate will become cooler or warmer?
3. What human activities are contributing to the potential changes in temperature and precipitation patterns?
4. Identify the major climatic controls that influence your geographic area.
5. Explain how fluctuations in solar output and the Earth-sun relationship may account for climatic changes.

PART 4

GEOLOGICAL COMPOSITION AND PROCESSES

*I*n the eighteenth century, James Hutton, called by many the father of geology, recognized that our planetary surface is dynamic. Since the time of his observations and insights, we have learned much about the composition of and processes that shape the solid and not-so-solid Earth. Aided by extensive laboratory and fieldwork and by remote sensing, geologists have discovered much about the solid components of our planet, their distribution, and their interactions.

At the *End of Part 4, You Will Be Able to:*

1. Identify the variable compositions of minerals and rocks.
2. Infer the distribution of elements in and on our planet.
3. Identify and illustrate the internal processes that shape the planet's ocean basins and continents.
4. Recognize how plate-tectonic theory accounts for numerous geological phenomena.
5. Distinguish the surface processes that shape the landscape.

The *Brocade of the Mountain*

from Tokaido by Ichiryusai Hiroshige (1797–1858)

As little by little the autumn mists
Cleared away in the skies,
I saw the mountain's bright brocade
Woven up before mine eyes.

Chapter 7

Earth Materials

Chapter Outline

Wizard Island in the caldera of Crater Lake, Oregon.

INTRODUCTION

The solid Earth upon which we walk and from which we obtain our building materials and mineral resources is composed of various kinds of rock. The rock runs deep beneath our feet, in some places as much as 80 or 100 kilometers (50 or 60 mi) before a somewhat different type of material is encountered. The general nature and broad origins of rock are well known, and the hundreds of varieties resolve themselves into a few clusters of similar types. Rocks, in turn, are composed of combinations of atoms and molecules that form substances called minerals. Like rocks, the thousands of identified varieties of minerals can be separated into a small number of groups based on chemical and physical similarities.

Almost everyone has heard of minerals in association with foods; for example, some cereal boxes proclaim the product to be "full of essential vitamins and minerals." Such "minerals" include zinc oxide, manganese sulfate, and potassium chloride, and they represent combinations of elements that allow our bodies to maintain their forms and functions. While essential to the well-being of organisms, they are not, in themselves, organic. While it is increasingly commonplace to supplement foods with "minerals" during processing, nature has been doing this for millions of years, and organisms through countless generations have evolved to a state of equilibrium with and dependence on what nature provides. To the earth scientist, however, the term *mineral* has a much broader meaning.

MINERALS

Minerals are nature's building blocks. Rocks are made of minerals, and rocks form Earth's outer shell. Earth scientists—specifically, mineralogists—have named and described more than 3,000 different minerals, and they are always on the lookout for new varieties. Some minerals, such as halite and quartz, are common and familiar; others, like gem minerals, are rare and either of great value or unfamiliar (or both). Regardless of their abundance or scarcity, minerals all share certain features, as the following definition specifies: *A mineral is a naturally occurring inorganic element or compound, with a definite internal arrangement of ions (i.e., a solid) and a chemical composition that is fixed or that varies within narrow limits.*

Minerals are "naturally occurring" because they form as a result of natural processes, rather than as a product of human laboratories and factories. Thus, we would exclude from consideration as minerals such materials as steel, cement, glass, and, if we carried this line of reasoning to its logical conclusion, synthetic rubies, even though such rubies would be identical to those that form naturally.

In legal documents, such as deeds, and in newspaper and magazine articles, coal, oil, and natural gas are often referred to as mineral fuels. Such fuels represent the remains of once-living organisms (e.g., microscopic marine organisms or trees and ferns in ancient swamplands). Consequently, they are *organic* (the result of life processes) in origin, rather than *inorganic*. Mineral fuels are often considered part of a state or country's mineral resources, but under the strict definition, they are not minerals.

Because a mineral can be either a single element or a molecular compound, mineralogists express a mineral's composition precisely with standard chemical symbols. For example, a single molecule of the mineral halite, or common rock salt, is written as NaCl, meaning that it consists of a single ion of sodium (Na^+) and a single ion of chlorine (Cl^-). Figure 7.1a represents an ionic model of NaCl. The ions, shown in their relative sizes, are held together by the attractive force of their opposite electrical charges. The expanded view shown in figure 7.1b depicts the ions in their relative positions and also isolates the basic structural unit that is repeated to form the mineral.

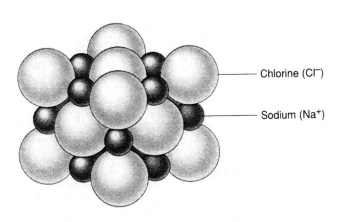

(a)

Chlorine (Cl⁻)

Sodium (Na⁺)

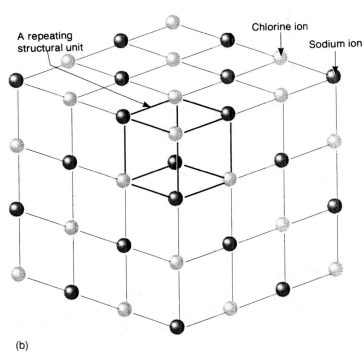

A repeating structural unit

Chlorine ion

Sodium ion

(b)

Figure 7.1   (a) Ionic model of the chemical compound NaCl (the mineral halite). The ions, shown in their relative sizes, are held together by the attractive force of their electrical charges. (b) Lattice model of NaCl expanded to show the positions of the Na and Cl ions but not their relative sizes.

Composition and Classification

While there are 92 naturally occurring elements, only 8 form the great bulk of the minerals at or near Earth's surface (table 7.1). Perhaps surprisingly, the most abundant of the 8 is oxygen, which, when uncombined with other elements, occurs as a gas. In combination with other elements, however, oxygen helps to form a variety of minerals, some of which are valuable natural resources (discussed in chapter 16). An example of a valuable oxygen mineral is magnetite, an important source of iron. A more familiar oxygen mineral is ice.

The chemical nature of minerals also provides earth scientists with a convenient method to sort them into smaller groups, a common procedure known as classification. Some minerals are formed of ions of a single element. These are the uncombined, or *native, elements* (fig. 7.2a). Some minerals are formed by combining various elements with oxygen, the *oxides;* with sulfur, the *sulfides;* or with one of the family of halogen elements (chlorine, iodine, fluorine, bromine), the *halides.* Other minerals are formed by combining certain elements with the carbonate complex ion, CO_3^{2-}; the sulfate complex ion, SO_4^{2-}; or the phosphate complex ion, PO_4^{3-}.

TABLE 7.1	The Most Common Elements in Earth's Crust
Element	**Average Weight Percent**
Oxygen	46.6
Silicon	27.7
Aluminum	8.1
Iron	5.0
Calcium	3.6
Sodium	2.8
Potassium	2.6
Magnesium	2.1
Other elements	1.5

Source: Data from B. Mason and C. B. Moore, *Principles of Geochemistry,* 4th ed. Copyright ©1982 John Wiley & Sons, Inc.

(fig. 7.2b). Table 7.2 lists examples of minerals in each of a number of important chemical mineral groups.

The Silicate Minerals

Easily the most diverse and abundant of all the groupings is the family of minerals known as the **silicates.** These minerals combine various elements with a basic building block of one ion of silicon and four ions of oxygen, known as the silicon-oxygen tetrahedron (fig. 7.3a). Minerals of increasingly complex composition and structure can be formed when two or more of these tetrahedra share oxygen ions (fig. 7.3b, c, and d).

Included within the silicate group are such common minerals as quartz and feldspar (fig. 7.4). In fact, so common are these minerals that the silicates are collectively known as the rock formers. More than 90% of all minerals found in nature belong to the silicate group, and these minerals, in turn, account for more than 90% of the rocks in Earth's outer shell.

Mineral Formation

Minerals form in nature by a process known as **crystallization.** That is, individual ions present in natural solutions join together to form molecules of solid compounds that grow larger by the addition of more ions. Some crystals form in the moderate temperatures at Earth's surface. Water molecules, for example, join together in the atmosphere to form the ice crystals we call snowflakes. Evaporating seawater causes dissolved ions of sodium (Na^+) and chlorine (Cl^-) to come close enough to attract one another and form solid particles of halite. Most of the common minerals, however, form from neither air nor water solutions but rather from rock solutions—that is, liquid masses formed from mineral matter at high temperatures deep within Earth. This liquid material is known as **magma.**

As magma cools, the individual ions that have been moving about in the magma lose energy and slow down. As the ions slow,

(a)

(b)

Figure 7.2 Mineral specimens. (*a*) Graphite (carbon), an example of a native, or uncombined, element. (*b*) An intergrowth of the light-colored carbonate mineral calcite ($CaCO_3$) and the dark-colored halide mineral fluorite (CaF_2).

TABLE 7.2 Classification of Minerals

Mineral Group	Mineral Name	Chemical Formula	Important Use
Native elements	Copper	Cu	Electrical applications
	Sulfur	S	Drugs, chemical industry
	Diamond	C	Jewelry, drills, saws
	Graphite	C	Lubricant, pencils
Sulfides	Pyrite	FeS_2	Sulfuric acid
	Galena	PbS	Lead ore
	Sphalerite	ZnS	Zinc ore
	Cinnabar	HgS	Mercury ore, thermometers
	Chalcopyrite	$CuFeS_2$	Copper ore
Sulfates	Gypsum	$CaSO_4 \cdot 2H_2O$	Plaster
	Anhydrite	$CaSO_4$	Plaster
	Barite	$BaSO_4$	Petroleum drilling mud
Halides	Halite	NaCl	Seasoning, chemicals
	Sylvite	KCl	Potash (fertilizer)
	Fluorite	CaF_2	Steel making
Oxides	Hematite	Fe_2O_3	Iron ore
	Magnetite	Fe_3O_4	Iron ore
	Corundum	Al_2O_3	Abrasive, jewelry (ruby, sapphire)
	Cassiterite	Sn_2O_3	Tin ore
	Ice	H_2O	Solid water
	Spinel	$MgAl_2O_4$	Jewelry
Hydroxides	Limonite	$FeO(OH) \cdot nH_2O$	Iron ore
	Bauxite	$Al(OH)_3 \cdot nH_2O$	Aluminum ore
	Brucite	$Mg(OH)_2$	Magnesium ore
Carbonates	Calcite	$CaCO_3$	Cement
	Dolomite	$CaMg(CO_3)_2$	Cement
	Malachite	$Cu_2(OH)_2CO_3$	Copper ore, jewelry
	Smithsonite	$ZnCO_3$	Zinc ore
Phosphates	Turquoise	$CuAl_6(PO_4)_4(OH)_8$	Jewelry
	Apatite	$Ca_5(F,Cl,OH)(PO_4)_3$	Fertilizer
Borates	Borax	$Na_2B_4O_7 \cdot 10H_2O$	Cleansers
	Kernite	$Na_2B_4O_7 \cdot 4H_2O$	Medicine, soap, glass
Silicates	Quartz	SiO_2	Glass
	Amethyst		Jewelry
	Opal		Jewelry
	Agate		Jewelry
	Feldspar		
	Plagioclase	$NaAlSi_3O_8$; $CaAl_2Si_2O_8$	Ceramics
	Microcline	$KAlSi_3O_8$	Ceramics
	Pyroxene (enstatite)	$Mg_2(SiO_3)_2$	None
	Amphibole (hornblende)		None
	Mica		
	Biotite	$K(Mg,Fe)_3AlSi_3O_{10}(OH)_2$	Paper, filler
	Muscovite	$KAl_3Si_3O_{10}(OH)_2$	Electronic equipment
	Chlorite	$(Mg,Fe)_5(Al,Fe)_2Si_3O_{10}(OH)_8$	None
	Olivine	$(Mg,Fe)_2SiO_4$	Jewelry
	Garnet (pyrope)	$Mg_3Al_2(SiO_4)_3$	Abrasives, jewelry
	Talc	$Mg_3Si_4O_{10}(OH)_2$	Ceramics, paint

they come together and attach themselves to one another in a regularly repeated arrangement. This regular pattern of ions is known as a **crystal lattice,** and it continues to grow as long as the appropriate ions and sufficient space are available (fig. 7.1b). Eventually, the growing mineral is large enough to see—first with the microscope and then with the naked eye. This orderly internal arrangement of ions is the principal characteristic of solids; thus, minerals are solids. The internal ionic arrangement also gives rise to a regular external geometric form (e.g., a cube or a pyramid) that is bounded by smooth, plane surfaces. Such a feature is known as a **crystal,** and every mineral has its own characteristic crystal form. Normally, however, good crystal form only develops when the

crystal grows in a void or within a liquid mass so that its growth is not impeded by other solid crystals (fig. 7.5).

Ionic Substitution

The particular internal arrangement of ions for any mineral is governed by three factors: the availability of certain ions, the size of those ions (ionic radius), and the atomic charge on each ion. Any ion must be able to fit into the space for it in the growing crystal lattice. In addition, when crystal growth is complete, the resulting mineral must be electrically neutral. That is, just as many positive charges as negative charges must have gone into the mineral's formation.

(a)

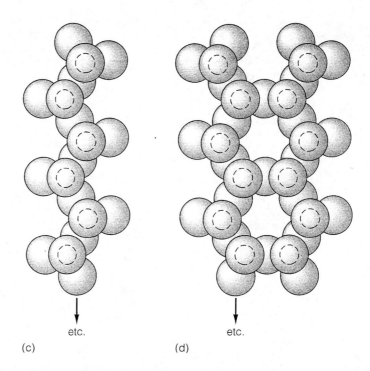

(b)

(c)

(d)

etc.

etc.

Figure 7.3 (*a*) The silicon-oxygen tetrahedron is the basic structural unit of all silicate minerals. It consists of a single silicon ion (charge =+ 4), surrounded by four oxygen ions (charge of each = −2). Connecting the centers of the oxygen ions forms a four-sided geometric figure known as a tetrahedron. Each of the four sides of the tetrahedron is an equilateral triangle. Variations in composition and complexity of silicate minerals are achieved by sharing of oxygen ions between adjacent tetrahedra. Examples shown are the (*b*) double tetrahedron, (*c*) single chain, and (*d*) double chain. Additional ions of other elements (not shown) attach themselves to complete a mineral's structure.

(a)

(b)

Figure 7.4 Feldspars, by far the most abundant rock-forming mineral group, are members of the silicate chemical mineral class. Pictured is the pink variety microcline (K-feldspar) (*a*) alone and (*b*) in combination with other silicate minerals in the rock granite.

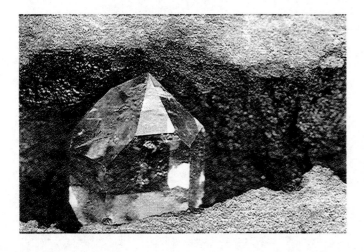

Figure 7.5 An example of the growth of a quartz crystal within a natural rock cavity. Such an environment, where the growing mineral is unconfined, is best for the development of the mineral's crystal shape.

Selected Minerals Displaying Ionic Substitution

Mineral Name	Chemical Formula	Substituting Ions
Plagioclase	$(Ca,Na)(Al,Si)AlSi_2O_8$	$(Na^+,Ca^{2+}),(Al^{3+},Si^{4+})$
Olivine	$(Mg, Fe)_2SiO_4$	(Mg^{2+},Fe^{2+})
Rhodonite	$(Mn, Ca)SiO_3$	(Mn^{2+},Ca^{2+})
Nepheline	$(Na,K)AlSiO_4$	(Na^+,K^+)
Biotite mica	$K(Mg,Fe)_3(OH)_2AlSi_3O_{10}$	(Mg^{2+},Fe^{2+})
Chlorite	$(Mg, Fe, Al)_6(OH)_8(Al,Si)_4O_{10}$	$(Mg^{2+},Fe^{2+},Al^{3+}),(Al^{3+},Si^{4+})$

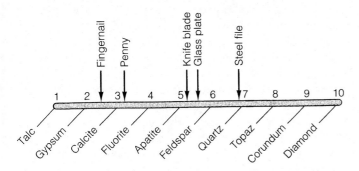

Figure 7.6 The Mohs hardness scale for minerals. The hardest of all natural substances is diamond, which is many times harder than corundum, the ninth mineral on the scale. A mineral that is higher on the scale "scratches" any mineral with a lower hardness value. Because hardness sets are usually not available in the field, hardnesses of some common items, which may be used in the identification process, are also shown on the scale.

The silicate mineral plagioclase feldspar can be used to illustrate this concept. Plagioclase exists in a sodium-rich variety ($NaAlSi_3O_8$) and a calcium-rich variety ($CaAl_2Si_2O_8$). This variation occurs because the calcium ion and the sodium ion are very similar in size, and either can fit in the appropriate place in the crystal lattice. That is, they can physically substitute for one another, a process known as **ionic substitution.** Calcium and sodium do not, however, carry equal electrical charges. The sodium ion has a charge of +1, while the calcium ion carries a charge of +2. To substitute calcium for sodium indiscriminately would lead to a mineral that is not electrically balanced. Consequently, if calcium is to substitute for sodium, a second, compensating substitution must occur that will return the mineral to electrical neutrality. The substitution of aluminum for silicon does that. The two ions are of similar size, but aluminum has a charge of +3, and silicon has a charge of +4. Thus, a paired substitution of calcium and aluminum (total charge of +5) for sodium and silicon (total charge of +5) leaves the resulting mineral electrically neutral. The effect of such a paired substitution can be seen in the chemical formulas for the sodium-rich and calcium-rich varieties of plagioclase.

This type of substitution is the rule in nature, rather than the exception. It also explains the last part of our mineral definition—that the chemical composition of a mineral is fixed or varies within narrow limits. The narrow limits are determined by the amount of ionic substitution. Variations in composition resulting from ionic substitution, as well as the presence of minor amounts of impurities within the mineral, account for some differences in physical

properties among individual specimens of the same mineral. For example, the sodium variety of plagioclase feldspar, known as albite, is always lighter in both color and weight than the calcium variety, anorthite.

Now that you are familiar with the principles of ionic substitution and electrical neutrality in minerals, return briefly to a consideration of the silicates. It was stated that the silicon tetrahedron consists of a combination of one silicon ion and four oxygen ions. The electrical charges on these ions are +4 and –2, respectively. If we add the charges on the four oxygen ions, they total –8 (compared to the +4 of the silicon). What this means is that the silicon tetrahedron by itself cannot be a mineral because it has a surplus of –4 charges and is electrically unbalanced. To form a mineral, other ions with charges totaling +4 must be added to the simple tetrahedron. In nature, this can be accomplished by the addition of ions such as Fe^{2+} or Mg^{2+}. The result is the mineral olivine, $(Mg,Fe)_2SiO_4$. As more complex silicate minerals form, these same rules of substitution and electrical neutrality must be maintained. Table 7.3 gives examples of minerals that are characterized by ionic substitution.

Mineral Identification

The properties of minerals are identifiable through certain field and laboratory tests even a novice can make. One of the tests is based on a scale of **hardness** devised in the eighteenth century by German mineralogist Friedrich Mohs (fig. 7.6). This test compares the hardness of an unknown mineral sample to that of the minerals on the hardness scale by "scratching" the unknown specimen. Each of the 10 minerals on the scale is assigned a hardness value, with talc (1) being the softest and diamond (10) the hardest. Commercial sets containing all of the scale minerals (with the exception of diamond) are available. Harder minerals will scratch softer minerals, and the hardness of the unknown can be bracketed between the hardness values of minerals on the scale. For example, the unknown specimen may be scratched by quartz (hardness = 7) but not by feldspar (hardness = 6). Therefore, the unknown specimen has a hardness value somewhere between 6 and 7. While not a definitive method of identification, this technique does narrow the possibilities significantly. Neither earth scientists nor interested amateurs commonly carry Mohs scale sets with them. Nevertheless, hardness approximations can be made by using some readily available materials, such as a fingernail, a penny, a knife blade, or a piece of glass. Hardness, in general, is a function of the strength of the chemical bonds that hold the ions together within the mineral: the stronger the bonds, the greater the hardness.

Minerals normally display a predictable range of colors, which is determined by both major elements and trace elements within the minerals. Many minerals also exhibit a characteristic called **streak,** which is the color of a chalklike mark the mineral makes when rubbed on a hard, unglazed ceramic plate known as a *streak plate.* The streak of a particular mineral (actually, a powdered sample of that mineral) may not be the same color as the specimen as a whole. For example, the brassy appearance of pyrite, or "fool's gold," is different from its dark streak. An advantage of using streak for identification purposes is that its

(a)

(b)

(c)

Figure 7.7 Crystal faces, fracture, and cleavage. (a) Smooth crystal faces on quartz. Note the irregular fracturing where this specimen was broken near its base. (b) Cleavage surfaces on a broken fragment of calcite. (c) Calcite always "cleaves" along three sets of planes oriented at constant angles to one another. All cleavage surfaces comprising one of the "sets" are parallel to one another (as are the top and bottom of a box). Thus, calcite is said to possess three cleavage "directions." (From R. D. Dallmeyer, *Physical Geology Laboratory Text and Manual,* 2d ed. Copyright © Kendall/Hunt Publishing Company, 1978. Used with permission.)

color tends to be more consistent than the variety of colors often displayed by different specimens of the same mineral. A major drawback is that the streaks of the vast majority of minerals are white and, therefore, not distinctive. For those minerals with characteristic streaks, such as the iron oxides hematite (reddish

brown) and limonite (yellowish brown), however, this feature can be most useful.

Related to color and streak is the physical property called **luster,** which is the way in which a mineral's surface reflects light. Since mineralogists use as many as 20 different terms to describe the surface appearances of minerals, just the recognition that a mineral might be described as metallic, glassy, or dull can be useful in identification.

All minerals possess mass and therefore **density** (mass per unit volume). In the laboratory, precise measurements of this density are compared to that of an equal volume of water, a property known as **specific gravity.** Mineral density (and specific gravity) are functions of two variables: the atomic weight of the constituent ions and the degree to which they are packed together. While such precise measurements are impossible to make in the field, simply comparing the weight, or "heft," of a mineral to that of an approximately equal-sized piece of a common mineral, such as quartz or feldspar, may be useful in identification. Many metallic-ore minerals, for instance, feel heavy.

Some minerals possess a characteristic known as **cleavage,** whereby they split smoothly in certain directions. Such directions are related to planes of weakness within the crystal structure. Planes of weakness are often associated with the type of bonds holding the ions together. Covalent bonds are generally strong and give rise to poor cleavage. Ionic bonds are weak and are often associated with well-developed cleavage directions. Because minerals most commonly occur as large clusters of many crystals, it is important when examining a specimen for cleavage to look at how a single crystal breaks. Often, breaking the mass of crystals simply separates them. When minerals break other than along smooth cleavage planes, they are said to **fracture.** While fracture is usually considered to be an uneven, random breakage, some minerals exhibit peculiar types of fracture that may aid in identification. Large crystals of the mineral quartz, for instance, often exhibit smooth, curved breakage surfaces known as *conchoidal fracture.*

As noted, every mineral assumes its own particular crystal shape whenever sufficient space is available during the growth process. Because these shapes are geometric forms bounded by smooth surfaces, they, too, may be useful for identification. Two notes of caution must be sounded here, however. First, most minerals as they are found within rocks did not have sufficient room to grow and filled in whatever irregular spaces were available; thus, they exhibit an irregular form. Second, even an expert may have difficulty differentiating smooth crystal faces ("growth" surfaces) from smooth cleavage ("breakage" surfaces). Often, the only way to be certain is to break the specimen, a technique that is obviously both destructive and costly. Figure 7.7a and b illustrate the crystal faces of quartz and the cleavage planes of calcite.

Some minerals can be identified by special properties. For example, the mineral magnetite, Fe_3O_4, is naturally magnetic and is attracted to a small magnet, making it easily identifiable. The mineral calcite, $CaCO_3$, "fizzes," or effervesces, when a drop of dilute hydrochloric acid (HCl) is placed on it. Calcite's close relative, dolomite, $CaMg(CO_3)_2$, likewise effervesces in HCl, but only if the acid is placed on a powder formed by scratching the specimen. Box 7.1 describes minerals with luminescence: They glow in the dark.

Box 7.1

LUMINESCENCE: MINERALS THAT GLOW IN THE DARK

Luminescence is a property possessed by certain minerals that causes them to emit light during and after exposure to some external energy source, usually electromagnetic radiation. The radiant energy causes the electrons in the atoms that are normally at their lowest energy level (ground state) to be raised to a higher energy level (excited state). While excited, and as they return to the lower energy level with the removal of the external energy source, the electrons radiate energy. For most minerals, the energy given off is the same wavelength as that of the external source. For some, however, the radiant energy is of a longer wavelength than the external source. If these minerals are exposed to electromagnetic radiation in the visible portion of the spectrum, they radiate some energy in a wavelength beyond the visible so that we do not see it. If exposed to radiation of a shorter wavelength than visible light, such as ultraviolet (UV), they radiate in the longer wavelength, visible portion of the spectrum.

Minerals that give off light during exposure to UV radiation are said to be *fluorescent*, from the mineral fluorite, which "glows" with a blue color, due to the presence of small amounts of rare earth elements. Such elements that are present as the impurities that cause fluorescence are called activators, and some minerals that do not normally fluoresce can be made to do so by adding activators to the crystal structure. The light of fluorescent minerals disappears when the UV source is withdrawn. A few minerals that continue to give off light even after the UV source is withdrawn are said to possess *phosphorescence*. Their color only fades gradually. If the external energy source is heat, rather than electromagnetic radiation, the same type of visual effect is produced in certain minerals (and in the filament of an ordinary electric light bulb). This is called *thermoluminescence*. Some minerals, including fluorite and sphalerite, give off light when scratched or rubbed, a phenomenon known as *triboluminescence*. Many museums house special "darkroom" displays to illustrate the effects of luminescence.

Apply Your Knowledge

1. Besides fluorite, what are some other fluorescent minerals? What is the activator of each?
2. Cite some examples of phosphorescent minerals. Cite examples of thermoluminescent minerals.
3. Explain the thermoluminescent effect of an ordinary incandescent light bulb.

ROCKS

The study of minerals is essential to the understanding of **rocks** because rocks are aggregates of minerals that make up a significant portion of planet Earth. Before beginning our examination of the various types of rocks and their origins, a brief examination of our planet and its characteristics on the broadest scale would be useful. That Earth is a solid body, or nearly so, is substantiated by the analysis of earthquake waves that pass through it—a topic that will be considered fully in chapter 8. Within Earth, three major, distinct layers can be identified, each of which, in turn, can be subdivided into smaller units. From inside out, the three major units are the core, mantle, and crust (fig. 7.8). The **core** consists of two subunits designated the inner core and the outer core. Both are thought to be composed of a mixture of metallic iron and nickel (sometimes called kamacite). They differ in that the inner core is solid, whereas the outer core, based on earthquake wave behavior, is considered to be

Inner Core
Solid iron-nickel

Outer Core
Molten iron-nickel
(some lighter
elements, such as
Si, S, O)

Base of mantle to
about 5,100 km
depth

Crust
Variable thickness
~ 10–50 km
(thickest under continents)

Highly variable chemically

Low in density; solid

Mantle
From base of crust to
2,900 km depth

Silicate minerals in upper
mantle: oxides of Fe, Mg,
and Si below

Localized partial melting within
upper mantle above ~ 250 km;
otherwise solid

Figure 7.8 Simplified view of Earth's interior.

liquid. The liquid state of the outer core has further implications for earth scientists because movement of material within this layer almost certainly gives rise to Earth's magnetic field, an idea that will be developed in chapter 9.

Above the core lies the **mantle,** which constitutes approximately the outer half of Earth. This zone is a solid that approximates the composition of the igneous rock *peridotite,* a mixture of the minerals olivine and pyroxene. Within the mantle are pockets of melted rock. As we shall see later in this chapter, this melted rock is the material from which igneous rocks (volcanic and plutonic) are generated.

Above the mantle lies the **crust,** Earth's rocky outer shell. On the scale of Earth, the crust is a very thin layer, but because it is the closest zone to us, we know far more about its rocky composition than we do about the deeper Earth layers. Broadly speaking, the rock that composes the crust can be divided into two types: granite and basalt. The former underlies the continental areas, whereas the latter forms the foundations of the ocean basins.

A few of the rock types that make up our solid Earth are *monomineralic,* consisting of grains or crystals of but a single mineral. Some sandstones consist wholly of quartz grains, and pure limestone is an accumulation of crystals or fragments of calcite. Most rocks, however, are *polymineralic* in that they are physical mixtures of two or more minerals. The common rock granite, often used for a memorial stone, is normally a mixture of quartz, potassium feldspar, biotite mica, and minor amounts of plagioclase feldspar.

You may better picture the place of rocks in nature by considering the following simple analogy: The 92 naturally occurring elements might be likened to the 26 letters of our alphabet. They are the fundamental building blocks. In isolation, most letters make little sense. Combining elements in different ways forms chemical compounds, including minerals, just as the combining of letters in meaningful ways forms words. Words by themselves may have little meaning until they occur in sentences. Similarly, minerals bound together form rocks. Just as it takes an educated person to read sentences, the educated earth scientist can interpret much of Earth's history by properly "reading" the rock record. Only 26 letters can be combined to form hundreds of thousands of words, and those words can form an indefinite number of sentences. Likewise, the number of possible rock types based on the potential combinations of more than 3,000 minerals staggers the imagination. Fortunately, for those involved with interpreting the rock record, only seven groups (or mineral families) account for a very large percentage of the volume of rock (table 7.4). Note that, of the seven mineral families, six belong to the silicate, or "rock-former," class.

In reality, the possible variety of rocks is limited by the nature of the rock-forming processes. Under various conditions of rock formation, only certain minerals are compatible. For example, of the minerals shown in table 7.4, members of the pyroxene family occur only rarely in quartz-bearing rocks because quartz crystallizes under relatively low-temperature conditions, while pyroxene crystallizes in a high-temperature environment.

An analogy for crystallization temperatures exists in the melting temperatures of butter and chocolate. Placed in similar pots and heated equally, butter melts before chocolate, and upon cooling, chocolate hardens before butter. Some minerals crystallize at very high temperatures, while others are still hot liquids. When experimenter N. L. Bowen melted minerals and allowed them to cool under controlled laboratory conditions, he found that certain minerals crystallized before others. From his experiments, Bowen derived a crystallization-temperature series, which indicates the order of crystallization of igneous minerals and the common associations of minerals that form when liquid rock cools and hardens (fig. 7.9). Quartz and olivine, for example, occur at opposite ends of the crystallization spectrum, making their association in rocks unlikely, or at best, very limited. A corollary to this is the realization that those minerals that form at high temperatures are least stable in Earth's low-temperature surface environment and

TABLE 7.4	The Seven Important Rock-Forming Mineral Groups	
Mineral Family	**Chemical Class**	**Principal Origin**
Feldspars	Silicate	Igneous
Quartz	Silicate	Igneous
Micas	Silicate	Igneous
Pyroxenes	Silicate	Igneous
Amphiboles	Silicate	Igneous
Clays	Silicate	Sedimentary
Calcite (+ dolomite)	Carbonate	Sedimentary

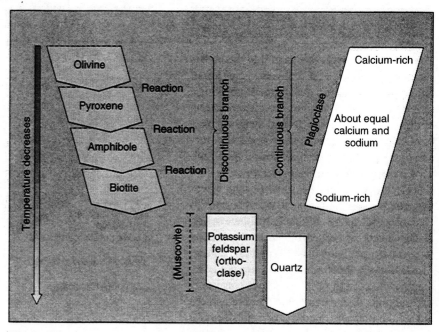

Figure 7.9 Bowen's reaction series. "Continuous" reactions (e.g., in plagioclase) involve continuous ionic substitution between the cooling magma and the growing mineral crystals. The mineral remains the same. In a "discontinuous" reaction (as from olivine to pyroxene), the earlier-formed mineral no longer continues forming and reacts with the remaining magma.

break down on contact with water, oxygen, and other atmospheric chemicals (the process of weathering, covered later in this chapter). Thus, olivine and pyroxene are uncommon in the sedimentary rocks that form on or near Earth's surface, while quartz is a dominant constituent of these rocks.

Just which minerals will form from a cooling rock liquid is a complex matter. In a general way, those minerals with relatively simple internal structures and that require little rearrangement of the constituent ions form earlier than those with more complex ionic arrangements. Obviously, the availability of necessary ions within the rock liquid also governs which minerals can or cannot form.

The Classification of Rocks

Just as they classify minerals, earth scientists also classify rocks. Their task here, however, is somewhat more difficult. Each mineral has a distinct chemical composition that automatically relegates it to a particular category. Rocks, consisting of physical mixtures of varying proportions of different minerals, cannot be sorted as easily on the basis of chemical composition. In fact, rocks with totally different mineral compositions and origins, such as granite and shale, might have very similar bulk chemical compositions.

Because earth scientists attempt to interpret Earth's history from clues provided from the rock record, they prefer to employ a classification that is based on rock origins. The traditional approach is such a "genetic" one. It is not perfect, but it has withstood the test of time. Under this scheme, the rocks, with few exceptions, fall naturally into one of three groups. The **igneous** ("fire-formed") **rocks** are those that crystallize from magma. **Sedimentary rocks** form by the accumulation and consolidation of loose rock and mineral material and/or by the accumulations of fossils and salts. **Metamorphic** ("changed-form") **rocks** are formed by the alteration of preexisting rocks in the solid state by the application of heat and pressure and the introduction of chemical fluids. The relationships between these three rock types are shown by the rock cycle.

The Rock Cycle

The **rock cycle** is the traditional visual vehicle for portraying the origins of and relationships between the three basic rock types (fig. 7.10). Note that each rock type is formed from a preexisting rock type. For example, sedimentary rocks are formed by the weathering and erosion of igneous, metamorphic, or other sedimentary rocks. Metamorphic rocks are formed by the **metamorphism,** or solid-state alteration, of sedimentary, igneous, or other metamorphic rocks. Igneous rocks are formed by the melting of sedimentary, metamorphic, or other igneous rocks. The rock cycle does not represent a truly "closed system," because some material is added from deep within Earth, and some is added from the atmosphere and even outer space. The cycle does involve, however, the constant recycling of much the same material. Mineral grains that are now present in a sandstone might have been in a granite millions of years ago and millions of years from now might be in a metamorphic schist.

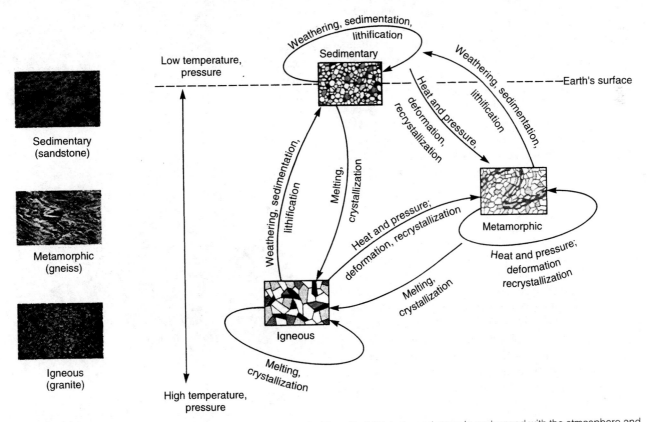

Figure 7.10 The rock cycle. While some new material is added from Earth's interior and some is exchanged with the atmosphere and the oceans, much of the same mineral material is refashioned and recycled again and again. Igneous rocks can form both above and below ground.

IGNEOUS ROCKS

Igneous rocks form by the crystallization of their constituent minerals from magma, which lies below Earth's surface, or from **lava** on Earth's surface. The distinction between magma and lava is primarily one of location. All evidence indicates that there is no worldwide layer of magma within easy reach of Earth's surface and that the source of magma must be in deep, isolated pockets produced by local melting. The melting of solid rock is caused by an increase in temperature under constant pressure, a decrease in pressure under constant temperature, or a combination of the two.

Heating the rock causes the constituent ions to vibrate more energetically in their lattice positions. If the vibrations become violent enough, the bonds between ions break, the lattice collapses, and the solid material changes to liquid. To some extent, high pressure counteracts the effect of elevated temperature by holding the ions in place and not allowing them to separate. Decreasing pressure, even without elevating the temperature, could allow the solid to melt if the rock was already at a sufficiently high temperature. Elevated temperatures within Earth might be generated by the decay of locally concentrated radioisotopes. Pressure could be significantly reduced when a mass of heated rock is raised by internal Earth forces toward the surface, and overlying rock layers are eroded away. Additionally, the presence of water, as in the pore spaces of sedimentary rocks, significantly lowers the melting points of rocks and minerals.

Once rock melts, the resulting magma becomes less dense than the surrounding solid rock and rises. It works its way upward through systems of cracks and crevasses, pushing aside, melting, and warping any overlying layers of rock. Some of the magma reaches the surface to be erupted as lava in **volcanic** (or **extrusive,** because it "comes out of") activity. The bulk of the magma, however, cools and crystallizes long before reaching the surface and, consequently, is emplaced as **plutonic** (or **intrusive**) rock. Such rock can only be exposed much later, when erosion removes the overlying rock layers. This difference in origin, which is reflected in mineral composition and certain physical characteristics, provides a convenient way to subdivide igneous rocks and, indeed, to provide names for individual igneous rock types.

Igneous Rock Textures

The most obvious physical characteristic of igneous rocks, as a response to differences in origin, is the size of the individual crystals in the rock. In general, the more slowly magma cools, the more time the mineral crystals have to grow and the larger they become. Conversely, rapid cooling leads to a matrix of many small crystals. Slow cooling in nature would most likely occur beneath Earth's surface, where heat loss is very slow because of the insulating effect of the overlying rocks. Lava erupted onto Earth's surface loses heat very rapidly to the atmosphere or, in oceanic eruptions, to the hydrosphere. Thin and/or shallow intrusive igneous bodies may also cool rapidly.

The size, shape, and arrangement of mineral grains or crystals in any rock is referred to as its **texture.** The mass of large (visible to the naked eye) crystals produced by the slow cooling of a magma is referred to as a **phaneritic (coarse) texture** (fig. 7.11*a*). The matrix of tiny crystals formed by the rapid cooling of a lava or a shallow intrusive is an **aphanitic (fine) texture** (fig. 7.11*b*). Under conditions of very rapid cooling, ions may not have time to arrange themselves into even the smallest crystals. The result is a *glassy texture*. Recall that a glass, though rigid, is not a true solid because it lacks an orderly internal arrangement of ions. The ions are simply "frozen" into random positions.

Other textures may develop under special circumstances, as when the upper portion of a lava flow hardens around escaping gas bubbles, leaving the rock with a **vesicular (porous) texture.** Some vesicular igneous rocks are very lightweight because of the holes, or vesicles, in them. For example, masses of the porous rock pumice have been reported floating on water. A magma often begins the crystallization process even as it rises toward the surface. This means that some crystals grow large slowly over a long period of time. When the mixture of large, solid crystals and still-liquid magma is erupted onto Earth's surface, the remaining liquid

(a)

(b)

Figure 7.11 (*a*) Coarse-grained (phaneritic) igneous rock texture, representing slow cooling and crystal growth at some depth beneath Earth's surface. (*b*) Fine-grained (aphanitic) texture developed by rapid cooling and solidification in the low-temperature environment at Earth's surface.

crystallizes rapidly as a "background" mass of fine crystals, resulting in a mixture of crystals of distinctly different sizes. Such a **porphyritic texture** normally indicates two stages of cooling: a slow early stage and a later rapid stage. The resulting rock is referred to as a *porphyry.* Its complete name is formed by adding the rock term that best describes the finer-grained fraction—for example, "basalt porphyry" or "andesite porphyry."

Sometimes, late in the crystallization of granitic magma, rock bodies with unusually large crystals may form a coarse-grained, **pegmatitic texture.** The resulting rock is called a pegmatite. While the bulk mineralogy of pegmatites is quartz and K-feldspar, a number of unusual minerals, including the gemstones ruby and sapphire, can also be found in them. The very coarse texture is usually attributed to the high percentage of water at this stage of the crystallization process, which allows for easy migration of ions to the sites of mineral formation. The percentage of water is high at this stage because the crystal structures of most early-formed minerals do not allow for its inclusion.

Igneous Rock Composition

The second important factor in classifying igneous rocks is the rock's mineral composition. Reference was made earlier to N. L. Bowen's laboratory experiments, which substantiated the idea previously held from field experience that crystal formation is not a random process. Rather, the various minerals that crystallize from a magma do so in a specific order as the temperature of the magma decreases. Thus, the igneous rock basalt is composed only of minerals, such as Ca-plagioclase and pyroxene, that crystallize early at high temperatures. Granite, on the other hand, is formed of late-crystallizing, low-temperature minerals. Coincidentally, many of the early-forming minerals, such as olivine, amphiboles, and pyroxenes, are rich in iron and magnesium (and called **ferromagnesian minerals**) and tend to be dark in color, while most late-forming minerals (quartz, K-feldspar, and muscovite) are light-colored. This means that igneous rock color can be used as a reasonable approximation to mineral composition. This is especially helpful in the identification of fine-grained rocks, the tiny crystals of which can only be identified under the microscope.

Figure 7.12 is a simplified classification scheme for the most common igneous rocks. The bottom portion of the diagram shows the names assigned to each combination of texture (vertical axis) and composition or color (horizontal axis). Although each of the basic rock types is given equal space in the diagram, the actual abundances in nature are far from equal. Granite and closely related rock types account for more than 90% of the total volume of intrusive igneous rocks, whereas basalt and its near relatives account for more than 90% of all extrusive igneous rocks. This distribution is not mere coincidence. Basaltic magma is much more fluid than granitic magma, and its greater mobility gives it a better chance of rising all the way to Earth's surface before it solidifies. You might liken the consistency of basaltic magma to a heavy motor oil and that of granitic magma to toothpaste. This "consistency," or resistance of the magma (or any fluid) to flow, is called *viscosity,* and we can characterize granitic magmas as being more viscous than basaltic magmas.

Figure 7.12 Classification scheme for igneous rocks, based on mineral composition and texture.

The upper part of figure 7.12 shows the approximate temperature range across which each of the important igneous rock-forming minerals crystallizes. Just as in the old expression "birds of a feather flock together," minerals that crystallize at relatively high temperatures (such as Ca-plagioclase, olivine, and pyroxene) can normally be found together in a rock, but are not found with low-temperature minerals (such as quartz, potassium feldspar, and muscovite), which form very different rock types. Because rocks are physical mixtures of minerals that can come together in varying proportions, unexpected mineral combinations may on occasion occur. Thus, the mineral percentages used to establish boundaries to separate one rock type from another (e.g., granite from diorite) are arbitrary and used by earth scientists for convenience.

An economically important aspect of igneous rock formation occurs during the latest stages of the process. When most of the common rock-forming minerals have already crystallized to form, for example, a granite, and even the pegmatites have formed, the residue of the original magma is a watery solution at several hundred degrees Celsius. Such a **hydrothermal,** or "hot water," **solution** contains an abundance of ions of rare metals that find no lattice positions to fill in such common minerals as quartz, feldspar, and mica. Instead, they are incorporated into and concentrated in rare

(a)

(b)

Figure 7.13 Mount St. Helens in the Cascade Range of Washington State (*a*) before and (*b*) after its spectacular eruption of May 18, 1980.

and unusual minerals. The economic importance of these hydrothermal solutions and the minerals that crystallize from them is discussed further in chapter 16.

Volcanoes

Most igneous rocks form beneath the surface of the continents or beneath the sea—thus, away from our direct observation. Only when overlying rock layers are removed by erosion or the rocks are moved above sea level do we see them. Nature does, however, provide scientists with at least one type of aboveground occurrence where igneous rock in the process of formation is visible: the volcanic eruption.

A **volcano** is normally, but not exclusively, a cone-shaped topographic feature composed of accumulations of igneous rock and ash material that have been extruded through an opening, or **fissure,** in Earth's surface. As these features grow, material is extruded either from a central vent at the cone's summit, the **crater,** or from fractures on the volcano's flanks. Because volcanoes can vary significantly in rock composition, history, and general appearance, earth scientists have subdivided and named the different types. Two general approaches to volcano classification are common: that based on eruptive history and that based on appearance (shape) and composition.

The volcano classification based on eruptive history recognizes three loosely defined categories: (1) volcanoes that were *active* and erupted in historic times; (2) those that have no historical record of eruption but are "fresh" looking with little sign of erosion and are

thus regarded as only "sleeping," or *dormant;* and (3) those that are *extinct* because they are highly eroded and show no sign of any activity. Because this approach depends on the very short period of human experience compared to the enormity of geologic time, we have often been tragically mistaken in our assessment of a particular volcano's capacity for violent eruption. One such instance was the reawakening on May 18,1980 of Mount Saint Helens, one of the peaks of the Cascade Range in Washington State. In a violent eruption that literally "decapitated" the volcano, the surrounding landscape was altered, with the tragic loss of 60 lives (fig. 7.13).

An even more devastating event shook the ancient Roman world almost 2,000 years ago: the eruption of Mount Vesuvius on the Bay of Naples in A.D. 79. Known to the Romans of that day as Monte Somma, this volcano had been quiet throughout the several hundred years of recorded human habitation in the area. Several years prior to its eruption, frequent small earthquakes in the area indicated that Somma was stirring. The A.D. 79 eruption was so violent that day was turned to night by thick clouds of volcanic ash. The port city of Pompeii was buried beneath many meters of rapidly falling ash, and the city of Herculaneum was buried by massive mudflows generated by the eruption. Both cities were lost in time only to be unearthed by archeologists in the last century. The death toll at Pompeii and Herculaneum can never be known, but the impressions of many bodies preserved in the surrounding ash indicate that events overwhelmed the inhabitants, leaving them little chance to escape. Since that time, Vesuvius has been one of Earth's most active volcanoes, with dozens of recorded eruptions.

The volcano classification based on topographic form, or appearance, recognizes three major volcano types and several minor types of features. The first is the **shield volcano,** so-called because it is rounded with a low topographic profile that resembles the shape of shields carried by warriors of old (fig. 7.14*a*). Such volcanoes are built up primarily by successive flows of basaltic lava. The slopes of the shield volcano are made gentle by the lava itself, which tends, while still in the fluid state, to flow down even the most gentle of slopes and to spread out. The foundation of the shield volcano is typically so broad, however, that even with its very gentle slopes, this feature can be built to an overall height of thousands of meters. Such is the case in Hawaii, where the volcanic shields have been built up from the seafloor, which is approximately 5,100 meters (17,000 ft) deep at that locality, to elevations in excess of 3,900 meters (13,000 ft) above sea level: a total height of more than 9,000 meters (30,000 ft). With its great height as measured from the seafloor and its size, the shield volcano Mauna Loa is the largest mountain on Earth. It is not, however, the largest in the Solar System. That distinction belongs to the shield volcanoes on Mars, including Olympus Mons, which was discussed in chapter 3.

A second volcano type, the **stratovolcano,** is built up of successive layers, or "strata," of alternating lava flows (usually of andesite rock) and solid volcanic particles (fig. 7.14*b*). The solid particles vary in size from fine dust to large blocks and are collectively called **pyroclastic** ("fire fragment") **debris.** Because andesitic lava is not as fluid as basaltic lava, and because the solid particles can form steeper slopes than lava, stratovolcanoes tend to be steeper-sided and to rise much more abruptly and spectacularly from their surroundings than do

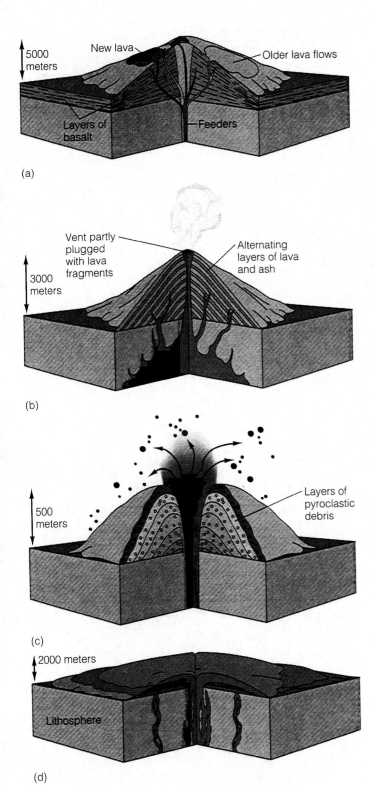

Figure 7.14 Types of lava extrusions. (a) Shield volcano.
(b) Stratovolcano. (c) Cinder cone. (d) Basalt plateau (flood basalt).

shield volcanoes. In general, the andesitic lava flows broaden the base of the volcanic cone and the pyroclastic debris builds it higher. Most of the world's most striking and beautiful volcanoes, such as Mount Fujiyama in Japan, Mount Kilimanjaro in Africa, Mount Mayon in the Philippines, and the peaks of the Cascade Range in the U.S. Pacific Northwest, fall into this category.

Less spectacular than the others, but interesting in its own right, is a third type of volcano known as a **cinder cone** (fig. 7.14c). Cinder cones are small, normally rising less than 450 meters (1,500 ft) above their surroundings, and often occur in groups. They consist almost exclusively of pyroclastic debris, which means that they are steep-sided, but their behavior is often modified late in their life cycles to include basaltic lava flows. Part of the fascination of cinder cones is that they appear to have very short life spans, on the order of 10 to 20 years. Earth scientists have, therefore, been able to study fully and to document completely cinder cones' cycles of growth.

Other related volcanic features include maars, spatter cones, and calderas. A *maar,* which often contains a lake, is a broad volcanic crater of low relief formed by multiple explosions. *Spatter cones* are small, basaltic cones, a few meters in height and formed from hardened accumulations of lava ejected as flying masses through fissures. **Calderas** are wide, deep depressions, many times larger than craters, that are the remnants of volcanic cones that erupted violently. The explosive eruption pulverizes much of the upper part of the cone and causes a good part of the remainder to collapse into the partially empty magma chamber below (see box 7.2). The best example of such a feature in North America is Crater Lake in southern Oregon (see the photo at the beginning of this chapter). Crater Lake formed by an explosive eruption of a volcano, now referred to by geologists as Mount Mazama, approximately 6,600 years ago. The result was a circular depression 8 kilometers (5 mi) in diameter and as much as 1,200 meters (4,000 ft) deep. Subsequent rain and snowmelt have filled the caldera to a depth of 600 meters (2,000 ft), forming the lake.

Basalt Plateaus

Very fluid basaltic lava can erupt out of many closely spaced vents, rather than from a single vent. When this happens, the lava spreads out to form a thin but widespread horizontal layer of basalt. Subsequent eruptions pile additional layers on top of the first until a sequence of many flows totaling a thousand meters or more in thickness has accumulated over the course of several million years. Such an accumulation of horizontal layers of basalt is called a **basalt plateau** (fig. 7.14d). In the United States, the most prominent such feature, the Columbia River plateau–Snake River plain, lies in the states of Washington, Oregon, and Idaho and includes much of the area drained by these two river systems. In places, the Columbia River plateau consists of a thickness of basaltic rock layers in excess of 1,500 meters (5,000 ft) that has been built up over the last 30 million years. Similar massive accumulations are found in the Parana River basin of Brazil and the Deccan Plateau of western India.

BOX 7.2

THE LONG VALLEY CALDERA: WILL HISTORY SOON REPEAT ITSELF?

The Long Valley Caldera, an oval depression covering 600 square kilometers (170 sq. mi), is located on the edge of the Sierra Nevada in east central California (fig. 7.A). The caldera came into existence as the result of a violent eruption approximately 730,000 years ago. The eruption buried a 1,475-square-kilometer (570-sq.-mi) area with ash and pumice accumulations up to 1,350 meters (4,500 ft) thick and left a 3.2-kilometer-(2-mi) deep depression. The thick blanket of volcanic ash is known to geologists today as the Bishop Tuff (fig. 7.B). Smaller-scale periods of eruption occurred again about 50,000 and 10,000 years ago, and volcanic activity has occurred as recently as 500 to 600 years ago at the nearby Mono Craters.

The most recent activity at Long Valley, however, has not been volcanic but seismic. In 1980, the town of Mammoth Lakes, California, a recreation center, began to experience earthquakes. This activity culminated on May 27, 1980, when four shocks of magnitude 6.0 were recorded. Over the next 2 years, the pattern of earthquake activity was so like that which preceded the Mount Saint Helens eruption that the director of the U.S. Geological Survey issued a notice of potential volcanic hazard for the region. Overall, the pattern of earthquakes, supplemented by other data, led seismologists to believe that the earthquakes were caused by the movement of magma toward the surface and that a mass of magma 4 kilometers (2.5 mi) across lies less than 8 kilometers (5 mi) below the ground surface.

Two important issues are emerging from the work done at Long Valley. The first relates to the area as an important recreational resource. Warnings of impending volcanic eruptions can be devastating to a local economy based on tourism. The problem is compounded by the fact that the area's very remoteness would make a hurried evacuation, should the need arise, difficult. On the positive side, regions with near-surface magma chambers such as Long Valley hold tremendous potential for geothermal ("earth heat") energy. Under the auspices of the U.S. Department of Energy, drilling was begun in 1989 on a 6,500-meter-(20,000-ft.) deep exploratory well within the caldera (fig. 7.A). The purpose of this well is to test the feasibility of tapping the magma's heat energy for electrical power generation. While the results of this $8 million project will not be known for some time and the commercial use of this type of geothermal energy is still a number of years away, the prospects are certainly interesting to contemplate.

Apply Your Knowledge

1. What might be some problems in trying to tap the thermal energy of a near-surface magma chamber for electric power generation?
2. What social and economic problems might arise from a governmental announcement of an impending major volcanic eruption? Consider both the short and long term.

Figure 7.A   Location map showing Long Valley Caldera and drill site for energy exploration well.

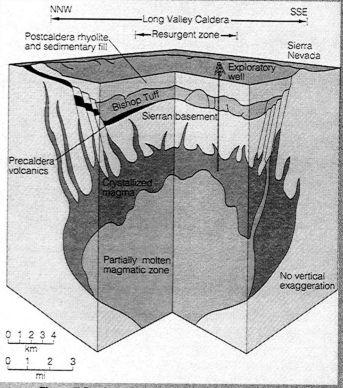

Figure 7.B   Cross section showing subsurface geology through the Long Valley Caldera.

Plutonic Features

Those masses of magma, many of them granitic in composition, that crystallized before reaching Earth's surface are found preserved in an array of sizes and shapes. All are referred to by the generic name **pluton,** after Pluto, the Roman god of the lower world (fig. 7.15). Some plutons are intruded between and parallel to the surrounding rock layers. These are **concordant.** Others intrude across the surrounding rock layers and thus are considered **discordant.** If a pluton has a shape that resembles a tabletop—that is, relatively thin compared to its length and width—it is called a **tabular pluton.** Any other shape is a **nontabular pluton.** These two characteristics are used to describe and name the several types of plutons (table 7.5). For example, a tabular, discordant pluton is a **dike,** while a tabular, concordant pluton is a **sill.** A concordant pluton made nontabular by a pronounced thickening that "arches up" the overlying rock layers is a **laccolith.** A similar concordant feature, but with a distinctive downward "bow," is a **lopolith.**

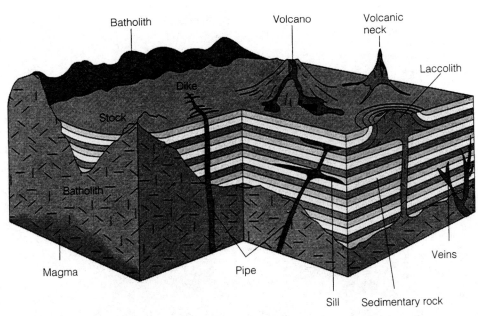

Figure 7.15   Igneous plutons. The laccolith shown in the diagram is exposed at the surface because overlying layers of rock have been eroded.

TABLE 7.5   Summary of Igneous Plutons

Pluton	Tabular or Nontabular	Concordant or Discordant	Common Compositon	Other Characteristics
Dike	Tabular	Discordant	Granite	
Sill	Tabular	Concordant	Gabbro	
Laccolith	Nontabular	Concordant	Granite	Thickened upward
Lopolith	Nontabular	Concordant	Gabbro	Thickened downward
Stock	Nontabular	Discordant	Granite	< 100 sq. kilometers
Batholith	Nontabular	Discordant	Granite	> 100 sq. kilometers

The largest pluton, by far, is the discordant, nontabular **batholith.** A batholith is usually composed of granite and/or related rock types and may occur over an area of hundreds of thousands of square kilometers. It must, however, by definition, have an exposed surface area of no less than 100 square kilometers (40 sq. mi). A similar feature with less surface exposure, regardless of the size of its underground dimensions, is called a **stock.** Elevated by forces operating within Earth, batholiths and stocks have been carved by the processes of weathering and erosion into some of the world's largest and most spectacular mountain ranges (fig. 7.16a). The classic example in the United States is the Sierra Nevada of eastern California, a mountain system stretching some 650 kilometers (400 mi) in length and averaging 80 kilometers (50 mi) in width (fig. 7.16b). Similar bodies in North America are found in central Idaho, southern California, and coastal British Columbia.

As a magma intrudes preexisting rock, pieces of the older rock may fall into the chamber to become "frozen" in the crystallizing magma. These pieces, called **xenoliths,** can be small fragments or as large as a house (fig. 7.17).

WEATHERING AND SEDIMENTS

Most igneous and metamorphic, as well as some sedimentary, rocks form deep in Earth's interior in an environment of high temperatures and pressures. When ultimately exposed at Earth's surface by the wearing away of overlying rock layers, these deeply formed rocks find themselves in a "hostile" low-temperature environment in which they are unstable. Additionally, they come in contact with such chemicals as oxygen, water, carbon dioxide, and various acids. Chemical reactions between these substances and the minerals in the rocks lead to rock breakdown in a process known as **weathering** (fig. 7.18).

This physical and chemical breakdown of rock material fulfills several important functions. Weathering prepares rock or any earth material for movement by converting large masses into smaller, more manageable particles that can be picked up and transported by air, water, and ice. With this subsequent removal of earth materials, weathering gradually wears down and lowers Earth's surface. Weathering is also partly responsible for the formation of soil on which not only plants but ultimately all life depends. Because of their importance as natural resources, soils will be considered in some detail in chapter 16.

Figure 7.16   (a) Representation of how batholiths and stocks are exposed at Earth's surface by the removal of overlying rock layers by erosion. The inclusions (xenoliths) are pieces of country rock broken off and surrounded as the liquid magma works its way upward. (b) The Sierra Nevada of California, a batholith exposed and carved into a rugged mountain range by erosion.

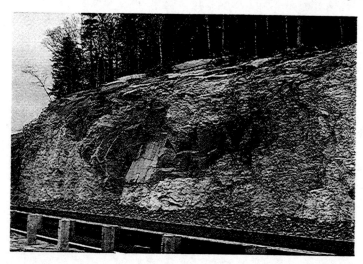

Figure 7.17   A large xenolith (dark mass) within a light-colored granite (White Mountains, New Hampshire). Xenoliths are distinguishable by color, texture, and composition.

(a)

(b)

Figure 7.18 Examples of weathering. (*a*) Marble (composed of the mineral calcite) tombstone, highly susceptible to weathering (dissolution) in a humid climate. (*b*) "Spheroidally" weathered igneous boulder.

Physical Weathering

Weathering is normally considered to occur in two fundamentally different yet related ways. The first is the purely mechanical breakdown of rock masses into smaller pieces without any change in chemical or mineralogical composition, a process known as **physical weathering,** or *disintegration.* For example, a large piece of granite may be broken into smaller pieces of granite or separated into its component minerals (fig. 7.19*a*). The reduction in particle size not only allows for easier movement, but, more importantly, exposes more rock and mineral surface area to attack by chemical weathering agents.

Physical weathering is a mechanical change that is brought about in several ways. The expansion of water as it freezes in cracks in the rock exerts tremendous pressure on the rock, often sufficient to break off large pieces (fig. 7.19*b*). Called **frost wedging,** this process is particularly important at high altitudes, where nighttime temperatures fall below freezing even during summer. Indeed, some landscapes above the treeline in mountainous regions are literally covered by angular rock boulders that have been dislodged by this process (fig. 7.19*c*). Plant roots, as they work their way into rock cracks and grow, eventually pry loose rock fragments. Burrowing animals may also contribute to this overall process. In some regions, even alternate wetting and drying of mineral material or the expansion and contraction due to temperature changes may contribute to the process of disintegration.

Some igneous rocks, particularly granites, that formed at great depths expand due to relaxation of pressure when overlying rock layers are stripped away by erosion. This expansion leads to the development of fractures parallel to the ground surface, since this is the direction of least resistance and, therefore, of easiest movement. Weathering then strips off these rock layers, like peeling an onion, in a process known as **exfoliation** (fig. 7.20). Mountainous masses with unique curved shapes that have been formed by this process are referred to as **exfoliation domes.** Yosemite National Park in the Sierra Nevada of California is especially noted for these features.

Chemical Weathering

More important than the mechanical breakdown of rock material are the chemical and mineralogical changes, known collectively as **chemical weathering,** or *decomposition,* that occur when rocks are exposed at Earth's surface (table 7.6). Chemical weathering, with its formation of new minerals, finally brings the rock material into a state of chemical equilibrium with the surface environment. Such changes brought about by reactions with water (*hydrolysis*) and carbon dioxide (*carbonation*) are especially important in converting the most abundant igneous mineral feldspar into clay and dissolved silica. These latter two minerals form the basis for most soils and for the abundant sedimentary rocks shale and sandstone. The red, tan, or brown color of most rocks exposed at Earth's surface is the result of the chemical reaction of iron-bearing minerals in the rocks with the oxygen and water in the atmosphere, a natural *oxidation,* or "rusting," process.

Climate is the overriding factor that governs the weathering process. In arid regions, where little water is available, physical

Figure 7.19 Physical (mechanical) weathering. (*a*) Physical weathering reduces particle size (without decreasing its overall volume), thereby increasing the amount of rock area exposed to chemical weathering. (*b*) Ice, expanding as it freezes in rock cracks, breaks off pieces of rock, a process known as frost wedging. (*c*) The results of frost wedging at high altitudes.

Figure 7.20 Exfoliation. (*a*) Batholith at depth. (*b*) Pressure reduction due to erosion of overlying rock layers causes upward expansion in granite and fractures parallel to the ground surface. (*c*) Exfoliation at work in the White Mountains of New Hampshire.

TABLE 7.6	The Chemical Weathering of Common Rock-Forming Minerals	
Original Mineral	**Major Mineral Product**	**Other (mostly soluble) Products**
K-feldspar	Clay minerals	SiO_2, K^+
Plagioclase feldspar	Clay minerals	SiO_2, Na^+, Ca^{2+}
Muscovite mica	Clay minerals	SiO_2, K^+
Biotite mica	Clay minerals	SiO_2, K^+, Mg^{2+}, Fe oxides
Hornblende (amphibole)	Clay minerals	$SiO_2, Na^+, Ca^{2+}, Mg^{2+}$, Fe oxides
Augite (pyroxene)	Clay minerals	$SiO_2, Na^+, Ca^{2+}, Mg^{2+}$, Fe oxides
Quartz	Quartz	
Calcite	—	$Ca^{2+}, Mg^{2+}, (HCO_3)^-$

weathering dominates over chemical weathering, soil development is curtailed, vegetation is sparse, and bedrock lies at or near the ground surface, producing a stark, "angular" terrain. In humid regions, with abundant moisture, the land becomes blanketed with a covering of soil and vegetation and develops a "smoother," more gently rolling appearance. Contrast, for example, the steep cliffs of the arid Grand Canyon region with the more gently rolling terrain of the humid Appalachians of north-central Pennsylvania (fig. 7.21). The underlying rocks are basically the same. It is largely the effect of climate that distinguishes the two areas.

(a)

(b)

Figure 7.21 (a) The Grand Canyon of the Colorado River in Arizona. (b) Pine Creek Gorge, the "Grand Canyon of Pennsylvania." Both canyons have been cut through horizontal sedimentary rock layers. The "smoother" topography of Pine Creek Gorge is attributable to the more intense chemical weathering and vegetation cover of "humid" Pennsylvania.

SEDIMENTARY ROCKS

Most earth material, once dislodged by weathering, begins another step in the endless rock cycle. It is picked up (eroded) and transported by water, wind, or ice until it finally is deposited and comes to rest. This loose material is called **sediment,** and it is most commonly deposited in nearly horizontal layers in the shallow waters at the edges of the continents, into which most large rivers ultimately drain. Successively younger layers deposited on top of older layers add to the sedimentary mass.

Because of the pressure of the overlying layers and the precipitation of mineral material within the body of sediment by circulating water, the loose sediment, over the course of millions of years, is converted into hard sedimentary rock. Because such rocks form at or near Earth's surface, they are the most common types found there and form a relatively thin veneer across approximately 75% of continental surfaces. Bear in mind that, although originally deposited in shallow seas, many of these rocks are eventually exposed when the seafloor is elevated or the seas drain off the continental surfaces.

Sedimentary Rock Types

The mineral material that makes up sedimentary rocks is transported and utilized in ways that give rise to three basic types of sedimentary rocks. The most common, by far, are those that form as the result of the movement by streams of rock and mineral particles of various sizes, ranging from fine clay to large boulders (see box 7.3). When deposited, buried, compacted, and hardened, or *lithified,* this material forms **clastic** ("fragmental") sedimentary rocks. This category includes such familiar rock types as conglomerate, sandstone, siltstone, and shale (fig. 7.22).

Box 7.3

Further Consideration

THE WENTWORTH-UDDEN SCALE: HOW LARGE IS A SAND GRAIN?

We all have an intuitive sense of the size of such common particles as sand grains and pebbles, and usually, such a sense is sufficient for our purposes. The professional earth scientist, however, often must be more precise about the nature of sedimentary particles. Consequently, several particle-size scales have been developed over the years. One of the oldest, but still the most widely used, is the Wentworth-Udden scale, first developed by J.A. Udden in 1898 and modified and expanded by C.K. Wentworth in 1922 (table 7.A).

This geometric scale has two distinct advantages over arithmetic scales, where each interval is of equal value. First, the boundaries for particle-size classes differ from one another by a constant ratio, or multiplier—in this case, one-half. For example, the upper limit of the "granule" category is a diameter of 4 millimeters. The lower limit of the "granule" category is 2 millimeters (4 x 1/2). Second, a geometric scale expands the fine-grained end of the scale and compresses the coarse-grained end of the scale. The advantage of this is that small changes in grain diameter at the clay-silt end of the scale can be very significant, whereas even large changes in particle diameter at the boulder-cobble end of the scale are probably of little significance.

Although the boundaries for the sand category seem to contradict the constant ratio of one-half for determining such boundaries, they indeed do not. Such categories can be subdivided, using the constant ratio as shown along the right-hand portion of the chart.

Apply Your Knowledge

1. Subdivide the "pebble" category as was done for the "sand" category and give appropriate names for each subdivision. Do the same for the "silt" category.

2. How does the expansion of the fine-grained end of a geometric scale and the compression of the coarse-grained end of the same scale differ from what would occur using an arithmetic scale?

TABLE 7.A   The Wentworth-Udden Scale

Particle Diameter (mm)	Name	Sand Particle Diameters (mm)
Greater than 256	Boulder	
256–64	Cobble	2–1 = Very coarse sand
64–4	Pebble	1–1/2 = Coarse sand
4–2	Granule	1/2–1/4 = Medium sand
2–1/16	Sand	1/4–1/8 = Fine sand
1/16–1/256	Silt	1/8–1/16 = Very fine sand
Less than 1/256	Clay	

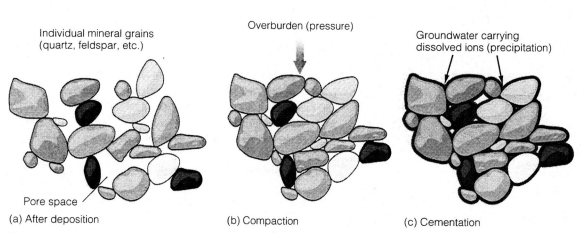

Individual mineral grains (quartz, feldspar, etc.)

Pore space

(a) After deposition

Overburden (pressure)

(b) Compaction

Groundwater carrying dissolved ions (precipitation)

(c) Cementation

Figure 7.22   (*a*) Mineral particles immediately after deposition. (*b*) Mineral grains squeezed closer together by the weight of overlying sediment. (*c*) Deposition of mineral material by circulating water that cements the mineral grains together, completing the lithification process.

Texture			Rock name	Mineral composition
Clastic	Finer than sand (< 1/16 mm)	"Gritty" / Smooth	Shale	Clay
			Siltstone	
	Sand size (1/16 to 4 mm)		Graywacke	Mica
			Arkose	Quartz / Feldspar / Rock fragments
			Quartz sandstone	
	Coarser than sand (> 4 mm)	Rounded grains	Conglomerate	
		Angular grains	Breccia	
Nonclastic			Chert	
			Rock gypsum	Gypsum
			Rock salt	Halite
			Dolostone	Dolomite
			Lithographic limestone	Calcite
Bioclastic			Fossiliferous limestone	
			Coal	Plant debris

Figure 7.23 A general classification scheme for sedimentary rocks, based on particle size (for just the clastic rocks) and mineral composition.

A third category of sedimentary rocks is the **nonclastic,** or *crystalline,* rocks, which precipitate directly out of solution, usually as the water in which their constituent ions are dissolved evaporates. Because this process is similar to how minerals form from magma, the minerals in nonclastic rocks form a tight texture of interlocking crystals. This category includes some limestones and the chemically similar dolostone (consisting of the mineral dolomite), but it also encompasses an economically important subgroup known as the **evaporites.**

The evaporation process removes only pure water, so that when a restricted body of seawater in an arid climate slowly dries up, the dissolved salts become increasingly concentrated in the water that remains. Eventually, the salts become so concentrated that they can no longer all remain in solution, and the less-soluble ones begin to precipitate out as horizontal rock layers on the floor of the shallow sea or lagoon. Three of the most important such salts are gypsum ($CaSO_4nH_2O$), widely used in plaster and plasterboard; halite ($NaCl$), or common table salt; and sylvite (KCl), an important source of potassium (K) for fertilizer. During the Permian Period (approximately 250 million years ago), a large sea that covered much of western Texas and eastern New Mexico gradually dried up and, in the process, left a blanket of evaporite deposits hundreds of meters thick over an area of more than 250,000 square kilometers (100,000 sq. mi). Such thick deposits imply a delicately balanced situation. Once the process of salt precipitation began, just enough seawater was able to enter the area of restriction to replace that which was being lost, leading to continuous precipitation of salts.

Compared to igneous rocks, sedimentary rocks are compositionally very simple, with many being monomineralic. Three rock types, shale (clay minerals + quartz), sandstone (quartz), and limestone (calcite), probably account for more than 99% of the volume of all of the sedimentary rocks. Rocks such as dolostone, gypsum, and rock salt may have local economic importance, but their quantity is insignificant. Figure 7.23 is a general classification scheme for the sedimentary rocks, based on particle size (for just the clastic rocks) and mineral composition.

Some weathered material is not carried in the form of particles but rather as dissolved ions. These ions may be removed from solution by animals to construct their shells, as clams and oysters do, or by plants for their growth. The accumulated shell remains of many generations of animals, mostly living in the world's oceans, give rise to the rock limestone, whose chief mineral constituent is calcite. The accumulation of dead plant material, mostly in swampy environments, forms coal. Both of these rocks are clastic in the sense that they consist of fragments. Since the fragments are of biological origin, however, they are more commonly considered **bioclastic** rocks. Because of its importance as an economic resource, coal receives additional consideration in chapter 16.

Clues to Earth's Past

Although simple in composition, sedimentary rocks contain a wealth of information that has allowed earth scientists to piece together much of what we know about Earth's history. The very fact that they form in almost horizontal layers tells us much about the nature of the formative processes and the environments in which they occur. *This horizontal layering, or stratification, is, in fact, the single most characteristic feature of sedimentary rocks.*

Fossils, the direct evidence of past life, also represent significant information. Fossils most commonly are in the form of hard animal parts, such as shells, teeth, and bones, which can withstand the rigors of erosion and transport. The rare preservation of imprints of animal soft body tissues, footprints, burrows,

(a)

(b)

(c)

Figure 7.24 Examples of the variety of fossils. (*a*) The shells of marine animals preserved in limestone. (*b*) Leaf impressions in shale. (*c*) Petrified wood.

and plant leaf impressions, however, can provide even more valuable information (fig. 7.24). The abundance of fossil material varies with rock type. Some limestone consists wholly or in large part of animal shell remains. Fine-grained limestones and shales provide the best media for the preservation of the various types of impressions. Sandstones often are lacking in fossil material because the constant pounding by waves in the beach environments where many form destroys the fragile shell material.

Mud cracks, formed on tidal mud flats and in other environments subject to alternate wetting and drying, can also be preserved in the lithified rock. They develop when wet mud shrinks upon drying. During the next submergence of the surface, other sediment carried in by the water may fill in the cracks, preserving them (fig. 7.25). Other features commonly preserved in sedimentary rocks are the sand ripples (**ripple marks),** formed by the movement of sand particles on the surfaces of dunes and sandbars, and the small-scale, inclined sand layers (**crossbeds)** within the bodies of the same features. Under certain circumstances, ripple marks and crossbeds tell earth scientists the direction of wind or water movement tens or hundreds of millions of years ago.

METAMORPHIC ROCKS

The third major group of rocks, the metamorphics, have been altered while in the solid state in response to changes in temperature, pressure, and the chemical environment. The significance of "solid-state" changes is that, once rock melts, the mineral matter crosses the boundary into the igneous domain. Generally, the metamorphic processes are the opposite of the weathering processes. During weathering, high-temperature, high-pressure rocks are exposed to the elements at Earth's surface. During metamorphism, low-temperature, low-pressure sedimentary rocks are made unstable by being buried deep in Earth, where temperatures and pressures are high. Although any rock can be metamorphosed, sedimentary rocks are the most easily changed.

Whereas elevated temperatures can bring about significant changes in sedimentary rocks (as the alteration of clay to mica and chlorite in hornfels), pressure is responsible for the most obvious changes. In some instances, as along fault zones (chapter 8), where

(a)

(b)

Figure 7.25   (a) Fresh mud cracks form as mud dries. (b) Mud cracks preserved in rocks that are more than 1 billion years old.

Figure 7.26   Response of mineral grains to increasing pressure. (a) Original open sedimentary texture. (b) Pressure pushes grains closer together (eliminating open space) without altering grains' shape or size. (c) With all open space eliminated, grain shape changes to form interlocking network. (d) A few large grains form from many small ones (with or without a change in composition), thereby reducing overall volume. The final step is a process known as recrystallization.

rocks move against each other, the rock may be altered by crushing and grinding to form a new rock of angular fragments cemented together, known as a *fault breccia.*

More significantly, however, pressure affects all sedimentary rocks by first squeezing mineral grains closer together, thus eliminating open spaces and expelling fluids (fig. 7.26 *a* and *b*). As pressure continues to increase, the mineral grains form a very tightly interlocking mosaic of crystals, much like a rock wall or fireplace, where irregularly sized and shaped rocks have been fitted tightly together. At still higher pressures, small mineral grains reform into fewer, but larger, grains in the process called **recrystallization.**

During recrystallization, the mineral may remain unchanged, or a new mineral may form. In the latter case, the new mineral is of higher density than the old one because recrystallization, like all of the responses to increased pressure, reduces the mineral matter to a smaller volume (fig. 7.26*c* and *d*). Pressure may also cause newly formed mineral grains, especially the elongated ones of the amphiboles and the flat ones of the micas, to be oriented so that their long or flat dimensions lie perpendicular to the direction of maximum pressure. This process imparts to the metamorphic rock a distinct alignment of linear minerals (**lineation**) or layering (**foliation**) in the case of flat minerals. Foliation is an important characteristic used in the classification of metamorphic rocks and is discussed more fully in that context.

A rock's "chemical environment" is largely determined by the presence of water carrying an abundance of dissolved ions, which come in contact and react with the changing rock. The source of such fluids is threefold: (1) groundwater that fell as precipitation and works its way downward through soil, sediment, and rock; (2) water that was trapped in the pore spaces of the sediment at the time of deposition—in a sense, "fossil" seawater; and (3) leftover, or residual, fluids associated with the final stages of igneous rock crystallization, which, as previously stated, often represent an important source of metallic ore minerals.

Types of Metamorphism

The term *metamorphism* really encompasses a broad group of related processes that operate at different intensities under different conditions. These variations in processes and conditions give rise to a number of categories of metamorphism. For our purposes, however, only two such varieties need be considered: **contact metamorphism** and **regional metamorphism.**

Contact metamorphism occurs in association with lava flows and shallow igneous intrusions. It involves the alteration of the rock that surrounds the intrusion (usually referred to as the **country rock**) by the high temperatures and chemical fluids associated with the intrusion. Thus, the effects are normally those produced by heat and chemical reaction. Pressure is often negligible. Alteration is localized in a "halo," or **metamorphic aureole,** surrounding the intrusion and extending only a few meters to a few tens of meters into the country rock. Just how far is normally a function of the difference in temperature between the intrusion and the country rock and the permeability

of (ease of passage of fluids through) the country rock. Permeability is discussed in more detail in chapter 11. In general, as the distance from the intrusion increases, the intensity of metamorphism decreases and does so rapidly (fig. 7.27).

Regional metamorphism, as the name implies, occurs across vast areas and normally at great depth in association with the deep burial of sediments and massive igneous batholiths. While heat, pressure, and chemical fluids all play major roles in regional metamorphism, pressure becomes particularly important because of the great depths involved. Evidence indicates that, in some instances, the igneous granite bodies are not the cause of the associated metamorphism, but rather, the result of it (see box 7.4).

Metamorphic Rock Classification

Metamorphic rocks are initially separated and classified on the basis of whether or not they possess foliation (figs. 7.28 and 7.29). Those rocks that do are called **foliated.** A secondary subdivision is based on grain size, with increasing pressure leading to progressively larger grain size. If we examine the progression of rocks formed in response to increasing pressure, we find that they possess large amounts of mica because the flat crystals of the members of this mineral group accommodate themselves well to high pressure. Shale, the most common sedimentary rock, consists mostly of clay minerals. These minerals are converted to micas under even relatively low pressures. The result is a fine-grained rock in which all of the minute mica crystals are oriented with their flat surfaces parallel to one another. This parallelism provides directions of weakness in the rock, along which the rock easily splits, or cleaves. This rock is a *slate,* and the quality whereby it splits is called **slaty cleavage,** a variety of foliation.

With increased pressure, the mica crystals become enlarged, and although still too small to be distinguished by the naked eye, they are large enough to reflect light, thereby giving a shiny appearance to the surfaces along which they split. A rock with this characteristic is called a *phyllite* and is easily recognizable by these shiny surfaces and its sometimes crenulated, or "wavy," appearance. At still higher pressures, the mica crystals become large enough to be distinguished with the unaided eye. The rock with such distinctive layering is called *schist,* and the foliation is **schistosity.** One other type of foliated rock–*gneiss* (pronounced "nice")—commonly forms under the highest metamorphic temperature and pressure conditions. Gneiss is coarse-grained and has much the same mineralogy and appearance as granite, except that the minerals are segregated into distinct bands dominated alternately by light and dark minerals. This distinct banding is the variety of foliation known as **gneissosity.**

We have considered only the characteristic of foliation in naming the metamorphic rocks, and indeed, this is the dominant characteristic. Metamorphic rocks are, however, as varied or more varied in their mineralogical composition than igneous rocks. While the basic rock name is determined by the type of foliation and by the texture (grain size), a more complete name can be formed by using compositional terms as modifying adjectives. For example, we might refer to a "granite gneiss" or a "biotite schist" and thereby present a meaningful image of the rock under consideration.

Figure 7.27 A metamorphic halo, or aureole, developed in sedimentary country rock in response to temperatures and chemical fluids associated with igneous intrusion. Total depth of metamorphic penetration may vary from a few meters to several tens of meters, depending on intensity of heat and permeability of the country rock.

Zone of intense metamorphism
Zone of slight metamorphism
Country rock unmetamorphosed

Movement of heat and chemical fluids

Further Consideration

Box 7.4

GRANITIZATION: WHERE DID ALL THAT GRANITE COME FROM?

A further consideration of metamorphism not only adds new information to the subject but also illustrates an important point about the nature of scientific inquiry and of scientific debate. Thus far, we have used the term *metamorphism* to describe all solid-state changes that occur in rocks. Specialists, however, would distinguish between metamorphism, which involves no fluids (or fluids already within a rock mass), and *metasomatism,* in which fluids carrying dissolved ions enter the rock mass from outside.

This concept of metasomatism is at the heart of a long-standing controversy dealing with the origin of granites. To this point, we have accepted that granite is of igneous origin. Some geologists argue, however, that some granites form by a specific type of metasomatism called *granitization.* They envision fluids carrying dissolved ions passing through a rock mass. Chemical reactions between these ions and the minerals already present convert the original rock to one with the mineralogy and texture of a granite.

What evidence could be cited to substantiate this radically different concept? First, the margins of some granite masses show no signs of the alteration of the country rock, which should have been caused by the heat of liquid magma. Second, some sedimentary and/or metamorphic features present in the country rock can be traced *into* the "granite" mass before disappearing completely. Third, proponents of an igneous origin for granite have always been at a loss to resolve what is usually referred to as the "space problem." If massive granite batholiths were intruded into the country rock, they would have had to displace hundreds of cubic kilometers of material. Where did this material go?

On the other side of the argument, specialists point to the numerous cases in nature where distinctive evidence for the forceful intrusion of hot, liquid magma can be cited. Which side is right, and which is wrong? As with so many questions in the sciences, there is no clear-cut answer. Most earth scientists would probably acknowledge that both origins for granite are possible.

Apply Your Knowledge

1. Do you think that metamorphism or metasomatism is the more common process? Why?
2. What do you think might have happened to the rock material displaced by the intrusion of a granite batholith? Approximately how much rock material (in cubic kilometers) was displaced by the intrusion of the Sierra Nevada batholith? (Consult a map of California.)
3. If both magmatic and metasomatic origins are possible for a magma, which do you think is the more common? Why?

Texture (identifying feature)			Rock name	Metamorphism		Dominant mineral composition	Original rock
				Dominant kind	Degree		
Foliated	Fine grained	"Smooth" "Fractured"	Slate	Regional	Low grade	Clay	Shale
Foliated	Fine grained	"Shiney" "Layered"	Phyllite	Regional	Medium grade	Chlorite / Mica	Shale
Foliated	Coarse grained	"Banded" "Layered"	Schist	Regional	Medium grade	Quartz / Amphibole / Feldspar	Shale
Foliated	Coarse grained	"Banded" "Layered"	Gneiss	Regional	High grade		Shale or granite
Nonfoliated	Fine grained		Hornfels	Contact	Medium to high		Shale
Nonfoliated	Coarse grained	No reaction with HCl	Quartzite	Contact or regional	Medium to high		Quartz sandstone
Nonfoliated	Coarse grained	Reaction with HCl	Marble	Contact or regional	Medium to high	Calcite	Limestone or dolostone

Figure 7.28 General classification scheme for metamorphic rocks.

Figure 7.29 Metamorphic rock textures. (*a*) Nonfoliated (marble). (*b*) Foliated (slate).

The second broad group of metamorphic rocks is the **nonfoliated** rocks. Such rocks are either formed under low pressures, as when shale is "baked" around the margins of igneous intrusions to form the dark, fine-grained rock known as hornfels (which is easily mistaken for basalt), or where the minerals present are not flat and do not lend themselves to the development of good foliation. In the latter category are the important nonfoliated rocks marble and quartzite. Marble is metamorphosed limestone (calcite) or dolostone (dolomite), and quartzite is metamorphosed quartz sandstone. Marble has been used since antiquity for statues, monuments, and buildings because it is abundant, can be worked with relative ease, and is reasonably resistant to the elements.

FURTHER THOUGHTS: TAKING THE GOOD WITH THE BAD

The mineral- and rock-forming processes summarized by the rock cycle have both positive and negative aspects. The rock material, formed and reformed over billions of years, provides us with the solid rock platforms on which we live. The same processes are still creating habitable surfaces in places like Hawaii and Iceland through volcanic eruptions, which add land area to those growing islands, and in deltaic regions, where the land is building outward into the sea. In other areas, similar processes form features of scenic wonder, such as the volcanic peaks of the Cascade Range and the sculpted batholiths of the Sierra Nevada. Natural concentrating processes have formed mineral accumulations of economic significance that have been exploited by human beings for thousands of years.

Too often, however, human beings and other organisms have been caught up in those same volcanic eruptions, earthquakes, and floods, with tragic results. The processes that formed economic concentrations of minerals may have left the soils and waters in certain regions with excessively high concentrations of certain elements or may have depleted the soils of vital plant nutrients. For the most part, however, human beings have learned to adapt to and live with this environment. When we cross the boundary into areas where we should not be or fail to care for what we have, nature has a way of catching our attention.

SIGNIFICANT POINTS

1. A mineral is a naturally occurring, inorganic element or compound with a definite internal arrangement of ions and a chemical composition that is fixed or that varies within narrow limits.

2. The silicates are the most abundant of all the mineral groupings. The basic silicate structural element is the silicon-oxygen tetrahedron.

3. Minerals form by crystallization from either magma or water.

4. Substitution of ions of similar charge and size within a crystal lattice of a mineral is the rule rather than the exception in nature.

5. While all minerals possess many physical and chemical properties, proper recognition of just a few of these is usually sufficient to identify each mineral.

6. Rocks are aggregates of mineral grains that make up a significant portion of Earth's outer shell. The three principal groups are igneous, sedimentary, and metamorphic, and they are interrelated through the rock cycle.

7. Igneous rocks form by the crystallization of mineral material from magma (intrusive) or lava (extrusive).

8. The size, shape, and arrangement of the mineral grains in a rock form the rock's texture.

9. Early-forming igneous minerals tend to be dark in color, while late-forming minerals are light. Mixing of early and late minerals in a rock is rare.

10. Basaltic magma is more fluid than granitic magma; therefore, basalts and related rocks dominate the volcanic (extrusive) rocks, while granites and their kin dominate the plutonic (intrusive) rocks.

11. Pegmatites and hydrothermal veins form late in the crystallization process of a granitic magma.

12. The more intense chemical weathering that is characteristic of humid regions leads to a topography that is smooth, whereas that of arid regions tends to be sharp and stark.

13. Sedimentary rocks form by the accumulation and consolidation of loose sediment at or near Earth's surface, where they are the most common rock type.

14. Sedimentary rocks are subdivided into clastic, bioclastic, and nonclastic on the basis of texture.

15. Metamorphic rocks form by the alteration of preexisting solid-state rocks, largely through a process known as recrystallization.

16. Metamorphic rocks are foliated if they possess a noticeable layering. They are nonfoliated if such layering is not apparent.

17. Contact metamorphism usually occurs on a small scale around the margins of intrusive igneous rock bodies. The principal metamorphic agents are heat and chemical fluids. Regional metamorphism occurs on a large scale, usually at great depth and in association with batholiths. Heat and pressure are the dominant metamorphic agents.

Essential Terms

mineral *157*
silicates *158*
crystallization *158*
magma *158*
crystal lattice *159*
crystal *159*
ionic substitution *161*
hardness *161*
streak *161*
luster *162*
density *162*
specific gravity *162*
cleavage *162*
fracture *162*
rock *163*
core *163*
mantle *164*
crust *164*
igneous rock *165*

sedimentary rock *165*
metamorphic rock *165*
rock cycle *165*
metamorphism *165*
lava *166*
volcanic (extrusive) *166*
plutonic (intrusive) *166*
texture *166*
phanteritic (coarse) texture *166*
aphanitic (fine) texture *166*
vesicular (porous) texture *166*
porphyritic texture *167*
pegmatitic texture *167*
ferromagnesian mineral *167*

hydrothermal solution *167*
volcano *168*
fissure *168*
crater *168*
shield volcano *168*
stratovolcano *168*
pyroclastic debris *168*
cinder cone *169*
caldera *169*
basalt plateau *169*
pluton *171*
concordant *171*
discordant *171*
tabular pluton *171*
nontabular pluton *171*
dike *171*
sill *171*
laccolith *171*

lopolith *171*
batholith *171*
stock *171*
xenolith *171*
weathering *171*
physical weathering *173*
frost wedging *173*
exfoliation *173*
exfoliation dome *173*
chemical weathering *173*
sediment *175*
clastic *175*
bioclastic *177*
nonclastic *177*
evaporite *177*
fossil *177*
mud crack *178*

ripple mark *178*
crossbed *178*
recrystalization *179*
lineation *180*
foliation *180*
contact metamorphism *180*
regional metamorphism *180*
country rock *180*
metamorphic aureole *180*
permeability *180*
foliated *180*
slaty cleavage *180*
schistosity *180*
gneissosity *180*
nonfoliated *182*

Review Questions

1. What is the basis for mineral classification? What are some of the categories?

2. How does a crystal differ from a crystal lattice?

3. What is meant by "ionic substitution" in minerals? Give at least one example.

4. What are some of the important characteristics used in mineral identification?

5. How does cleavage differ from fracture? How do cleavage surfaces differ from crystal faces?

6. What are the major zones that comprise Earth?

7. What are the three major categories of rocks?

8. What are the principal igneous rock textures? Under what conditions does each form?

9. What is a volcano? How are volcanoes categorized according to eruptive history?

10. How do the three principal types of volcanoes differ from one another in terms of size, shape, and composition?

11. What is a caldera?

12. What are the important concordant plutons? What are the important discordant plutons? What is the largest of all plutons?

13. How do chemical and physical weathering differ?

14. What are some examples of clastic sedimentary rocks? Of bioclastic rocks? Of nonclastic sedimentary rocks?

15. What is a fossil? Give some examples.

16. What are some examples of foliated metamorphic rocks? of nonfoliated metamorphic rocks?

Challenges

1. Examine some of the rocks exposed in road cuts in your area. Are they generally igneous, sedimentary, or metamorphic? Photograph or sketch several typical exposures. Identify and describe the rock types, indicating particularly the characteristics that aided in your identification.

2. Make a collection of rocks and/or minerals that can be found near your home or that you have picked up on a trip.

3. Select several mineral specimens that you found or bought or that were made available to you by your instructor. Examine each in terms of the identifying properties described in this text. Note on a checklist which features or properties you can

observe on the specimens and which ones you cannot observe.

4. Examine a single (or several) rock specimen you have found or is provided by your instructor. Describe it as completely as you can, particularly with reference to those characteristics that tell you something about the rock's origin and history.

5. Select a volcano that is located in your state (if none exists, select one from anywhere). With the use of reference materials available in your college or public library, write a complete history for that volcano. Pay particular attention to type, severity, and frequency of eruptions.

Chapter

8

Earthquakes, Geologic Structures, and Earth's Interior

Large scale rock folding, Convict Lake, California.

INTRODUCTION

All of us are aware of atmospheric disturbances, such as tornadoes and hurricanes, that periodically sweep across Earth's surface, not only disrupting our daily routines but frequently putting life and property at risk. Events such as the Loma Prieta ("World Series") earthquake that rocked the San Francisco area in October 1989 (see chapter 1) likewise serve as periodic reminders that planet Earth is not only an unstable platform drifting through space but also an often hazardous place to live. Earthquakes are not only reminders of our precarious foothold on the planet today. Examination of the twisted and broken rocks exposed at many locations at or near Earth's surface verifies that forces of unimaginable strength have been at work throughout all of geologic time.

In recent years, however, the passage through Earth of the energy associated with these forces has painted a picture of the planet's interior for scientists who have learned to read earthquake records. Without such information, we would know little about Earth's interior beyond what could be observed in deep mines or in well bores. Such knowledge has unlocked secrets related to the movement of continents and the formation of ocean basins, discussed in chapter 9. Indeed, it has laid the groundwork for theories that explain the origin of many mineral resources, as well as the historical evolution and development of our planet.

EARTHQUAKES

More than 1 million earthquakes are recorded each year (an average of almost two per minute). Fortunately, most of these are minor tremors detectable only by sensitive instruments, but in an average year, 20 are strong enough to cause severe damage and loss of life. Typically, at least one earthquake each year is catastrophic.

Simply put, an **earthquake** is a trembling, shaking, or vibration of the ground surface caused by the passage of energy, in the form of waves, through the rocks of Earth's outer shell. The most common cause of the release of this energy and, thus, of the vibrations is the breaking and shifting of rocks in Earth's outer zones. This breaking and movement of rocks is a process known as **faulting.** Thus, the immediate cause of most earthquakes is faulting.

Hazards Associated with Earthquakes

In addition to the shaking of the actual earthquake are associated phenomena that are the direct consequences of the earthquake and that often account for more damage and loss of life than the earthquake itself. In urban areas, with their development and high population densities, fires resulting from overturned appliances, broken electrical cables, and ruptured natural gas pipelines represent a deadly hazard. Once started, the fires are difficult, or even impossible, to control because of broken water mains and streets clogged with rubble that restricts access to the affected areas by firefighters and emergency crews. During the Loma Prieta earthquake, fire damage was restricted to a relatively small district because of a farsighted system that employed seawater for fire-fighting purposes (fig. 8.1). The emergency procedures that prevented widespread destruction in 1989 were not in place during the 1906 San Francisco earthquake. Consequently, during that earlier earthquake, approximately 80% of the city was destroyed, mostly by fire. As in the aftermath of many earthquakes, firefighters stood by helplessly until the fires burned themselves out.

Perhaps the most tragic example of devastation wrought by fire occurred as the result of a major earthquake that struck Japan in 1923. Open cooking fires easily engulfed the paper and wood structures and set up whirlwinds of fire driven by their own heat. The fires consumed oxygen, causing people to die by the thousands from suffocation. Even those who sought refuge in the rivers and shallow coastal waters did not survive. Hardest hit were the cities of Tokyo and Yokohama. In all, 150,000 people lost their lives, most from the firestorms, and approximately 80% of Tokyo and virtually all of Yokohama were destroyed—almost 400,000 buildings.

At 5:46 A.M. on January 30, 1995, Japan was devastated once again when an earthquake shook Kobe, the country's sixth largest city and second largest port. Kobe, located on the southwest coast, was thought to be relatively safe from the earthquakes that have plagued Tokyo and other parts of Japan. When the devastation could finally be assessed, 5,100 people were dead, almost 27,000 were injured, and 20% of the city's 1.5 million inhabitants were homeless. More than 100,000 buildings were destroyed, and estimates of the costs to rebuild were in

Figure 8.1   Fire, triggered by the October 1989 earthquake, caused significant damage in the Marina District of San Francisco.

Figure 8.2   Collapsed section of the Kobe-Osaka elevated highway.

excess of $100 billion. Many of the homes and buildings that collapsed predated important engineering advances and improved building codes. Most newer buildings survived intact, but some structures that were designed to be "earthquake-proof" were spectacular losses. The high-speed rail line to Tokyo was cut. A 500-meter (1,630-ft) stretch of the Kobe-Osaka elevated highway rotated onto its side when numerous supporting piers collapsed (fig. 8.2). As in 1923, hundreds of fires broke out as gas mains ruptured and cooking stoves overturned. Broken water lines made fire fighting difficult, but unlike in 1923, these blazes were responsible for relatively little loss of life. With 70% of the city's water supply gone, however, major sanitation problems arose.

In mountainous regions, where slopes are already unstable, rockslides and other earth movements generated by earthquake vibrations represent another major hazard. This type of event was responsible for the greatest natural catastrophe in history: a series of earthquake-generated movements of unconsolidated wind-deposited material in northern China in 1556. Whole villages were buried beneath masses of sediment, and an estimated 830,000 lives were lost. In more recent times, a massive avalanche of snow and rock debris, triggered by a major earthquake off the Pacific coast of South America, roared at high speed down a series of valleys in the Andes Mountains and buried the cities of Yungay and Ranrachirca, Peru. An estimated 70,000 people died. Compounding the tragedy was the memory of a similar, but smaller, event that had struck the same area only 8 years earlier, leaving more than 3,500 dead (see fig. 10.13).

Along coastlines and within the ocean basins occurs yet another earthquake-induced event: the *tsunami*, or seismic sea wave, described in more detail in chapter 13. These waves, generated by sudden motion when the seafloor is displaced by an earthquake, radiate outward from the point of disturbance. They can do great damage along low-lying shorelines even thousands of kilometers distant (fig. 8.3).

The movement of portions of the seafloor, such as those that generate seismic sea waves, can also have profound effects if they occur along a coastline. During the so-called Good Friday earthquake, which rocked Alaska on March 27, 1964, some 207,000 square kilometers (80,000 sq. mi) of seafloor rose as much as 15 meters (50 ft) to form new land (fig. 8.4). In other areas, the coastal land sank below the water, carrying shoreline structures with it.

Smaller-scale features and changes of less consequence and less danger also accompany earthquakes. One such common feature involves the liquefaction of saturated soils and their eruption through ground cracks as features known as *sand spouts*.

Regardless of the damage done by fires, landslides, and seismic sea waves, the earthquake is first and foremost a series of vibrations. If severe enough, these vibrations do considerable damage to human structures. Apart from the strength of the earthquake, which is considered later in this chapter, several factors govern how much damage an earthquake causes. An important and obvious factor is the distance a structure is located from the earthquake's point of occurrence. Earthquake energy is dissipated, and the resulting vibrations are reduced with distance from the

Figure 8.3 (*a*) Boats carried inland at Kodiak by seismic sea waves during the 1964 Alaskan earthquake. (*b*) Seismic sea waves, or tsunami, are very long wavelength waves generated by volcanic eruptions, earthquakes, or any sudden displacement of the seafloor.

Figure 8.4 Portion of the seafloor at Cape Cleare, Alaska, elevated more than 8 meters (26 ft) by movement associated with the 1964 Alaskan earthquake.

Box 8.1

Investigating the Environment

Earthquake Engineering: "Bracing" for the Big One

For buildings constructed on the same type of foundation materials, an important factor in the different levels of earthquake damage sustained is the type of construction employed. In general, buildings are designed to withstand vertical stress—that is, the weight of the upper floors must be supported by the lower floors. In Kobe, where older structures were built without regard to earthquake resistance, most of the loss of life resulted from the collapse of wooden houses that could not support the weight of their heavy tile roofs during the earthquake vibrations. It is more difficult to design a building to withstand horizontal stress: whiplash, shifting, and rotational motion that might be equal to the weight of the building itself. As ground motion moves the lower floors of a multistory steel-frame building, the upper floors lag behind. When the lower floors move back, the "whiplash effect" may actually snap the upper floors off the lower floors. With increased building height, the likelihood of this whiplash actually decreases because the drift angle (amount of lateral displacement of the top of the building/building height) decreases. Thus, a 40-story building would be safer than a 10-story building.

The history of earthquake engineering is relatively short and not overly successful. Some of the early, taller buildings in San Francisco that were designed to withstand strong winds also survived the great earthquake of 1906, probably for the same basic engineering reasons. After 80% of the buildings in Tokyo were destroyed in the Great Kwanto earthquake of 1923, building codes were established that, among other things, required the use of reinforced concrete in certain buildings and limited building height to 160 meters (525 ft). Following the Long Beach earthquake of 1933, in which a number of schools were severely damaged, the California legislature passed the Field Act, requiring rigid building standards for all public buildings. In subsequent years, specialized seismographs were developed to study

and understand ground motion, and "shakers" were attached to buildings to determine their critical frequencies of vibration. The studies show that low buildings (two to four stories) are most susceptible to short-term, high-frequency vibrations, whereas taller buildings are more likely damaged by prolonged, lower-frequency vibrations. The studies also resulted in the development of a number of construction techniques for minimizing structural damage.

In *ductile-frame construction,* the building's framework is designed to absorb energy by permanently bending and cracking *but not collapsing.* During the 1971 San Fernando earthquake in southern California, the Olive View Hospital, which employed ductile concrete columns, swayed and moved 46 centimeters (18 in) out of plumb, but it did not collapse. The columns had been wrapped in wire, which trapped the fractured concrete and prevented its disintegration. Columns on freeway overpasses had not been so treated, and their collapse was common. Likewise, the collapse of untreated supporting columns of the upper level of I-880 (the Nimitz Freeway) in Oakland, California, led to the greatest loss of life during the 1989 Loma Prieta earthquake.

Another construction technique used to a limited extent is *base isolation,* in which the building is mounted on a series of blocks, each consisting of alternate layers of rubber and steel. The blocks are designed to move and absorb earthquake energy. This technique is not suitable for tall buildings because they might become top-heavy and capsize. It is being used more frequently in hospitals, however, and was recently installed at the city hall in Oakland, California, and the J. Paul Getty Museum of Art in Malibu, California.

Many buildings have been reinforced by cross-braces, which are probably the most common engineering strategy to date. In *shear wall construction,* a building's walls consist of a number of smaller, triangular steel or concrete components

that are free to shift when subjected to earthquake stress. Friction between the moving components absorbs most of the energy. The walls bend and crack but do not collapse.

A more recent approach to building design is called *active resistance.* In this approach, computer-driven machinery alters the building's structure many times per second by moving braces and weights to counteract ground motion and earthquake-induced stresses.

The bottom line on structural integrity is whether or not a building survives a major earthquake. The relatively low death tolls for Loma Prieta and Northridge—62 and 61, respectively—are in stark contrast to the loss of life measured in the tens of thousands for recent earthquakes of similar magnitude in Armenia and Iran. These low totals must be due, at least in part, to extensive engineering research and development over the years.

Building codes in most states require only that a structure resist collapse during an earthquake, not that it remain in usable condition. What this means is that buildings should be "earthquake-resistant" rather than "earthquake-proof." If people are able to evacuate a building safely during and after an earthquake, then the building designers have done their job successfully.

Apply Your Knowledge

1. You are considering the construction of a 10- to 12-story office complex in the San Francisco area. What environmental factors would you take into account? Which engineering techniques would you consider using? (Don't forget the cost factor.)
2. Your company transfers you to a city in a known seismic area. What questions would you ask realtors as you looked for a home? What agencies and other sources might you contact to obtain this type of information?

Source: Data from Charles C. Plummer and David McGeary, *Physical Geology,* 5th ed. Copyright ©1991 Wm. C. Brown Communications, Inc., Dubuque, Iowa.

point of occurrence. This general relationship, however, is subject to modification by other factors, including the nature of the rocks through which the earthquake waves pass. At the location of any structure in the path of the waves, the nature of the rocks becomes even more important. Because soil and loose sediment amplify the earthquake waves much more than solid bedrock, buildings with foundations in such loose material are subject to much stronger vibrations and, consequently, much greater damage than those built on bedrock. Studies of damage to similar buildings after the 1906 San Francisco earthquake indicated that structures built on loose sediments suffered damage up to 12 times greater than those built on solid bedrock. (See box 8.1 for a discussion of earthquake engineering.)

Structural damage is also dependent on the duration of the earthquake. In most small earthquakes, the vibrations last but a few seconds. In larger earthquakes, however, structures may be subjected to vibrational swaying for up to several minutes (1906, San Francisco, 1 minute; 1964, Alaska, 3 minutes). A building that resists damage when vibrating for a few seconds may collapse from the accumulated stress of several minutes of vibrations. Those structures that do not collapse outright may be so weakened that they must be condemned, or they may collapse during subsequent earthquake stresses. The last case introduces the point that an earthquake does not occur in isolation.

The Nature of an Earthquake

Any earthquake is preceded by a series of small, but measurable, tremors. Such *foreshocks* are not dangerous but have been, in recent years, the focus of one line of investigation into the prediction of the larger earthquakes with which they are associated (see box 8.2). Of more concern to earthquake survivors are the tremors that invariably follow a major shock. These are *aftershocks,* some of which are almost as large and destructive as the main event. This is particularly true when buildings are already weakened. While some buildings may survive the main shock, the additional stresses of the aftershocks, occurring over the next few hours or days, are enough to bring the buildings down.

What are the causes of earthquakes? While some small earthquakes result from the pushing and movement of rock layers by liquid magma as it works its way up toward Earth's surface, the large, destructive earthquakes are the result of other stresses applied to Earth's outer layers. Such stresses are explored in more detail later in this chapter and in chapter 9. For now, we will focus on the consequences of these forces.

As stress is applied to rock, the rock initially stretches and deforms, much like a rubber band that is stretched at both ends. The more the rubber band is stretched, the more stress it is under. With continued stretching, more energy accumulates in the system. There is a limit to how much a rubber band can be stretched and how much energy it can accumulate. When this limit is reached, the rubber band breaks, as the loose ends move rapidly apart and then snap back (rebound), releasing the stored energy (fig. 8.5). When the limit of rocks' resistance to stretching is reached, they, too, break and move rapidly, creating a **fault,** a break in rocks of Earth's crust or mantle along which movement has taken place. In the process, the energy that has accumulated in the rocks for hun-

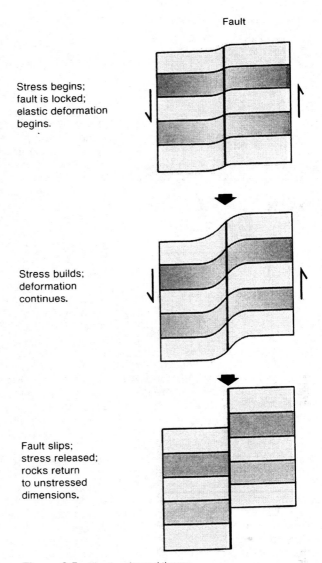

Fault

Stress begins; fault is locked; elastic deformation begins.

Stress builds; deformation continues.

Fault slips; stress released; rocks return to unstressed dimensions.

Figure 8.5   Elastic rebound theory.

dreds or thousands of years is suddenly released and travels outward through the surrounding rocks as high-speed waves. The passage of these waves, in turn, generates the series of vibrations that is the earthquake.

The actual location, or zone, at or below Earth's surface where faulting occurs is the **focus** (sometimes called the *hypocenter*) of the earthquake. If the focus is below the surface, then the point on the surface directly above the focus is termed the **epicenter** of the earthquake. The epicenter provides a geographic reference point for describing the earthquake's location (fig. 8.6). The depth to the focus is a useful criterion for the classification of earthquakes, which are often described as *shallow focus, intermediate focus,* or *deep focus* (table 8.1).

An interesting observation is that the frequency of earthquakes diminishes with depth. Shallow-focus earthquakes are the most common, while deep-focus earthquakes are the least common. Indeed, no earthquake foci have ever been recorded below a depth of approximately 700 kilometers (435 mi). At least two physical conditions might be cited to help explain this observation.

Box 8.2

Earthquake Prediction: Where, When, and How Big?

Of the ten natural disasters that have taken the highest tolls in human life, six have been earthquakes. As world population grows, the press of people into earthquake-prone areas becomes ever greater. These two perspectives—one historical and other current—make the accurate prediction, and even prevention, of earthquakes an increasingly desirable scientific goal.

Four nations—China, Russia, Japan, and the United States—are active to varying degrees in the field of earthquake prediction. To date, China has both the best and worst examples of predictions. On February 4, 1975, a magnitude 7.3 earthquake destroyed 90% of the city of Haicheng in northeast China, as well as many surrounding towns. Fortunately, 9 1/2 hours earlier, the government had ordered several million people living in this region to leave their homes and move temporarily into open areas. This governmental directive, resulting from the prediction of an imminent earthquake, probably saved tens or even hundreds of thousands of lives. Eighteen months later, on July 28, 1976, an earthquake in excess of magnitude 8.0 leveled most of the city of Tangshan, 150 kilometers (93 mi) south of Beijing. Loss of life was in the hundreds of thousands. While Chinese scientists had predicted that a major earthquake would occur in this region sometime within a 2-month period, this lack of immediacy was virtually the same as no warning, so no preventive actions were taken.

Scientists have identified a number of events that may be related to the imminent occurrence of an earthquake. These are referred to as *precursor phenomena*. Among those most actively investigated are the occurrence and frequency of foreshocks (as at Haicheng), changes in ground level (either swelling or tilting), changes in the degree to which the ground conducts or retards (resistivity) the flow of electrical currents, rock density changes,

increases in the amount of the radioactive gas radon in well water, anomalous animal behavior (such a snakes leaving their holes in winter and restlessness of livestock), and even changes in atmospheric pressure or the alignment of the planets.

In addition to looking for and monitoring precursor events, scientists are also studying the statistical probability of earthquakes of certain magnitudes occurring along specific faults (or segments of faults) within a given period of time. One outgrowth of this last approach has been the recognition of *seismic gaps:* segments of active faults where the buildup of stress in the rocks has not been reduced by the almost continuous slight displacements known as creep. Stress continues to build until the rocks can no longer withstand it, and all of the accumulated energy is released suddenly to cause a large earthquake. As logical as this sounds, however, some recent studies indicate that "low-risk" zones have had up to five times as many earthquakes.

No type of precursor is universally accepted as the most fruitful avenue for further research. Likewise, no model that accounts for all phenomena leading to an earthquake is accepted by everyone. One such model, however, the *dilatancy model*, probably has more adherents and accounts for more of the observed phenomena than all of the others. The dilatancy model holds that rocks within the fault zone continue to accumulate stress until the stress is relieved by the fracturing of the rock along a network of countless microscopic cracks. This cracking results in a phenomenon known as *dilatancy hardening* and, at least temporarily, relieves some of the accumulated stress. This period of dilatancy hardening can be recognized by the fact that P-waves from minor seismic events or those artificially induced move through the rocks in the vicinity of the fault zone with lower-than-normal velocities. (A more common method of expressing this change in seismic velocities is a reduction in the ratio of P-wave to S-wave velocities.) Over a period of time, even as stress continues to be applied to the rock, groundwater moves in to fill the fracture system and seismic-wave velocities gradually increase. When the velocities reach their normal values, the hardening effect is canceled, and an earthquake can be expected at any time. What studies have been made of these seismic-velocity changes also suggest that the longer the anomaly, the larger the earthquake will be.

An earthquake prediction attempt at Parkfield, California, has been highly publicized. This town, located on the north end of the Parkfield segment of the San Andreas Fault, has experienced earthquakes of approximate Richter magnitude 6 every 22 years, on average, for more than a century. Based on this history, seismologists predicted that a similar earthquake would happen here again by mid-1991. To date, such an earthquake has not occurred. Although the prediction would have to be classified as a failure, it relied on substantial scientific data and may have been subject to unexpected events. One suggestion that has been offered is that the regional stress many have been altered by a recent earthquake at nearby Coalinga, California.

In general, U.S. seismologists have adopted in recent years a more conservative approach to earthquake predictions. This involves stating probabilities of occurrence within a rather wide time window for earthquakes in a seismically active area. One other recent approach related to this is what has come to be called *paleoseismology*. This basically involves digging trenches within the soil to look for disrupted soil and rock layers that could be related to a particular seismic event. The layers are then dated to give an indication of the frequency with which such events have occurred in that particular region.

An earthquake prediction would ideally include three factors: time, location, and magnitude. As desirable as such an end result would be, however, success will not be simple, nor will it come without a price.

Apply Your Knowledge

1. Discuss the significance of being able to determine in advance *how big* an earthquake will be.
2. Discuss the economic and social implications of the prediction of an imminent earthquake for a major metropolitan area. Consider how long people might have to stay at home and how long they might have to avoid freeways and public buildings.
3. Under what conditions might you recommend the evacuation of a metropolitan area? Consider the time factor.
4. Discuss the consequences of an erroneous prediction in terms of economics, disrupted lives, and future credibility. Who would be responsible (morally and legally) for these consequences?

Figure 8.6   Earthquake focus and epicenter.

| TABLE 8.1 | Shallow, Intermediate, and Deep Earthquakes | | |

Earthquake Type	Depth From	To	Percentage of Total Earthquake Energy
Shallow focus	Surface	70 km (43 mi)	85
Intermediate focus	70 km (43 mi)	300 km (187 mi)	12
Deep focus	300 km (187 mi)	700 km (435 mi)	3

Source: Charles C. Plummer and David McGeary, *Physical Geology*, 6th ed. Copyright © 1993 Times Mirror Higher Education Group, Dubuque, Iowa.

First, rock distortion and faulting occur when the stresses applied to the rocks are unequal (i.e., stronger in one direction than in others), so the rock is "stretched." With increasing depth, rock pressures become more uniform and equal-sided, just as do water pressures. Second, rocks at increasing depths are hotter than at the surface, so hot that, in some cases, they melt to form magma. Even without melting, however, they may lose their brittleness and become more **plastic.** Thus, rather than snapping and breaking, they stretch and deform slowly.

Although the generally accepted origin for earthquakes works well for shallow-focus earthquakes, it has never been particularly satisfying with respect to intermediate-focus and deep-focus earthquakes (approximately 20% of all earthquakes). Because rocks cannot be brittle under the temperature and pressure conditions that prevail at these depths, sliding along fault surfaces is not likely. Lubrication by water brought downward from the surface in minerals and sediments might account for some intermediate-focus earthquakes, but in the last several years, earth scientists have turned to alternative explanations for deep-focus earthquakes. The most commonly accepted idea today involves a change in the structure of olivine, the most common mineral in the upper part of the mantle. It is believed that, at a depth of 400 kilometers (250 mi) and below, the structure of olivine crystals collapses to form the denser mineral spinel. This sudden change, which would cause the rock to collapse and energy to be released, would only occur where slabs of surface rock are being forced downward to great depths. Because this type of faulting involves the transformation of one mineral into another, it is referred to as *transformational faulting.*

As evidence of the dynamic nature of science, recent evidence already has cast a shadow of doubt on this very young theory. This evidence is in the form of two deep-focus earthquakes: one beneath the South American country of Bolivia in June 1994, and the other beneath the Pacific island of Tonga in March 1994. The difficulty presented to the transformational faulting theory is that these earthquakes occurred across large fault zones (30×50 km [19×31 mi] and 30×40 km [19×25 mi], respectively). Most earth scientists feel that transformational faulting would occur on a much smaller scale. One other possible explanation for deep-focus earthquakes is that they occur along old faults and zones of weakness within the descending crustal units called *plates* (see chapter 9).

Another important observation about earthquakes is that they are not randomly distributed about Earth's surface. For the most part, they are confined to certain distinct geographic zones (fig. 8.7). Most earthquake epicenters lie in a linear zone around the margin of the Pacific Ocean basin, the Circum-Pacific belt, which coincides with the major zone of volcanic activity that has led to the designation "Pacific ring of fire." Both earthquakes and volcanoes arise from the same underlying causes and are related to the position of boundaries between adjacent plates. A second major earthquake trend can be traced from southern Europe and Asia to the islands of Indonesia. This is the Mediterranean-Himalayan belt. The third major trend follows the axis of the submarine oceanic ridge system, which can be traced for tens of thousands of kilometers through all of the ocean basins. It is interesting to note that only shallow-focus earthquakes are recorded along the oceanic ridge system, where magma is forcing its way into the crustal rocks at or just below the surface of the ocean basin. Deep-focus earthquakes are known only in association with the deep-sea trenches of the ocean basins, where crustal plates are being forced as rigid slabs to great depths within Earth (figs. 8.8 and 8.9).

Measuring Earth Tremors

Earlier in this chapter, we noted that earthquake strength varies and that variation is an important factor in the amount of damage associated with any particular earthquake. How, then, is earthquake strength assessed? The answer is in two ways: intensity and magnitude.

Intensity is a measure of earthquake strength in terms of structural damage and human perception. Information needed to determine earthquake intensity is gathered by field examination of damage, photographic assessment, personal interviews, and analysis of questionnaires. The most widely used intensity scale, the **Modified Mercalli scale,** assigns numerical values of strength from I to XII based on such qualitative assessments and perceptions (table 8.2). Results of such analyses are often portrayed for easier interpretation in the form of an *intensity map* (fig. 8.10). Note on the map that intensity values vary from place to place, and that, in a general way, the closer a location is to the earthquake epicenter, the greater is the earthquake intensity.

The second measure of earthquake strength, **magnitude,** is a calculation of the amount of energy released during the earthquake, as determined from seismic records. Any earthquake releases only

Figure 8.7 Worldwide distribution of earthquake foci between 1961 and 1967.

Figure 8.8 Distribution of earthquakes with foci between 100 and 700 kilometers (62 and 435 mi) and their relationship to deep-sea trenches.

a certain amount of energy; thus, each earthquake has only a single magnitude value. It does not matter where an individual was during the earthquake, how strongly an individual perceived the earthquake, or whether that person felt it at all: The earthquake has only a single magnitude value.

Magnitude values are measured on the open-ended **Richter scale.** This scale is familiar because the media use it in news accounts of earthquakes. The Richter scale is a logarithmic, rather than linear, scale, meaning that numerical increments on the scale are not of equal value but increase by some multiple. Each whole-number

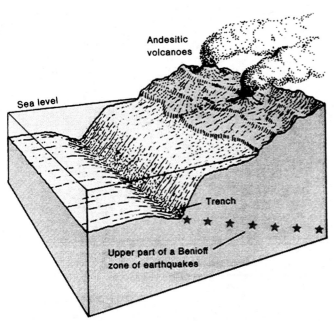

Figure 8.9 Topography and structure of the seafloor along a deep-sea trench. The dipping trend of the earthquake foci outlines a feature known as the Benioff zone and delineates a downward-moving tectonic plate (see chapter 9 for a fuller explanation).

Figure 8.10 Seismic intensity map for the 1886 Charleston, South Carolina, earthquake. (Source: Data from U.S. Geological Survey.)

TABLE 8.2	**Damage and Perception for Each Value on the Modified Mercalli Scale of Earthquake Intensity**

I.   Not felt by humans except under very unusual circumstances.

II. Possibly felt by persons at rest on the upper stories of buildings. Swinging of some suspended objects, such as lights.

III. Noticeable indoors, especially on higher stories of buildings. Might be mistaken for the vibrations of passing trucks.

IV. Some sleepers awakened. During the daytime, felt indoors by most, outside by a few. Stationary automobiles rocked noticeably. Sensation of heavy impact like a truck striking the building. Dishes rattle; walls creak.

V.   Felt by most people. Many sleepers awakened. Dishes and windows broken and plaster walls cracked. Unstable objects overturned, and poles and trees disturbed. Pendulum clocks stop.

VI. Felt by all. Many frightened people leave buildings. Some furniture moved. Plaster and poorly constructed walls cracked. Some chimneys damaged.

VII. Most people leave buildings. Chimneys broken. Noticed by people in vehicles. Damage to poorly constructed (adobe) houses. Some cracks develop in buildings of ordinary construction.

VIII. Heavy damage to buildings of poor or even ordinary construction. Some collapse. Even well-designed buildings damaged. Disturbance of people in moving automobiles. Heavy furniture overturned. Chimneys, columns, and monuments collapse. Mud spouts, and the level of the water table changes.

IX. Well-designed buildings thrown out of alignment. Some damage to specially constructed buildings. Poorly constructed buildings destroyed. Heavy damage to ordinary buildings. Conspicuous ground cracks. Underground pipelines broken.

X.   Most masonry and frame structures destroyed. All structures severely damaged. Extensive ground cracking. Railroad rails bent. Landslides common along stream banks and steep slopes, with water slopping over the banks.

XI. Few masonry structures left standing. Extensive bending of rails and collapsing of bridges. Broad, open cracks in the ground. Underground pipelines completely out of service. Slumps and landslides common.

XII. Total destruction. Waves visible on the ground surface. Sight and level lines distorted. Objects thrown into the air.

Source: Compiled from C. F. Richter, *Elementary Seismology*, copyright © 1958 W. H. Freeman, and other sources.

increase in Richter magnitude actually represents an increase in energy released of 31.5 times the previous value (table 8.3). By convention, an earthquake with a Richter magnitude value of 7.0 or greater is considered a major earthquake, while one of 8.0 or greater is catastrophic. The 1906 San Francisco earthquake is estimated to have had a Richter magnitude of 8.2 (the Richter scale had not been devised at that time). In the same year, an earthquake in Peru is estimated to have been of magnitude 8.9. The 1964 Alaskan earthquake had a magnitude of approximately 8.4, and in 1993, the Japanese island of Hokkaido was shaken by a magnitude 7.8 earth-

TABLE 8.3 Earthquake Magnitude Values

Earthquake Magnitude	Frequency (per year)	Conventional Explosives Equivalent	Area Felt (sq. km)	Distance (km)	Approximate Mercalli Intensity
1.0	10,000,000	122 gm (6 oz)	—	—	none
2.0	1,000,000	5.85 kg (13 lb)	—	—	I–II
3.0	200,000	178.65 kg (397 lb)	—	—	II–III
4.0	30,000	5,400 kg (6 tons)	1,950	25	IV–V
5.0	3,500	179,000 kg (199 tons)	7,770	50	V–VI
6.0	500	5.64×10^6 kg (6,270 tons)	38,850	115	VII–VIII
7.0	50	1.79×10^8 kg (199,000 tons)	130,000	200	IX–X
8.0	5	5.64×10^9 kg (6.27×10^6 tons)	520,000	400	XI–XII
9.0	≤ 1	1.8×10^{11} kg (2.0×10^8 tons)	2,072,000	800	XII

quake that killed more than 160. No earthquake has ever been recorded with a magnitude value greater than 8.9, for the simple reason that rocks are unlikely to be strong enough to store the tremendous amounts of energy that must necessarily be released to cause earthquakes of this magnitude.

Currently, some earth scientists are using a different version of magnitude, the *moment-magnitude scale*. Moment-magnitude values are thought to be a more precise measure of the energy released in an earthquake and are calculated by multiplying the area of the rupture surface by the amount of displacement along the fault. Richter magnitude values of 8.4 and 6.8 for the Alaskan and Kobe earthquakes, respectively, translate into moment-magnitude values of 9.2 and 6.9.

Figure 8.11 The ground particle motion of (a) Rayleigh and (b) Love surface earthquake waves.

Earthquake Waves

When rocks break during the process of faulting, they release energy that has been accumulating for many years. The energy travels outward from the point of the disturbance in the form of waves, which vibrate and displace the rocks through which they travel. The disturbance creates two categories of waves—surface waves and body waves—and their formation and movement might be compared to what occurs when a pebble is tossed into a quiet pond. The most obvious result of the impact of the pebble is a series of ripples that spread outward across the surface of the pond from the point of the disturbance. In the same manner, energy travels from the earthquake focus to Earth's surface and then outward on the surface from that point. The ground is thrown into a series of waves by its passage; these are **surface waves.**

If the earthquake is strong enough, such surface-wave motion is actually visible to observers near the epicenter. Some of the fans

standing in the parking lot outside Candlestick Park reported seeing cars rise and fall in a sequence across the lot during the 1989 Loma Prieta earthquake. During a series of earthquakes that rocked a large area centered on the small southeastern Missouri town of New Madrid in late 1811 and early 1812, whole forests were uprooted, and the Mississippi River flowed backward for a short time and had its course permanently altered.

Surface waves are actually of two types (fig. 8.11): *Love waves* cause the ground to rock back and forth in a side-to-side motion. *Rayleigh waves* cause ground particles to move in elliptical orbits, similar to the movement of water particles with the passage of an ocean wave (chapter 13). In Rayleigh waves, however, orbital motion is vertical and counterclockwise with respect to the direction of wave movement, as opposed to the clockwise motion that occurs in water waves.

A listening device placed on the bottom of the pond into which a pebble is thrown detects the sound caused by the pebble's impact. This is because the sound travels downward through the water in wave form, much as it does through air. The passage of sound en-

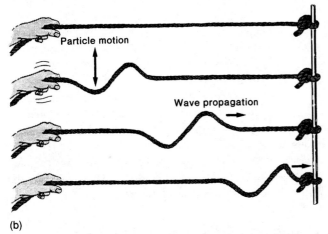

(a)

(b)

Figure 8.12 (*a*) A toy "Slinky™" (actually, a long, coiled spring) illustrates the back-and-forth (push-pull) motion of the passage of a P-wave. (*b*) A rope attached to a wall and given a shake shows the up-and-down particle motion associated with S-waves.

ergy disturbs and displaces the water particles. In the same way, earthquake energy in wave form travels downward through the solid Earth, disturbing and displacing rock and mineral particles. Because these waves travel through the "body" of Earth, rather than on its surface, they are called **body waves.**

Body waves are also of two types, differentiated because they displace the rock particles through which they pass in different ways. The first of these are **P-waves (primary waves),** so-called because they are the fastest of all waves and arrive first at any recording station. "P" might also stand for "push-pull," which describes the compressional motion by which they form. Such motion might best be visualized by imagining a flexible spring (or a child's "Slinky™" toy) with one end attached to a wall or doorknob and the other end in your hand (fig. 8.12*a*). Stretching the spring horizontally and giving it a sharp push inward causes some of the coils of the spring to compress together in a sequence. To compensate for the area of compression, coils in the adjacent portions of the spring stretch, or expand. The zone of compressed coils moves down the length of the spring (followed by the expanded zone) until it reaches the wall. Each push generates another series of compressions and expansions (also called *rarefactions*). The

coils of the spring are not, of course, moving from your hand to the wall; only the energy imparted to the spring makes this journey. The coils travel only a short distance back and forth as the energy passes each part of the spring. As P-waves pass through the coils (or through rock particles in Earth's crust), the back-and-forth movements, parallel to the direction in which the waves are moving, are identical to sound waves. Thus, like sound waves, they are capable of being transmitted through any medium: gas, liquid, or solid.

The second type of body wave is the **S-wave (secondary wave),** so-called because it travels more slowly than the P-wave and, consequently, arrives at any recording station "secondarily," or after, the P-wave. "S" might also stand for "shake" (or, more technically, *shear*), which describes the motion of these waves. S-waves act similarly to a rope attached at one end to a stationary point and shaken (fig. 8.12*b*). The individual particles that the rope is composed of do not travel from hand to wall; only the energy travels this course. At most, the rope particles move a short distance up and down as each wave passes that part of the rope. This type of up-and-down particle motion, perpendicular to the direction of wave movement is possible only in bodies that are "rigid"—that is, in solids. In gases and liquids, the energy is dissipated, and the wave motion dies.

The Movement of Waves through Earth

The action of S-waves provides an important key to interpreting the structure of Earth's interior. Solid layers within Earth allow the passage of both P-waves and S-waves. Any liquid layer within Earth, however, only transmits P-waves. (A gaseous layer cannot exist within Earth because of the high pressures found there and the compressibility of gas.)

Observations of the loss of S-wave energy within Earth have led *seismologists,* those earth scientists who specialize in the study of earthquakes, to conclude that at some depth lies a major zone that is liquid rather than solid. They have identified zones on Earth's surface some distance from any earthquake's epicenter where the S-wave energy from that earthquake is not received. Such zones are called **shadow zones,** and their occurrence is shown in figure 8.13. The explanation for the shadow zones is that a deep liquid layer has caused any S-wave energy that impinges on it to die out.

A further examination of figure 8.13 shows that numerous small refractions of both P-waves and S-waves impart to them generally curved paths as they travel downward through Earth. This bending brings them back to the surface at locations closer to the epicenter than if they had followed straight line paths through Earth. Because P-waves are slowed dramatically at the upper boundary of Earth's liquid zone, the bending is accentuated. This leads to the formation of a P-wave shadow zone.

Seismic-wave velocities vary as they travel through different kinds of rock units. As they pass through the different rock layers, their changing velocities cause them to be refracted to varying degrees. Wave velocities and the amount of refraction are governed by rock characteristics, such as rigidity, density, and elasticity. These, in turn, are controlled by temperature, pressure, and mineralogical composition.

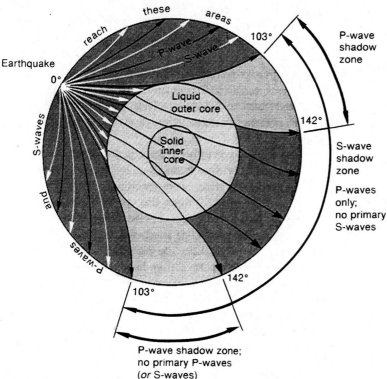

Figure 8.13 S-wave shadow zone on the side of Earth away from the earthquake epicenter results from the liquid composition of the outer core, which does not allow for the passage of such waves. The P-wave shadow zone results from the P-waves slowing and being refracted as they pass through this zone.

Instrumentation for Measuring Seismic Activity

Earth scientists use a network of instruments to measure and record movements of the ground surface during the passage of seismic energy. The primary instrument for recording these movements is the **seismograph,** or *seismometer.* Although modern seismographs are complicated and sophisticated instruments, the basic principle on which they operate is simple (fig. 8.14a). A weight suspended by a slender spring from a rigid support firmly anchored in bedrock holds a pen or a light source. In front of the pen, and in contact with it, is a clock-driven, rotating drum covered with paper (photosensitive paper in the case of a light source). As the drum rotates in front of the weight, the pen traces a straight line on the paper. When earthquake waves reach the seismic station, the ground, the support, and the rotating drum begin to shake. Everything vibrates except the suspended weight, because the slender spring cannot transfer enough energy to overcome the weight's inertia and cause it to move.

The simple act of carrying a cup of coffee illustrates this energy transfer. If you attempt to walk with a cup firmly gripped in your hand, you will probably spill a good portion of your coffee by the time you reach your destination. Much of the energy associated with the movement of your body travels through your hand and to the cup, causing the coffee to vibrate violently and splash out. If you carry the cup with only your thumb and forefinger, however, you decrease the area of contact between your hand and the cup, transferring less energy to the cup and reducing the movement of the coffee.

When earthquake waves vibrate a seismograph, the rotating drum moves in front of the stationary weight that holds the pen, and the normal straight line being drawn becomes a series of small to large deflections on the paper. These deflections constitute a **seismogram,** the written record of the passage of the earthquake waves (fig. 8.14b). The first deflection represents the arrival of the first P-wave, which took the most direct route from the focus to this station. This is followed by other small deflections, which indicate the subsequent arrivals of additional P-waves, which took longer routes. The arrival of the first S-wave is followed by more deflections, indicating the arrival of additional P-wave and S-wave energy. Time markings on seismograms allow scientists to determine precisely when the first P-wave and the first S-wave arrived at a station. This time difference is extremely important in determining the location of the earthquake epicenter. The largest deflection on the seismogram marks the arrival of the first surface wave. The large deflection is a testimony to the impact of surface waves. In fact, their large-scale vibrations are responsible for most earthquake damage.

Depending on a number of factors, seismogram deflections range from small to large. One important factor in this equation is the direction from which the waves emanate. Because this is variable, most modern seismic stations have at least three seismographs. One is oriented to record east-west displacements, another records north-south displacements, and the third records vertical displacements of the ground.

Determining the Earthquake Epicenter

Shortly after the 1989 Loma Prieta earthquake, seismologists pinpointed the epicenter near the town of Santa Cruz and Loma Prieta peak in the Santa Cruz Mountains, south of San Francisco. How did they arrive at their conclusion so rapidly?

Because seismologists have compiled and tabled the seismic velocity data from thousands of earthquakes, they now know the time intervals required for P-waves and S-waves to travel given distances. Examples from this data in table 8.4 show that a P-wave taking the most direct route requires 4 minutes, 6 seconds to travel from the focus to a seismic station 2,000 kilometers (1,242 mi) away. An S-wave leaving the focus at the same time and following the same route requires 7 minutes, 25 seconds to reach the same station. The P-wave obviously travels much faster than the S-wave. This situation is analogous to two automobiles leaving the same location at the same time but traveling at different speeds. The faster automobile reaches any given destination before the slower one. Furthermore, the farther the destination is from the starting point, the greater the time interval between the two arrivals. In the same manner, the P-wave pulls farther ahead of the S-wave as they travel farther from the focus. Therefore, the difference in arrival times (S − P) of the two types of waves at any recording station can be used as a measure of the distance from the focus to that station.

Armed with the type of information given in table 8.4, seismologists can easily pinpoint an epicenter through the cooperative

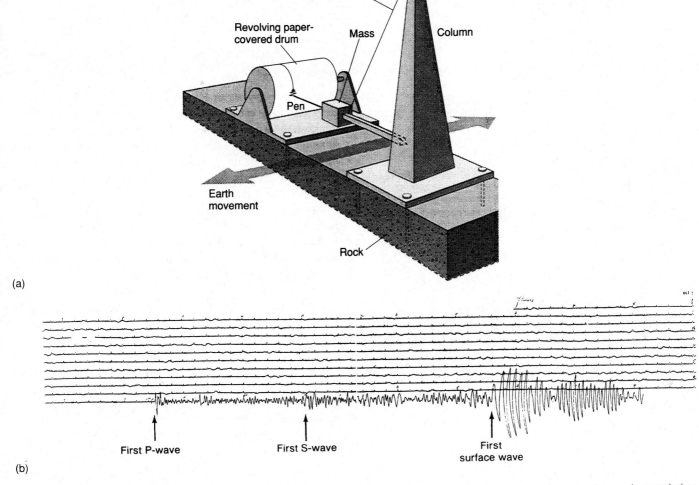

(a)

(b)

First P-wave   First S-wave   First
surface wave

Figure 8.14   (a) A seismograph for recording horizontal ground motion. Movement of the paper-covered drum as the ground moves is recorded as a series of lines in front of the stationary mass. The same station would also have a seismograph for recording vertical ground displacements. (b) A typical seismogram. The small "tic" marks represent time in minutes. The longer the time lag between the arrival of the first P-wave and the arrival of the first S-wave, the greater is the distance from the seismic recording station to the earthquake epicenter. (Source: Seismogram courtesy of University of California, Berkeley.)

TABLE 8.4   Sample Seismic Velocity Data

Distance from Source (km)	Travel Time				Interval between P and S arrivals (S–P)	
	P-wave		S-wave			
	Minutes	Seconds	Minutes	Seconds	Minutes	Seconds
2,000	4	06	7	25	3	19
4,000	6	58	12	36	5	38
6,000	9	21	16	56	7	35
8,000	11	23	20	45	9	22
10,000	12	57	23	56	10	59
11,000	13	39	25	18	11	39

Source: Data from S. Judson and M. Kauffman, *Physical Geology,* 8th ed., p. 185 Copyright © 1989 Prentice-Hall, Inc.

efforts of at least three seismic stations (fig. 8.15). Assume that a seismograph at station 1 records the data described in the previous paragraph. Seismologists at that station, by consulting their table of travel times, know that the earthquake epicenter lies 2,000 kilome-

ters (1,242 mi) from their station. To locate the epicenter, they first draw a circle on a map, centered on station 1, with a radius equal to 2,000 kilometers. The earthquake epicenter must lie somewhere on the circumference of that circle because those are all of the points

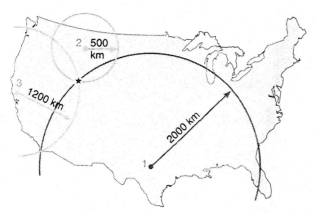

Figure 8.15   The epicenter of an earthquake is located by drawing circles centered on each of three seismic stations. The radius of each circle is the distance that the station is from the epicenter as determined from S-wave minus P-wave velocity data. The intersection of the three circles is the location of the epicenter.

Figure 8.16   Relationship of seismic-wave paths to earthquake focus and receiving stations. The deeper the focus and the more distant the stations, the shorter the paths of the P- and S-waves, compared to the surface waves.

on Earth's surface that are exactly 2,000 kilometers from station 1. By itself, the circle is relatively useless, but in conjunction with circles drawn on the basis of information provided by seismologists at other stations, it becomes the first step in the locating process.

Seismologists at station 2, a site closer to the epicenter than station 1, provide travel times that allow the plotting of a second circle, one with a radius of 500 kilometers (311 mi) and centered on station 2. The two circles intersect at two points. The epicenter must be one of these two points because these are the only two locations on Earth's surface that satisfy the conditions: 2,000 kilometers from station 1 and 500 kilometers from station 2.

Determining which of these points is the epicenter requires data from a third station. If the distance to the epicenter from station 3 is 1,200 kilometers (745 mi), a circle of that radius and centered on station 3 is drawn. This third circle should intersect one of the two earlier determined points or come very close to it. This is the earthquake epicenter: the only location on Earth's surface that is 2,000 kilometers from station 1, 500 kilometers from station 2, and 1,200 kilometers from station 3.

The circles often do not meet precisely at a point because of several influences. The most important of these is that distances from an epicenter to any seismic station are measured across Earth's surface, while the waves take a "shortcut" from the focus through Earth (fig. 8.16). In addition, seismic wave velocities in-

crease with depth, so waves traveling more deeply in Earth travel faster than those following shallower paths. For example, as the distance from an epicenter to a station doubles, the S and P travel times do not double but are less than that amount (table 8.4).

GEOLOGIC STRUCTURES

That Earth undergoes an extraordinarily high number of tremors and earthquakes each year was earlier cited as evidence that Earth is a restless body. Earth scientists can cite additional evidence to support the contention that Earth has always been restless. For example, rocks containing the fossil remains of animals that once lived in the sea have been raised to such heights that they now make up portions of some of our highest mountains. In addition, layers of coal, known to have been formed at or above sea level, have been pushed downward to depths of hundreds or thousands of meters below sea level. Surely, extraordinary forces must have been at work over long periods to bring about such changes. As compelling as these examples are, geologists can point to even more commonplace rock features that tell much the same story. These features, which were produced when strong, deforming forces were applied to the rocks, may be grouped together as the **geologic structures.**

The geologic structures can be broadly separated into two categories, principally on the basis of how the rocks respond to stresses: They break if they behave as brittle solids, and if they respond plastically, they bend. Structures that form when rocks break can be further subdivided into two types: *faults* and *joints*. If rocks respond plastically, they form *folds*. The process by which all geologic structures are formed is called **diastrophism.**

Faults

Faults are of several types. When the movement is predominantly in a horizontal, or sideways, direction, they are referred to as **lateral faults** (or as *strike-slip, transcurrent,* or *transform faults*). This group includes the famous San Andreas Fault in California, movement along which was responsible for the 1906 San Francisco earthquake as well as the 1989 Loma Prieta earthquake. During the 1906 event, a portion of the San Andreas Fault underwent an instantaneous horizontal slippage of 6.4 meters (21 ft), a remarkably large displacement for a single instance of movement.

When the movement along a fault is predominantly vertical, geologists normally employ a pair of terms that have been adapted from coal miners: *hanging wall* and *footwall* (fig. 8.17). The diagonal line on the front of the block represents a fault plane, which reaches from Earth's surface to some undetermined depth. If you could walk down the fault plane and into Earth's interior, you would have to place your feet on the right-hand side (or block of rock), while the left-hand side would "hang" overhead. Because of this relationship, the right-hand block is referred to as the footwall, while the left-hand block is the hanging wall.

Figure 8.18 depicts the several types of faults with displacements recognized by earth scientists. In the instance where the hanging wall has moved downward *relative* to the position of the footwall, the resulting fault is called a **normal fault** (an

Figure 8.17 The hanging wall block (which would be above an observer's head) and the footwall block (on which the observer would stand) in relation to the fault plane.

form when rocks of Earth's crust are subjected to a stretching force (referred to by earth scientists as *tension*). Where blocks of Earth's crust are raised or lowered between pairs of faults, *horsts* and *grabens,* respectively, are recognized.

If the hanging wall block is forced upward relative to the position of the footwall block (the reverse situation from what caused the normal fault), the result is a **reverse,** or **thrust, fault.** If the fault plane is inclined at a low angle to the horizontal, an **overthrust fault** is formed. Portions of the southern Appalachians as well as the northern Rockies have been moved tens of kilometers from their original positions by overthrusting. Both reverse faults and overthrusts occur when the rocks are subjected to squeezing, or *compression.* Figure 8.19 shows the front (fault scarp) and back of a major overthrust in northern Montana.

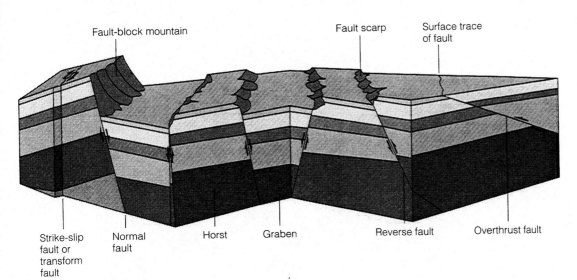

Figure 8.18 Various types of faults.

Joints

The second major type of structure resulting from rock breakage is the **joint,** a break in the rock along which *no movement* has taken place. Joints are, by far, the most common type of structural feature found in rocks. They usually form from the release of stress, rather than from its direct application. That is, when deeply (or even shallowly) buried rocks are brought to or near Earth's surface by uplift and erosion of overlying rocks, the lower-pressure environment allows for a certain amount of expansion. When expansion occurs, cracks develop in the rocks. Such cracks, or joints, almost always occur in parallel sets, spaced centimeters or meters apart. Joints may also form in rocks by contraction rather than expansion, as when igneous rocks cool.

unfortunate application of terminology, because this type of fault is no more or less "normal" than any other type). Understand the importance of the term *relative* displacement. As far as the *actual* movement is concerned, there are really five distinct possibilities:

1. The hanging wall may have indeed moved down, while the footwall remained stationary.
2. The footwall may have moved up, while the hanging wall remained stationary.
3. The footwall may have moved up, while the hanging wall moved down.
4. Both blocks may have moved up, with the footwall moving farther.
5. Both blocks may have moved down, with the hanging wall moving farther.

During faulting, and for a period of time after, the upthrown block may stand topographically higher than the downthrown block, with the steep surface separating the two called a *fault scarp.* In time, however, the processes of weathering and erosion wear down the elevated block and restore a uniform surface. The evidence of past movement remains, however, in the broken and displaced rock layers visible on the front of the block. Normal faults

Folds

Rocks may respond to deforming stresses by behaving plastically. This flowlike behavior produces a group of structural features known as **folds.** Although earth scientists recognize a variety of folds, the two fundamental types are anticlines and synclines. Both result from the application of strong, compressive stresses. **Anticlines** form when rocks are bent, or arched, upward (fig. 8.20). The name derives from the fact that the rock layers on either side of the fold center, or *axis,* are "inclined" away from or "against" (*anti-*) each other and the fold axis. In an anticline, the axial area is also referred to as the *crest.* The very action of pushing the rocks upward carries older rocks nearer the surface, where they may be exposed by erosion. Indeed, if you examine the ages of rocks in the

(a)   (b)

Figure 8.19 (*a*) Front (facing the fault scarp) and (*b*) backside of an overthrust fault in the Sun River Canyon area of Montana. Massive limestone units have been pushed up and over much younger shale beds for a distance of several kilometers.

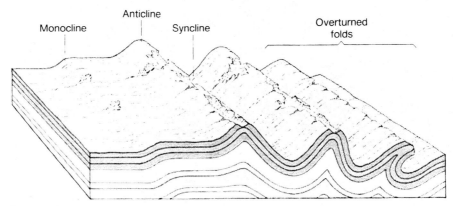

Figure 8.20 Simple folds: anticlines and synclines.

(a)   (b)

Figure 8.21 (*a*) The Tremont Syncline along I-81 in Pennsylvania. (*b*) Alternating anticlines and synclines in western Maryland.

Box 8.3

Further Consideration

SIDELING HILL: NOT YOUR ORDINARY REST STOP

The expenditure of public money to build a museum dedicated to the geology exposed in a road cut is anything but a common occurrence. Not only was it done in Maryland at Sideling Hill, but it has been an uncommon success. The deep cut made for the passage of I-68 through Sideling Hill in the western mountainous portion of Maryland revealed one of the finest exposures of a major geologic feature in the northeastern United States: an almost perfectly developed, tightly folded syncline (fig. 8.A). Within the syncline are exposed a sequence of sandstones, siltstones, shales, conglomerates, and coals that were laid down as sedimentary deposits some 340 million years ago, when this area was alternately dry land and shallow seas. The synclinal structure was formed approximately 240 million years ago, the result of intense compression caused by the collision of Africa and North America during the Alleghenian Orogeny.

Located 9.7 kilometers (6 mi) west of Hancock, Maryland, this spectacular cut is visible on a clear day from as far away as South Mountain, 60 kilometers (37 mi) to the east. It took 16 months to excavate the cut, which was completed in August 1985, and required the removal of 3.4 million cubic meters (4.5 million cu. yd) of rock. The cut is 216 meters (720 ft) wide at the top, 60 meters (200 ft) wide at the bottom, and 102 meters (340 ft) deep.

Work began on the Sideling Hill Exhibit Center in 1990 and was completed 1 year later. The center, with its tourist information, rest area, and walkway across I-68, was officially opened to the public on August 2, 1991, by Governor William Donald Schaefer. It includes 20 exhibits, which explain the geologic setting and the geologic history of the Sideling Hill area. Some of the exhibits are outdoors, some are "hands-on," and there is a block model of the cut available for the visually impaired. In the first year, more than a half million people visited the exhibit center.

Apply Your Knowledge

1. What benefits (economic, social, and educational) can you cite in support of the establishment of a facility such as that at Sideling Hill, Maryland?
2. Would you support the expenditure of public funds for the construction of similar geological museums in your state? Why or why not?

Figure 8.A Aerial view showing Sideling Hill road cut and the Sideling Hill Exhibit Center.

eroded core of an anticline, you find the oldest exposed layer along the axis, with progressively younger rocks exposed in either direction away from the axis.

The opposite situation occurs in a **syncline,** or downfold, where younger rocks, originally near the surface, are pushed downward to greater depth. As a result, younger rocks are found near the axis, or *trough,* of a syncline, with increasingly older rocks exposed outward on the fold flanks (fig. 8.21). Synclines are so-named because the rock layers on either side of the axis are "inclined" toward, or "with" (*syn-*) one another (see box 8.3).

Anticlines and synclines vary greatly in scale, ranging from microscopic to whole mountains or mountain ranges. For example, the individual ridges of the Allegheny Mountains of Pennsylvania and Maryland are individual, broad, anticlinal folds.

The large-scale structures described in this section are caused by hundreds or thousands of incremental movements occurring over millions of years. Each such movement causes the type of vibration and ground displacement characterized as an earthquake (see box 8.4).

Box 8.4

Further Consideration

At 4:31 A.M. on January 17, 1994, the Los Angeles area was rocked by an earthquake of magnitude 6.7 on the Richter scale. Centered near the city of Northridge in the San Fernando Valley (fig. 8.B), the earthquake left 61 people dead, 9,000 injured, 25,000 homeless, and 72,000 buildings damaged or destroyed. Ten bridges on three major freeways collapsed, including three on the Santa Monica Freeway, the nation's busiest, which handles 290,000 vehicles per day. Ironically, the overpasses on the Santa Monica Freeway were scheduled to be strengthened as part of a retrofitting program instituted after the 1971 San Fernando earthquake. In such a process, concrete columns are encased in steel to prevent their expansion and collapse during an earthquake. With 12,000 overpasses on the southern California highway network, not all could be done at once. Those that had already undergone retrofitting generally survived intact.

Some 300 schools were also seriously damaged, with damage estimates ranging to $700 million. Thousands of businesses were ruined. In the subsequent months, inspectors examined more than 100 steel-frame buildings (generally more than 5 stories high) that apparently survived the earthquake unscathed. Even here, however, they found that thousands of welds connecting horizontal beams to vertical columns were cracked and could pose a serious threat in another earthquake. In addition to the building inspection costs, repairs to each weld are estimated to cost between $500 and $15,000 per weld. Power was out across the entire metropolitan area, and the power network was affected as far away as Alberta, Canada. The most tragic aspect of the earthquake was the collapse of a portion of the Northridge Meadows apartment complex, in which 16 people lost their lives. The collapse caused the upper two stories to crush the first floor. Rescue techniques employed to search the rubble for survivors included fiber-optic cameras, inflatable bags capable of propping up 72 tons, special saws with diamond cutting blades, and search dogs. One ironic casualty of an earthquake-induced fire was the home of Charles Richter, developer of the Richter earthquake magnitude scale. All of this happened in just 40 seconds. The final tabulations showed this to be the costliest earthquake in U.S. history, with damage estimates in excess of $20 billion (some

NORTHRIDGE AND A BLIND THRUST FAULT

three times that of the Loma Prieta earthquake of 1989). By February 5th, 1,178 aftershocks had been recorded, the largest of which measured 5.7 on the Richter scale.

The rupture on the fault responsible for the Northridge earthquake occurred at a depth of 18 kilometers (11 mi) beneath the San Fernando Valley and rose to within 5 kilometers (3 mi) of the ground surface. Nearby Oat Mountain rose nearly 38 centimeters (15 in) and moved 20 centimeters (8 in) northwestward instantaneously as a result of fault displacement. The San Andreas Fault was not directly involved with the Northridge earthquake, although there is a historical connection. The rupture occurred on a fault that was unknown and unmapped prior to the earthquake, a variety newly coined by geologists as a *blind thrust fault*. Movement on such faults is up a very gentle slope angle (thrust), but the rupture does not reach the surface (blind). The surface manifestation of blind thrust faults is usually the formation of folded mountains, as around the margins of the Los Angeles Basin (Transverse Ranges, Santa Monica Mountains). With "young" blind thrust faults (as the one that caused the Northridge earthquake), surface folding is not yet evident. Almost certainly, all of the world's major fold and thrust belts also contain numerous blind thrust faults.

The San Andreas Fault runs for a distance of 1,200 kilometers (745 mi) through California, from the Salton Sea in the south to Cape Mendecino in the north, where it disappears out to sea. The San Andreas is the physical boundary between the Pacific plate to the west and the North American plate to the east. The Pacific plate has for millions of years been sliding northwestward past the North American plate at an average rate of approximately 5 centimeters (2 in) per year. Movement along most segments of the fault tends to occur in bursts, with the energy released by each burst being felt as earthquake vibrations.

Although the San Andreas is a relatively straight feature throughout much of its course, in the vicinity of Los Angeles, it forms a pronounced bend to the west. This "kink" in the fault causes it to hang up in the Los Angeles areas and to squeeze the Los Angeles Basin, a 9,325 square kilometer (3,600 sq. mi) area, reducing it in size by 1/2 acre every year. Pressure on the Los Angeles Basin has also caused the formation of dozens of blind thrust faults within the basin, any one of which is capable of moving and generating an earthquake of magnitude 7.0 (or larger, if two or more faults are activated at the same time). Nine of these blind thrust faults have produced earthquakes of magnitudes greater than 4 since 1971.

Because faults are so numerous and because individual ones may be difficult to identify, some geologists are referring to the Los Angeles area as simply the "Transverse Ranges Compression Zone" and considering it one big danger zone. Seismic surveys are attempting to identify and map as many of these blind thrust faults as possible, but the faults are so numerous that assessing the earthquake potential of any one probably would be impossible. Another new initiative is underway to deploy a network of 250 to 300 stations and to employ the Global Positioning System (GPS) to monitor precisely any small crustal movements throughout southern California. Scientists believe that the stress building on the San Andreas Fault was probably not relieved by the Northridge earthquake, meaning that "the big one" could still occur along this fault in the near future.

What can be done if one lives in an earthquake-prone area such as Los Angeles? For many years, one answer was to purchase earthquake insurance. Currently, however, such insurance is almost prohibitively expensive for most home owners and small business owners, and in many cases is no longer even available. A few simple precautions are recommended: Avoid building on unconsolidated sediments in or near known fault zones. Houses should be bolted to their foundations to prevent movement. Have a store of fresh water and food, as well as fresh batteries for flashlights and a portable radio, on hand and accessible. In homes that use gas heat and appliances, tape a wrench to the gas shutoff valve so that the gas supply can be turned off in the case of a line break.

Figure 8.B   Map of the Los Angeles area, showing the epicenter and the principal damage locations from the Northridge earthquake. (Source: Data from Associated Press, January 18, 1994.)

MOUNTAINS

Mountains comprise a category of Earth's surface features that result from one or more of the tectonic processes that we have been considering. While difficult to define precisely, **mountains** normally are landforms that rise significantly above their surroundings (300 meters [1,000 ft] is sometimes taken as a standard), with limited surface areas at their summits. Distinctions between mountains and hills are similarly difficult to define and often are a matter of local custom and usage. Features in areas of low relief that might be called "mountains" would probably be considered "hills" in areas of more rugged terrain. Differences in relief are also a function of age because, as we shall see in chapter 10, erosion wears down areas of high elevation so that younger mountain systems, such as the Himalayas, also tend to be the highest.

Mountains form in a variety of ways, all of which we have now considered. Whereas classifications and categories may vary somewhat, for our purposes, we recognize six types: *volcanic mountains, fault-block mountains, folded mountains, domal mountains, residual mountains,* and *complex mountains* (fig. 8.22). While generally designated as one of these six types, mountains most commonly form by a combination of processes, and the vast majority develop along subduction zones and other places where tectonic plates converge with consequent high heat and crustal thickening (see chapter 9).

Many of the world's volcanic mountains are associated with subduction zones. These mountains usually occur in linear belts of isolated cones that rise spectacularly above the surrounding terrain. Examples include the Aleutian Islands, which stretch southwestward from Alaska; the Andes of South America; and the Cascades of the Pacific Northwest.

Fault-block mountains result from vertical displacement along steeply dipping fault planes. Weathering and erosion carve the uplifted crustal blocks into a series of separate but related peaks (see the photo at the beginning of this chapter). Horsts, blocks uplifted along major faults on either side of the block, are similarly carved into mountain peaks. The Grand Tetons of Wyoming are,

Time

Young   Old

Domes (Black Hills, SD)

Fault-block mountains (Tetons, WY)

Folded mountains (Central Appalachians, PA-MD-VA)

Residual (complex) mountains (Sierra Nevada, CA; St. Francois, MO)

Volcanoes (Cascades, WA-OR; Aleutians, AL)

Figure 8.22 Types of mountains and their alteration through time.

perhaps, the most spectacular example of these types of mountains in the United States, with uplift along the faulted side of 2,000 meters (6,000 ft) or more. Many of the small, isolated mountain ranges of Nevada are also of this variety and are thought to have formed as Earth's crust was stretched above a large mass of magma that is working its way upward from depth. In the southern Appalachians (Tennessee and Virginia) and the northern Rockies (Montana and British Columbia), mountains have been formed not along high-angle faults, but from rock masses moved great distances (tens of kilometers) along low-angle faults (see fig. 8.19).

Folded mountains result from the compression of crustal rocks during the converging of tectonic plates. The rocks are forced into a series of anticlines and synclines (see fig. 8.20). Initially, the mountains, or ridges, coincide with the anticlines, and intervening valleys coincide with synclines. Erosion, over the course of many years, may alter this simple pattern (see chapter 10). Sideling Hill (see fig. 8.A), for instance, is a syncline that now stands as a topographic high capped by resistant rock layers. It lies within the best example of folded mountains in the United States—indeed, perhaps in the world: the Valley and Ridge Province of Pennsylvania, Maryland, and Virginia.

Similar to folded mountains, but consisting of a single, broad upwarp are domal mountains. One of the better examples of this type of mountain system in North America is the Black Hills of western South Dakota. As this rock mass was moved upward, it weakened the overlying sedimentary rocks that covered this area and exposed them to weathering and erosion. These rocks have now been stripped off the top of the Black Hills dome, but remnants still remain as upturned edges along the dome margins. Similar examples are the Front Range of the Rockies in Colorado and the Bighorn Mountains of Wyoming.

Residual mountains are formed when more easily erodible rocks have been removed from an area, leaving a core of resistant igneous and metamorphic rocks that are carved by streams and glaciers into a series of mountain peaks. The Saint Francois Mountains of the Missouri Ozarks and the Sierra Nevada of eastern California (see fig. 8.16) are examples of this type. One might also use the Sierra Nevada to illustrate complex mountains because they have also been elevated some 3,040 meters (10,000 ft) along a major high-angle fault.

EARTH'S INTERIOR

Since most of Earth, of course, is not directly observable, we must rely on the techniques of remote sensing and extrapolation to determine its composition and structure. For many years, scientists have used evidence from meteorites and seismic studies to piece together a picture of Earth's interior.

Evidence from Meteorites

Scientists have derived a theory of Earth's composition from some of the millions of *meteoroids* that impinge on Earth from space each year. Most of these are consumed by the frictional heat generated by their passage through the atmosphere, which produces the brilliant, moving light displays called *meteors.* Some, however, survive this ordeal and reach Earth's surface, where scientists collect and study them as *meteorites* (so-called once they are found on Earth's surface). Years of collecting and study have led to two basic classifications based on meteorite composition: those that are metallic (an iron-nickel mixture) and those that are "rocky" or "stony." Some scientists suggest that meteorites represent the remains of a disintegrated planet that once occupied an orbit between Mars and Jupiter (the present site of the *asteroid belt*). Such a planet, they reason, could have been similar to Earth.

Meteorites, then, would be samples of the interior of some planet that approximated the composition of Earth's deep, unsampled interior. This analogy seems reasonable when used in conjunction with other data and, indeed, helps us to explain some of the other data.

Seismic Studies of Earth's Interior

In recent years, seismologists have been analyzing Earth's interior three-dimensionally, much as doctors do when studying the human body with CAT (computerized axial tomography) scan. Such studies applied to Earth are referred to as *seismic tomography* and are done by analyzing tens of thousands of high-quality seismic (earthquake) records. As noted earlier, seismic-wave velocity depends upon rock density, rigidity, and elasticity, which, in turn, are dependent upon temperature, pressure, and mineralogical composition. A vertical traverse through Earth indicates that compositional changes may be responsible for distinctive boundaries and layers. Laterally within any layer, the principal distinctions are mainly the result of temperature variations, with high seismic-wave velocities associated with cold, heavy, sinking rock masses and low seismic-wave velocities associated with hot, buoyant, rising rock masses. (The terms *cold* and *hot* are used here in a relative sense because all rock temperatures at these depths are many times greater than temperatures at Earth's surface.)

Earlier, as a prelude to the study of rocks and minerals (see chapter 7), we offered a brief description of the four major zones that constitute Earth: inner core, outer core, mantle, and crust (fig. 8.23). The first of these, the **inner core,** occupies approximately the inner 1,255 kilometers (780 mi) of Earth's radius and is thought to consist of a mixture of iron and nickel, called *kamacite.* This high-density metallic material probably worked its way toward Earth's center as lighter material became segregated toward the surface during the formative stage in Earth's history. Because of the very high pressures that must exist at this depth, and also because of P-wave characteristics, the kamacite in the inner core is considered to be in a solid state.

From the boundary with the inner core to approximately 3,475 kilometers (2,159 mi) out from Earth's center is the **outer core.** Although somewhat less dense, this zone is thought to consist of the same mixture that constitutes the inner core. This is the deep layer, as discussed earlier in this chapter, where the energy associated with S-waves becomes lost and the velocity of P-waves is drastically reduced. To the seismologist, this means that the material of the outer core is a liquid rather than a solid.

The liquid composition of Earth's outer core has further important implications for scientists. Because liquids flow, heat-driven currents of metallic material likely exist within this zone. Such movement would constitute an electrical current, and an important principle of physics is that electrical currents generate and surround themselves with magnetic fields. Thus, the outer core is a likely source for Earth's magnetic field. This idea is explored in some detail in chapter 9.

The next zone out from the center, the **mantle,** occupies approximately the outer half of Earth. With the exception of isolated pockets of magma in its upper portion, the mantle is assumed, because of its seismic behavior, to be in the solid state. Unlike the metallic core, the mantle is considered by scientists to be a rocky

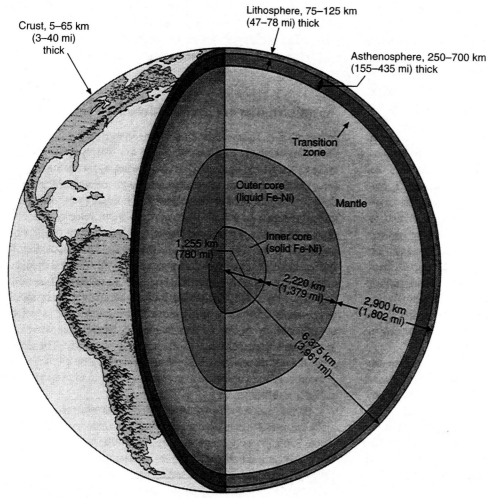

Figure 8.23 Cutaway view showing the major zones of Earth's interior.

layer. While opinion differs on its exact composition, which almost certainly varies significantly from place to place, a gross approximation might be that of the igneous rock *peridotite,* a mixture of the iron- and magnesium-rich minerals olivine and pyroxene. A variety of peridotite known as *kimberlite* is usually associated with the diamonds of South Africa and elsewhere. Both the fragmented nature of the kimberlite rock and the high-pressure origin of diamonds suggest that this rock was forced up from some depth in the mantle.

Seismic tomography has recently revealed distinctive zones within the mantle. Two major global boundaries (discontinuities) can be distinguished at depths of 400 kilometers (248 mi) and 670 kilometers (416 mi). Other discontinuities can be recognized intermittently at depths of approximately 60, 80, 220, 330, 710, and 2,640 kilometers (37, 50, 137, 205, 441, 1,640 mi, respectively). The two global discontinuities appear to represent phase transitions from olivine to spinel (see the discussion of deep-focus earthquakes earlier in the chapter), with the 670 kilometer discontinuity generally recognized as the boundary between the upper and the lower mantle (fig. 8.24).

Laterally within the upper mantle, "cold," descending slabs of material are identified beneath subduction zones. Some of the sinking slabs are deflected laterally and accumulate at the core-mantle boundary (CMB); others penetrate the boundary for up to several hundred kilometers. Which of these happens is probably a function

of velocity and angle of descent. As slabs of lithosphere accumulate at the base of the upper mantle, they may sink into and ultimately through the lower mantle in some places.

"Hot," buoyant rock areas coincide with material rising to form volcanic hot spots, approximately 40 of which have been identified worldwide. These remain stationary as the lithospheric plates move above them (see chapter 9). Thus, some of the volcanics of Washington and Oregon were formed over the hot spot that now lies beneath Yellowstone Park in Wyoming.

Just above the CMB are areas of fast seismic velocity that lie below areas of extensive historical subduction. Apparently, subducted slabs of oceanic lithosphere have "piled up" here over hundreds of millions of years. Other areas with low seismic velocities lie beneath major hot spots. These large areas of "hot" and "cold" material above the CMB are sometimes referred to as grand structures.

Seismic tomography has mapped out a grand, convective cycle of material constantly moving between Earth's surface and the CMB. This cycle takes the form of descending slabs of oceanic lithosphere and rising plumes of hot, buoyant rock. The driving force for the cycle may be the subducting slabs, but the system is fed by energy from Earth's cooling core as well as from the decay of radioactive material within the mantle. Such a cycle probably requires several hundred million years to run its course.

As kimberlite (or any other material) moves upward from the mantle, it must pass through a last zone, the **crust,** Earth's outer rocky shell. On the scale of Earth, the crust is an extremely thin layer, varying from a minimum of about 5 kilometers (3 mi) thick beneath the ocean basins to a maximum of about 65 kilometers (40 mi) thick beneath the continents. These thicknesses have been determined by a number of seismic studies. Although small in volume and thickness, the crust is of immense importance to us. Because of its relative accessibility, it is the zone about which we know the most.

Figure 8.25 portrays both the composition and the dynamics of the crust. Two dominant types of crustal material are recognized. The first is essentially granite in composition and underlies only the continents (including the shallow, submerged seafloor around continental margins). Because of its location and its composition, this material is referred to as either the *continental crust* or the *granitic crust.* Because the minerals that compose a granite are rich in silicon (Si) and aluminum (Al), this material has also been referred to as *sial,* or *sialic crust,* but this terminology is not in vogue in newer texts. The thickness of granitic crust is highly

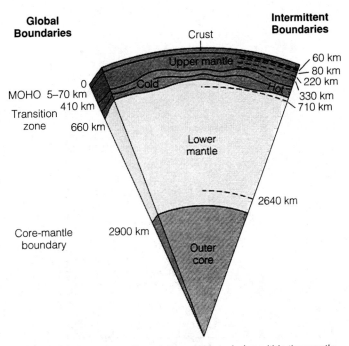

Figure 8.24 Locations of some internal boundaries within the mantle that are recognized from seismic studies. (Source: *Geotimes,* June 1994, p. 13, American Geological Institute.)

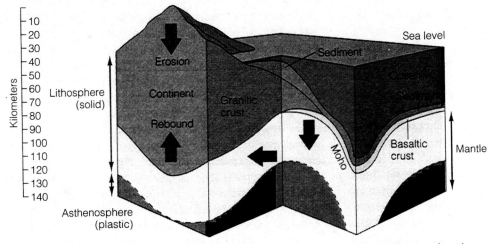

Figure 8.25 Expanded view of Earth's crust and uppermost mantle. As the continent is worn down by erosion, the base of the continental crust rises to maintain balance. Material moves laterally to replace it.

of the granitic crust, as determined through seismic studies, its high position, and its low average specific gravity (2.7) compared to the materials of the other earth zones, appears to substantiate a view long held by earth scientists that the continents represent a light "scum" that has accumulated on Earth's surface throughout the planet's development.

The ocean basins are underlain by a very different material: rocks rich in the ferromagnesian minerals best represented by volcanic basalt and its plutonic counterpart, gabbro. These comprise the second dominant type of crustal material. Because of its location and its composition, this material is often referred to as *oceanic crust* or *basaltic crust.* Its composition, dominated by silicate minerals rich in magnesium and iron, has led in the past to the designation *sima,* an abbreviation of silicon (Si) and "mafic," a term used to describe dark minerals and rocks.

The basaltic crust is not as restricted as the granitic crust, and some seismic evidence suggests that it forms a continuous layer stretching beneath the continents as well as the ocean basins. If it does lie below the granitic crust in continental areas, it is because of its greater specific gravity (3.0). Unlike the granitic crust, the basaltic crust maintains an approximately uniform thickness of between 4 and 5 kilometers (2.48 to 3.1 mi).

Because seismic-wave velocities are functions of the physical properties of the rock layers through which they travel, seismic waves undergo a marked increase in velocity as they pass downward from the crust into the mantle, where specific gravity increases markedly (fig. 8.26). Such an abrupt velocity increase represents an important boundary that was first recognized in the early twentieth century by Croatian seismologist A. Mohorovicic. Earth scientists now refer to this seismic representation of the crust-mantle boundary as the *Mohorovicic discontinuity,* the *M-discontinuity,* or simply, the **Moho.**

Seismologists have found that the downward increase in seismic-wave velocity through the crust (including the sharp increase at the Moho) continues through the uppermost part of the mantle. At a depth of approximately 100 kilometers (62 mi), however, seismic-wave velocities not only stop increasing, they actually slow somewhat. This depth represents the top of a zone that extends downward to an average depth of approximately 220 kilometers (136 mi). Because of its seismic characteristics, this is referred to as a *low-velocity zone.*

Material in this layer is apparently still solid, but not brittle and rigid. Rather, it is likened to plastic, which may be distorted in shape and caused to flow over long periods of time. Thus, occasional reference is made to a "plastic layer" in the upper part of the mantle. What could cause such plastic behavior in seemingly solid rock? The best explanation is that the material within this layer is

varied; it is absent beneath the ocean basins and in direct proportion to elevation in the continents. That is, it is thickest beneath high, mountainous regions and thinnest beneath low-lying plains. This distribution leads to comparisons of continents to icebergs, where the ice mass hidden beneath the water is in direct proportion to that visible above the water. As the exposed ice melts and its surface is lowered, the bottom of the iceberg rises to compensate for this loss of mass.

As mountains wear down by erosion, the base of the granitic crust is thought to rise to keep this system in balance, so that the continents are, in a sense, "floating and bobbing" on the underlying mantle. This system of balance with respect to the rising and lowering of continents is referred to as *isostasy.* The varying thickness

Figure 8.26 (*a*) P-wave velocities within the crust and upper mantle. Note the progressive increase in velocity through the crust and the pronounced velocity decrease in the low-velocity zone in the upper mantle. (*b*) Interpretation of the nature of the crust and upper mantle, based on seismic-wave data.

probably very hot—not hot enough to melt, but close enough to its melting point that some of its solid characteristics are altered. Because of the loss of solid characteristics, this layer is referred to as the **asthenosphere** (from the Greek *asthenes,* meaning "weak"). The more rigid material above the asthenosphere, consisting of the continents, the ocean basins, and the uppermost layer of the mantle, acts as a single unit in most geologic processes. This unit is called the **lithosphere** (from the Greek *lithos,* meaning "rock"). As important as the discovery of the Moho was, the recognition of the distinction between the asthenosphere and the lithosphere is what really has helped to answer questions that had for so long seemed unanswerable.

For example, what is the source of magma for volcanic eruptions? If the material of the asthenosphere is indeed very close to its melting point, then a decrease in pressure or the application of a small amount of additional heat would be enough to melt the rock and form magma. Indeed, plots of successive earthquake foci have tracked the upward movement of magma from the upper part of the asthenosphere just prior to its eruption at the surface. If material is, in fact, moving vertically at or near the surface (as in the "floating and bobbing" of the continents), there must be a "cushion" at depth that has sufficient flexibility to allow for such

movement. A plastic layer would provide the necessary flexibility. It could also account for the continuing "rebound" of Earth's crust following the melting away of the continental glaciers of North America and Europe. The formation of massive ice sheets in excess of 3.25 kilometers (2 mi) thick placed an enormous strain on Earth's crust, literally pushing it downward. The melting of the ice, a relatively rapid geological event, left the crust out of isostatic balance. Since the melting (approximately 8,000 to 10,000 years ago), the crust has been slowly recovering to its former position. Evidence for such rebound, particularly in high-latitude regions, is in the form of elevated beach ridges and a continuing decrease in coastal tide gauge readings.

Lastly, a plastic layer, capable of flow, would provide a plausible mechanism for the movement of large segments of lithosphere. They could be carried along as rafts. Long a shortcoming of the old theory that the continents had somehow drifted from ancient sites to their present positions, the "continental drift" theory now holds that the continents move as integral parts of larger, "floating" lithospheric units, called *plates,* whose movements can now be logically explained. This new theory, the topic of the next chapter, is called *plate tectonics.*

FURTHER THOUGHTS: ADAPT TO WHAT CANNOT BE CONTROLLED OR CHANGED

*E*arthquakes have played a significant role throughout all of human history. Historians and archeologists have suspected that they may even have contributed to the decline and demise of whole civilizations. Scientists now understand the causes and mechanisms of earthquakes, but while major efforts are made to predict their occurrence, no reliable system has as yet been developed. The

prospect of eventually being able to control them is remote. Perhaps the best that can be achieved is to learn to live with earthquakes in a sort of uneasy truce. Avoid them if possible, but where you cannot, exercise good judgment by following the advice of professional earth scientists and engineers.

SIGNIFICANT POINTS

1. Planet Earth is a restless body undergoing constant change, as attested to by the more than 1 million earthquakes recorded each year.

2. An earthquake is the sudden movement or vibration of Earth caused by the passage of energy in wave form released by faulting. The energy accumulates in the rocks as the result of the application of stress over many years.

3. Structural damage resulting from an earthquake is a function of earthquake strength and duration, distance from the epicenter, and type of foundation material.

4. The location of energy release (faulting) is the focus of the earthquake. The point on Earth's surface directly above the focus is the epicenter.

5. Earthquakes are classified as shallow, intermediate, or deep, based on their depth of focus. This is also their order of abundance in that earthquake frequency diminishes with depth.

6. Deep-focus earthquakes, which occur in the upper portion of the mantle, are thought to be caused by the change, or transformation, of olivine into the denser mineral spinel.

7. Earthquakes are, for the most part, confined to distinct geographic zones: the Circum-Pacific belt, the Mediterranean-Himalayan belt, and the oceanic ridge system.

8. Earthquake intensity is measured by the Modified Mercalli scale and is a qualitative assessment based on property damage and human perception, which vary from place to place. Magnitude, as designated by values on the Richter scale, is a measure of the amount of energy released. Each earthquake is assigned only a single magnitude value.

9. Energy is transmitted by surface waves and body waves. The two types of body waves are P-waves and S-waves.

10. P-waves are the fastest of all earthquake waves, they are compressional in origin, and they travel through solids, liquids, and gases. S-waves are shear waves and are transmitted only through solids.

11. Shadow zones for both P-waves and S-waves have been interpreted to mean that Earth has a liquid outer core.

12. The basic instrument for recording the passage of seismic waves is the seismograph, which operates on the principle of a stationary mass. The "written" record of an earthquake is the seismogram.

13. The epicenter of an earthquake can be determined by plotting the distances as reflected by travel time differences for P-waves and S-waves (S − P) to any three seismic stations.

14. Faults and joints develop when rocks respond as brittle solids to earth stresses, while folds result from plastic rock behavior. All are grouped together as geologic structures.

15. Fault movements may be dominantly horizontal or vertical in nature. The former gives rise to lateral faults, while the latter forms normal or reverse faults.

16. Normal faults result from tensional stresses, reverse faults from compressional stresses.

17. Joints involve no rock movement but form from the release of stress or from the cooling of igneous rock.

18. Folds are of two types: anticlines and synclines. Both are of compressional origin.

19. Blind thrust faults have no surface expression in their early stages of development and are therefore difficult to locate and map.

20. The principal categories of mountains are volcanic, fault-block, folded, domal, residual, and complex.

21. The nature of Earth's interior has been deduced largely from the analysis of seismic waves and the study of meteorites.

22. Four major zones are recognized within Earth: inner core, outer core, mantle, and crust.

23. Seismic tomography has identified large, cold, sinking slabs of lithosphere beneath subduction zones and hotter, lighter, rising masses of material that probably give rise to volcanic plumes or hot spots.

24. Crustal material is of two types: granitic, associated with the continents, and basaltic, associated with the ocean basins.

25. The crust and uppermost mantle act as a single unit, called the lithosphere, which is divided into a number of segments called plates.

26. Below the lithosphere is a plastic layer of low seismic-wave velocity known as the asthenosphere. Heat-driven currents within the asthenosphere are thought to be responsible for plate movements and a number of other geologic phenomena.

ESSENTIAL TERMS

earthquake *185*
faulting *185*
fault *189*
focus *189*
epicenter *189*
plastic *191*
intensity *191*
Modified Mercalli
  scale *191*

magnitude *191*
Richter scale *192*
surface wave *194*
body wave *195*
P-wave (primary
  wave) *195*
S-wave (secondary
  wave) *195*
shadow zone *195*

seismograph *196*
seismogram *196*
geologic structure *198*
diastrophism *198*
lateral fault *198*
normal fault *198*
reverse (thrust) fault
  199
overthrust fault *199*

joint *199*
fold *199*
anticline *199*
syncline *201*
mountain *204*
inner core *205*
outer core *205*
mantle *205*
crust *206*

Moho *207*
asthenosphere *208*
lithosphere *208*
plate tectonics *208*

REVIEW QUESTIONS

1. What is an earthquake, and what is its origin?
2. What are some of the potentially deadly side effects of an earthquake?
3. What are the factors that determine the extent of earthquake damage?
4. What is the potential for damage of foreshocks? of aftershocks?
5. What is the difference between the focus and the epicenter?
6. What is the relationship of earthquake frequency to depth of focus?
7. Where do most earthquakes occur?
8. Why are deep-focus earthquakes only associated with deep-sea trenches?
9. What is meant by transformational faulting, and where does it occur?
10. How does intensity differ from magnitude?
11. How do surface waves differ from body waves? How do P-waves differ from S-waves?
12. What is the origin of the shadow zones?
13. How do seismologists determine the epicenter of an earthquake? What are some potential sources of error in such a determination?
14. How does the occurrence of the various types of faults and folds relate to whether the applied stresses were tensional or compressional?
15. How does a normal fault differ from a reverse fault?
16. How does an anticline differ from a syncline?
17. What are blind thrust faults, and why do they occur in the Los Angeles area?
18. In what geologic setting do mountains most commonly form?
19. How might the composition of meteorites tell us something about the composition and structure of Earth's interior?
20. How do we know that Earth's inner core is solid and its outer core is liquid?
21. At what depths in the mantle have two global boundaries been identified? Which is considered to be the boundary between the upper and the lower mantle?
22. What are the differences between the continental crust and the oceanic crust?
23. Why is the asthenosphere referred to as a "low-velocity zone," and what is the geologic significance of this?

CHALLENGES

1. Consider the area in which you live. Are you aware of or can you find any reference (oral or written) to a history of or potential for earthquakes? Consider your immediate neighborhood. What are some of the potential earthquake hazards you might encounter there? How would you rate your home with regard to its potential to withstand a moderate to severe earthquake?
2. Suppose you were given the task of assessing the intensity of an earthquake that occurred in or near the area where you live. How would you go about it? What lines of evidence would you pursue?
3. How would you construct a simple seismograph? What materials would you need? What difficulties would you encounter in terms of potential sources of error? (Hint: Consider other sources of vibrational energy.)
4. Examine some exposures of bedrock in the area where you live (in road cuts, stream valleys, etc.). Photograph or sketch any geologic structures (faults, joints, or folds) that you can identify.
5. Examine a world map that includes the major relief features of the continents and the ocean basins. What other mountain systems, besides the Rockies and the Appalachians, can you identify? Can you discern any major plateaus? Where are some extensive low-lying plains? What are some of the names applied to major segments of the oceanic ridge system?

9 Chapter

Plate Tectonics: A Unified Theory of Earth

Aerial photograph of the San Andreas Fault as it crosses the Carrizo Plain between San Francisco and Los Angeles.

INTRODUCTION

If the ultimate goal of the earth sciences is a holistic view of the planet and its processes, then the single most unifying theory currently available is one based on the interactions between Earth's interior and its outer shell. This theory, now called **plate tectonics,** began as a series of *hypotheses,* or topics for investigation, which became progressively interrelated as scientists in different fields gathered observational data. The evolutionary history of this unified view of Earth traces a series of purposeful and accidental discoveries that a few insightful scientists used to develop a new model of the planet. The transformation of this perspective from hypothesis to theory is a good example of how science often works. Not just the product of researchers in laboratory coats, scientific discovery and theory often begin with straightforward observations of the obvious, such as observations you can make.

The initial tenet of plate-tectonic theory was simple: The continents are changing units on a changing lithosphere. They move, break up, collide, and even form new continents. The movement creates oceans where breakup has occurred, mountain ranges where collisions take place, and numerous volcanoes and earthquakes wherever the lithosphere releases heat and relieves stress. All of the movements depend on activity within Earth's asthenosphere, a zone in which heat generated through radioactivity, pressure, and friction causes convectional movements that press against the bottom of the lithosphere.

Casual Observations, Unsubstantiated Conclusions

When you look at a map of the world, you might notice a linearity in the mountain systems. The lines of mountains, often called ranges or ridges, occur on every continent. Among some of these linear systems are extensive tracts of volcanoes, also "lined up," making volcanic chains and, in some instances, volcanic islands. What could cause such linear systems to form?

The question is compounded by another seeming coincidence. Earth scientists have long noted that not only the mountains and volcanoes exhibit this trend, but earthquakes, too, generally follow patterns in narrow zones across Earth's surface (fig. 9.1).

The location and origin of our planet's surface features, such as mountains, have long generated numerous hypotheses about the evolution of Earth's surface, but many of these have been based more on imagination than on accurate observations and sampling. At the beginning of the twentieth century, for example, the prevailing idea was that mountains formed when a cooling Earth contracted and wrinkled. Many held that view even though no scientific observations supported it.

Scientific Observations

After World War II, scientists adapted a number of military technologies to earth science research and, armed with instruments appropriate for their objective studies, began to make accurate observations of Earth that were not possible before the war. Earth scientists soon had sound observational data on which to base their hypotheses about continental movements.

Some of the major scientific advances of the postwar explorations occurred in 1958, the International Geophysical Year (IGY), during which the concerted efforts of several cooperating countries led to the discovery of mountain systems hidden in the depths of the oceans, systems that are also linear. The technology that made their discovery possible was an adaptation of sonar, the sound reflection device used to detect submarines. Sound vibrations, which pass through water just as they pass through air and solids, can be bounced off the ocean floor to reveal its **bathymetry**—that is, its depth and configuration. Signals sent to the bottom are timed, and any differences in successive return times indicate varying distances to the ocean floor. A shorter return time for signals means shallower water, whereas longer returns indicate deeper water (fig. 9.2).

THE BEGINNING OF A UNIFIED THEORY

The discovery of the undersea volcanic mountains led a Princeton University scientist, Dr. Harry Hess, to speculate that the oceans are actually the birthplace of oceanic crust. He believed that hot material from the mantle wells up to form new crust and creates the large linear volcanic systems called oceanic ridges (fig. 9.3). Hess's speculations were preceded by those of British scientist Arthur Holmes, who had suggested that rising cells of hot mantle material upwelled to "stretch," or thin, the ocean floor and move the continents apart, but he believed that the ocean floor and the continents were similar in composition. Because of the information IGY scientists had provided, Hess knew that *the basaltic ocean floor differs from the predominantly granitic continental rocks.* In Hess's view, the oceanic ridges on the ocean floor were volcanic areas where the crust formed. Although Hess had little proof for his speculations, he helped to renew scientific interest in an older notion, one proposed early in this century by German meteorologist Alfred Wegener.

Wegener's Idea of Continental Drift

If you look at a world map for nothing more than the shapes of the continents, you will notice that some of the continental units have coastlines that would, if merged, fit into one another like the interlocking pieces of a puzzle. This "fit" caught the attention of some thinkers shortly after the first crude maps of coastlines were published. The idea of connected continents somehow separating did not generate research in the earth sciences, however, until Wegener examined a growing body of evidence that suggested that formerly linked continents had moved from their previous positions.

When Wegener suggested in his 1915 work, *The Origin of the Continents and Oceans,* that the continents had moved from their initial locations, his fellow scientists ridiculed the idea. As a theorist, Wegener worked with limited information, but he saw convincing evidence for what he called "continental drift." To Wegener, the world was a changing place, and the changes were much larger than most scientists had imagined.

Wegener's Proofs for Continental Drift

The impetus for Wegener's work initially came from a common-sense examination of the coastlines on either side of the Atlantic.

(a)

(b)

Figure 9.1 (*a*) The locations and linearity of the world's major mountain systems. (*b*) Plot of earthquake epicenters and active volcanoes shows the linear arrangements of these systems.

(a)

(b)

Figure 9.2 (*a*) Surveying underwater topography (bathymetry) by means of shipborne sonar. (*b*) Bathymetry as portrayed on a typical echo-sounder record. The "scattering layer" may be due to a water temperature anomaly. (Source (*b*): Courtesy of Peter A. Rona, NOAA.)

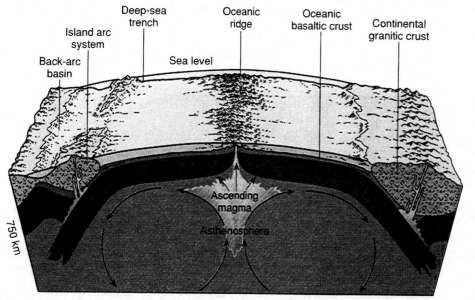

Figure 9.3 Magma rising from the asthenosphere forms new oceanic crust at the oceanic ridges.

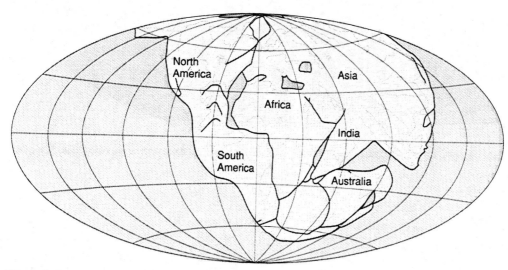

Figure 9.4 Wegener's Pangaea.

You may have noticed that the western edge of Africa and the eastern edge of South America make the two continents look remarkably like two separated puzzle pieces. Unlike the casual observer, Wegener followed his geologic impressions with fact finding.

He found that the Atlantic continental shelf edges of Africa and South America match even more closely than the present shorelines, which are subject to erosional and depositional changes as well as to changes in worldwide sea level. The edge of each continental shelf (see chapter 15), called the *shelf break*, represented the "true" continental boundary in his view. Wegener used such boundaries to reassemble the continents cartographically into one united landmass, the supercontinent he called **Pangaea,** or "all lands" (fig. 9.4).

Fossils played a key role in Wegener's research. He knew, for example, that fossilized palm trees occur in the rocks of Spitsbergen, an Arctic Ocean island covered by ice. The island houses fossils of temperate plants, too. Relatives of oak, maple, and beech trees also once grew in what must have been dramatically different climatic conditions on Spitsbergen. For Wegener, the presence of the fos-

Figure 9.5
(*a*) Fossil remains of the small, freshwater reptile *Mesosaurus*. (*b*) Artist's drawing of *Mesosaurus*.

Figure 9.6 (*a*) Fossil remains of the land plant *Glossopteris*. (*b*) Artist's drawing of *Glossopteris* leaves.

sils was evidence that the island had moved from tropic through temperate to its current boreal climate.

Wegener also used occurrences of similar fossils on the opposite sides of oceans to support his claim. Two groups of fossils in particular seemed to confirm his theory: fossils of a small reptile known as *Mesosaurus* (fig. 9.5) and fossils of the leaves of the plant *Glossopteris* (fig. 9.6).

The occurrence of similar fossils on different continents is significant because most animals and plants live in specific climates and habitats. *Mesosaurus,* for example, appears to have been a shallow-water swimmer, inhabiting lakes and estuaries similar to Chesapeake and Hudson Bays. Its lifestyle and habitat are inferred from its body structure and the types of rock in which it was fossilized. *Mesosaurus* apparently did not have the capability to cross a wide, deep ocean like the Atlantic, so its

range would have been limited. Although many animals do have wide ranges, the distribution of a species over Earth is usually limited by geologic and climatic barriers, such as ocean basins and deserts. *Mesosaurus* appears to have encountered no such barriers between the two continents—evidence, perhaps, that the continents were once linked and not separated by an ocean (fig. 9.7).

Plants are especially sensitive to climatic change. The redwoods of Oregon and California, for example, do not grow along the beaches of Florida, and palm trees do not grow in the Adirondacks. *Glossopteris* and related plants (collectively called the *Glossopteris* flora) grew in temperate, humid areas, probably in swampland, as long ago as the Permian Period, a geologic interval that began 285 million years ago and lasted 40 million years. Also, plants of similar age and distribution called

Figure 9.7 Distribution of *Mesosaurus* and *Glossopteris* fossils on a reconstructed southern supercontinent called Gondwanaland.

the *Gangamopteris* flora flourished before the supercontinent rifted into various landmasses. Today, these plant fossils occur in rocks found in areas with climates ranging from tropical to polar. These two floras have left fossils of 58 species of seed plants as evidence of continental separation and climatic change.

Regardless of the proof that both the shapes of continents and fossils provided, Wegener had difficulty convincing others of his theory of continental drift because he had proposed no credible mechanism, or process, that might have moved the landmasses. Without such a mechanism, the theory languished in the annals of science as an imaginative, but foolish, proposal. Continental drift received a further setback as late as the 1950s with the discovery of the undersea ridges. If the continents had drifted, some argued, their movements would have destroyed these large mountain systems.

Other Early Proofs for Continental Drift

Even the scientific efforts of Australian geologists, who accepted the theory of continental drift and the breakup of a southern supercontinent, called **Gondwanaland** by Edward Suess, did not convince the scientific community at large. Scientists from countries

(a)

(b)

Figure 9.8 (*a*) Location of evidence of late Paleozoic glaciation in the lands of the Southern Hemisphere. Arrows show direction of ice movement. Patterns in several instances indicate movement of ice from the oceans onto the surfaces of the continents, an impossible situation. (*b*) Glaciation patterns on the southern continents in their premovement locations. Glaciers moved outward from a central location on the reconstructed Southern supercontinent called Gondwanaland.
(Source: Arthur Holmes, *Principles of Physical Geology,* 2d ed. Copyright 1965 Ronald Press.)

in the Northern Hemisphere were particularly skeptical because geological evidence for continental movement was not striking there. South African geologist Alex du Toit also proposed the breakup of a supercontinent. Du Toit's evidence consisted of similarities he observed in the rocks and fossils of South Africa and Brazil and from a pattern of glacial till that encompasses parts of several Southern Hemisphere landmasses (fig. 9.8). Like Wegener, du Toit had no acceptable mechanism for the continental splitting and movement.

CONFIRMATION OF THE THEORY

Regardless of its quality, the work of Wegener, du Toit, and others during the early decades of the twentieth century remained in the background of mainstream earth studies until the late 1950s. Then, an explosion of information about Earth's crust became available through the concerted efforts of many scientists. In fact, investigating hypotheses about the dynamic nature of Earth's crust became an international cause for financing earth studies.

The Deep-Sea Drilling Project

One scientific breakthrough that earth scientists needed to accept the existence of ancient supercontinents and continental breakup came with the initial voyage of a research ship capable of drilling in deep water to recover cores of sediments and rocks. The Joint Oceanographic Institutions for Deep Earth Sampling (JOIDES) launched the *Glomar Challenger,* its primary research vessel, in March 1968, to begin a series of explorations of the ocean floor called the *Deep-Sea Drilling Project* (fig. 9.9).

Through their initial voyages, the ship's scientific crews provided two new bits of indirect, but convincing, evidence that the continents had moved. The first evidence was that the ocean floor was geologically young, everywhere less than 180 million years old. By comparison, some continental rocks approach 4 billion years in age. (Zircon crystals found in 1984 in the Acasta gneisses of Canada's Northwest Territories were radiometrically age-dated at 3.96 billion years.)

The second bit of evidence came from the relative dating of different areas of the ocean floor. The rocks and sediments that scientists cored near the axis, or center, of the oceanic ridge system appeared to be younger than those at increasing distances from the ridge—that is, the ocean floor became increasingly older away from the ridge axis. Apparently, the geologically young ocean floor was almost new at the ridge axis (fig. 9.10).

Seafloor Spreading: The Missing Mechanism

Harry Hess's proposal of crustal birth seemed to offer the mechanism that explained the ages of ocean floors and the movement of the continents. The apparent continental drift was the result of **seafloor spreading,** as it was termed in 1961 by R. S. Dietz, Hess's colleague. As new crustal material wells up from the mantle, the older material is pushed aside, constantly renewing the igneous rock at the axis by replacement.

Figure 9.9   The *Glomar Challenger.* This vessel had six computer-controlled engines that held it precisely on station over a drilling site. After 15 years of service, the *Challenger* was decommissioned and replaced by the JOIDES *Resolution.*

0–5 million years	38–53 million years
5–23 million years	53–65 million years
23–38 million years	65–135 million years

Figure 9.10   Plot of ages of oceanic crust in the southern Atlantic. The crustal rocks, cored by such ships as the *Glomar Challenger* and its successor, the JOIDES *Resolution,* have been dated through radiometric methods. Note the symmetrical distribution of ages about the central youngest rocks. (Source: After W. C. Pitman III, R. L. Larson, and E. M. Herron, Geological Society of America.)

Figure 9.11 Rifting of a continent. (*a*) Pressure from the upward movement of magma forms an area of upwarping within the continent. (*b*) Continued pressure generates a series of grabens and half-grabens (down-faulted blocks) that eventually fill with lava flows and volcanoes. (*c*) Movement of continental fragments and intrusion of oceanic crustal material (basalt and gabbro) form a small basin subject to flooding. Continued movement further enlarges (perhaps greatly) this embryonic ocean basin.

The seafloor spreading that moves the continents begins when a section of the crust succumbs to pressure from beneath, pressure exerted by a rising segment of a partially molten upper mantle. The uplift breaks, or "rifts," the crust, allowing volcanic flows and mountains to form in fault-bordered structures called *grabens* and *half-grabens* (fig. 9.11). The rifts occur on both seafloors and continents. When the latter occurs, a large continent can separate into two or more smaller landmasses, allowing seawater to fill the intervening, low-lying gap. A series of such rifts divided Wegener's Pangaea into today's continents. One of the larger rifts opened the Atlantic by separating the Americas from Africa and Europe, and another created the Indian Ocean. Aware of the consequences of rifting, contemporary earth scientists now study both continental and oceanic rift valleys to determine their

dynamic nature, the forces operating within the depths of the crust, and the history of crustal movements responsible for distributing the landmasses.

Two Rifts You Can Visit

One of the most studied crustal rifts occurs on Iceland, a land of significant volcanic and geothermal activity. The rift of the Mid-Atlantic Ridge extends through the Reykjanes Peninsula from southwest to northeast toward the Krafla shield volcano (fig. 9.12). Earth scientists, using lasers for precision in yearly surveys, have carefully measured the rate at which the rifting widens Iceland: Their studies reveal that Iceland is growing longitudinally about 1 centimeter per year. At its current rate of growth, Iceland will be 10 kilometers (6.2 mi) wider in a million years!

Iceland has been growing simultaneously with the formation of the Atlantic Ocean. A look back in time, therefore, reveals a world without the Atlantic and Iceland. Iceland formed through a series of volcanic eruptions that raised the oceanic ridge above sea level. In 1963, an example of Iceland's formation manifested itself in the eruption of Surtsey. Now a volcanic island just south of Iceland, Surtsey is a part of the oceanic ridge that stands above sea level (fig. 9.12). Continued volcanism in its vicinity could eventually produce another island similar to Iceland, one that will grow by the slow accumulation of basaltic lavas.

The East African rift system extends along the East African Plateau as a two-armed split in the continent (fig. 9.13). The western rift differs somewhat from its eastern counterpart, called the Kenya rift, generally as a result of an age difference. The Kenya rift opened about 23 million years ago, with the first volcanic events near the central plateau, according to C. J. Ebinger of the Massachusetts Institute of Technology. The western rift appears to be younger, about 12 million years old. Both arms seem to have propagated north to south, and both have associated volcanism in historic times. The Kenya rift includes the famous Mount Kilimanjaro of Tanzania. The western rift is filled with large lakes, including Lake Tanganyika. If the rifting continues for millions of years, seawater will eventually inundate the rift system, forming a new sea similar to the Red Sea.

Rifting and seafloor spreading appear to answer a number of questions, particularly those surrounding the occurrences of similar fossils on different continents and the varying ages of seafloor rocks. They do not, however, explain how the continents move without breaking into disparate pieces, all unconnected and grossly deformed.

CRUSTAL UNITS

If massive, rigid continents move, would they not constantly break into random pieces, even within their interiors? The theory that accounts for continental movement without much catastrophic destruction is the product of research by Daniel P. McKenzie and Robert L. Parker.

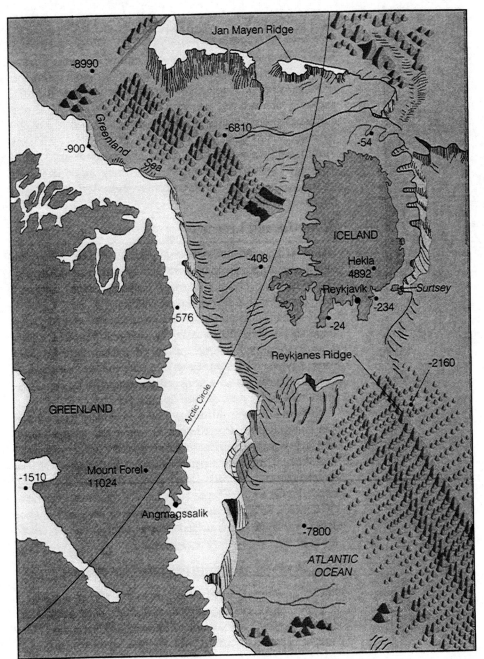

Figure 9.12 Iceland is located on the Reykjanes Ridge, a part of the Mid-Atlantic Ridge system. The small, recently formed volcanic island of Surtsey lies off the southeast coast. Elevations above sea level as well as bathymetry are indicated in feet.

The Plates

McKenzie and Parker postulated that the lithosphere consists of a series of movable, interlocking segments, which they named **plates.** These plates are of varying thicknesses: Some carry oceanic crust solely, while others underlie both oceanic and continental crust. The approximate thicknesses have been determined more recently through *seismic tomography,* which gives a three-dimensional view of Earth's interior (see chapter 8). The lithosphere has also been imaged through *electromagnetic induction* methods that use electrical conductivity, which is influenced by temperature, pore fluids, and the presence of conducting materials.

Plate Interactions: Divergence, Lateral Sliding, and Convergence

Plates can interact in one of three ways (fig. 9.14). In the first kind of interaction, plates separate from each other, or *diverge,* such as those on either side of the Reykjanes Peninsula and the East African rift. Divergence also occurs along the length of the oceanic ridge systems, such as the Mid-Atlantic Ridge (plate 1) and the Southwest Indian Ocean Ridge (plate 2).

In the second type of plate interaction, two plates laterally slide past each other, which is the geologic condition in California typified by the San Andreas Fault (see fig. 9.22). This type of interaction, generally known as transform faulting, produces numerous earthquakes that relieve the stress built up by the passing plates, whose rocks break along linear zones. Because plate boundaries can be complex, earthquakes in transform fault zones occur along many related faults, including some overthrust faults, such as the one that damaged Northridge, California (see chapter 8).

The third type of plate interaction involves plates colliding, or converging, driving massive sections of crust together, as the Nazca and South American plates do on the western side of South America (see fig. 9.25). Where an oceanic plate like the Nazca collides with the continental material of the South American plate, the denser oceanic crust underthrusts, or dives beneath, the continental crust in a process known as **subduction** (from the Latin for "lead under").

As the subducting crust moves beneath overlying material, it releases water to the overlying rock. Sources of water include water-bearing minerals (with hydroxyl groups), such as hornblende and the micas, that are present in subducting crustal material and that give up their water at temperatures between 700 and 1,300° C in a process known as "dewatering." Marine sediments and saturated crust being carried downward on the subducting plate also add water that enhances this "wet melting." Another "volatile" compound that contributes to the melting of rock is carbon dioxide. Much of the partial melting occurs in the plastic layer known as the asthenosphere. This chemically uncombined water penetrates the overlying rock and reduces its melting temperature. In response to this infiltrating water, the overlying rock partially melts. Because of different constituent minerals and varying pressures, the

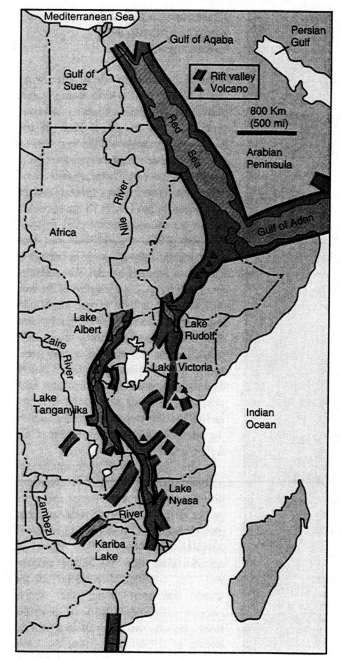

Figure 9.13 The East African rift is actually a bifurcated (two-branched) rift.

Plate Tectonics: A Unifying Theory

Each movement of the crustal plates "builds" a geologic feature. This building led to another refinement of the initial continental drift theory, which is now known as plate tectonics because of the geologic "architecture" generated by plate movements. In plate collisions, mountains (Himalayas), volcanic chains (Cascades), volcanic islands (Aleutians), and deep-sea trenches (Marianas) form. Finally, in the lateral sliding that moves one plate past its neighbor, faults act as the slip surfaces along which sections of rock pass others in the spastic earth movements we know as faulting (San Andreas Fault).

Tectonics and Linearity

The linearity evident in mountain systems, volcanic chains, and earthquake zones now makes sense in light of plate movements. The linearity is a reflection of plate boundaries, where divergence, convergence, and sliding occur (fig. 9.15).

To outline plate positions, McKenzie and Parker used plots of moderate and large earthquakes for a 10-year period. The locations demonstrated the linear nature of most earthquake zones. Since they assumed that plate movement generated earthquakes, both men suggested that seismic activity outlined plate boundaries, where most of the tectonic activity would occur.

The movements of the plates seemed evident wherever the plates separated. Charles Richter, for whom the seismic magnitude scale is named, and Beno Gutenberg noted that the axis of the Mid-Atlantic Ridge is the site of numerous earthquakes. Because the orientation of the rifts along a central axis generally extends perpendicular to the direction of seafloor spreading, scientists could more easily plot the trends for some of the plates, such as those of the South American and African plates, which figure 9.10 shows in successive stages of separation.

Past, Present, and Future Plate Movements

Other plates, however, did not appear to move so predictably, or their boundaries were questionable. Because plate interactions cause earthquakes and volcanism, knowing the orientation of the boundaries provides scientists with information relevant to the prediction of regions with a potential for disasters. Present plate movements also provide clues to both past and future movements. For scientists, however, predictions are an inadequate substitute for the truth. Determining the past movements of the plates, particularly the movements of the continents, required the approach of a new scientific discipline: *paleomagnetic studies.*

Paleomagnetism and Plate Movements

Evidence for the continental movements came in a roundabout way from the study of Earth's magnetic field and the magnetism captured in rocks. As magma cools, individual mineral crystals form and grow in the magma. When the temperature of the cooling mass falls below a certain temperature for that mineral, known as the *Curie point,* the magnetic properties of the growing mineral crystals become fixed, aligned parallel to the direction of Earth's magnetic field as it occurs at that time. Each individual mineral has its own

melting is not complete. Physical evidence for partial, rather than total, melting comes from the passage of seismic S-waves that would die out if they encountered a completely liquid layer.

Partial melting may lead to the formation of large magmatic intrusions and to volcanoes (fig. 9.14*e*). In this manner, the andesitic volcanoes of the Aleutians, the Japanese islands, the Andes, and the Cascades have formed. Large batholiths like the Sierra Nevada of California and the White Mountains of New Hampshire have also been emplaced because of subduction and the consequent partial melting.

Figure 9.14   Plate boundaries. (*a*) Divergent-oceanic. (*b*) Divergent-continental. (*c*) Continent-continent convergent. (*d*) Ocean-continent convergent. (*e*) Ocean-ocean convergent. (*f*) Transform fault. In (*e*), the downgoing slab loses water in a process called dewatering. The released water reduces the melting point of the overlying rock, which then undergoes a partial melting, becomes lighter, and rises to form volcanoes.

Plate 1   Atlantic Ocean floor. (World Ocean Floor map by Bruce C. Heezen and Marie Tharp, 1977. Copyright © 1977 Marie Tharp. Reproduced by permission of Marie Tharp, 1 Washington Ave., South Nyack, N.Y. 10960.)

Plate 2   Indian Ocean floor. (World Ocean Floor map by Bruce C. Heezen and Marie Tharp, 1977. Copyright © 1977 Marie Tharp. Reproduced by permission of Marie Tharp, 1 Washington Ave., South Nyack, N.Y. 10960).

characteristic Curie point. Once the entire rock mass solidifies, the orientation of the magnetic domains within the mineral crystals can no longer change, even if the orientation of Earth's magnetic field changes. The direction of Earth's magnetic field at the time of rock formation thus becomes imprinted on the rock and preserved for millions of years. This ancient magnetism is called **paleomagnetism** (from the Greek *palaio,* meaning "ancient"). The individual mineral crystals not only point the direction to the magnetic poles, but they also are inclined to the horizontal because the lines of magnetic force that compose Earth's magnetic field change ori-

entation with respect to the horizontal as one follows them from magnetic equator to magnetic pole. They are horizontal at the magnetic equator and are inclined ever more steeply toward the poles, becoming vertical at the magnetic poles. (An ordinary compass needle behaves the same way. At any location within North America, for example, the needle would be pointing downward at some angle. The needle remains horizontal within the compass case only because one end has been weighted to counteract the normal downward tendency.)

Plate 3   Pacific Ocean floor. (World Ocean Floor map by Bruce C. Heezen and Marie Tharp, 1977. Copyright © 1977 by Marie Tharp. Reproduced by permission of Marie Tharp, 1 Washington Ave., South Nyack, N.Y. 10960).

Figure 9.15   Crustal plates and their relative movements (indicated by arrows). Plate movements have been determined on a large scale, but "microplates" may operate in such areas as southern California and Central America. (Source: After W. Hamilton, U.S. Geological Society.)

Figure 9.16   Earth's magnetosphere and the magnetic lines of force. A volcanic eruption on the equator (location *1*) produces lava, the iron-bearing minerals of which align themselves parallel to the lines of magnetic force of the dipole magnetic field. The dip of the lines of magnetic force, and thus of these minute "compass needles," increases toward the poles, as can be seen at locations *2* and *3*.

The Magnetic Recording Mechanism

The oxide magnetite, a common mineral found in many rocks, aligns itself on the atomic level to Earth's prevailing magnetism. The alignment can occur during the formation of plutonic and volcanic rocks as they cool through magnetite's Curie point (578° C or 1,072° F). It can also result from the orientation that settling flakes of magnetite take when they are washed into the sediments of quiet waters, such as lakes.

Earth acts like a giant *dipole* magnet, with the lines of force exiting the Southern Hemisphere, where the south magnetic pole is located, and entering at the north magnetic pole (fig. 9.16). The lines are invisible, but they are the force that directs a compass needle toward the north magnetic pole, which is located on Bathurst Island in northern Canada. Thus, following a compass needle does not lead you to the North Pole on the axis of planetary rotation, but it does take you to magnetic north. The magnetic force lines encompass the planet as an

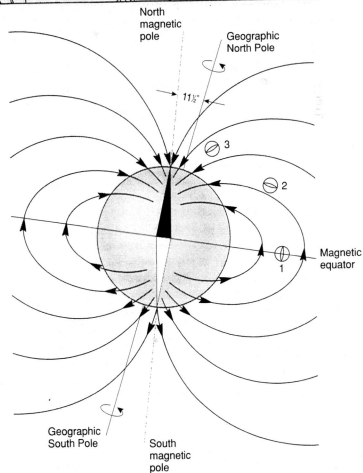

asymmetrical *magnetosphere*. (It is this magnetosphere that directs the solar wind to generate the northern lights, while the sun's corpuscular radiation shapes the field lines into an asymmetrical form.)

A hardened lava in the vicinity of the equator should exhibit an almost horizontal magnetic alignment, while one in British Columbia should reveal a dipping alignment. The direction of dip depends on the relative locations of the magnetic poles and the hardening magma. Exceptions to this general rule on magnetic alignment do occur, however, and these exceptions are highly significant.

In numerous instances throughout the world, older rocks have shown magnetic alignments, or *declinations,* that are *not* parallel to the lines of force in Earth's magnetosphere. Using magnetometers to study the magnetism captured in rocks of various types and ages, scientists discovered a magnetic mystery. Not only do some rocks exhibit an alignment oriented away from the present magnetosphere, but they also point magnetically to the Southern Hemisphere.

Anomalous Magnetic Readings and Magnetic Reversals

A number of earth scientists took up the challenge of explaining the strange magnetic readings of some rocks. Among them were three Americans—Brent Dalrymple, Allan Cox, and Richard Doell—who asked themselves whether or not the magnetism captured by the rock was the result of special minerals that would adopt a magnetic alignment opposite that of the prevailing field. They soon realized that the minerals were not in themselves responsible for the differences in magnetic alignments. Instead, they recognized that the geomagnetic field had reversed itself: *The north magnetic pole had actually lain in the Southern Hemisphere* (fig. 9.17).

By dating the volcanic rocks through radiometric methods, these American scientists and others around the world set out to determine the time of the most recent *magnetic reversal*. According to the best estimates, the north magnetic pole was actually in the Southern Hemisphere about 800,000 years ago. At that time, it appears to have reversed itself, or flipped, into the Northern Hemisphere. The time of the "flip," which includes the present, has been called the Brunhes Normal epoch. Throughout geologic time, each reversal has ushered in a new geomagnetic epoch, which the rocks have recorded (fig. 9.18).

Remember that the development of plate-tectonic theory required the work of numerous scientists in different fields. The work on paleomagnetic reversals was just one more step in the transformation of hypothesis to theory. It provided the framework that allowed scientists to tie a number of discrete facts together in a unified theory. The geomagnetic reversal scale made possible another discovery, which supported the seafloor-spreading theory, and helped to trace the paleodirections of the plates and their continents.

Polar Reversals As Evidence for Seafloor Spreading

When British scientist Drummond Matthews made a magnetic map of an oceanic ridge—the Juan de Fuca Ridge—by trailing a magnetometer behind a ship, he discovered something unexpect-

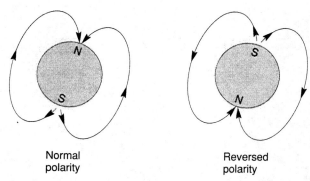

Normal polarity   Reversed polarity

Figure 9.17   (*a*) The current (normal) geomagnetic field and (*b*) a reversed field.

Figure 9.18   Geomagnetic polarity time scale for the past 4.5 million years. Ages have been determined by the potassium-argon (K-Ar) age-dating technique. (Reprinted with permission from Allan V. Cox, "Geomagnetic Reversals," *Science* 163:240, 1969. Copyright 1969 The American Association for the Advancement of Science.)

Figure 9.19 Magnetic anomalies of the Juan de Fuca Ridge. The alternating black and white zones represent the magnetic readings for strips of ocean floor rock. The "zebra" pattern shows a set of magnetic and nonmagnetic stripes.
(Source: After A. D. Raff and R. G. Mason, "A Magnetic Survey of the West Coast of North America, 40N to 52½° N," *Bulletin of the Geological Society of America,* vol. 72, 1260.)

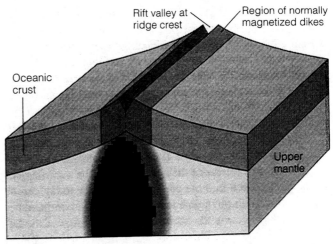

(a) Time of normal magnetism

(b) Time of reverse magnetism

(c) Time of normal magnetism

Figure 9.20 Formation of magnetic "anomalies" by the process of seafloor spreading. (*a–c*) Oceanic crust is continuously moved away from the oceanic ridge axis as new crustal material is emplaced.

ed. The magnetic map of the ocean floor was mystifying to Matthews and others because it recorded "stripes" of apparently nonmagnetized rock (fig. 9.19). The nonmagnetized rock, lying next to the magnetized rock, seemed inexplicable, so the magnetic readings for these apparently nonmagnetized rocks were called "magnetic anomalies," and they remained a mystery for about 10 years.

Typical of the interrelationships found among the various earth science disciplines, those between geomagnetic research and the budding studies of seafloor spreading led to an important discovery. When Allan Cox and others defined the magnetic reversals, they laid the groundwork for the resolution of the irregular magnetism Drummond Matthews had found. Taking the paleomagnetic evidence of reversals and the model of seafloor spreading devised by Harry Hess, British researcher Fred Vine determined that the stripes the magnetometer had recorded were actually evidence for seafloor spreading and magnetic reversals.

According to Vine, as the newly formed crust captured the prevailing geomagnetic field, it was moved aside, giving way to more crust, which recorded a different magnetism. The mapping stripes were actually magnetizations aligned to the two hemispheres. Those that align to a north magnetic pole in the Northern Hemisphere are *normally* aligned, whereas those pointing to a north magnetic pole in the Southern Hemisphere are *reversely* magnetized (fig. 9.20).

The credence that Vine's explanation of the magnetic anomalies lent to the seafloor-spreading hypothesis was only part of the benefit derived from his work. Vine also provided scientists with a mechanism for determining the relative motions of the continents.

Still called anomalies in spite of his explanation, the magnetic stripes of different ocean-floor rocks established the pathways for the movements of the crustal plates. The separation of Wegener's Pangaea into the continents we know today can be traced backward through time to recreate the supercontinent before its breakup during the Mesozoic Era, or the Age of the Dinosaurs (see fig. 9.10). The colors in figure 9.10 are parallel on either side of the spreading center, or ridge axis, because the rocks emerged simultaneously from the central rift, and as they cooled, captured the prevailing geomagnetic field. Radiometric dating of the rocks permits the assignment of the ages shown.

THE MOVEMENT OF INDIA: A TECTONIC HISTORY

The complexity of plate movements is nowhere more evident than in the path of the Indo-Australian plate, which carries the two landmasses for which it is named. Since the breakup of Pangaea, India has rotated and moved at varying rates on an eventual collision course with southern Asia (fig. 9.21).

Beginning about 70 million years ago, the Indian subcontinent moved northward relatively quickly for about 15 million years. Rapid movement in tectonic terms is about 15 centimeters (5.85 in) per year. During the ensuing 15-million-year period, its movement slowed, as India probably encountered an island arc in its path. From about 55 to 40 million years ago, according to Australian earth scientist C. McA. Powell, the subcontinent rotated counterclockwise toward Africa. For some unknown reason, India resumed its northward movement about 40 million years ago and, at the same time, changed the direction of its rotation. During this renewal of movement, the northwestern boundary of the Indo-Australian plate progressed northward at about 3 centimeters (1.2 in) per year. Some 20 million years ago, India's convergence with Asia was expressed in a squeezing of Iran and Afghanistan, two smaller continental masses that lay to the northwest between India and more massive continental material. Sporadic seafloor spreading over millions of years produced the current configuration of the Indian Ocean.

Turning an Ocean Basin into a Mountain Range

The convergence of India and Asia continues even today as the subcontinent builds the Himalayas higher and causes earthquakes throughout Asia. The earthquake and mountain-building activities, however, are just part of India's 70-million-year history. The path of the Indo-Australian plate carried India 2,000 kilometers (1,243 mi) and over the site of an ancient tropical sea, the **Tethys**, closing it and elevating the rocks of the converging plates to form the mountain range that includes the world's two highest peaks: Mount Everest and K2.

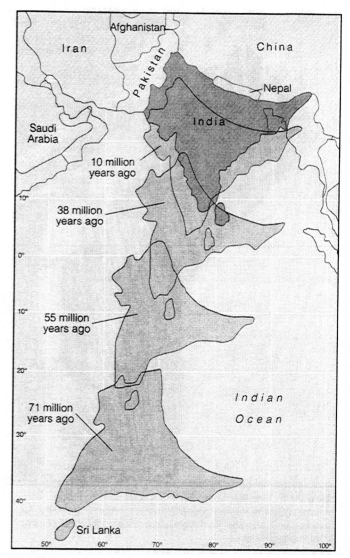

Figure 9.21 Movement of the Indian subcontinent over the past 70 million years, based on the magnetic anomalies in the Indian Ocean floor. (Drawn with permission from P. Molnar, "Cenozoic Tectonics of Asia: Effects of a Continental Collision" in *Science,* vol. 189, pp. 419–26, 1975. Copyright 1975 American Association for the Advancement of Science.)

Producing the mountains required shortening and buckling Earth's crust. Forming the Himalayas, therefore, probably resulted in 300 to 500 kilometers (186 to 310 mi) of *crustal shortening.* In Pakistan, the energy of India's movement shortened the crust by producing a belt of folded mountains. You can visualize this process by placing a sheet of paper on a table, then sliding its two ends toward each other. The "fold" in the paper is analogous to the shortening and mountain-building process.

As the Indo-Australian plate continues its northward movement, it pushes itself beneath the southern end of Asia in the process of underthrusting called subduction. If the plate were fully oceanic (basaltic), it would tend to sink into the mantle. Because India is continental and of a lower density than basalt, however, it has a tendency to "float on" rather than sink into the asthenosphere. The convergence that is forcing northern India downward, therefore, has created a continuously thickening continental area and raised the height of the Himalayas. Continental thicknesses average about 35 kilometers (21.7 mi), but the Tibetan Plateau is now approximately twice that thickness.

Additional Evidence for India's Movement

Evidence for India's movement lies in both the earthquakes that shake China and in a series of ocean-floor and continental features. India's northward movement has generated devastating earthquakes in China. One of the most catastrophic of these occurred in 1976, when the city of Tangshan was hit by an earthquake with a magnitude of 7.6 (see box 8.2). Because the Indo-Australian plate continues to move, other, similarly catastrophic earthquakes will occur within the region.

This release of kinetic energy is not the only proof for the plate's movement. Features on the ocean floor and on the subcontinent of India also provide evidence for tectonic activity. The Indian Ocean, like the Pacific and the Atlantic, has a curving oceanic ridge that trends from south to northwest; then its rift valley exits the Indian Ocean and enters the Gulf of Aden, the Red Sea, and the Dead Sea. On the eastern side of this spreading center is an oceanic plateau that traces the subcontinent's movement. The basaltic Chagos-Laccadive Plateau is a series of volcanic piles that formed over a magma chamber as the plate moved northward. Its slightly curved shape may reflect India's counterclockwise rotation and mark an ancient transform fault. The Deccan Traps (see chapter 7), a high basaltic plateau on India, also appears to be related to the plate movement. The basaltic flows spread over the land through fissures in response to the rifting of Pangaea. Similar flows of basaltic magma occurred in the Americas during the initial rifting of the supercontinent.

TRANSFORM BOUNDARIES

Crustal units can also slide past each other in a movement that has dire consequences for inhabitants along the interplate boundaries. In 1906, such sliding devastated San Francisco, and a similar action caused the October 1989 Loma Prieta earthquake.

In fact, one of the best examples of lateral sliding between plates occurs in California, site of the famous San Andreas Fault, the division between the North American and Pacific plates. The San Andreas is the main fault in a system of faults that begins where Baja California separates from the mainland of Mexico. The fault system extends past Los Angeles and then exits the continent north of San Francisco. It is a deep split, developed vertically into the crust, between two plates. Its vertical extent was highlighted during the 1989 earthquake, when scientists traced the focus of the Loma Prieta earthquake to a depth of 16 kilometers (10 mi).

The San Andreas belongs to a class of faults known as *transform faults*. These faults, first identified in 1965 by Canadian geologist J. Tuzo Wilson, are the locations of lateral movements between adjacent plates. Most transform faults lie along the ocean-

Figure 9.22   San Andreas Fault system.

ic ridges and extend perpendicular to the ridge axis, but some do not have a conspicuous relationship with a spreading center. One of those faults not readily associated with an oceanic ridge is the San Andreas. The Pacific plate moves northwestward relative to the North American plate along the San Andreas Fault, producing earthquakes, subsidiary faults, and mountains (fig. 9.22).

SEAFLOOR FEATURES AND PLATE TECTONICS

A number of seafloor features associated with plate tectonics have been identified through detailed mapping beginning with and subsequent to the IGY.

Patterns of Volcanism

At some localities on the ocean floor itself, volcanoes form a similar linear series on either side of a spreading center. The volcanoes are progressively older away from the spreading center (fig. 9.23). The interpretation of the origin of these features is that they form from magma that is brought up from depth and erupted along the axis of the spreading center. New material coming from depth and emplaced along the axis pushes the older material (volcanoes) away from the oceanic-ridge axis (spreading center). With time, the volcanoes are moved progressively farther away from the ridge axis in both directions.

(a)

(b)

Continental crust

Oceanic crust

(c)

Figure 9.23 (*a–c*) Volcanoes become progressively older as they are carried away from their site of formation along the oceanic ridge (location *1*).

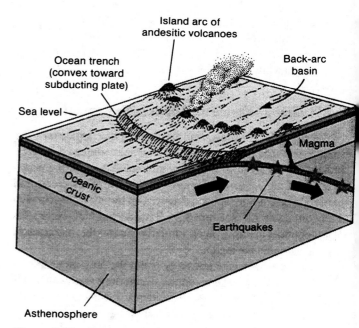

Figure 9.24 The generalized scheme of any island arc/trench system. On the landward side of the island arc lies a back-arc basin, which receives sediments from the continent.

Bathymetry

Because upward pressure is greatest directly beneath the spreading center, the crust is upwarped most where the ridge buildup occurs. Away from the rift, the seafloor begins to subside. John G. Sclater and others have postulated that four factors are responsible for this subsidence:

1. The movement away from the concentrated upward pressure beneath the ridge axis reduces the upwarping.
2. The volcanic crustal rock cools and contracts.
3. The great volume of volcanic and plutonic rocks piled onto a young and thin oceanic crust initiates a downwarping.
4. The oceanic rock is the recipient of sediments that originate as the hard parts of life-forms in the pelagic waters. The

sediments accumulate slowly, with maximum rates rarely exceeding 21 meters (69 ft) per million years; yet, over many millions of years, they can add up to a considerable weight on the crust.

Trenches

Convergence of oceanic crust and continental crust usually leads to the destruction of the thinner and denser oceanic material through subduction. The subduction zone is associated with frequent earthquakes along deep **trenches** (fig. 9.24). The sinking crust begins to break up and partially melt beneath the lighter and thicker continent. The partially melted crust shudders at all levels, and earthquake foci show a pattern of increasing depths beneath the adjacent continent. A good example of such activities occurs along the western coast of South America in the vicinity of the Peru-Chile Trench (fig. 9.25). The trench exceeds a depth of 6.5 kilometers (4 mi) and is the site of the shallowest earthquakes. Farther inland beneath South America and the Andes Mountains, the foci are deeper.

Trenches vary in bathymetry, and the Peru-Chile Trench shoals in some places, notably where an oceanic plateau like the Juan Fernandez Ridge lies off the coast. The significance of trenches lies in their role in seafloor destruction. It is subduction in trench areas that eliminates "old" ocean floor.

Island Arcs

In some instances, particularly on the western and northern edges of the Pacific plate, a subduction zone is bounded on the landward side by a series of volcanic islands in an arc. The **island arcs** of the Pacific include the Tonga-Kermadec Islands, the Japanese Islands, and the Aleutians. The islands are subject to numerous earthquakes

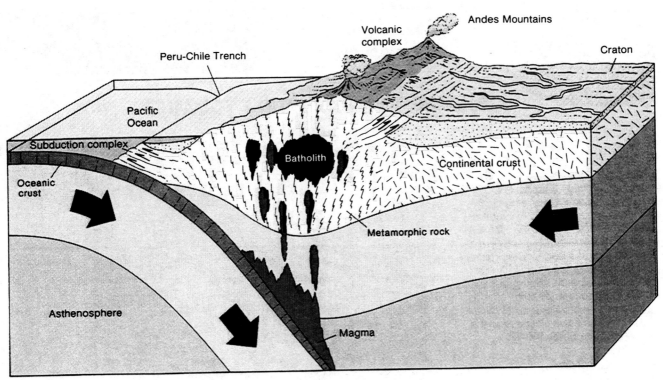

Figure 9.25   The Peru-Chile Trench is part of the grand architecture of plate movements.

Figure 9.26   The Emperor Seamounts and the Hawaiian Island chain. The most recent volcanism occurs on Hawaii and on an undersea volcano called Loihi. As the Pacific plate continues to move toward the northwest, the Hawaiian Island volcanoes Kilauea and Mauna Loa (noted with triangles in the inset) will move off the hot spot, leaving Loihi to be built above sea level as the next island in the chain. (Source: After I. McDougall, 1964, *Geological Society of America Bulletin*.)

and eruptions, such as the most recent volcanic activity in the Aleutians. Generally, the island arcs are built from the andesitic lavas that result from the partial melting of oceanic rock and sediments in the subduction zones. Such lavas are intermediate in composition between rhyolite and basalt. (See box 9.1 on page 232.)

Seamounts

Another product of plate activity are **seamounts,** which are volcanic piles that do not reach the ocean surface. Most seamounts occur in groups, such as those off the eastern coast of North America, and some make up linear systems, such as the Emperor Seamounts of the western Pacific. At one time, some of these seamounts may have been islands, but the inevitable subsidence of the oceanic crust caused all to sink below sea level.

The linearity of the Emperor Seamounts begins at the end of the Hawaiian Island chain, just northwest of Midway Island (fig. 9.26). The Hawaiian system is also linear, but both it and the Emperor Seamounts lie on the Pacific plate, far from the plate's edges, where volcanism and earthquake activity is most likely. Why, then, are these volcanic piles where they are?

Box 9.1

Investigating the Environment

LISTENING TO AN ERUPTING VOLCANO

On January 19, 1993, scientists using SOFAR channel (see chapter 14) hydrophones located near Oahu, Hawaii, detected intense acoustical activity centered on a site about 200 kilometers (124 mi) southwest of the western side of the Rivera fracture zone (figs. 9.A and 9.B). Acoustic signals are now being used to identify submarine volcanic activity throughout the Pacific. Hydrophones located at the Laboratoire de Géophysique in Tahiti recently discovered a new volcano near the Eltanin fracture zone (54°S, 140°W).

Apply Your Knowledge

1. Would volcanic activity be common or rare on the ocean floor?
2. Why would some areas of the ocean floor be more likely sites of volcanic activity than others?

Figure 9.A   The volcanic activity detected by hydroacoustic instruments is associated with a chain of seamounts.

Figure 9.B   Eruption signals from suspected submarine volcanic activity in the Islas de Revillagigedo region at about 18.75° N, 110.8° W. These signals were recorded on January 19, 1993, by a SOFAR channel hydrophone (Kaneohe hydrophone 13SP) near Oahu at a distance of about 4,400 kilometers (2,728 mi) from the suspected eruption site. The intense episodes of unusual activity lasted for about 1 hour.

Hot-Spot Volcanoes

Just as the Chagos-Laccadive Plateau appears to mark the path of the Indo-Australian plate and the subcontinent of India, so the Hawaiian Islands and the Emperor Seamounts may plot the direction of the Pacific plate's movements. Since no rift valley is associated with these features in either ocean, however, another mechanism must be responsible for the string of volcanoes.

The Kilauea volcano on the island of Hawaii has erupted almost continuously for the past 40 years. After a few inactive years, the volcano releases great quantities of lava through fissures along its flanks, building the shield ever larger. Kilauea's sister volcano, Mauna Loa, the largest mountain on Earth, has also erupted recently. Both lie at the southeastern end of the

Box 9.2

COULD SEAFLOOR SPREADING INITIATE AN EL NIÑO EVENT?

In box 6.2, you learned about the El Niño/Southern Oscillation (ENSO) and associated changes in world weather patterns. It now appears that seafloor-spreading activity may be related to the warming of ocean water that is known as El Niño. Scientists aboard the *RV Melville* recently discovered 1,133 seamounts and volcanic cones covering 88,700 square kilometers (34,238 sq. mi) in the vicinity of Easter Island (fig. 9.C). According to Dr. Ken Macdonald of the University of California at Santa Barbara, two or three of the volcanoes could be active simultaneously.

The southeastern Pacific location of these volcanoes suggests that they may have some effect on the ENSO phenomenon. When a volcano erupts, it pumps heat into the surrounding environment. Numerous erupting volcanoes may sufficiently warm ocean water to initiate a change in the Southern Oscillation and to begin an El Niño event.

Apply Your Knowledge

1. What oceanic ridge is associated with the Easter Island volcanoes?
2. How could scientists keep track of underwater volcanic activity?
3. How could scientists relate an ENSO event and volcanic activity?

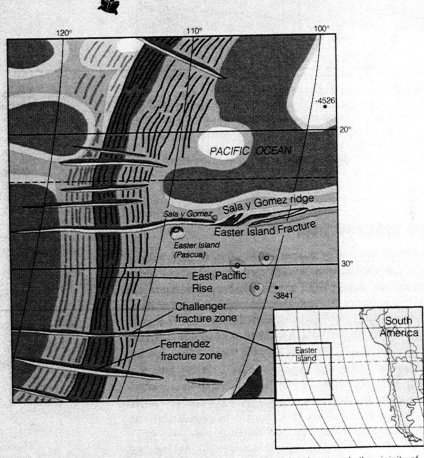

Figure 9.C   Scientists have discovered seamounts and volcanic cones in the vicinity of Easter Island.

Hawaiian Island chain. Yet, on Midway Island, one of the most northwesterly islands of the chain, no volcanism has occurred for more than 20 million years.

The explanation for both the linearity and the volcanism lies in stationary **hot spots,** magma chambers located in the asthenosphere. As a plate passes over a hot spot, the rising magma produces a sequence of volcanoes in a line that traces crustal movement. The great depth of the magma chamber can be inferred from its stationary nature: Plate movement seems to have no effect on the hot spot's location. Because the vol-

canoes sit on the plate, they move with it, passing away from their source of lava. Midway, a relatively low island, is more than 25 million years old, and its volcanism ceased when it moved off the hot spot responsible for its formation. Prior to the formation of the Hawaiian Island chain, the Pacific plate must have moved more north than west, as evidenced by the orientation of the Emperor Seamounts. The date for the directional change in plate motion would coincide, therefore, with the oldest features of the Hawaiian Island chain and the youngest of the Emperor Seamounts. (See box 9.2.)

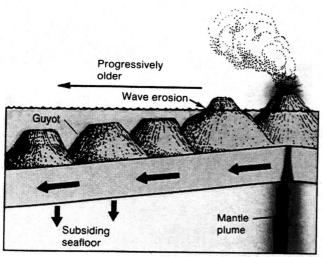

Figure 9.27 Movement of a plate across a mantle plume produces a linear succession of volcanic cones. The upper portions of the cones may be planed off by wave erosion. When combined with the continued subsidence of the seafloor, this erosion forms a flat-topped, submerged feature known as a guyot. In tropical climates, coral development takes place when the volcanic cone is still above, at, or just below sea level.

Guyots and Coral Atolls

As volcanoes move off a hot-spot locality, they begin to subside and to be attacked above sea level by the processes of weathering and erosion (see chapter 10). The islands in the northwestern part of the Hawaiian chain are much lower and more eroded than those in the southeastern part. Unseen beneath the water are former islands that have subsided through the zone of wave action in these tropical waters. Coral reefs formed on the fringes of the volcano tops when the islands were close to sea level. As the volcanoes subsided, these coral reefs formed islands called **atolls** (see chapter 15). With further subsidence, the underlying volcanoes carried their carbonate caps too deep for coral life, becoming relatively flat-topped, subsided features, now called **guyots** (fig. 9.27). Wherever subsided volcanoes formed in waters too cold for coral development, no carbonate cap tops the guyots.

TERRANES AND THE GROWTH OF CONTINENTS

One of the consequences of plate movements is the welding of different crustal pieces called **terranes.** Geologists have identified a series of adjacent, but unrelated, rock units from the northwestern United States to Alaska (fig. 9.28). The types of rocks, fossils, and ages for these units are so radically different that their only explanation must lie in diverse origins.

Plate movements frequently combine pieces of crustal rocks and add to the size and volume of the continents. Western North America is largely a product of such crustal welding, but other areas, such as Newfoundland, have also grown through the addition of terranes. The probable sequence for the accretion of the terranes begins in the movement of the continent itself. As North

Figure 9.28 Terranes of western North America.

America moved against the ancestral Pacific Ocean, it collided with a series of island arcs, each of which lay on the landward side of a subduction zone. The oceanic rocks of western Idaho, which now lie hundreds of kilometers inland, represent one of the ancient boundaries between the ocean and the continent. Similar collisions have added to the size of other continents. Therefore, locating the boundaries of the terranes also means finding the ancient coast of a continent.

Along the western side of the Sierra Nevada in California (see fig. 7.16b) is an elongate region called the Foothills terrane (fig. 9.29). This terrane exemplifies the difficulties that terranes can pre-

Figure 9.29 The Foothills terrane of the central Sierra Nevada contains rocks of varying ages and compositions. The youngest rocks are 114 million years old, whereas the oldest are plutonic rocks 151 million years old. The complexity of the terrane's composition and history makes geologic interpretation difficult. Gabbro, granite, schist, sandstone, and volcanic rocks all lie in close proximity. Fault zones, such as the Bear Mountains fault zone and Melones fault zone, add to the complexity. Island arc rocks, marked by a "V" pattern, lie north and south of the Santa Cruz Mountain pluton. "Ma" indicates millions of years ago.

sent to earth scientists trying to interpret an area's past tectonic activity. The Foothills terrane consists of igneous, metamorphic, and sedimentary rocks that appear to have been, at least in part, associated with an island arc. Some of the terrane's igneous rocks are volcanic, whereas others are plutonic; some are basaltic, while others are granitic. Metamorphic rocks in the Foothills terrane also vary greatly, indicating a complex baking process. Faults and other geologic structures make this approximately 250-kilometer-(155-mi) long stretch of land very difficult to interpret geologically. The complexity of the Foothills terrane does provide a lesson. Past tectonic activity, just like the current activity, is not a simple process involving a few large plates moving in an orderly fashion.

PLATE TECTONICS AND MINERAL RESOURCES

One of the most studied terranes lies in the Mediterranean Sea on the island of Cyprus. The Troodos Massif is an *ophiolite*, or a section of ocean crust that was broken off from the subducting

plate and emplaced onto the island in a process called *obduction*. Evidence for its identity as a fragment of the ocean floor lies in both rock type and form: Some of the igneous rocks of the massif are basaltic lavas of submarine origin.

Since Roman times, the Troodos Massif has been a mining site for copper and other metals. The occurrence of the metals seems to be associated with the origin of the rock itself. Whenever tectonic activity is associated with magma chambers, metallic salts are precipitated out of hot fluids to form **hydrothermal deposits** (see chapter 16). Seawater circulating through cavities near the magma chamber dissolves these minerals and carries the ions away from the hot rock, to deposit them later.

Knowing where ancient sites of convergence and divergence occurred gives clues to the presence of mineral resources. The reverse can also be helpful. For example, Alfred Wegener used similarities between the diamond mines of Brazil and South Africa to provide evidence for his continental drift theory.

Figure 9.30 This deep-sea hydrothermal vent discharges water, dissolved minerals, and metals into the surrounding environment. The discharges of some vents are black, while others are white or clear.

The discovery of deep-sea volcanic fissures and vents, where water in excess of 300° C (572° F) boils up through chimneys of sulfide deposits, confirmed the role of tectonics in metallic deposit formation (fig. 9.30). The vents are active for a few hundred years at most, but during their short lives, they act as release valves for heated water, which circulates through the ocean's volcanic floor. The hot water picks up dissolved mineral matter and redeposits it in the vicinity of the vent. Some of the metals may circulate throughout the bottom water of the ocean to precipitate elsewhere in the form of oval or spherical *nodules* and encrustations rich in manganese, iron, copper, and other metals.

FURTHER THOUGHTS: A PARADIGM

*R*ejection of the hypothesis of continental drift by his contemporaries did not deter Alfred Wegener from pursuing a scientific explanation for Earth's features. Unfortunately, much of his work received the same response from the following generation, and our current scientific explanations for the shapes and locations of the continents and oceans did not gain acceptance until the second half of the twentieth century.

Wegener's experience with rejection was not an exception in the history of science. Almost every advance in scientific understanding has met similar rejection because each upset the intellectual status quo. Once a model of Earth gains acceptance, it offers a secure basis on which humans can organize the diversity of the planet. Wegener laid the groundwork for a **paradigm,** a model so significant that it overturned the organizing principles of a previous scientific explanation. Because the plate-tectonic model of Earth does not explain all features and processes, it may eventually give way to another paradigm. When that paradigm is offered, will it encounter the same scientific inertia that Wegener's idea of continental drift met?

SIGNIFICANT POINTS

1. Plate tectonics is currently the most unifying geophysical theory of the planet. It is based on the interaction between Earth's interior and its outer shell.

2. A series of hypotheses formulated by scientists of diverse fields combined interrelated observational data to create a new model of the planet.

3. The basic principle of plate-tectonic theory is simple: Lithospheric plates move, break up, collide, and slide past one another to form new continents and oceans.

4. The result of plate movement is the creation of oceans where continents rift. Mountain ranges, volcanic islands, and deep-sea trenches result where collisions take place.

5. Plate movement is a direct result of convection currents within Earth's asthenosphere exerting pressure against the bottom of the lithosphere.

6. The idea of continental drift (continents moving from their initial positions) was suggested by Alfred Wegener, a result of his observation that the Atlantic continental shelf edges of Africa and South America matched closely.

7. Each continental shelf, or shelf break, represents the "true" continental boundary, since shorelines are subject to erosional and depositional changes. Wegener used such boundaries to reassemble the continents cartographically into one united landmass, the supercontinent he called Pangaea.

8. The occurrence of similar fossils on different continents is significant, since the distribution of a species is limited by geologic and climatic barriers.

9. The oceanic floor is geologically young in comparison to continental rock. The youngest rocks and sediments are near the axis of the oceanic ridge systems. Rocks increase in age with distance from the ridge axis.

10. The various ages of the seafloor and the movement of continents are a direct result of seafloor spreading. As new crustal material wells up from the mantle through rifts, older material is pushed aside, forming large, linear volcanic systems called oceanic ridges.

11. Continental rifting occurs as the continent begins upwarping because of rising pressure from below. A series of grabens and half-grabens form and eventually fill with lava flows and volcanoes. The rift allows seawater to enter, creating two or more smaller landmasses separated by a growing body of water.

12. The lithosphere is composed of movable interlocking segments called plates. Some plates carry oceanic crust solely, while others underlie both oceanic and continental crust.

13. Plates interact in one of three ways: divergence, convergence, and lateral sliding.

14. Partial melting occurs above a subducting crustal slab after the slab releases water. The water changes the melting temperature of the overlying rocks.

15. Mountain ranges, volcanic chains, and earthquake zones occur as linear systems in narrow zones across Earth's surface. The linearity is a reflection of plate boundaries.

16. As magma cools and crystallizes to form igneous rock, its magnetic properties align parallel to Earth's magnetic field.

17. Dating of volcanic rocks along the seafloor through radiometric methods has provided evidence that magnetic north has shifted repeatedly between the Northern and Southern Hemispheres.

18. Magnetic anomalies form during the reversal of the magnetic north and south poles.

19. Where oceanic crust and continental crust converge, the thinner and denser oceanic material is subducted beneath the lighter and thicker continental crust. The result of this convergence is volcanic activity and earthquakes.

20. Volcanoes, island arcs, and seamounts are features of the ocean floor that result from plate activity.

21. Stationary hot spots are magma chambers that extend downward to the asthenosphere. As a plate passes over the hot spot, the rising magma produces a chain of volcanoes that record plate movement.

22. The accretion of terranes along the western part of North America is the result of the North American plate's collision with island arcs as it moved in its northwesterly direction.

23. Whenever tectonic activity is associated with magma chambers, metallic salts are precipitated out of hot fluids to form hydrothermal deposits.

ESSENTIAL TERMS

bathymetry *212*	plate *219*	trench *230*	atoll *234*	hydrothermal deposit *235*
Pangaea *214*	subduction *219*	island arc *230*	guyot *234*	paradigm *236*
Gondwanaland *216*	paleomagnetism *223*	seamount *231*	terrane *234*	
seafloor spreading *217*	Tethys *228*	hot spot *233*		

REVIEW QUESTIONS

1. What are the proofs Alfred Wegener used to establish his continental drift theory?

2. How have earth scientists used fossils to reassemble continental masses cartographically?

3. What is the name of the southern supercontinent?

4. How does the age of oceanic rock serve as evidence for seafloor spreading?

5. Where can you go to visit a rift valley on dry land?

6. In what ways do the plates interact with one another? What are the results of these interactions?

7. Name examples of the following: divergent plate boundary, convergent plate boundary, transform plate boundary.

8. What are magnetic anomalies? How do they record the movements of oceanic crust?

9. What processes destroy oceanic crust? Where do these processes occur?

10. Why is the San Andreas Fault the site of numerous earthquakes?

11. What is the origin of the Hawaiian Islands?

12. How do guyots and atolls form?

13. How is plate divergence associated with metallic mineral deposits?

CHALLENGES

1. How far is your home from a plate boundary? Would you expect to experience earthquake or volcanic activity in your area because of divergence, convergence, or transform faulting?

2. How could the redistribution of continents affect climate? (See chapter 6 for clues.)

3. Using the plate motion map in figure 9.15, determine the possible tectonic future of Athens, Greece; Los Angeles, California; Tokyo, Japan; and Dar es Salaam, Tanzania. What lies in the tectonic future of your area?

4. Are island arcs always associated with subduction?

5. How could the evolution of life be affected by seafloor spreading?

Chapter

10

Geologic Work and Mass Wasting

Exfoliation, Enchanted Rock State Natural Area, Texas.

INTRODUCTION

During the course of an ordinary human life, Earth appears to change very little. Its surface features and processes seem constant to the casual observer. Hills continue to stand above the lowlands, streams steadily run through their channels, and waves lap endlessly at the shorelines. Our perceptions notwithstanding, Earth's surface is constantly changing. Streams undercut their banks and carry the resulting sediment away. Rock and mineral particles dislodged from the hills move downslope, gradually lowering the hills and leveling the land. Along the shore, the sand migrates up or down the beach under the influence of wind and water. These and other subtle changes slowly reshape the landscape as we go about the daily business of our lives.

From time to time, however, such major natural events as floods, hurricanes, volcanic eruptions, and earthquakes radically alter a locality, sometimes within a matter of minutes or even seconds. After a nineteenth-century earthquake, the citizens of New Madrid, Missouri, had to relocate their town because the old site was inundated when the Mississippi River shifted its course. The 1980 eruption of Mount Saint Helens, in a matter of seconds, removed the upper one-third of the mountain, pulverizing the rock material and converting it to immense clouds of airborne dust and devastating mudflows (see chapter 7).

GEOLOGIC WORK

All change, whether in life or in geology, involves work. This and the three chapters that follow will emphasize over and over again that the landscape we see is the product of countless small changes compounded over thousands of years. Each surface agent that we will consider operates in its own way to produce unique landscape features. The common theme among all of them, however, is that they do geologic work.

Energy and Change

Geologic work, or the movement of material, requires the expenditure of kinetic energy. In every instance of change, some force releases potential energy and causes it to be converted to kinetic energy. This energy may be stored in millions of tons of volcanic sediments and glacial ice perched high on a mountain or in rocks undergoing stress along faults. It may be released suddenly during a volcanic eruption or an earthquake. In other instances, energy release occurs slowly as streams, glaciers, and wind move rock and mineral material from one place to another on Earth's surface.

While gravity directly influenced the energy expenditure that changed Mount Saint Helens and its environment, it was not the sole physical cause of the event. Energy from the sun, traversing the vacuum of space in the form of electromagnetic radiation, was also involved. Solar energy differentially heats the surfaces of our planet (see chapter 4), causing wind and driving the hydrologic cycle (fig. 10.1). The massive water supply that was locked in glacial ice on Mount Saint Helens was the product of the hydrologic cycle and the weather conditions associated with high altitudes. In its rush downhill, the water in the mudflows worked to complete the cycle, by moving back toward the sea from which it had originally evaporated. Because sediment was moved by the water, the result was geologic work.

Geologic Agents and Geologic Work

The external processes that constantly reshape Earth's surface involve the concentrated movements of air, water, and ice. These substances in motion comprise the six primary **geologic agents:** streams, groundwater, glaciers, wind, waves, and currents.

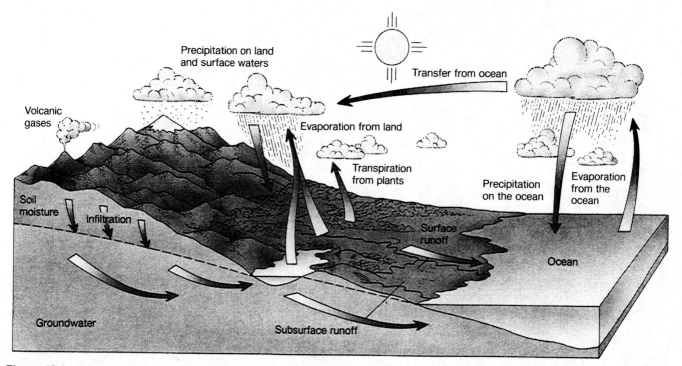

Figure 10.1 The hydrologic cycle. The diagram shows the possible paths taken by water, most of which is initially evaporated from ocean surfaces.

Geologic agents expend energy on a landscape under the guiding influences of atmospheric pressure and gravity.

All of the geologic agents do work by moving earth materials from one place to another. Their task has three basic components: (1) the picking up of rock material, or **erosion**, (2) the actual movement of rock material, or **transportation**, and (3) the ultimate laying to rest of rock material, or **deposition**. Each component differs from the others in its expenditure of energy. Consider the energy required to move a heavy box across a room. The work done in bending over and picking up the box differs from the work necessary to carry it across the room. Compare these two actions to dropping the box in a corner. Bending over and picking up the box uses more energy than carrying it, and dropping the box requires none at all. This is analogous to the work of the geologic agents. More energy is expended in erosion than in transportation, while deposition requires no energy. Deposition is the natural consequence of the earlier actions, since any material will eventually come to rest, even though that rest may be geologically temporary.

The energy that powers this endless cycle of landscape change has one of two possible sources: internal or external. **Endogenous** (internal) **processes,** manifested in crustal uplift, mountain building, and volcanism, in general build Earth's surface higher. Energy is provided by the decay of unstable radionuclides, or it may be residual from an earlier, hotter stage in Earth's history. The **exogenous** (external) **processes** are powered by energy from the sun. As we shall see, this solar energy works in concert with gravity to gradually lower Earth's surface, wearing away mountain ranges in the process.

Erosional and Depositional Landforms

We only need to look at Earth's landscapes to see the results of the geologic agents' work in the series of individual features known as **landforms.** Each landform is shaped by either the erosional or depositional work of one of the six agents. A valley, for example, is a stream erosional feature, whereas a sinkhole is a groundwater erosional feature, and a moraine, a pile of rock debris, is a glacial depositional feature. Landforms are products of the geologic agents, and studying them in conjunction with the agents will reveal the interrelationship between process and product.

The Role of Weathering

Chapter 7 briefly discussed the nature of the weathering processes, both physical and chemical. **Weathering** is the sum of Earth's surface processes that bring rock and mineral material into equilibrium with their low-temperature, low-pressure surface environment. It is a preparatory step that readies material to be moved about Earth's surface by gravity, water, wind, and ice. The result of this movement, as we shall see, is the formation of landforms of both erosional and depositional origin.

Mass Wasting: The Preliminary Step

Before beginning a study of the six external geologic agents and their resultant landforms, we must consider mass wasting, a set of related natural processes that normally occur in the alteration

of landscapes prior to the work of the geologic agents. **Mass wasting** is the downslope movement of earth material under the direct pull of gravity. While gravity gives direction to the downward movement of the geologic agents, it is, in the case of mass wasting, often sufficient by itself to move materials downslope. Rock and mineral matter broken loose by one of the weathering processes may begin the downhill movement without the intervention of streams, glaciers, or wind. A pebble broken loose from a conglomerate rock may roll down a slope for a short or a long distance before it temporarily comes to rest. A large mass of bedrock forming part of a cliff face may break loose and fall under the pull of gravity to the valley floor below. There is a variety of such movements—some very slow and others virtually instantaneous. Some movements are barely perceptible, while others are highly visible and even destructive. At times, dry rock masses will move, but often, the movement requires some lubrication by water or ice. Generally, the steeper the slope, the less lubrication required for movement and the more rapid the movement will be.

Mass wasting performs at least three important functions: (1) it is directly responsible for some landforms, (2) it is a dominant process in soil erosion, and (3) with stream erosion, it is the dominant shaper of Earth's surface (fig. 10.2). As we shall see in chapter 11, a stream functions much like a conveyor belt at the foot of a slope. Rock and mineral material that moves downslope under the pull of gravity eventually arrives at the slope base, where it is picked up by the stream, incorporated into the moving water, and carried away.

For a number of years, earth scientists have attempted to categorize and classify mass movements. No single such classification scheme is universally accepted, but in general, scientists tend to use the same variables when they discuss mass movements, and by one route or another, most arrive at the recognition of the same basic types of movement. Variables usually considered include type of material moved (mud, soil, rock, etc.); speed of movement; moisture content and type (water or ice) within the moving mass; and whether or not movement is along a discrete, recognizable surface, such as a joint or fault. Figure 10.3 is an attempt to summarize in one diagram the important types of mass movement.

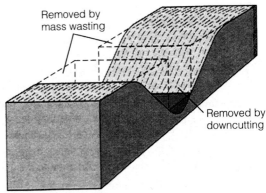

Figure 10.2 Vertical column above the stream channel represents the earth material removed from the valley directly by stream erosion. The remainder of the missing material was delivered to the stream by mass wasting.

Figure 10.3 Classification scheme for mass movements. Mass movements are described and classified primarily on the basis of two variables: moisture content of the moving mass and relative velocity of movement. No attempt is made in the diagram to assign actual water content or velocity values.

Creep

On all slopes, regardless of climatic regime, individual soil, rock, and mineral particles work their way downward. Such movement is usually very slow, with the results noticeable only after months or years of observation. This gradual movement is called **creep**. In many regions, the most common cause of creep is the alternate freezing and thawing of water in the soil. As the water freezes, it expands and lifts individual soil particles. When the ice melts, it contracts and drops the lifted particles. As a solid, heated ice expands before melting, further lifting the particles, then dropping them as it melts. Although the lift is perpendicular to the ground's surface, the drop is vertical under the direct pull of gravity toward Earth's center. On a sloping surface, the directions of lift and drop do not coincide. This process of alternate freezing and thawing with the consequent downslope displacement of mineral grains is known as **frost heaving** (fig. 10.4). The results of frost heaving

and creep can be seen in curved tree trunks, displaced cemetery headstones, tilting utility poles, and crooked fence lines (fig. 10.5). On some slopes, creep produces narrow, parallel, flat surfaces, called **terracettes** (fig. 10.6), that animals use as trails across the slopes. A variety of creep called **rock creep** is evidenced by the overturning in a downslope direction of the exposed edges of thin rock layers that had been in a vertical or near-vertical orientation (fig. 10.7).

Although slow, undramatic, and seemingly unimportant, creep is the most significant of all mass movements because it occurs on most slopes and affects the shallow surface zone where humans live and build structures. Designers of homes, barns, retaining walls, and highways must take into account this inevitable movement. One way this is done is by pouring concrete "footers," which serve as a base for concrete block walls, to a depth below the normal frost level of the soil.

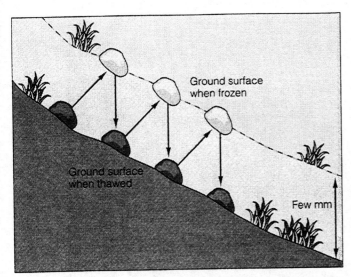

Figure 10.4 Slow progress of a rock particle downslope as a result of the alternate freezing (expansion) and thawing (contraction) of water in the pore spaces of the soil. This process is known as frost heaving.

Figure 10.5 Evidence of soil creep.

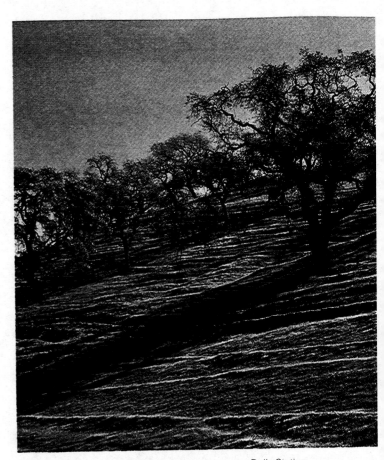

Figure 10.6 Terracettes formed on a slope near Bells Station, California, by the process of soil creep.

Figure 10.7 Edges of near-vertical sedimentary rock layers overturned in the downslope direction as a result of rock creep.

Rockslides, Rockfalls, and Avalanches

Far more spectacular, but geologically much less important, are **rockslides** and **rockfalls.** Such movements are virtually instantaneous and involve the displacement of rock masses down very steep or vertical slopes. Rockslides and rockfalls are common and dangerous in mountainous areas. They are, nevertheless, limited in scope and do not normally affect large numbers of people.

Figure 10.8   A rockslide blocks the highway at Boone, North Carolina.

Rockslides occur along a sloping surface that is less than vertical (fig. 10.8). (The popular term *landslide* includes all movements, such as rockslides, debris slides, and earth slides, where essentially dry material moves rapidly down an inclined surface.) Notable landscape features that result from rockslides are the slope scar that represents the location from which the material moved, the landslide debris pile at the foot of the slope, and an up-valley lake formed by the debris pile's damming of natural drainage.

Rockfalls, on the other hand, are essentially free falls of material down a vertical or near-vertical cliff face. Angular rock fragments from numerous small rockfalls accumulate in piles at the base of the cliff. This loose rock debris is called **talus,** or *scree*, and its most common form is as cone-shaped mounds known as **talus cones.** Individual talus cones often merge to form a continuous series known as a **talus slope,** or *talus apron* (fig. 10.9), at the cliff base.

Earth scientists sometimes divide the factors that contribute to slides and falls into two categories: *basic* and *active*. Basic factors are features present at the site that make a slope inherently unstable. These include potential slip surfaces, such as **bedding planes** (natural breaks between adjacent layers of sedimentary rock), joints, and fault surfaces; rock that has been weakened by weathering and decomposition; steep slopes; and lack of a protective cover of vegetation. Active factors are those that may initiate, or trigger, a slide

or fall. The two most common active factors are earthquake vibrations and heavy rainfall. Others include the removal of slope support by mining, the placement of additional weight on the slope by building construction, and the lubrication of slip planes by unnatural sources, such as leaking swimming pools.

Rock on a steep slope is inherently unstable. Often, large rock masses are held in place above a fracture surface or a sedimentary bedding plane only by friction. If an event occurs that reduces the frictional resistance, the unstable mass above the surface may begin to move. Historically, the shaking and vibrations associated with earthquakes have been the major culprits in triggering rockslides and rockfalls. Such was the case on August 17, 1959, when a major earthquake in the vicinity of Yellowstone National Park caused the movement of more than 30 million cubic meters (more than 1 billion cu. ft) of rock material from the steep walls of the Madison Canyon into the valley bottom, where the rock dammed the Madison River and formed an 8-kilometer-(5-mi) long lake, Earthquake Lake (fig. 10.10). Eventually the U. S. Army Corps of Engineers dredged a spillway through the natural dam to drain off excess water, and a balance was affected.

Heavy rainfall can also induce landslides by infiltrating fractures and lubricating the slide surface, thereby reducing frictional resistance. In addition, water adds more weight to an already unstable slope. A classic example was the 1903 slide at Turtle

Figure 10.9   Talus cones. Death Valley National Monument, California.

Figure 10.10   Madison Canyon landslide scar and debris pile. Earthquake Lake (foreground) was formed when the Madison River was dammed by the slide debris.

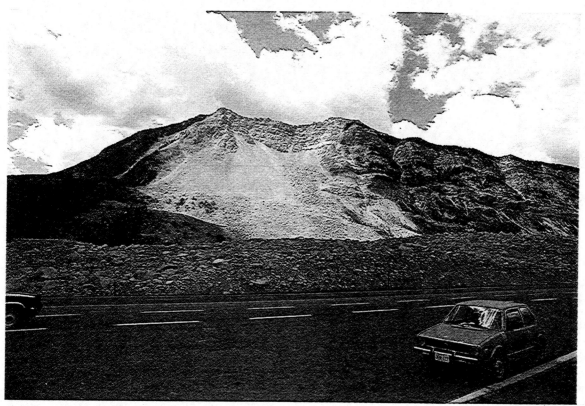

Figure 10.11 Turtle Mountain slide. Frank, Alberta, Canada.

Figure 10.12 Beginning of a snow avalanche.

Mountain above the town of Frank, Alberta, Canada (fig. 10.11). Some 70 million tons of limestone broke loose from the southern shoulder of the mountain and slid, then fell, a total distance of 900 meters (3,000 ft). At the base of the mountain, the limestone spread out, and moving at speeds up to 100 kilometers (60 mi) per hour, overwhelmed a part of the town. In all, 70 lives were lost. A group of miners trapped in a coal mine at the base of the mountain were able to dig themselves out by tunneling through the soft coal. While heavy rainfall was the initiating factor at Turtle Mountain, the slope stability had been reduced by coal mining.

Closely related to rockfalls and rockslides are **avalanches.** An avalanche normally incorporates a large quantity of snow and ice with the rock debris. Indeed, many avalanches consist exclusively of snow and ice. Avalanches are common in the Alps, and many an unwary skier has fallen victim to them (fig. 10.12). A particularly devastating avalanche occurred in the Andes Mountains of South America on May 31, 1970. Triggered by a powerful earthquake, a mass of rock and ice, estimated to have a volume of between 50 and 100 million cubic meters (65 and 130 million cu. yd), was loosened from a high peak, Nevados Huascarán, and came roaring down the valley for a distance of approximately 15 kilometers (9.3 mi). The debris almost completely buried the towns of Ranrahirca and Yungay, Peru, which lay at the base of the mountain (fig. 10.13) More than 40,000 lives were lost. The debris mass was estimated to have moved with a velocity approaching 300 kilometers (186 mi) per hour. It could only have achieved such a high velocity by literally riding a layer of compressed air that formed beneath it as it fell, since the ordinary frictional drag along the rocky valley floor would have slowed it appreciably. An ironic footnote to this tragedy is that an almost identical event had occurred in this same location only 8 years earlier. Then, 3 million cubic meters (3.9 million cu. yd) of material covered part of the same area, with a loss of 3,500 lives. This event undoubtedly will recur with a similar result because the area remains inhabited and unstable. (See box 10.1.)

Slumps and Earthflows

On a somewhat smaller scale and commonly in hilly regions, masses of soil and bedrock slip along curved surfaces in a natural rotational movement. This results in the variety of mass wasting known as **slump.** The upper portion of a slump is characterized by an exposed, steep, curved slip surface. Toward the base of the moving mass, movement becomes more irregular, and the discrete slip surface becomes less recognizable. The heterogeneous mass of moving material at the base of the slope is called an **earthflow** and is almost always associated with slump (fig. 10.14). Such movements commonly threaten highways or other structures near the base of the slope. Slopes that are susceptible to slumping and earthflow are easily recognizable by numerous small ground-surface breaks, or *scars,* and rough topography.

Figure 10.13   Debris avalanche in the Peruvian Andes, 1970. The cities of Yungay (*left*) and Ranrahirca (*right*) were virtually wiped out.

(a)   (b)

Figure 10.14   Slumps in soil. (*a*) The component parts of the (*b*) actual movement.

Box 10.1

ENGINEERING AGAINST MASS MOVEMENTS

Humans' attempts to combat and control the several types of falls and slides have met with varying degrees of success. Perhaps the earliest and simplest technique employed was the erection of *retaining walls* or *fences* at the base of a slope. Newer variations on this are the use of metal screens to cover an entire steep rock face and of **gabions**—literally, wire baskets filled with stones that are placed at the foot of a slope or along a drainage channel. Rock bolts, several tens to several hundreds of centimeters in length, are used to anchor loose surface rock layers to more stable rock layers below. Systems of pipes and French drains are used to remove excess water from slope materials that are susceptible to flowage when wet. For especially deep road cuts, engineers normally design the cut as a series of terraces, or *benches,* rather than a single steep slope. The benches allow for periodic access to remove fallen rock material. Figure 10.A shows examples of all of these engineering techniques.

Apply Your Knowledge

1. What slope stabilization techniques have you observed?
2. How might you rank the relative costs of the techniques described? How might you rank their relative effectiveness?

(b)

(a)

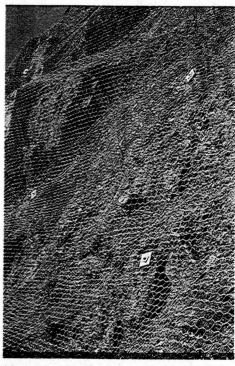

(c)

Figure 10.A Engineering techniques used to reduce slumps and slides on unstable slopes. (*a*) Fences. (*b*) Gabions. (*c*) Rock bolts and metal screens. (*d*) Benches (terraces) along a road cut.

Figure 10.15 Slumping at Calvert Cliffs, Maryland, along the western shore of Chesapeake Bay.

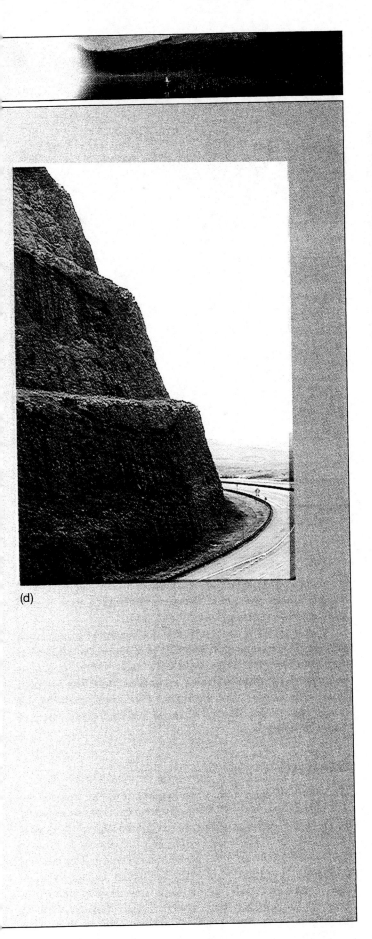

(d)

Slumps of unstable material also regularly occur along coastlines as a result of wave and current erosion (fig. 10.15). Related mass movements that occur along the continental slopes in the marine envroment give rise to the downslope movement of turbid masses of water, known as *turbidity flows,* into the deeper parts of the ocean basins. These movements and their significance will be discussed in chapter 15.

Mudflows

Residents of the hills and canyons of southern California are plagued by another variety of mass wasting, the **mudflow.** Mudflows are common in arid and semiarid regions or anywhere where rainfall is highly seasonal and torrential when it does occur. Southern California has very dry summers. Brushfires strip the hillsides of their covering of vegetation. When the heavy rains come during the winter, the water picks up the unprotected soil to form masses of mud that follow the natural stream channels through the hills and out onto the flat lands below. Widespread destruction of the expensive homes that line the canyons and cover the flats is as common as the change of seasons (fig. 10.16).

Mudflows form part of a continuum with streams. As the amount of water present increases, a stream will form. Decreasing, but still significant, amounts of water give rise to a mudflow.

Rainfall is the most common cause of mudflows, but on occasion, that rainfall may be related to volcanic eruptions. Condensation of water vapor from the erupting volcano, plus melting snow and ice, provide moisture that mixes with loose volcanic debris on the volcano's upper slopes. The resulting masses of mud, known as **lahars,** follow natural passageways downslope. The A.D. 79 eruption of Mount Vesuvius, near present-day Naples, Italy, caused massive mudflows that literally buried the Roman city of

Figure 10.16   These men are standing on the roof of a home buried in a mudflow at La Crescenta, California, February 1978.

(a)

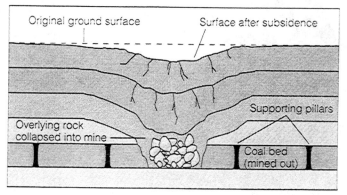

(b)

Figure 10.18   (*a*) Grocery store in Belle Vernon, Pennsylvania, damaged by subsidence of the ground surface over an abandoned coal mine. (*b*) Subsidence caused when a coal seam is mined, leaving the overlying rock layers and ground surface without sufficient support.

Figure 10.17   A portion of the town of Aberfan, Wales, was covered by a debris flow from the coal refuse pile in the background in 1966.

Herculaneum (even as neighboring Pompeii was being buried by volcanic ash). Herculaneum was only rediscovered near the end of the nineteenth century. In recent times, the 1980 eruption of Mount Saint Helens in Washington State was characterized by lahars that filled the stream valleys and adjacent lake basins. In 1986, a lahar rushed off the summit of Colombia's Nevada del Ruiz volcano at 160 kilometers (100 mi) per hour toward the town of Armero, 48 kilometers (30 mi) distant. By the time the flow stopped, more than 41 square kilometers (16 sq. mi) of the Lagunilla River valley

and some 20,000 people (all but 3,000 of the town's inhabitants) had been buried beneath a 30-meter-(100-ft) thick layer of mud (see the photo at the beginning of chapter 10).

Human carelessness can also lead to material flowage, often with tragic consequences. Unstable spoil-bank deposits above the town of Aberfan, Wales, the refuse of many years of coal mining, were mobilized by heavy rainfall in 1966. The material flowed downslope, covering a part of the town, including the school (fig. 10.17). Dozens of people lost their lives, many of them schoolchildren.

Subsidence

Mass wasting also occurs when humans or nature disturbs the rock balance underground. Such a disturbance causes **subsidence,** the vertical collapse or settling of the ground surface. A number of human activities have been responsible for subsidence. In some regions of Pennsylvania, the deep mining of coal and the ensuing subsidence have caused millions of dollars in damage to buildings, homes, and roads (fig. 10.18*a*). Consider the mining of a 3-meter-(10-ft) thick seam of coal in a mine 90 meters (300 ft) deep. If the roof collapses under the weight of the overlying rock layers, 0.3 meter (1 ft) or more of vertical displacement may occur

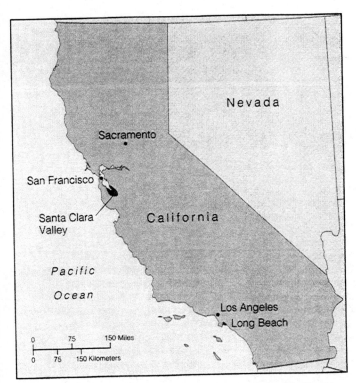

Figure 10.19   Map of California, showing the locations of the Santa Clara Valley and Long Beach, two areas of significant ground subsidence.

(a)

(b)

Figure 10.20   (*a*) Collapse of the ground surface into a cavern in limestone to form a sinkhole. (*b*) The sinkhole formed at Winter Park, Florida, May 8, 1981.

at the ground surface (fig. 10.18*b*). A full 3 meters (10 ft) of displacement will not occur at the surface because, as the overlying rock layers break up and settle, they will expand and occupy a larger volume than they did prior to subsidence.

In other areas, subsidence is caused by pumping groundwater and petroleum from loose sands. Without the water or oil's support, the sand grains compact, reducing the overall rock volume and causing the ground surface to sink. In such major metropolitan areas as Houston, Texas; Venice, Italy; and Mexico City, Mexico; severe surface subsidence has resulted from extensive overpumping of groundwater to meet the demands of increasing populations and industries. At Venice, subsidence combines with a rising sea level and high storm tides to produce periodic flooding of the historic squares, monuments, and buildings (see box 10.2 on page 252).

Subsidence due to groundwater withdrawal is not only a problem in rapidly growing urban areas; it is, perhaps, even more widespread in areas where groundwater is relied on heavily for irrigation. Such an area is the Santa Clara Valley, just south of San Francisco Bay, where groundwater irrigation has been practiced throughout most of the twentieth century, resulting in what is probably the most extensive area of subsidence in the world (fig. 10.19). In some parts of the valley, subsidence between 1934 and 1967 alone was in excess of 2.5 meters (8 ft). Flooding from the southern end of San Francisco Bay has required constant remediation.

Extensive groundwater use in areas of limestone bedrock is also thought to be a major contributor to subsidence in those areas. Although the bedrock in such cases is well indurated, solution of the rock over thousands of years has led to the formation of extensive networks of underground caverns. In those places where caverns lie just beneath the ground surface, a high water table may help to support that surface. If the water table is drawn down, the support is removed, and the ground surface may suddenly collapse (see fig. 10.20 and chapter 11).

Box 10.2

VENICE: WHERE (MORE AND MORE) LAND AND WATER MEET

World attention became focused on Venice, Italy, on November 4, 1966, when a storm surge from the Adriatic Sea submerged more than 80% of the city. The water rose 1.9 meters (6 ft) above its normal high level. Saint Mark's Square lay beneath 1 meter (3.3 ft) of water. Total damage was estimated at $70 million. The November 1966 event was but one of an increasingly frequent series of floods that are causing the city's historic palaces, libraries, and museums to deteriorate at an alarming rate.

Venice was founded in the fourth century A.D. by refugees from the Italian mainland on a group of low-lying islands that occupy a part of a 10-kilometer-(6-mi) wide lagoon (fig. 10.B). The daily tide, with a range of approximately 0.65 meter (2 ft), moves into and out of the lagoon through three inlets. This flow of water has always provided a natural flushing action for the lagoon and the city's complex of canals. In an early attempt to preserve the city's environment, the ruling magistrates of the sixteenth and seventeenth centuries had three rivers that fed into the lagoon diverted to reduce the amount of siltation. Over the years, seawalls were built for protection from storms. Only in the twentieth century was the city linked to the mainland by railroad and highway bridges.

The problems of Venice represent an example of the interrelationship of the several earth sciences. The city's location in a shallow lagoon adjacent to the Po River delta sets the stage. Meteorological and climatic factors lead to the storm surges and submergences. Sharp drops in atmospheric pressure are capable of raising sea level by as much as 30.5 centimeters (12 in). Heavy, concentrated precipitation during the winter months can raise water levels from 10 to 20 centimeters (4 to 8 in). Southeastern winds, known as *siroccos,* push water northward up the narrowing Adriatic Sea toward Venice. Like all coastal cities, Venice is also affected by the general rise in sea level, estimated at 10 centimeters (4 in) during the twentieth century, due to glacial melting.

The increasing frequency and severity of flooding can generally be attributed to human causes. Because of the heavy pumping of groundwater in the first two-thirds of the twentieth century, the ground surface has subsided significantly. The situation was alleviated somewhat by a 1969 ban on the drilling of new wells. Production of natural gas from wells in the Po River delta and the weight of new factories and other buildings may also have contributed to the subsidence. Filling of portions of the lagoon for urban expansion and the Marco Polo Airport and the sealing off of other sections for fishponds have reduced the lagoon's overall volume, leaving the incoming water nowhere to go but *up.* Deterioration of the seawalls and enlargement of the three natural inlets to accommodate shipping have also led to greater influxes of water. The net result of all of this is that average high-tide levels have increased some 35 centimeters (10 in) since the beginning of the twentieth century.

What can be done to save Venice for future generations? Plans have been drafted to construct additional barriers to the sea as well as inflatable storm gates that could be raised from positions on the floor of the lagoon to block the tidal inlets during times of very high water. Any solution that restricts the free flow of tidal water, of course, decreases the natural cleansing action of the tides.

Figure 10.B
Location of the Lagoon of Venice and the city of Venice (Venezia), Italy, at the northern end of the Adriatic Sea.

Apply Your Knowledge

1. Will the problems of Venice worsen as a result of the increasing greenhouse effect? Why?
2. What coastal regions of the United States might be particularly susceptible to rising sea level as a consequence of excessive building and filling of estuaries and lagoons?
3. Discuss the pros and cons of measures you would consider applying to control the flooding problem at Venice if you were in a position of responsibility there.

Figure 10.21 The Long Beach Naval Shipyard has been affected considerably by subsidence caused by the removal of oil from unconsolidated sands beneath the city..

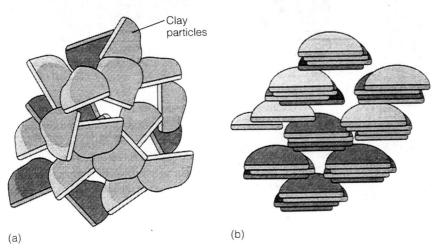

(a) (b)

Figure 10.22 Quick clay. (*a*) Clay particles in random orientations prior to disturbance. (*b*) Vibrations reorient particles, leading to rapid flowage.

From the 1920s to the 1960s, the city of Long Beach, California (fig. 10.19), suffered as much as 8 meters (27 ft) of subsidence as a result of the extraction of oil and natural gas from the sands beneath the city. Because it lies along the coast, any drop in elevation subjected Long Beach to flooding (fig. 10.21). Over the years, the city spent millions of dollars to construct seawalls and levees to hold back the sea. In the early 1960s, subsidence in the Long Beach area was significantly reduced by the pumping of seawater under pressure into the sands from which oil had been extracted. The water became a substitute support system, and the companies profited from increased productivity, as the pressurized water forced additional oil from the sands.

Quick Clay

Quick clays are seemingly solid bodies of fine-grained mineral material. When subjected to sudden stresses, however, they liquify and undergo rapid lateral flow. Vibrations set up by pile drivers and bulldozers may be sufficient to cause this change. Natural phenomena, such as earthquakes, likewise may serve as triggering mechanisms.

Quick clays can occur in a number of natural environments, but they are especially associated with areas that were at one time submerged beneath marine waters. Such areas include major river valleys that were inundated by a rising sea level during interglacial times. Dissolved salts in the seawater bind together the individual platelike clay particles in an open, random orientation (fig. 10.22*a*). Subsequently, after the seas have withdrawn, fresh

(a)

(b)

Figure 10.23 (*a*) The Tuve area, Gothenburg, Sweden, prior to the February 1977 quick-clay movement. (*b*) Tuve, after the displacement.

groundwater moving through the deposit leaches out the dissolved salts and thereby weakens the clay structure, leaving it susceptible to a reorientation of the constituent particles and sudden movement when disturbed (fig. 10.22*b*).

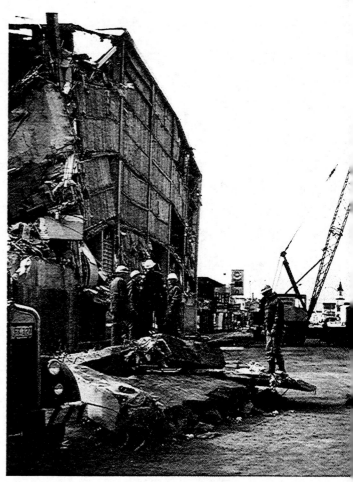

Figure 10.24 Ground displacement during the Good Friday earthquake of 1964 in the retail district of Anchorage, Alaska included severe damage to the J.C. Penney store.

Areas along the St. Lawrence River in the Canadian province of Quebec have historically suffered from quick-clay movements, as have parts of Norway and Sweden (fig. 10.23). Individual movements may be sufficiently large to encompass dozens of structures, displacing them in some instances hundreds of meters. A number of coastal areas in Alaska, most notably the city of Anchorage, experienced these types of movement during the devastating Good Friday earthquake of 1964 (fig. 10.24).

Quicksand

Quicksand differs from quick clay, not only in that the deposit consists of mineral grains of larger size than clay particles, but also in that quicksand has no inherent strength. It is unable to support a body or structure at any time. Quicksand forms where water constantly flows upward through a sandy deposit, as a type of natural spring. The flowing water pushes individual sand grains apart. A lack of grain-to-grain contact means that the mineral grains are free to move apart. Thus, any weight that is added to the surface of the deposit meets no solid resistance. Slowly, or sometimes rapidly, the surface object settles through the quicksand, much as an object slowly sinks downward in water.

Quicksands are most commonly associated with areas of high water tables, such as swamps, lakes, and springs and along

Figure 10.25 Permafrost.

Figure 10.26 Solifluction on a slope in an area of permafrost. Denali National Park, Alaska.

some stream courses. Streams of the Great Plains region in the central and western United States are notable for the occurrence of quicksands. This is due, at least in part, to the large quantities of sandy sediments that have temporarily accumulated along these stream channels.

Mass Wasting in Areas of Permafrost

Arctic and subarctic climates favor a unique set of surface processes that, in turn, lead to the development of distinctive landforms. The major influence on these processes and landforms is a permanently frozen ground layer known as **permafrost.** At high latitudes and altitudes, the short summer season permits the ground to thaw to only a certain depth. Below that level, the ground remains permanently frozen to a depth as great as 600 meter, (2,000 ft) (fig. 10.25). The depth to the permafrost is highly variable, but in a general way, it decreases with increasing latitude and altitude. The presence of a continuous permafrost layer is also more likely at higher latitudes.

During the short summer melting season, the thawed surface layer becomes saturated with meltwater; the frozen layer beneath is impermeable and does not allow the water to drain through. The surface layer of saturated soil is then free to flow down even the most gentle slopes, a process known as **solifluction.** The result of solifluction is often defined by the presence of distinct lobes of flowing material known as *solifluction lobes* (fig. 10.26).

The alternate freezing and thawing of water in the pore spaces of soil in permafrost regions also is thought to act as a sorting mechanism to separate and concentrate coarse rock debris from finer rock material. The coarser material usually forms a series of adjacent rings, with the finer material within each ring. These features, which may be 10 meters (33 ft) or more in diameter and are visible from the air, are referred to as **stone rings,** or *stone polygons*. On sloping ground, gravity will pull the rock debris downslope and, in the process, stretch the stone rings into **stone stripes.** These and related features are collectively referred to as **patterned ground** (fig. 10.27).

A **periglacial** (associated with the margins of a glacier) feature characteristic of high elevations is the **rock glacier** (fig. 10.28). These landforms have the shape of ordinary glaciers in that they are tonguelike deposits of rock debris that move downslope confined within the walls of a former stream valley. They differ from glaciers in that rock particles, which may be up to several meters in diameter, are the dominant components, rather than ice. Some ice is present, however, between the rock masses, and this serves as a lubricant to facilitate movement. Rock glaciers up to a kilometer (0.6 mi) long and 50 meters (170 ft) thick are known from the Andes, Rocky Mountains, and other mountain systems.

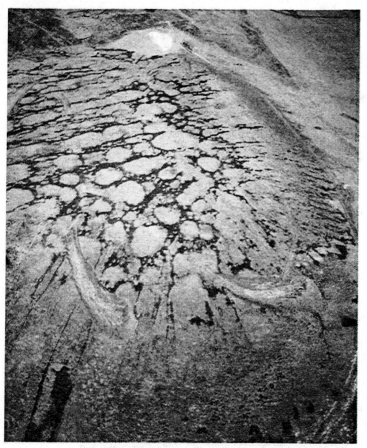

Figure 10.27 Patterned ground near Klamath Falls, Oregon.

Figure 10.28 Rock glacier. Chugach Range, Alaska.

FURTHER THOUGHTS: HUMAN BEINGS, THE ULTIMATE GEOLOGIC AGENTS

The natural processes of weathering and mass wasting described in this chapter have operated throughout most of Earth's history, presumably in much the same way as they do now. It is fair to assume, then, that the surface features similar to those that we note today have been formed over and over again. Throughout most of history, human beings present in small numbers and living at subsistence level or just above had little impact on the land surface, except for the large-scale clearing of forests in some areas. In the last few centuries, however, humans have developed the capability to modify Earth's surface dramatically. Such modifications may be direct, by applying explosives and heavy earth-moving equipment, or indirect, by constructing along streams and coastlines engineering works that accelerate or alter natural surface processes. As world population increases exponentially and underdeveloped countries adapt modern engineering techniques, the pace of conflict can only increase, with potentially dire consequences.

SIGNIFICANT POINTS

1. Earth's surface constantly changes. Any geologic change involves work—the movement of earth material—with an expenditure of energy.

2. Earth's surface is shaped by six geologic agents doing geologic work, which consists of erosion, transportation, and deposition of earth materials. Ultimately, these agents obtain their energy from solar radiation and their direction from gravity.

3. Endogenous processes generally raise Earth's surface to higher elevations. Exogenous processes wear the surface down.

4. The result of geologic work is the production of surface features called landforms.

5. The prelude to action by surface agents is a gravity-driven process called mass wasting, which includes a variety of downslope movements.

6. Important variables in defining types of mass movements are type of material moved, speed of movement, moisture content, and slippage surfaces.

7. Creep, the slow, downslope movement of earth materials, is commonly caused by the alternate freezing and thawing of water in the soil. It is the most important and widespread of the mass movements.

8. The most important basic factors in initiating slides and falls are steep slopes, weathered rock, the presence of slide surfaces, and lack of vegetation, while the primary active factors are earthquake vibrations and heavy rainfall.

9. Slump, a rotational movement of soil and bedrock along curved slip planes, is common on many slopes. It is usually associated with earthflow.

10. Retaining walls, gabions, rock bolts, and terracing are some of the techniques commonly employed to stabilize slopes.

11. Mudflows are characteristic of arid and semiarid regions, where the covering of vegetation is sparse and the infrequent rainfall is torrential.

12. Mudflows associated with and caused by volcanic eruptions are lahars.

13. Subsidence is the vertical displacement or collapse of the ground surface.

14. Subsidence may be natural in areas of limestone bedrock, but it is commonly induced by such human activities as mining, groundwater withdrawal, and pumping of oil and gas.

15. A quick clay is a clay deposit capable of collapsing and flowing when disturbed by earthquake or other vibrations.

16. Quicksand is a sedimentary deposit that lacks strength to support objects.

17. Permafrost, a permanently frozen ground layer, is common at high latitudes and altitudes. Summer melting of ice in the surface layer results in a type of flowage called solifluction.

Essential Terms

geologic work 240
geologic agent 240
erosion 241
transportation 241
deposition 241
endogenous processes 241

exogenous processes 241
landform 241
weathering 241
mass wasting 241
creep 242
frost heaving 242
terracette 242

rock creep 242
rockslide 243
rockfall 243
talus 244
talus cone 244
talus slope 244
bedding plane 244
avalanche 246

slump 247
earthflow 247
gabion 248
mudflow 249
lahar 249
subsidence 250
quick clay 253
quicksand 254

permafrost 255
solifluction 255
stone ring 255
stone stripe 255
patterned ground 255
periglacial 256
rock glacier 256

Review Questions

1. What are the six geologic agents? How do they do work?
2. What are the three principal components of geologic work?
3. What are endogenous processes? What are exogenous processes?
4. What is a landform?
5. What is mass wasting? What are some important variables used to identify and distinguish the types of mass wasting?
6. State three important functions of mass wasting.
7. How does the process of creep occur? What are some of the evidences for the occurrence of creep?
8. What is the difference between a rockslide and a rockfall?
9. What is a "landslide"?
10. How do talus cones form?
11. What are some of the basic factors involved in slides and falls? What are some of the active factors?

12. How does an avalanche typically differ from a rockslide or rockfall?
13. What are the characteristic features of a slump?
14. How does an earthflow relate to a slump?
15. Under what conditions do mudlfows most characteristically occur?
16. What is subsidence?
17. What are some of the common causes of subsidence?
18. How does quick clay differ from ordinary clay? What does "quick" mean in this context?
19. How does quicksand differ from ordinary sand?
20. What is permafrost? Where does it occur?
21. What is solifluction?
22. How does patterned ground form?

Challenges

1. Look around your neighborhood and town. What examples of change or potential change brought about by geologic agents can you identify?
2. Give some examples from nature of potential energy being converted to kinetic energy. Describe the geologic work being done in each case.
3. What laws could be enacted to protect citizens from the dangers of lahars?
4. Cite some examples of mass movements that you can identify in the vicinity of your home.

Chapter

11

Chapter Outline

Water on and Beneath the Land Surface

Oxbow lakes, meander scars, cutoffs, and floodplain
scrolls along the Pecatonica River, Winnebago County, Illinois.

INTRODUCTION

Throughout history, and even during prehistoric times, streams played an important role in all aspects of human existence and endeavors. They were accessible sources of drinking water, easy avenues for transportation, sources of water for crops, and physical barriers between enemies. Most early cities and many entire civilizations developed along or at the mouths of major rivers. Streams remain important, even today, for the same reasons.

The ancient Egyptians and other early Middle Eastern cultures developed shallow, hand-dug wells and distribution systems of tunnels and clay pipes to use water from beneath the land for irrigation purposes. In more recent times, humans have utilized subsurface water on an enormous scale for agriculture and industry, and for the support of major urban populations in areas where little or no surface water exists. Some understanding, therefore, of these precious freshwater resources, their place in nature, and the constraints that exist on their use is important.

STREAMS

Streams, the channelized flow of continental surface water, are the most important geologic agents. They do more work than any other agent—perhaps more than all other agents combined. Even in arid regions, where few permanent streams flow, the bulk of sediment is removed during those short periods when running water occupies the otherwise dry channels, known locally as "arroyos" or "washes" in the southwestern United States and as "wadies" in the Middle East and North Africa.

General Characteristics

Streams result from precipitation over land. Moisture that is not immediately evaporated, taken up by plants, or absorbed by the ground begins to run off the land surface under the influence of gravity. For a short distance, this flow is in the form of a very thin sheet. Soon, however, the sheet of water begins to divide, and the water becomes concentrated into small channels, or **rills.** As the water flows downslope, these small channels merge to form larger channels, and streams form. In this manner, streams of increasing size come together to form an interconnected system. Although there is no defin-

itive lower limit, the large streams in such systems are often designated as **rivers.** Even as streams enlarge and grow, they maintain a relationship with their smaller **tributaries,** or feeder streams. Indeed, the main stream and its system of tributaries can conveniently be considered a distinct entity, a system that is responsible for carrying away the precipitation that falls within a particular geographic area. This area is the stream system's **drainage basin,** or **watershed.** Drainage basins exist at any scale, from a few square kilometers for a small creek to millions of square kilometers for a major river system.

A drainage basin, regardless of size, is separated from each of its neighboring basins by an area of high ground, a **drainage divide.** On the scale of continents, where divides separate the drainage basins of major river systems, such as the Mississippi and the Colorado, the divides are usually referred to as *continental divides* (fig. 11.1). Precipitation falling on a given side of the divide will flow through the basin on that side of the divide, whereas precipitation falling on the other side of the divide will flow

Figure 11.1 Limekiln Hill, Montana, part of the Continental Divide.

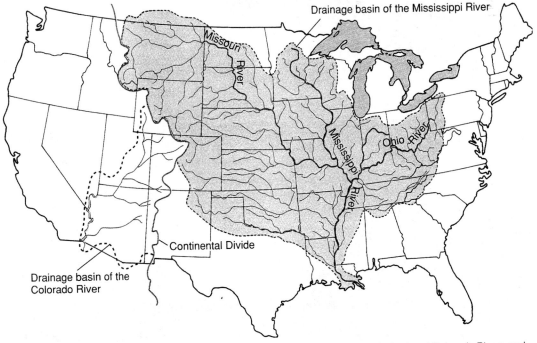

Figure 11.2 Map of the United States, showing the drainage basins of the Mississippi and Colorado Rivers and the western Continental Divide.

through the basin on that side. The continental divide that can be traced through the central and southern Rocky Mountains separates drainage that will flow through the Mississippi River system eventually to the Gulf of Mexico from drainage that will flow through the Colorado River system to the Gulf of California and the Pacific Ocean. Figure 11.2 shows the drainage basins of the Mississippi and Colorado Rivers and the continental divide that separates them.

Within a stream channel, the water may move in either of two ways: as laminar flow or as turbulent flow. In **laminar flow,** the water literally moves as thin sheets, or *lamina*, over one another. Such flow is possible only where channel walls are relatively smooth (as within a water pipe) and velocity is low. As velocity increases and/or the channel sides and bottom become rougher, the flow pattern becomes more irregular, or **turbulent,** with eddying and swirling within the water mass (fig. 11.3).

All streams flow downslope, regardless of the geographic direction. They drop in elevation as they flow from their point of origin, or **stream head,** to their end point, or **stream mouth.** The drop in elevation as a stream flows a certain distance is called the **stream gradient** and is measured in meters dropped for each kilometer traveled—that is, meters per kilometer (or ft/mi). Normally, this drop in elevation is not constant over a stream's course. Rather, the stream drops most steeply near its head and least steeply near its mouth. Consequently, streamflow is usually turbulent in the high ground where the stream originates and sluggish in the channel near the mouth, resulting in different expenditures of energy over the stream's length. Energy is available for erosion on the steeper slope,

but reduced energy leads to extensive deposition near the mouth. Figure 11.4 shows the **long (longitudinal) profile** of a stream— literally, a cross-sectional (side) view from its head to its mouth. Note that the profile is "concave upward," indicating diminished gradients toward the stream's mouth.

The seemingly lazy flow and dominant deposition that occurs along a stream's lower course can be misleading in terms of stream velocity. Because of the large volume of water that must be moved through the stream channel near its mouth, flow velocity is usually much higher there than in the more turbulent portion of the stream near its head, where turbulence actually imparts a local backward component to the movement. The volume of water passing any point on a stream in a given interval of time is called the **discharge** and is normally measured in cubic meters per second (or cu. ft per sec). Discharge for any stream varies significantly with the seasons, usually being high during the spring months and at its lowest in late summer or early fall. During times of flood, of course, the stream will have exceptionally high discharge.

Floods

Floods occur whenever the water volume in a stream exceeds the amount that can just be contained within the stream's banks (*bank-full stage*). At this time, the excess flow spreads out across the stream's **floodplain,** the broad, flat area between the stream channel and the valley walls. As during the midwestern floods of 1993 (see box 11.1), heavy rainfall beyond the capacity of a drainage basin and/or stream to absorb it is the most common cause of flooding. The floods that ravaged California in January 1995 and then again in March of that year were, in a sense, "climatic floods." Winter is the rainy season in the Mediterranean-type climate of southern and central California (see chapter 6). Predictably heavy rains occur at this time virtually every year. Their predictability, however, does not make them more welcome or tolerable.

A special type of flood occurs when dams, both natural and artificial, fail. In this category is the deadliest flood in U.S. history, which took place on May 31, 1889, along the valley of the Little Conemaugh River, culminating at Johnstown, Pennsylvania. More than 2,200 people lost their lives, including almost 800 who were

Figure 11.3 Water flow passes from laminar to turbulent with increasing velocity and channel roughness.

Figure 11.4 The long, or longitudinal, profile of a stream—literally, a cross-sectional view from the head to the mouth. Note that the profile is "concave upward," indicating diminishing slopes (gradients) as you follow the stream from point A to point B.

never identified. The flood caused an estimated $17 million in property damage, a significant amount at that time.

The Johnstown Flood illustrates what can happen when humans interfere with natural processes. Johnstown, at that time a manufacturing city of approximately 30,000 people, lies on the narrow floodplain of the Little Conemaugh River, where it is joined by Stony Creek to form the Conemaugh River. The floodplain is constricted by hills on each side, a common topographic configuration in this part of the Appalachians. An unusually heavy rainfall occurred within the drainage basin of the Conemaugh River onto already-saturated ground. Approximately 24 kilometers (15 mi) up the Little Conemaugh River valley and at an elevation more that 135 meters (450 ft) higher than Johnstown was a large earthen dam measuring 270 meters (900 ft) wide by 21 meters (70 ft) high. The dam impounded what at one time was the largest artificial lake in the United States, South Fork Lake. South Fork Lake had for some time been the private domain of a group of wealthy sportsmen from Pittsburgh, who had formed the South Fork Hunting and Fishing Club. Over the years, scant attention had been given to the care and maintenance of South Fork Dam, and by 1889, it was no longer structurally sound. In addition, overflow channels designed to carry away excess water had become clogged and nonfunctioning.

As the rains came down through the night of May 30th and into the following morning, the water level in the lake rose, sometimes at the rate of 2.5 centimeters (1 in) every 10 minutes. With no functioning overflow system to drain off the rising waters, pressure on the dam built, and eventually, water began to pour over the top of the dam. Once the earthen dam was topped, it eroded quickly, leading to its eventual collapse in the early afternoon of May 31st. An estimated 18 million metric tons (20 million tons) of water poured downslope within the confining walls of the narrow valley in the form of a 12-meter (40-ft) high wall of water that leveled and then incorporated everything in its path. Flow rates for the water varied as it worked its way past temporary obstructions, but the main mass of water arrived at Johnstown 57 minutes after the dam collapse. The flood carved a path of destruction three blocks wide through the city and formed a 30-acre accumulation of wreckage from buildings and downed trees as it ponded against a large stone bridge that resisted collapse. The mass of wreckage formed a temporary haven for trapped survivors until it caught fire, killing an additional 80 people.

Occasionally, humans have deliberately taken advantage of the awesome power of flooding rivers to serve their own purposes. The Yellow River of China, one of the largest and historically most destructive rivers on Earth, flows along much of its course through a series of embankments, both artificial and natural. At some places, the river is confined 9.1 meters (30 ft) above the surrounding terrain. In June 1938, as the invading Japanese army was advancing across northern China, Chiang Kaishek, leader of the Chinese forces, ordered that sections of the river's embankments be de-

stroyed to release the river's waters onto the surrounding plain. So extensive was the resulting flood that the river changed its course significantly. Militarily, the maneuver was a success in that a large part of the Japanese army, along with much of its heavy equipment, was destroyed, and the remainder was forced to shift its military operations to the south. For this military victory, however, the Chinese people paid a great price. Tens of thousands of square kilometers of fertile farmland were lost to cultivation, and close to 1 million people drowned. Incidents of this type, as well as hundreds of natural floods through the centuries, have caused the Yellow River to be referred to as "China's sorrow."

Controlling Floodwaters

For almost as long as humans have had organized civilizations, they have attempted to harness stream water, both for their use and to prevent destruction. Historically, such efforts have taken two main forms: dams and levees. One purpose of dams and their attendant reservoirs is to store excess water temporarily and to release it gradually into the river system as conditions permit (fig. 11.5). This is done routinely with success, but sometimes, the volume of water is too great to be retained and must be released at other than optimum times. Because streams deposit their sediment loads in quiet waters, the reservoirs gradually (sometimes rapidly) become filled with sediment, which diminishes their holding capacity for water. When this occurs, the reservoirs must either be abandoned or the sediments dredged and removed. Most large dams and reservoirs serve functions other than just flood control, including hydroelectric power and recreation.

Sometimes, dams serve other unique functions. A case in point is the Thames River Barrier. Located at Woolwich, 13 kilometers (8 mi) downstream from central London, the barrier is designed to protect that part of London and its environs that lie on the Thames floodplain. The principal threats to this area are tidal surges that

Figure 11.5   Dam and reservoir on the White River, Arkansas.

Box 11.1

Investigating the Environment

The Midwest Floods of 1993

The Midwest flood of the summer and fall of 1993 have taken their place in history as the worst of all U.S. floods in terms of flood crest height; economic loss, estimated at $10 billion ($7 billion in property damage and $3 billion in crop losses); and area inundated—more than 44,000 square kilometers (17,000 sq. mi, or 12 million acres). Eight states (Illinois, Iowa, Missouri, Kansas, Nebraska, Minnesota, South Dakota, and Wisconsin) bore the brunt of the flooding. The flood magnitude exceeded the 300-year flood (the magnitude of flooding that would be expected, on average, only once every 300 years) at many localities, and at Hannibal, Missouri, it exceeded the 500-year flood. Fortunately for that city, a newly completed $8 million floodwall prevented significant damage. The Mississippi River peaked at 2.1 meters (7 ft) above flood stage at Davenport, Iowa, and 4.9 meters (16 ft) above flood stage at St. Louis, Missouri. Residents of Davenport had declined some years back to construct a floodwall because it would detract from the appearance of their waterfront. They paid the price (fig. 11.A). Across the river, the citizens of Rock Island, Illinois, had built a floodwall, and that city was spared any major flooding. For a distance of 320 kilometers (200 mi) along the Mississippi, no bridges were open between Illinois and Missouri. The lack of bridges disrupted rail transportation, and the Mississippi was closed to barge traffic for several months.

It is remarkable, given the extent of devastation, that the death toll from this event only reached 26. Among the reasons for this were extensive early warning systems and evacuation plans. Because there were no flash floods and the river rose slowly, people had time to evacuate. Also, over the years, many of the large population centers had developed extensive systems of levees and floodwalls that, for the most part, did the job for which they were intended. It was mostly in the rural areas and smaller towns, where the quality of flood-control works was much lower, that levee breaks and extensive flooding occurred.

The Mississippi River and its tributaries, a system that drains approximately 40% of the conterminous United States, has a long history of devastating floods. Over the years, in an attempt to control the river, the

U.S. Army Corps of Engineers (that branch of government service that is charged with maintaining this country's navigable waterways) constructed 29 locks and dams on the Mississippi and 36 dam-reservoir systems on its tributaries. For the most part, these have worked, but from time to time, an event of such a magnitude occurs that it cannot be controlled.

An unusual set of circumstances was responsible for the 1993 midwestern floods. The Mississippi River normally

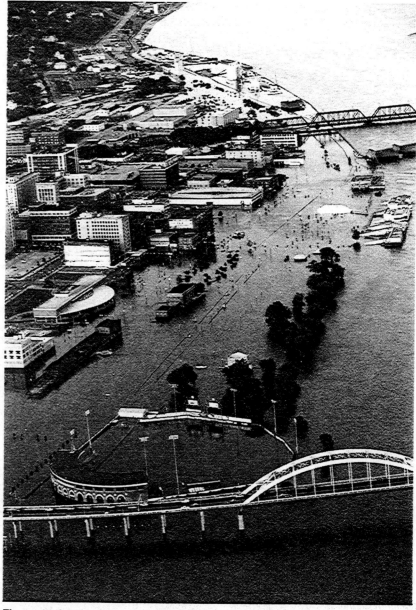

Figure 11.A   Flooding in downtown Davenport, Iowa, 1993.

floods during the late winter or early spring, allowing farmers sufficient time to replant if necessary. The autumn of 1992 was unusually wet in the Midwest, and winter snowfalls that year were very heavy. Consequently, by the spring of 1993, the ground within the Mississippi drainage basin was largely saturated. During July, there was an unusual and protracted period of heavy rainfall throughout the region. The state of Iowa recorded measurable precipitation for 33 consecutive days. For 5 weeks, a high-pressure system (an expanded Bermuda High) sat over the southeastern United States, causing warm, moist air from the Gulf of Mexico to move northward up the Mississippi River valley to collide with cold Canadian air in the Upper Midwest. This led to frequent thunderstorms and attendant heavy precipitation.

Few problems occurred and little damage was done along the Mississippi valley south of Cairo, Illinois, where the Ohio River joins the Mississippi. The Mississippi widens considerably in this area, and the flow added by the Ohio was relatively low that year. The valley was more than able to accommodate the total flow.

The causes and occurrences of flooding are parts of natural cycles, but across the years humans have done much to exacerbate the situation. The natural wetlands and forests that flank rivers, have always acted as a "sponge" to absorb excess water. When the natural vegetation is cleared for conversion of the land to agricultural use, however, this safety valve is lost. In addition to absorbing excess water through infiltration, wetlands also absorb industrial and agricultural toxins and provide animal habitats. So important are the wetlands, in fact, that an innovative program, developed as a result of the 1993 midwestern flood will allow the U.S. government to take long-term leases from the owners of floodplain property, with the intention of converting the property back to wetlands. During the term of such leases, the owners will not be permitted to build on or cultivate the land.

In some cases, it has even been suggested that relocating flood-prone communities off the floodplain may be more cost effective than trying to provide them with flood protection. This is a significant change in policy from that of the federal flood insurance program, which all too often encouraged people to remain on the floodplains by providing cheap insurance against disaster. Figure 11.B shows satellite views of the Mississippi River during a period of normal flow and during the flood of 1993.

Apply Your Knowledge

1. How does a high-pressure system over the Atlantic Ocean influence rainfall in the Midwest?
2. What happens to the flow rate when water from a wide channel is forced through a narrow one created by artificial levees?

Figure 11.B   Satellite views of the Mississippi River in the vicinity of St. Louis. (*a*) Period of normal flow. (*b*) During the flood of July 1993.

occur with some regularity from the North Sea. Constructed between 1974 and 1982 at a cost of half a billion dollars, and first used in February 1983, the system consists of 10 movable gates that, during times of low water, lie on the riverbed. The gates can be rotated 90° to the vertical position in 20 minutes to form a barrier 18 meters (60 ft) high. Figure 11.6 shows one of the nine units that stand above river level and house the machinery that operates the gates.

The second principal engineering technique for controlling stream water is the construction of **levees,** embankments of earth or stone along the stream channel to confine the stream by raising its banks and increasing the channel volume (fig. 11.7). The Mississippi River and its tributaries have 11,270 kilometers (7,000 mi) of levees constructed by the U.S. Army Corps of Engineers. Just as streams deposit their sediment loads in reservoirs, so they also gradually fill their channel bottoms with sediment. Thus, raising the height of the levees is necessary to keep pace with the rising river channel. Levees, however, have some unfortunate consequences. While confining the river (usually where it passes through major urban areas), the levee system may not be able to accommodate all of the water and acts as a bottleneck. The result is that the water backs up, causing serious *upstream flooding.*

A related technique, **channelization,** involves the deepening and straightening of a stream channel. Channelization enhances navigation and allows the movement of a greater volume of water through that part of the channel in a shorter period of time. Unfortunately, however, the increased water volume cannot be accommodated downstream from the channelized segment, and significant erosion and *downstream flooding* may result.

Urbanized areas, which levees, **floodwalls** (steel, stone, or concrete walls designed to contain a stream), and channelization are designed to protect, themselves contribute to flooding problems. Large areas of towns and cities are paved over or built upon, thereby not allowing precipitation to infiltrate the ground. Water is instead forced to flow across the ground surface directly to streams. This adds a large volume of water to the stream network in a very short time.

Where conditions permit, providing a river with additional channels to carry off some of the excess flow may be feasible. A large part of the Mississippi River discharge can be diverted around the city of New Orleans by opening floodgates and sending some of the river's flow through a series of "floodways" and, ultimately, into the Gulf of Mexico and Lake Pontchartrain (fig. 11.8). Although redirecting water alleviates periodic flooding, this causes some of the river's sediment load to be deposited in the Gulf or in Lake Pontchartrain, thus depriving the Mississippi Delta of its normal sediment. Consequently, portions of the delta are subsiding and being reclaimed by the sea.

One other approach to avoiding flood damage and loss of life is to stay out of harm's way. Over the years, however, all cultures have been drawn to the fertile soils and flat topography of floodplains. Because we now better understand how rivers work, federal, state, and local statutes prohibit the construction of most structures within those portions of a river's floodplain that are most susceptible to flooding. However, many structures and farms were located on perilous sites prior to the enactment of these laws.

Figure 11.6 One of the nine units that controls the raising and lowering of the Thames River barrier.

Figure 11.7 Artificial levee dikes along the Missouri River (right bank).

Stream Erosion

Streams do not flow indefinitely. At some point, they end, either by flowing into another stream, a lake, or an ocean. In arid regions, they may simply dry up or infiltrate the ground. When a stream reaches an ocean, its water is dispersed, and it is no longer capable of doing geologic work. Sea level is thus the lowest point to which a stream can erode its valley. This downward limit of erosion for all streams is called **ultimate base level.** Rare exceptions to sea level as base level for stream systems are isolated arid

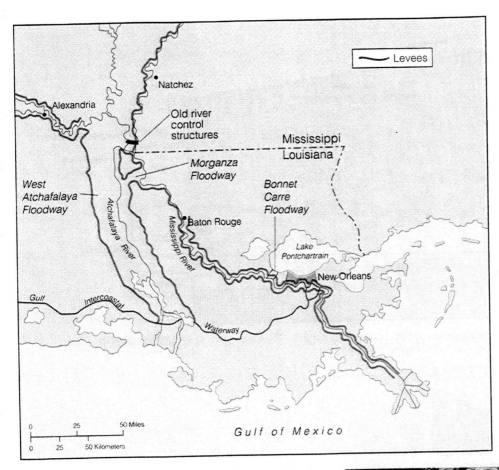

Figure 11.8 Location of floodways along the course of the lower Mississippi River. (Source: Coates, *Environmental Geology,* copyright © 1981 John Wiley & Sons.)

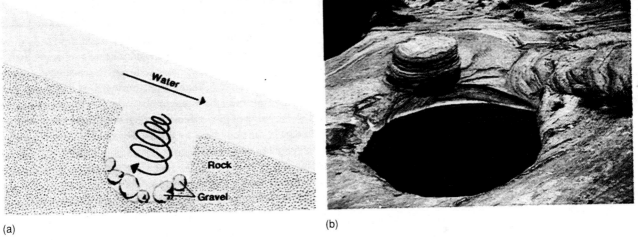

(a)

(b)

Figure 11.9 Pothole formation. (*a*) The process. (*b*) A pothole scoured into the bedrock floor of a stream channel.

basins, such as Death Valley in California and the Dead Sea in Israel and Jordan. These areas are cut off from the oceans and were dropped below sea level by faulting (see chapter 8). Throughout its life and length, every stream reaches base level by eroding its channel and the surrounding landscape. Although the world's oceans serve as the ultimate base level for all stream systems, the downward erosion by individual streams may be controlled by the lakes or larger streams into which they flow. Such base-level control is considered to be *local* (*temporary*) *base level.*

Erosion by streams involves a multifaceted expenditure of energy. On the smallest scale, the work entails the picking up of loose sediment delivered downslope by mass wasting and added to the stream's load by caving stream banks. As these mineral and rock particles move downstream, they bump against one another. The bumping process gradually reduces the sizes of the particles in the downstream direction. In addition, any sharp edges or corners on the particles undergo a chipping that smoothes, or rounds, them. The particles also bump against the stream banks, dislodging other particles. In streams that flow over bedrock channels, turbulence and eddying may move pebbles and even larger rocks in a rapid, swirling motion at certain points on the bedrock channel floor. These moving rock particles act much like a drill, scouring circular depressions known as **potholes** into the channel floor (fig. 11.9).

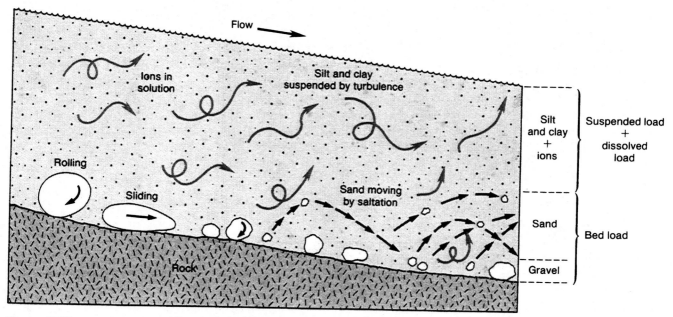

Figure 11.10 Transport of dissolved ions and sediment in a stream under turbulent flow. The coarser part of the bed load remains at rest except during periods of high stream flow (discharge) and consequent high energy.

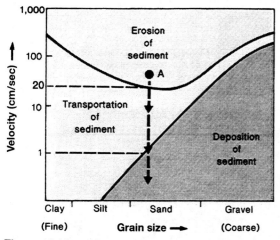

Figure 11.11 Modified version of the Hjulstrom diagram, which relates stream velocity to sediment particle size. To pick up (erode) a sand-sized particle such as *A*, stream velocity must exceed 20 centimeters/second. The same particle could be kept in motion until the velocity drops below 1 centimeter/second, at which time it would be deposited.

On the largest scale, the erosive work of streams cuts **valleys,** or linear depressions (V-shaped in profile), into the landscape. The valley is the principal stream erosional feature and is probably the most common of all landforms (see box 11.2). It is a standard geological principle that valleys are the products of the streams that occupy them, although streams can also occupy valleys originally cut by other streams and/or that have been extensively modified by glaciers. A stream's tendency to erode vertically under the pull of gravity is responsible for the deepening of stream valleys. Valleys are widened by a combination of lateral migration (the process of meandering, discussed later in the chapter) and mass wasting of material down the valley sides to the stream flowing along the valley floor (see chapter 10). Box 11.3 describes a series of changes that occur through time as a result of stream erosion.

Stream Transportation

Streams transport sediment of different sizes in different ways. Because of chemical weathering, some earth materials move through a stream system as dissolved ions that are invisible to us. More apparent, especially in times of high flow, when the stream more actively erodes its banks, is the movement of silts and clays. They are transported by **suspension,** riding in the water column of the moving stream. Whenever these particles are present in abundance, the stream looks brown or muddy. Larger particles, sand, pebbles, and even boulders move only under high-volume, high-energy flows during a stream's **flood stage.** Too large for suspension, these particles skip and bounce (a process known as **saltation**) or roll along the stream bottom during transport. During times of low stream energy, they remain motionless on the channel bed (fig. 11.10).

Valley Floor Deposition

A variety of depositional landforms, created by the loss of stream energy and the dropping of sediment, form within stream valleys. Streams transport and deposit material selectively. Depending on its velocity, a stream carries or drops gravel, sand, silt, and/or clay. With greater energy, a stream can carry larger particles. When a stream loses its energy by slowing down, it deposits its materials, starting with the largest particles, followed by progressively smaller ones. Eventually, even the clay-sized sediments settle where the flow is very slow or the stream loses its identity. This action leads to the separation, or **sorting,** of stream sediment deposits by size. These relationships are illustrated by the Hjulstrom diagram (fig. 11.11).

Box 11.2

Further Consideration

STREAM EROSION ON MARS

For many years, the best-known physical attributes of the planet Mars were the straight, linear features known popularly as "canals." Many scientists, including Sir Percival Lowell, the nineteenth century's most prominent astronomer, considered these the marvelous engineering works of a long-dead civilization. Closer views in photographs taken by the several *Mariner* and *Viking* space probes show no evidence of the canals' existence, and they are generally regarded now as optical illusions. What the 1972 *Mariner 9* probe did reveal, however, was strong evidence for large-scale water erosion on the Martian surface. Because of the extremely low temperatures found there, liquid water cannot exist on the surface of Mars today. In addition, the atmosphere of Mars is so thin and holds so little water vapor that rainfall cannot occur. The evidence for surface erosion by running water, therefore, requires the existence of very different climatic and environmental conditions at some time in the past.

Water-carved channels on Mars come in all sizes. The largest, the Valles Marineris (named for the *Mariner* probe), measures 4,500 kilometers (2,800 mi) long, has a maximum width of 600 kilometers (370 mi), and is up to 7 kilometers (4.4 mi) deep. If superimposed on the United States, it would stretch from New York to California. The principal origin was probably the rapid melting of large quantities of buried ice, which gave rise to a series of catastrophic floods. Such occurrences are known on Earth. During the Pleistocene Ice Age (see chapter 12), glacial ice dams burst, releasing the impounded waters of lakes in floods of almost unimaginable proportions.

On Mars, eroded channels of intermediate size are sinuous and range from as much as 56 kilometers (35 mi) to as little as 90 meters (288 ft) in width (fig. 11.C). They possess short, blunt tributaries forming dendritic patterns, as well as meandering channels, braided channels, islands, and terraces. The numerous small channels occur mostly on crater rims and look like the channels and rills that form by runoff from rainfall and spring outflow on Earth.

The water that caused channel erosion on Mars probably was absorbed into the ground, where it is stored as ground ice, as in the permafrost regions of Canada and Alaska. Whatever their origin, the channels on Mars are remarkably similar to stream channels on Earth and offer unique challenges to scientific interpretation.

Apply Your Knowledge

1. Describe the characteristics of the stream system shown in figure 11.C.
2. Which appears to be younger—the stream system or the impact craters?
3. What possible explanations can you offer for the melting of ice on Mars that led to stream channel erosion?

Figure 11.C   Dendritic valley system on Mars that has been cut deeply into the old cratered terrain. North is toward the top.

All stream deposits are collectively known as **alluvium.** The landforms created by accumulations of alluvium include natural levees, backswamps, and point bars. **Natural levees** are low, parallel ridges on either side of a channel that form as a result of repeated floods. After leaving the confinement of its channel, a stream quickly loses energy and begins to deposit its sediment. The largest particles (sand and silt) and the greatest volume of sediment settle first, in the area adjacent to the channel, forming more massive accumulations than those farther out on the floodplain. The silts and clays, deposited some distance out on the floodplain, form a waterproof seal that prevents the water from draining into the soil. The result is the formation of **backswamps** between the natural levees and the distant valley walls. Because alluvium deposits on the floodplain are mostly formed as the stream overflows its banks, they are also referred to as *overbank deposits.* Figure 11.12 illustrates these relationships.

Figure 11.12   Water velocity drops as soon as the water leaves the confinement of its channel and spreads out across the floodplain. Drop in velocity causes immediate deposition (coarsest material first). The accumulation of large amounts of coarse sediment along both stream banks forms ridges called natural levees.

(a)

(b)

Figure 11.13   (*a*) Erosion occurs on the outside bank of each meander, with deposition occurring on the inside bank. The deposits are called point bars. Continued moving and "stretching" of the meanders eventually leads to their being cut off and isolated (usually during flood stage) as oxbow lakes. (*b*) A floodplain in Florida showing meanders, oxbow lakes, and point bar deposits.

Natural streams never travel in straight lines for any significant distance. Instead, they follow curving, or *meandering*, paths. As the water flows around each bend, or **meander,** it travels faster on the outside of the curve than on the inside because of the greater distance to be traversed. Greater velocity means more energy. Thus, the outside of the curve undergoes erosion, while the inside of the curve, where less energy is available for work, re-

ceives an accumulation of sediment. The deposit on the inside of the meander is called a **point bar.** Eventually, erosion of the outside bank lengthens the meander and narrows its neck to the point where it may be cut off, as a shorter route for the water is formed (fig. 11.13a). This event normally occurs during flood stage, when water flow is fast and high, the stream possesses extra energy, and a portion of the water leaves the stream channel. What remains is a horseshoe-shaped, detached segment of the former channel that fills with water to form an **oxbow lake** (fig. 11.13b).

Some streams carry such great sediment loads that deposition occurs at many places *within* the stream channel. Consequently, the stream breaks up into a series of small channels that weave in and out between numerous sand and gravel bars (fig. 11.14). These **braided streams** typically are found where glacial meltwater streams carry large volumes of sediment down valleys away from the ice front (see chapter 12). Whether a stream, or a segment of a stream, is straight, meandering, or braided describes its **channel pattern** (see box 11.3).

Deltas

When a stream enters a standing body of water (lake, pond, reservoir, or ocean), it disperses and drops its load of sediment. If the shoreline is relatively free of wave and current motion, that sediment may accumulate at the mouth of the stream, forming a sedimentary deposit called a **delta.** As additional sediment is transported to the stream mouth, the delta is extended farther out into the water body. Forced to travel through its own deposits, the stream lengthens and often divides into a series of smaller channels known as **distributaries,** so-called because they distribute the stream's flow. Each distributary seeks its own route across the delta surface to reach base level. Figure 11.15 illustrates delta formation and structure, and figure 11.16 is a satellite view of the most actively building portion of the Mississippi Delta. Deltaic environments will be discussed in more detail in chapter 15.

Figure 11.14 High-altitude view of the Brahmaputra River, India, a braided stream.

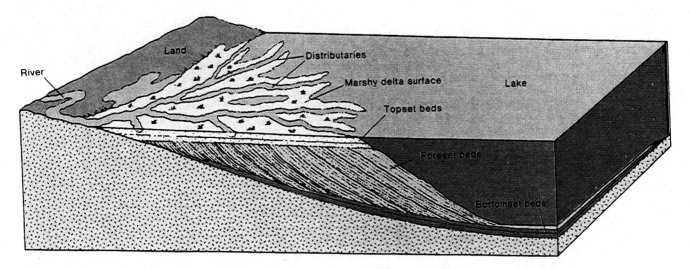

Figure 11.15 General form and internal structure of a delta.

Box 11.3

Further Consideration

THE STREAM EROSION CYCLE

For many years, earth scientists have recognized that landscapes and the geologic agents that form them change slowly over long periods of time. By analogy with the life cycle of organisms (including humans), they have come to recognize these stages of development in landscapes and streams that may be characterized as *youth, maturity,* and *old age* and that together comprise the **stream erosion cycle.** Each stage, whether of an individual stream or an entire landscape, has its own recognizable characteristics. In fact, a stream of any significant length might well have segments in all three stages of development.

A youthful stream might best be envisioned as the small, rushing mountain torrent with highly turbulent flow, steep gradient, and numerous rapids along its channel. Such a stream expends most of its energy in cutting its channel downward, driven by gravity toward the ultimate goal of base level; therefore, it lacks significant floodplain development. Although such streams do not flow in straight lines, they have not as yet developed any meanders of note. The youthful landscape (fig. 11.Da) is characterized by broad divides separating adjacent valleys, to the point where most of the region might be described as *upland surface.* Such upland areas, being broad and flat, often are the sites of lakes and swamps, not having as yet been drained by the newly formed streams.

The mature stream is one with a more moderate gradient; few, if any, rapids; notably less turbulence; and the development of a pronounced pattern of meanders. In many mature regions, streams are numerous and form well-integrated networks that have extensively eroded the region so that the upland divides are now much narrower (fig. 11.Db). In fact, most of the area is now in *slope,* with little flat upland surface and relatively narrow floodplains flanking the stream channels. The local relief of the area has reached its maximum, and con-

tinued erosion of the uplands will lower them and lessen relief. Vertical stream erosion has declined, to be replaced by lateral erosion, with consequent valley widening and significant stream deposition.

Streams in old age have a sluggish appearance, characterized by low gradients and extensive patterns of meandering across wide floodplains. Broad, flat *valley bottoms* (largely floodplains) are the dominant features of the region (fig. 11.Dc). The floodplains possess all of the normally attendant features, including natural levees, backswamps, abandoned meanders, and oxbow lakes. Little erosion is taking place; rather, deposition has become the dominant process. Stream divides, where they can still be recognized, are low and rounded, and streams are large, but few in number. Relief in this stage is minimal because the upland surfaces have been almost completely worn down. The resulting broad surface of very low relief is referred to as a **peneplain** (literally, "almost a plain"). The occasional areas of higher relief rising above the peneplain are called **monadnocks,** after Mount Monadnock in southern New Hampshire, and represent upland remnants that have temporarily escaped elimination by erosion.

The cycle of stream erosion just described is doubtless an oversimplification. No one knows just how the process may proceed (or, indeed, if it does at all) because the time for such a cycle to run its course must be measured in tens of millions of years. Whether Earth's crust would remain stable long enough for the cycle to be completed is doubtful. In fact, evidence in the form of entrenched meanders indicates that such stability often does not persist. **Entrenched meanders** are highly sinuous segments of streams that are found within steep valley walls (fig. 11.E). Little or no floodplain exists. In these cases, a highly meandering old-age stream apparently became *rejuvenated* and began to cut downward as that portion

(a)   Youth

(b)   Maturity

(c)   Old age

Figure 11.D Stages of the stream erosion cycle. (*a*) Youth. (*b*) Maturity. (*c*) Old age.

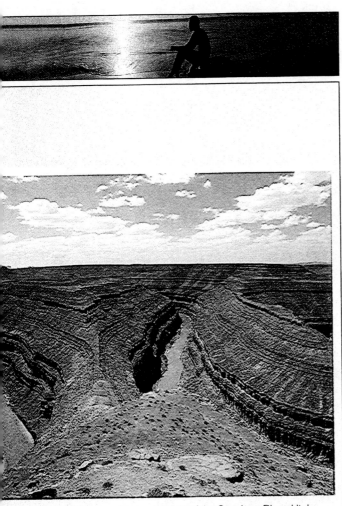

Figure 11.E Entrenched meanders of the San Juan River, Utah.

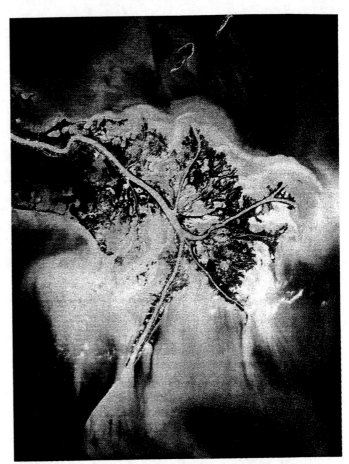

Figure 11.16   A *Landsat–1* view of a part of the Mississippi River delta from an altitude of 914 kilometers (568 mi). Barrier islands, distributaries, and interdistributary bays are clearly visible, as is the light-colored plume of sediment in front of the delta.

of Earth's crust was uplifted, with the rate of downcutting just keeping pace with the rate of uplift. As a result, the meanders became entrapped within the steep gorge that they cut, and the stream is no longer able to straighten its course as it normally would.

Although the cycle of stream erosion is, at best, hypothetical, the terms *youth, maturity,* and *old age* provide a graphic method whereby earth scientists can succinctly describe for one another the appearance of any stream or region.

Apply Your Knowledge

1. If you live near a stream, can you identify any characteristics that would enable you to classify it as youthful, mature, or old?
2. Why is a classification of stream development difficult to apply to all streams?

Alluvial Fans

Somewhat analogous to the formation of deltas in standing bodies of water is the formation of **alluvial fans** at the foot of mountains, most commonly in arid or semiarid regions. Streams that flow down steep gradients through mountains slow abruptly as they move out onto the relatively flat surfaces along the mountain front. Such a change in velocity brings a corresponding change in the stream's sediment-carrying capacity that results in deposition, first of the coarsest, then the finest sediment. The result is a cone-shaped sediment deposit at the mouth of the stream canyon that is progressively built out from the mountain front (fig. 11.17). The depositional process is also enhanced as the flow of water spreads laterally across the unconsolidated sediments of the fan and some water "soaks" into these very porous and permeable materials. In the arid climatic regime, the sediments of the alluvial fan, which are capable of storing large quantities of water, may represent important economic resources.

Figure 11.17 Alluvial fan. Death Valley National Monument, California.

Stream Patterns

From head to mouth, a stream system of tributaries and main channels make a pattern on the landscape that is usually only evident from above. Among the most common of these stream patterns are the dendritic, trellis, radial, and parallel (fig. 11.18).

In an area of horizontal sedimentary rocks or homogeneous igneous rocks, streams appear to branch out randomly in all directions. This **dendritic stream pattern** evolves because no control, other than the ever-present pull of gravity, mandates a particular flow direction. The randomness of the downslope flow of tributaries into the main channel gives the aerial appearance of a branching tree.

Where surface rocks are not of equal resistance to weathering and erosion, streams erode through zones of weakness, particularly in areas of alternate belts of weak and resistant rock units. By following the zones of weak rock, streams take the paths of least resistance and have less work to do in eroding their channels. The resulting stream system has a **trellis pattern,** wherein parallel major valleys alternate with intervening ridges.

On volcanoes, streams adopt a **radial pattern.** Water falling on the higher elevations takes the shortest routes downslope. Because this occurs almost evenly on all sides of the volcano, the pattern, when viewed from above, looks much like the spokes on a wheel.

Similar to the radial pattern is the **parallel pattern,** where streamflow is determined by the general slope of the ground surface in a single direction. Parallel patterns are found along sections of the coastal plains of the Atlantic and Gulf coasts, where the land surfaces slope gently toward the ocean.

(a) Dendritic

(b) Trellis

(c) Radial

(d) Parallel

Figure 11.18 Some common stream patterns and their relationship to the underlying geologic structure. (*a*) Dendritic—uniform resistance to weathering and erosion of the rocks exposed at the surface. (*b*) Trellis—alternate weak and resistant rock zones. (*c*) Radial—uniform slope in all directions from a central high point. (*d*) Parallel—streamflow down an inclined, or sloping, surface.

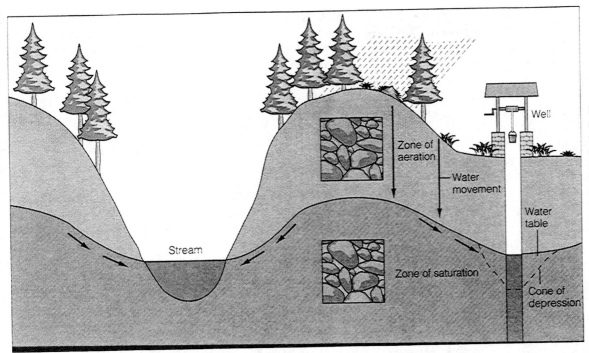

Figure 11.19 Zone of saturation (phreatic water zone), zone of aeration (vadose water zone), and the water table, which separates them. Where the water table intersects a stream channel, groundwater feeds and sustains the stream. If this situation persists year-round, the stream is perennial. If the water table periodically drops below the stream channel, the stream goes dry and is considered to be intermittent.

Figure 11.20 (*a*) A spring forms where water moving along the upper surface of an impermeable shale bed emerges at the ground surface. (*b*) A series of springs developed within a sequence of alternating sandstones and shales in southwestern Pennsylvania.

GROUNDWATER

Like streams, groundwater has its origin in precipitation. Some of the rain and melting snow sinks into, or *infiltrates,* the soils and underlying rocks. Moving from space to space between and around mineral grains, this water is pulled slowly downward by gravity.

The Water Table and Other Features

In the uppermost ground layer that water traverses in its downward movement, the spaces between mineral grains are partly filled with air and partly occupied by water. This is the **zone of aeration,** or the *vadose water zone.* This zone may be subdivided into three smaller units: a *surface belt of soil moisture,* where water is held by plant roots and mineral grains; an *intermediate belt,* where water is actively transiting downward; and a *capillary fringe,* where water is rising by *capillary action* (an attractive force between water and mineral grains) from the zone of saturation below.

Within the **zone of saturation,** or the *phreatic water zone,* the pore spaces of the rocks and soil are completely filled with water (fig. 11.19). The upper surface of this zone, or the boundary between the aerated zone and the saturated zone, is called the **water table.** The water occupying the pore spaces within the saturated zone is **groundwater.** The depth of the water table is largely a function of climate. In arid regions (B climates, see chapter 6), the water table may be 100 meters (328 ft) or more deep, whereas in more humid regions, it is very near the surface. The water table also rises and falls seasonally. During the wettest time of year in some locations, it can actually lie at the ground surface. In fact, when we look at a lake, a marsh, or a large river, we are really looking at the water table. The water table also intersects the ground surface on steep slopes or along fracture systems to form seepages of water called **springs** (fig. 11.20).

In areas of alternating rock layers of varying types, a rock layer often acts as a local impediment to the downward movement of water toward the regional water table. As a result, some water is held in a saturated rock layer above this barrier. Because it lies above the regional water table, this localized saturated zone has its own water table, a surface referred to as a **perched water table** (fig. 11.21). A succession of such features can give rise to a series of vertically arranged springs.

With the exception of streams flowing through caverns in areas of limestone bedrock, groundwater moves slowly from opening to opening through the saturated zone. Typical velocities of groundwater flow lie between a few meters per day and a few meters per year. The ease and speed of this movement depends largely on the **permeability** of the rock or soil—that is, the extent to which pore spaces are interconnected. Rock or sediment bodies, such as sand, gravel, and cavernous limestone, that allow relatively easy passage of water are called **aquifers**. Aquifers, such as the Dakota Sandstone discussed in box 11.4, are important economic resources. The amount of water that can be stored in an aquifer is a function of the percentage of open space within that body, known as the **porosity**. Rock or sediment bodies with low permeability preclude the passage of water and are called **aquicludes**.

Groundwater Problems

Groundwater's very slow movement is a major difficulty in areas dependent on wells for their water supply. If groundwater is pumped from a well faster than it can be replaced by water mov-

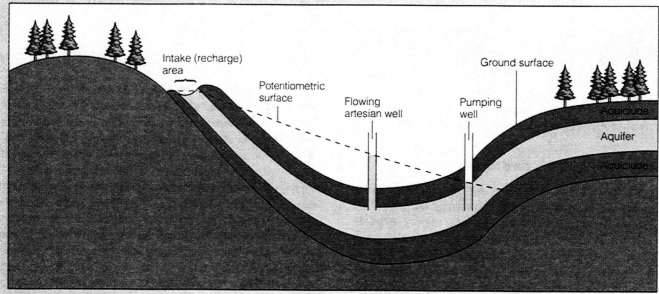

Box 11.4

Further Consideration

ARTESIAN WATER SYSTEMS

An **artesian aquifer** system consists of an inclined aquifer enclosed above and below by impermeable rock layers. If the aquifer is exposed at the ground surface (intake, or recharge, area) at a sufficiently high elevation and if a significant volume of water is taken in, pressure within the aquifer becomes much greater than atmospheric pressure. When the aquifer is penetrated by a well or when a natural system of fractures is present, the water rises through the opening, driven by the weight (pressure) of the water in the aquifer. Theoretically, the rise of the water should be to the same elevation as the location of the intake area. In practice, the water loses some energy to friction during its passage through the aquifer, and the rise is somewhat less. In general, the farther the water travels through the aquifer, the less it rises through the well or fracture

Figure 11.F A simplified natural artesian system.

ing through the aquifer, the water table surrounding the well drops. This cone-shaped depression of the water table centered on the well is called a **cone of depression** (see fig. 11.19). If pumping continues unabated, the point of the cone will fall below the bottom of the well, and the well will go dry.

In coastal areas, heavy drawdown of wells often leads to saltwater contamination of the water supply. Under normal conditions, the slope of the water table is from the land toward the sea. If the water table is locally lowered enough, the slope of the water table and, consequently, the direction of water flow is reversed, and wells begin to produce salt water.

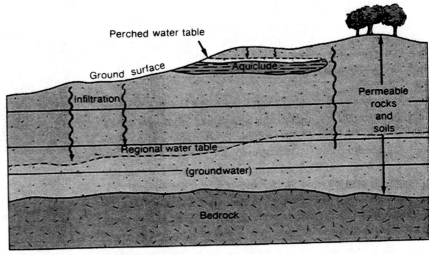

Figure 11.21 A perched water table.

system (fig. 11.F). The surface defined by the level to which the water rises in all the associated wells or fracture systems is the **piezometric (potentiometric) surface.**

If the **hydraulic gradient** (elevation difference between the intake area and the ground at the surface opening or well site) is sufficient, water rises to the ground surface and flows out as an **artesian spring** or **artesian well.** If the gradient is less, water must be pumped from the well.

The artesian system operates much like a municipal water system. Here, water

flows through a network of pipes (the "aquifer") and into the plumbing systems of homes and businesses under the gradient produced by the high location of the water reservoir or water tower (fig. 11.G).

In the United States, an important artesian aquifer is the Dakota Sandstone, which underlies a large area of the Great Plains region from South Dakota to Texas. The intake area for the Dakota Sandstone is in western South Dakota, where the upturned edges of the sandstone are exposed around the Black Hills. For thousands of years, water accumulated

within and flowed slowly southward through the Dakota Sandstone. In the last 150 years, however, more than 10,000 wells have been drilled into this unit to tap the water for irrigated agriculture in this semiarid region. The result is that this water resource has literally been "mined"—that is, removed at a far greater rate than nature can replace it. Consequently, both the volume of water remaining in the aquifer and the pressure within the aquifer have dropped drastically. Most of the wells still producing from the Dakota Sandstone must now be pumped.

Apply Your Knowledge

1. What are the components of an artesian system?
2. Can you find references in the geological literature to any other important aquifers (besides the Dakota Sandstone) in the United States or Canada?
3. What are the progressive changes brought about in an artesian aquifer, such as the Dakota Sandstone, by the overmining of the groundwater?

Figure 11.G A simple municipal water system operating under the same principles as an artesian system.

The movement of water from pore space to pore space within the soil, a process known as *percolation,* is also important for homes with septic systems. The percolation rate must be rapid enough to permit the movement of fluid wastes quickly away from the house, yet slow enough to permit the filtering of contaminants out of the water.

Groundwater *contamination* has increased as more communities have turned to groundwater as a source of *potable water,* water suitable for human consumption. Two measures of contamination are normally used. **Water purity** is a measure of the degree of contamination by microorganisms. **Water quality** is a measure of chemical content (i.e., the amount of dissolved mineral material). Water with large amounts of dissolved calcium and magnesium is referred to as *hard water.* Hard water typically forms scaly mineral deposits in pipes over a period of time and leaves rings in bathtubs and sinks. *Soft water* has a lower mineral content and is recognizable by its ability to form lather readily with soap. Commercial water softeners remove calcium and magnesium from the water and replace them, in part, with sodium.

An even more serious problem affecting groundwater supplies today is *depletion.* Not only does urbanization increase the demand for groundwater, but the building over of the ground surface robs the groundwater system of much of its natural recharge area. **Recharge** occurs as precipitation infiltrates the ground, replacing any water that has been removed. To compensate for lost recharge area, some communities on Long Island, New York, have drilled recharge wells into which water that has been removed (principally for air-conditioning systems) can be pumped back into the ground after use.

The Relationship of Groundwater to Streams

Whereas some groundwater may eventually emerge at the ground surface as a spring, a large amount seeps into the channels of nearby streams. This seepage provides the water that allows **perennial streams,** typical of humid regions with high water tables, to flow year-round. Such streams are also referred as **effluent streams** (fig. 11.22*a*). Frequently, the water table falls below the beds of smaller streams, causing the stream channel to become dry and creating a flow called an **intermittent stream.** Intermittent stream channels carry water during the wetter times of the year but are dry during other times. A third type of flow regime is an **ephemeral stream,** which is characteristic of streams in arid regions. Ephemeral stream channels carry water only during and shortly after a period of intense rainfall. In arid regions, such an event might occur several times a year or once every several years. Because in arid regions the water table is very deep, groundwater rarely flows into a stream. Rather, when water flows through the stream channel, it infiltrates the channel bed and ultimately seeps down to the water table. These streams, in which the flow of water is from stream channel to water table, are **influent streams** (fig. 11.22*b*).

(a)

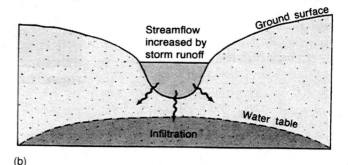

(b)

Figure 11.22 (*a*) Effluent stream, typical of humid regions. Groundwater flows into the stream channel. (*b*) Influent stream, typical of arid regions. Water flows from the channel (after a storm event) into the ground.

Groundwater Erosion and Deposition

As an agent of erosion, groundwater performs most of its geologic work by *dissolution.* When it comes in contact with the soil and bedrock during its slow movement, groundwater dissolves some of the minerals and transports them in solution. Because it moves so slowly and through such tiny openings, groundwater rarely transports suspended silts and clays.

Acid rainfall produced by industrial and automobile pollution tends to increase groundwater erosion. Groundwater becomes acidic by absorbing carbon dioxide from the atmosphere and the soil. Increased acidity enhances groundwater's capacity to do geologic work in areas of soluble limestone bedrock. So effective is this work that large masses of limestone may be removed, leaving subsurface voids known as **caverns.** Without its bedrock support, the ground surface above these voids occasionally collapses to form surface depressions called **sinkholes** (see chapter 10). The collective occurrence of surface and subsurface features of groundwater origin, including caverns and sinkholes, is called **karst topography,** after a limestone plateau along the northeastern coast of the Adriatic Sea where such features are especially well developed (fig. 11.23). In addition to the presence of limestone bedrock, three other conditions contribute to karst formation: (1) a humid climate, (2) fractures in the otherwise impermeable limestone to provide passageways for the downward movement of water, and (3) a major stream in the area that provides a base-level control for downward-moving water.

Figure 11.23 Development of groundwater (karst) features in an area of limestone bedrock.

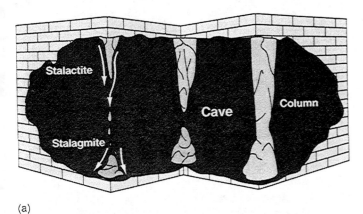

(a)

Figure 11.24 (*a*) Formation of stalactites, stalagmites, and columns within a cavern. Arrows show movement of water carrying dissolved calcium carbonate. (*b*) Dripstone features. Carlsbad Caverns, New Mexico.

As groundwater progresses through the soils, sediments, and bedrock, some of its dissolved minerals precipitate out of solution. Near Earth's surface, this deposition occurs chiefly in two locales: (1) among loose sediment, where the precipitating mineral matter serves as a cement that binds the individual grains and converts the sediment into rock; and (2) as calcite-rich and clay-rich layers within the soils of arid and humid regions, respectively (see chapter 16).

When groundwater saturated with dissolved mineral material seeps out of fractures in the roof of a cave, it undergoes a reduction in pressure, loses some of its carbon dioxide, and becomes less acidic, which reduces its ability to retain calcium carbonate in solution. Some of this mineral material then precipitates to form delicate, icicle-like projections, called **stalactites,** from the roof of the cave (fig. 11.24). Continuing its downward movement, some of the water drops onto the cave floor, where it deposits more mineral material. This accumulating material builds up a cone-shaped feature known as a **stalagmite** from the cave floor. Often stalactites and stalagmites merge to form **columns.** Mineral deposits formed in caves in this manner are collectively known as **dripstone.**

(b)

Further Thoughts: The Pervasiveness of Water

In addition to being a critical element of our daily existence, water pervades much of our planet and occupies an important position in the study of Earth. In earlier chapters dealing with meteorology and climatology, we learned how water is distributed by air currents and why it collects in abundance in some localities and minimally in others. It even plays an important role in the formation of magma, as you read in chapter 9. This chapter dealt with the characteristics of water's liquid form—both on and beneath Earth's land surfaces. An important component of this is how water expends energy to erode, transport, and deposit rock material, thereby altering the appearance of the land. Later chapters focus on the ocean, that vast water reservoir that is the ultimate source of the water found on and beneath the land. We consider in chapter 16 the importance and distribution of water as a natural resource, including how humans, to satisfy their needs, have in the past and still are today altering water's natural distribution. Water was the birthplace for life. Its inundation of the land and its ability to hold suspended substances and dissolved solids and gases added to the development of our planet, giving Earth the special designation "the water planet."

Living on a water planet, we must acknowledge water's importance to our lives. Yet, many individuals, organizations, and industries have used this valuable resource and returned it in a polluted state to the environment. Maintaining the purity of our water supplies is essential because supplies are limited for many cultures and because a variety of physical ailments have been linked to polluted water. If we continue our careless ways, we may find ourselves very much like Samuel Taylor Coleridge's ancient mariner, proclaiming, "Water, water, everywhere, nor not a drop to drink."

Significant Points

1. Streams are the most important of the geologic agents, doing more work than all of the others combined.

2. A stream is the channelized flow of water across the land surface.

3. A stream and its system of tributaries drain an area of land known as the drainage basin, or watershed. Adjacent drainage basins are separated by a drainage divide.

4. Water moving slowly across a smooth surface moves by laminar flow. As velocity increases and/or the surface becomes rougher, the flow becomes turbulent.

5. Discharge is the amount of water moving past a point in the stream channel in a given interval of time.

6. Floods occur when the volume of water in a stream exceeds the capacity of the stream channel to contain it.

7. The most common flood-control techniques are dams and reservoirs, levees, floodwalls, and channelization.

8. The downward limit of erosion for all major streams is sea level, or ultimate base level. For smaller streams, local base level may be a lake, a desert basin, or a larger stream.

9. The stream-eroded valley is probably the most common of all landforms.

10. Streams transport material in solution, in suspension, or by saltation.

11. Stream deposition occurs when a stream loses energy. The largest particles are dropped first, followed by progressively finer material. This process leads to the sorting of stream sediments, or alluvium.

12. Streams never travel in straight lines for any significant distance. Rather, they follow curving, or meandering, paths across their floodplains.

13. Point bars, meanders, backswamps, oxbow lakes, and natural levees are features found on a typical floodplain.

14. A delta may form when a stream flows into a standing body of water, where wave and current activity is not excessive.

15. Alluvial fans form at the mouths of stream canyons, where the streams flow out onto a more gently sloping surface.

16. Streams and landscapes may be qualitatively described as youthful, mature, or old.

17. Stream patterns are the composite areal arrangement of a group of streams. Common patterns are dendritic, trellis, radial, and parallel.

18. The surface that separates the zone of aeration above from the zone of saturation below (or, simply, the top surface of the zone of saturation) is the water table. The water occupying the saturated zone is the groundwater.

19. The intersection of the water table with the ground surface along slopes or fracture zones forms springs.

20. Rock and soil units that are sufficiently permeable to allow the passage of groundwater are called aquifers. Those that are impermeable to the passage of groundwater are called aquicludes.

21. Water purity is a measure of the contamination of water by microorganisms, whereas water quality is a measure of water's dissolved mineral content.

22. Perennial streams maintain their flow year-round, while intermittent streams go dry when the water table drops below the bed of the stream channel. Perennial streams are fed constantly by groundwater and are effluent.

23. Ephemeral streams, typical of arid regions, carry water only during and immediately after a period of rainfall. They lose water to the subsurface by infiltration through the streambed and, thus, are influent.

24. Groundwater does most of its geologic work by dissolution.

25. Groundwater dissolution of limestone leads to the formation of karst topography, which is characterized by caverns, sinkholes, and other solutional features.

26. Groundwater depositional features occurring in caverns are collectively known as dripstone and include stalactites and stalagmites.

27. .In an artesian system, water from an aquifer rises toward the ground surface through wells or fractures, driven by the weight (pressure) of the water in the aquifer.

ESSENTIAL TERMS

stream *259*
rill *259*
river *259*
tributary *259*
drainage basin
  (watershed) *259*
drainage divide *259*
laminar flow *260*
turbulent flow *260*
stream head *260*
stream mouth *260*
stream gradient *260*
long (longitudinal)
  profile *260*
discharge *260*
flood *260*
floodplain *260*
levee *264*

channelization *264*
floodwall *264*
ultimate base level *264*
pothole *265*
valley *266*
suspension *266*
flood stage *266*
saltation *266*
sorting *266*
alluvium *268*
natural levee *268*
backswamp *268*
meander *269*
point bar *269*
oxbow lake *269*
braided stream *269*
channel pattern *269*
delta *269*

distributary *269*
stream erosion
  cycle *270*
peneplain *270*
monadnock *270*
entrenched
  meander *270*
alluvial fan *271*
dendritic stream
  pattern *272*
trellis stream
  pattern *272*
radial stream
  pattern *272*
parallel stream
  pattern *272*
zone of aeration *273*
zone of saturation *273*

water table *273*
groundwater *273*
spring *273*
perched water
  table *274*
permeability *274*
aquifer *274*
porosity *274*
aquiclude *274*
artesian aquifer *274*
cone of depression *275*
piezometric
  (potentiometric)
  surface *275*
hydraulic gradient *275*
artesian spring *275*
artesian well *275*
water purity *276*

water quality *276*
recharge *276*
perennial stream *276*
effluent stream *276*
intermittent stream *276*
ephemeral stream *276*
influent stream *276*
cavern *276*
sinkhole *276*
karst topography *276*
stalactite *277*
stalagmite *277*
column *277*
dripstone *277*

REVIEW QUESTIONS

1. What is a stream? How does it differ from a river (or does it)?
2. What is a drainage basin? What is a drainage divide?
3. How does laminar flow differ from turbulent flow? Under what conditions does each occur?
4. What is a stream gradient? How does it normally change along a stream's course? In what units is it measured?
5. What is a flood? What is a floodplain?
6. What is the principal purpose of dam-reservoir systems? What other functions do they often fulfill?
7. What is an artificial levee? What is its purpose?
8. What is the purpose of channelization? Does this technique typically lead to upstream or downstream flooding? Why?
9. What is base level? What is the difference between ultimate and local base level?
10. What is the principal stream erosional landform?
11. What is meant by a stream sorting its sediment?
12. By what mechanism does meandering occur?
13. What are some of the stream depositional landforms typically found within a valley?
14. Describe a braided stream channel pattern. How does this pattern form?

15. How and where do deltas form?
16. How and where do alluvial fans form?
17. What are some of the common stream patterns, and why do they form?
18. What are some common characteristics of each of the three stages of the stream erosion cycle?
19. How do entrenched meanders form?
20. How does the zone of aeration differ from the zone of saturation? What surface separates the two zones?
21. What is a spring?
22. What is the difference between an aquifer and an aquiclude?
23. What is a cone of depression, and how does it form?
24. What is meant by water purity? What is meant by water quality?
25. What is the difference between a perennial and an intermittent stream?
26. Where would one typically find ephemeral streams?
27. What are the characteristics of an artesian system?
28. Under what conditions does karst topography form?
29. What are some of the erosional and depositional features associated with karst topography?

CHALLENGES

1. Describe the potential for a major (or minor) flood event for your town or city.
2. If a stream flows near where you live, make a list of flood-control measures that have been taken to protect the community.
3. By visual observation and notes or by photographs, keep a record over a period of months of changes in water level of a stream near your home.
4. What type of water-supply system feeds your home? What analogies can you make between this system and an artesian system?

Chapter 12

The Work of Glaciers and Wind

Glacial meltwater from the base of
Athabasca Glacier. Jasper National Park, Alberta, Canada.

In this chapter, we will consider two geologic agents that, at first glance, appear to be more dissimilar than similar: glaciers and wind (ice and air, respectively, in motion). Closer examination, however, leads to the discovery of some interesting similarities. Both glaciers and wind, like other geologic agents, shape the land surface through the processes of erosion and deposition. The result in each case is spectacular and unique scenery. Both are associated with extremely inhospitable regions, where human populations are very low and/or migratory. Both are intensely related to extreme climates. For example, deserts, where the work of wind is most noticeable, are the result of a paucity of rainfall. Glaciers also develop in climates with low precipitation, but in which low temperatures have allowed snow and ice to accumulate. Although we cannot actually see the wind, we can feel its presence and see its results. While glaciers today cover only 10% of the land surface, as recently as 20,000 years ago, 30% of the land area was covered by ice sheets up to 4 kilometers (2.5 mi) thick. That as much as 75% of the world's total land area was affected directly or indirectly by these ice sheets can be inferred from abundant geological evidence. Finally, both glacers and wind will figure prominently in Earth's future as global warming and human mismanagement of the environment lead to melting polar ice caps and desertification.

GLACIERS

When annual snowfall exceeds an area's climatic ability to melt, evaporate, and sublimate it, the accumulation can create ice fields, from which, in turn, glaciers form. As geologic surface agents, **glaciers** are thick masses of ice that move as their weight responds to gravity and to pressures within. An estimated 75% of the world's fresh water is locked up in the ice of glaciers, and 95% of this ice is contained in the massive ice sheets on the continent of Antarctica and the island of Greenland.

Types of Glaciers

Two kinds of glaciers transform landscapes. Glaciers that move primarily in response to gravity are long, linear, and confined to stream valleys within mountainous regions. They are variously referred to as *ice streams, alpine glaciers, mountain glaciers,* or **valley glaciers** (fig. 12.1*a*). Glaciers that move from areas of high pressure (thick ice) to areas of low pressure (thin ice) are *ice sheets, ice caps* (sometimes considered a smaller version of an ice sheet), or because they may be geographically very large, **continental glaciers** (fig. 12.1*b*). Such

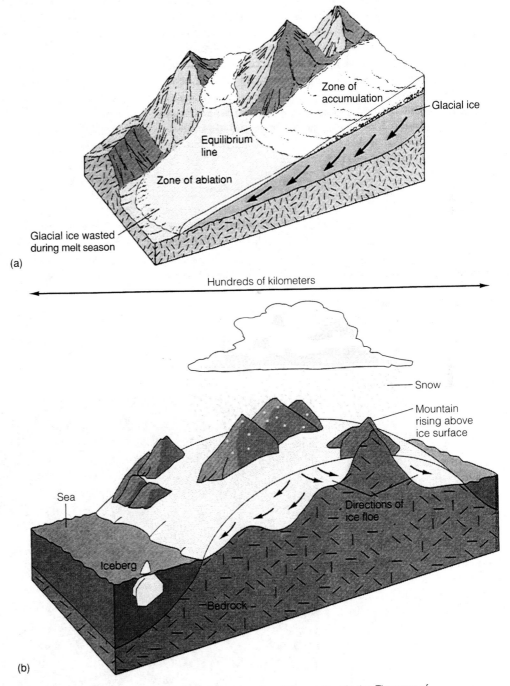

Figure 12.1 (*a*) Ice movement in response to gravity within a valley glacier. The zone of accumulation is the area of the glacier where more snow and ice accumulate each year than are lost by melting or other causes. In the zone of ablation, annual loss exceeds annual accumulation. The equilibrium line separates the two zones. (*b*) Ice within an ice sheet (continental glacier) flows outward in all directions from the region of high pressure (thick ice) to the zones of lowest pressure (thin ice).

glaciers are formed at high latitudes, are unconfined by topography, and may have surface areas measured in millions of square kilometers and thicknesses in excess of 3 kilometers (2 mi).

Other types of glaciers are variations on these two fundamental types. Individual ice streams, as they emerge from valleys, may coalesce at the foot of mountains to form a small ice sheet. Because of its location, such an ice mass is referred to as a **piedmont** (literally, "foot of the mountain") **glacier.** Other valley glaciers have shrunk back to the point where they merely occupy the high-altitude basins in which they first formed and are now called **cirque glaciers.** These glaciers tend to be best preserved on the north and east sides of mountain peaks, where the ice is most protected from melting. In the Northern Hemisphere, the sun lies to the south, leaving shady northern slopes. East-facing slopes are exposed to the rising sun during the colder part of the day, whereas west-facing slopes are exposed to the sun during the warmer afternoons. Another type of glacier occurs on Greenland, where the ice sheet occupies a central depression ringed by mountains. Pressure in the central ice cap forces streams of ice outward through low passes in the mountains, where they eventually enter the sea. These glaciers, varieties of ice streams, are **outlet glaciers.**

Anatomy of a Glacier

New ice forms across the entire area of a glacier when fallen snow changes by melting and refreezing to a granular form called **firn.** Even as new ice forms, older ice is lost. That portion of a glacier where accumulation of new ice exceeds loss of old ice (usually at higher elevations or latitudes) is the **zone of accumulation.** That part of the glacier where loss of ice exceeds gain is the **zone of ablation** (see fig. 12.1*a*). The line separating the zone of accumulation from the zone of ablation is the **equilibrium line.** Ice loss, or **ablation,** may be by melting, sublimation (the direct change from the solid to the gaseous state), or **calving,** the breaking off of ice masses that extend into a body of water. The calving process is responsible for the formation of **icebergs,** or floating masses of ice (fig. 12.2), that have become detached from the glacier because the water into which it moves is not able to support the weight of the ice as the land surface does. If the addition of new ice exceeds that lost to ablation, the front of the glacier advances across the landscape. If ablation exceeds accumulation, the ice mass shrinks, and the ice front retreats. In both cases, ice movement within the glacier is *forward: it is only the glacier's front that moves forward or backward.* Like groundwater, glaciers fluctu-

ate with the seasons and move very slowly, at rates generally between a few meters per day and a few meters per year.

Ice becomes a glacier only as it undergoes movement in response to gravity and/or internal pressure. More specifically, that movement manifests itself in several ways (fig. 12.3). In the upper 30 to 60 meters (100 to 200 ft) of the glacier, where pressures are generally low, the ice usually fractures, opening up large surface cracks, or **crevasses.** This is the **fracture zone.** Fracturing displaces blocks of ice downslope or toward areas of lower pressure. Deeper within the glacier, where pressures are high, fracturing is inhibited, and the ice flows slowly as a plastic solid (**plastic zone**). Within this zone, individual ice crystals are deformed, slide past one another, and undergo melting and refreezing (recrystallization). Along the glacier's base, the ice slips across the ground surface. This movement is greatly enhanced by the lubricating effect of abundant meltwater. Such basal slippage is particularly important in the **temperate glaciers** of milder climatic regimes, where temperatures are at or just below the melting point of the ice. In more severe climatic zones, as in the thick, polar ice caps, extremely low temperatures preclude melting, and the ice of these **polar glaciers** adheres to the ground beneath. Movement along the base of the glaciers in this case is by the physical plucking of the underlying bedrock.

Unusual buildup of basal meltwater is the apparent cause of the glacial phenomenon known as **surging,** or relatively rapid ice movements within a short time period. Why such buildups occur is not known, but the phenomenon may be related to blocking and unblocking (changes in direction) of meltwater streams within and beneath the glacier.

Glaciers As Geologic Agents

The geologic work of glaciers is limited today because glaciers cover only about 10% of the land. In the recent geologic past, however,

Figure 12.2 Iceberg off Anvers Island, Antarctica.

glaciers covered as much as 30% of Earth's land surface, and many areas still bear the imprint of glaciation in the form of distinctive landscape features. As noted earlier, most of the volume of today's glaciers is contained in large ice sheets on Antarctica and Greenland. Much smaller ice sheets occur on Iceland, and ice streams are found in many of the higher mountains, even at equatorial locations.

Glacial Erosion

Glaciers are very powerful agents of erosion. They grind and push their way downslope and across the ground surface, scraping up loose sediment, plucking fragments from masses of solid rock (**quarrying**), polishing bedrock by abrasion, and cutting linear grooves (**striations,** or *glacial striae*) into the bedrock surface (fig. 12.4). These striations are particularly useful in determining past directions of glacial movement. In mountainous regions (fig. 12.5),

(a)

(b)

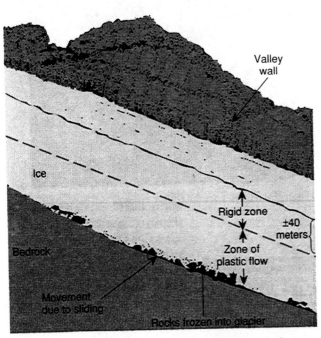

Figure 12.3 Types and zones of movement within a glacier.

Figure 12.4 Glacial striations and polish on bedrock. South Australia.

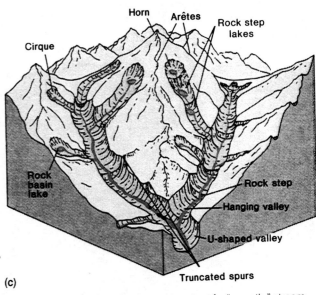

(c)

Figure 12.5 Modification by glacial erosion of a "smooth," stream-formed landscape to a "sharp," glacial landscape: (*a*) Prior to glaciation. (*b*) During glaciation. (*c*) After glaciation.

Figure 12.6   Horns, arêtes, and cirques in Mount Reynolds at Logan Pass, Montana.

Figure 12.7   U-shaped glacial trough. Glacier National Park, Montana.

where their erosive power is best displayed, glaciers carve the higher elevations into a series of sharp peaks, called **horns** (after the famous Matterhorn in the Swiss Alps), and narrow ridges, called **arêtes,** that often connect the horns (fig. 12.6). At their points of origin, they scour flat-floored, semicircular depressions called **cirques** that often fill with water to form small lakes, or **tarns,** after the glacier melts. Valley glaciers also broaden and deepen the valleys they occupy. When the ice melts, such valleys are left with a characteristic U-shaped cross profile, making them easy to identify (fig. 12.7). Glacially eroded valleys, or **troughs,** lack the smooth downslope profile characteristic of unglaciated stream valleys. They consist of a series of flat, steplike surfaces, each of which may contain a basin-like depression. These basins, when filled with water, form a linear series of small lakes, known as **paternoster lakes,** extending down the glacial trough.

Figure 12.8 Hanging valley and waterfall, Yosemite Valley, California.

Figure 12.9 Fiord on the coast of British Columbia.

The rate of downcutting by a tributary stream of water is governed by the level of the main stream into which it flows, an example of local base-level control. Consequently, at their junction, the tributary stream and the main stream are at the same elevation. Ice streams, however, behave much differently. They erode proportionately to their thickness, with large glaciers eroding more deeply than small glaciers. When the glacial ice melts and streams once again occupy the valleys, the smaller tributary streams flow through **hanging valleys** above the level of the main stream. To join the main stream, the tributaries must flow down steep rapids or over waterfalls (fig. 12.8). Bridal Veil Falls and Yosemite Falls in Yosemite National Park, California, are well-known examples of such features.

Because glaciers are solid masses, they are not governed by the base-level control of sea level that acts as a downward limit for stream erosion. Along coastlines, glaciers can erode their troughs well below sea level. When the ice melts away, the sea moves in to occupy the troughs, giving rise to narrow, deep, steep-sided embayments known as **fiords** (fig. 12.9). The coastlines of Norway, Greenland, New Zealand, and New England are famous for their spectacular fiord development.

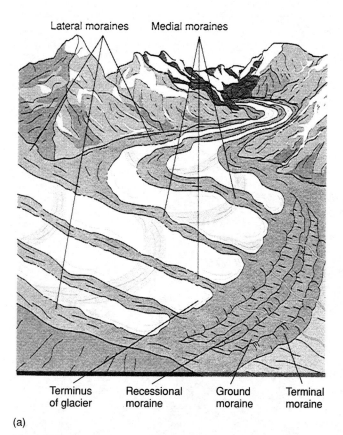

Lateral moraines   Medial moraines

Terminus   Recessional   Ground   Terminal
of glacier   moraine   moraine   moraine

(a)

(b)

(c)

Figure 12.10   (*a*) Positions of the several types of moraines commonly associated with valley glaciers. (*b*) The lateral and medial moraines on a typical valley glacier. (*c*) Lateral, terminal, and recessional moraines remain as topographic features after the glacier has melted away. Note the general "sharpness" of the glacially eroded topography.

Glacial Deposition

Sediment picked up by scraping and quarrying, as well as material that falls onto the ice surface from overhanging valley walls (*avalanching*), is incorporated into the moving ice mass or carried on top of it. Because ice is a solid and can support the weight of material even when not moving, sediment is not deposited when the ice slows down, only when it melts. The sediment dumped by the melting ice is called **glacial till.** Because ice lacks the sorting capability of running water, glacial till is a mixture of all sizes of particles, from fine clay to large boulders.

Landforms produced by the accumulation of glacial till are called **moraines,** and they occur in a variety of shapes and sizes (fig. 12.10). Some are low, linear ridges formed at the end, or terminus, of the glacier. These **end,** or **terminal, moraines** are crescent-shaped, like the lobate form of the ice front.

Rock debris that falls from overhanging valley walls and accumulates along the sides of a valley glacier forms **lateral moraines.** Where two valley glaciers come together, the lateral moraines merge to produce an elongated ridge of glacial till on the ice surface and, later, in the center of the valley, called a **medial moraine.** As a glacier melts back, it may pause for a period of time in its retreat so that a ridge of glacial till accumulates along the ice front, forming a **recessional moraine.** This type of moraine most commonly occurs as one of a group of such features paralleling the terminal

moraine that lies down-valley. Recessional moraines mark the locations of successive pauses in the glacier's general retreat. If conditions permit the glacier to advance once again, the recessional moraines are highly modified or obliterated by the advancing ice. As continental glaciers retreat, terminal and recessional moraines, respectively, also form at the line of furthest advance and at locations of pauses.

Between terminal and recessional moraines, especially where large ice sheets cover relatively flat areas, the glacial till is deposited as a broad blanket with little topographic relief, known as a **ground moraine.** In fact, deposition of the ground moraine will fill in low portions of the preglacial topography, effectively obliterating it (fig. 12.11). In areas of extensive coverage by continental glaciers, such as the midwestern United States, terminal and recessional moraines may represent the only significant topographic features standing above a flat, monotonous plain.

In general, deposition is a process more characteristic of continental glaciers than valley glaciers. The deposition of glacial till by continental glaciers imparts a smoothness to the landscape that contrasts with the sharp erosional landforms of mountain glaciation.

Other landforms are also characteristic of regions of continental glaciation. Sediment carried by streams flowing within or

Figure 12.11 Ground moraine. Kettle Moraine State Park, Wisconsin.

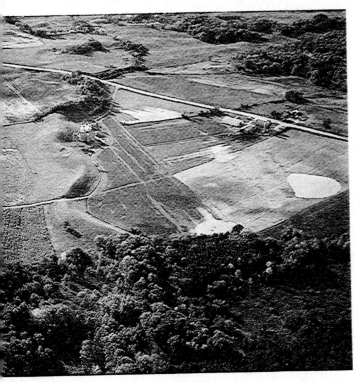

Figure 12.12 Esker near Dundee, Wisconsin.

beneath the ice may be deposited when ice movements block the stream channel. Such deposits, known as **eskers,** remain after the ice sheet has melted (fig. 12.12). These curving linear ridges mimic the meandering pattern of the stream channel in which they were deposited. An advance of an ice sheet or the flow of meltwater across previously deposited till may shape those deposits into a series of hills, or **drumlins,** that are elongated parallel to the direction of ice movement (fig. 12.13).

Streams of meltwater may pick up sediment deposited along the ice front and carry it down the valley away from the ice front. This transported sediment is **glacial outwash.** The meltwater sorts and deposits this material in a geologic action typical of streams. Some of this sediment has been pulverized to such a fine size that it is referred to as *rock flour*. Because rock flour stays easily suspended in meltwater streams, it gives the streams a cloudy appearance. Meltwater deposits, if spread across a broad area by numerous migrating streams, form an **outwash plain.** If, rather, they are concentrated as linear deposits along individual stream valleys, they are **valley trains.**

All glacially deposited sediment was at one time referred to as **drift.** This was an allusion to the idea that all such sediment was transported by drifting icebergs, which, upon melting, set free their sediment loads. While we now know that the greatest amount of glacial sediment does not have such a history of transport, some does. Recent work on deep-sea sediment cores, in fact, has enabled scientists to date rather accurately times when large numbers of icebergs drifted into the North Atlantic and released their load of rafted sediment onto the seafloor as they melted. These

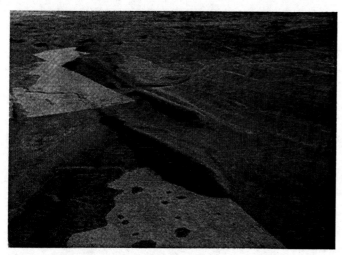

Figure 12.13 Drumlin near Jameson Lake, Washington.

Figure 12.14 Large transported boulder (glacial erratic) on Cape Cod, Massachusetts.

periods of intense iceberg formation were, perhaps, the result of climatic changes or changes in oceanic current patterns.

Most of the finer material within glacial till consists of local bedrock that is ground and pulverized by the action of the glacier; hence, one deposit of till may differ significantly from other deposits in composition and texture. For instance, many of the tills of the midwestern United States consist largely of fine material, with relatively few larger pebbles and boulders. This is because the underlying bedrock in this region is largely limestone and shale, weak rocks that are easily pulverized. By contrast, many tills in New England, northern Wisconsin, and other states and provinces contain numerous large boulders, some the size of small buildings (fig. 12.14). These tills consist mostly of igneous and metamorphic rocks, the local bedrock types, and they are not easily reduced to fine-grain sizes. In the midwestern United States and Canada, the soils derived from till are easily worked by farmers. In New England and other areas of rocky till, generations of farmers had to remove the boulders from their fields by hand. Demonstrating their ingenuity, however, the farmers used the boulders to construct homes, barns, and fences.

Not all components of till are of local origin, however. Glaciers that traveled hundreds of kilometers from the area of original ice accumulation often incorporated pieces of rock from the source area and from locations along their routes. These may then have been deposited long distances from their bedrock sources. Because such rock fragments are now found far removed from their places of origin, earth scientists refer to them as **erratics** (meaning that they are "wanderers" or out of place). Aspiring "rock hounds" can often accumulate a fine collection of different rock types simply by hunting through a single deposit of glacial till.

Some very rare minerals with significant economic value have even been found in glacial deposits. In 1876, a large, rough diamond was found in a till deposit in southwestern Wisconsin. Since that time, similar finds have been made in Minnesota, Michigan, Illinois, Indiana, and Ohio. Amateurs as well as professionals have attempted to trace these diamonds back to their source, thus far with no success. Tracing the path of the glaciers only indicates a possible source area near James Bay, a southward projection of Hudson Bay. To the north and west, however, diamonds were discovered in the glacial deposits of the Northwest Territories of Canada in 1991. This led to a frenzied period of exploration in this remote wilderness area (see box 12.1). Figure 12.15 illustrates the principal depositional features associated with an ice sheet.

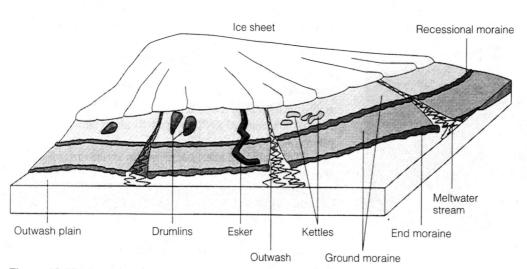

Figure 12.15 General assemblage and locations of characteristic features associated with continental glaciation. All are of depositional origin, and the resulting topography is "smooth" and gently rolling.

Further Consideration

Box 12.1

THE GREAT NORTHERN DIAMOND RUSH

Diamonds occur in minute amounts in a variety of dark igneous rock known as kimberlite (see chapter 16). Kimberlite forms under intense pressure within Earth's mantle and is literally exploded through the overlying crust in pipe-shaped bodies. More than 3,000 such pipes have been identified in South Africa, making it the world's principal source of diamonds for the last 100 years. The South African mining giant, DeBeers Consolidated Mines Limited, mines approximately 50% of the world's diamond production and controls most of the rest through a cartel arrangement that limits the number and quality of diamonds that reach the market, thereby determining world diamond prices.

In 1991, however, diamonds were found in the glacial tills of Canada's Northwest Territories (fig. 12.A). They were brought and distributed there by glaciers that had eroded exposed diamond pipes. These transported diamonds have been traced back to their source area between Great Slave Lake and Great Bear Lake. Since the diamond discovery, almost 300 companies have staked claims to more than 195,000 square kilometers (75,000 sq. mi) of

land, carried out numerous aerial surveys, and taken thousands of samples. The results of this work are highly encouraging. With 100 high-quality diamond pipes already discovered, some believe that this could be Earth's richest source of diamonds.

Exploiting this diamond bonanza will not be easy. This is a barren and hostile land of tundra, permafrost, thick ice, temperatures that reach −75° C (−100° F), and winds of hurricane velocity. Roads are nonexistent. The ecological balance is fragile. There are potentially conflicting claims with Native Americans, the Inuits. Nevertheless, the first mine is expected to be in production soon, probably at a cost in excess of $500 million. While development costs are high, the deposits are

thought to be rich enough to recoup the investment in a very few years. What this will do to the diamond market that has been carefully controlled by DeBeers for more than a century is difficult to predict. That the market will be disrupted is virtually certain.

Apply Your Knowledge

1. What would be some of the practical difficulties encountered in trying to establish and develop diamond mines in the Northwest Territories?
2. How might this new source of diamonds affect the world supply of diamonds and the industry's pricing structure?

Figure 12.A   Location of major diamond discovery near Lac de Gras, Northwest Territories, Canada.

Figure 12.16 Kettle formation (*a*) Detached mass of glacial ice partially or totally covered by till and outwash. (*b*) Ice melts, leaving hole that may or may not fill with water.

Figure 12.18 Locations of some major pluvial lakes that existed in the western United States during the most recent period of glaciation. Great Salt Lake is a remnant of Lake Bonneville.

Figure 12.17 Landsat satellite photograph of the Finger Lakes region, New York State.

Figure 12.19 Varves from a glacial lake. Light-colored layers are summer deposition; dark-colored layers are winter deposition. Each pair represents a 1-year cycle of deposition.

Glacial Lakes and Rivers

Occasionally, large chunks of ice become detached from the main glacier, stagnate, are buried by glacial outwash, and then melt. This process causes the ground surface, now composed mainly of glacial outwash, to subside. The depression created by the subsidence is called a **kettle** (fig. 12.16). Filled with water, the kettle becomes a **kettle lake,** or *kettle pond* (see figs. 12.11 and 12.13). In glaciated areas, such water bodies may occur by the hundreds or

thousands. Once covered by continental ice sheets, Minnesota is now the "land of 10,000 lakes" because of its vast number of kettle lakes.

Kettle lakes are not normally very large. Some lakes associated with glaciation, however, were (and are) extremely large. The Great Lakes occupy deep basins that were gouged out by the passage of glaciers down broad, preglacial lowland areas. As the glaciers retreated and melted away, lakes occupied parts of these basins, constantly changing size and shape as the location of the

Figure 12.20   The present pattern of the upper Mississippi drainage system is shown in red. The preglacial drainage pattern is shown in yellow. (Source: Arthur L. Bloom, *Geomorphology*, 2d. Copyright 1991 Prentice-Hall.)

margin of the adjacent ice sheet changed. The Finger Lakes of central New York State (fig. 12.17) formed in a similar way, but on a smaller scale. Large glacial lakes formed by ice dams include Lake Agassiz in south-central Canada (the remnants of which are Lake Winnipeg, Lake-of-the-Woods, and a number of smaller lakes) and Lake Missoula in the Pacific Northwest. As the ice dams melted or broke, immense volumes of water were released from these **ice-marginal lakes** in catastrophic floods that quickly eroded and altered the landscape over which they passed and raised sea level by a significant amount.

Great Salt Lake in Utah is the remnant of a once much larger lake, Lake Bonneville, that existed in glacial time. At its maximum extent, Lake Bonneville covered some 50,000 square kilometers (19,300 sq. mi) and was as deep as 300 meters (1,000 ft). Lake Bonneville did not develop adjacent to glacial ice but formed because the climate in that region was much more humid during glacial times (fig. 12.18). Lakes of this type, which were common throughout the western United States during the recent glacial epoch, the Pleistocene (see box 12.2), are called **pluvial,** from the Latin word for "rain."

Sediment is deposited in glacial lakes, as it is in all standing bodies of water. Small lakes, whose surfaces are susceptible to freezing over each year, are characterized by an interesting type of

sediment known as **varves** (fig. 12.19). Each varve is a pair of thin sedimentary layers formed during one annual cycle of deposition. A light-colored layer represents fine sediment carried in by streams that settles out during the summer months. During the winter months, when influx of new sediment may be diminished by frozen streams and when the ice-covered lake surface ends wave activity (causing very quiet water conditions), the finest sediment, including an abundance of suspended organic material settles out to form a thin, dark layer. Because each pair of layers represents one year of deposition, the age and history of such lakes can be interpreted by counting and examining varves in sedimentary core samples taken from the lakes.

Major ice sheets moving south from Canada had a profound effect on the primary preglacial rivers of North America. The upper Ohio River drained to the north in preglacial times and into the Gulf of St. Lawrence. When the ice sheet blocked this northern route, a new pattern of drainage formed, first flowing parallel to the ice front and eventually emptying into the Mississippi River. In the west, the northward-flowing upper Missouri River system was likewise diverted to a southeastward path paralleling the ice front and eventually became a part of the Mississippi River system (fig. 12.20).

Box 12.2

Further Consideration

SUSPECTED CAUSES OF THE PLEISTOCENE ICE AGE

Approximately 2.6 million years ago, great ice sheets began to form at high latitudes and high altitudes. A long interruption in the hydrologic cycle meant that water that evaporated from the oceans and precipitated onto the land did not return to the seas in the period normally associated with such an exchange. As the glaciers grew, they advanced toward lower latitudes and lower elevations, profoundly altering the landscape in the process. At their maximum extent, the ice sheets covered millions of square kilometers (fig. 12.B) and were as much as 3 kilometers (2 mi) thick. All of New England was covered, and the ice extended as far south as the southern tip of Illinois. At least four times, the ice sheets formed, expanded, shrunk, and then melted away. Superimposed upon this cycle were numerous minor ice advances and retreats.

For almost the past 200 years, since it was first recognized that glaciers must at some times in the past have been much more extensive than they are at present, scientists and naturalists have pondered and debated the possible cause(s) of ice age episodes. Of the numerous hypotheses advanced, none has won universal acceptance on the basis of evidence, but a consensus may be reached on an explanation based upon both long-term and short-term observations.

While glaciation is an uncommon event in Earth's history, apparently seven previous ice age episodes have occurred. Evidence in the form of striated rocks, indurated glacial till deposits (tillite), and fossils that suggest significant ecological changes can be found in the geologic record at approximately 2.2 billion, 1.2 billion, 960 million, 750 million, 670 million, 430 million, and 270 million years ago. Admittedly, it is not known whether these were worldwide events, but the evidence has persisted for very long periods. Apparently, the onset of Pleistocene glaciation was the culmination of a long-term period of cooling that began about 50 million years ago. Prior to that time, Earth's average temperatures were more than 10° C higher than at present.

On the short-term scale of the last 2.6 million years, not only the cyclical nature of glacial and interglacial events must be explained, but also changes in precipitation patterns to form the ice and in temperatures cool enough to allow heavy winter snowfalls to survive the summer melting. During the glacial events, temperatures may have averaged as much as 5 to 7° C cooler than present temperatures. That these short-term fluctuations were worldwide events is substantiated by the ice advances and retreats that occurred simultaneously in the Northern and Southern Hemispheres.

In their attempt to trace the cause(s) of glaciation, scientists have looked at both terrestrial and extraterrestrial processes. The latest terrestrial explanations center on the unifying theory of plate tectonics. Tectonic activity provides us with a possible explanation of the onset of Pleistocene glaciation and, perhaps, the long-term periodicity of glaciations. This explanation, which has gained increased acceptance, relates the declining temperatures of the Cenozoic and the onset of glaciation to the arrival of Antarctica in a position over the South Pole and of the Northern Hemisphere continents to high-latitude positions surrounding the shallow Arctic Ocean and the North Pole. This continental configuration also would have altered oceanic currents. It would have deflected the warm-water Gulf Stream (see chapter 14) away from the polar regions, leaving them colder than they had been throughout most of geologic time. Altered oceanic currents and wind patterns might also have led to an increase in precipitation sufficient to nourish the growing ice sheets.

During the last 50 million years, the continents have been elevated by the formation of mountains, and their areal extent has been greater than at any previous period. The significance of increased land surface exposure, among other things, is that it provides an increase in *albedo,* or the reflection of solar energy, compared to the darker water surfaces. Increased albedo has a cooling effect in that solar energy is reflected back out to space, rather than being absorbed by Earth's surface. This is a positive feedback system in that, as the glaciers form and expand, they have even higher albedos than the land surface, so that the cold becomes even more pronounced.

It is becoming ever more likely that the short-term changes within the last 2.6 million years are related not to plate tectonics but, rather, to cyclic changes in the orientation of Earth's axis of rotation and in the shape of Earth's orbit around the sun (see chapter 4). The tilt of Earth's axis of rotation, currently 23.5°, actually varies from 22° to 24° on a cycle of approximately 41,000 years. In addition, the axis of rotation undergoes a slow wobbling motion such that it describes a cone-shaped figure in space and completes one circuit every 26,000 years. This movement is known as *precession.* The orbit of Earth's revolution around the sun varies from its current elliptical shape to essentially circular through a period of approximately 90,000 years. This change in eccentricity brings Earth closer to or farther from the sun at various times of the year. (Currently, Earth is at its farthest point from the sun during the Northern Hemisphere summer.) Early in the twentieth century, Yugoslavian mathematician and engineer M. Milankovitch first postulated that these three natural changes in Earth's normal rhythm should once every 100,000 years or so bring about conditions that would favor the formation of the great ice sheets. His calculations include two critical factors: (1) The total amount of incoming solar insolation need not change, but its distribution should be different, and (2) lower radiation levels at approximately 65°N latitude (rather than at the pole), combined with increased moisture, should trigger the formation of ice sheets. This 100,000-year cycle has recently been confirmed by the analysis of changes in microscopic organisms in deep-sea cores.

It appears, then, that long-term changes associated with plate movements are necessary to initiate a glacial period and that short-term changes associated with astronomical cycles cause the alternation of glacial and interglacial events. While all of this seems to make considerable sense, the questions have not been totally answered. In fact, other suggestions over the years also merit mention, if not detailed consideration. An increase in cloud cover would cause an increase in the reflection of solar energy and lower Earth's temperatures. Increased levels of atmospheric dust, either from volcanic eruptions or meteorite impacts, would produce the same result. A difficulty with the dust theory, however, is that the effects of such increases are not long-term; nor do they occur with regularity. Increased sunspot activity has been suggested as a mechanism to affect climatic change, but the current level of increase is much too low to cause significant climatic changes on Earth, and the cycle of change is much too short (only 11 years). The possibility of longer-term cycles is a theory that can probably never be tested. The rise of the Himalayas, Andes, and Alps, and their effect on wind patterns and moisture distribution have been suggested as contributing factors to, if not direct causes of, glaciation, as has the raising of the Isthmus of Panama approximately 3 million years ago. This last event would affect oceanic currents, oceanic mixing, and water salinity.

Apply Your Knowledge

1. Why are the sites of ice accumulation and glacier formation to the south of the North Pole, rather than directly over the pole?
2. Why would it be difficult to test the theory described here for the initiation of one of the earlier glacial episodes?
3. How might human activities be affecting the warming or cooling of Earth?

Figure 12.B   Maximum extent of glaciation in North America during the Pleistocene.

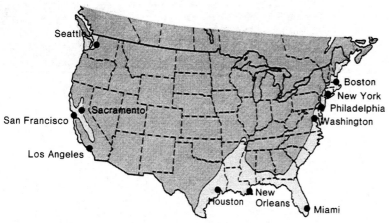

Figure 12.21 The area of the United States (blue) that would be submerged by a 65-meter (215-ft) rise in area level associated with the melting of the present glacial ice caps.

Lakes and rivers were not the only water bodies affected by the formation of the Pleistocene ice sheets. Massive amounts of water must have been withdrawn from the world's oceans to form the ice. As a result of this withdrawal, worldwide sea level at the time of maximum glaciation is estimated to have been some 130 meters (400 ft) lower than it is today. Thus, coastal cities, such as New York, would have been far inland, with the Atlantic shoreline lying some 50 to 80 kilometers (30 to 50 mi) to the east. Significantly lower sea level also exposed the seafloor in shallow water areas and connected landmasses that had previously been separated by water. Notable examples are a dry land connection between England and continental Europe and a similar **land bridge** between Siberia and Alaska at the current location of the Bering Strait. This allowed for the slow, but steady, migration of land animals, including humans, from continent to continent.

Between major glaciations, when all or parts of the ice sheets on Antarctica and Greenland melted, sea level may have stood as much as 65 meters (215 ft) higher than at present. Low-lying coastal areas, including the sites of many of the world's major cities, would have been submerged. All of the state of Delaware and much of the state of Florida would have been under water. The seas would have advanced up the low-lying Mississippi River valley as far as southern Illinois (fig. 12.21).

WIND

The effect of wind as a geologic agent is often overrated. Although the wind is present everywhere, it is usually effective in performing geologic work only under certain circumstances. Wind is most effective when loose, dry, fine-grained sediment is exposed at the ground surface. Although exceptions occur (see box 12.3), particles larger than fine sand are normally too big to be picked up and transported by the wind's energy. Wet sedimentary particles tend to bind together, inhibiting the wind's lifting potential. Because the vegetation common to humid climates shields sediment from the wind's action, the wind is most effective in arid and semiarid regions. Wind-borne sediment and wind-formed features are referred to as **eolian,** after the Greek god Aeolus, who was thought to control the winds. Before examining the erosional and depositional results of wind's work, we consider briefly the

realm in which wind is most effective—that is, the world's deserts.

Deserts

Deserts form for a variety of reasons, and while difficult to define precisely, they have at least one unifying characteristic: lack of moisture. Although they are often depicted as blistering hot, they actually develop in subtropical, temperate, or polar climatic regimes. Deserts with the highest temperature characteristics, the *subtropical,* are associated with the subtropical high-pressure belts (see chapter 6), where air masses are descending from higher altitudes to become significantly warmer. As they warm, these air masses do not yield moisture, but their capacity to evaporate and hold additional moisture is greatly enhanced. *Temperate* deserts normally form because they lie in the *rain shadow* of a topographic mountain barrier or are far removed from any major moisture source. In the case of the former, as air rises on the windward side of a mountain range, it cools and gives up its moisture. As it descends on the leeward side, it warms and is capable of evaporating and holding additional moisture. The Sierra Nevada of California and the associated Mojave Desert to the east is an example of this type of system. The Gobi Desert of central Asia is an example of a desert formed because of its distance from a major body of water. *Coastal* deserts can be either subtropical or temperate. They form under the influence of cold coastal currents (see chapter 6). *Polar* deserts, as in Antarctica, form under polar high-pressure systems because the air is so cold that it contains very little moisture.

In deserts, both weathering and stream behavior differ from that of more humid regions. The presence of water in humid regions enhances chemical weathering. The relative absence of water in arid regions gives physical weathering processes a more dominant role. These differences in weathering processes form soils with very different characteristics (see chapter 16).

With a much lower water table than in humid regions, deserts are characterized by few streams. Those that do exist are either exotic or ephemeral. **Exotic streams,** like the Nile River and the Colorado River, normally arise in a more humid region and then maintain their flow across hundreds or thousands of kilometers of desert with the addition of few, if any, tributaries. Such streams are called "exotic" because they are alien to desert regions. Within deserts, rainfall, when it does occur, is usually torrential, leading to *flash floods.* The water flow will normally subside in such short-lived, or **ephemeral,** flows in a matter of hours, as the water infiltrates the channel bed or is carried into basins surrounded by mountains. Because these short-lived streams never flow to the oceans but often end in temporary lakes occupying the basin floors, the drainage is referred to as *internal* (it does not leave the immediate area). The lakes themselves, known as **playa lakes** (fig. 12.22), have high evaporation rates and may periodically dry up, leaving behind precipitated salts, some of which, like borax, have significant economic value. Wagons pulled by 20-mule teams that hauled borax to the railhead from deposits in Death Valley, California, late in the nineteenth century became famous commercial television symbols.

Box 12.3

Further Consideration

THE SLIDING ROCKS

A strange phenomenon occurs on the surface of a playa known as the Racetrack: sliding rocks. The Racetrack lies near the northern end of Death Valley in California. The rocks, which weigh up to 320 kilograms (700 lb), move across the playa's flat surface, leaving shallow tracks in their wake (fig. 12.C). The tracks have been measured for distances of over 250 meters (820 ft). No one has ever seen the rocks move, so no one knows for certain how they do it. Most earth scientists attribute the movement to extremely strong winds pushing the rocks across a surface made slippery by one of the infrequent rainfalls. Velocities of a meter (3.28 ft) per second have been postulated for the sliding rocks.

Figure 12.C One of the "sliding rocks" of the Racetrack Playa, Death Valley, California. Note the irregular path that the rock has taken.

A recent corollary to the movement hypothesis is that it may occur across a thin film of ice formed on the playa surface after a winter rainfall.

Apply Your Knowledge

1. What is your opinion of the proposed explanation for the "sliding rocks"? Can you think of any other possibilities?
2. Can you find references to the occurrence of this phenomenon in any other location besides Death Valley?

Figure 12.22 Surface of playa (lake). Death Valley, California.

Desertification

Human influence can form or expand deserts. This process is known as **desertification,** the change of marginally productive lands into deserts, with the consequent loss of their ability to support human and other populations. Whereas human mismanagement of the land is the principal cause of desertification, natural factors, such as prolonged, or even short, periods of drought usually initiate the process. Desertification is recognized by the destruction of the scanty natural vegetation by overgrazing and overforaging (usually for firewood), followed by wind erosion of the usable soil cover. Packing of the soil by the hooves of grazing animals also makes the ground impermeable to moisture infiltration from the infrequent rainfalls. The result is the progressive lowering of the water table. In addition, because irrigation practices employ the use of water that has some dissolved mineral content, both the groundwater and the soil become progressively more saline.

Desertification is a worldwide problem. An estimated 600 million people live on arid lands, at least 10% of which are currently undergoing desertification. As many as 70 nations are affected by this problem, including parts of the Great Plains and the southwestern United States. Each year, 70,000 square kilometers (27,000 sq. mi) of usable land turns to desert. By the end of the twentieth century, fully one-third of the world's once arable land likely will have lost its agricultural usefulness.

The term *desertification* conjures up images of mass migrations of humans and other animals and, occasionally, of mass starvation. Nowhere has this process been more pronounced in recent years than in the region of central Africa, south of the Sahara Desert, known as the Sahel (Arabic for "border") (fig. 12.23). This is a marginal land, where for centuries humans have existed on the edge by nomadism and irrigated agriculture. Rainfall in the region is unreli-

able, and droughts are common. The current cycle of desertification began in 1970—a year in which no rain fell. Ironically, it was the preceding 35 years of greater-than-normal rainfall that actually set the stage for disaster. During this time of plenty, people were drawn to the Sahel from other sections of Africa to graze their herds and to practice limited agriculture. This influx, combined with a decrease in the infant mortality rate, led to a doubling of the population between 1935 and 1970, and herd sizes increased proportionately.

The 1970s and 1980s were decades of lower-than-normal precipitation in the Sahel. Between 1970 and 1976, some 3 million people and up to 70% of the livestock are estimated to have died as a direct consequence of the drought. By 1985, some 10 million people had abandoned their homes and their nomadic way of life to seek food and work in countless refugee camps and the few large cities. In addition to the starvation, malnutrition, and disease, civil wars racked several of the Sahel countries. A return to near normality and an end to widespread death and suffering were only accomplished through massive international relief efforts. Meanwhile, the Sahara Desert continued to expand southward several kilometers each year. A total of 650,000 square kilometers (250,000 sq. mi) is estimated to have been added to the Sahara in the last 50 years.

Wind Erosion

Erosion by wind occurs in two ways: (1) lifting and carrying away particles in a process called **deflation,** and (2) the sandblasting of rock by wind-borne sediments in a process called **abrasion.** In some areas, deflation creates broad, shallow depressions called **deflation basins (blowouts)** (fig. 12.24). These are particularly common in the American Great Plains region of Nebraska and eastern Colorado and in the High Plains of northeastern New Mexico and the Texas

Figure 12.23 The Sahel region, sub-Sahara Africa.

Panhandle. They serve as collection basins for water during periods of rainfall and as natural waterholes for bison and other forms of wildlife that once populated these areas in vast numbers. Some blowouts are large and spectacular. The Richat Hole in the African country of Mauritania measures 32 kilometers (20 mi) in diameter and is 610 meters (2,000 ft) deep (fig. 12.25). The Qattara Depression in Egypt, formed by a combination of faulting and deflation, is 320 kilometers (200 mi) long and up to 80 kilometers (50 mi) wide, and has a floor 134 meters (420 ft) below sea level.

Wind abrasion and deflation, working in combination with weathering, have also carved the spectacular rock arches in Arches National Monument in eastern Utah. Individual sand grains are loosened by percolating groundwater and frost wedging from the thick sandstones in which the arches form. The loosened particles are picked up by the wind and transported away.

In some areas, the deflation process has, over a period of many years, removed most of the fine sediment from the ground surface, leaving behind the larger pebbles and cobbles that could not be lifted. This coarser material that has "lagged behind" is called **lag gravel** (fig. 12.26a). Sometimes, these larger particles make up an almost continuous surface, referred to as **desert pavement** (fig. 12.26b) because of its resemblance to paving stones, a common street material in years past. Individual large particles may be so abraded by the action of smaller wind-borne particles that they become smooth on their exposed sides. As they are gradually eroded, they may become unstable in their current positions and eventually topple over,

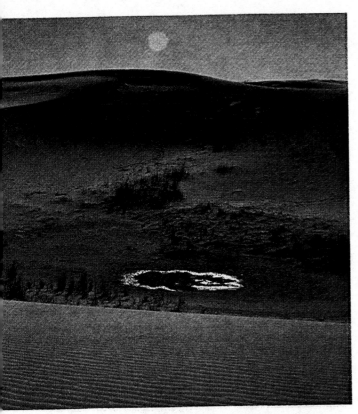

Figure 12.24 Blowouts in Sand Hills State Park, Monohans, Texas.

Figure 12.25 Satellite view of the Richat Hole, a blowout of enormous proportions. Mauritania, Africa.

(a)

(b)

Figure 12.26   (a) Lag gravel deposit. A mixture of fine and coarse particles is still exposed at the surface. Finer material is in the process of being eroded away. (b) Desert pavement. Fine sediment has been completely removed by deflation, leaving the armored surface of larger rock masses.

exposing yet another side to the wind's abrasive action. Such wind-smoothed rocks are **ventifacts** (literally, "wind-formed").

Box 12.4 on pages 300-301 describes the classic example of wind erosion in the United States: the American Dust Bowl of the 1930s.

Wind Deposition

Like streams, the wind is a highly selective transporter of sediment. The size of the particle that can be moved depends on wind velocity. Because air is not very dense, however, it is capable of lifting only the finest particles to significant heights. Even fine sand particles can only be lifted a meter or two and are primarily transported by bouncing and skipping along the ground surface. Fine, wind-borne dust, on the other hand, may be carried to heights of thousands of meters and stay suspended for months or even years.

When wind velocity diminishes, sediment is progressively deposited, coarsest first and finest last, to make depositional landforms. The most common and best-known of wind-generated features are **dunes,** accumulations of sand that either are migrating or have migrated but are now stabilized by a protective covering of vegetation.

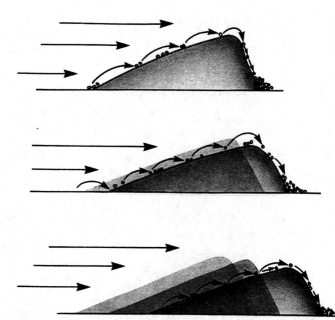

Figure 12.27   Dune formation and movement. The wind moves sand, grain by grain, up the windward side of the dune. The grains tumble down the leeward side and come to rest. The net movement is downwind.

Dunes form wherever there is sufficient sand and where the wind is almost constantly blowing in the same direction. The wind moves the dune's sand grains by rolling and bouncing them on the upwind (windward) side of the dune toward the peak, or *crest,* of the dune, where they then tumble onto and down the downwind (leeward) side. The effect of all the individual sand grain movements is the transport of the entire dune (fig. 12.27). Although dunes are often envisioned as desert features, they are equally common along coastlines (as along the southern shore of Lake Michigan and the eastern shore of Cape Cod, Massachusetts) and some stream courses, especially in the Great Plains region.

Dunes can be classified into several types, based largely on their shapes and to a lesser degree on their sizes and modes of origin (fig. 12.28). *Barchans* are individual, isolated, crescent-shaped dunes, with "horns" that extend in the downwind direction. They may reach heights of a few tens of meters and have a maximum spread of a few hundred meters. Barchans normally form on rocky desert floors, where the sand supply is limited, and in response to a relatively constant wind direction. *Parabolic dunes* require abundant sand, constant wind conditions, and vegetation to anchor the "points" of the dune, which extend upwind. Parabolic dunes are essentially blowouts, with the central portion of the sand mass scooped out. *Star dunes* are complex in both origin and appearance, but they normally have a higher central core, from which ridges of sand radiate outward in several directions. They appear to require changing winds that blow periodically from different directions and are common constituents of the dune fields of North Africa and Saudi Arabia. *Transverse dunes* are parallel ridges of sand that form perpendicular to the dominant wind direction. They occur commonly along shorelines and often cover large areas, but in all cases, they require an abundant sand supply and a constant wind direction. *Longitudinal dunes* are ridges of sand elongated in the direction parallel to the wind and are common in desert regions. They require an abundant sand supply, the presence of little or no vegeta-

(a)

(b)

(c)

(d)

(e)

Figure 12.28 Types of dunes. (*a*) The barchan forms when the sand supply is limited and the wind direction is constant. (*b*) The parabolic dune requires abundant sand, constant wind, and anchoring vegetation. (*c*) Star dunes require an abundant sand supply and highly variable winds. (*d*) Transverse dunes, which require abundant sand and constant winds, often develop along coastlines. (*e*) Longitudinal dunes, or seifs, require abundant sand, a fairly constant wind to elongate the dune, and an occasional crosswind to bring in more sand.

Figure 12.29 Attempts to stabilize dunes along the New Jersey shore by the planting of dune grass.

tion, strong prevailing winds to elongate the dune, and occasional crosswinds to add sand to the growing dune. They normally are a few meters high and stretch for a few tens of meters. In the Sahara and Arabian Deserts, however, some longitudinal dunes are as much as 100 meters (328 ft) high and can be traced for hundreds of kilometers. Such extremely large dunes are called *seifs* (from the Arabic, meaning "sword"). In these same deserts can be found extremely large dune fields known as *ergs,* which are, literally, seas of sand. Fully one-third of Saudi Arabia, approximately 1 million square kilometers (386,000 sq. mi), is covered with dunes.

Dunes, by their very nature, are mobile features, and their locations are temporary. Such mobility often conflicts with humans' desire to build on or otherwise utilize the land. Consequently, efforts to stabilize and halt dune movement, particularly in coastal areas that are important recreational resources, are widespread and ongoing. These efforts commonly involve the placement of sand fences (to break up and slow the wind currents) and the planting of vegetation (usually, some variety of grass) to hold the sand (fig. 12.29).

Accumulations of silt-size sediment, known as **loess,** are most closely associated with glacial till deposits. Along the eastern side of the Mississippi River valley, loess deposits have been laid down by the prevailing winds that blow across the surface of the glacial till deposits, pick up the fine sediment, and carry it in a downwind direction until it is deposited. Because the silt-size grains have a tendency to interlock, loess is capable of standing in near-vertical slopes. These slopes are extremely unstable, however, and subject to collapse and flowage if disturbed by earthquake vibrations or heavy precipitation. The most extensive loess deposits in the world

BOX 12.4

THE GREAT AMERICAN DUST BOWL

One of the best-known examples in history of wind erosion occurred in the 1930s across much of the Great Plains region. Dubbed the "Dust Bowl" by an enterprising reporter, the affected area stretched from Montana to Texas but was especially severe in the panhandle regions of Oklahoma and Texas. These were storied times. Indeed, one of the classics of American literature, John Steinbeck's *The Grapes of Wrath,* chronicled the movement of one Oklahoma family as family members worked to overcome their tribulations.

The storms of the Dust Bowl began in 1932 and lasted until the end of the decade. Low, boiling, thick clouds—the infamous "black blizzards"—rolled down from the north. During March 1936, parts of Texas and Oklahoma recorded 22 days of dust storms (fig. 12.D). The greatest storm of the decade raged for 4 days during May 1934, when a 2,400-kilometer- (1,500-mi) long dust cloud, covering 3.5 million square kilometers (1.35 million sq. mi), stretched from Canada to Texas and from Montana to Ohio. As the storm moved eastward, day turned to night in cities along the eastern seaboard. When it was over, an estimated 272 million metric tons (300 million tons) of soil had been blown away. The dust that formed each storm was so pervasive that it could not even be escaped indoors. It would sift through the finest openings around windows and doors, leaving a coating on every surface, including sleeping human beings. Piles of dust would accumulate unseen in attics until their weight caused ceilings to collapse. One particularly bad day, April 14, 1935, became known as Black Sunday. An immense dust cloud rolled through Kansas, Oklahoma, and Texas. Dodge City, Kansas, was in total darkness for 40 minutes. So terrifying was the phenomenon that many thought that the end of the world was at hand.

(a)

(b)

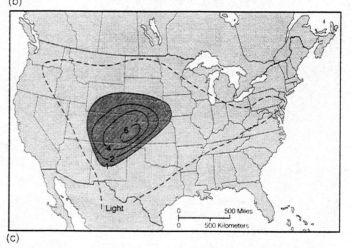

(c)

Figure 12.D   The sequence of maps shows the number of days with dust storms in the United States for the months of (*a*) March, (*b*) April, and (*c*) May 1936.

Folksinger Woody Guthrie, so the story goes, was so awed by this event that he began to compose his classic song, "So Long, It's Been Good to Know You."

What caused a once highly productive agricultural region to be turned into a part of the great American desert? This portion of the Great Plains was, in a sense, a victim of its own success. The soils of these endless prairies, under normal conditions, were protected from erosion by the dense root system of the native grasses. When this part of the United States was opened by the federal government for homesteading in the late 1800s, farmers (the so-called "sod busters") broke up this natural sod armor with their plows, converting natural grasslands to wheat farms. During World War I, tractors came into large-scale use in this region for the first time, and in a matter of a few years, the amount of prairie under cultivation increased dramatically.

As long as rainfall was plentiful, wheat grew in abundance, and the region prospered. The good times, however, could not last in a region that has historically been subjected to periodic droughts. The year 1932 began a 6-year period in which rainfall averaged little more than half of the normal amount. As a result, the wheat crops failed. With no vegetation to bind and hold the soil particles, the winds that blow almost ceaselessly across the prairies were able to pick up and carry away the soil and, with it, the hopes and dreams of many farm families. With crop failures came farm mortgage foreclosures and unemployment.

Although the Dust Bowl days of the 1930s are the best known, they have not been the only times of drought in the Great Plains during the twentieth century. Similar conditions occurred in the mid-1950s, the mid-1960s, and the mid-1970s (fig. 12.E). Wind erosion was also notable in 1981. During the drought of the 1950s, Congress passed legislation creating the Great Plains Conservation Program. Under this program, individual farmers and ranchers planned, scheduled, and contracted with the U.S. Department of Agriculture for a conservation plan to be instituted over a 3- to 10-year period. Technical help was available from the Soil Conservation Service, and the federal government paid from 50 to 80% of the cost of the work. This federal investment has made a significant difference in terms of decreased erosion and increased agricultural income.

Apply Your Knowledge

1. Examine figure 12.E. Does there seem to be a cycle to the recurrence of periods of intense wind erosion in the Great Plains? What year was characterized by the greatest loss of soil acreage to wind erosion?
2. What human activities might lessen the frequency and/or degree of future "dust bowl" periods?

Figure 12.E Wind damage to croplands in the Great Plains by years. In addition to the damage in the mid- to late 1930s, note the high instances of soil erosion in the mid-1950s and late 1970s. Wind erosion was also noticeable in 1981 and during other years of the 1980s. (Source: Soil Conservation Service, *America's Soil and Water: Condition and Trends*, U.S. Department of Agriculture.)

are found in north central China, where they cover 635,000 square kilometers (245,000 sq. mi) and are up to 100 meters (328 ft) thick. The origin of this loess is not glacial, but rather from winds blowing constantly out of the vast Gobi Desert that lies to the north. Caves scooped out of the loess deposits were used as dwelling places for many generations (fig. 12.30). Collapses of these deposits due to earthquake vibrations and other causes have left a sad history of large losses of life in China.

Figure 12.30 Human shelters hollowed out of vertical loess cliffs in China.

FURTHER THOUGHTS: LOOKING ON THE BRIGHT SIDE

Although glaciers and deserts are generally considered inhospitable environments, they have and still do provide humans with resources and benefits. The material that forms the soils of the U.S. Midwest, as well as other areas of the world, was laid down by melting glaciers. During the past 8,000 to 12,000 years, weathering converted these thick blankets of glacial till to soils of remarkable fertility that continue to sustain an exploding world population.

Many of the world's deserts are the locations of significant mineral resources. In addition, their many days of sunshine provide the potential for widespread utilization of solar power. In the desert countries bordering the Mediterranean and Red Seas, this power could be harnessed to operate desalinization plants, which, in turn, would provide the fresh water necessary for irrigation. The vast expanses of flat desert land also would allow for the harnessing of wind energy. Pilot projects to develop wind energy have been carried out in a number of desert locations around the world, including the southwestern United States.

SIGNIFICANT POINTS

1. A glacier is a thick body of ice that moves in response to gravity or to pressures generated by its own mass. The two principal forms of glaciers are ice streams (valley, outlet, and cirque glaciers) and ice sheets (continental and piedmont glaciers).

2. If more ice is added to a glacier than is lost by ablation, the front of the glacier advances. If ablation exceeds accumulation, the ice front retreats.

3. The upper part of a glacier moves by fracturing, whereas the lower part moves by plastic flow. In temperate glaciers, there is also significant sliding along the underlying bedrock, which does not tend to occur in polar glaciers.

4. Landforms associated with valley glaciers are predominantly erosional in origin and include horns, arêtes, cirques, troughs, and hanging valleys. They may also be depositional, in the form of lateral, medial, and terminal moraines.

5. Glacial till is sediment deposited directly by melting glacial ice. It is unsorted and unstratified. Glacial outwash is sediment that has been transported away from the ice front by meltwater streams, and when deposited, it is sorted and stratified like any stream-deposited sediment.

6. Landforms associated with continental glaciers are predominantly depositional in origin and include terminal, recessional, and ground moraines; drumlins; eskers; outwash plains; and kettles.

7. The flat farmland and fertile soils of the central United States and Canada are the direct result of widespread continental glaciation.

8. During the Pleistocene, major lakes formed along the ice margins, as well as in regions that at that time were much more humid than they are today.

9. The formation of the Pleistocene ice sheets profoundly affected sea level and preglacial river systems.

10. The recent period of Pleistocene glaciation is thought to have been initiated by the movement of landmasses into polar and near-polar positions. The alternation of glacial and interglacial episodes may result from short-term, cyclical changes in the tilt and precession of Earth's rotational axis, as well as from changes in Earth's orbit of revolution around the sun.

11. Wind as a geologic agent is most effective where the ground surface consists of fine, loose sediment unbound by moisture or vegetation.

12. Deserts may possess any temperature characteristics, but all are characterized by low, infrequent, and unpredictable precipitation. The principal varieties of deserts are subtropical, temperate, and polar.

13. Desertification is the change of marginally productive land into desert, with the result that the land can no longer support human populations. The process may be initiated by a natural event, such as drought, but the major causes are overpopulation, overgrazing of animals, and general mismanagement of the land.

14. Fine surface sediment may be lifted and carried away, resulting in deflation basins, or blowouts. Some of these are of enormous size. Abrasion is the sandblasting of rock by wind-borne sediments.

15. A dune is an accumulation of sand that is either mobile or has moved in the past. Dunes form wherever sand is available and wind conditions are suitable: usually in deserts, along shorelines, and along stream courses.

16. Dune type depends on the abundance of sand available and the constancy (or inconstancy) of the wind.

ESSENTIAL TERMS

glacier *281*
valley glacier *281*
continental glacier *281*
piedmont glacier *282*
cirque glacier *282*
outlet glacier *282*
firn *282*
zone of
   accumulation *282*
zone of ablation *282*
equilibrium line *282*
ablation *282*
calving *282*
iceberg *282*

crevasse *282*
fracture zone *282*
plastic zone *282*
temperate glacier *282*
polar glacier *282*
surging *282*
quarrying *283*
striation *283*
horn *284*
arête *284*
cirque *284*
tarn *284*
trough *284*
paternoster lake *284*

hanging valley *285*
fiord *285*
glacial till *286*
moraine *286*
end, terminal, moraine
   286
lateral moraine *286*
medial moraine *286*
recessional
   moraine *286*
ground moraine *286*
esker *287*
drumlin *287*
glacial outwash *287*

outwash plain *287*
valley train *287*
drift *287*
erratic *288*
kettle *290*
kettle lake *290*
ice-marginal lake *290*
pluvial lake *290*
varve *291*
land bridge *294*
eolian *294*
exotic stream *294*
ephemeral stream *294*
playa lake *294*

desertification *296*
deflation *296*
abrasion *296*
deflation basin
   (blowout) *296*
lag gravel *297*
desert pavement *297*
ventifact *300*
dune *300*
loess *301*

REVIEW QUESTIONS

1. What is a glacier? What are the principal varieties of glaciers?

2. How does a glacier move?

3. What is a horn? What is an arête? What is a cirque?

4. What is the name of the sediment deposited directly by melting glacial ice? What landform does it produce? What is the name for stream-deposited glacial sediment?

5. How does a lateral moraine form? How does a medial moraine form? How does a recessional moraine form?

6. What is an esker? How does it form?

7. When and how were the Great Lakes formed?

8. What is the name given to the large ice-marginal lake that once existed in south-central Canada? What are some of its remnants?

9. What was the largest pluvial lake in North America? Where was it? What is the name of its remnant?

10. How were the various components of the Mississippi River drainage system altered by Pleistocene glaciation?

11. What are thought to be the long-term and short-term causes of glaciation?

12. What is a desert? What are the major types of deserts? Why does each form?

13. What are the characteristics of streams in arid regions?

14. What is desertification? Where might this be a problem in North America?

15. What is desert pavement? How does it form?

16. What is the principal wind depositional landform? In what environments does it occur? What are some of the varieties of this feature?

17. Under what conditions would barchans form? Under what conditions would transverse dunes form? Under what conditions would star dunes form?

18. What is loess? What are possible origins for deposits of this material?

CHALLENGES

1. Was the area in which you reside glaciated during the Pleistocene? What local features can you identify to substantiate this?

2. Examine a map of North America, and list those cities that would probably be inundated by a rise in sea level caused by the melting of the ice caps on Greenland and Antarctica.

Determine from a world map some other major cities that would be similarly affected.

3. If you live in or visit an area that was glaciated, collect different rock types that you find in a local deposit of glacial till.

4. What is the climate where you live? Assess the potential for desertification there.

Chapter 13

Waves and Coastal Currents

Surface zone at San Simeon along California coast.

INTRODUCTION

Waves and currents are characteristic of standing bodies of water, and both serve to transfer energy. As geologic agents, they differ fundamentally in their orientation to the energy that generates them. In general, energy transfer in a fluid medium induces movements in two directions: one relatively perpendicular to the passage of energy and another relatively parallel to it. The circular or elliptical *rise-and-fall* movement perpendicular to the passage of energy in water is called a **wave.** A *flow* aligned to the passage of energy within a body of water is a **current.** Unless they "break," as they do along beaches, waves displace water only slightly. Currents, however, transfer water, as well as energy. Waves and currents may jointly affect coastal areas, performing geologic work on unconsolidated sediments, rocks, and coastal communities. Waves may also induce currents, and currents may induce waves. One source of energy for both is wind.

WIND-INDUCED WAVES AND CURRENTS

The immediate source of energy for most waves and currents is wind, which transfers its energy to surface water. Water, however, is almost 1,000 times denser than air, so wind must blow continuously in contact with water to transfer sufficient energy to maintain waves and currents. As a result of this density difference, water currents move at less than 5% of the speed of winds that generate them.

The extent of the water surface over which a wind blows is called its **fetch.** With increasing fetch and duration, wind transfers more of its energy to water, amplifying waves and strengthening currents. As you learned in chapter 5, strong winds result from steep pressure gradients. Storms over the oceans can generate some of the strongest winds on Earth, but ocean winds can vary from breezes to gales. Thus, waves and currents vary in duration and size.

WAVE FEATURES AND BEHAVIOR

Figure 13.1 illustrates the motion of individual water particles as they respond to the passage of energy. Each water particle describes a circular or elliptical path, temporarily returning close to its original position before repeating the motion. The diameters of these paths decrease with depth until the energy no longer influences the water at a depth called the **wave base.**

Above the wave base, the passage of energy is reflected in a cyclical changing of surface elevation and identifiable features (fig. 13.1). The top of the circular motion in a mass of water forms a ridge of water called a

crest. The bottom forms a valley called a **trough.** The difference between the elevations of crest and trough yields the **wave height.** The distance between successive crests is the **wavelength,** and the time required for two successive crests to pass a point is the **wave period.** Because waves in open water cycle through successive crests and troughs, or "oscillate," they are **waves of oscillation.**

Open ocean surface waters may be subject to the energy from more than one storm system. As it transmits the energy from multiple sources, the sea surface often becomes chaotic. The crest of a wave may coincide with either the crest or the trough (or any part between) of another wave. Whenever crests randomly meet, they enhance each other, sometimes creating peaks and sprays called *whitecaps.* As crests meet troughs, they tend to cancel each other.

Individual **wave trains,** or wave systems, fall into two categories based on water depth (fig. 13.2). Waves that occur in water deeper than one-half their wavelength (D > 1/2 L) are the **deep-water waves** characteristic of the open ocean. Waves that occur in water shallower than one-half their wavelength (D < 1/2 L) are the **shallow-water waves** characteristic of the near-shore coastal zone. Because wavelengths associated with different wave trains vary, wave base changes for any location, and *shallow water* is a relative term.

As they enter a *shoaling,* or shallowing, zone, waves lose energy by friction with sediments and rocks along the bottom. The result is an increase in wave height and a decrease in wavelength. The tops of the waves, not slowed by friction, move forward over the leading troughs, where the water has no support. In a water zone that closely parallels the shoreline, the crests then "break" by falling or spilling into their landward troughs. This breaking water is the **surf zone** (fig. 13.2). Because the water in the surf zone rushes forward and no longer oscillates, its waves are called **waves of translation.** These waves transfer (translate) their energy both to surrounding water and to bottom, cliff, or beach surfaces.

As a wave train impinges upon a shoaling bottom at any angle except 90°, successive crests exhibit a bending when they approach the shore. Because of a loss of energy to friction in shallow water, each crest may break in a moving sequence along the beach.

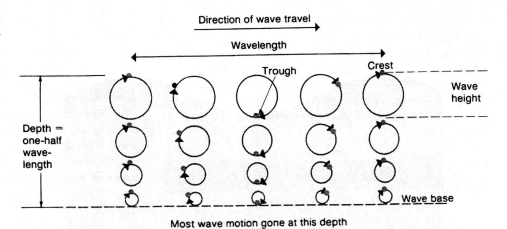

Figure 13.1 Waves of oscillation. Each water particle that is disturbed by the passage of a wave describes a circular or elliptical path, returning close to its original position before the arrival of the next wave. The diameter of the path decreases with depth until at a water depth equal to one-half wavelength (wave base), such motion, for all practical purposes, ceases. Waves are a surface phenomenon.

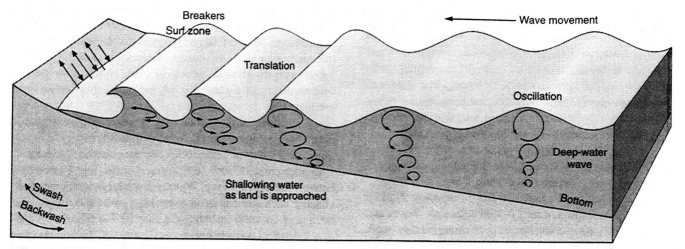

Figure 13.2 As a wave approaches a shoreline, the sea bottom begins to interfere with the orbital motion of the water particles. The orbital paths are distorted, the bottom of the wave is slowed relative to the top, the wave becomes unstable, and eventually, it collapses (breaks). Water rushes up the beach face as swash and flows back down as backwash.

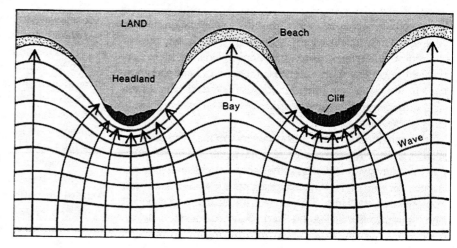

Figure 13.3 As they approach a shoreline, waves "feel bottom," are slowed, and are refracted first in front of the projecting headlands. Energy associated with the wave (shown as lines, or "rays," perpendicular to the wave fronts) is concentrated on the headlands, causing their erosion and retreat.

This bending, or **wave refraction,** enables surfers to ride continuously in front of the crest. It also initiates a process by which waves can perform geologic work on natural and artificial coastal materials and structures (fig. 13.3).

One other type of wave bending occurs. Whenever waves encounter a fixed obstacle in the water, they bend into the water behind the obstacle in a process known as **wave diffraction.** Diffraction enables water to do work in coastal areas protected by walls from the breaking waves of the surf zone.

WORK OF WAVES

Wherever the energy of waves intersects the floor of a basin, a beach face, or a cliff, waves perform geologic work by eroding, transporting, and depositing sediments and rock. The work of waves can be destructive, as when waves erode natural and artificial materials; or constructive, as when they build sedimentary structures like beaches.

Wave Erosion

By erosion, waves can alter a sandy shoreline in a relatively brief time. When the waves of Hurricane Gloria struck the beach of Ocean City, Maryland, in 1985, they removed more than a meter (3.25 ft) of beach material from several miles of beach. During the twentieth century, waves have caused some sandy cliffs on Cape Cod, Massachusetts, to retreat almost 100 meters (328 ft).

Waves use more than water as tools of destruction. Carried by the waves, sediments become abrasive materials that can wear away bedrock exposed along cliffs or lying at shallow depths. Waves also erode rock by alternately compressing (sometimes under tons of water) and releasing air in crevices. As the water falls out of the crevices, the air expands rapidly, driving water upward and eroding rock.

Transferring energy, waves of translation lose their momentum in a final rush against a cliff or up a beach, carrying any loose sediment with them or breaking away weak rock and depositing these materials elsewhere. The end of this landward movement of a wave on a beach is called the **swash** (see fig. 13.2). It is the last

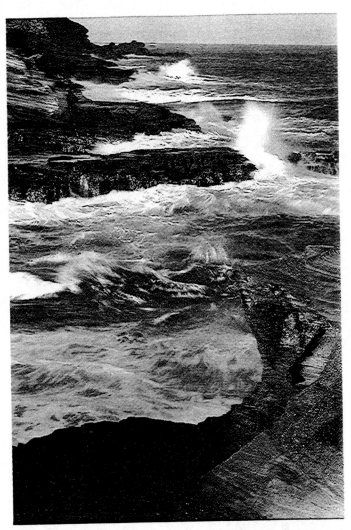

Figure 13.4 Splash-and-spray zone on Oahu's basaltic shore.

stage in the predominantly *horizontal* transfer of energy. Against a cliff or seawall, where the landward movement ceases abruptly with the compression of trapped air, a **splash-and-spray zone** develops (fig. 13.4). Splash and spray end in both a horizontal and *vertical* transfer of energy that is sufficient at times to erode and displace solid rock and to cut notches and caves into seaside cliffs (the term *cliff* originally meant "sea cliff").

Finally, robbed of its energy, the water that is thrown onshore then flows downslope under the pull of gravity as the **backwash** (see fig. 13.2). Like the swash, the splash, and the spray, the backwash can move sediment, carving channels. Whereas the swash carries sediment up a beach face in the direction of incoming waves, backwash carries it directly downslope. Wherever the backwash scours narrow channels, a **rip current** develops. Rip currents can be dangerous zones for swimmers, who are pushed seaward by the channelized fast flow of large volumes of water. The net result of all stages in waves of translation is a transportation of sediment landward, seaward, and also along a beach by each incoming wave, a process known as **beach drifting.**

Along irregularly shaped coasts, wave refraction concentrates the energy of incoming waves on the **headlands,** those parts of the land that stand farthest seaward (fig. 13.5). Shoals directly seaward of the headlands slow approaching waves, but the deeper

(a)

(b)

(c)

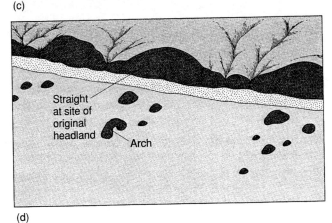

(d)

Figure 13.5 (*a–c*) With time, the headlands along irregular shorelines are worn back. (*d*) The shoreline becomes straightened, but sea cliffs mark the former headland positions.

Figure 13.6 Sea arch along the coast at Point Lomas, near La Jolla, California.

Figure 13.7 Wave-cut platform along the coast at Point Fermin, near San Pedro, California.

action, headlands (and cliffs) erode. In their landward retreat, they leave trailing subaerial ("under air") sloped areas called **ramps** and subaqueous ("underwater") terracelike surfaces called **wave-cut platforms** (fig. 13.7). In tectonically active areas, these platforms may rise above sea level to make a steplike coast of **marine terraces** (fig. 13.8). Such steps can be seen along the coasts of Oregon and northern California and in other areas associated with earthquakes and tectonic uplift.

Eventually, an irregular shoreline tends to straighten, with low areas, marking sites of former bays, alternating with sea cliffs at the locations of former headlands (see fig. 13.5). Because of changing sea levels, tectonic activity, and types of material, the process is ongoing, so coasts may develop a subsequent irregular appearance. Cliffs continue to erode largely by mass wasting because waves **notch,** or cut, cliff bases, as they have at Brookings, Oregon (fig. 13.9). With underlying support removed, a cliff retreats, as its material slides or falls into the sea, where it is removed by continuing wave action. Above sea level, a constant wetting and drying helps to weather rock, but wave energy, rock composition and strength, and climate all play a role in cliff erosion. Whenever a straight coast becomes irregular through the erosion of softer, overlying material (such as glacial drift), the new irregular landscape cut into the bedrock is called a **contraposed shoreline.**

Generally, greater wave energy means greater erosive power. Whenever storms produce large waves, shorelines undergo the

water to each side has less effect on wave velocity, so the waves refract. The sides of the headlands become the terminus of the incoming wave energy. In many instances, waves first cut **sea caves** into sides of the headlands. When the caves meet, a **sea arch** forms (figs. 13.5 and 13.6). As support for the arch lessens, it falls, isolating the most seaward part of the headland as a **sea stack** similar to the small rocky "islands" shown in figures 13.5 and 13.8. These features are especially well developed along the Pacific coast of North America, but they also occur along the rocky coasts of New England and eastern Canada. Attacked by continuing wave

Figure 13.8 Along the coast near Pacific Valley, California, marine terraces develop when wave-cut platforms are uplifted (or when sea level falls). On some marine terraces, isolated sea stacks stand as dry-land remnants of former headlands.

Wave Deposition

Even during erosive storm events, individual waves lose their kinetic energy by striking fixed objects and transporting sediments. From the Hjulstrom diagram (see fig. 11.11), you know that, as energy decreases, larger particles settle out before smaller particles. On beaches with pebble- and cobble-sized sediments, waves construct steep ridges of these materials at the high-water mark. Because storm waves move farther up-beach than ordinary waves, the highest ridge usually marks the water level of the most recent storm. Its orientation to the water also reveals the direction from which the waves approached the beach.

Figure 13.9 Wave-cut notch at Brookings, Oregon.

removal of sediments. The energy that a particular wave train expends upon a shoreline eventually diminishes, because waves lose energy in loosening and transporting materials. As energy decreases, waves enter a constructive phase that exhibits itself in a variety of short-lived sedimentary structures.

With less energy available for transport, sand-sized sediments form small, deltalike accumulations, beaches, and elongate mounds of sand called **bars.** Sandbars move onshore (landward)

Figure 13.10 Landsat satellite image of Padre Island, Texas, a barrier island. Reddish colors indicate its vegetation.

or offshore (seaward), depending on the available wave energy. Strong waves move beach sands offshore, whereas gentle waves usually build up a beach. Typically, stronger wave systems occur in winter, especially along North America's West Coast, and beaches are usually narrow during that season. Nor'easters (blizzards arriving from the northeast) also produce larger wave systems during winter along North America's East Coast (see box 13.1 on page 314). The tropical storms and hurricanes (typhoons) of summer and fall can generate powerful wave trains that move large quantities of sediment offshore. Under the normally calmer waves of summer, however, beaches widen as sands migrate onshore.

Sandbars are also subject to the daily rise and fall of sea level associated with the tides (discussed later in this chapter). The change in sea level alters the site of the surf zone. Thus, sandbars can migrate even under calmer conditions.

Very large offshore bars have formed parallel to the coastline and separated from it by narrow (tens to hundreds of meters) lagoons along much of the Atlantic and Gulf coasts of the United States (fig. 13.10). These narrow bars are called **barrier islands,** or *barrier bars,* and may extend for many kilometers (fig. 13.11). Because they offer wide, sandy beaches, they have become the sites of many coastal communities and resorts, including Ocean

Figure 13.11 Barrier island complex.

City, Maryland; Gulf Shores, Alabama; Galveston, Texas; and Miami Beach, Florida (fig. 13.12). Barrier islands are exposed to the fury of the sea, however, and a heavy price must be paid to protect them from the onslaught of storm waves.

WAVE-INDUCED CURRENTS AND DEPOSITIONAL FEATURES

Wave trains rarely approach the shore straight on. Their refraction in shallow water, however, aligns crests almost parallel to the shoreline. Because the refraction is rarely complete, the wave fronts strike the shore at an angle other than perpendicular, resulting in a pushing of the water along the shore away from the incoming waves. This action of waves in the surf zone creates a zigzag flow of water that trends parallel to the shoreline. Called the **longshore current,** this flow picks up, carries, and drops beach materials (fig. 13.13). Along both coasts of North America, longshore currents move hundreds of thousands of cubic meters of sediment past many locations annually.

Movement of sediment within the surf zone by longshore currents is called **longshore transport.** Such transport occurs continuously along the submerged portions of beaches. Wherever the longshore current encounters an embayment in the shoreline, however, it carries its sediment across the opening to form a **spit,** an elongate extension of the beach into the bay (fig. 13.14). A spit ends in the deeper, open water of a bay when the current cannot deposit enough sediment to remain above water. If a spit's continued accretion blocks the seaward opening of a shallow bay, however, it becomes a **baymouth bar.** Unless it is breached by storm waves, such a feature prevents further exchange between bay and open water. Once formed, the bar also traps sediment brought into the bay by streams. With time, the accumulated sediment behind the bar converts the bay first to marsh and then, with the help of colonizing plants, to land. Deposits of this type also may be built up as a connection between the mainland and an offshore island or sea stack, forming a **tombolo** (fig. 13.15).

Figure 13.12 Miami Beach, Florida, a resort city built on a barrier island.

Figure 13.13 Formation of longshore and rip currents.

Figure 13.14   A spit.

Figure 13.15   A tombolo develops where wave energy is diminished by an offshore barrier, such as an island or sea stack. Sand accumulates behind (on the landward side) of the stack.

BEACH ENGINEERING

Natural objects, such as sea stacks, or any artificial offshore structure can rob the beach of the incoming wave energy necessary to sustain longshore transport. Where there is a deficit of wave energy, sand piles up and builds seaward. Many communi-

ties have attempted to provide calm anchorages for pleasure boats or to protect their beaches from erosion by constructing engineering works of various kinds, often with unexpected and undesirable results. The most common of these structures are *breakwaters, jetties, groins, seawalls,* and *riprap.*

A **breakwater** performs the function its name suggests: As a structure of natural or artificial material, it breaks up (by dissipating their energy) the incoming waves to create a quiet, protected zone for navigation or anchorage. Some breakwaters are connected to the land, whereas others are detached from it. Some are fixed walls of stone or concrete; others are floating devices. Often, the area that a breakwater protects becomes choked by accumulated sediments trapped without the energy for further transport. The usual solution to the problem of clogged waterways is dredging. Such is the case at Santa Barbara, California, where a large, connected breakwater has caused a large spit to form. The spit developed in the harbor from the sediment in the longshore current and because of subsequent wave diffraction around the breakwater. A series of detached breakwaters has become the protective structure of choice for Presque Isle State Park at Erie, Pennsylvania, as the state government attempts to reduce wave erosion along the popular beach.

A **jetty** is a wall built perpendicularly to the shore. Usually constructed in pairs, one on either side of a channel or river mouth, jetties help to keep a passage open to navigation. They do this by diverting the flow of longshore currents to deeper water, thereby causing sediment deposition away from the channel or river mouth (fig. 13.16*a,c*)

A **groin** is similar to a jetty in that it stands perpendicular to the shoreline, but its purpose is to capture sand in its migration and to prevent beach erosion. These structures reduce the energy available for transport on their up-current sides. As the current moves in

Figure 13.16 (*a*) and (*c*) Jetties designed to keep the mouth of a stream or channel free of sediment. (*b*) and (*d*) A system of groins placed to prevent shore erosion.

Figure 13.17 The seawall at Galveston, Texas.

a deflected path around the end of the groin, it has less than its normal load of sediment, making it capable of eroding sediments away from the down-current side. Because the down-current sides of groins are starved of replenishing sands, engineers usually design a series of these structures to capture sand in the longshore current and widen beaches (fig. 13.16 *b, d*).

Although expensive to construct, groins are nevertheless common where communities attempt to control the flow of beach sand. Miami Beach's waterfront hotels still have beaches today, in part, because of the construction of groins but also because of another

technique commonly used to maintain beaches: **beach nourishment.** With this technique, sand is continuously applied to a beach to replenish that carried away by longshore transport and storm waves. The source of sand may be offshore dredging, channel dredging, or some distant location from which sand must be trucked to the site.

A **seawall** is a breakwater that is fully connected to the land, built of stone or concrete, and designed to give protection from direct wave erosion (fig. 13.17). Because of the direct contact between waves and wall, beaches usually do not occur at the wall

Box 13.1

*Investigating the
Environment*

CHATHAM: PROPERTY AS STABLE AS THE SHIFTING BEACH SANDS

The charm of Cape Cod in Massachusetts is one that few people can miss. The cape was shaped by glaciers and their meltwater, ocean currents, waves, storms, and human activities. The result of natural processes is a stretch of beaches, sandy barrier islands, sand dunes, and high cliffs of unconsolidated sediments. Human activity has built communities, such as Chatham on the southeastern end of the cape.

Chatham is a model Cape Cod community, with an architecture that has been copied elsewhere in North America. Its Cape Cod–style homes were built on a moderately high, sandy beach in a lagoon behind a narrow barrier island. On January 2, 1987, storm waves from a Nor'easter broke through the offshore bar in the Nauset Beach area, allowing wave energy to strike the shoreline in the residential area. In the short span of a few months, more than 19 meters (65 ft) of the beach area, including homes perched along the low cliff, were washed away.

Figure 13.A shows the southern end of Cape Cod, with Chatham on the upper left. Since the breakthrough occurred, sediments have moved to cut off Pleasant Bay from the water north of the break. The loss of their homes has motivated many to seek legal recourse because Massachusetts does not allow artificial structures, such as rock barriers, along the Chatham area. In a desperate attempt to protect homes, some citizens have placed boulders at the base of the sandy cliff. This attempt to save property is, in reality, futile. The boulders will move whenever the sands beneath them are washed away (fig. 13.B).

Cape Cod will always be subject to the movement of its unconsolidated sediments. The Marconi Wireless Station, a set of four tall radio towers that received the SOS call from the *Titanic,* is only a historical marker now. The high cliff on which it sat, north of Chatham, has been eroded back beyond two of the tower base pads, a distance of more than 50 meters (164 ft).

Apply Your Knowledge

1. How does a barrier island protect a mainland?

Figure 13.A   Aerial view of southern Cape Cod, with Chatham in the upper left.

Figure 13.B   Erosion at Chatham.

2. Why might riprap be an ineffective protective structure on the sandy cliffs of Cape Cod?

Figure 13.18 Riprap on the beach at Chatham, Massachusetts (Cape Cod).

base. Often, even with the addition of protective groins that act as artificial headlands, waves undercut the wall, leading to its collapse. Some seawalls have uncemented materials (stones or star-shaped concrete slabs) at their bases to absorb the wave energy. Loose stones have also been used to make a protective barrier of **riprap** at the base of sandy cliffs (see fig. 13.18 and box 13.1).

TECTONICALLY INDUCED, OR SEISMIC, SEA WAVES

A **seismic sea wave,** or **tsunami** (Japanese for "port-," or "harbor-wave"), is a large-scale wave system generated by an earthquake, volcanic eruption, or large avalanche, rather than by the wind. These waves have very long wave lengths and travel at speeds of several hundreds of kilometers per hour. In the open ocean, tsunamis are not distinguishable from other ocean waves, so putting to sea is one way to avoid the dangers associated with them. As they change from waves of oscillation to waves of translation, however, seismic sea waves can perform more geologic work than storm waves. When they approach a beach, seismic sea waves can steepen to heights of tens of meters. They have the energy to lift and move boulders and to destroy buildings.

Seismic sea waves have been responsible for thousands of deaths in and around the Pacific Ocean basin, where earthquakes and volcanic eruptions are common. Tsunamis generated by the eruption of the Indonesian volcano Krakatoa in 1883 caused an estimated 30,000 deaths as they inundated low-lying coastal villages. In July 1993, tsunamis with wave heights exceeding 9 meters (30 ft) were responsible for most of the deaths associated with

a severe earthquake that struck the northernmost of the Japanese islands. In villages and towns along the shore, the tsunamis washed people seaward and tossed boats onto the land.

The work of seismic sea waves is short-lived but significant. They have left their mark on the geologic landscape, and their effects from millions of years ago have been studied for evidence of major geologic events, such as a possible comet impact in the ocean that may have caused a mass extinction that ended the age of dinosaurs.

GRAVITY-INDUCED WAVES AND CURRENTS: THE TIDES

The largest of the shallow-water wave systems are the **tides.** Driven by centrifugal force on a rotating planet and the gravitational attraction primarily of the moon but also of the sun, these waves have crests and troughs that encompass whole oceans. Because their wavelengths far exceed the water depth, they are, essentially, shallow-water waves.

The gravitational pull of the moon and the sun affects the continents, all water bodies, and the atmosphere. Although the sun exerts an attraction on Earth's center almost 200 times greater than that exerted by the moon, its attractive force on individual objects on Earth is less than that exerted by the moon. This difference in tide-generating forces is a product of distance (gravity decreases as distance between two objects increases). The mean distance from Earth to the moon is only 384,404 kilometers (238,587 mi), whereas the mean distance from Earth to the sun is 149,600,000 kilometers (93,000,000 mi). Remember, also, that Earth exerts a gravitational

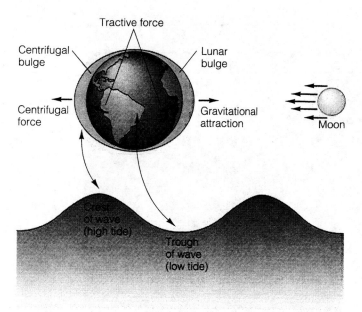

Figure 13.19 The tides are basically waves with exceptionally long periods (approximately 12 hours) between successive wave crests (the high tides). The diagram shows the effect of the moon's gravitational pull (the sun's effect is not considered here) on Earth's waters. As Earth rotates on its axis and the moon moves in its orbit around Earth, high tide is experienced at the point on Earth's surface directly facing the moon and at the same time at the opposite point on the other side of Earth.

(a) **Neap tide**

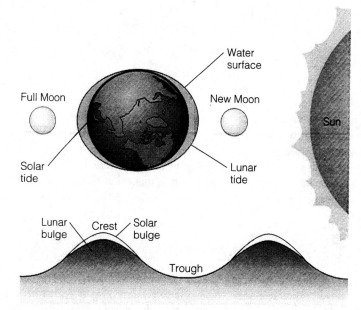

(b) **Spring tide**

Figure 13.20 (*a*) When the sun and moon are oriented at right angles with respect to Earth (as when the moon is in the first and third quarters), their gravitational attractions are operating in different directions and partially cancel one another. The result is a neap tide, a lower-than-normal tidal range (i.e., lower-than-normal high tides and higher-than-normal low tides). (*b*) When the sun and the moon pull in the same direction (during times of the full and new moons), gravitational attraction is reinforced. The result is a spring tide, a greater-than-normal tidal range (i.e., higher-than-normal high tides and lower-than-normal low tides).

pull on all objects that lie on its surface and that Earth is much more massive (about 80 times larger) than the moon.

The consequence of the nearby mass of the moon is a bulge of water almost directly beneath the moon at a changing location called the **sublunar point.** Because Earth rotates and the moon revolves around our planet, and because continents act as obstacles to the progression of the bulge, the tidal crest actually occurs 1° east of the sublunar point (i.e., it lags behind the sublunar point). Two tidal bulges are generated by a lateral flow of water toward the sublunar point and to a point on the opposite side of Earth. This lateral flow results from a dragging that is the **tractive force** exerted by the moon. This tractive, or horizontal, force is zero at the sublunar point and at 180° from the sublunar point, and is strongest 45° east and west of these two points (fig. 13.19). Because the moon's attractive force is smallest at 180° from the sublunar point, centrifugal force enhances a bulge of water on the side of Earth facing away from the moon.

These bulges of ocean water are crests called **high tides** (fig. 13.19). Between tidal crests are troughs called **low tides.** The difference between the elevations (relative to mean sea level) of the high and low tides (wave height) is called the **tidal range.** As Earth rotates on its axis and the moon moves in its orbit around Earth, locations along the track of the sublunar point have high tides approximately twice each day. The moon rises 50 minutes later each day, so Earth turns beneath each bulge once every 12 hours and 25 minutes, and tides have periods of this same length. Friction with the continents, the shapes of water bodies such as bays, and latitude with respect to the sublunar point all act as controls on the

(a)

(b)

Figure 13.21 (*a*) High and (*b*) low tides in the tidal creeks of a saltwater marsh along the South Carolina coast.

height of the tidal crest for a given locale. The elongate Bay of Fundy between New Brunswick and Nova Scotia, Canada, for example, has a tidal range of 16 meters (52.5 ft), and Passamaquoddy Bay (United States and Canada) has a range of 15 meters (49.2 ft). These two bays have the greatest tidal ranges on Earth.

Along some coasts, high tide produces a rapidly advancing wall of water called a **tidal bore** (or a *mascaret* in France). Tidal bores may travel 10 meters per second (33 ft per sec), performing geologic work on riverbanks and stream deposits. Because of the great tidal range in the Bay of Fundy, the landward rush of water reverses flow in the St. John's River, with white water alternatively moving landward and seaward. Elsewhere, a tidal bore has been used to generate electricity. At the Rance Estuary on the English Channel Coast of France, where the tidal range is about 8 meters (26 ft), a dam with reversible turbines can be opened to let water flow upstream into a reservoir. Then, with the reversing tide, the water flows seaward and back through the turbines, generating about 0.5 billion kilowatt-hours annually by converting about one-fifth of the kinetic energy in the moving water to electricity.

Another control on the elevation of tidal crests is the spatial relationship among the sun, moon, and Earth. Twice each month, when these three bodies lie in a straight line, the tide-generating force of the sun amplifies that of the moon. The enhanced tidal crest is called a **spring tide,** and it is offset by a deeper trough, producing a lower-than-normal low tide (fig. 13.20*a*). Alternatively, when the sun and moon are oriented perpendicularly to each other with respect to Earth, high tides are lower than normal, and low tides are higher. This is the **neap tide** (fig. 13.20*b*).

Tides control the surface against which waves can perform geologic work. On gently sloping coasts close to sea level, large tidal ranges make the areal extent of wave influence great. On steeply inclined shorelines, greater tidal ranges mean greater notching. Tides also affect the extent of tropical and Nor'easter storm damage.

When a hurricane approaches the land, its low pressure pulls the water up. If this uplift of water, combined with the push of the winds, coincides with the crest of a spring tide, the water may inundate the land to a great extent (tens of kilometers), and the storm's waves may perform work on sediments they would not ordinarily affect. Along low-lying coasts, such as that of Bangladesh on the delta of the Ganges River, this combination of factors has historically led to massive influxes of water far inland across the islands of the delta, with death tolls measured in the hundreds of thousands. One recent such occurrence, in 1985, took an estimated 20,000 lives.

Tides also influence marshlands, such as those found in New Jersey and South Carolina. The rising water flows up tidal channels, spreads out over the marsh, and moves clay and silt particles among the marsh grasses (fig. 13.21). Within the tidal channels, the flow can be swift, but the marsh grasses act like baffles to dampen the energy and slow the shallow water over the marsh. The twice-daily flow of water into and out of the marshes has the important effects of moving nutrients into the environment and carrying out pollutants. These marshes are important breeding grounds for fish and invertebrates (see chapter 15).

Further Thoughts: Your Vacation Home, My Tax Dollar

Owning a home on the shore is a chancy economic venture. Storms inevitably occur. Waves steepen. Houses, motels, and restaurants fall into the onrushing water. When it is someone else's home or restaurant, a neighbor may have two emotions: one of sadness for the victims of storm damage and another of relief (or even joy) that the waves did not strike a few meters farther up-beach or inland.

The problem with the "I'm sorry it was you, but I'm glad it wasn't me" mentality is that it allows us to assume an invulnerability that is both temporary and imaginary. It ignores certain economic realities. Taxpayers put their money into a common treasury, and that treasury may be one source of funding for refurbishing, remodeling, or restoring a community devastated by storm waves. In other words, we all pay when a storm victimizes some of us.

The measures that coastal communities usually take to ward off further storm damage or to reclaim inundated land are mostly stopgap. They are measures undertaken to recover from immediate damage or to prevent similar damage. In some instances, such as at Galveston, Texas, where an extensive seawall protects a city once subject to severe damage, the measures are sufficient. In many other instances, the remediation is too little, too late.

Governments responsible for the maintenance of coastal communities have an obligation to the inland citizenry. They need to take responsible action based on knowledge of how the ocean can affect their community. Their foresight and commitment to safety and prudence will save everyone money.

Significant Points

1. Waves and currents transfer energy in standing bodies of water.
2. A wave of oscillation is a circular or elliptical rise and fall of water in response to the passage of energy.
3. A current is a streamlike flow of water on or within a standing water body.
4. Most waves and currents are induced by winds.
5. Water is about 1,000 times denser than air; thus, wind must blow continuously in contact with water to maintain waves and currents.
6. Fetch is the distance over the water that the wind blows.
7. A wave of translation is a breaking wave that transfers energy to a beach or a cliff.
8. As waves approach a shoreline, they refract. When they strike an object, they diffract.
9. Water piled onto a beach by incoming waves flows downslope as the backwash or as rip currents.
10. Wave refraction concentrates wave energy on headlands, where waves carve sea caves, sea arches, and sea stacks.
11. Wave-cut platforms can be raised by tectonic activity to become marine terraces.
12. Bars are usually elongate mounds of sand-sized particles formed by the processes responsible for beach drifting.
13. Barrier islands are large offshore bars separated from the mainland by narrow (tens to hundreds of meters) lagoons.
14. Wave refraction produces a shoreline current called the longshore current.
15. The longshore current transports beach materials, resulting in the migration of sands and the formation of spits and baymouth bars.
16. Breakwaters and seawalls are designed to protect coastal properties from wave erosion.
17. Groins built perpendicularly to seawalls protect the walls by absorbing wave energy. Those that stand perpendicular to shorelines capture migrating sands to stabilize and widen beaches.
18. Seismic sea waves, called tsunamis, radiate from the epicenters of earthquakes, volcanic eruptions, and large avalanches. They can cause widespread damage to coastal areas and have sometimes been responsible for thousands of deaths.
19. Tides are gravity-induced, shallow-water waves with periods of 12 hours and 25 minutes.
20. The tidal crest is the product of the moon's tractive force, which is strongest 45° from both the sublunar point and a point on the opposite side of Earth.
21. Tidal range is the difference in elevation between the high and low tides. Tidal range is controlled by location with respect to the sublunar point, by the shape of a water body, by the Earth-sun-moon orientation, and by friction with the continents.
22. Earth's greatest tidal ranges occur in the Bay of Fundy and in Passamaquoddy Bay.
23. Large tidal ranges can produce a tidal bore.
24. Spring tides occur whenever the sun, moon, and Earth lie in a straight line. Neap tides occur when the sun, moon, and Earth make a right angle.
25. Storm surges that coincide with a spring tide inundate land to a greater extent.

ESSENTIAL TERMS

wave   *305*
current   *305*
fetch   *305*
wave base   *305*
crest   *305*
trough   *305*
wave height   *305*
wavelength   *305*
wave period   *305*
waves of oscillation
   305
wave train   *305*
deep-water wave   *305*

shallow-water
   wave   *305*
surf zone   *305*
waves of translation
   305
wave refraction   *306*
wave diffraction   *306*
swash   *306*
splash-and-spray
   zone   *307*
backwash   *307*
rip current   *307*
beach drifting   *307*

headland   *307*
sea cave   *308*
sea arch   *308*
sea stack   *308*
ramp   *308*
wave-cut platform   ·*308*
marine terrace   *308*
notch   *308*
contraposed
   shoreline   *308*
bar   *309*
barrier island   *310*
longshore current   *311*

longshore
   transport   *311*
spit   *311*
baymouth bar   *311*
tombolo   *311*
breakwater   *312*
jetty   *312*
groin   *312*
beach nourishment   *313*
seawall   *313*
riprap   *315*
seismic sea wave
   (tsunami)   *315*

tide   *315*
sublunar point   *316*
tractive force   *316*
high tide   *316*
low tide   *316*
tidal range   *316*
tidal bore   *317*
spring tide   *317*
neap tide   *317*

REVIEW QUESTIONS

1. Does a wave of oscillation result in a significant horizontal movement of water?
2. What is the difference in density between air and water? How does this difference affect the transfer of energy between air and water?
3. What causes a wave of oscillation to become a wave of translation?
4. What causes wave refraction?
5. What causes wave diffraction?
6. Why is a rip current potentially dangerous to swimmers?
7. How does a sea arch form?
8. Is a crescent-shaped beach an indication of wave erosion or deposition?
9. Why are bars shifting features?
10. Why are barrier islands economically important?

11. How can coastal communities protect themselves from the erosive power of waves?
12. How can coastal communities widen their beaches?
13. What causes a tsunami?
14. Why are tsunamis dangerous to coastal communities?
15. Why are the tides called shallow-water waves?
16. Why does the moon have a greater influence on tides than the sun?
17. Where is the tractive force of the moon greatest?
18. What causes the tidal bulge on the side of Earth that faces away from the moon?
19. What is the tidal range in the Bay of Fundy?
20. How can tides help to reduce a country's dependence upon oil and coal as sources of energy? Would this reduction be feasible for all coastal countries?

CHALLENGES

1. What concerns would you have about docking your boat in the Bay of Fundy?
2. Research a coastal community's (such as Nags Head, North Carolina) procedures for protecting against or recovering from storm beach erosion.
3. How would a coastal plain community that has no native outcropping of rock construct an economically viable breakwater?

4. If you live near or visit regularly a shoreline (lake, bay, ocean), examine the effect of engineering structures. Can you determine the effect that each of them has on erosion or deposition?
5. How do waves and currents compare with other geologic surface agents in performing short-term geologic work? in performing long-term geologic work?

PART 5

OCEAN WATERS AND ENVIRONMENTS

*T*he ocean waters *and* their basins are the most important controls on Earth's surface systems. Seafloor spreading is the starting point for most magmatic processes because it results in the movements of lithospheric plates that redistribute and reshape landmasses and ocean basins. Extensive ocean currents move heat, affecting climates, storms, and the hydrologic cycle. Gas exchanges between atmosphere and oceans can diminish or enhance greenhouse warming, and salt exchanges between seawater and life can multiply sediments and increase coral reefs.

The complexity of ocean systems is a reflection of interconnectedness. Thus, marine geology is inseparably related to marine chemistry, and both are tied to atmospheric processes, continental evolution, and life.

At the *End* of Part 5, You Will be Able to:

1. Relate the nature and significance of water.
2. Identify and integrate the controls on seawater and its circulation.
3. Illustrate air-sea interactions.
4. Interpret ocean environments and their relationships to life.

from William Shakespeare's The Tempest, *V, i*

I'll deliver all;
And promise you calm seas, auspicious gales,
And sail so expeditious that shall catch
Your royal fleet far off.

Chapter

14

Ocean Waters

Soft coral. Nigali Pass, Gau, Fiji.

INTRODUCTION

More than 1.3 billion cubic kilometers (312 million cu. mi) of water fill the ocean basins to overflowing, inundating the continental shelves and intruding upon low-lying coastal areas. In fact, only 29.1% of Earth's surface lies above the average level of seawater, as the **hypsographic** (from the Greek *hypsos*, meaning "height," and *graphein*, meaning "to write") **curve** in figure 14.1 shows. The oceans contain 98% of the world's water and anchor the hydrologic cycle. They are largely responsible for the latitudinal distribution of solar heat, the amount of water vapor available for weather systems, and the storage and exchange of gases, such as carbon dioxide (CO_2). The ocean waters, particularly in the large hurricanes they generate, also extend their influence to coastal geology and human structures. Along the ever-changing shorelines, ocean currents and waves move unconsolidated sediments, erode cliffs, and undercut buildings, roads, and bridges.

With their rich supply of dissolved gases and nutrients, the oceans harbor vast quantities of life. Marine photosynthesizers and sulfide-reducing bacteria serve as the base of the food chain, making the oceans a supplier of protein for both marine and terrestrial organisms. Birds, terrestrial mammals, reptiles, and amphibians along coasts and island shorelines act as foraging marauders who invade the seawater for their sustenance. Even humans derive millions of tons of protein from sea life.

The Sink

Geologically and chemically, the oceans are the ultimate sink because they are so deep. Gravity insures that much of what is above water is destined to be washed into some sea or ocean through the continuous processes of weathering, erosion, and transport. Although lakes and floodplains may trap sediments for millions of years, they serve merely as temporary stopovers. A few dry inland basins (e.g., Death Valley) are lower than sea level or restricted by surrounding highlands, which allows local sediments to collect. Eventually, however, tectonic activity opens pathways to the sea or uplifts an area to initiate erosion and sediment transport. The pollutants in our streams, the soils on our farms, even the upper bedrock of the continents are all seaward bound. The process may take tens, or even hundreds of millions of years, but it is inevitable. And yet, because Earth is dynamic, the oceans are themselves only temporary repositories and parts of larger chemical and physical cyclic systems on Earth.

Oceanographic Studies

The complexity of ocean studies is manifested by the different kinds of scientific activities in which oceanographers engage. Marine geophysicists, geologists, and coastal geomorphologists research and explain the composition, evolution, and processes of the seafloor and basin boundaries, and they work to locate, exploit, and protect marine resources. Physical oceanographers study air-sea interactions, surface and deep-water dynamics, and ocean temperatures and salinities. Chemical oceanographers analyze the surface and deep water for distributions of the more than 70 elements that influence marine life and sediments. Almost half of those dedicated to understanding the oceans are marine biologists, who study the varied flora and fauna that reside above, on, in, and under the water column. Finally, ocean engineers design ships, drilling and research platforms, and coastal structures, such as seawalls, docks, and jetties. As you can see, oceanography is among the most interdisciplinary of subjects.

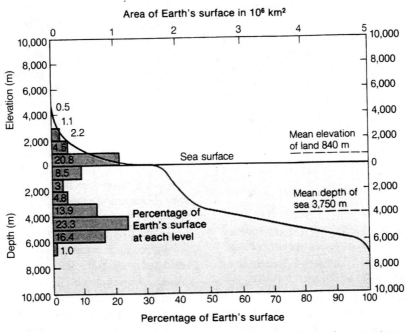

Figure 14.1   A hypsographic curve. The cumulative curve indicates the percentage of Earth's surface above any elevation on the curve. (Sverdrup/Johnson/Fleming, *The Oceans,* © 1942, © renewed 1970, p. 19. Adapted by permission of Prentice-Hall, Upper Saddle River, New Jersey.)

Water is the most important compound on Earth. It is also Earth's most characteristic compound, since the oceans cover most (71%) of Earth's surface. Thus, references to Earth as the *watery planet* are well founded.

The Significance of Water's Liquid State

Earthbound observations and data from such spacecraft as *Voyagers I* and *II* reveal that *no other planet in our Solar System maintains a liquid water ocean.* Water may have once flowed elsewhere in the Solar System, such as on Mars (see chapter 11), but ice (a solid) and water vapor (a gas) are the forms water takes outside Earth. Evidence of erosion by water on Mars shows that planet to have lost its liquid surface water billions of years ago. At 450° C (842° F), the surface of Earth's sister planet, Venus, is too hot for liquid water, and the other inner planet, Mercury, is a barren, cratered wasteland baked by a sun only 53 million kilometers (33 million mi) away. The Jovian planets are mostly gaseous balls, but Jupiter's moon Ganymede may house a liquid ocean mantle, and the rings of Saturn, Jupiter, and Uranus appear to be composed primarily of ice particles. Our planet is unique because of its liquid water.

A delicate orbital balance keeps Earth just the right distance from the sun for water to exist in a liquid state. If our planet were about 16 million kilometers (10 million mi) closer to the sun, it would be too hot for liquid water to occur on Earth's surface. If Earth were 16 million kilometers farther from the sun, all the surface water would be ice. This significant balance between freezing and boiling water has existed for more than 3 billion years, resulting in the continued occurrence of oceans, rivers, lakes, and groundwater.

The long-term presence of liquid water has influenced the origin, composition, and evolution of life. Life most likely originated in association with water, and water is necessary for its preservation. Organisms are composed chiefly of water, which comprises as much as 80% of a living cell. In dry climates, life collects at oases and on the windward sides of mountains. In humid climates, such as those in the eastern half of North America, the land is ubiquitously covered with life, whose presence is made possible by water.

The Nature of Water

What is this substance that makes up almost 97% of the oceans? **Water** is a compound of hydrogen and oxygen that exists through the sharing of electrons (see chapter 2). Although atoms are electrically neutral and balanced, they can be thought of as being incomplete whenever their most remote energy levels do not hold their full potential of electrons. This incompleteness enables many atoms to react or to bind into molecules. Oxygen, an element with eight electrons, has an incomplete outer energy level, where six of its eight electrons are located. Hydrogen, the simplest of all elements, has only one electron in its single energy level, which can

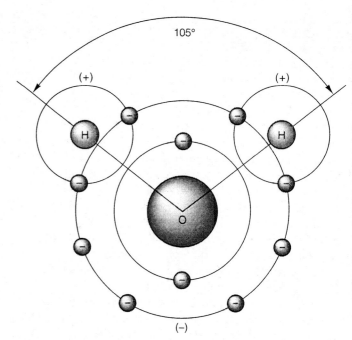

Figure 14.2 Arrangement of H and O ions in a covalent bond to form the water (H_2O) molecule. The molecule has a net positive charge on the H end and a negative charge on the O end because of its asymmetry.

potentially hold two. In the sharing of electrons, the hydrogen and oxygen both receive and lend electrons from their outer energy shells, and they make a covalent bond. The arrangement known as H_2O, therefore, completes the respective outer energy levels of the three atoms (fig. 14.2). The resultant molecule is unstable at best, breaking up and reforming as many as a million times each second and accounting for water's liquid nature.

Many kinds of water result from combinations of different isotopes (see chapter 2) of hydrogen and oxygen, and they possess different properties. The most common form of hydrogen contains a single, positively charged proton and a negatively charged electron (^1H). The balance of charges makes the atom electrically neutral. Other forms of hydrogen exist, however. Deuterium (^2H) is hydrogen with a neutron in its nucleus, and tritium (^3H) has two neutrons. Oxygen has isotopes with eight (^{16}O), nine (^{17}O), and ten (^{18}O) neutrons in their nuclei. The most common type of water is $^1H_2^{16}O$, but other forms, such as $^2H_2^{16}O$, or deuterium oxide, do occur in nature. Deuterium oxide is called *heavy water*. It does not behave the same as common water, and it does not quench your thirst. Nuclear reactors use heavy water as a moderator to slow the velocity of neutrons, resulting in an increase in fission.

The arrangement of atoms in the molecule gives water a special dipole (*di*, meaning "two") property, much like a bar magnet's north and south poles. The hydrogen end of the water molecule exposes two protons, while the oxygen end is dominated by electrons. The isolated charges result from the pull of eight protons in the oxygen nucleus. For the electrons in the molecule, these more numerous protons exert a stronger tug than the two isolated hydrogen nuclei. This arrangement results in a positive hydrogen end and a negative oxygen end of the molecule. The positive end of one water molecule binds to the negative end of another, and so on,

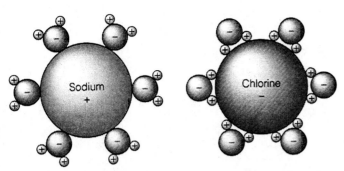

Figure 14.3 Water molecules surrounding and separating ions of sodium (Na) and chlorine (Cl) during the process of hydration.

TABLE 14.1 The Most Common Elements in Seawater and Their Residence Times (where appropriate)		
Element	Concentration (mg/l)	Known Residence Time (yr)
Oxygen	857,000	
Hydrogen	108,000	
Chlorine	19,400	
Sodium	10,800	2.6×10^8
Magnesium	1,350	4.5×10^7
Sulfur	885	
Calcium	413	8.0×10^6
Potassium	387	1.1×10^7
Bromine	68	
Carbon	28	
Strontium	8.1	1.9×10^7
Boron	4.5	
Silicon	3	8×10^3
Fluorine	1.4	
Nitrogen	0.5	

making a glass of pure water virtually a single molecule. The lining up of opposite charges also makes pure water incapable of conducting an electrical current.

Hydration

The dipole water molecule can act electrically to dissociate weakly bound molecules like sodium chloride, or common salt, which water separates into its component Na^+ and Cl^- ions. In a process known as **hydration,** water molecules surround the component elements by binding to them in molecular form as the oxygen end of water molecules isolate the sodium and the hydrogen ends surround the chlorine (fig. 14.3). The significance of this process lies in the production of *dissolved salts* and water that is *saline,* or salty.

Seawater

Seawater is composed of both water and dissolved salts. The salt water of the oceans contains the dissolved ions of more than 70 elements, the most abundant of which are listed in table 14.1. A swimmer who swallows seawater drinks potassium, magnesium, silicon, and common salt, among other dissolved substances. More than 3% of the oceans is composed of these invisible salts, but they do not add to the ocean's volume because they are contained between water molecules.

A small experiment demonstrates the relationship between volume and dissolved salt. Partially fill a glass with water, and mark the water level on the outside of the glass. Then add salt to the water until a few of the salt crystals fall to the bottom of the glass without dissolving. You now have a *saturated solution,* or one in which there is no additional capacity for hydrating salt ions. A check of the water level against the mark should show no increase in water volume after you add the salt.

Residence Time

Elements pass into and out of the oceans because of physical, chemical, and biochemical reactions. Seashells predominantly consist of calcium carbonate extracted from the water by certain enzymes in organisms. Coral reefs are the product of a similar extraction. Thus, some ions do not reside permanently in the water but, rather, may become incorporated into marine sediments and rocks upon the deaths of the extracting organisms. Some of these materials may be returned to the water through dissolution, but many undergo burial and inclusion in the rock cycle. The time an element spends in the oceans is called its **residence time** (see table 14.1).

SEAWATER SALINITY

Oceanographers measure dissolved salts in parts per thousand (‰, read "parts per mille"). So, in a liter of seawater, the saltiness might yield a reading of 34.5‰, meaning that 34.5 grams (or 3.45%) are dissolved substances. In 1902, an international commission defined saltiness, or **salinity,** as the amount of solid matter in grams contained in a kilogram (1,000 g, or 2.2 lb) of seawater after any carbonate has been converted to an oxide, any bromine and iodine have been replaced by chlorine, and any organic matter has been oxidized. To find salinity, oceanographers can use a *salinometer,* which is an instrument that determines salinity on the basis of electrical conductivity. Or they titrate (determine the quantity of dissolved salts by causing a chemical reaction) a water sample with silver nitrate. This process precipitates bromides, iodides, and chlorides, resulting in the *chlorinity,* or the total amount of chlorine. They then convert chlorinity to salinity through the following formula:

$$\text{salinity} = 1.808 \times \text{chlorinity}$$

Figure 14.4 Average July surface water salinities in parts per thousand (‰).

The salinity of seawater differs with latitude and depth, location in open ocean or restricted water bodies, climate, stream runoff, and ice formation and melting. However, except for locally influenced waters along coastlines, the relative *constituent proportion of the various dissolved substances in seawater remains the same.*

Controls on Surface Salinities

Oceanic surface salinities change with the seasons and with variations in precipitation amounts and evaporation rates. In equatorial zones, the surface salinity of the open ocean is relatively low because of dilution from rain, whereas in the subtropics, the salinity of the surface water is higher because of evaporation. The July surface salinities shown in figure 14.4 reveal generally lower salinities in high latitudes than in low latitudes. Increased rainfall, runoff, and ice melt dilute the higher-latitude waters. The low equatorial readings that derive from excessive rainfall are shifted slightly to the north during the Northern Hemisphere summer and to the south during its winter.

Latitudinal salinity patterns established by climates can be offset by local seasonal influences in coastal waters. In restricted lagoons and bays, such as Laguna Madre along the Texas coast, for example, fluctuating salinities reflect wet and dry periods (fig. 14.5).

Salinity Profiles

The salinity of open ocean water varies with depth. The vertical record of this change is a **salinity profile.** The starting points for salinity profiles of vertical water columns are the surfaces of the seas and oceans. Wherever the profile reveals a rapid change in salinity with depth, it marks the **halocline** (from *halo,* meaning "halite"; and *cline,* meaning "transition"). A clearly defined halocline does not form throughout the oceans. In the equatorial regions, for example, the surface water salinity averages less than that for the subtropics. High-latitude surface salinities are actually lower than those in deep water, so a salinity profile reveals a slight increase in salt content down a high-latitude water column. Ultimately, mixing at depths overcomes local effects, resulting in deep water of a relatively constant salinity. Figure 14.6 reveals the salinity characteristics for generalized water columns.

OCEAN TEMPERATURES

Ocean temperatures vary. Vacationers on beaches in the Bahamas experience different water temperatures from those who attempt to swim along the coastal waters of Oregon, Washington, and British Columbia. These temperature differences result from controls not much different from those that affect atmospheric temperatures.

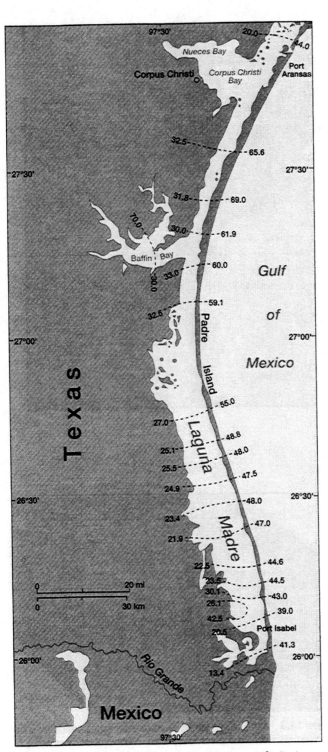

Figure 14.5 The salinity variations (in parts per mil [⁰/₀₀]) of Laguna Madre, a large lagoon along the south Texas coast. The extreme values at each end of the short, dashed lines indicate the annual range at each location: higher during the dry season and lower during the wet season. (After G.A. Rusnick, *Recent Sediments Northwest Gulf of Mexico*, ed. by Shephard and Moore, p. 155. Copyright 1960 American Association of Petroleum Geologists, Tulsa, Oklahoma. Reprinted by permission.)

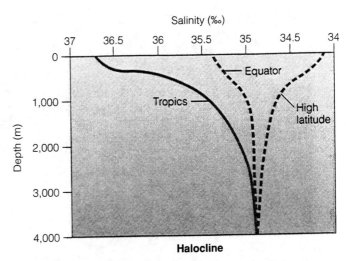

Figure 14.6 Haloclines at various latitudes. Note that the most pronounced change occurs in the tropical seas because of high evaporation rates but low precipitation.

Controls on Ocean Temperatures

Latitude is the chief control on ocean surface temperature. Ocean waters in high latitudes, for example, receive less solar energy per unit area than low-latitude waters. Seasonal changes in the amount of solar energy available also affect changes in temperature. Another control on temperature is depth, because deep waters are not influenced by the warming sun.

Typically, low-latitude surface water is warm, and high-latitude surface water is cold, but these terms are only relative. Figure 14.7 shows average isotherms for surface waters during August, revealing very low temperatures in polar regions. Precise temperature readings by oceanographers and merchant marine sailors have enabled scientists to map not only the surface but also the deep-water temperatures and to draw temperature profiles.

Temperature Profiles

Vertical profiles of ocean temperatures show varying patterns for different latitudes and indicate a zone of rapid temperature change with depth, called the **thermocline.** In equatorial and tropical waters, the thermocline is well developed because the surface temperatures are relatively high (fig. 14.8). Temperatures drop rapidly in the top kilometer of these two water columns. In high-latitude surface waters, however, temperatures can fall below freezing (0° C, 32° F), so the change in temperature down the water column is not great.

The deep waters of the oceans are not universally cold. Along oceanic rifts with active volcanism, water that circulates near shallow magma chambers becomes very hot. Some of this water reaches 500° C (932° F) and exits the ocean floor through vents. Plumes of hot water then spread out over the ocean floor in localized areas, gradually cooling by contact and mixing with the ambient cold water of the deep ocean.

Figure 14.7 Mean oceanic surface water temperatures during August (°C).

Figure 14.8 Thermoclines at various latitudes. Note that the sharpest change occurs in equatorial seas because of intense solar heating of the surface waters.

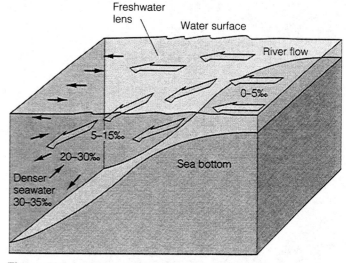

Figure 14.9 A freshwater lens rides above denser seawater for some distance until natural mixing processes bring about homogeneity.

SEAWATER DENSITY

Density is weight per unit volume, usually given in grams per cubic centimeter. Our ordinary experiences give us a good sense of density. A block of wood, for example, is not as heavy as a similarly sized mass of iron. Of course, the atomic mass number (see chapter 2) of iron is higher than that of any constituent atom in the wood. Water, as you now know, can be made of different oxygen and hydrogen isotopes, some of which are heavier than others. But the most significant controls on seawater density are salt and temperature.

Salinity and Density

At 4° C (39° F), pure water weighs 1 gram per cubic centimeter. Because salt water is heavier than pure water, seawater averages about 1.025 grams per cubic centimeter. Wherever rains or inflows

Figure 14.10 The relationship of temperature to water density. At 20° C, water molecules are separated, with few attached to one another. As temperature decreases to 4° C, the molecules are slowed and packed tightly together. This is the densest configuration. Below 2° C, the water molecules attach themselves together in a crystalline pattern to form solid ice. Because there is a specific spacing between ions in the crystal lattice, they separate from one another as they link up, thus lowering the density. (Redrawn from *Introductory Oceanography*, Fifth Edition by Harold V. Thurman. Copyright © 1988 Macmillan Publishing Co. Used by permission of Prentice-Hall, Inc., Upper Saddle River, NJ.)

of river water dilute ocean salinity, the local surface water becomes less salty, and its density decreases. Many large river systems, such as the Amazon, for example, flow *onto*, rather than into, the ocean, forming a *freshwater lens*, which is a body of lighter, lens-shaped water that slowly mixes with the seawater (fig. 14.9).

Temperature and Density

Like salinity, ocean temperatures vary with latitude and depth. Surface waters in equatorial regions can exceed 30° C (86° F), whereas those of high latitudes can fall below 0° C (32° F). The water in the depths of the oceans can fall below 0° C. That water is not frozen on the ocean bottoms is the result of three factors:

1. It is salt water, which does not freeze at 0° C.

Figure 14.11 (*a*) Sea ice in an early stage of formation. (*b*) An iceberg in the polar sea.

2. Ice floats because it is less dense than water.
3. Even though water is not very compressible, it is under great pressure on the ocean bottom, as much as 1,000 times the average sea-level pressure. The increase in pressure with greater depth causes a slight adiabatic warming.

Pure water is densest at 4° C (39° F). Although salt water is denser, on average, than fresh water, temperature exerts an even greater control than salinity on water density. Water warmer than 4° C is less dense because of more rapidly vibrating molecules. But 4° C marks a *pivotal point* in the density of pure water. Between that temperature and the initial freezing point, water decreases in density with the formation of partial and complete hexagonal ice crystals that add volume without adding mass (fig. 14.10). Relatively stable ice crystals make a latticework, which incorporates empty spaces because the angle between the hydrogen atoms in the water molecule increases to form hexagonal crystals.

As a consequence of the density differences between ice and water, ice floats. *Ice floes* form directly on the sea's surface (fig. 14.11*a*). *Icebergs*, which are *calved* (or broken) pieces of glaciers, drift with currents, becoming hazards to shipping in high latitudes (fig. 14.11*b*). A collision with an iceberg sank the *Titanic*, the world's largest passenger liner, on her maiden voyage in 1912. Even larger ice accumulations can occur. The Arctic Ocean is covered by a number of moving *ice islands* of considerable size, and in the South Atlantic, some tablelike icebergs attain an area equal to the size of Rhode Island.

Figure 14.12 A sigma-t diagram, showing variation in water density with temperature and salinity.

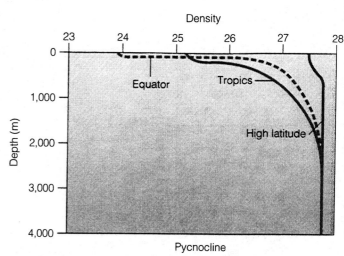

Figure 14.13 Pycnoclines at various latitudes. The most pronounced density changes occur in equatorial seas.

The density of ice also influences organisms. Life on the ocean bottom is effectively protected by this density difference. If ice were denser than liquid water, the oceans would freeze from the bottom up, and marine organisms would have no secure habitat. A layer of seawater ice insulates the water below from subfreezing atmospheric conditions. In addition, frozen seawater contains very little of the salt from its original liquid state. The absence of salt in icebergs has even led some to speculate about towing them to desert countries like Saudi Arabia for a large freshwater supply. Any melting in transit would be offset by the great volume of ice.

The Sigma-t Diagram

Oceanographers use a special graph to plot the combined effects of salinity and temperature. This graph, called the **sigma-t** or **T-S diagram** (s = salinity; t = temperature), enables scientists to establish density characteristics for particular water masses (fig. 14.12). Earlier, you learned that pure water at 4° C has a density of 1 gram per cubic centimeter. The addition of salt or a change in temperature alters density. Seawater is always salt water, and it has, therefore, a slightly higher density than pure water, varying from about 1.025 to about 1.028 grams per cubic centimeter. On the sigma-t diagram, 1 gram is subtracted from each of the readings, which is then multiplied by 1,000, making, for example, 1.0255 grams per cubic centimeter read as sigma-t 25.5 at 1 atmosphere of pressure. Figure 14.12 reveals that warm, less-saline water is less dense than cold, saline water.

The vertical density profiles for both the equatorial and subtropical water columns show a rapid change in density with depth, called the **pycnocline** (fig. 14.13). Temperature, rather than salinity, has a greater effect on water density. The warm surface waters

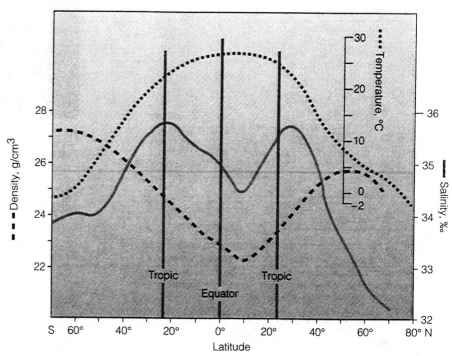

Figure 14.14 Latitudinal variation of temperature, salinity, and density of surface waters.

of equatorial and tropical oceans are relatively light, making the pycnoclines mimic the pattern of the thermoclines for these regions, as a comparison of figures 14.8 and 14.13 shows.

GENERALIZED SURFACE PROFILE

By examining the surface water characteristics between 80°N and 60°S, which are plotted in figure 14.14, you can see the relationships among temperature, salinity, and density. Where temperatures are high and salinities are low, density is lower. In the subtropics, the warm water temperatures are balanced by the higher salinities derived from excessive evaporation, yielding higher densities.

Further Consideration

Box 14.1

DID THE MEDITERRANEAN SEA DRY UP?

In the December 1972 *Scientific American,* author Kenneth J. Hsü reported evidence that the Mediterranean Sea had once dried up. The evidence was part of a multiple working hypothesis, one that adopted the findings of numerous scientists working in several research disciplines. Hsü's multiple evidence derived from deep-sea drilling by the crew on board the *Glomar Challenger,* from the studies of microfossils, from accounts of seismologists, and from other sources. Although other scientists had worked on the data from Leg XIII of the *Glomar Challenger* voyages, only Maria Cita and Bill Ryan, who were members of the scientific cruise, agreed with Hsü on the validity of a dessicated Mediterranean.

In particular, Hsü and his co-workers found layers of halite below the marine sediments of the western Mediterranean's Balearic Basin. The halite, which was associated with anhydrite ($CaSO_4$), appears to have been produced by the evaporation of relatively shallow seawater. That it was found under 3 kilometers (approximately 2 mi) of Mediterranean water seemed to indicate that the sea had once been very shallow.

Corroborating evidence from drill sites on land came in the form of newly discovered canyons that lie buried beneath current stream systems, such as the Rhône in Europe and the Nile in Egypt. These canyons indicate a downcutting that reached below present sea level by thousands of meters. Because streams attain their erosive power through gravity, the base level of these streams must have been lower during the downcutting.

In addition, beneath deep water south of Greece is the large Mediterranean Ridge. This ridge also shows a downcutting that could not have occurred under deep-water conditions. Apparently, Atlantic seawater rushed in to fill the dried-up basins partly through the Mediterranean Ridge, eroding and cleaving the ridge in the process (fig. 14.A)

The time of this desert Mediterranean has been estimated at 6 million years ago, and coinciding with this estimate is a change in the fauna that inhabited the region. A dry Mediterranean allowed the passage of animal life previously blocked by a deep sea. With fossil evidence supporting the theory, Hsü speculated that the Mediterranean opened and closed repeatedly at the Straits of Gibraltar. Each time the basin was flooded, a spectacular waterfall more than 1,000 times the volume of Niagara Falls spilled into the Mediterranean.

Apply Your Knowledge

1. What happens when you allow a glass of salt water to evaporate?
2. Is there any mechanism other than erosion by running water that could explain the cleft in the Mediterranean Ridge?

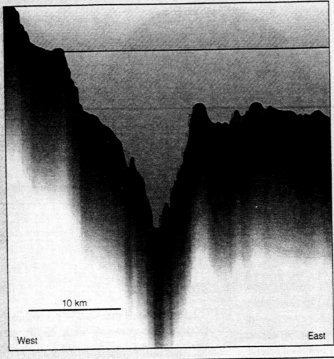

Figure 14.A Seismic profiling showed a deeply eroded valley in the Mediterranean Ridge that formed as Atlantic water flowed into the Mediterranean basins. (From Hsü Kenneth J., *The Mediterranean Was a Desert.* Copyright © 1983 by Princeton University Press. Reproduced by permission of Princeton University Press.)

10 km

West   East

THERMOHALINE CIRCULATION

The combined effects of temperature and salinity generate vertical currents in the oceans. Dense water falls below less-dense water. Thus, the cold surface waters of high-latitude seas sink because of their relatively high density. Similarly, water from climatically dry regions in midlatitudes sinks because of increased salinity. The movement of ocean water driven by density differences is called **thermohaline circulation.**

Water Masses

Oceanographers and sailors have measured salinity and temperature for many years, and the compilation of their data has enabled scientists to characterize **water masses,** which are large, three-dimensional bodies of water with identifiable boundaries.

In the Mediterranean, evaporation is high, and rainfall is seasonal. From its volume of 4.2 million cubic kilometers (1 million cu. mi) of seawater, the Mediterranean loses 1,235 cubic kilometers (296 cu. mi) through evaporation annually. (Box 14.1 describes evidence that the Mediterranean Sea once dried up.) The

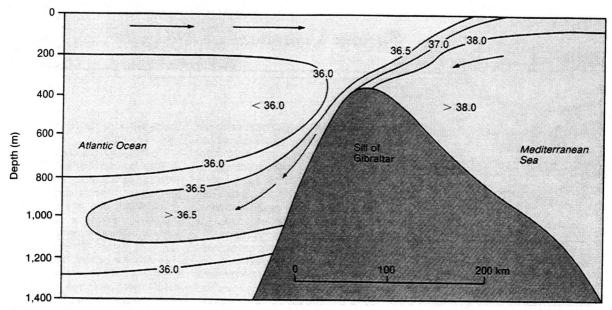

Figure 14.15 Cross section shows movement of dense Mediterranean water over the sill of Gibraltar and into the deep Atlantic Ocean basin. Figures within diagram indicate water salinity (⁰/₀₀). (John A. Knauss, *Introduction to Physical Geography*, ©1978, p.168. Adapted by permission of Prentice-Hall, Upper Saddle River, New Jersey.)

Figure 14.16 Major water masses and their origins.

surface water that does not evaporate becomes increasingly more saline and, obviously, more dense. As the surface water sinks under its own weight to make bottom currents, it exits the sea at an estimated flow rate of 1,750,000 cubic meters (61,775,000 cu. ft) per second through the Straits of Gibraltar, mostly beneath incoming, less-dense Atlantic surface water that replenishes the sea (fig. 14.15). Once in the ocean, the great volume of Mediterranean water becomes an intermediately deep layer of water in the Atlantic, spreading laterally and eventually mixing with water sinking in the Norwegian Sea.

Because of its temperature, water from the Norwegian Sea sinks even lower than Mediterranean water and becomes the *North Atlantic Deep Water* (*NADW*). At the bottom of the ocean lies a cold layer, *Antarctic Bottom Water* (*AABW*), derived largely from the Southern Ocean, that surface body of water that encircles Antarctica. AABW is very cold (–0.4° C, 31.3° F) and very dense (sigma-t over 27.8).

Downwelling

The formation of the AABW presents a good lesson on the complexity of the ocean systems. As the prevailing westerlies blow across the Southern Ocean, they drive different bodies of surface water together. Because water cannot form mountains at such a confluence, some of the converging water sinks. At the surface, the Southern Ocean averages 0.5° C (33° F), with a salinity of 34.68‰. This **downwelling** water merges with sinking shelf water that averages –1.9° C (28.58° F) and 34.62‰ to make the AABW water mass at a depth of 4 kilometers (2.48 mi). The AABW, with a characteristic temperature of –0.4° C (31.3° F) and a salinity of 34.66‰, is among the densest of all water masses.

The autonomous characteristics of various water masses like the AABW make the ocean more or less *stratified*. The less-dense surface waters are underlain by moving layers of *intermediate, deep,* and *bottom waters*. Just like air masses, each of these water

Figure 14.17
Stratification of water masses in the South Atlantic.

Figure 14.18 Principal areas of upwelling along coasts.

masses derives from a particular source region (fig. 14.16). A water mass can vary within its boundaries and, depending on neighboring densities, can extend upward or downward through other masses (fig. 14.17).

Upwelling

The downward movements of water masses must be offset by upward moving water. Wherever surface water bodies are separated by prevailing winds, they diverge. Because a liquid such as water cannot have a permanent "hole," water from below rises to take the place of the displaced water. The result is oceanic **upwelling,** a mechanism that returns sunken water to the surface. Upwelling occurs both in the open ocean, where wind-driven currents diverge, and along coastlines, where prevailing winds blow seaward (fig. 14.18).

Along the western coast of South America, an important upwelling brings cold, nutrient-filled water to the surface to replace

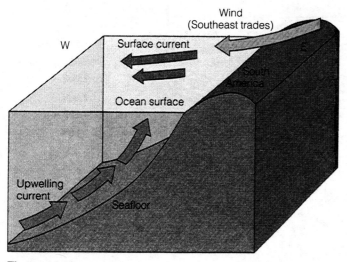

Figure 14.19 Upwelling along the western coast of South America.

water driven westward by the trade winds (fig. 14.19). The nutrient-rich water that upwells has traveled from as far away as the Atlantic, where it sank to become deep water, carrying the elemental remains of organisms with it into the Pacific. Bolstered by the influx of phosphates and nitrates, compounds that are essential to plant growth, the upwelling waters off the west coast of South America support a rich flora comprised of algae, which, in turn, feed an abundance of fish. The Peruvian fishery is, as a result, one of the largest in the world.

The vertical movements of water turn the ocean over about once every 2,000 years. That means that ocean-dumped pollutants, such as radioactive wastes, will resurface to plague future generations of sea life and humans. Possibly, dilution from mixing will minimize the effects, but the same hazards will still exist, especially exposure to those toxic wastes with long half-lives.

Horizontal Circulation

Even though thermohaline circulation is important to the movement of seawater, the overriding influence on the surface is wind. The greatest volume of downwelling seawater results from converging currents driven by prevailing winds. The winds, in fact, also produce a planetwide surface circulation. In your study of meteorology earlier in this text, you learned that six major wind systems scour Earth's surface. These winds obey the dictates of the Coriolis force by veering to the right in the Northern Hemisphere and to the left in the Southern, and their latitudinal boundaries migrate north and south with the seasons. The winds can also fade and intensify, or, as they do under the influence of changing pressure patterns, even reverse themselves locally, like those that respond to monsoonal changes over the Arabian Sea.

Currents and Gyres

The general circulation of the atmosphere transfers some of its energy to the surface waters, pushing them along in relatively narrow bands called *currents*. Generally, these surface currents veer to the left in the Southern Hemisphere and to the right in the Northern, though

there are some exceptions in high latitudes. They also maintain identifiable characteristics. As the currents turn throughout the oceans, they appear, on the largest scale, to run in **gyres,** or large, somewhat circular, clockwise and counterclockwise patterns that almost mirror the movements of the atmosphere (fig. 14.20). The water flow is not exactly the same as the winds because the ocean currents can veer up to 45° from the direction of the winds. Since water is a more viscous fluid than air and its inertia makes it travel more slowly than winds (see p. 299), it is subject to an amplification of the Coriolis force.

Because of the configurations of the continents and the interruptions to flow caused by large islands and capes, currents do not always conform to an ideal, smooth pattern. More like the surface winds influenced by friction than like the high-altitude jet stream, ocean surface waters give only a general semblance of the "ideal" movements. No ideal basin boundaries exist, so the currents often diverge from the expected pathway and meander through the surrounding surface water.

Geostrophic Flow

As Northern Hemisphere currents flow, they trend toward the right, and water pealing off equatorial and subtropical surface currents mounds up. The oceanic mound acts just like a hill on land with water falling down its slopes, offsetting the Coriolis force and establishing a continual flow along the mound's base. This continual movement establishes the gyres, and even in the absence of winds, it would continue under the influence of Earth's spinning to make a turning current called a **geostrophic flow** (fig. 14.21).

The Ekman Spiral

As the wind blows across the ocean surface, it pushes against the more viscous water, which resists the flow with a greater inertia and veers, in the Northern Hemisphere, 45° to the right. Below the "pushed" surface water, the progressively deeper water moves more slowly and even more to the right. Eventually, the water runs opposite the surface flow and 225° (180° plus the 45° of deflection from the driving wind) to the wind that initiated the surface movements. This deflection that increases with depth is termed the **Ekman Spiral** (fig. 14.22).

Types of Surface Currents

Oceanographers classify surface currents according to their relative temperatures. Usually, the designation accounts for movements across latitudinal boundaries, so that surface flows traveling away from or along the equator are termed *warm currents,* and those traveling from high latitude to lower latitude or longitudinally at high latitudes are called *cold currents* (see chapter 6). Figure 14.20 shows the warm currents in red and the cold currents in blue. The latitudinal position of the currents is not as important in this classification as is the direction of travel. Thus, the Alaska Current, which flows northward along the coast of northern British Columbia toward Alaska, is a warm current because it flows from warmer (lower) to colder (higher) latitudes. The Canary Current, which runs southward off the western coast of North Africa, is a cold current, carrying cooler water equatorward.

Figure 14.20 Major surface currents of the world's oceans.

Figure 14.21 Geostrophic flow around a mound of surface water. (F_g = Gravity force; F_c = Coriolis force.)

Figure 14.22 The Ekman Spiral.

Typically, warm surface currents are fast, narrow, and deep, and cold currents are slow, wide, and shallow. These are, of course, comparative terms. At 35°N, the **Gulf Stream,** which is the most intense warm current in the Atlantic Ocean, averages 150 centimeters per second (3.35 mph). That may not seem fast, but at that rate, the current carries more than 50 million cubic meters (1.75 billion cu. ft) per second across its approximate 75-kilometer (46.6-mi) width and 2-kilometer (1.24-mi) depth. By comparison, off the West Coast, the Pacific's cold California Current, a broad sheet of water that travels little more than 10 kilometers (6.2 mi) per day, transports about 10 million cubic meters (350 million cu. ft) per second across its almost 1,000-kilometer (621-mi) width and 500-meter (1,640-ft) depth.

Oceanographers also classify surface currents as either *western* or *eastern boundary currents*. With the exception of high latitudes, warm currents run along the western sides of the oceans; cold currents, along the eastern. In addition an intensification of western currents makes them flow faster in narrow bands against the continental margins.

The Western Intensification

The intensification of western boundary currents is the product of several influences. The trade winds move the North and South Equatorial Currents across the oceans to collide with such landmasses as South America. At Recife, Brazil, the continent juts into a wedge and divides the equatorial flow of the Southern Hemisphere into two directions: southwest and northwest. The latter component moves water across the equator. In the Northern Hemisphere, some of the water flows into the Caribbean Sea through the southern Antilles, and the rest, because it veers right, moves northward along the windward islands. The water that enters the Caribbean eventually moves into the Gulf of Mexico and exits between Cuba and Florida, as the *Florida Current.*

The Florida Current presents a good lesson on the *Bernoulli theorem,* which states that channeling a moving fluid increases its rate of flow. The narrow strait between Cuba and Florida channels the water, and the flow increases just as it joins the windward *Antilles Current.* At about the latitude where the two currents merge, the trade winds give way to the prevailing westerlies, and a vortex of winds at the convergence, plus the shape of North America, give impetus to the Gulf Stream. The large subtropic gyre called the *Sargasso Sea* also adds a geostrophic flow and helps intensify the current through the addition of water in a continuous flow.

At the equator, the Coriolis force is zero, so the equatorial currents have a greater tendency to move longitudinally than do higher-latitude return currents on the northern end of the Sargasso Sea. The Sargasso Sea, therefore, tends to pinch the Florida Current and the southern end of the Gulf Stream toward the continent,

Figure 14.23 (*a–d*)   Eddies, or rings, form along the western boundary of the warm Gulf Stream Current.

with the consequence of channeling the flow. A channeled flow is a faster flow, and the Gulf Stream reaches its peak rate at about 35°N, as it is squeezed against the southwestward-moving *Labrador Current* and shelf waters.

The Gulf Stream

The most studied current in the oceans is the Gulf Stream, the giant river of water described in the preceding section. As a climatic control, the current transfers heat from low latitudes toward boreal regions and separates northern colder water from warmer water to the south. In this latter regard, the Gulf Stream acts like the high-altitude jet stream, which also serves as a fast-moving boundary between warm and cold air. Recent studies have shown that the Gulf Stream does not reach the shores of Ireland and England, as long thought. Instead, the stream becomes very complex in the northern Atlantic, and the *North Atlantic Current* transfers heat to the *Norwegian Current.* Then, north of Scandinavia, the *North Cape Current* prevents sea ice from forming along the coast to the port of Murmansk, Russia.

The Gulf Stream does, however, influence the weather of the North Sea and eastern Atlantic countries. Denmark is a rainy land, and Britain occasionally has heavier rains when the current warms the western Atlantic more than usual. The heat that the Gulf Stream transfers to other North Atlantic currents also makes southern Ireland's climate milder than one would expect for its high latitude (see chapter 6).

One of the most intriguing aspects of the Gulf Stream is its meandering. As the current moves northward, it twists itself into loops and cutoffs very much like a terrestrial old-age stream that leaves oxbow lakes on an alluvial plain. As fluid expressions, the loops and cutoffs of the Gulf Stream do not create oxbows. Instead, the meanders isolate bodies of water from either the Labrador Current or from the neighboring Sargasso Sea. These isolated, spinning bodies of water are called **eddies,** or rings (fig. 14.23). As the loop closes on Sargasso Sea water from the south, it pinches off on the northern side of the current, making a *warm-core ring.* The opposite happens as the Gulf Stream loops around cold water from the Labrador Current. Thus, *warm eddies spin off north of the current, and cold eddies spin off to the south* (fig. 14.24).

The Return Water

Just as upwelling balances downwelling, return currents resupply surface areas that lose water and keep the ocean water from piling up against and spilling onto the continents. The largest of the return currents is the Pacific's *Cromwell Current.*

The Cromwell Current is an equatorial *countercurrent* that transports an estimated 25 million cubic meters (875 million cu. ft) per second toward the eastern Pacific. Reports from tuna fishers in the early 1950s revealed that their lines drifted to the east below the surface while the prevailing Equatorial Current flowed west. The fastest speeds (150 cm/sec, 4.88 ft/sec) of this current occur at the 10-meter (32.8-ft) depth, so the surface current is superimposed on an opposite, shallow undercurrent. At the 350-meter (1,150-ft) depth, the current moves more slowly, indicating that it is truly a surface phenomenon. The Cromwell Current, which results from the wind's piling up water in the western Pacific, is a good example of water flowing down a water hill, and it acts to return water driven away from the eastern Pacific.

The return of water across an ocean or along the sides of gyres shows that the ocean currents describe a closed system. The system operates within the basinal confines established by seafloor spreading, moving continents, and, as might have occurred during the last glacial advance, the buildup of ice that creates temporary barriers to flow.

Figure 14.24   A cold eddy (1) and a warm eddy (2) that have spun off of the Gulf Stream south of Georges Bank in the western Atlantic.

AIR-SEA INTERACTIONS

Although the currents make a closed system, the ocean and the atmosphere cross their mutual boundary through an exchange of gases vital to several of our planet's systems. Chief among the interchanges is the exchange of water vapor, the point of departure for the hydrologic cycle. About 334,000 cubic kilometers (80,160 cu. mi) of water evaporate from the ocean surfaces each year to enter the atmosphere as a significant gas. This water vapor captures heat that radiates from the surfaces of both land and water. It also adds energy to storm systems through the latent heat of vaporization and supplies the atmosphere with water for precipitation. As a consequence, oceans have weather and climate.

Another exchange of gas occurs when the oxygen produced by floating photosynthesizers leaks from the surface waters into the atmosphere. Since light is essential for plants and since darkness prevails below 1,000 meters (3,280 ft), photosynthesis is mostly a surface phenomenon. Plants also require phosphates and nitrates for growth. Wherever these nutrients are plentiful, such as within upwelling waters, the oceans house great abundances of Thallophyta, the plant subkingdom that includes the algae, dinoflagellates, bacteria, and fungi. Because of their relative abundance, the algae, particularly the **diatoms,** are the most important oxygen producers in the sea, with population densities exceeding 200,000 per liter (800,000 per gal) in the North Pacific (fig. 14.25).

Figure 14.25   Siliceous shell of a diatom magnified hundreds of times.

Some higher plants, members of the subkingdom Embryophyta, also produce oxygen. One of these is the plant *Zostera,* the eel grass that grows in shallow coastal waters. Typically, oxygen production from photosynthesis varies with sun angle, which is a control on light intensity and duration. It also varies with the availability of nutrients.

The exchange of carbon dioxide at the ocean-atmosphere interface has led to a controversy about the role the oceans play in moderating the greenhouse effect (see chapter 1). Water has the ability to store dissolved gases, but its temperature and pressure control its storage capacity. An analogy lies in carbonated beverages (soda pop, beer) that go "flat" after their containers are opened and their temperatures rise. Streams of rising bubbles attest to the loss of dissolved gas, and warmer temperatures speed up the rate of loss. Because cold water and water under high pressure can hold more dissolved gas than low-pressure warm water, the heated surface waters of the Bahamas hold less carbon dioxide than the cold waters off Antarctica. The vertical profiles of oxygen and carbon dioxide show opposite trends as respiration removes oxygen from the water and produces carbon dioxide, and photosynthesis does just the opposite (fig. 14.26).

With the increase in atmospheric carbon dioxide from the burning of fossil fuels (coal, natural gas, and oil), some scientists have taken different sides of an important issue: whether or not the oceans can act as a sink for the additional carbon dioxide. If the oceans have the capacity to accept the gas, then the greenhouse effect may be stabilized or even reduced. But if they are incapable of siphoning off the gas from the atmosphere, then worldwide atmospheric temperatures will increase. The warmer temperatures of the atmosphere will also mean warmer surface waters and a further diminished capacity to hold dissolved gas, compounding the problem.

Warmer surface waters lying under the influence of a warmer atmosphere would have an increased evaporation potential. Cloud cover might increase as a result, and world temperatures may be affected by blocked, reflected, and diffracted sunlight.

LIGHT IN WATER

The peculiar color of our blue planet derives from the dominant substance on its surface: water. In general, the oceans are blue for the same reason that the skies are blue. The shortwave end of the spectrum is scattered more than the longwave end, so blue light, as well as ultraviolet light, scatters most. The red end of the spectrum, which comprises longer waves than the blue end, is absorbed more readily, particularly by the water molecule (fig. 14.27).

To say that the ocean is "blue," however, is to miss the great variety of color reflected by the oceans. The deep ocean does appear a deep blue, but subtropical and tropical coastal waters have colors varying from light green to dark green (fig. 14.28), and cold Arctic waters look "oily."

The color of water is in part influenced by the angle of the sun's rays and by the roughness of the water surface. The low angle of incidence in high latitudes means less penetration (or more reflectivity). At low latitudes, high angles of incidence over calm seas mean greater penetration and less reflectivity.

Another influence on water color is the amount of suspended matter. In coastal waters, plumes of sediment can make the water green or light brown by reflecting or absorbing light. In some areas, extraordinarily high concentrations of floating plants and animals also influence water color, as can the colors of the bottom in shallow water.

Figure 14.27 Representative penetration depths in clear water for the several wavelengths (colors) of the light spectrum.

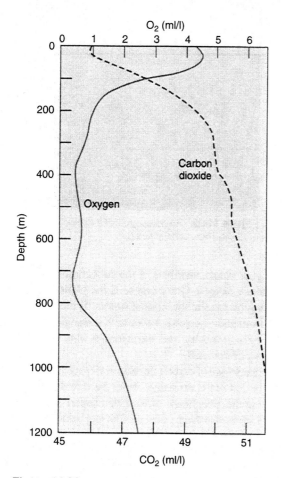

Figure 14.26 Oxygen and carbon dioxide profiles.

Figure 14.28 Water color change in the Bahamas.

SOUND IN WATER

One of the most intriguing discoveries made by marine biologists is that whales can communicate with one another over great expanses of ocean. Their "songs" carry hundreds of kilometers in the modern oceans, and some speculate that, prior to the advent of noise pollution by mechanized ships and the sounds of machinery, those songs could carry across whole oceans.

Water is an efficient transmitter of sound. In water, sound travels more than four times faster than it does in air, but variations occur because of differences in temperature, salinity, and pressure. By analogy, sound bends at density boundaries, just as light bends in water, a phenomenon that makes a utensil or a pencil look broken when half of it is submerged in a glass of water.

Submarine crews use this bending of sound whenever they attempt to hide their vessels. They know to look for the thermocline, since it represents a zone of rapid density change. Because surface ships use sonar to locate submarines, the best place to hide is wherever sound bends radically because it changes speed (fig. 14.29). For every degree Celsius that seawater increases in temperature, there is a corresponding rate increase of 4.5 meters (14.75 ft) per second for sound. The overall effect within a well-developed thermocline is to establish an apparent, but false, location of the submarine as the sonar signal returns to the surface ship.

Sound can also be trapped in a "channel" by bending. The SOFAR (SOund Fixing And Ranging) channel is the product of sound bending as it moves through the water. The faster-moving sound has a tendency to bend toward lower-velocity zones (fig. 14.30). Thus, sound from above and below a low-velocity zone bends to become trapped and channeled. Because little energy is lost in this low-velocity zone, sound can travel great distances, potentially thousands of kilometers. This channel once enabled the whales to project their mating calls over entire oceans. Today, rescue operations often include the use of the SOFAR channel to locate those lost at sea.

Sound is an important tool in imaging the ocean bottom. The newly designed SEABEAM system uses sound to paint an accurate picture of oceanic bathymetry, revealing seafloor features as small as 100 meters (328 ft).

OCEAN WATER AND BOTTOM ZONES

Oceanographers classify the waters of the deep ocean and the continental shelves into zones based on location, depth, and the penetration of light. The most landward of these encompasses the water over the continental shelf and is called the **neritic zone** (fig. 14.31). This relatively shallow zone extends from the high-water mark (high tide) to the edge of the continental shelf, so that at its deepest, it reaches about 200 meters (656 ft). The shoreline between high and low tide is the **littoral zone.** The littoral lies between the **supralittoral** (the beach and dune area), and the **sublittoral** (the sea bottom immediately below the low-water (low-tide) mark).

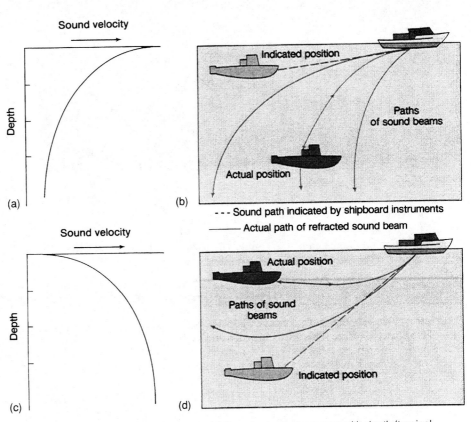

Figure 14.29 Hiding in the thermocline. (*a*) Sound velocity decreases with depth (tropical waters). (*b*) Refraction causes indication of target at shallow depth. (*c*) Sound velocity increases with depth (polar waters). (*d*) Refraction causes indication of target at deep depth.

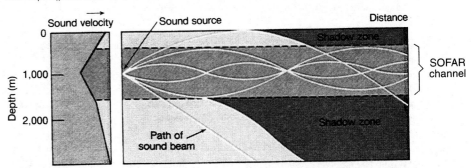

Figure 14.30 The SOFAR channel. (*a*) Sound velocity in seawater is at minimum in a zone centered on a depth of 1,000 meters (3,280 ft) because of changes in temperature, salinity, and pressure. (*b*) Refraction causes some sound waves to be trapped within the channel and other waves to bypass certain areas (shadow zones) through which the sound never passes. (Redrawn from Lawrence E. Kinsler and Austin R. Frey, *Fundamentals of Acoustics,* 2d ed. Copyright © 1962 John Wiley & Sons, Inc., Reprinted by permission of John Wiley & Sons, Inc.)

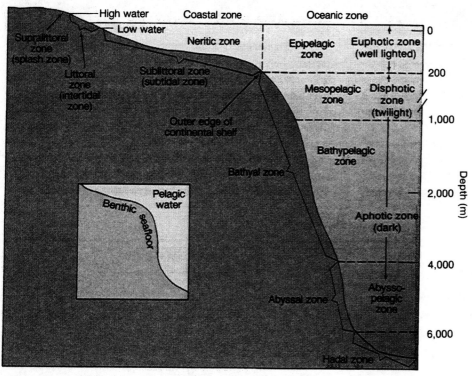

Figure 14.31 The ocean zones.

meaning "light"). The epipelagic is a layer with high primary productivity. Diatoms and other photosynthesizers have ample light for growth in this zone. From 200 meters (656 ft) to 1,000 meters (3,280 ft), the light attenuates rapidly, making the **mesopelagic zone,** the middle zone, one of "twilight." In this semidark, *disphotic* region are fish with *bioluminescent* spots very much like the chemical light of fireflies. Light does not penetrate beneath the mesopelagic, making all the water below 1,000 meters (3,280 ft) dark, or *aphotic* (*a,* meaning "without"). The uppermost lightless zone is the **bathypelagic,** which extends to 4,000 meters (2.5 mi). Along the bottom of the ocean is the **abyssopelagic,** the water column above the abyssal plains. As you learned in chapter 9, the deepest ocean water lies in the trenches. This water overlies the **hadal zone,** after the Greek underworld of Hades. One other ocean zone has been identified, the **bathyal zone** of the continental slope, running from shelf to continental rise. Many of the organisms that inhabit the aphotic zones are believed to have evolved from inhabitants of bathyal waters.

The water beyond the continental shelf is classified as **pelagic water.** The upper 200 meters (656 ft) of the open ocean is the **epipelagic** (*epi,* meaning "on") **zone.** This zone is well-lit and, as such, is also called *euphotic* (*eu,* meaning "true"; *phot,*

FURTHER THOUGHTS: THE OCEAN-ATMOSPHERE SYSTEM

*E*arth's oceans are geographically connected because they cover 71% of the planet's surface. This interconnection allows the exchange of water among water bodies, which enables one ocean to influence another. In the Norwegian Sea, for example, cold water sinks and begins a flow back toward the Altantic as deep water. Although water that downwells initially carries nutrients to greater depths, it eventually upwells, taking those nutrients to the surface, where they once again provide plants—and, eventually, animals via the food chain—with material for growth. The constant circulation of the ocean waters beneath the "ocean" of atmosphere also leads to exchanges of matter, such as the incorporation of dissolved

carbon dioxide in seawater or the incorporation of water vapor in the atmosphere.

Knowing the interactions between atmosphere and oceans provides us with a warning. These highly interconnected systems can spread far beyond our local boundaries whatever we choose to dump into either air or water. Oceans affect human life in many ways, including the diet of inland peoples. The pollutants that spew from our factory smokestacks or that run off farms into streams headed for the oceans may eventually end up on factory workers' or farmers' tables as part of their imported seafood.

SIGNIFICANT POINTS

1. Oceans cover 71% of Earth's surface, leading to the term *watery planet.*

2. The compound called water forms when two hydrogen atoms combine with an oxygen atom through the mutual sharing of electrons.

3. The salinity of seawater differs with latitude and depth, location in open ocean or restricted water bodies, climate, stream runoff, and ice formation and melting.

4. Salinity profiles of ocean waters reveal a change in salinity with depth. Wherever the profile reveals a rapid change in salinity with depth, it marks the halocline.

5. Temperatures of the oceans vary with latitude and depth. The zone of rapid temperature change with depth is called the thermocline.

6. That water is not frozen on the ocean bottom is the result of three factors: it is salt water, which does not freeze at 0° C; ice floats; and the water is under great pressure.

7. The sigma-t diagram is a graph used to plot the combined effects of salinity and temperature to establish density characteristics for particular water masses.

8. The combined effects of temperature and salinity generate vertical currents in the oceans. This vertical movement of ocean water driven by density differences is called thermohaline circulation.

9. Downwelling seawater is the product of convergent currents driven by prevailing wind. Similarly, upwelling seawater is the product of divergent currents, also driven by prevailing winds.

10. The general circulation of the atmosphere transfers some of its energy to the surface waters, pushing them along in relatively narrow bands called currents.

11. Generally, surface currents veer to the left in the Southern Hemisphere and to the right in the Northern, with some exceptions in high latitudes.

12. Surface currents are classified as warm or cold according to their relative temperatures. The latitudinal position of the currents is not as important in this classification as is the direction of travel.

13. Typically, warm surface currents are fast, narrow, and deep, and cold currents are slow, wide, and shallow. With the exception of high latitudes, warm currents run along the western sides of oceans; cold currents, along the eastern.

14. The Bernoulli theorem states that channeling a moving fluid increases its rate of flow.

15. Just as upwelling balances downwelling, return currents resupply surface areas that lose water and keep ocean water from piling up against and spilling onto the continents.

16. The return of water across an ocean or along the sides of gyres shows that ocean currents describe a closed system. The system operates within the basinal confines established by seafloor spreading, moving continents, and the ice buildup, that may have created temporary barriers to flow during the last glacial advance.

17. The ocean and the atmosphere cross their mutual boundary through an exchange of gases. Three important gases that interchange are water vapor, oxygen, and carbon dioxide.

18. Water has the ability to store dissolved gases, but its temperature and pressure control its storage capacity.

19. Cold water and water under high pressure can hold more dissolved carbon dioxide than low-pressure warm water.

20. The color of water is influenced by several factors: the angle of the sun's rays, the roughness of the water surface, the amount of suspended matter, and in shallow water, the colors of the bottom.

21. Since water is an efficient transmitter of energy, sound travels more than four times faster in water than it does in air. The rate at which sound travels in water varies because of differences in temperature, salinity, and pressure.

22. Sound can also be trapped in a "channel" by bending toward a zone of less resistance. Faster-moving sound has a tendency to bend toward lower-velocity zones, becoming trapped in the SOFAR channel.

23. Sound in the SOFAR channel can travel great distances because little energy is lost in this low-velocity zone.

24. Waters of the deep ocean and the continental shelves are classified into zones based on location, depth, and penetration of light.

25. The most landward zone encompasses the water over the continental shelf and is called the neritic zone.

26. The water beyond the continental shelf is classified as pelagic water.

ESSENTIAL TERMS

hypsographic curve *323*
water *324*
hydration *325*
seawater *325*
residence time *325*
salinity *325*
salinity profile *326*

halocline *326*
thermocline *327*
density *328*
sigma-t (or T-S) diagram *330*
pycnocline *330*
thermohaline circulation *331*

water mass *331*
downwelling *332*
upwelling *333*
gyre *334*
geostrophic flow *334*
Ekman Spiral *334*
Gulf Stream *335*
eddy *336*

diatom *337*
neritic zone *339*
littoral zone *339*
supralittoral zone *339*
sublittoral zone *339*
pelagic water *340*
epipelagic zone *340*
mesopelagic zone *340*

bathypelagic zone *340*
abyssopelagic zone *340*
hadal zone *340*
bathyal zone *340*

REVIEW QUESTIONS

1. How do water molecules react with common salt?
2. What controls the salinity of pelagic surface waters?
3. What prevents the ocean bottom waters from freezing?
4. Why is Mediterranean water denser than the surface waters of the Atlantic?
5. What distinguishes the cold from the warm currents?
6. How and why do the oxygen and carbon dioxide profiles differ?
7. What is the role of ocean waters in the control of global carbon dioxide?
8. Why is the ocean blue? What controls ocean colors?
9. Why do submarine captains look for the thermocline?

CHALLENGES

1. Would you put hazardous materials in the oceans? Why?
2. If an oil spill occurs just north of the Yucatan Peninsula in Mexico, will the coastline of Texas be affected?
3. Using an atlas, find the southern boundary of sea ice in the Northern Hemisphere. Why does this boundary assume its particular shape? How does this boundary affect shipping?
4. What factors control the direction and intensity of the ocean surface current known as the West Wind Drift?
5. How do the oceans interact with the atmosphere to influence climate?

Chapter

15

Marine and Nearshore Environments

Tidal marsh at Wood End Light, Cape Cod National Seashore.

INTRODUCTION

Wherever plants and animals reside in the seas, they both affect and are affected by the physical, chemical, and geologic systems of the oceans. In fact, these interrelationships are an example of the interdependence between the inanimate and animate worlds. Even humans, who are temporary visitors to the deep, but permanent inhabitants of coastal regions, can affect and are affected by the oceans.

An extreme example of humans affecting the oceans occurred during the 1991 Persian Gulf War. The intentional spilling of more than 3 million barrels of Kuwaiti oil into the Persian Gulf brought havoc to the marine environment and demonstrated how catastrophic human actions can be (fig. 15.1). The seabirds, mammals, and fishes of the Persian Gulf were subjected to the world's greatest oil spill, one that eventually stretched along the entire western coastline and jeopardized sea life and humans from Kuwait to Qatar. By contrast, an event such as Hurricane Hugo's storm surge, with its devastation of the Charleston, South Carolina, area (see chapter 1), demonstrates how the oceans affect humans.

These interactions, however, are not always negative. Although many countries have increased their consumption of seafood, adding an important source of protein to the human diet, some seafood companies have acted to protect such animals as dolphins from becoming victims of commercial fishing methods. For many years, dolphins have been caught in drift seine netting used to surround and capture fish. An internationally signed agreement, called Marpol V, restricts this killing of dolphins. Within the past 10 years, a worldwide public awareness has led to greater protection of the oceans and marine life, largely through the efforts of those who have objectively observed, described, and modeled the marine environments.

Defining the interrelationships among marine and terrestrial environments and between marine environments and life is a holistic task that requires information obtained through the efforts of many scientists. Among these are different kinds of oceanographers, whose work benefits both human and nonhuman life. Whereas ocean engineers and physical oceanographers work to control the coastal environment for millions of human inhabitants, marine biologists monitor the ecological effects of human activities and artificial structures. Because of a high population density along the coastlines of many countries, engineers must design seawalls, direct sediment dredging operations in ship channels, and protect and enhance the beauty of resort areas, where seasonal influxes of tourists impinge upon the stability of local ecologies (fig. 15.2).

Chemical oceanographers and marine geologists also analyze interactions between life and environment in the seas. The chemistry of seawater is, in part, controlled by organisms that remove dissolved substances to construct biological "hard parts" like shells. Marine sedimentation is also a product of life processes that produce those hard parts, which, upon the deaths of the organisms, settle to the ocean floor. That oceanographers devote so much effort to understanding these interrelationships among environments and life is an acknowledgment of the complexity in the oceans.

Marine environments exhibit a diversity of compositions, features, and processes. They extend from the shallow intrusions of water in salt marshes and estuaries, across the gently dipping continental shelf, over the continental slope and rise, onto the

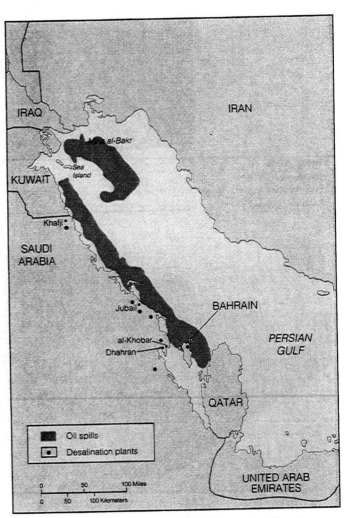

Figure 15.1 The extent of surface pollution from the deliberate release of crude oil during the 1991 Persian Gulf War.

Figure 15.2 Dredge clearing ship channel in the Bahamas.

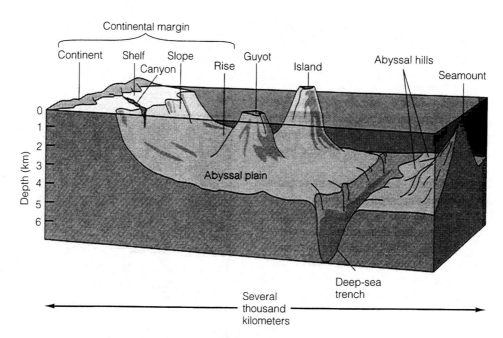

Figure 15.3 A summary of marine environments and seafloor features.

Figure 15.4 Side-looking (side-scan) sonar image obtained over the Siqueiros Transform Fault. (From D.J. Fornari, D.G. Gallo, M.H. Edwards, J.A. Madsen, M.R. Perfit, and A.N. Shor, "Structure and Topography of the Siqueiros Transform Fault System: Evidence for the Development of Intra-Transform Spreading Centers," *Marine Geophysical Researches*, 11:263–99, 1989. © Kluwer Academic Publishers.)

abyssal plains, and into the trenches (fig. 15.3). Many of these environments are hidden from human inspection unless inquisitive scientists expend money and energy in the risky endeavor of underwater exploration. Peering into the environments of the deep ocean requires oceanographers to use submersible ships, such as the *Alvin*, which can carry three crew members, or robot submersibles, such as *Jason*. Both types of vessels enable humans to see, for example, the hydrothermal deep-sea geysers that vent heated water and steam from a volcanically active oceanic ridge system (see chapter 14). Describing the marine environments has also meant using *side-looking sonar*, instrumentation that bounces

sound energy off the ocean floor from an oblique angle to get detailed images on a scale that cameras cannot provide in the darkness of the ocean bottom (fig. 15.4).

SALT MARSHES: THE MOST LANDWARD EXTENT OF THE SEA

One of the most short-lived marine environments is the **salt marsh,** a low-lying, constantly wet area of silt, sand, and organic material at the boundary between land and sea, found mostly in temperate regions. Poised in a delicate balance, the salt marsh is a fragile

Figure 15.5 Housing development in the wetlands of Barnegat Bay, New Jersey.

Figure 15.6 Tidal marsh and channels near Jacksonville, Florida.

and floods the adjacent flats. Since the tides are a daily phenomenon and the marshes occur in temperate climates where evaporation cannot keep pace with wetting, *salt marshes do not become dry,* even in the warmest weather.

Salt marshes are more likely to occur on a tectonically passive continental margin characterized by gentle gradients, rather than on an active one with steep gradients, where the movement of land from earthquake activity changes local sea level. Consequently, the Atlantic and Gulf of Mexico coasts, which have a more stable land-sea margin, have more area in salt marsh than does the Pacific coast of North America. However, valley marshes are not uncommon along the coasts of California, Oregon, Washington, and British Columbia, where streams enter the ocean through narrow valleys, and their mouths come under the influence of the tides.

The marshes along the U.S. eastern seaboard have suffered from the intrusion of urbanization (fig. 15.5). Builders of housing and recreational complexes constantly encroach upon marsh areas. Along the coast of both Carolinas and Georgia, for example, recreational and retirement communities are growing rapidly, and a transient population of tourists strains the stability of the salt-marsh environment.

Typically, a salt marsh is a geologically quiet environment, receiving the influx of the tides across its flats of fine particles and *cordgrass (Spartina)* and channeling the ebb and flow in tidal channels, where the larger sand and silt sediments collect. The *tidal range* is the difference between the heights of the water surface during high and low tides. As the water rises, it flows up tidal channels and then spreads out over the salt marsh (fig. 15.6). The result of this inflow makes the mean depth of water greater during low tide, when the water lies only in the channels, than during high tide, when the water makes a shallow layer over a wide area. Additionally, water that fans out over the marsh slows as it

environment, one easily disrupted by human activities and by changes in **sea level,** which is the relative position of the ocean surface with respect to the land.

Because the ocean surface reached its approximate current level only within the past 5,000 years, *current salt marshes are geologically young.* They will disappear—or move—whenever sea-level changes either inundate them completely or leave them as higher, drier land.

The constantly wet condition of the marshes derives from the daily inflow of the tides through **tidal channels,** which act like streams in reverse during the tidal flow. As the tide moves into the marsh, it exceeds the capacity of the meandering channel system encounters cordgrass and other plants, which act as baffles to dampen the energy of the tidal current. The reduced flow rate causes suspended sediments and organic debris to settle through the relatively quiet water. This is one way in which life directly affects the shallow marine environment.

The daily ebb and flow of shallow water make a tidal marsh a nutrient-rich, euphotic (well-lit), shallow-water zone that enhances photosynthesis and provides food for many organisms. Among the most numerous inhabitants of the salt marsh are crabs,

Figure 15.7 Crabs on a surface exposed at low tide.

which are relatives of lobsters and crayfish. With their five pairs of legs, these *crustaceans* manuever easily over a mud-supported surface of silts and sands that adheres to shoes and makes human passage difficult (fig. 15.7). The presence of crabs also indicates the abundance of *detrital food,* or fragments of other organisms, including parts of local plants that settle once the water ebbs. Crabs intensively burrow the marsh and, along with other burrowers like worms, *bioturbate,* or overturn, the sediments. As the marsh develops, constant bioturbation eliminates most traces of the marsh's initial sedimentary *laminae,* the thin layers of small particles laid down by successive tides.

ESTUARIES

Many salt marshes border **estuaries,** partially open bodies of water that lie between the fresh water on the continents and the salt water of the oceans. Bays, lagoons, deltas, and river mouths all exhibit estuarine characteristics. Like the marshes, estuaries are geologically ephemeral features, with the persistence of even the largest measured in thousands of years, a relatively short geological span. Estuaries disappear when river sediments fill them or changing sea level either isolates them or drowns them in the relatively deeper water. Seas have inundated continents throughout Earth's history and, during certain periods like the Devonian (395 to 345 million years ago) and Cretaceous (136 to 65 million years ago), have covered more than 50% of continental areas. Usually, these **epicontinental** ("on the continent") **seas** were shallow, with depths often no greater than 50 meters (164 ft). Both Hudson Bay

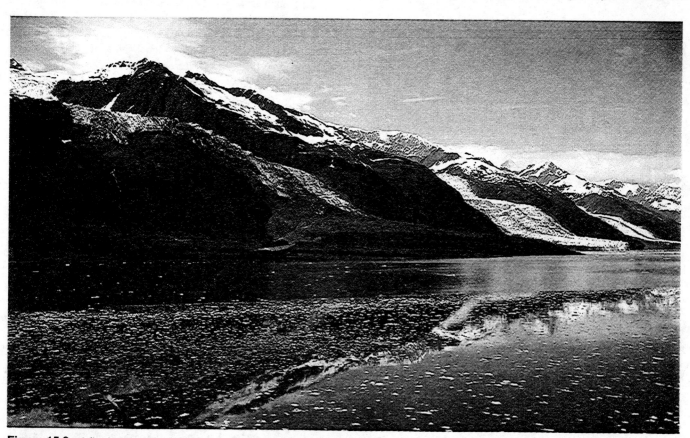

Figure 15.8 A fiord, a glacially deepened estuary, along the coast of Alaska.

Figure 15.9   Satellite image shows Chesapeake Bay (*center*), a drowned river system. Delaware Bay is the smaller embayment to the *right*. Red areas indicate vegetation in this false-color image.

and the North Sea are examples of recent **transgressions,** or intrusions, of seawater onto continental areas, and both have led to the development of estuaries along their boundaries. In fact, *all modern estuaries are related to the most recent rise in sea level,* which resulted from the melting of vast continental glaciers. After the retreat of the ice from its last advance over the Northern Hemisphere's landmasses, sea level rose rapidly, reaching an elevation close to present values between 6,000 and 5,000 years ago.

Essentially, the position and size of estuaries depend on sea level, local topography, and the configurations of river mouths or distributary channels. Whenever sea level rises in response to land subsidence or to an influx of water from ice melt, seawater encroaches on river mouths, drowning the lower part of the river and typically making a shallow estuary. Where streams empty into the lagoonal water behind barrier islands, shallow, elongate estuaries run parallel to the coast. If an alpine glacier retreats from a coastal valley cut below sea level, a *fiord* develops (fig. 15.8). The deepest estuary along the eastern coastline of the continental United States lies at the mouth of the York River, which is actually part of a larger, shallow estuarine system known as Chesapeake Bay, often described as a *drowned river system* (fig. 15.9).

A special kind of circulation occurs when the fresh waters discharging from rivers mix with the saltier seawater arriving through the open end of the estuary (fig. 15.10). This **estuarine circulation** results when the less-dense fresh water becomes **brackish,** or

Figure 15.10   The zone of interaction between river flow and ocean tides in an estuary. The *bottom* portion of the diagram shows the relative abundance of riverine and marine sediments at various locations.

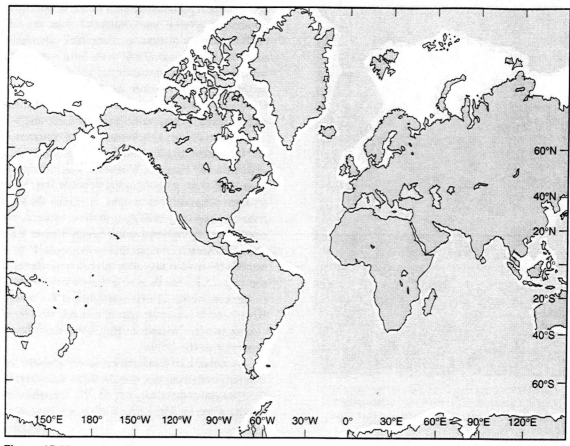

Figure 15.11 Distribution of continental shelves (white areas).

slightly salty, as it acquires some salts through mixing with the seawater. Both the fresh and the brackish water flow seaward over denser salt water, which flows landward along the estuary bottom. The landward flow traps suspended sediments that settle out of the discharging river mouths and enhances the filling of the estuary by blocking the exit of sediments. The flow also supplies plants with nutrients that flow off the land. Estuarine circulation dominates the northeastern coastline of the United States and the southeastern coastline of Canada.

CONTINENTAL SHELVES

The shoreline so familiar to tourists and coastal residents is neither the edge of the continent nor the beginning of the oceanic basin. Instead, water overfills the basins and spills onto the continents, drowning a narrow area called the **continental shelf.** Inundated continental borders underlie about 7.5% of the total ocean surface, but because they are not deep, shelf waters comprise only 0.15% of the total volume of seawater (fig. 15.11).

The structural tendency of continental shelves is a seaward **dip,** or incline. This dip resulted from two processes. After the breakup of Pangaea, the trailing edges of continents, like the eastern coast of North America, began to subside in response to a decrease in tectonic activity along their trailing edges. As the continents moved away from the spreading center, they also moved away from the upward push of rising plumes of magma. In addi-

tion, many continental margins have been the sites of sedimentary deposition. The thicknesses of sediments deposited over millions of years can be measured in kilometers, and the sediments' great weight has caused compaction and subsidence.

On average, the continental shelves dip 0.1°, but they exhibit a variety of bathymetric profiles. For example, on some shelves lying in tropical waters, extensive, organically produced, calcium carbonate buildups called coral reefs have altered the original bathymetry. Nowhere is this more evident than along the northeastern coast of Australia, where the Great Barrier Reef has covered the basement rock with an elongate, though irregular, carbonate platform and carbonate islands. Reefs are discussed later in this chapter.

Shelf Characteristics

Shelves can also be divided into *inner* and *outer shelf provinces.* Inner continental shelf areas have depths between sea level and 65 meters (213 ft). Depths on the outer shelf provinces range from 65 to 150 meters (492 ft), although some shelves have isolated depths exceeding several hundred meters. The average depth for the **shelf break,** or shelf edge, is 132 meters (433 ft). During the last glacial advance, just under 20,000 years ago, sea level was an estimated average of 135 meters (443 ft) lower than it is today, exposing most of the shelves to wind and river erosion. At that time, most rivers found their ultimate base level in the proximity of the shelf edges, so the currently urbanized eastern seaboard of the United States would have been tens of kilometers more distant from the sea.

Figure 15.12   Possible origins for continental shelves. (*a*) Faulting. (*b*) Folding, or downwarping. (*c*) Coral reefs. (*d*) Volcanic. In most cases, some structure (reef, volcanic cone, etc.) acts to trap terrigenous sediment, leading to infilling of basins and a gently sloping surface.

The continental shelf is frequently the location of a large **terrigenous** (derived from the land) sedimentary wedge, or sediment accumulation, derived from the continents and sometimes called a *geosyncline*. Geologists have for years argued about the definition of a geosyncline, essentially described as a U-shaped depression filled with sediment or sedimentary rock. The characteristic U-shape of this definition does not apply to most of the wedge-shaped continental shelf deposits, but the term still finds its supporters. A commonly used subcategorization of geosyncline defines those continental margin deposits that contain no volcanic rock as *miogeoclines* (or miogeosynclines) and those with volcanic rocks as *eugeoclines* (or eugeosynclines).

The weight of thousands of meters of sediment on these **depositional centers** has led to crustal subsidence and the further accumulation of sediments on the downwarped crust. Figure 15.12 shows a series of possible origins for the world's continental shelves. Continental shelves may vary because of differences in original topography, in climatic conditions controlling erosion, and in the availability of source material. Climatic conditions, though apparently unrelated to the *subaqueous* (submerged) geology of the shelves, can be a significant contributor to the delivery of sediments. Humid source areas typically deliver more sediments to continental shelves than do arid ones.

The Inner Shelf

The chief delivery system for terrigenous systems is river discharge. River water carries both dissolved and suspended sediments. Moving downslope along the bottom of a channel system is the *bed load*, which migrates by traction and saltation (see chapter 11). The quantity of sediments arriving yearly at the land-water interface and available to migrate onto and off the shelves ranges

TABLE 15.1	**Approximate Average Sediment Discharge for Selected Rivers**
River System	**Discharge (millions of tons per year)**
Ganges-Brahmaputra	1,600
Huang Ho (Yellow)	1,000
Amazon	900
Chang (Yangtze)	475
Irrawaddy	280
Magdalena	225
Mississippi	200
Orinoco	200
Hong Ha (Red)	150

in the billions of tons. Nine river systems, in fact, annually channel more than 5 billion tons toward the shelves (table 15.1). The Ganges-Brahmaputra system in India and the Huang Ho (Yellow) River in China, the foremost transporters of sediment, carry more sediment than the other seven rivers in the table combined. The ultimate destinations of the sediments from these two rivers are somewhat different. The Ganges-Brahmaputra flows onto the continental shelf at the Bay of Bengal, where the sediments migrate downslope and onto the floor of the Indian Ocean (fig. 15.13*a*). The Huang Ho empties into a marginal basin behind an island arc and two peninsulas, where there is no access to the deep ocean. If an access through these barriers were available for the sediments of the Huang Ho, they would spill into the trench system that borders the island arc (fig. 15.13*b*).

Figure 15.13 Depositional centers for the (*a*) Ganges-Brahmaputra system in the Bay of Bengal (Indian Ocean). (*b*) Depositional centers for the Huang Ho (Yellow) River system in the Yellow Sea.

The sediments delivered to the continental shelves have been shaped by wind and water into both subaerial and subaqueous features. Where rivers deposit their silts and sands into the longshore transport system on relatively broad shelves, sediments can form a number of unconsolidated sedimentary features associated with coasts.

Sandy islands along the inner continental shelves develop as barriers to incoming wave energy from the open sea. These **barrier islands** have complex histories associated with local and worldwide sea-level fluctuations, sediment supply, and longshore transport (fig. 15.14). Sands move parallel to and along the seaward side of barrier islands in the longshore current, and they also move perpendicularly to the barrier island as wave energy increases or decreases (see chapter 13). During periods of low-wave energy, sands migrate beachward. An increase in wave energy usually moves the sands seaward by gouging the unconsolidated particles on the beach face, causing a subsequent migration in offshore bars. Large storm waves can also move sands, often those piled into dunes, across the narrow width of the barrier island to form fanlike deposits called **overwash deltas** in the adjacent lagoon (fig. 15.15).

Unconsolidated barrier islands can be altered by human activities. Whenever shipping lanes or boating inlets are needed to allow passage through the barrier system, dredging moves sands from their natural, if temporary, resting place and changes the movement of water. With freedom to circulate into the lagoon behind the barrier island, water picks up and moves sediment, piling it elsewhere, often as an obstruction to boating and shipping and usually creating the need for further dredging. Construction of jetties, groins, and seawalls also changes the natural movement of unconsolidated material, and structures designed to protect a coastal community on a barrier island sometimes have an opposite, and detrimental, effect (see chapter 13).

One place where human activities have altered the movement of sands and changed the environment is Ocean City, Maryland, and Assateague Island. A jetty built along the inlet at the southern end of Ocean City has affected the movement of sands in the longshore current. Sands that used to replenish the northern end of Assateague Island now migrate seaward and farther to the south. As a consequence, the northern end of the island has been starved of its sediment supply and has changed its location and shape (fig. 15.16).

Barrier islands are also the sites of *dune complexes*. Because they are mounds of sand piled asymmetrically in arcing layers by the wind, beach dunes change easily with alterations in wind speed and direction, the movement of storm waves, and human trespassing. As *eolian* (wind-driven) deposits, they contain relatively uniform particle sizes, and they exhibit layering in cross section (see chapter 12).

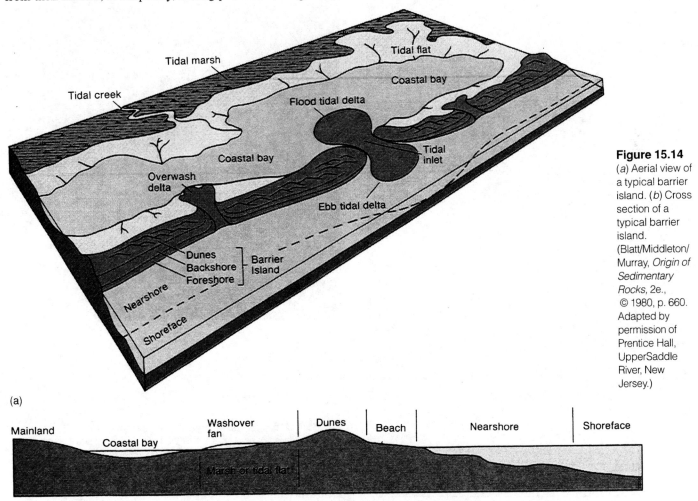

Figure 15.14
(*a*) Aerial view of a typical barrier island. (*b*) Cross section of a typical barrier island. (Blatt/Middleton/Murray, *Origin of Sedimentary Rocks*, 2e., © 1980, p. 660. Adapted by permission of Prentice Hall, UpperSaddle River, New Jersey.)

Figure 15.15   An overwash delta, or fan, at North Beach, Cape Cod, Massachusetts.

(a)

(b)

Figure 15.16   (*a*) Map and (*b*) photograph show offset of north end of Assateague Island as a result of the construction of jetties at the end of neighboring Fenwick Island. The southward-moving longshore currents are starved of sediment as they flow along Assateague, and, consequently, erosion has been considerable. Total offset has been more than 500 meters (1,640 ft).

Figure 15.17   Sand dunes along the New Jersey shore have been posted and planted to retard erosion.

Figure 15.18   Sand moved by storm waves from Hurricane Gloria in 1985 filled the parking lot at Ocean City, Maryland.

Dunes can be relatively stabilized by vegetation. The initial plant colonizers, however, have only the most easily disturbed surfaces on which to grow, and even small animals can dislodge the roots. To protect the easily eroded dunes in some areas, "snow" fences have been erected, and signs prohibiting walking on the dunes or the driving of dune buggies have been posted (fig. 15.17). Plants can proliferate and, over time, build soil fertile enough for woody bushes and, eventually, trees.

Dune sands can also be dislodged during severe weather. The storm waves of Hurricane Gloria in 1985, for example, removed 1.2 meters (4 ft) of sand from the beach at Ocean City, Maryland (fig. 15.18).

MARGINAL SEAS

Because sea level has risen about 130 meters (425 ft) since the last glacial advance, the continental shelves house a number of **marginal seas.** Most, like the North Sea, are drowned continental shelf areas, but bordering the shelves in tectonically active areas is a number of marginal seas with complex origins. Some, such as the Sea of Japan, are thought to be the product of seafloor spreading.

Eustatically Formed Marginal Seas

The Atlantic shelf of Europe underlies shallow marginal seas, the Baltic and North Seas (fig. 15.19). Both of these seas are sub-

Figure 15.19   The floors of the Baltic and North Seas.

merged parts of the continent, and both were overlain by ice during the last glacial advance. After the recession of ice, worldwide changes in sea level, known as **eustatic changes,** resulted in a transgression of shelves. The sediment of these seas is topped by a layer of glacial rock debris, and a few of the islands of Denmark, such as Fyn (or Funen), are dominated by glacial till. The water between the North and Baltic Seas is shallow enough for bridges to connect islands and mainland. Sweden and Denmark are now

Figure 15.20   The Gulf of Maine, bordered on the south by Cape Cod.

Figure 15.21   Satellite photo of the Nile Delta. Dark color indicates vegetation.

connected by such a bridge, and the Danish peninsular connection with Germany and the continent is joined by a bridge to the island of Fyn.

On the opposite side of the Atlantic lies a marginal water body called the Gulf of Maine (fig. 15.20). This shallow sea currently is, and has been since colonial days, an important fishery. The southern end of the Gulf of Maine is bordered by Cape Cod, a glacially constructed feature that typifies in composition the kind of rock debris that lies over most of the floor of this water body.

Tectonically Formed Marginal Sea

The origin of the Sea of Japan is still a partial mystery for earth scientists. It differs from a eustatically formed marginal sea in several respects. First, its basement depth (the water depth plus the sedimentary layers) is considerably greater than pelagic ocean floor of similar age. Second, the water depth at places within the Sea of Japan is greater by an order of magnitude than the depths of marginal seas on the continental shelves. Third, it overlies a subducting section of the Pacific Ocean floor. All of this indicates that tectonic activity played a significant role in the formation of this marginal sea.

Deltas

Deltas form at the mouths of rivers along coasts where average wave energy is rather small and where subsidence of sediments under their own weight is matched by the influx and buildup of new river deposits. As accumulations of sediments at river mouths, deltas build the land seaward in a process known as **progradation.** The buildup of sediments can form a variety of shapes. The name of this accumulation form derives from the Greek letter Δ because the most prominent delta in ancient western civilization, the Nile Delta, has an approximate triangular outline (fig. 15.21). Other shapes are pos-

sible, however, and the Mississippi Delta has been described as a bird's-foot delta (see fig. 11.16).

Sediments deposited in deltas can accumulate to make a number of related sedimentary deposits, including migrating channel sands, fan-shaped sand and silt deposits beside levees, mud layers within bays, bars of sands at stream mouths, silt deposits at the sea's edge, and muddy, subaqueous deposits.

Distributaries are streams that carry water from the alluvial valley through the delta and into the ocean. They are branches that receive water from the main channel, and they extend through the delta as channels in the very sediment they deposit. Distributaries can be numerous and ephemeral because rivers will seek the most direct and least resistant path to the ocean, the ultimate base level. Whenever the channels receive an excess of water, they flood, breaching the natural levees and depositing sandy, fan-shaped *splays* of sediment more or less perpendicular to the channel (fig. 15.22).

As the river lays down its deposits during floods, the distributaries encounter sediments that block and alter their paths. The changing pattern of these streams leads to a varied development along the delta's seaward edge. In the case of the Mississippi Delta, seven different "lobes" of the delta have prograded the coastline over the continental shelf during the last 7,000 years. The typical pattern of development takes five steps.

In the first step, a distributary bifurcates. The two newly formed channels establish an approximate parabolic shape open to the sea, creating an *interdistributary bay* with marine sedimentation characterized by muds and burrowing organisms. The second step requires a flood that breaches the channel boundaries or natural levees, allowing silts and sands to migrate into the bay between the two channels. A third step involves the buildup of terrigenous sedimentation in the interdistributary bay, the water body between the distributary channels. An eventual shift in the channel chokes the flow of silt and sand in the fourth step. Fifth in the cycle of steps is subsidence of the bay, producing a marine environment.

Figure 15.22 Principal features developed along a distributary channel of a delta.

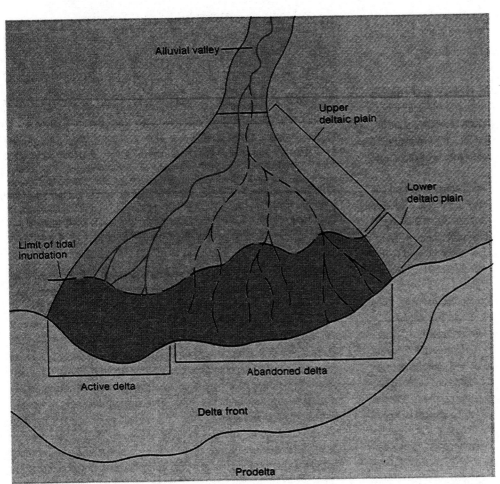

Figure 15.23 Diagrammatic view of a delta, showing its principal features. (Source: J.M. Coleman and L.B. Wright, *Analysis of Major River Systems, Their Deltas, Procedures, and Rationale,* Coastal Studies Institute Technical Report 95, Louisiana State University.)

A delta progrades differentially seaward. While abandoned areas subside under their own weight, other accumulations build toward the shelf edge. At the leading edges of the delta lie deposits of sands called *distributary mouth bars.* Seaward of the bars, silts form a convex-upward feature called a delta front. At depth and farther seaward lies a fine-grained, muddy accumulation known as a **prodelta** (fig. 15.23).

A delta is a rapidly changing environment that exhibits both marine and terrestrial features. It is one of the most ephemeral of Earth's features, and its form and development depend on the flow of fresh water through distributary channels, changes in sea level, the amount and type of sediment carried by the distributaries, and the intensity of wave energy. The largest of deltas can stretch across the shelves to the shelf break.

CORAL REEFS

A predominantly biogenic (derived from life) subenvironment on the continental shelves and on stable platforms is the **coral reef.** Reefs form slowly by the layered accumulations

(a)

(b)

Figure 15.24 (*a*) Cross section through a typical coral reef. (*b*) Development of surge channels through the reef.

Figure 15.25 The origin of three common types of reefs, as first postulated by Charles Darwin. The progression from fringing reef to atoll is evolutionary a subsiding ocean floor. In the first stage, a volcano has risen to an elevation above sea level in tropical waters. A fringing reef forms close to the mountain the second stage, the volcano, having subsided and undergone weathering, separated from the reef by an intervening lagoon. As the volcano subsides below sea level in the third stage, the reef continues to build upward to stay the warm, well-lit water, making an atoll that surrounds a subaqueous crater

of calcium carbonate, mostly generated by sack-shaped animals called coral polyps. Because coral polyps live symbiotically with algae known as zooxanthellae, coral reefs form in warm, shallow, clear water with a slightly elevated pH. Mixed into this environment are algae, numerous fish, sponges, echinoderms, molluscs, and arthropods.

Reefs occur in all sizes and in a number of shapes, but all exhibit certain common features, including *reef flat, reef crest,* and *reef slope* (fig. 15.24). The slope is a seaward precipice leading to deep water that absorbs most of the incoming wave energy. In violent storms, however, the reef crest and the reef flat behind it also feel the impact of wave energy. Typically, water over the crest and flat is well lit and shallow.

Despite their seeming diversity, reefs can be grouped into three fundamental types: (1) *fringing,* or those linked closely to the land surface with little or no intervening lagoon; (2) *barrier reefs* with large lagoons separating the reef structure from its associated landmass; and (3) *atolls,* or circular reef structures built around a central lagoon with no associated landmass visible at the surface (fig. 15.25). In the mid-nineteenth century, the naturalist Charles Darwin postulated that these three reef types often represent an evolutionary sequence associated with subsidence of the ocean basin floor (see also chapter 9). He reasoned that, as the associated landmass (usually an island) was gradually carried downward with the ocean floor, the reef continued to be built upward by corals and other organisms, its position being maintained at or just below sea level. The reef would begin its growth at the shoreline, attached to the land. Vertical growth of the reef, combined with sub-

sidence of the island, would result in a larger lagoon and smaller island. Eventually, the island would be completely submerged, leaving an atoll surrounding an empty central lagoon (fig. 15.25).

The entire reef complex is home to many species, some of which are very colorful. Unseen by most human visitors to the reef are the *cryptic,* or hidden, *fauna,* possibly many as yet unnamed species. The reef is a relatively fragile system, and changes in temperature, amount of terrigenous sediment, and pollution can diminish its growth or cause it to die, leaving deposits of sterile carbonate rock and sand.

Ancient reefs, such as the one in figure 15.26, can serve as clues to the marine settings of the geologic past. Other, larger reefs that yield clues to the past lie in Texas and in the Canadian Rockies. Their presence indicates a different, warmer climate than that found in either setting today.

The oceans contain many carbonate environments. Among the most notable are the Great Barrier Reef of Australia and the

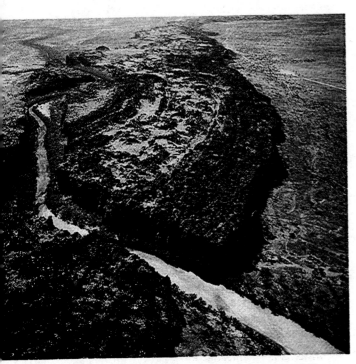

Figure 15.26 Dry season aerial view of fossilized coral reef. The Kimberleys, Windjana Gorge National Park, Western Australia.

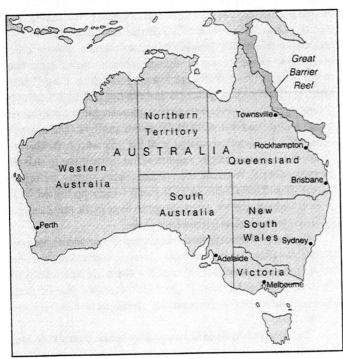

Figure 15.27 Location of the Great Barrier Reef along the northeastern coast of Australia.

Figure 15.28 Eroded reef rock on a Bahamian cay.

tially collections of carbonate sediments or portions of older reef rock that now lie above sea level. Some have extensive deposits of concentrically developed, carbonate sand grains called *oolites*. Figure 15.28 reveals the rough surfaces of eroded older reef material that makes up part of a small island in the Bahamas.

CONTINENTAL SLOPES

Continental slopes are the sites of sporadic, but highly effective, geologic work. Essentially areas bypassed by deposition, the slopes house spectacularly large canyons and, at their bases, piles of terrigenous sediment (fig. 15.29).

Turbidity Flows and Submarine Canyons

Turbidity flows develop along continental slopes whenever dense, sediment-filled water migrates under gravity downslope within another, larger body of water. The flow is characterized by a chaotic movement of water and sediment in a dense "plume," with a leading edge called a *head*. Behind this head trails the rest of the flow as an identifiable body with a thinning *tail* of turbulent water and sediment. The speed of the flow, which has been estimated to reach up to 35 kilometers (21.7 mi) per hour, generally depends on the height of the head.

As massive volumes of sediment move occasionally off the continental shelf, they slide over and erode the continental slope, which has an average 6% gradient, dropping 100 meters for every kilometer seaward (325 ft/0.62 mi). Channeled turbidity flows appear to be responsible for cutting some **submarine canyons** into continental slopes and for making large and extensive deposits at slope bases.

The discovery of canyons in continental slopes led initially to speculation that the canyons were primarily the product of gouging by migrating river sediment. Further analysis of the distribution of these features, however, revealed that many canyons seem to have no associated river.

Apparently, sediments emplaced by ancient rivers migrate to the shelf break, where, under the stress of earthquake temblors or gravity, they move rapidly downward in turbidity flows toward the deep ocean floor. The arrival of such sediments at the

islands of the Bahamas. The Great Barrier Reef is the largest structure ever made by life (fig. 15.27). It is more than 1,000 kilometers (620 mi) long and consists of numerous individual carbonate reefs in different stages of development. In the warm waters of the Gulf Stream, reefs have developed on a stable platform called the Bahama Banks. The abundant reef material in the warm, shallow waters has accumulated in both unconsolidated and consolidated forms, making individual islands called *cays*. The cays are essen-

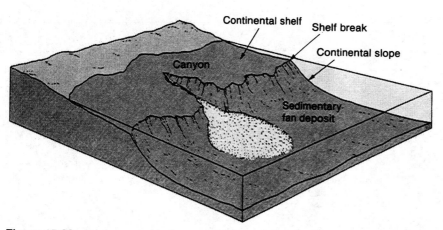

Figure 15.29 Canyon carved in the continental slope with a fanlike accumulation of sediment at its mouth.

shelf break is hardly a mystery. The Mississippi Delta has prograded to the outer shelf. At times of lower sea level, all rivers wend their way to reach their base level farther seaward across exposed shelves.

Deep-Sea Fans, Turbidites, and Mounds

As turbidity flows reach the bottom of continental slopes, they lose energy, and their sediments settle into a *fan,* or *cone,* lying against the base of the slope and extending onto the deep ocean floor. Ensuing flows of sediment can cut distributary channels and build levees in this accumulation of sediment. Numerous adjacent and connected fans make a sediment accumulation with a gentle gradient called the **continental rise.** The finer sediments of a turbidity flow settle out to become *distal* (for "distant") *turbidites* tens to hundreds of kilometers from the flow source. Coarser grains make up the *proximal* (for "near") *turbidites,* which settle out of a turbidity flow closer to the point of flow origin.

In addition to turbidites, moundlike structures dot environments from the continental shelves to the deep ocean floor. Some of these result from the growth of corals that do not require warm water, sunlight, and the symbiotic zooxanthellae. These coral mounds lie as deep as 5 and 6 kilometers (3.1 and 3.7 mi). Other mounds, called *mud mounds,* apparently develop when microbes form bafflelike structures that block the transport of fine sediments. Mud mounds can rise more than 100 meters (328 ft) above the surrounding seafloor.

THE DEEP OCEAN FLOOR

It was only with great difficulty and great expense that humans learned anything about the deep ocean floor. Early attempts to discover just what lies on the ocean bottom included dragging metal cages and boxes over the floor. As technology advanced, crews in submersibles dived to the ocean bottom, where, with the help of artificial lighting and robotic arms, they were able to photograph and take samples of the sediments, rocks, and animals of the deep.

The oceanic deep is the site of the **abyssal plains,** vast areas with relatively little change in elevation (relief), except for volcanic seamounts (see chapter 9), islands associated with submarine plateaus, and upwardly warped features of several origins

called *diapirs.* In the Pacific, the abyssal floor is dotted by many seamounts and island mountains, such as the Hawaiian Island chain, the Emperor Seamounts, and the Tuamotu Archipelago. In the Atlantic, the relatively flat Hatteras Abyssal Plain along the tectonic trailing edge of North America is the recipient of distal turbidites and hard parts of sea life.

The sediments of the deep, which overlie the predominantly volcanic oceanic crust, include the following:

1. The siliceous and calcareous hard parts (bone and shell) of mammals, fish, and plants (such as diatoms)
2. Cosmic particles
3. Fine eolian sediments
4. Terrigenous sediments from turbidity flows and from melting ice rafts calved from glaciers
5. **Hydrogenous sediments,** which are metal-rich accumulations in the form of encrustations and nodules

In the cold environment of the abyssal plains are holothurians (sea cucumbers), clams, worms, and fish, all adapted to the darkness and the great pressure. In contrast with the fisheries of the epipelagic, the abyssal environment apparently has smaller food sources. One of those sources is a detrital rain of organic material and nutrients that falls through the water column. Another source of nutrients ample enough to support a community of varied lifeforms is the hydrocarbon seeps found on the floor of the Gulf of Mexico. The community that prospers in the vicinity of the seeps is dependent on *chemosynthesizers,* microscopic organisms that can manufacture food without the aid of sunlight. These organisms, initially found associated with the volcanic, hydrothermal vents of the oceanic ridges, require sulfur or methane to start the chemosynthesis. Whereas the volcanic vents supply sulfur dissolved from the volcanic rocks through which the heated water passes, the hydrocarbon seeps appear to furnish the raw materials for food synthesis through methane leaks.

Typically, chemosynthetic-dependent communities are populated by clams, crabs, and tube worms. Some deep-sea fishes, including grenadiers, or rattails, swim in the vicinity of these ecological havens. Figure 15.30 shows one of these chemosynthetic-based communities photographed by the crew of the *Alvin.*

The deep ocean floor is covered by accumulations of fine-grained, organically produced muds derived from various microorganisms. Oceanographers call these muds **oozes** and identify them on the basis of their composition. *Calcareous oozes* are usually white or dirty-white muds dominated by accumulations of calcium carbonate in the form of whole and broken hard parts from many organisms (fig. 15.31*a*). Some of the organisms that contribute to oozes are microscopic unicellular foraminifera, small molluscs called pteropods, and algae known as Coccolithophoridae. *Siliceous oozes* are muds dominated by hard parts of opaline silica (fig. 15.31*b*). Diatoms (see chapter 14) and unicellular radiolarians are important sources of these deposits. Extensive diatom oozes occur beneath the cold waters of high latitudes (fig. 15.32). See box 15.1.

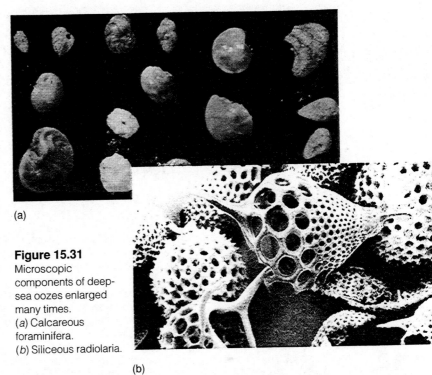

(a)

Figure 15.31
Microscopic components of deep-sea oozes enlarged many times.
(*a*) Calcareous foraminifera.
(*b*) Siliceous radiolaria.

(b)

Figure 15.30   Tube worms and other organisms dependent on chemosynthesis in the deep-sea environment cluster around a thermal vent.

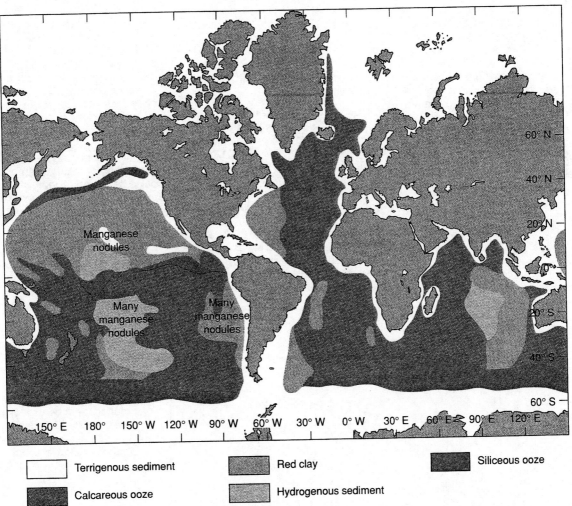

Terrigenous sediment

Red clay

Siliceous ooze

Calcareous ooze

Hydrogenous sediment

Figure 15.32   Distribution of the principal sediment types in the world's oceans. Manganese nodules are predominantly fist-size accumulations of chemically precipitated metallic oxides and hydroxides.

Investigating the Environment

CARBONATE SEDIMENTS ON THE DEEP OCEAN FLOOR

Numerous coral reefs, oolitic sands, and seashells lying in warm, shallow water may give the impression that, with the exception of small coral mounds, carbonate buildups generally do not occur in deep, cold water. On the *Glomar Challenger,* during the cruise labeled Leg XVI in the equatorial Pacific Ocean, however, scientists mapped a large bulge of carbonate sediments on the deep-sea floor. The bulge exceeds a thickness of 500 meters (1,640 ft) in its elongate central portion just south of the Clipperton fracture zone (fig. 15.A). The presence of the bulge in cold water enabled scientists to develop a model that combined a number of oceanic and biological processes.

The carbonate bulge in the equatorial and north equatorial Pacific is a knot that ties together the threads of upwelling along the Peru (Humboldt), Equatorial and Cromwell Currents, the food chain, detrital sedimentation, and ocean chemistry. The bulge reflects a number of interrelationships:

1. Upwelling water enriches surface waters with nutrients.
2. Surface currents spread the nutrient-rich water generally westward.

3. Organisms extract calcium, carbon, and oxygen from the water to build hard parts of calcium carbonate.
4. Floating organisms die and sink, with their journey to the bottom aided when larger organisms ingest and then excrete them in heavier, fecal-pellet form.
5. Lower pH and a higher concentration of dissolved carbon dioxide in the bottom waters lead to the dissolution of calcium carbonate unless more matter than can be dissolved falls in a detrital rain.
6. The Pacific plate carries sediments from the East Pacific Rise into deeper water away from the ridge crest.

Upwelling water beneath the Peru (Humboldt) Current supplies nutrients to the microscopic organisms of surface waters (see chapter 14). The Cromwell Current is also a nutrient-rich current, and a divergence of surface water along its northern boundary allows some of the countercurrent water to upwell. Thus, the epipelagic waters just north of the equator can support an abundance of life. The fertility of these waters and the abundance of life diminishes occasionally when a warming trend called El Niño caps the upwelling with a layer of warm water (see chapter 6).

For millions of years, however, these nutrient-rich waters have supported organisms that produce hard parts of calcium carbonate.

Because the planktonic organisms are light and have disproportionally large surface areas, they tend to sink slowly unless they are ingested and then excreted by larger organisms. Incorporation in fecal pellets enhances the fall through the water column. As the hard parts and their associated organic matter sink, they undergo attack by bacteria and by more acidic water, which reduces them to their molecular and elemental states. The hard parts collect on the bottom, where they undergo further dissolution or become part of the seafloor sediment.

Bottom water is not conducive to the preservation of calcium carbonate because of a lower pH that is controlled by the presence of dissolved carbon dioxide. At a variable depth in the oceans, the rate of dissolution of calcium carbonate exceeds its depositional rate. This depth of excessive dissolution is called the calcite compensation depth (CCD). In the vicinity of the carbonate bulge, according to oceanographers Tjeerd H. van Andel and G. Ross Heath, the CCD lies between 4,700 and 4,800 meters (15,416 and 15,744 ft). Below this depth, there is no accumulation of calcium carbonate, and the bulge becomes siliceous oozes made primarily of radiolarians. Because the detrital rain of carbonate sediments falls on a moving and subsiding plate, those sediments that accumulate west of the East Pacific Rise are destined to ride into deeper water toward the north and west (see chapter 9). With subsidence, the carbonate passes below the CCD.

Apply Your Knowledge

1. How would the CCD of the equatorial and north equatorial Pacific be affected by a decrease in surface productivity?
2. What would a cross section of seafloor sediments look like along a line from the Marquesas Islands past the eastern Hawaiian Islands to the Aleutian Islands?

Figure 15.A
Sediment thickness (in meters) in a portion of the eastern Pacific. The numbered dots represent core sample locations.

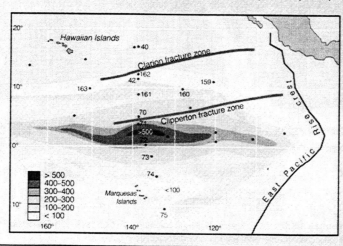

Beneath the gyres of the Pacific Ocean lie the *red clays*. These fine-grained sediments are terrestrial aluminosilicates that have settled out of the water column after transport in currents. Some clays may also result from the chemical alteration of the basaltic seafloor.

TRENCHES

The deepest points from the surface to the ocean bottom lie at the bottom of **trenches,** those V-shaped sites of subduction. Along the western coastline of South America, the trench system reaches depths in excess of 6 kilometers (3.7 mi). At 11 kilometers (6.8 mi) below sea level, the Mariana Trench in the western Pacific is the world's deepest feature. Even this hostile environment of high pressure and cold water is home to holothurians and rattails. Since trench exploration is very dangerous, additional knowledge about the life in trench waters is scarce.

EPIPELAGIC WATERS

The temperatures and salinities of the epipelagic environment vary widely (see chapter 14). These variations act as controls on some organisms, though other organisms appear unaffected by such changes. Those organisms that can tolerate a wide range of salinities are called *euryhaline;* those capable of tolerating wide temperature ranges are *eurythermal*. Animals restricted by narrow salinity and temperature ranges are *stenohaline* and *stenothermal*, respectively.

Sunlight penetration of the upper 200 meters (656 ft) of open ocean water enhances the proliferation of life wherever nutrients are adequate. The food chain begins with tiny photosynthesizers like the Coccolithophoridae and ends, with the exclusion of humans, in fast-swimming fishes and mammals. Tunas, billfishes, various sharks, and whales, all euryhaline animals, move with great speed throughout the epipelagic zone, feeding as they go from surface waters into the upper layers of the mesopelagic.

Generally, the large ocean gyres are not as nutrient-rich as coastal waters and areas of divergent currents. Consequently, the epipelagic zones of these gyres are not known as fisheries, and the gyres are called the ocean's deserts. The gyres are not, however, devoid of life, just as continental deserts are not without a variety of life-forms.

The epipelagic zone of upwelling waters, however, serves as an abundant fishery. Fast-swimming tunas provide a good example of organisms at the top of the food chain in this fishery. Tunas have fusiform (bullet-shaped) bodies that enable them to cut through the water with hydrodynamic ease. Almost every part of their bodies enhances rapid movement, including tiny finlets that decrease turbulence (fig. 15.33). Tunas also exhibit warm-bloodedness through a network of arteries and veins that act as heat exchangers.

Figure 15.33 Tuna is an important food source in the world's oceans. The tuna has a body shape designed for constant cruising in search of prey. It reaches a maximum length of approximately 1.25 meters (5.13 ft).

Of the large mammals that inhabit the epipelagic zone, whales survive by following one of two feeding strategies: Some whales are plankton feeders, using baleen strainers to capture small organisms within the mouth. A large humpback whale that opens its mouth may spread its jaws more than 4 meters (13.1 ft) to take in both food and water. By ejecting the water through its baleen, the whale captures its food. Toothed whales like the sperm whale follow a different strategy for food and seek out prey as deep as the mesopelagic. Other toothed whales, such as the killer whale, frequently attack smaller sea mammals, such as seals, that swim near the surface.

MESOPELAGIC WATERS

The twilight of mesopelagic waters fades to darkness with depth. Some species of fish have adapted to the absence of light in this environment by acquiring organs that generate chemical light, or *bioluminescence*. The light apparently serves two purposes: reproduction and food acquisition. Light spots on some fish serve as lures to attract both mates and prey (fig. 15.34).

Generally, mesopelagic organisms are relatively weak swimmers, compared to those of the epipelagic. Life in the mesopelagic also rises and falls in daily and monthly cycles, making a mass of protein available for deep-diving epipelagics. Sonar waves scatter when they encounter this zone of the ocean, which is now known as the *deep scattering layer*.

Figure 15.34 Examples of fish adapted to life in the deep sea.

FURTHER THOUGHTS: HUMAN INFLUENCE ON MARINE AND NEARSHORE ENVIRONMENTS

*O*ur knowledge about marine and nearshore environments is uneven. We know more about nearshore environments than about marine environments because of accessibility. Many seaside dwellers and transient vacationers are familiar with some features and life in the nearshore environments. That familiarization has meant the intrusion of humans into the natural processes of those environments, often with adverse effects on life that depends on the sea. Our pollution of fragile environments like salt marshes and estuaries has spread into marginal seas and the epipelagic realm. For several decades prior to the 1990s, for example, Europeans allowed unchecked pollution of the Elbe River, which annually emptied thousands of tons of pollutants into the North Sea. Even for this relatively shallow environment, however, no one has completely assessed the effects of the Elbe's polluted water. But common sense tells us that pumping heavy metals into nearshore and marginal-sea environments is not without adverse influence.

Most of the fish taken for human consumption come from waters that lie no farther than 350 kilometers (217 mi) from coastlines. One particular disaster associated with methyl mercury pollution in the 1950s emphasized the changes humans can force on the nearshore environments. At that time, Japanese, who

consumed fish and shellfish from Minamata Bay, ingested enough mercury from a local industrial complex to cause birth defects that included both mental retardation and deformities.

In the Caribbean and the Gulf of Mexico, two pollutants attack the environment: petroleum and sewage. The heavy tourist traffic in and around the Caribbean places burdens on sewage systems, and many shellfish ultimately incorporate pathogens dangerous to humans in their tissues. Petroleum enters the Caribbean and the Gulf of Mexico from seeps, spills, and pipeline leaks. In 1978, a blowout beneath an offshore drilling platform owned by a Mexican oil company released approximately 500,000 tons of petroleum into the sea.

The conclusion that we are changing both marine and nearshore environments is unavoidable, but the oceans are large and may be capable of absorbing and cycling many of our pollutants. Because they are complex, no one fully understands all the interrelationships within the oceans and between the oceans and other Earth systems. Until we gather more information, we can only hope that the ocean's capacity to absorb and cycle will prevent us from detrimentally affecting Earth's ability to support human life.

SIGNIFICANT POINTS

1. Life is both affected by and affects marine and nearshore environments.
2. The chemistry of seawater is, in part, controlled by organisms.
3. Marine sedimentation is, in part, the product of life processes that produce hard parts, such as shells.
4. The salt marsh is an ephemeral environment dependent for its survival on sea level. Salt marshes do not become dry, even in the warmest weather.
5. The mean depth of water in a salt marsh is greater during low tide, when the water lies in the tidal channels, than it is at high tide, when water spreads over the entire marsh.
6. Constant bioturbation disrupts the sediments of a salt marsh.
7. Estuaries include bays, lagoons, deltas, and river mouths in which salt water meets fresh water.
8. All modern estuaries are related to the most recent rise in sea level.
9. In estuaries, both fresh and brackish water flow seaward over denser salt water, which flows landward along the estuary bottom in estuarine circulation.
10. The continental shelves serve as depositional centers.
11. Barrier islands have complex histories related to sea-level fluctuations, modern currents, sediment supply, storms, and urbanization.
12. Marginal seas have two origins: Some form from eustatic changes, others through tectonic processes.
13. Deltas are built up by sediment carried in distributaries.
14. Coral reefs are warm-water complexes dominated by the calcium carbonate deposits of coral polyps. Numerous kinds of animals are present in the reef environment.
15. Turbidity flows carry sediment downslope toward the abyssal plains. In the process, they erode the continental slope, cutting submarine canyons.
16. Red clays dominate the sediments beneath the ocean gyres. The ocean floor also has coverings of siliceous and calcareous oozes.
17. Trenches are the lowest points on Earth's surface. The Mariana Trench in the western Pacific is Earth's deepest point.
18. Epipelagic waters consist of the well-lit upper 200 meters of the ocean beyond the continental shelf.
19. Mesopelagic waters lie immediately below the epipelagic zone and constitute a "twilight" zone to a depth of 1,000 meters.

ESSENTIAL TERMS

salt marsh 344	estuarine circulation 347	terrigenous 349	progradation 354	abyssal plain 358
sea level 345	brackish 347	depositional center 349	prodelta 355	hydrogenous sediment 358
tidal channel 345	continental shelf 348	barrier island 351	coral reef 355	ooze 358
estuary 346	dip 348	overwash delta 351	turbidity flow 357	trench 361
epicontinental sea 346	shelf break 348	marginal sea 353	submarine canyon 357	
transgression 347		eustatic change 353	continental rise 358	

REVIEW QUESTIONS

1. What instruments enable oceanographers to "see" the features of the ocean floor?
2. Does a salt marsh ever dry out?
3. Why does water flow in a tidal channel?
4. What is a tidal range? ·
5. How does a fiord form?
6. What characterizes estuarine circulation?
7. What is a miogeocline?
8. What is an overwash delta?
9. How did the North Sea form?
10. How did the Sea of Japan form?
11. What is the difference between the shapes of the Nile and Mississippi Deltas?
12. How does an interdistributary bay form?
13. What is the composition of the prodelta? Where does it form?
14. What are zooxanthellae?
15. Do coral structures form in deep water?
16. What is a distal turbidite?
17. How do chemosynthesizers differ from photosynthesizers?
18. What is the composition of an ooze?

CHALLENGES

1. Which North American coastlines favor the development of barrier islands? Why?
2. Why are dunes fragile? How do human activities adversely alter dunes?
3. What road construction problems associated with the nature of the feature do engineers face in deltaic environments?
4. What major canyons lie along the continental slopes of North America?
5. Select a coastal community. What pollution problems must be solved? What construction or use along the coast would disturb the naturally formed features?

PART 6

APPLYING THE EARTH SCIENCES

According to a 1938 speech by Karl Taylor Compton, "Science really creates wealth and opportunity which did not exist before." Knowledge of the composition and processes of our planet has led to the discoveries of many useful materials. These materials now make up an annual worldwide value worth hundreds of billions of dollars.

At the End of Part 6, You Will be Able to:

1. Distinguish between renewable and nonrenewable resources.
2. Identify the difficulties associated with discovering new sources of raw materials.
3. Classify soils.
4. Identify the types and sources of metallic and nonmetallic resources.
5. Identify the types and sources of fossil fuel resources.

Job 28: 1–6. The New Oxford Annotated Bible

(Revised Standard Version)

Surely there is a mine for silver
and a place for gold which they refine.
Iron is taken out of the earth,
and copper is smelted from the ore.
Men put an end to darkness,
and search out to the farthest bound
the ore in gloom and deep darkness.

Chapter

16

Earth Resources

Open pit copper mine at Bingham Canyon, Utah.

INTRODUCTION

The culmination of earth studies is knowledge about the planet's use and care. In this sense, all of us must read the Earth's package instructions, or the lessons drawn from the work of earth scientists. Earth is our home, and living in any home means using it repeatedly. Generations of humans must reuse the planet, and that use will require the extraction of minerals, some of which are abundant and some of which are scarce.

Earth has undergone many natural changes that have radically altered the environment. In the process, continents have been constructed, broken up, and moved, and certain substances that humans find either necessary or desirable have been emplaced within Earth's crust. Life, too, has added to the accumulation of valuable substances in Earth's crust, in the form of natural oils, energy-rich coals, and enriched soils. These and other resources are the materials we need to live on Earth. The word *resource,* appropriately, comes from the Old French for "to arise anew."

When humans began using their home, they found a well-stocked food supply and more than enough materials for construction, decoration, and energy. Because of the careless and sometimes wanton use of Earth's resources, however, generations to come may find a home with few amenities and diminishing necessities.

NATURAL RESOURCES

A **natural resource** is anything drawn from Earth to support life or a way of life. Earth-derived resources are normally considered either renewable or nonrenewable. **Renewable resources** are materials that can be regenerated within a relatively short span of time (crops, timber) or reused (air, water). This chapter focuses on nonrenewable resources.

Nonrenewable resources (rocks, minerals, and fossil fuels) are found in nature in finite quantities. Their formation within Earth involves such extraordinarily long periods that new supplies could not form in hundreds or even thousands of years. The discovery and assessment of these resources have traditionally been the special concerns of earth scientists. No matter where or how they may have formed, all nonrenewable resources share three fundamental characteristics, all resulting from an increased human population and its more widespread industrial and technological advancement: (1) increasing rates of consumption, (2) diminishing supplies, and (3) diminishing rates of discovery of new supplies.

Determining the quantity of any resource ultimately available for use involves making educated guesses. The significance of data that relate to making such assessments is often difficult to judge. For example, the number and size of new discoveries of *ore bodies* (economically significant mineral concentrations) over a period of years must be estimated. Another consideration is that technological advances in ore processing may allow for use of low-grade ores that have already been discovered but as yet are not economically exploitable. In addition, new uses for any commodity that increase consumption rates will lower the expected life of that resource. Changing economic and technological conditions, as well as political, social, and environmental pressures, also impact significantly on the useful life of a resource.

Despite the uncertainty inherent in evaluation, a portion of each known resource has already been discovered and measured with some accuracy by earth scientists or engineers. Such measured quantities available for immediate use are designated as **reserves**: the measured, evaluated, and currently exploitable portion of a resource.

WATER

Water is essential to all life-forms. For thousands of years, people have camped, farmed, and built villages and cities near sources of fresh water. Essential to life, water is used for transportation, irrigation, waste disposal, and industrial development, and is an ecological habitat for many of our food sources. Of the total abundance of water, fully 97% is found in the world's oceans and, because of its dissolved salt content, is not usable for drinking or agriculture. Two-thirds of the remaining 3% is locked up in glacial ice. Subtracting the groundwater leaves only the 0.008% of all water that is present in lakes and streams. Even so, this is an extraordinarily large amount, with worldwide stream runoff estimated to be between 31,000 and 47,000 cubic kilometers (7,525 and 11,410 cu. mi) per year. Average rainfall in the conterminous United States is 76 centimeters (30 in) per year, of which two-thirds is consumed by vegetation and one-third is returned to the oceans, with an average daily runoff of 4,540 billion liters (1,200 billion gal).

Water Distribution

Even though the percentage of available fresh water is only a small part of the water total, this in itself is not really a problem. Supplies are still sufficient to satisfy our needs. The more significant factor is that freshwater distribution varies greatly, both seasonally and geographically. Southern Arizona, for example, receives most of its annual precipitation in thunderstorms during the summer months, when temperatures and evaporation rates are extremely high. Australia, likewise, experiences 65% of its runoff during its summer (January through March). Over the years, humans have attempted to modify this cycle by constructing dams and reservoirs to store water for the drier times of the year. Today, more than 36,000 dams over 15 meters (49 ft) high impound approximately 5,000 cubic kilometers (1,215 cu. mi) of water.

Geographically, freshwater distribution exhibits great disparities. In California, for example, two-thirds of the annual runoff is north of San Francisco, leading to a water surplus, whereas two-thirds of the water use is south of San Francisco, causing a deficit. The world's annual renewable water resources average 7,420 cubic meters (262,370 cu. ft) per capita. Table 16.1, however, shows the inequity of the distribution of this resource, ranging from a per capita value of only 50 cubic meters (1,768 cu. ft) for citizens of Egypt to 653,850 cubic meters (23,120,136 cu. ft) per year for residents of Iceland. The rivers of Brazil alone contain approximately 13% of the world's freshwater supply. In the United States, approximately 7.57 million liters (2 million gal) of pure water are available for each person every year. The problems are that too many people have become concentrated in urban areas, and too many have moved into arid environments.

TABLE 16.1	Annual Per Capita Renewable Water Resources in Cubic Meters (1992 data)
Egypt	50
Saudi Arabia	140
United Arab Emirates	180
Mauritania (Africa)	190
Jordan	240
United States	9,710
Brazil	33,680
Canada	106,000
Gabon (Africa)	132,580
Guyana (South America)	298,270
Suriname (South America)	456,620
Iceland	653,850

Source: *World Resources*, 1994–95. World Resources Institute. Oxford University Press, 1994.

Water Usage

Globally, agricultural irrigation is, by far, the largest consumer of fresh water, accounting for 69% of all usage. Between 1900 and the year 2000, agricultural consumption is expected to have increased by six times, to 3,250 cubic kilometers (790 cu. mi) annually. Unlike industrial and household use, which returns most of the water to the natural waterways, agricultural use is *consumptive*. The water is either evaporated, transpired by plants into the atmosphere and lost, or incorporated into the vegetation mass. One acre of corn is estimated to transpire 11,355 to 15,140 liters (3,000 to 4,000 gallons) of water per day into the atmosphere. While water use for irrigation has continued to increase in Mexico and Canada, it has actually declined by 49.2 billion liters (13 billion gal) per day, from a peak of 570 billion liters (150 billion gal) per day, in the United States. Water returned to natural drainage systems is often degraded by sediment and salts from soil erosion, chemical wastes from industry, and increased temperature. In many parts of the United States, agricultural use of water is subsidized by government agencies, keeping the price artificially low and encouraging excessive use and waste.

Efforts to make sufficient fresh water available to growing populations take a number of forms. The most basic is simply to cut usage and conserve. In agriculture, this might mean a shift to crops that require less water; a shift to dryland farming or grazing (or in some cases, abandonment of the land); night irrigation, when cooler air temperatures mean less evaporation; covered irrigation canals; or use of the more efficient "drip irrigation," where water is distributed in the fields through pipes with pinhole-size openings, rather than through open ditches. A 15% reduction in the amount of water used for irrigation in California, for example, would double the amount available for urban and industrial use. **Desalinization** of seawater, or the removal of dissolved salts, either by *filtration* or *distillation,* is used in some localities and circumstances. With seawater filtration is less effective than distillation because the filters become easily clogged. On the other hand, unless solar energy is used, distillation requires an expensive fuel source. Other techniques employ bigger dams, deeper wells,

or pipelines to more distant sources. In the last case, however, such sources are either not readily available, or the water already belongs to someone else.

On a grander scale, schemes have been proposed that would transfer vast quantities of fresh water from one part of a continent to another. For example, the North American Water and Power Alliance (NAWAPA), proposed in 1964 at a projected cost of $100 billion, would move water from Alaska and the Northwest Territories of Canada to the southwestern United States and northern Mexico. More imaginative schemes have also been proposed. One, for instance, calls for the towing of large icebergs from the Antarctic region to Saudi Arabia and neighboring states.

Water usage also has a political aspect. Many streams and larger lakes are shared by more than one state, province, or nation, either necessitating agreements (national and international) and cooperation or instigating conflicts. In fact, more than 2,000 treaties currently deal with water rights and development (see box 16.1). In the case of streams, upstream users often maintain their right to withdraw as much water from the stream as they wish; while downstream users expect the streamflow to be maintained in both quantity and quality. At least one factor that precipitated the 1967 Arab-Israeli conflict was the perception that Israel might divert the headwaters of the Jordan River for its exclusive use. On the other hand, India and Pakistan have been able to share in the development of the Indus River, and Brazil and Argentina have jointly developed the Parana River.

SOILS

Soils are a vital natural resource (see box 16.2). Without soils, land plants could not grow, and without those plants, the food sources on which we and many other animals depend would not be available.

Soils may be defined and classified in a number of ways, depending on who defines them and the purpose of the classification. An engineer, for example, considers soil to be any unconsolidated material overlying bedrock at Earth's surface. The engineer's principal concern is the ease of soil removal or the soil's ability to support any structure built upon it— not its ability to sustain plant life. This latter consideration is, however, of primary importance to the agronomist and, from the standpoint of soil being an "earth resource," to the earth scientist.

In this text, **soil** is defined as that portion of the loose material at Earth's surface capable of supporting plants with root systems. A number of schemes of varying complexity have been proposed to describe soils in terms of their origin, occurrence, and characteristics. The classification most commonly used today by specialists is called the *7th Approximation* (see appendix G). For the nonspecialist interested only in understanding the general characteristics of soils and their broad patterns of distribution, this scheme is unnecessarily complex.

Soils found in most areas of North America typically possess a layered structure, with each layer developed to a greater or lesser degree, depending on climate and the length of time the soil-forming processes have been operative. Each of the layers is

Box 16.1

Investigating the Environment

Laws that govern the use and ownership of water have evolved over time in response to supply and demand. Although in the United States, most such laws have been formulated at the state level, reflecting geography and climate, they are all one of two types: *riparian doctrine* or *prior appropriation doctrine*. Riparian (from the Latin for "bank") doctrine derives from English common law and finds its greatest application in the humid eastern United States, where fresh water is generally abundant (fig. 16.A). In essence, riparian doctrine states that the owner of the land adjacent to a stream has the right to make reasonable use of the water in the stream, provided that the water is returned to the stream undiminished in quantity or quality before it leaves his or her property. In turn, that owner has the right to receive the undiminished flow of water from the upstream land owner. Riparian water rights are part of the owner's property rights. That means that the water in the adjacent stream and the right to use it contribute to the value of the owner's property. The land owner does not, however, actually own the water, only the right to use it. While access to and use of the water is a valuable part of the estate, it cannot be transferred or sold. Rather, the water benefits, whether they are used or not, stay with the land. This doctrine is also referred to as the "rule of reasonable use."

THE OWNERSHIP OF WATER

In the prior appropriation doctrine, first usage of the water is the most important factor. This doctrine derives from Spanish law and practice and is most widely used in the more arid western part of the United States. Prior appropriation leads to usage that is highly consumptive, in that water is not normally returned to the stream channel but is used for some purpose (usually irrigation) at a considerable distance from the stream. The result is that streamflow may be greatly diminished downstream. Unlike riparian rights, the water can be bought and sold like any other real property. In addition, once beneficial use of the water by the owner ceases (abandonment), prior appropriation rights are lost.

Groundwater rights generally follow the same pattern as surface water rights, both in terms of doctrine and geographic locality. Because the water is not visible in discrete channels, however, the situation is usually more complex and difficult to monitor. Withdrawal of groundwater by a property owner leads to a lowering of the water table not only under that property, but under all adjacent properties. Also, water cannot be easily returned to the supplying aquifer.

California, because of its large population and general deficiency of water, has developed the most complex and inclusive system of water rights. In the California doctrine of *correlative rights*, the surface watershed or groundwater aquifer system is the basic unit for purposes of planning. This has led to the development of Water Conservation Districts, self-governing entities with respect to water use and allocation. In addition, California also practices large-scale water resource planning, which involves the reallocation of water resources from one part of the state to another. A consequence of such action is that the state can limit the water supply within both the supplying and the receiving areas.

Apply Your Knowledge

1. Which doctrine of surface-water ownership rights applies where you live?
2. Why is the prior appropriation doctrine so important in the western United States?
3. Why did the state of California adopt a compromise approach to the development of a water ownership doctrine?

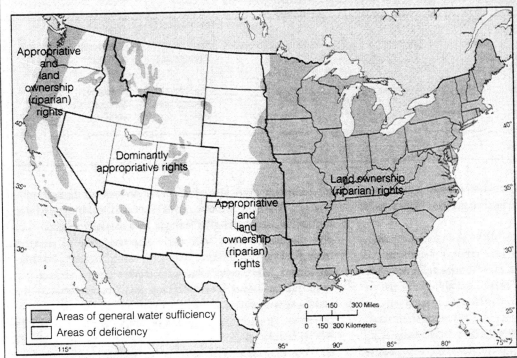

Figure 16.A Distribution of water law practices in the United States. (Source: U.S. Bureau of Reclamation, 1977.)

Box 16.2

Investigating the Environment

AGRICULTURAL CAPABILITY UNITS: HOW BEST TO USE THE LAND

The rationale for including soils among Earth's ural resources is that they have been used for a cultural purposes for thousands of years. No soils are equally suited for such use, however. W thousands of soil types have (or can be) describ having a method whereby the agricultural use ness of any soil can be quickly assessed and co municated is beneficial. Such a system is tha *agricultural capability units*, as defined by the L Department of Agriculture (table 16.A). The ei

TABLE 16.A Agricultural Capability Units

	Class	Land Quality (soils)	Slope	Drainage	Productivity (cultivation)	Precautions	Primary Uses	Secondary Uses
Farmland	I	Excellent	Flat	Well drained	Easily cultivated, very productive	None	Agriculture	Pasture, recreation, wildlife
Farmland	II	Good (some sandy)	Gently sloping	Less well drained	Productive but smaller range of crop suitability	Some (contour farming)	Agriculture, pasture	Recreation, wildlife
Grazing Land	III	Moderately good	Sloping	Less well drained	Regularly cultivated, much less crop diversity (rotation)	Special erosion prevention	Agriculture, pasture, watershed	Recreation, wildlife
Grazing Land	IV	Fair (thin or sandy)	Steeper slopes	Poorer drainage	Cultivated only occasionally, very little diversity	Requires careful management	Pasture, tree crops	Recreation, wildlife, watershed
Grazing Land	V	Low fertility	—	Wet	Unsuited for agriculture	Requires good management	Forest, range, watershed	Recreation, wildlife
Limited-Use Land	VI	Very low (shallow soil)	Steep and easily eroded	—	Completely unsuited for agriculture	Requires careful management	Forest, range, watershed	Recreation, wildlife
Limited-Use Land	VII	Very low (shallow and/or sandy)	Steep	Low rainfall	Pasture and forest	Very careful management	Watershed, recreation, wildlife	Forest, range
Limited-Use Land	VIII	Absent or thin	Steep	Extremely wet or dry	Scenery or recreation	Little return for management input	Recreation, watershed, wildlife	—

Source: U.S. Department of Agriculture.

referred to as a **horizon,** and each has evolved through thousands of years of weathering. The total vertical sequence of horizons is the **soil profile** (fig. 16.1).

The uppermost few centimeters of the soil consist of abundant decaying organic material mixed with some minerals and are referred to in most soil descriptions as the **O-horizon.** Immediately below this thin surface layer is the first true soil horizon, the **A-horizon.** Because weathering proceeds from the ground surface downward, the A-horizon is the most intensely weathered zone. Water moving downward through this horizon dissolves and carries away certain soil minerals, especially calcite, but also iron ox-

ides and clay particles (which move downward through minute cracks). This downward removal process is **leaching,** and the A-horizon is characterized by being at least partially leached of mineral material. The A-horizon is also the zone of maximum biological activity, housing burrowing animals, plants, and microorganisms. Many generations of plants live, grow, and die in this uppermost soil layer. Dead plant material is broken down by chemical processes and microorganisms in the soil, resulting in a concentration of dark, fine-grained organic material called **humus,** which colors the A-horizon dark brown or even black. This nutrient-rich, dark surface layer is what we also know as the **topsoil,** classes are characterized in terms of such factors as slope, erodibility, and drainage, with Class I being the best suited for agriculture and Class VIII the least suitable (fig. 16.B). Subdivisions of these classes may be formed by indicating with a lowercase letter the specific limitation: e for erosion, w for wetness, s for shallow, and c for climate. A class IV soil, for example, with an extreme risk of erosion would be designated IVe.

Apply Your Knowledge

1. Which of the eight classes in this scheme best describes the land in your immediate vicinity?
2. Can you cite an example from your own knowledge of a location that would be considered Class II? Can you cite an example of Class V?
3. Cite examples from anywhere in the world where humans have modified the natural environment or adapted crops to areas where you would not normally expect agriculture to occur.

Figure 16.B   Agricultural capability units.

an incredibly important natural resource but one highly susceptible to loss through erosion.

Below the A-horizon is the **B-horizon,** or the **subsoil.** While the A-horizon is considered the **zone of leaching,** the B-horizon is the **zone of accumulation,** because some of the less-soluble minerals, such as the clays, are redeposited in this layer. Concentrated zones of these minerals are known as *hardpan* because they are tough and not easily worked. In humid climates, the soluble calcite remains in solution and is completely removed from the soil by downward-moving water. In arid climates, however, the water does not always pass down through the soil but may be drawn back up

to the ground surface and evaporated. As the water evaporates, the calcite is precipitated in the soil or, often under true desert conditions, as a white mineral crust on the ground surface. This hard, calcium carbonate crust is called *caliche.* The **C-horizon** represents a transition zone between the weathered horizons above and the unweathered **parent material** (usually bedrock) below, from which the soil has developed.

Five factors are important in the formation of any soil and in the development of different soil characteristics: time, parent material, topography (slope and drainage), climate, and organisms. Of these, the most fundamental is climate. Regardless of which soil

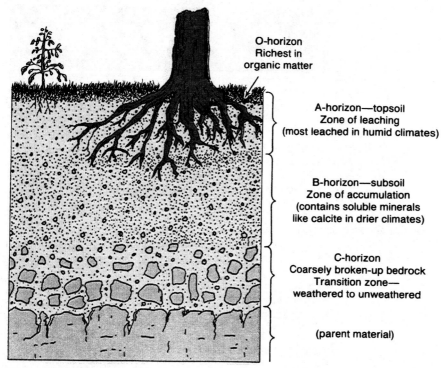

O-horizon
Richest in
organic matter

A-horizon—topsoil
Zone of leaching
(most leached in humid climates)

B-horizon—subsoil
Zone of accumulation
(contains soluble minerals
like calcite in drier climates)

C-horizon
Coarsely broken-up bedrock
Transition zone—
weathered to unweathered

(parent material)

Figure 16.1 Generalized soil profile in a humid climate.

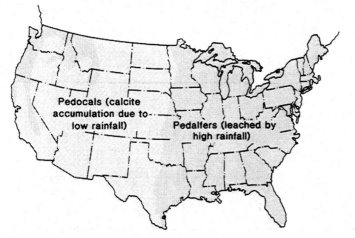

Pedocals (calcite
accumulation due to
low rainfall)

Pedalfers (leached by
high rainfall)

Figure 16.2 Simple subdivision of soils in the United States. (Source: U.S. Department of Agriculture.)

classification scheme is employed, the broad regional differences in soil types are determined by the climatic factors of temperature and moisture. Figure 16.2 shows a very simple but useful subdivision of soils in the United States that is based on precipitation. The north-south line that divides the United States into two nearly equal parts is the 64-centimeter (25-in) annual *rainfall line* (approximately 100°W). The area to the east of this line receives, on average, more than 64 centimeters of rainfall each year, and the area to the west of the line (with the exception of some of the higher mountains and coastal regions) receives less than 64 centimeters annually.

Soils in the east are loosely grouped as **pedalfers** (*ped,* meaning "soil"; *Al,* for aluminum; *Fe,* for iron). The pedalfers are characterized by humus-rich A-horizons and clay-rich B-horizons that have been completely leached of calcite. For agricultural purposes,

these soils have to be regularly treated with anhydrous ammonia and lime to counteract the *acidity* that results from the leaching of calcite. Soil horizons in pedalfers are well defined, and under natural conditions, these soils support both broadleaf and coniferous forests.

West of the 64-centimeter (25-in) annual rainfall line lie the **pedocals** (*ped,* meaning "soil"; *cal,* from calcite). Generally, the farther west, the drier the climate and the less complete the covering of vegetation. Because of the drier climate, leaching has not been totally effective, and calcite remains in or on the soils. As a result, the soils are naturally *alkaline* rather than acidic. With little vegetation, humus accumulation is less significant, and the horizons become more difficult to distinguish from one another. Under natural conditions, the pedocals support grass or scrubby desert vegetation.

Laterites are the soils of the humid tropics. Because they have been subjected to intense chemical weathering for a very long time, they may be tens of meters thick. This same intense weathering has leached these soils of most minerals and left them as little more than reddish concentrations of iron and aluminum oxides. Abundant soil microorganisms break down and destroy the vegetation immediately; thus, humus does not accumulate, and individual horizons are virtually impossible to distinguish. While the laterites seem to support lush vegetation in the form of tropical rain forests, they are, in fact, very infertile soils. Much of the natural vegetation grows in a litter of decaying vegetation on the forest floor and not within the true soil. When such soils are cleared for intensive agriculture, grazing, or timber, as they have been in the Amazon Basin of South America, they very quickly dry up and become bricklike (and, indeed, have historically been used as building stone in parts of southeast Asia).

METALS

Metals are those elements characterized physically by the properties of malleability, ductility, and conductivity (discussed later in this section) and chemically by having the tendency to lose outer shell electrons and form positively charged ions. The metals used in industry may be classified for discussion in various ways. A useful first subdivision is by their relative abundance in nature. Such abundances have been determined by chemical analysis of thousands of rock and mineral samples. On this basis, metals are arbitrarily separated into those that are **abundant** (average abundances greater than 0.01% of Earth's crust) and those that are **rare** (abundances less than 0.01%). This difference in abundance leads to a fundamental distinction between the groups. When natural processes concentrate the abundant metals just a few times above their average abundances, an economically exploitable **ore mineral** results. Indeed, the definition of an ore mineral is one that can be mined and refined at a profit. A rare metal must generally be concentrated hundreds or even thousands of times above its average abundance to be profitably worked.

Abundant Metals

The two best known of the abundant metals are very different in terms of their histories of exploitation and can be used to illustrate most of the characteristics of this group, as well as some significant differences between group members. Aluminum, the most abundant metal and the third most abundant element (after oxygen and silicon) in Earth's crust, was until the twentieth century merely a scientific curiosity. Its use in the nineteenth century was so rare that Napoleon III is reported to have given his nephew an aluminum rattle worth thousands of dollars. Iron, the second most abundant metal and fourth most abundant element, on the other hand, has been used by humans for thousands of years.

Aluminum The chemical element aluminum is found in nature in many minerals but especially in the feldspars and clays. Both of these mineral families are, in turn, extremely abundant, with the feldspars forming the bulk of most igneous rocks and the clays the most common minerals in sedimentary rocks. This would seem to indicate that a ready supply of aluminum ore is present virtually everywhere at Earth's surface. This, however, is not the case. Abundance alone does not make an ore. Minerals must be mined and refined at a profit to be considered ores. If the desired metal cannot be extracted easily and cheaply from the enclosing mineral, then that mineral is not an ore. Such is the case for aluminum in both feldspars and clays. These are silicate minerals in which the aluminum ions are very tightly locked in the mineral structure and from which they cannot be easily removed. Therefore, the abundance of these minerals is of little consequence from the standpoint of aluminum production.

Although other aluminum-bearing minerals are much less abundant than either the feldspars or clays, some can be more easily processed. One of these is the important ore *bauxite,* which is a complex mixture of aluminum oxide and hydroxide minerals. Bauxite formed as a tropical weathering product and may be considered "fossil" soil (fig. 16.3). Because they formed in Earth's surface environment, bauxite deposits are shallow and can normally be mined by large-scale, low-cost, open-pit operations.

The separation of aluminum ions from oxygen requires extraordinary amounts of electrical energy. Thus, the availability and cost of electrical power is a controlling factor in the profitability of aluminum production. For this reason, aluminum ore has historically been transported from the tropical areas where it is mined (Jamaica, South America, West Africa) to areas of abundant, cheap, hydroelectric power (western Canada, Scandinavia, the United States) for processing. This procedure is very different from that employed for most metals, for which considerable processing is done in the immediate vicinity of the mine before the upgraded ore is sent to the final processing location (smelter, refinery, blast furnace). Because of the high cost of electricity, it has been cheaper to ship the raw aluminum ore, still mixed with large amounts of waste material, thousands of kilometers for processing.

More than any other event, the invention of the airplane led to widespread use of aluminum. This metal is strong, yet light-

Figure 16.3 Formation of the ore mineral bauxite by the weathering of aluminum-rich source rocks under humid tropical conditions.

weight, a requirement for anything that is going to get off the ground. In addition to its use in the transportation industry in general (decreased weight means decreased fuel requirements), which accounts for 24% of total usage in the United States, aluminum is also used extensively in packaging (31%), in the building industry (20%), and in the electrical industry (10%) as a cheaper, but generally less effective, substitute for copper. Numerous other uses account for the remaining production (1991 data).

Recycled scrap metal has become an increasingly important source of aluminum, accounting for approximately 20% of annual metal production. On average, 50% of the aluminum used in beverage cans is now recycled, and in those states with beverage container deposit laws, the percentage recycled is much higher. Recycling uses far less electrical energy than the electrolytic processing of raw ore.

Iron Iron has been the mainstay of industry since humans first (probably accidentally) refined iron ore by placing it in a fire. Iron ores, most commonly as the oxide minerals hematite, limonite, and magnetite, are abundant and widespread. Hematite is found concentrated in certain ancient sedimentary rock layers, limonite in tropical laterites and other soils, and magnetite in many, but especially dark, igneous rocks. By far, the most important type of iron ore, exceeding all others combined, is a sedimentary ore known as **banded iron formation (BIF),** or *taconite* (fig. 16.4). This is a low-grade ore in which iron (in the form of hematite and magnetite) is concentrated in dark layers that contrast with light, iron-poor, quartz-rich layers, giving the rock an overall banded appearance. All BIF deposits, including those of the Lake Superior region, are geologically very old. They are thought to represent chemical precipitates formed in ancient seas on or at the margins of the original continents. The iron was transported to the oceans dissolved in streams at a time when Earth's atmosphere contained much less oxygen than it does today. The soluble iron, therefore, was not converted (oxidized) during this period of transport to the insoluble oxidized variety that dominates Earth's surface environment today.

Because BIF is a low-grade ore, it is mined almost exclusively in large, open pits within the iron ranges of the western Lake Superior region. Because the ore is transported some distance to the iron and steel mills, located closer to the coal and limestone deposits necessary for its refining, it must be upgraded. Before being transported, most BIF ores are crushed, and the iron-rich minerals are magnetically separated from the waste rock.

(a)

Figure 16.4 (*a*) Locations of important banded iron formation (BIF) deposits. (*b*) Mass of BIF on display outside of the Smithsonian Institution.

(b)

The iron-rich material is then mixed with special clays and crushed limestone and rolled into pellets, which are transported to steel mills and fed directly into blast furnaces.

Iron ore processing is simple and cheap, compared to the processing of aluminum ore. It requires only that the oxygen be burned, thereby freeing the iron. This is done in a blast furnace by burning *coke,* a form of coal from which the gases have been driven by heating in special ovens (fig. 16.5). To the iron ore–coke mixture are added limestone and a small amount of manganese. These materials act as scavengers, picking up oxygen, sulfur, and other impurities from the iron ore and coke. The limestone forms waste material, or *slag,* which floats on top of the liquid iron and is removed. Disposal of large volumes of slag has always been a major envi-

ronmental problem. One solution in recent years has been to build on top of these layered and compacted slag piles (fig. 16.6).

The molten iron produced from the blast furnace is *pig iron,* so-called because early iron workers were reminded of a sow and her piglets when the molten iron from the furnace ran into molds. Most pig iron, or *cast iron,* is moved in liquid form to nearby oxygen, open hearth, or electric furnaces, where it is converted to *steel.* Steel is formed by the addition of carbon and one or more metals. *Plain carbon steel,* which accounts for more than 90% of steel production and is the backbone of the construction and automobile industries, contains about 1.5% carbon and small amounts of manganese and silicon. *Stainless steel* contains between 12% and 60% chromium.

Figure 16.5 Diagrammatic representation of a blast furnace.

Figure 16.6 Commercial development (shopping center) on a slag dump south of Pittsburgh.

TABLE 16.2	The Principal Ferroalloys and Their Uses		
Ferroalloy	**Steel Type**	**Characteristic**	**Ore Mineral**
Chromium	Stainless steels, high-speed tool steels	Strength, hardness, corrosion resistance	Chromite
Cobalt	Magnet steels	Hardness at high temperatures, magnetism	By-product of copper mining
Manganese	Carbon steels	Removes oxygen and sulfur, resistance to wear	Pyrolusite
Molybdenum	Molybdenum steels	Hardness, strength, corrosion resistance	Molybdenite
Nickel	Nickel stainless steels	Corrosion and stain resistance	Pentlandite
Tungsten	Tungsten steel	Hardness, high-speed cutting tools	Scheelite, wolframite
Vanadium	High-temperature steels	Tarnish, strain, and fatigue resistance; grain size control	Carnotite

Source: U.S. Department of Agriculture.

Manganese, chromium, and several other metals are routinely mixed, or **alloyed,** with iron to give steel certain desirable qualities. Chromium, for example, in addition to providing corrosion resistance ("stainless"), also gives strength. Nickel makes steel more wear-resistant. Manganese, the most important of the alloying metals, lengthens crystal size and hardens the steel, as do molybdenum and tungsten. Because these metals are produced principally for use in the steel industry, they are grouped together under the name of **ferroalloys** (table 16.2).

Most nations possess some iron ore deposits. What many lacked was the infrastructure (roads, railroads, ports, etc.) necessary to develop and exploit those deposits. This situation has now changed, and steel industries have developed in many countries, much to the detriment of that in the United States. Because of higher labor costs, aging facilities, lack of government subsidies, and environmental constraints, the U.S. steel industry is in many cases no longer economically competitive in the world market.

Iron and steel account for approximately 95% of all the metal products consumed worldwide. The construction (31% of 1991 usage in the United States), transportation (27%), machinery (18%), and appliance (7%) industries have their foundations in iron and steel. Other metals could substitute for iron and steel, but all are more expensive. The abundant and widespread iron ore deposits are not likely to be exhausted in the foreseeable future. A far more immediate constraint, at least from the standpoint of the United States and Canada, is the rather limited and unevenly distributed supplies of the important ferroalloys. The United States is self-sufficient only in molybdenum, and Canada possesses significant quantities only of nickel and cobalt. The other ferroalloys must be imported, sometimes from politically unstable or otherwise unreliable sources.

Russia is the world's leading steel producer, followed by Brazil. In 1991, the United States produced approximately 6% of the world's total. While the United States possesses enough reserves to be self-sufficient in steel production, it nevertheless imports both raw ore (from Canada) and approximately 15% of the finished steel it uses. The U.S. steel industry is intensely localized. Because of the proximity of major coal and limestone deposits and the ease of transportation afforded by the Great Lakes for ore from the great iron deposits in northern Minnesota, 47% of the steelmaking capacity has been concentrated in the Illinois-Indiana-Michigan area. An additional 31% is located in Ohio and Pennsylvania.

Rare Metals

The rare metals, which include copper, tin, gold, silver, lead, zinc, and a number of others, must be concentrated to many times their average abundance by natural processes to be economically exploited. As with the abundant metals, two examples—copper and gold—are considered here to illustrate the important characteristics of this group.

Copper   Copper plays an important role in our everyday lives because of its reasonable cost and peculiar characteristics. Copper is *malleable* and *ductile;* that is, it can be shaped and drawn out into fine wire. While not as good an electrical conductor as gold or silver, it is still effective enough for most purposes and is considerably cheaper. Its widespread use in the electrical industry (about 60% of the total usage of this metal), in a sense, makes copper responsible for our high standard of living, with its many labor-saving devices. Copper has also found applications in the plumbing and transportation industries, in coins, and in munitions. Copper mixes easily with other metals and has been alloyed with zinc to form *brass* and with tin and zinc to form *bronze.*

The element copper occurs in well over 100 minerals, but the most important ore mineral is *chalcopyrite,* a copper-iron sulfide. Most importantly, chalcopyrite is found disseminated as small grains and concentrations in large masses of granitelike rock known as *porphyry copper* deposits. These rock bodies are geologically young (less than 225 million years old) and invariably parallel to subduction zones. They occur throughout the western United States and southward into the Andes Mountains of Peru and Chile. They are especially common in Montana, Utah, and southern Arizona, the latter state accounting for more than half of total U.S. copper production.

Porphyry copper deposits formed from hydrothermal solutions that worked their way through cracks and crevices in the now solidified granite and the surrounding country rock (fig. 16.7). As these fluids cooled, metal-bearing minerals, usually in a matrix of quartz, were precipitated. These small, irregularly shaped bodies, called **veins,** contain not only copper-bearing minerals but also minerals bearing gold, silver, tin, mercury, molybdenum, beryllium, and many other metals. The metallic ions could not be accommodated in the structures of the abundant rock-forming minerals that crystallized earlier. Thus, they were concentrated in many rare minerals, in far above average abundances.

Figure 16.7   Formation of hydrothermal mineral deposits.

The porphyry coppers are low-grade deposits, meaning that the percentage of copper present in the ore body is very low, often less than 0.5%. Consequently, very large tonnages of material must be mined to derive relatively small amounts of copper. Even so, staggering wealth has resulted over the years from some of these mines. The city of Butte, Montana, lies on top of what has been called "the richest hill on Earth." More than $3 billion worth of metals have been extracted from the mines at Butte. But even this pales when compared to the open-pit mine at Bingham Canyon, Utah, the largest mine in the world (fig. 16.8). At Bingham Canyon, where the average copper content is only 0.65%, more than $15 billion worth of metals (mostly copper, but also gold and silver) have been removed from a mine 1.7 by 2.5 kilometers (1.0 by 1.5 mi) in area and a little over 1 kilometer (0.6 mi) deep.

Because U.S. reserves of copper ore are relatively low, copper conservation and recycling efforts have been strong for a number of years. Today, approximately 20% to 25% of annual U.S. copper production is recycled metal. Ironically, world reserves of copper are actually increasing, not just because of the discovery of new deposits, but also because of the replacement of copper by glass fiber optics in transmission lines.

Gold   Gold is not only a rare metal, but because of its high economic value (measured in dollars per ounce), it is also, along with silver and the members of the platinum group, considered a *precious metal.* Gold derives its long history of use from its beauty, and rarity, and from the fact that it is virtually indestructible. With the exception of that in sunken Spanish treasure ships on the seafloor, much of the gold that has been mined throughout history, an estimated 95,000 metric tons (105,000 tons) is still in circulation. Its principal use today is as a backing for the world's monetary systems, and consequently, an estimated 32,600 metric tons (36,000 tons) are stored in vaults, such as that at Fort Knox, Kentucky. Other important uses are in jewelry, dentistry, plating, coinage, electronics, and the aerospace industry.

Like chalcopyrite, pure gold and rare gold-bearing minerals occur primarily in hydrothermal vein deposits. A secondary source is in small sedimentary units known as **placer deposits,** which are distributed along stream channels and shorelines. Placer deposits

Figure 16.8
This open-pit copper mine at Bingham Canyon, Utah, is the largest mine in the world.

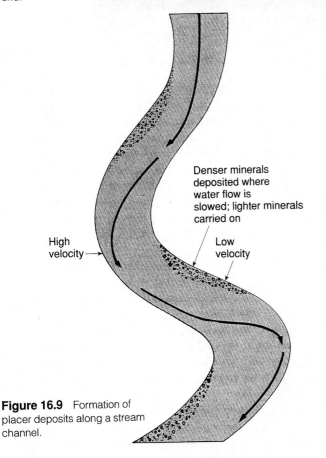

Denser minerals deposited where water flow is slowed; lighter minerals carried on

High velocity

Low velocity

Figure 16.9 Formation of placer deposits along a stream channel.

represent the accumulation of heavy mineral grains that were eroded from the primary vein deposits, transported some distance downstream, and then dropped when the stream currents lost energy and could no longer carry them (fig. 16.9). The largest gold-bearing deposits, those in the Witwatersrand District of the Union of South Africa (known as "the Rand"), are found in ancient bodies of metamorphosed conglomerates. These have the appearance of placer deposits, but because their size is so much larger than normal placers, their exact origin remains a mystery. South Africa possesses approximately half of the world's gold reserves and has led the world in gold production since the late 1800s. Other important gold-producing countries include Russia, Australia, Canada, and the United States.

The United States currently produces approximately 35% of its own needs. About 10% of this gold is a by-product of the refining of other metals, principally copper, (see box 16.3), and the remainder represents primary mine production and recycled metal. Most gold mines today are open-pit operations that produce large tonnages of very low-grade ore. Indeed, the great increase in the number of such mines in recent years has led to a major controversy within the metal ("hard-rock") mining industry and within the halls of Congress (see box 16.4).

Box 16.3

Further Consideration

BY-PRODUCTS: A USE FOR EVERYTHING

While large mining operations are often developed for the production of a single metal resource, such as iron or copper, the much lower natural concentrations of many other metals preclude the expenditure of large capital to develop specific sources for them. They are retrieved from Earth entirely, or in large measure incidentally, during the mining and/or processing of ores of other metals—that is, as *by-products.* In some instances, the by-product metal is present in a mineral that is intimately associated with the principal ore mineral and must be separated from it before processing begins. In other cases, the by-product metal is present within the principal ore mineral and must be separated during the refining process or from the refinery wastes.

Of the ferroalloys, only manganese and nickel are produced as primary products. Cobalt is mostly a by-product from the waste (gangue) minerals associated with copper ores and from nickel-bearing laterites. Vanadium is primarily retrieved from uranium ores and titaniferous magnetite deposits. Large deposits of molybdenum ore are located at Climax, Colorado, but much of the production of this metal comes as a by-product of copper ores be-

cause of the large quantities of copper that are processed.

Silver, a precious metal, is rarely produced as the primary metal but is separated from lead, copper, and zinc ores after smelting. Consequently, the production rate of silver is dependent on the production of these other metals. The amount of silver held within the ore of lead (galena) is dependent on the presence of bismuth; thus, bismuth becomes a by-product of lead refining as well. While there is some primary production of the platinum-group metals in Russia and South Africa, most comes as a by-product of nickel refining.

Many rare elements important to today's technology are retrieved only as by-products from the wastes of ore processing. Rhenium comes from the flue dust of molybdenite smelters and, along with gallium, from coal ash. Germanium,

thallium, and indium are retrieved from zinc refinery residues and flue dust. Cadmium is salvaged from lead smelter dust, and selenium and tellurium from the slimes (residues) of copper refining. Hafnium is recovered during the production of zirconium metal, and scandium from fluorspar wastes.

If two or more metals of approximately equal value are produced by working the same deposit, they are referred to as *co-products.* Examples include the joint production of zinc and lead from deposits at many localities and of copper from many nickel and tin deposits.

Apply Your Knowledge

1. Why is it not feasible to produce many of the rare elements as primary ores?
2. Discuss the economic and technological problems associated with the production of materials as by-products.
3. What is an environmental benefit of the processing of refinery and manufacturing wastes for their by-product content?

INDUSTRIAL MINERALS

Because all industrial minerals are abundant in nature, they are classified by use, rather than by abundance. In this text, we recognize three categories of industrial minerals, with some subdivisions: raw chemicals, fertilizers, and construction materials.

Raw Chemicals

The raw chemical products are dominated by two mineral substances: halite (common salt) and sulfur. Halite (NaCl) is one of a group of economically important mineral products, known collectively as *evaporites,* that formed when large portions of ancient seas underwent periodic isolation and evaporation. Seaways or small basinal areas may have been detached for an extended period of time from the main ocean basin by uplift of the seafloor, the building of reef masses, or some other natural process. Intense evaporation left the isolated waters greatly enriched in dissolved mineral material, to the point where these minerals could no longer remain in solution and precipitated out to form layers on the seafloor. The seaway need not have dried up completely (although this perhaps occurred on occasion). The concentration of

dissolved mineral matter only had to exceed some critical level at which the water was saturated with salts. As such a level was reached and exceeded for each member of the mineral group, that mineral came out of solution (see chapter 14). In North America, significant deposits of halite and related evaporites occur in lower Michigan (the Michigan, or Salina, Basin) and stretch east and southeast to underlie parts of Ohio, Pennsylvania, and New York; in West Texas, eastern New Mexico, and western Kansas (the Permian Basin); in western North Dakota, eastern Montana, and southern Canada (the Williston Basin); and in belts paralleling the Gulf Coast (fig. 16.10).

Along the Gulf Coast, the salt deposits show a unique characteristic. The salt layer, buried at great depth, has been subjected to the enormous pressure exerted by the weight of thousands of meters of overlying sedimentary rocks. As a result, the salt has slowly flowed and has been squeezed upward to form hundreds of vertical pillars, many of which reach the surface. These **salt domes,** not only form important sources of halite but also are the location of other important resources, such as oil, natural gas, and sulfur (fig. 16.11).

Salt has been an important commodity for thousands of years, as evidenced by the English word *salary,* which derives from the Latin for salt. It has served as a basis for economic wealth, trade,

Box 16.4

Further Consideration

THE GENERAL MINING LAW OF 1872: TOO MUCH OF A BAD THING?

A major controversy boils today in the field of mineral resource development over a movement to repeal or modify in a significant way the General Mining Law of 1872. This law was one of a series of acts designed to provide an economic stimulus following the Civil War by opening the 260 million square kilometers (100 million sq. mi) of federally owned land in the western United States to development. That it has been a success is a matter of historical record. That it has been (and still is) abused is equally certain.

The basic provisions of the law are such that any U.S. citizen can file claim to an 8-hectare (20-acre) (placer claim) or 457-meter-by-183-meter (1,500-by-600-ft) (lode claim) area of federally owned land for the expressed purpose of developing a mineral deposit. The only costs to the claimant are a $100 annual maintenance assessment and a $2.50 per acre (placer claim) or $5.00 per acre (lode claim) fee paid at the time of application for patenting. Receiving the patent to the land provides the claimant with full title to the land, but even if the patent is never applied for or is refused, the claimant still retains full rights to the mineral resource as well as unre-

stricted use of the land surface, provided that such use is even remotely related to mining activity. Thus, for a $100 annual fee, a significant tract of land could be easily diverted to recreation or some other activity. Further, any minerals that are taken from the claim are not subject to the federal government royalties that must be paid for coal, oil, natural gas, and other nonmetallic resources.

Proponents of reform have suggested three fundamental changes: First, they would impose a significant annual "rent" on a standardized claim size of 16 hectares (40 acres) that would rise from $800 in each of the first 5 years to $12,800 after 25 years. Second, they would impose a leasing-royalty payment system of perhaps 8%. Third, any new law or major revision would include stringent provisions to protect the environment, something that was not a concern when the law was originally formulated.

Those who argue against changing the provisions of the law as they apply to the "hard-rock" (metallic) mineral industry—primarily those who work in that industry—offer the following counterarguments: The hard-rock mining industry needs the eco-

nomic incentive provided by this law to compete in an international minerals market where foreign mining companies may operate with significant government subsidies. Although no royalties are paid on minerals produced, the economic benefits in the form of jobs and taxes more than outweigh such potential royalties. The General Mining Law has no provisions for maintaining the environment, but all mining on federal land falls within the purview of other environmental legislation, including the National Environmental Policy Act (NEPA), the Clean Air Act, and the Clean Water Act.

Regardless of the outcome of this debate, it provides an opportunity to examine an important and controversial subject in the earth sciences from opposite viewpoints and to evaluate the merits of the arguments raised by both sides.

Apply Your Knowledge

1. Take a stand on this issue, and defend your position.
2. Regardless of your current position on this issue, do you think that the law when it was passed was justifiable on economic and social grounds? Why?
3. Should the mining of "hard-rock" metals be treated differently from other mineral resources? Why?
4. Research the policy on public lands and mining adopted in any of the Canadian provinces.

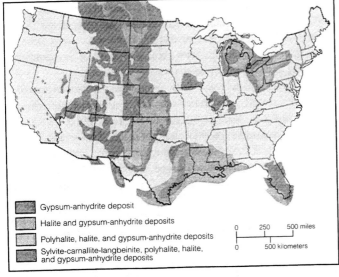

Gypsum-anhydrite deposit

Halite and gypsum-anhydrite deposits

Polyhalite, halite, and gypsum-anhydrite deposits

Sylvite-carnallite-langbeinite, polyhalite, halite, and gypsum-anhydrite deposits

0   250   500 miles

0   500 kilometers

Figure 16.10   Locations of various types of marine evaporite deposits in the United States.

and taxation. Its value has made it subject to government monopolies (as in India and China today). Approximately 50% of the salt used in the United States is consumed by the chemical industry, where 96% of this amount is manufactured into chlorine-based bleaches, polyvinyl chloride, and caustic soda (NaOH). De-icing of highways accounts for 26% of the salt consumed, with most of the remainder used in food seasoning and preservation, water treatment, ceramic glazes, fertilizers, medicines, and insecticides.

In the United States, the world's leading salt producer, 55% of production is from *brines*, highly saline groundwater (natural or formed by injecting water) found in the pore spaces of sedimentary rocks; 29% is from the mining of rock salt deposits; and 15% is produced by solar evaporation from shallow ponds, as at Great Salt Lake in Utah and along San Francisco Bay. There are no

Figure 16.11 Typical Gulf Coast salt dome with associated sulfur and petroleum deposits. Gypsum can also be found in association with salt domes.

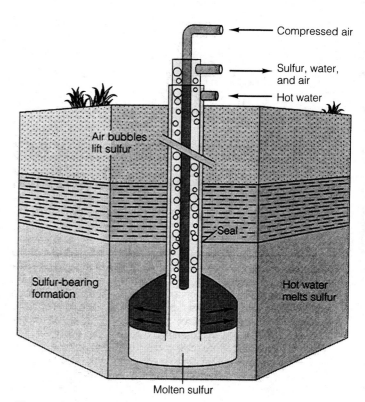

Figure 16.12 Recovery of sulfur by means of the Frasch process.

economic substitutes for salt. Fortunately, world resources of salt, including the waters of the oceans, are limitless.

In its pure form, sulfur is often found in veins and filling fractures in rocks at the tops of salt domes. It forms from the alteration of the mineral *anhydrite* ($CaSO_4$) by anaerobic, sulfate-reducing bacteria. Anhydrite is another evaporite mineral usually associated with halite. Texas and Louisiana together account for 55% of U.S. sulfur production and also lead the world in this area.

For much of the twentieth century, most sulfur was produced by the *Frasch process*. In this method, air and hot water are pumped down separate pipes in a well bore and into the sulfur-bearing formation. Under pressure, they dissolve the sulfur to form a foamy mixture that is pumped to the surface through the same well bore (fig. 16.12). Sulfur produced by this technique is extremely pure (99.8% sulfur). In recent years, the percentage of sulfur produced by the Frasch process has declined to approximately 35%. This reduction is being made up by a dramatic increase in the amount of sulfur recovered from oil and natural gas, currently 53% of U.S. production. While the sulfur supply that can be obtained by the Frasch process and from natural gas is limited, that which could be produced from the sulfate minerals gypsum and anhydrite is virtually limitless.

Most of the sulfur produced in the United States goes into the making of sulfuric acid (H_2SO_4), and of that, 60% goes to the production of fertilizer. Sulfuric acid is reacted with phosphate rock to yield phosphatic acid (H_2PO_4), the basis for the phosphate-based fertilizers discussed in the next section. Sulfur is also used in plastics, paper, synthetic fabrics, explosives, medicines, and insecticides.

Fertilizers

Modern intensive agriculture places great stress on soils. As crops are harvested, nutrients that plants extract from the soil and incor-

porate in plant tissue are lost to the soil. If a soil is to remain a useful resource, capable of sustaining future generations of plant growth, these nutrients must be replaced. This is done in large measure by the use of inorganic **fertilizers,** chemical resources taken from Earth in one form and returned to it in a form usable by plants. Three nutrients essential for plant growth are the elements potassium, nitrogen, and phosphorus.

Potassium (for marketing purposes referred to as *potash*) is one of the most common elements found in the rocks and minerals of Earth's crust. Although it does not occur as elemental potassium in nature because it reacts readily with water, potassium is an important constituent of micas, feldspars, and clays. As is the case in the processing of aluminum, these abundant silicate minerals are **refractory,** or difficult to break down, and the potassium in them is not easily released. Consequently, a better but less abundant source of potassium for fertilizer is the mineral *sylvite*. Sylvite (KCl) forms in the same manner as halite, and thus, it, too, is classified as an evaporite mineral. Sylvite, however, is even more soluble than halite, and an even greater amount of evaporation is required before it precipitates onto the seafloor.

In the Permian Basin (West Texas, eastern New Mexico, and western Kansas), a blanket of subsurface evaporite deposits covers more than 260,000 square kilometers (100,000 sq. mi). Conventional underground mining of these deposits accounts for almost 90% of U.S. potash production. Even larger deposits of potash are known in central Europe, Russia, and western Canada, with these last two countries being the world's leading producers. Approximately 95% of the potash marketed in the United States goes directly into the manufacturing of fertilizer. The remaining 5% finds various applications in the chemical industry. World reserves of potassium salts are enormous and are certainly sufficient to last for several centuries.

For many years, until the time of World War I (1914–18), the world's demand for nitrogen salts was supplied almost exclusively from vast deposits in the Atacama Desert of Chile. These Chilean nitrate deposits, consisting primarily of sodium nitrate ($NaNO_3$), were formed by the evaporation of groundwater and the consequent precipitation of soluble salts under arid conditions, forming a type of caliche. During the war, these deposits were more important for the manufacturing of explosives than they were for fertilizers. When British naval blockades prevented German ships from reaching these nitrates, German scientists developed methods whereby nitrogen could be *fixed*, or extracted from the air by combining chemically with other elements, and used in the munitions industry. These same techniques were subsequently employed for the manufacturing of nitrogen-based fertilizers, and the Chilean nitrate deposits eventually lost their significance. The major difficulty with using what is an essentially inexhaustible supply of atmospheric nitrogen is the large energy requirement of processing.

Most of the fixed nitrogen produced in the United States is in the form of ammonia (NH_3), with the hydrogen derived from natural gas. The United States produces most of the fixed nitrogen products that it consumes, with 60% of that production coming from the states of Texas, Oklahoma, and Louisiana, the sites of large natural gas fields. Approximately 80% of the nitrogen goes to the fertilizer industry for manufacturing into the anhydrous ammonia that is applied to fields in liquid form. The remaining ammonia is used in synthetic fabrics, in plastics, and in explosives.

Like nitrogen and potassium, the potential reserves of phosphorus for use in fertilizers are enormous. Most of these reserves are in marine sedimentary rocks. Florida and North Carolina produce almost 90% of the phosphate rock in the United States, with Idaho, Montana, Tennessee, and Utah producing much of the remainder. Vast amounts of phosphate-rich sediment have been identified on the continental shelf off the eastern coast of the United States and almost certainly will be mined someday. The United States is the world leader in the production of phosphate rock, followed by Russia, Morocco, and Israel. More than 90% of the world's production of phosphate rock goes to the fertilizer industry. The remainder is used in the manufacturing of products as varied as scouring powders, insecticides, and ceramics.

Construction Materials

Construction materials represent the largest tonnage of all of the natural resources produced, with an aggregate value in 1991 of more than $11 billion in the United States alone. The simple reason for this is that virtually every rock type can be used for building something. Such usage is governed largely by local supply because high transportation costs preclude the long-distance transport of these large tonnage materials, except when needed for specialized applications. A convenient subdivision of building materials separates them into two categories: natural products and prepared products.

Natural Products   Natural products are those rocks and minerals that require a minimal amount of preparation for use. Such preparation normally consists of cutting, polishing, crushing, sorting, and/or washing. Humans have always used locally available materials, fashioned to the desired size and shape, for the construction of dwellings and monuments. Architecturally, all such building stone is referred to as **dimension stone.** The most commonly used dimension stones are various coarse-grained igneous rocks generically termed "granite" (52% of usage in the United States) and limestone (28%). Because brick and concrete are far cheaper, use of dimension stone for most construction purposes has diminished. Exceptions to this trend are as decorative facing in building lobbies and other interior areas, where quality dimension stone is locally available, or where considerations of local or national pride outweigh considerations of cost.

At one time, the metamorphic rock slate, because it splits easily along parallel surfaces, was widely used for roofing. Asbestos shingles have now almost totally replaced it for that purpose. Slate is still widely used, however, for billiard tables, blackboards, and countertops.

Indiana (limestone) and Georgia and Vermont (granite) together account for 40% of U.S. dimension stone production. Resources of dimension stone are inexhaustible, but specific varieties are limited on a local or regional basis.

Crushed stone, used primarily as aggregate in highway construction and maintenance (52% of usage) is generally whatever rock material is available locally that can be crushed easily to the desired size. In the coal-producing areas of Pennsylvania and West Virginia, driveways, country roads, and parking lots are often covered with a material known locally as "red dog," shale rock that has been hardened and given a reddish color by the combustion of coal mine waste deposits, or "gob" piles. It is available and cheap, and it serves the purposes of communities and individuals who do not wish to bear the costs of using more expensive materials. In addition, using the red dog helps to eliminate unsightly debris piles. Crushed rock is mined from quarries in 48 of the 50 states, with the most commonly used rock types being limestone and dolostone (71% of usage), granite (14%), and basalt (8%). Crushed rock also presents a relatively new and interesting example of recycling. Increasingly, when a highway is resurfaced, the old aggregate is saved and reconstituted into new aggregate material.

Sand and gravel, which generally are washed free of their fine-grained impurities and sorted by size, are available virtually everywhere. They particularly occur as glacial, stream channel, and beach deposits. Sand and gravel have many of the same uses as crushed rock, and like crushed rock, they have a low cost per ton value. This means that they must be mined close to their points of consumption, usually in or near urban areas. This proximity often leads to environmental problems associated with noisy and dirty quarrying operations and heavy truck traffic. There are, however, notable examples of sand and gravel pits that, when exhausted, were converted into community assets by wise planning and the expenditure of some money. Indeed, one location in the city of Denver, Colorado, was used sequentially for gravel pits, for sanitary landfills, and finally, for a stadium parking lot complex.

Prepared Products   Prepared products are manufactured, usually by mixing, heating, and/or chemical conversion. Such products include (among many others) cement, clay products, and glass. **Cement** is the binding material in concrete. It is formed by roasting a crushed

TABLE 16.3	The Various Categories of Clay and Their Uses	
Clay Type	**Use**
Common clay (illite-rich)	Bricks, tiles, pipes, cement
Kaolin "china clay" (includes kaolinite and halloysite)	Chinaware, refractories (furnace lining)
Montmorillonite	
Bentonite	Drilling mud (oil industry)
Fuller's earth (includes attapulgite)	Absorbent (grease, etc.)
Ball clay	Tiles and refractories
Fire clay	Refractories

Source: U.S. Department of Agriculture.

Figure 16.13   Glass sand quarry near Berkeley Springs, West Virginia.

mixture of limestone (or dolostone) and clay (or shale) in a kiln at a temperature of approximately 1,500° C (2,732° F). This drives off the water present in the clays, as well as the carbon dioxide generated in the roasting process. The end product is *clinker*, which is ground to the desired size and mixed with a small amount of gypsum to form the final cement. Unfortunately, a considerable quantity of fine cement dust is also given off in the process. This dust is vented high into the atmosphere through a very tall stack, or chimney, so that its dispersal occurs across a broad area in the downwind direction, rather than accumulating in great quantity near its source.

Clay is the group name for a number of related minerals. All are hydrous aluminum silicates, and most have been formed by the weathering of igneous rocks. Because of compositional differences among clays, their chemical and physical properties vary, and each is best suited for certain applications. Clays are widely used not only in the making of cement but also in the manufacturing of bricks, ceramics, chinaware, and a host of other products (table 16.3). Reserves of most types of clay are enormous because the soils that cover the ground surface consist in large part of clay.

The principal component of *glass* is silica, in the form of quartz sand (fig. 16.13). The basic process of producing glass involves melting the silica at high temperatures and then cooling ("quenching") it quickly, so as to inhibit the growth of crystals. Although seemingly solid, glass is, in fact, a supercooled liquid, a material in which the individual ions have not arranged themselves into the orderly crystalline pattern that characterizes true solids. Various chemical substances are added to the silica to speed its hardening and to impart to the glass the desired qualities of color, weight, and resistance to heat and breakage. The U.S. reserves of the necessary raw materials for glass manufacturing are sufficient for the foreseeable future.

ABRASIVES AND GEMS

Abrasives and gems are considered together because they generally share the same characteristic of hardness and, in some cases, even represent the same mineral used for different purposes. Hardness is essential in abrasives because of the nature of their use. In gemstones, hardness is an asset because the cost of most gems makes it important that their useful lives be extremely long.

Abrasives

Abrasives include a variety of materials, natural and manufactured, that perform one of several functions either in industry or in the home: cleaning, polishing, grinding, cutting, or drilling. Although all lie toward the high end of the Mohs scale (see chapter 7), with respect to one another, they can be further categorized as hard, siliceous, or soft. This subdivision is based, in part, on their natural hardnesses but also, in part, on their compositions and on the form in which they are used. The principal abrasives included in the "hard" category are diamond, corundum, emery, and garnet.

Diamond is the hardest naturally occurring substance (10 on the Mohs scale) and is used in one of three size categories, from largest to smallest: stone, bort, or dust. Because the United States has no diamond deposits that can be exploited under current economic conditions, all natural diamond stone (60% of that consumed in the United States) is imported. The remainder is synthetic diamond. Natural industrial diamonds (those unsuited for gem use because of color or flaws) occur, like the gem variety, in the igneous rock known as kimberlite. Because of the tremendous pressure required to form diamond, this rock is assumed to originate at a depth of several hundred kilometers in Earth and is somehow intruded, perhaps explosively, through Earth's crust in cylindrical masses known as **diamond pipes** or kimberlites, after Kimberley, South Africa (fig. 16.14). Diamond stones are also typically found in placer deposits, either along stream courses or on beaches.

Bort consists of small fragments and, like stone, is used mostly in rock drill bits (approximately 75% of total usage). Diamond dust, used mostly for cutting and polishing gemstones, is formed from crushed synthetic diamonds. The United States manufactures more than enough diamond dust to satisfy its needs.

Corundum, the second hardest naturally occurring substance, and *emery,* a natural mixture of corundum and magnetite, are used mostly on paper or cloth for polishing and finishing or on grinding wheels. In addition, emery is widely used for nonskid surfaces on

Figure 16.14 Cross-sectional view of a South African diamond pipe.

Figure 16.15 Red patches of garnet in dark igneous rock. Barton Mines, North Creek, New York.

stairs and pavements. Corundum occurs in metamorphic rocks, and virtually all is imported into North America, chiefly from South Africa. The largest deposits of emery are found in Turkey, but minor deposits also occur around Peekskill, New York. Both corundum and emery are being replaced in many uses by synthetic alumina (Al_2O_3).

Garnet, primarily the variety almandine, is found in both igneous and metamorphic rocks. It is used mostly for sandblasting (45%); for the finishing of hardwoods, in which its cutting power is several times greater than that of sandpaper; and for cutting marble and slate. The United States possesses the world's greatest reserves of garnet and produces almost 50% of the world's annual supply. The principal garnet deposits currently being exploited are in the Adirondack Mountains near the town of North Creek, New York (fig. 16.15).

Sand and sandstone are examples of siliceous abrasives. Quartz sand is widely used as a sandblasting medium, while sandstone is shaped into grindstones, whetstones, and millstones. In fact, a sandstone unit in England that has been so used for hundreds of years is known as the "Millstone Grits." The use of siliceous rocks and sand for polishing and pulverizing has been replaced to a large extent by steel balls.

Among the soft abrasives are feldspar, fuller's earth, and diatomite. Feldspar, from granite pegmatites, is crushed and used in soaps and as scouring powders. *Fuller's earth,* a variety of clay, is used as a soft polishing medium for metals. *Diatomite,* or *diatomaceous earth,* is an accumulation of the siliceous remains of shell-secreting freshwater and marine algae (diatoms). It is used not only as an abrasive in polishes and toothpaste but as a filtering medium in water and waste treatment plants and as a filler in paints and plastics. The United States possesses the world's most important reserves of diatomite.

Gems

Gemstones, or **gem minerals,** are those natural substances that can be cut and polished to form **gems,** which, in turn, can be set in jewelry. With few exceptions, they possess the special characteristics of hardness (or durability), beauty (color, clarity, etc.), and rarity. (Box 16.5 looks at how gemstones are measured.) Many have been used for adornment for thousands of years. Others have found widespread usage only recently. The great majority of gem minerals have their geologic origin either in pegmatites (emerald) or in metamorphic rocks (ruby). Diamond is a significant exception to this, having formed, as noted earlier, in kimberlites. Because of the inherent hardness of the minerals in this group, many of them are also found as placer accumulations. A few materials, such as *amber* (hardened tree sap) and *pearl* (formed by secretions of oysters within their shells), do not fit the strict definition of a mineral but, because of their widespread use in jewelry, are included here.

Some gem minerals can be manufactured and are thus considered *synthetic gems.* Synthetic rubies are especially important as lasers, and synthetic diamonds and diamond dust are widely used as abrasives. *Simulated gems* are materials (cheaper stones or even glass) that have the appearance of one of the precious gems. Because these are readily available on the market, buyers must exercise caution to avoid confusing them with their more valuable namesakes. Certainly, gems marketed under a trade name, such as "Cape May Diamonds," are not real diamonds but inexpensive imitations (in this case, quartz crystals).

For convenience, gem minerals have long been divided into two basic groups: **precious gems** (diamond, ruby, sapphire, and emerald) and **semiprecious gems** (all others). Such a subdivision, seemingly based on economic value, is not necessarily foolproof. There are exceptions. For example, some specimens of alexandrite (the mineral chrysoberyl) from the Ural Mountains of Russia surpass emeralds in value.

Diamonds are, by far, the most important of the precious stones, accounting for approximately three-quarters of the world's gem trade. Until the eighteenth century, diamonds came

Box 16.5

KARATS AND CARATS

Precious metals and gemstones are dealt with in such small quantities that special units of measurement are necessarily employed. The precious metals are traded in dollars per troy ounce,* with gold being approximately 75 times more valuable than silver, and platinum somewhat more valuable than gold. Current values for the precious metals may be obtained from tables in the financial sections of most daily newspapers. The purity of precious metals, or objects made from them, is indicated in parts per thousand (*fineness*) or, in the case of gold, in number of parts per 24 (*karats*). Sterling silver, for example, has a fineness of 925, being alloyed with 75 parts of copper. Silver coinage, used for many years in the United States, was 900 fine, the other 100 parts being copper.

Gold, because of its inherent softness, is almost always alloyed with silver, platinum, copper, and/or nickel. Most commonly, gold alloys are 12K (12 karat), 14K, 18K, or 21.6K, meaning that they contain 12, 14, 18, and 21.6 parts of gold out of a total of 24, respectively. These alloys equate to fineness values of 500, 585, 750, and 900. Gold coins, when they were still minted by the U.S. government, were 21.6K, or 900 fine.

The *weight* (not parts or percentages) of gemstones is universally measured by the other *carat*. This "metric carat" is equal to 200 milligrams (0.2 g) and, in turn, is divisible into 100 *points*. The term *carat* is thought to derive from the "carob" tree (a member of the locust family), which is native to the Mediterranean region. Carob seeds were used from ancient times as a standard measure for gemstones, because the seeds are remarkably uniform in weight. Even so, there was always some slight variation in the value of the carat, because of the imprecise standard on which it was based. To end this confusion, the metric carat was adopted by France, Italy, and Germany in 1907, by the United States in 1913, and by most other countries by the 1920s.

Apply Your Knowledge

1. Is there any relationship between the carat and the karat?
2. Does the value of a gemstone increase arithmetically or geometrically as the carat size increases? Why?
3. Examine any gold or silver object to which you have access. How is its purity marked? If it is in karats, convert this to fineness, or vice versa.

*1 troy ounce = 31.1 gram = 1.09714 avoirdupois ounce (1/16 of a pound).

---

exclusively from alluvial deposits in Brazil and India. The latter went to the collections of local princes, and in some instances, such as the Hope diamond now in the Smithsonian Institution, became spoils of war. After the discovery of the diamond fields around Kimberly, South Africa, in 1871, that country became the world's leading diamond producer and held that position for many years. Recently, South Africa has been surpassed in output by Australia, Botswana, and Russia.

Ruby and *sapphire* are, respectively, the red and blue clear gem varieties of the mineral corundum. They typically occur in marbles and alluvial deposits formed from them. Large, blood-red rubies are extremely rare and command extraordinarily high prices. Both rubies and sapphires may contain tiny needles of the mineral rutile, which reflect light to give a six-rayed star pattern. These are the highly prized "star rubies" and "star sapphires." The most important production of both of these stones has been from placer deposits in Burma and Sri Lanka.

Emerald is the deep green variety of the mineral beryl. One of the most ancient of stones in terms of its usage, emerald mines were operated in Egypt as early as 1600 B.C. Emeralds occur most commonly in granite pegmatites and in the metamorphosed limestones into which they have been intruded. The most important deposits worked in recent years have been around Muzo, Colombia. Beryl may also be found in a lighter blue-green gem variety known as *aquamarine,* one of the semiprecious gems. The significant characteristics of aquamarine, as well as those of a number of other semiprecious gems, are listed in table 16.4.

FOSSIL FUELS

Coal, oil, and natural gas constitute the **fossil fuels.** These fuels represent solar energy used, stored, and preserved for millions of years in plant and animal tissues. While fossil fuels are not, strictly speaking, minerals because they are of organic origin, they are usually considered along with other earth materials as mineral resources or as mineral fuels. In small ways, humans have used fossil fuels for thousands of years. Such usage has increased enormously since the beginning of the Industrial Revolution in the mid-eighteenth century. Fossil fuels today represent the backbone of industry and the lifeblood of our technological society.

Coal

Coal formed from the accumulated remains of plants that once grew in vast coastal swamps (fig. 16.16). Generations of such plants lived, died, and were preserved in a thickening pile of debris beneath the shallow swamp waters. These waters must have lacked the dissolved oxygen necessary to sustain the chemical and biochemical processes that normally cause dead plant tissue to decay. Accumulations of hydrogen sulfide gas prevented the presence of organisms that consume dead vegetation. A modern analog of such an environment is the Great Dismal Swamp of Virginia and North Carolina.

Over hundreds of thousands of years, the geologic environment changed, with shallow coastal seas flooding the land, destroying the coastal swamps, and allowing for normal marine

TABLE 16.4   The Semiprecious Gems

Name	Origin	Hardness	Chemical Class
Amber	Organic	2–2 1/2	Organic
Apatite	Igneous	5	Phosphate
Beryl (aquamarine)	Igneous and metamorphic	8	Silicate
Chrysoberyl (alexandrite)	Igneous and metamorphic	8 1/2	Oxide
Feldspar (moonstone, amazonite, sunstone)	Igneous	6	Silicate
Garnet	Igneous and metamorphic	7–7 1/2	Silicate
Jadeite (jade)	Metamorphic	6 1/2	Silicate
Lazulite (lapis lazuli)	Metamorphic	5–5 1/2	Silicate
Malachite	Sedimentary	3 1/2–4	Carbonate
Nephrite (jade)	Metamorphic	5–6	Silicate
Opal (hydrous silica)	Sedimentary	5 1/2–6 1/2	Silicate
Pearl	Organic		Organic
Peridot (olivine)	Igneous	6	Silicate
Quartz (agate, jasper, smoky, rock crystal, amethyst, citrine, rose, tigereye)	Igneous and sedimentary	7	Silicate
Spinel	Igneous	8	Oxide
Topaz	Igneous and metamorphic	8	Silicate
Tourmaline	Igneous and metamorphic	7 1/2	Silicate
Turquoise	Sedimentary	4–6	Phosphate
Zircon	Igneous	6 1/2–7	Silicate

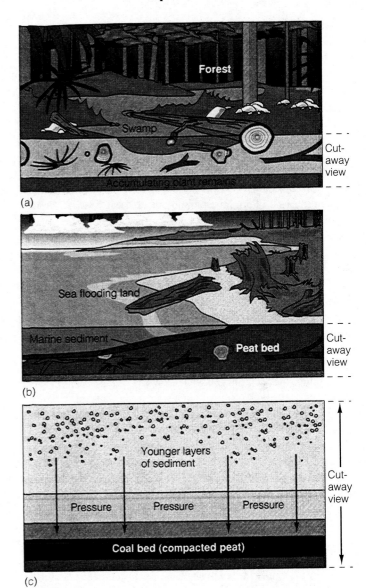

(a)

(b)

(c)

Figure 16.16   Coal formation. (*a*) Plant debris accumulates in the reducing environment of a coastal swamp. (*b*) Rising sea level floods the area and brings normal marine deposition. (*c*) The pressure (weight) of overlying sedimentary layers converts the vegetation to coal.

sedimentation processes. The weight of accumulating thicknesses of sandstones, shales, and limestones compressed and heated the underlying vegetation. The compression of the vegetation squeezed out most of the water and gases, which make up a large proportion of plant tissue, and left the remaining material enriched in carbon and a number of minor solid impurities.

This is a progressive process. As heat and pressure increase, vegetation, with a carbon content of approximately 50%, is converted to *peat* (carbon content, 60%), a substance in which the original vegetable material is still recognizable. Peat is widely used as a soil conditioner, and where better grades of coal are unavailable, it is burned as a fuel. Deeper burial of peat to still higher temperatures and pressures forms first *lignite* (carbon content, 70%), then *subbituminous coal*, and finally *bituminous coal* (carbon content, 80% to 85%). Bituminous, or *soft*, coal, is the common variety in the extensive coalfields of western Pennsylvania, Ohio, West Virginia, Kentucky, and Illinois. Lignite and subbituminous coal are common in the western states of Wyoming and Montana (fig. 16.17).

Increasing carbon content yields higher heat values as measured in British Thermal Units (BTUs). A coal with 28,600 BTUs per kilogram (13,000 BTUs per lb) is theoretically more valuable than one with a lower rating. The burning of coal, however, has an

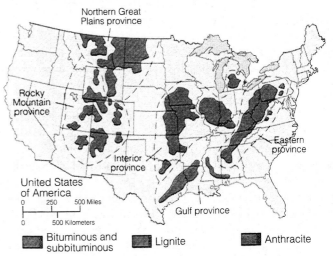

Figure 16.17   Distribution of coal fields and coal types in the United States.

environmental impact that must be taken into consideration. Unfortunately, many of the bituminous coals of the U.S. East and Midwest contain excessive amounts of sulfur and, when burned, yield sulfuric acid, a prime contributor to acid rainfall and other types of pollution. In general, the western coals, although lower in grade, contain less sulfur and occur at shallower depths and in thicker layers. These last two qualities make them exploitable on a large scale and at relatively low cost.

In northeastern Pennsylvania and in a few locations in Virginia, where the coal beds and other sedimentary rock layers have been subjected by continental collision to the additional pressures of intense folding, the bituminous coal has been metamorphosed to *anthracite (hard)* coal, with a carbon content of approximately 95% (fig. 16.18). Additional stress caused by very deep burial and/or intense folding would, presumably, lead to formation of the mineral graphite (pure carbon).

Even though coal formation is directly related to the growth of plants (a renewable resource), the quantity of plant material and the time involved make coal a nonrenewable resource. It requires an estimated 330 years of plant growth to form a 1-meter (3.3-ft) thick layer of peat and an estimated compression of 30 meters (100 ft) of peat to form a 1-meter (3.3-ft) layer of soft coal. Thus, a meter of soft coal requires the accumulated plant growth of almost 10,000 years. To form a 3-meter (10-ft) coal seam such as the Pittsburgh coal, a major economic resource in Pennsylvania, West Virginia, and Ohio, would require the accumulated plant growth of 30,000 years.

Although nonrenewable, coal still represents an abundant resource in the United States, as well as in many other parts of the world. Its distribution, however, is not uniform. Some 95% of the world's coal reserves lie in Asia, North America, and Europe. Little is found in the Southern Hemisphere, but two such occurrences are rather interesting. South Africa, a country poor in oil but rich in coal, has for many years chemically converted enough coal to petroleum to satisfy most of its oil requirements. Antarctica, a continent almost totally buried beneath an ice sheet thousands of meters thick, possesses coal deposits, indicating a far warmer climate at various times in the geologic past and providing one line of evidence for the idea that continental positions are not fixed but have changed.

The United States could be self-sufficient in its coal production and usage. Most coal produced today is burned in power plants to generate electricity (more than 50%) or, in the form of coke with its upgraded carbon content, burned in blast furnaces to produce iron and steel. Minor amounts of coal are still used for the direct heating of homes and for a variety of industrial purposes.

A number of environmental problems, besides that of acid rainfall, are traceable to the mining and burning of coal. **Strip mining,** the common method by which shallow coals are removed from the ground, requires excavation of the soil and overlying rock layers, or **overburden,** to expose the coal. This procedure destroys the vegetation cover, retards soil development, and disrupts groundwater flow. Soil erosion and stream siltation become significant problems unless great care is taken both during the mining activity and land reclamation. While the coal industry has made great strides in reclamation in recent years under the impetus of new federal and state laws, many parts of the old coal-mining regions of the U.S. East and Midwest still bear the scars of careless strip mining,

Figure 16.18 Location and geological setting of the Pennsylvania coal fields. High pressures associated with folding have converted bituminous coal to anthracite in the folded Appalachians.

Figure 16.19 Regraded and reclaimed area in eastern Ohio that was once stripped for coal.

Figure 16.20 Mine refuse, or "gob," pile in eastern Ohio.

as well as piles of waste rock from both surface and underground mines (figs. 16.19 and 16.20). New technologies for separating coal included in these waste dumps have made reclamation feasible. Screening and washing the waste rock in a water to which a special mud has been added allows the coal to float and separate from the waste in response to density differences.

The mineral pyrite (FeS_2), found both in the coals and in shale beds associated with the coals, is converted to sulfuric acid upon exposure to oxygen and water in the atmosphere and carried into the local stream drainage network. This condition, known as **acid mine drainage,** is a problem associated with both surface and deep coal mining. In addition to the acid, the iron present in the pyrite is oxidized and becomes a stream pollutant, coloring the water red, giving the water a disagreeable taste, and inhibiting plant and animal life.

Subsidence, an environmental problem specifically related to underground mining, was discussed as a form of mass wasting in chapter 10. An additional environmental problem, especially in the older coal-mining regions, is fire. Both the underground mines and the surface piles of waste rock that came from them are susceptible to catching fire either by lightning strikes or human carelessness. Mine fires can be most hazardous, and in extreme cases, they have led to the abandonment of buildings or even towns situated above the burning mine or adjacent to the burning spoil bank.

Petroleum

The other major fossil fuel is **petroleum.** While not a sedimentary rock in the sense that coal is, petroleum is found almost exclusively *in* sedimentary rocks. Petroleum is a complex mixture of hundreds of chemical compounds representing all three states of matter: solid (*asphalt* or *bitumen*), liquid (**oil**), and gas (**natural gas**). With the exception of some contaminants, these materials are all **hydrocarbon compounds**—that is, compounds composed predominantly of hydrogen and carbon.

The hydrocarbons are believed to represent the altered remains of microscopic organisms that lived in the seas. When the organisms died, their remains settled to the sea bottom, where they escaped complete decay and became incorporated into the accumulating sediment. With time, heat, and pressure, these remains

were converted to hydrocarbons, which were squeezed out of the rock layer, or **source rock** (usually shale), in which they originated to begin a slow migration upward through the surrounding rocks. As long as these rocks were permeable, the hydrocarbons continued to move. Eventually, however, they came up against impermeable rock that prevented further migration. The hydrocarbons then accumulated in environments that petroleum geologists refer to as **traps,** awaiting only the enterprising geologist (and driller) to discover their presence. Figure 16.21 shows some of the common petroleum traps, the geological origins of which have been considered in earlier chapters. The rock layer within which the petroleum eventually collects is called the **reservoir rock** and is most often a sandstone or a limestone.

Oil and natural gas (and the two almost always occur together) within the pore spaces of a rock layer thousands of meters deep are under extremely high pressure. When the reservoir rock is penetrated by a drill, it is very much like sticking a pin in an inflated balloon. The pressure difference between reservoir rock and ground surface causes oil and gas to rush up the borehole toward Earth's surface. If uncontrolled, the uprushing oil and gas may reach and destroy the drilling platform at the surface. This condition is known as a *blowout,* and modern drilling methods anticipate and prepare to counteract this. Under controlled conditions, then, oil and gas may flow all the way to the surface, where they are led through a series of valves into collecting lines and holding

Figure 16.21 Principal types of petroleum traps. (*a*) Fault. (*b*) Anticline. (*c*) Salt dome. (*d*) Stratigraphic, or "pinchout."

tanks. If oil in the reservoir rock is under less pressure, it may need to be brought to the surface by pumping.

Normally, 80% to 85% of the oil in the reservoir rock remains in place and does not flow or cannot be pumped to the surface. A number of ingenious methods, collectively called **enhanced recovery techniques,** have been devised to recover additional amounts of this oil. In one widely used and highly successful technique—the *waterflood*—water is pumped under pressure down a well bore and into the reservoir rock (fig. 16.22a). The hope is that this water will push some of the oil ahead of it to another well, from which the oil can be pumped. *Gas injection* techniques employing natural gas, carbon dioxide, or nitrogen can achieve the same result. In fact, natural gas that is normally produced with the oil can be separated and pumped back into the reservoir rock to force out additional oil. Other procedures attempt to make the oil more fluid and, therefore, more mobile, by heating it. This is accomplished by injecting steam into the reservoir (fig. 16.22b) or by igniting some of the oil in the reservoir, causing it to burn and heat the remaining oil. Newer methods, mostly still in the experimental or pilot stage, involve the use of chemical solvents to dissolve and remove the oil from the reservoir (fig. 16.22c).

While petroleum and natural gas have familiar uses in transportation, heating, and electric power generation, they also form the basis of the petrochemical industry and, as such, are the raw materials from which thousands of widely used products are manufactured. These products include plastics, medicines, fertilizers, explosives, synthetic fabrics (rayon, nylon, etc.), rubber, teflon, alcohol, antifreeze, and a host of others.

Most of the world's known reserves of petroleum lie in the Middle East (Saudi Arabia, Kuwait, Iran, and Iraq). The U.S. position with respect to these liquid fuels is less than desirable, but enormous deposits of hydrocarbon-rich rocks do lie beneath southwestern Wyoming, northeastern Utah, and northwestern Colorado. These are the so-called **oil shales** (fig. 16.23).

Figure 16.22 Enhanced oil recovery techniques. (*a*) Waterflood. (*b*) Steam injection. (*c*) Chemical solvents.

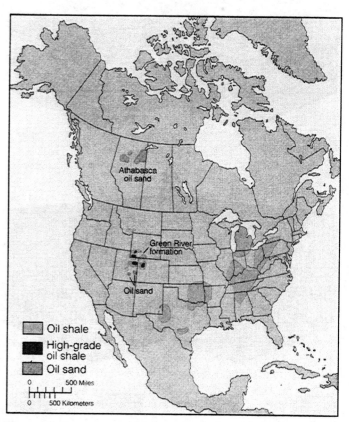

Figure 16.23 Oil shale and tar sand deposits in North America.

Although the potential for oil shale usage is enormous, the developers of these deposits will not only have to overcome problems of technology and economics but also those of a social and environmental nature. Several methods of exploiting the oil shales have been considered. Most likely, they would be mined by conventional strip (where overburden is not too thick) or deep mining techniques and the organic compounds converted to hydrocarbons by some type of retorting (heating) process. A difficulty with this approach is that the removal of the hydrocarbons leaves a pulverized waste rock that actually occupies a greater volume than the original mined rock. Thus, a significant waste disposal problem would exist. Processing of the oil shales would require a large quantity of water, which is not readily available in a semiarid region. Such water usage would have to compete with ranching and irrigated farming. Lastly, the infrastructure of this region would have to be developed and social problems related to housing, schools, and services for growing communities in an area of very low population density would have to be solved. Current economic conditions do not allow for the development of oil shale resources beyond the pilot feasibility stage. Whenever economic and social pressures outweigh the obvious environmental concerns about mining oil shale, the United States may resort to the exploitation of this valuable oil reserve.

A similar nonliquid petroleum resource is found in abundance along the Athabasca River in the Canadian province of Alberta. These are **tar sands,** sandstones impregnated with solid asphaltic hydrocarbons. These deposits have already been exploited for a number of years by strip mining. The mined rock is transported by an extensive system of conveyor belts to a processing plant, where the petroleum is separated from the rock, liquified, and sent by pipeline to conventional oil refineries around the city of Edmonton.

FURTHER THOUGHTS: CONSERVE, SO THAT ALL CAN SHARE

Earth, during its formation and throughout its history, was blessed with abundant resources. Largely untapped until recent years, these resources now are being consumed at varying, but generally very high, rates. In but the rarest of cases, nature cannot replace them. As world population increases and as developing countries attempt to reach the level of development enjoyed by the United States, Canada, and western Europe, these resources are being stretched perilously thin. Whether such development can ultimately extend to all of the peoples of the world is doubtful. What is certain is that we must be far more careful stewards of nature's gifts than we have been in the past. We must be less wasteful of what we use, and leave uncontaminated what we do not need. Care of the planet's resources can ensure an adequate supply of resources for future generations.

SIGNIFICANT POINTS

1. A natural resource is anything taken from Earth to support life or a way of life. Nonrenewable resources form over long periods of time and are present in finite quantities.

2. The most significant problem with fresh water is that it is not necessarily available where and when we need it.

3. A soil is that portion of the loose surface material that is capable of supporting plants with root systems. It evolves by weathering over thousands of years and typically consists of several distinct layers, known as horizons.

4. Of the factors that lead to soil development (time, parent material, topography, climate, and organisms), climate (temperature and rainfall) is the most important.

5. Metals, those elements characterized by the properties of malleability, ductility, conductivity, and the tendency to form positive ions are normally classified on the basis of their relative abundance.

6. The principal ore mineral of aluminum is bauxite, a tropical weathering product, that is mined from large, shallow, open-pit mines.

7. The most important iron ores are banded iron formations (BIF), or taconite, and are typified by those mined in the Lake Superior region. They consist of the oxides hematite and magnetite, mixed with quartz-rich rock.

8. The metal copper is widely used in the electrical, plumbing, and transportation industries.

9. Gold, diamonds, and other heavy, resistant minerals are found along stream channels and beaches in secondary sedimentary deposits known as placers.

10. Because the industrial minerals are all abundant in nature, they are classified by use, rather than by abundance.

11. Halite and sylvite, examples of industrial minerals, are classified as evaporites because they were precipitated from marine waters as those waters underwent evaporation.

12. Potassium (potash), phosphorus, and nitrogen are three elements necessary for plant growth that must be returned to the soil in the form of inorganic fertilizers.

13. Because a use can be found for virtually every type of rock and mineral, building products represent the largest volume production of all the natural resources.

14. Abrasives are characteristically hard minerals and are used for cleaning, cutting, grinding, polishing, and drilling.

15. Gems are natural substances that can be cut and polished and that are highly prized for their beauty, durability, and rarity.

16. Fossil fuels (coal, oil, and natural gas) are burned to provide heat and energy.

17. Coal formed from the compression of plant material that once grew in coastal swamps.

18. Petroleum is a complex mixture of hydrocarbon compounds formed from the organic remains of microorganisms that once lived in the seas. After being squeezed out of its source rock, it migrates through permeable rock strata until it is trapped in a reservoir rock by an impermeable rock barrier.

19. The oil shales of the western United States represent an important future petroleum resource if economic, technological, and environmental problems can be overcome.

20. The tar sands of northwestern Canada have been mined and processed for their petroleum content for a number of years.

ESSENTIAL TERMS

natural resource *367*
renewable resource *367*
nonrenewable resource *367*
reserve *367*
desalinization *368*
soil *368*
horizon *370*
soil profile *370*
O-horizon *370*
A-horizon *370*
leaching *370*

humus *370*
topsoil *370*
B-horizon *371*
subsoil *371*
subsoil profile *371*
zone of leaching *371*
zone of accumulation *371*
C-horizon *371*
parent material *371*
pedalfer *372*
pedocal *372*
laterites *372*

metal *372*
abundant metal *372*
rare metal *372*
ore mineral *372*
banded iron formation (BIF) *373*
alloy *375*
ferroalloy *375*
vein *376*
placer deposit *376*
salt dome *378*
fertilizer *380*
refractory *380*

dimension stone *381*
cement *381*
abrasive *382*
diamond pipe *382*
gemstone (gem mineral) *383*
gem *383*
precious gem *383*
semiprecious gem *383*
fossil fuel *384*
coal *384*
strip mining *386*
overburden *386*

acid mine drainage *386*
petroleum *387*
oil *387*
natural gas *387*
hydrocarbon compound *387*
source rock *387*
trap *387*
reservoir rock *387*
enhanced recovery technique *388*
oil shale *388*
tar sands *389*

REVIEW QUESTIONS

1. What features characterize all of the nonrenewable resources?
2. What type of usage is the largest consumer of fresh water?
3. What is the riparian doctrine of water usage? What is the prior appropriation doctrine of water usage?
4. What are the two fundamental soil types in the United States? What are their essential characteristics? How do they differ from one another? How do they relate to climate?
5. What are the soils of the humid tropics? How do they differ from those of the United States and Canada?
6. What is an ore mineral?
7. What scrap metals are commonly recycled?
8. Name the important ferroalloys. What is the principal use of each?
9. What is the principal ore mineral of copper? What is its geologic origin? Where are some important geographic occurrences?
10. Where and why do placer deposits typically form?

11. Describe the two common occurrences of the evaporite mineral halite.
12. What three essential plant nutrients are usually obtained from inorganic fertilizers?
13. What are the most commonly used dimension stones?
14. What are the most common uses of crushed rock and sand and gravel?
15. How do prepared rock products differ from natural rock products?
16. What is the most important physical characteristic of an abrasive mineral?
17. What are gemstones? What are the principal categories of gemstones? Give some examples.
18. What are some of the environmental problems associated with the mining and burning of coal?
19. What are some of the enhanced recovery techniques for petroleum?

CHALLENGES

1. Make a survey of your town and its environs to ascertain what metal processing plants, if any, exist there. (Hint: you might start by consulting the telephone directory.) You could pursue this further by talking with plant officials to determine where the raw materials (ore, fuel, etc.) come from.
2. Are there any mining operations near where you live? If so, investigate how the mining is done and what measures are taken to protect the environment. Do these measures meet the standards specified by federal, state (or provincial), and local laws?
3. Investigate any abandoned mining operations to determine whether they still pose a hazard to the environment and in what ways. If they still do, why has nothing been done about them?

4. What are some observable characteristics of the soil in your area? Can you identify its type from those characteristics? If you live in an agricultural region, ask the farmers what treatments are necessary to maintain the soil's fertility.
5. Is oil or natural gas produced near where you live? If so, consult with local geologists, petroleum engineers, or oil-field workers to compile a report that includes information about the reservoir rock, type of trap, amount of production, and any enhanced recovery techniques employed.
6. Pick a metal, and compile a report that deals with its geologic origin, mining, processing, and final manufactured products. Pay particular attention to the geography of where all of this occurs and what role the metal plays in the world economy.

Appendices

Figure A.1

Brooks and Roberts Modified
Van der Grinten Projection

A weather scientist or forecaster depends upon a number of important charts and maps to analyze the development and movement of weather systems. Such maps and charts display conditions at various levels of the atmosphere and cover areas as small as the local region to as large as the entire hemisphere. Included among these tools are analysis charts, prognosis charts, satellite imagery, upper-air charts, and extended forecast charts. The information for the maps and charts is collected by observers at approximately 500 National Weather Service offices located throughout the United States. Many of the offices use the Automated Surface Observation System (ASOS) to collect the data. The data are then converted to maps, charts, and text and distributed to the users, by wire, in a timely fashion by the National Weather Service.

The National Weather Service product that is most familiar to the general public is the Surface Analysis Chart, or "weather map." The many printed forms of this map range from the simplified version found in the daily newspaper to the Official Weather Map. Perhaps the map's greatest dissemination occurs through local and national television weather programs. Often, the focus of attention is the surface weather map used by the presenter to explain current weather patterns or to predict future weather conditions.

Codes and Map Plotting

For economy of space and speed of transmission, codes have been devised for sending the information and for plotting it on maps. A great deal of information is contained in a brief, coded weather message. If each item were named and described in plain language, a very lengthy message would be required, and the information would be confusing to read and difficult to transfer to a map. Use of a code permits the message to be condensed to a few five-figure numeral groups, each figure of which has a meaning, depending on its position in the message. Persons trained in the use of the code can read the message as easily as plain language.

The location of the reporting station is printed on the map as a small circle (the station circle). The data are placed around the station circle, in an arrangement called the station model (fig. B.1). When the report is plotted in these fixed positions around the station circle on the weather map, many of the code figures are transcribed exactly as sent. Noncoded entries may be actual values, or they may be symbols that graphically represent the element concerned. In some cases, certain of the data may or may not be reported by the observer, depending on local weather conditions. Precipitation and clouds are examples. In such cases, the absence of an entry on the map is interpreted as nonoccurrence or nonobservance of the phenomena.

The station model is based on international agreements. Through such standardized use of numerals and symbols, a meteorologist of one country can use the weather reports and weather maps of another country, even though he or she does not understand the language. Weather codes are, in effect, an international language, making possible complete interchange and use of worldwide weather reports.

An explanation of the symbols, with remarks on map entries, appears in figure B.2.

Many of the elements in the plotting model are entered in values that can be interpreted directly; however, some require reference to code tables. These tables are shown in figures B.3 to B.8.*

* Text exerpted from L. Moses and John Tomikel, *Basic Meteorology, An Introduction to the Science.* Copyright © 1981 Allegheny Press. Used by permission.

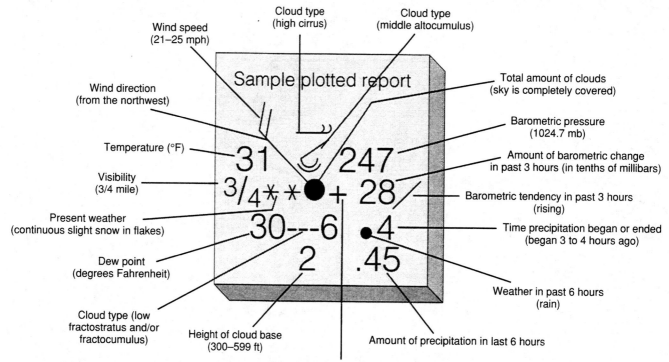

Figure B.1 Sample plotted report for a set of observations made at a single weather observing station.

Figure B.2 (Source for figures B.2 through B.8: Adapted from *World Meteorological Organization Code*.)

Cloud abbreviation	C_L		Description (abridged from W.M.O. Code)
St or Fs-Stratus or Fractostratus	1		Cu of fair weather, little vertical development and seemingly flattened
Ci-Cirrus	2		Cu of considerable development, generally towering, with or without other Cu or Sc bases all at same level
Cs-Cirrostratus	3		Cb with tops lacking clear-cut outlines, but distinctly not cirriform or anvil-shaped; with or without Cu, Sc, or St
Cc-Cirrocumulus	4		Sc formed by spreading out of Cu; Cu often present also
Ac-Altocumulus			
As-Altostratus	5		Sc not formed by spreading out of Cu
Sc-Stratocumulus	6		St or Fs or both, but no Fs of bad weather
Ns-Nimbostratus	7	- - -	Fs and/or Fc of bad weather (scud)
Cu or Fc-Cumulus or Fractocumulus	8		Cu and Sc (not formed by spreading out of Cu) with bases at different levels
Cb-Cumulonimbus	9		Cb having a clearly fibrous (cirriform) top, often anvil-shaped, with or without Cu, Sc, St, or scud

	C_M	Description (abridged from W.M.O. Code)		C_H	Description (abridged from W.M.O. Code)
1		Thin As (most of cloud layer semi-transparent)	1		Filaments of Ci, or "mares tails," scattered and not increasing
2		Thick As, greater part sufficiently dense to hide sun (or moon), or Ns	2		Dense Ci in patches or twisted sheaves, usually not increasing, sometimes like remains of Cb; or towers or tufts
3		Thin Ac, mostly semi-transparent; cloud elements not changing much and at a single level	3		Dense Ci, often anvil-shaped, derived from or associated with Cb
4		Thin Ac in patches; cloud elements continually changing and/or occurring at more than one level	4		Ci, often hook-shaped, gradually spreading over the sky and usually thickening as a whole
5		Thin Ac in bands or in a layer gradually spreading over sky and usually thickening as a whole	5		Ci and Cs, often in converging bands, or Cs alone; generally overspreading and growing denser; the continuous layer not reaching 45° altitude
6		Ac formed by the spreading out of Cu	6		Same as 5, but the continuous layer not exceeding 45° altitude
7		Double-layered Ac, or a thick layer of Ac, not increasing; or Ac with As and/or Ns	7		Veil of Cs covering the entire sky
8		Ac in the form of Cu-shaped tufts or Ac with turrets	8		Cs not increasing and not covering entire sky
9		Ac of a chaotic sky, usually at different levels; patches of dense Ci are usually present also	9		Cc alone or Cc with some Ci or Cs, but the Cc being the main cirriform cloud

Appendix   395

h	Height in feet (rounded off)	Height in meters (approximate)
0	0 - 149	0 - 49
1	150 - 299	50 - 99
2	300 - 599	100 - 199
3	600 - 999	200 - 299
4	1,000 - 1,999	300 - 599
5	2,000 - 3,499	600 - 999
6	3,500 - 4,999	1,000 - 1,499
7	5,000 - 6,499	1,500 - 1,999
8	6,500 - 7,999	2,000 - 2,499
9	At or above 8,000, or no clouds	At or above 2,500, or no clouds

Figure B.3

N	Sky coverage (total amount)
	No clouds
	Less than one-tenth or one-tenth
	Two-tenths or three-tenths
	Four-tenths
	Five-tenths
	Six-tenths
	Seven-tenths or eight-tenths
	Nine-tenths or overcast with openings
	Completely overcast
	Sky obscured

Figure B.4

N_h	Sky coverage (low and/or middle clouds)
0	No clouds
1	Less than one-tenth or one-tenth
2	Two-tenths or three-tenths
3	Four-tenths
4	Five-tenths
5	Six-tenths
6	Seven-tenths or eight-tenths
7	Nine-tenths or overcast with openings
8	Completely overcast
9	Sky obscured

Figure B.5

WW Present weather (descriptions abridged from W. M. O. Code)

	0	1	2	3	4
00	Cloud development NOT observed or NOT observable during past hour	Clouds generally dissolving or becoming less developed during past hour	State of sky on the whole unchanged during past hour	Clouds generally forming or developing during past hour	Visibility reduced by smoke
10	Light fog	Patches of shallow fog at station, NOT deeper than six feet on land	More or less continuous shallow fog at station, NOT deeper than six feet on land	Lightning visible, no thunder heard	Precipitation within sight, but NOT reaching the ground
20	Drizzle (NOT freezing and NOT falling as showers) during past hour, but NOT at time of observation	Rain (NOT freezing and NOT falling as showers) during past hour, but NOT at time of observation	Snow (NOT falling as showers) during past hour, but NOT at time of observation	Rain and snow (NOT falling as showers) during past hour, but NOT at time of observation	Freezing drizzle or freezing rain (NOT falling as showers) during past hour, but NOT at time of observation
30	Slight or moderate dust storm or sandstorm, has decreased during past hour	Slight or moderate dust storm or sandstorm, no appreciable change during past hour	Slight or moderate dust storm or sandstorm, has increased during past hour	Severe dust storm or sandstorm, has decreased during past hour	Severe dust storm or sandstorm, no appreciable change during past hour
40	Fog at distance at time of observation, but NOT at station during past hour	Fog in patches	Fog, sky discernible, has become thinner during past hour	Fog, sky NOT discernible, has become thinner during past hour	Fog, sky discernible, no appreciable change during past hour
50	Intermittent drizzle (NOT freezing) slight at time of observation	Continuous drizzle (NOT freezing) slight at time of observation	Intermittent drizzle (NOT freezing) moderate at time of observation	Continuous drizzle (NOT freezing), moderate at time of observation	Intermittent drizzle (NOT freezing) thick at time of observation
60	Intermittent rain (NOT freezing), slight at time of observation	Continuous rain (NOT freezing), slight at time of observation	Intermittent rain (NOT freezing), moderate at time of observation	Continuous rain (NOT freezing), moderate at time of observation	Intermittent rain (NOT freezing), heavy at time of observation
70	Intermittent fall of snowflakes, slight at time of observation	Continuous fall of snowflakes, slight at time of observation	Intermittent fall of snowflakes, moderate at time of observation	Continuous fall of snowflakes, moderate at time of observation	Intermittent fall of snowflakes, heavy at time of observation
80	Slight rain shower(s)	Moderate or heavy rain shower(s)	Violent rain shower(s)	Slight shower(s) of rain and snow mixed	Moderate or heavy shower(s) of rain and snow mixed
90	Moderate or heavy shower(s) of hail, with or without rain or rain and snow mixed, not associated with thunder	Slight rain at time of observation, thunderstorm during past hour, but NOT at time of observation	Moderate or heavy rain at time of observation, thunderstorm during past hour, but NOT at time of observation	Slight snow or rain and snow mixed or hail at time of observation: thunderstorm during past hour, but NOT at time of observation	Moderate or heavy snow, or rain and snow mixed or hail at time of observation, thunderstorm during past hour, but NOT at time of observation

Figure B.6-1

WW Present weather (descriptions abridged from W. M. O. Code)

	5	6	7	8	9
00	Haze	Widespread dust in suspension in the air, NOT raised by wind, at time of observation	Dust or sand raised by wind, at time of observation	Well developed dust devil(s) within past hour	Dust storm or sandstorm within sight of or at station during past hour
10	Precipitation within sight, reaching the ground, but distant from station	Precipitation within sight, reaching the ground, near to, but NOT at station	Thunder heard, but no precipitation at station	Squalls within sight during past hour	Funnel cloud(s) within sight during past hour
20	Showers of rain during past hour, but NOT at time of observation	Showers of snow, or of rain and snow, during past hour, but NOT at time of observation	Showers of hail, or of hail and rain, during past hour, but NOT at time of observation	Fog during past hour, but NOT at time of observation	Thunderstorm (with or without precipitation) during past hour, but NOT at time of observation
30	Severe dust storm or sandstorm, has increased during past hour	Slight or moderate drifting snow, generally low	Heavy drifting snow, generally low	Slight or moderate drifting snow, generally high	Heavy drifting snow, generally high
40	Fog, sky NOT discernible, no appreciable change during past hour	Fog, sky discernible, has begun or become thicker during past hour	Fog, sky NOT discernible, has begun or become thicker during past hour	Fog, depositing rime, sky discernible	Fog, depositing rime, sky NOT discernible
50	Continuous drizzle (NOT freezing), thick at time of observation	Slight freezing drizzle	Moderate or thick freezing drizzle	Drizzle and rain, slight	Drizzle and rain, moderate or heavy
60	Continuous rain (NOT freezing), heavy at time of observation	Slight freezing rain	Moderate or heavy freezing rain	Rain or drizzle and snow, slight	Rain or drizzle and snow, moderate or heavy
70	Continuous fall of snowflakes, heavy at time of observation	Ice needles (with or without fog)	Granular snow (with or without fog)	Isolated starlike snow crystals (with or without fog)	Ice pellets (sleet, U.S. definition)
80	Slight snow shower(s)	Moderate or heavy snow shower(s)	Slight shower(s) of soft or small hail with or without rain, or rain and snow mixed	Moderate or heavy shower(s) of soft or small hail with or without rain, or rain and snow mixed	Slight shower(s) of hail, with or without rain, or rain and snow mixed, not associated with thunder
90	Slight or moderate thunderstorm without hail, but with rain and/or snow at time of observation	Slight or moderate thunderstorm, with hail at time of observation	Heavy thunderstorm, without hail, but with rain and/or snow at time of observation	Thunderstorm combined with dust storm or sandstorm at time of observation	Heavy thunderstorm with hail at time of observation

Figure B.6-2 *(Continued)*

ff	Miles (statute) per hour	Knots
Calm	Calm	Calm
	1 - 2	1 - 2
	3 - 8	3 - 7
	9 - 14	8 - 12
	15 - 20	13 - 17
	21 - 25	18 - 22
	26 - 31	23 - 27
	32 - 37	28 - 32
	38 - 43	33 - 37
	44 - 49	38 - 42
	50 - 54	43 - 47
	55 - 60	48 - 52
	61 - 66	53 - 57
	67 - 71	58 - 62
	72 - 77	63 - 67
	78 - 83	68 - 72
	84 - 89	73 - 77
	119 - 123	103 - 107

Figure B.7

Code number	a	Barometric tendency
0		Rising, then falling
1		Rising, then steady; or rising, then rising more slowly
2		Rising steadily, or unsteadily
3		Falling or steady, then rising; or rising, then rising more quickly
		Barometer now higher than three hours ago
4		Steady, same as three hours ago
5		Falling, then rising, same or lower than three hours ago
6		Falling, then steady; or falling, then falling more slowly
7		Falling steadily, or unsteadily
		Barometer now lower than three hours ago
8		Steady or rising, then falling; or falling, then falling more quickly

Code number	W	Past weather
0		Clear or few clouds
1		Partly cloudy (scattered) or variable sky
2		Cloudy (broken) or overcast
		Not plotted
3		Sandstorm or duststorm, or drifting or blowing snow
4		Fog, or smoke, or thick dust haze
5	,	Drizzle
6	•	Rain
7	*	Snow, or rain and snow mixed, or ice pellets (sleet)
8	▽	Shower(s)
9		Thunderstorm, with or without precipitation

Figure B.8

TABLE 2.1 Climate Data for Selected Stations

Stations		Jan	Feb	Mar	Apr	May	June	July	Aug	Sept	Oct	Nov	Dec	Yea
1. Belém, Brazil	T	78.1	77.9	77.7	78.3	78.8	78.8	78.6	78.8	78.8	79.2	79.7	79.3	78.6
	P	12.52	16.02	17.17	15.04	10.43	6.50	6.34	4.57	4.72	4.13	3.54	7.76	108.7
2. Darwin, Australia	T	83.6	83.4	83.6	83.9	81.4	78.5	77.2	79.1	82.5	84.9	85.7	85.0	82.4
	P	16.18	12.37	11.18	3.08	.33	.09	.01	.02	.60	1.93	4.32	8.57	58.6
3. Darjeeling, India	T	40	42	50	56	58	60	62	61	59	55	48	42	53
	P	.8	1.1	2.0	4.1	7.8	24.2	31.7	26.0	18.3	5.3	.2	.2	121.7
4. Tripoli, Libya	T	53.4	55.9	59.4	64.6	69.1	74.8	78.1	79.3	77.9	72.3	64.8	56.3	67.1
	P	3.03	1.66	.97	.38	.20	.06	.02	.03	.39	1.42	2.66	3.76	14.5
5. Eucla, Australia	T	70.4	70.7	69.3	65.6	60.7	55.9	54.4	56.0	59.0	62.5	65.5	68.5	63.2
	P	0.73	0.78	1.18	1.09	1.13	1.10	0.89	1.05	0.51	0.73	0.70	0.66	10.5
6. Touggourt, Algeria	T	50.5	54.6	61.1	68.8	76.9	86.7	92.0	90.1	83.6	71.7	60.1	51.5	70.6
	P	.24	.24	.35	.12	.16	.04	.04	.04	.08	.20	.43	.24	2.2
7. Norfolk, Virginia	T	42.1	41.8	48.2	56.8	66.5	74.4	78.6	77.3	71.8	61.8	51.3	42.9	59.4
	P	3.2	3.5	4.0	3.4	3.9	4.2	5.8	5.5	3.7	3.4	2.5	3.4	46.4
8. Dublin, Ireland	T	40	41	42	45	49	55	58	57	54	48	44	47	48
	P	2.2	1.9	1.9	1.9	2.1	2.0	2.6	3.1	2.0	2.6	2.9	2.5	27.7
9. Santa Ines, Chile	T	51	51	50	48	45	43	42	42	43	45	47	49	46
	P	6.80	5.76	6.67	7.12	7.52	7.29	7.70	6.58	5.42	6.31	6.42	6.73	80.3.
10. Casablanca, Morocco	T	54.0	54.9	57.7	60.4	63.7	68.7	72.5	73.6	71.4	67.3	61.0	56.3	63.5
	P	1.97	1.89	1.93	1.54	.79	.24	.01	.03	.24	1.57	2.56	2.87	15.6
11. Capetown, Union of South Africa	T	70.7	71.1	68.9	64.6	59.5	56.7	55.2	56.7	58.5	62.4	66.4	68.7	63.1
	P	.67	.59	.87	1.93	3.70	4.29	3.70	3.27	2.28	1.57	1.02	.79	24.68
12. Wuhan, China	T	39	40	49	61	71	78	84	83	76	65	54	43	62
	P	2.1	1.1	2.8	4.8	5.0	7.0	8.6	4.6	2.2	3.9	1.1	.6	43.8
13. Addis Ababa, Ethiopia	T	60.8	62.8	64.6	63.9	64.8	61.9	59.7	59.4	60.3	60.3	59.5	59.5	61.3
	P	0.5	1.5	2.6	3.4	3.4	5.4	11.0	11.8	7.5	0.8	0.6	0.2	48.7
14. Chicago, Illinois	T	25.6	27.0	26.8	47.4	58.4	68.1	74.0	72.9	66.3	54.8	41.5	30.3	50.2
	P	2.1	2.1	2.6	2.9	3.6	3.3	3.4	3.0	3.1	2.6	2.4	2.1	33.2
15. Helsinki, Finland	T	22	21	25	35	46	56	62	61	53	43	35	28	41
	P	2.2	1.7	1.4	1.7	1.6	2.0	2.7	2.8	2.8	2.9	2.7	2.6	27.0
16. Norman, Canada	T	−19	−13	−2	19	41	54	59	54	41	24	−1	−15	20
	P	.4	.5	.6	.5	1.1	1.3	1.8	1.9	1.0	.8	.4	.4	10.7
17. Peking (Beijing), China	T	24	29	41	57	68	76	79	77	68	55	39	27	53
	P	.1	.2	.2	.6	1.4	3.0	9.4	6.3	2.6	.6	.3	.1	24.8
18. Pavlolar, Russia	T	0	1	13	36	55	66	71	66	54	37	19	5	35
	P	.4	.4	.6	.4	.7	1.7	1.7	1.9	.9	.8	.8	.6	10.0
19. Irkutsk, Russia	T	−5	1	17	35	48	59	65	60	48	33	13	1	31
	P	.6	.5	.4	.6	1.2	2.3	2.9	2.4	1.6	.7	.6	.8	14.6
20. Selagoncy, Russia	T	−42	−33	−14	11	33	54	59	51	37	13	−23	−38	9
	P	.3	.2	.3	.4	.9	1.4	2.0	2.4	.9	.9	.6	.5	10.9
21. Upernivik, Greenland	T	−8	−9	−6	6	25	35	41	41	33	25	14	1	17
	P	.4	.5	.7	.6	.6	.5	.9	1.1	1.1	1.1	1.1	.5	9
22. Ice Cap, Greenland	T	−41.8	−41.8	−31	−18.4	8.6	28.4	30.2	26.6	8.6	−11.2	−27.4	−36.4	−8.9
	P						NO DATA							

T = Temperature (° F)
P = Precipitation (in)

The World

Figure C.1   Numbers on the map show the location of the stations represented in Appendix C. (Source: Data from L.L. Moses, *Climatology Lab Manual*, copyright © 1979 Allegheny Press.)

Most of the heavens' brightest stars down to magnitude 4 are shown in figure D.1a–D.1c. The two polar charts (fig. D.1a and D.1b) include those portions of the celestial sphere that lie between 40° and 90° north and south declination. The equatorial-ecliptic chart (fig. D.1c) includes that portion of the celestial sphere between 40° north and 40° south declination. Right ascension is given on the horizontal axes of the equatorial-ecliptic chart and on the circumferences of the polar charts. The celestial equator horizontally bisects the equatorial-ecliptic chart, and the ecliptic circle makes an S-shaped curve about the celestial equator.

The positions and the magnitudes of the stars are indicated by a number from −1 to 4. All stars of magnitude 1 or greater are named on the charts. Some other stars of significance are also named (e.g., Polaris, Algol). Constellations are indicated by name and by tie-lines joining the brightest stars in each. The Milky Way is shown as an irregular, dark band crossing the charts.

If you live in the Northern Hemisphere, use the northern polar region chart (fig. D.1a) and the northern part of the equatorial-ecliptic chart (fig. D.1c). If you live in the Southern Hemisphere, use the southern polar region chart (fig. D.1b) and the southern half of the equatorial-ecliptic chart. Locate a prominent constellation in the sky (e.g., the Big or Little Dipper in the north or the Crux or Triangulum Australe in the south). Then, using a flashlight, locate the same constellation on the appropriate chart. Rotate the chart until the constellation is oriented the same way as it is in the heavens, and then the chart will be properly oriented for locating and identifying other features in the heavens.

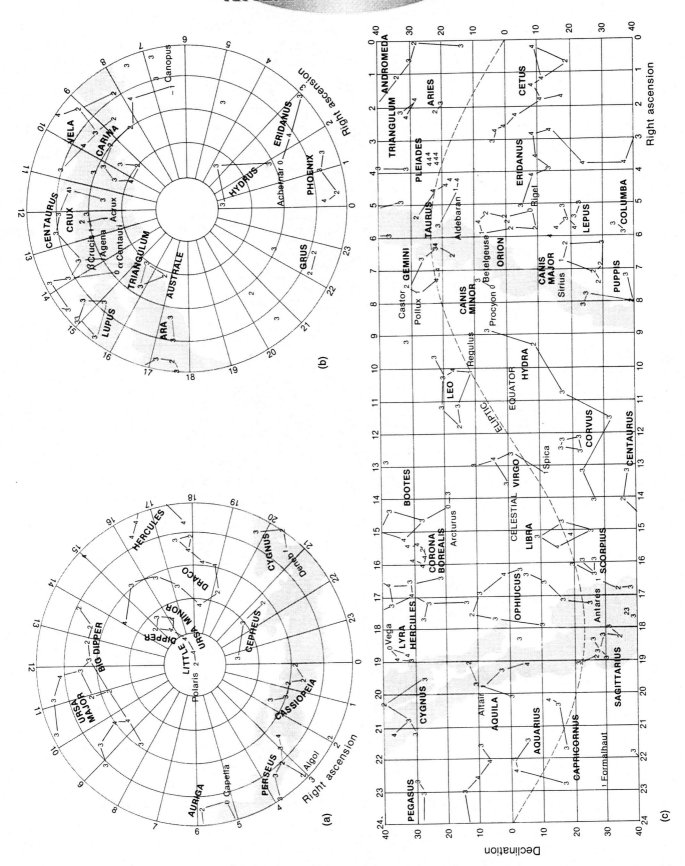

Figure D.1   Star charts of the (*a*) northern and (*b*) southern polar regions and of the (*c*) equatorial-ecliptic belt. (Text and star maps from David Laing, *The Earth System.* Copyright © 1991 Times Mirror Higher Education Group, Inc., Dubuque, Iowa. All Rights Reserved. Reprinted by permission.

Mineral Identification Flowchart

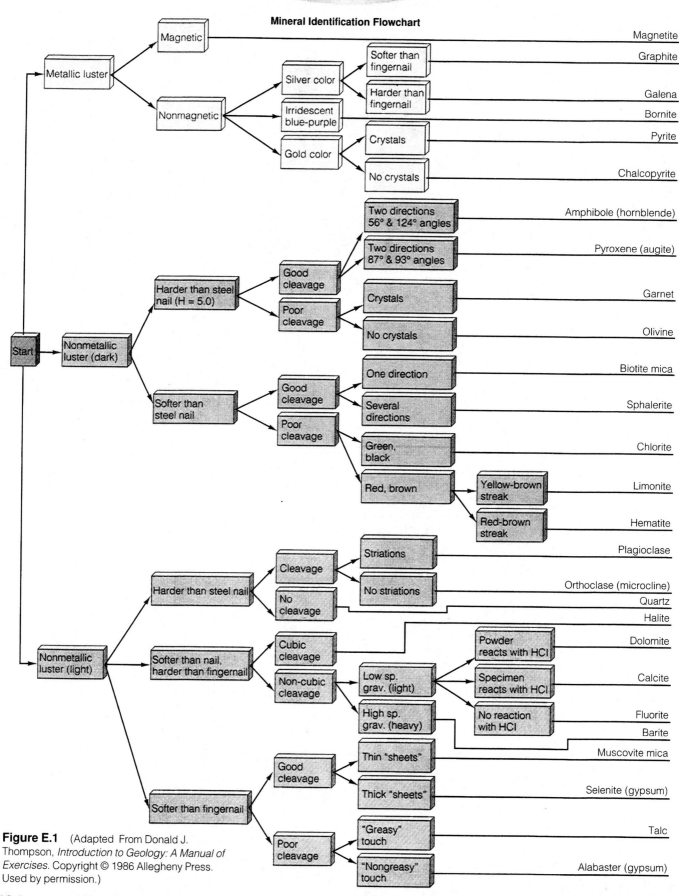

Figure E.1 (Adapted From Donald J. Thompson, *Introduction to Geology: A Manual of Exercises*. Copyright © 1986 Allegheny Press. Used by permission.)

Rock Identification Flowchart

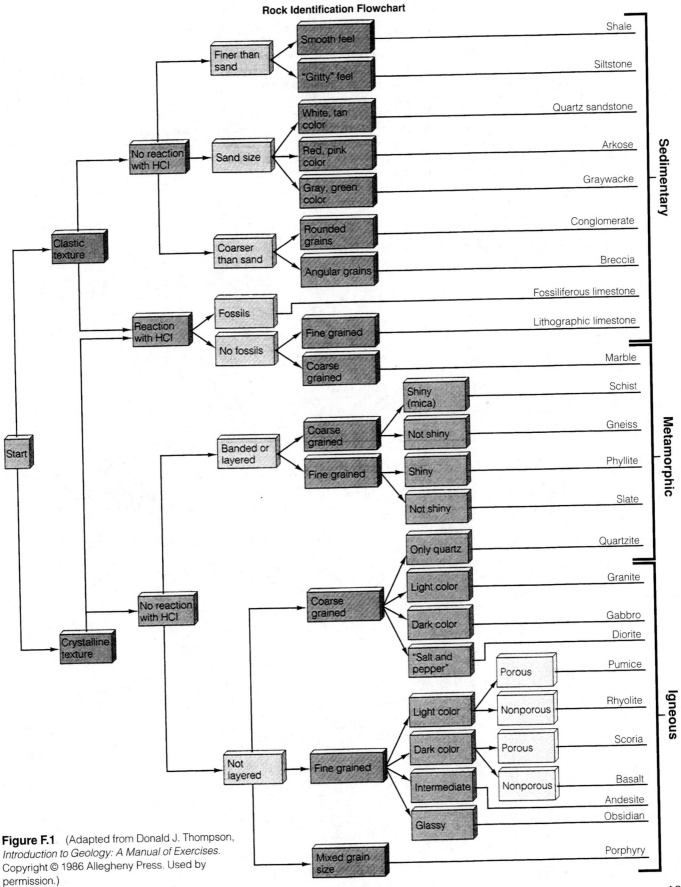

Figure F.1 (Adapted from Donald J. Thompson, *Introduction to Geology: A Manual of Exercises.* Copyright © 1986 Allegheny Press. Used by permission.)

APPENDIX G THE 7TH APPROXIMATION SOIL CLASSIFICATION

At the beginning of the twentieth century, the U.S. Department of Agriculture (USDA) adopted a system of soil classification developed by Russian soil scientists. This scheme included three major levels of classification: from highest to lowest, these are *orders, suborders,* and *great soil groups.* The three soil orders largely reflect the soil's degree of maturity: **Zonal soils** are mature and well-developed; **intrazonal soils** are developed in such places as bogs, where local drainage conditions preclude normal soil development; and **azonal soils** are young and immature. The 9 to 12 recognized suborders are largely a reflection of climate and include such categories as desert; cold, temperate forest; and mountain. The great soil groups

are soil varieties familiar to anyone with a rudimentary knowledge of soil. These include sierozems, chestnuts, podsols, prairie soil, and latosols. The great soil groups can be subdivided further into **soil families, soil series, soil types,** and **soil phases.**

Although the USDA system of classification underwent a number of modifications through the years, it was finally abandoned and replaced by a descriptive system that emphasizes observable physical and chemical properties, rather than the environment or the

soil-forming process. This **Comprehensive Soil Classification System (CSCS)** uses soil names of Greek or Latin derivation and consists of six levels of classification (fig. G.1). In descending order, these levels are: 10 **orders** (the names of which end in *sol*), 47 **suborders**, 185 **great soil groups**, 970 **subgroups**, approximately 4,500 **soil families,** and more than 10,000 **soil series.** Over the past 50 years, U.S. soil scientists have altered and modified this basic scheme through a series of **approximations,** each of which tries to relate the classification

Figure G.1 CSCS soil map of the world. (From Arthur H. Doerr, *Fundamentals of Physical Geography,* 2d ed. Copyright © 1993 Times Mirror Higher Education Group, Inc. Dubuque, Iowa. All Rights Reserved. Reprinted by permission.)

Oxisols

Ultisols

Vertisols

Alfisols

Spodosols

Mollisols

descriptions more closely to the soil as it is found in nature (fig. G.2). For example, the 4th approximation was developed and published in 1955. The 7th approximation, published in 1960 and subsequently modified, is the latest version. Descriptions of the 10 soil orders of the CSCS follow:

1. **Entisols** (*ent,* recent) Soils with no distinct horizon development (azonal). Little evidence of the work of most soil-forming processes. Usually young, immature soils.

Commonly developed on alluvial or eolian deposits. May form in any climatic regime. Erode severely when covering of natural vegetation is removed.

2. **Vertisols** (*vert,* turn) Characteristic of regions with distinct wet and dry seasons or those subjected to periodic drought. More than 35% swelling clay content. Soils expand during the wet season and shrink and crack during the dry season. Expansion often causes overturning of upper layers. Form under grass cover. High in organic and base content.

3. **Inceptisols** (*incept,* begin) Immature soils with weakly developed horizons. No clay enrichment in B-horizon. Develop from the Arctic to the tropics, often on glacial deposits or volcanic ash. Brown soils because of an abundance of organic material. Native vegetation is forest.

4. **Aridisols** (*aridus,* dry) Desert soils with thin, moderately developed horizons. Low organic content gives A-horizon a light color. Subsoil (B-horizon) may contain accumulations of calcite, salt, or gypsum. Other high-mineral concentrations may lead to plant toxicity. Strongly alkaline. With irrigation, these soils may be productive. These soils cover perhaps one-third of the world's land surface.

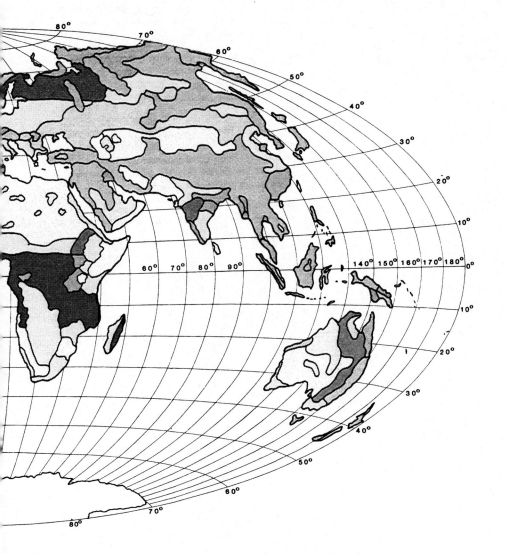

Aitoff's Equal Area Projection

- Aridisols
- Entisols
- Inceptisols
- Histosols
- Highlands

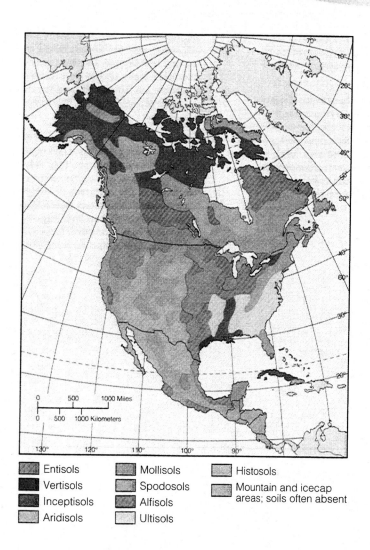

Entisols
Vertisols
Inceptisols
Aridisols
Mollisols
Spodosols
Alfisols
Ultisols
Histosols
Mountain and icecap areas; soils often absent

Figure G.2 CSCS soil map for North America.

5. **Mollisols** (*molli,* soft) Thick, dark, organic-rich A-horizon and a clay-rich B-horizon (prairie soils). Rich in bases (calcium, sodium, magnesium). Weakly alkaline. Semiarid to subhumid climates. Grasslands. Also include the chestnut and chernozem soils. Highly fertile with sufficient precipitation or irrigation. Dominant soils of the "grain belts."

6. **Spodosols** (*spodo,* wood ash) Ash-colored, sandy A-horizon over a brownish, clay-rich B-horizon. Amorphous aluminum and iron oxides and humus. Strongly acidic. Typically develop from sandy parent material in cool, humid climates and under forest vegetation. Relatively infertile. Include some podsols.

7. **Alfisols** (*alfi* from *pedalfer*) Thin, brown to gray-brown A-horizon over a clay-rich B-horizon. More than 35% base (calcium, sodium, magnesium) saturation. Common under forest vegetation in the humid midlatitudes. Moderate organic material, slightly acidic. Agriculturally productive. Include the gray-brown podsols.

8. **Ultisols** (*ulti,* ultimate) Red-yellow to red-brown color. Moist, clay-rich B-horizon. Less than 35% base saturation. Weakly acidic. Wet-dry tropical to subtropical climates. Develop by prolonged weathering of parent material. Include the red-yellow podsols. Low fertility. Productive only with proper management.

9. **Oxisols** (*oxi,* oxide) Thick, intensely weathered soils with poor horizon development. Highly leached of bases. Weakly alkaline. Dominated by clay and hydrated oxides of iron and aluminum. Common in the tropics (rain forests). Include the laterites (latosols). Infertile, dry to bricklike consistency when natural vegetation is stripped off.

10. **Histosols** (*histo,* tissue) Organic soils, including peat. Strongly acidic. Form in swampy areas, such as the Florida Everglades, and in cool, moist climates. Highly productive if drained. Fragile soils, easily eroded if disturbed.

BOUNDARIES

National

State or territorial

County or equivalent

Civil township or equivalent

Incorporated-city or equivalent

Park, reservation, or monument

Small park

LAND SURVEY SYSTEMS

U.S. Public Land Survey System:

Township or range line

Location doubtful

Section line

Location doubtful

Found section corner; found closing corner

Witness corner; meander corner

Other land surveys:

Township or range line

Section line

Land grant or mining claim; monument

Fence line

ROADS AND RELATED FEATURES

Primary highway

Secondary highway

Light duty road

Unimproved road

Trail

Dual highway

Dual highway with median strip

Road under construction

Underpass; overpass

Bridge

Drawbridge

Tunnel

BUILDINGS AND RELATED FEATURES

Dwelling or place of employment: small; large

School; church

Barn, warehouse, etc.: small; large

House omission tint

Racetrack

Airport

Landing strip

Well (other than water); windmill

Water tank: small; large

Other tank: small; large

Covered reservoir

Gaging station

Landmark object

Campground; picnic area

Cemetery: small; large

RAILROADS AND RELATED FEATURES

Standard gauge single track; station

Standard gauge multiple track

Abandoned

Under construction

Narrow gauge single track

Narrow gauge multiple track

Railroad in street

Juxtaposition

Roundhouse and turntable

TRANSMISSION LINES AND PIPELINES

Power transmission line: pole; tower

Telephone or telegraph line

Aboveground oil or gas pipeline

Underground oil or gas pipeline

CONTOURS

Topographic:

Intermediate

Index

Supplementary

Depression

Cut; fill

Bathymetric:

Intermediate

Index

Primary

Index Primary

Supplementary

MINES AND CAVES

Quarry or open pit mine

Gravel, sand, clay, or borrow pit

Mine tunnel or cave entrance

Prospect; mine shaft

Mine dump

Tailings

SURFACE FEATURES

Levee

Sand or mud area, dunes, or shifting sand

Intricate surface area

Gravel beach or glacial moraine

Tailings pond

VEGETATION

Woods

Scrub

Orchard

Vineyard

Mangrove

COASTAL FEATURES

Foreshore flat

Rock or coral reef

Rock bare or awash

Group of rocks bare or awash

Exposed wreck

Depth curve; sounding

Breakwater, pier, jetty, or wharf

Seawall

BATHYMETRIC FEATURES

Area exposed at mean low tide; sounding datum

Channel

Offshore oil or gas: well; platform

Sunken rock

RIVERS, LAKES, AND CANALS

Intermittent stream

Intermittent river

Disappearing stream

Perennial stream

Perennial river

Small falls; small rapids

Large falls; large rapids

Masonry dam

Dam with lock

Dam carrying road

Intermittent lake or pond

Dry lake

Narrow wash

Wide wash

Canal, flume, or aqueduct with lock

Elevated aqueduct, flume, or conduit

Aqueduct tunnel

Water well; spring or seep

GLACIERS AND PERMANENT SNOWFIELDS

Contours and limits

Form lines

SUBMERGED AREAS AND BOGS

Marsh or swamp

Submerged marsh or swamp

Wooded marsh or swamp

Submerged wooded marsh or swamp

Rice field

Land subject to inundation

Figure H.1 (Source: U.S. Geological Survey.)

The geologic time scale is the product of many minds, and earth scientists are still refining it. The scale evolved from studies of rocks and fossils in numerous locations, and it reads, in part, like a geography lesson. For example, the time between 360 and 250 million years ago is divided into the Mississippian and Pennsylvanian periods, based on significant occurrences of rocks of those ages in the upper Mississippi River valley and the state of Pennsylvania, respectively. The ensuing 45-million-year span is called the Permian period, from rocks of that age in the Perm Basin of central Russia. Other geographical names include the Cambrian period, after a Roman name for Wales, and the Jurassic period, for the Jura Mountains in France. The naming system is not, however, solely geographical. Some names reflect the character of the rocks themselves. For example, the name Cretaceous is derived from the Latin word *creta*, meaning "chalk," in reference to the chalk cliffs along the English Channel. Other names on the geologic calendar refer to the character or abundance of the life of that time, as expressed in the fossil record (e.g., *Mesozoic* means "middle life"). The geologic time scale now categorizes time, in descending order of magnitude, into eons, eras, periods, epochs, and ages (table I.1).

Geologists recognize two eons. The first is called Prephanerozoic (*pre*, meaning "before"; *phaneros*, meaning "visible"; *zoio*, meaning "animal") because it covers the time for which there is no sign of *metazoan*, or multicellular, life. The other eon is the Phanerozoic, an eon of metazoan life-forms. The Phanerozoic is further subdivided into three eras: the Paleozoic ("ancient life"), the Mesozoic, and the Cenozoic ("recent life"). The Prephanerozoic is also known as the Precambrian. The terms have evolved over the last 300 years and have provided scientists with those temporal reference points so necessary for the study of Earth's history.

From Earth's origin to the present is a very long time. To conceive of this 4.6-billion-year history, imagine running a 1-mile race with some of Earth's historical events standing along the race path. At the beginning of Earth history, 4.6 billion years ago, the full race course of 5,280 feet lies ahead of us. Some of the oldest crustal rocks, dated at 3.8 billion years, would be approached at the 4,361.8-foot mark. Primitive life-forms would lie at the 4,132.1-foot mark, some 3.6 billion years ago. The first fishes would be seen with 585 feet left to run in the race. Vascular plants, evolving 400 million years ago, would be visible at the 459.2-foot mark. The first birds, at 150 million years ago, would fly over us as we begin to run the last 172.5 feet. Dinosaurs became extinct about 65 million years ago, just 7.57 feet before the finish line. An ancient human ancestor, the bipedal primate called Lucy, would be standing just 4 feet from the finish line. *Homo erectus*, a closer ancestor living 750,000 years ago, would be seen with 10.3 inches left. Neanderthals, an even closer human ancestor, would stand at the 1.72-inch mark. As the ice of the last glacial event was in retreat, about 10,000 years ago, we would have only 0.14 inch left in our race.

TABLE I.1 The Geologic Time Scale

Eon	Era	Period	Epoch	Millions of Years before Present
PHANEROZOIC	Cenozoic	Quaternary	Holocene	Recent
			Pleistocene	1.6
		Tertiary	Pliocene	5.3
			Miocene	23.7
			Oligocene	36.6
			Eocene	57.8
			Paleocene	65
	Mesozoic	Cretaceous		144
		Jurassic		208
		Triassic		245
	Paleozoic	Permian		286
		Pennsylvanian		320
		Mississippian		360
		Devonian		408
		Silurian		438
		Ordovician		505
		Cambrian		543
		Vendian		563
		Ediacaran		700
PREPHANEROZOIC	Late Proterozoic			900
	Middle Proterozoic			1600
	Early Proterozoic			2500
	Late Archean			3000
	Middle Archean			3400
	Early Archean			3800
	Earth forms			4550

Glossary

ablation Loss of ice from a glacier through melting, sublimation, and calving; usually, a glacial ice loss that expresses itself as a thinning of the terminal end of a glacier.

abrasion Erosion by friction between glacial ice and rock or between bedrock and the rock embedded in passing glacial ice; also the wearing away of rock particles in transit within streams or in the wind.

abrasives Natural and manufactured materials used for cutting, sanding, grinding, or polishing.

absolute humidity Ratio of water vapor to the volume of a parcel of air.

absolute zero Temperature at which there is no molecular motion; 0 Kelvin.

abundant metal Metal with an average abundance greater than 0.01% of Earth's crust.

abyssal plain Usually extensive ocean floor area with relatively low relief.

abyssopelagic Water column above the abyssal plains; usually designated as the water below the bathypelagic and above the hadal zones.

acid mine drainage Waters that exit deep and strip coal mines; waters rich in sulfuric acid that originate from the weathering of pyrite in mined coal seams and coal refuse piles.

actualism A concept that qualifies uniformitarianism; the concept of the uniformity of natural law with the qualification of differences in the frequency and intensity of natural events.

adiabatic cooling Internal cooling process that results when a parcel of air ascends and expands.

advection Wind; essentially, horizontally moving replacement air.

advection fog Ground cloud that develops over land or sea, usually in the winter or spring, that results from the cooling of warm air as it passes over cold land or water.

aftershock One of a series of tremors or temblors that invariably follows an earthquake over a period of days, weeks, or months.

A-horizon Soil zone below O-horizon; uppermost of the true soil layers; soil layer that is dark by enrichment with humus and deficient in soluble minerals lost to leaching; synonymous with topsoil and zone of leaching.

air mass Body of air that can be identified by its temperature, pressure, and moisture characteristics.

air pressure Quantifiable result of molecular collisions within atmospheric gases and between gases and planetary surfaces as a function of the overall weight of the gases; expressed as pounds per square inch, in millibars, or in inches of mercury.

albedo Measurable reflectivity of any surface.

alloy Any mixture of two or more metals, such as bronze, brass, and steel.

alluvial fan A cone- or fan-shaped sediment deposit laid down at the base of a mountain front by a stream when the stream slows as it emerges from a steep canyon onto a more gently sloping surface.

alluvium The generic name for any sediment that has been moved and deposited by stream action.

alpine glacier *See* valley glacier.

amber Hardened tree sap.

ambient air Surrounding air.

anemometer Instrument that measures wind speed.

aneroid barometer Instrument that measures atmospheric pressure by means of an airless, corrugated container that expands and contracts to move a needle along a calibrated scale.

angle of incidence Measurement in degrees from overhead where the sun appears at any time of day.

anhydrite Evaporite mineral associated with very hot, evaporating conditions; $CaSO_4$.

anorthosite A plutonic rock dominated in composition by plagioclase.

Antarctic Bottom Water (AABW) Water that originates as cold water along Antarctica and sinks because of its increased density; a cold, moving water layer derived largely from the Southern Ocean.

anthracite Hard coal; metamorphosed bituminous coal.

anticline Arch-shaped or up-folded rock structure produced by compressive or mountain-building stress; arch-shaped rock structure with outward limbs that dip away from the axis, or crest.

anticyclone A downward and outward flow of air; a high-pressure system; a clockwise circulation of air in the Northern Hemisphere.

antimatter Matter composed of antineutrinos, positrons, antiprotons.

aphanitic (fine) texture Textural term, most commonly applied to igneous rocks, in which the individual fine crystals are too small to be seen by the naked eye; associated with rapid cooling of lava; fine-grained.

aphelion Orbital position that is farthest from the sun; Earth's orbital position in July.

aphotic Dark water zone; ocean water zones below 1,000 meters (3,280 ft).

apogee Position in an elliptical orbit where the orbiting body is at its greatest distance from the object it orbits.

aquiclude Rock, soil, or sediment that prevents the passage of groundwater; impermeable rock, soil, or sediment.

aquifer Rock, soil, or sediment that allows relatively easy passage of groundwater; permeable rock.

arête Narrow ridge caused by glacial erosion; narrow rock ridge between adjacent alpine glaciers.

artesian aquifer Groundwater system in which water, driven by the weight (pressure) of the water in the aquifer, flows to (or toward) the ground surface through a well or a system of fractures.

artesian spring Flow that occurs when water under pressure in a confined aquifer reaches the ground surface.

artesian well Type of well in which water from a confined aquifer is driven to the ground surface by the weight (pressure) of the water in the aquifer.

asphalt (bitumen) Solid or highly viscous component of petroleum.

asteroid One of numerous rocky bodies that occupy an orbit between Mars and Jupiter.

asthenosphere Zone in the upper mantle characterized by low seismic velocities and composed of very hot, near-molten material that behaves plastically.

astronomical unit (AU) Unit based upon Earth's average distance from the sun (150 million km or 93 million mi); used for measuring distances within the Solar System.

astronomy One of four earth science disciplines; the study of objects and processes beyond Earth.

atmosphere Sphere of gases that envelops a celestial body.

atoll Semicircular coral reef island that forms around subsided, tropical oceanic volcano.

atom A naturally occurring or synthesized unit of matter composed of a nucleus and orbiting electrons; the smallest indivisible form of an element that maintains that element's chemical characteristics.

atomic number Total number of protons in an atom of an element.

aurora borealis (northern lights) Light produced as solar wind encounters nitrogen and oxygen in the upper atmosphere.

avalanche A mass of snow, ice, and rock debris, common in many mountainous areas, that moves rapidly downslope under the pull of gravity.

backswamp Low-lying, marshy area created when floods on an alluvial plain deposit impermeable muds; marsh area of poor drainage and impermeable muds located between the natural levees of a stream and the valley walls.

backwash Downslope return water from waves breaking along a beach; the water that runs down the beach toward the surf zone.

banded iron formation (BIF) Low-grade ore (taconite) in which iron is concentrated in dark layers that contrast with light, iron-poor, quartz-rich layers, giving a banded appearance; also known as Lake Superior-type ore.

bar Elongate deposit of unconsolidated sediments that have been deposited by waves and near-shore currents; deposit of sand at the mouth of a distributary stream.

barograph A recording barometer.

barrier island Elongate coastal island that acts as a barrier to waves and tides, protecting the mainland and separated from it by a shallow lagoon.

basalt Dark, mafic volcanic rock generally characterized by a fine-grained texture.

basaltic crust The oceanic crust; that portion of Earth's crust that is dominated by volcanic rocks of mafic composition.

basalt plateau Accumulation of horizontal layers of basalt erupted from multiple fissures during a relatively brief geologic span.

batholith Large, discordant, nontabular plutonic mass that has a surface exposure of at least 100 square kilometers (40 sq. mi) and that may extend for thousands or tens of thousands of square kilometers; Stone Mountain, Georgia, and Half-Dome in Yosemite are parts of exposed batholiths.

bathyal zone Seafloor along the continental slope, running from shelf to continental rise.

bathymetry Depth and configuration of the ocean floor.

bathypelagic zone Uppermost aphotic zone in the ocean that extends from 1,000 meters (3,280 ft) to 4,000 meters (13,120 ft).

bauxite Principal aluminum ore, composed of two or more aluminum oxides and hydroxides; a "fossil" soil or a residual deposit that includes diaspore and gibbsite found in the tropics or in areas with lateritic soils.

baymouth bar Spit that has closed off the open ocean entrance to a bay.

beach Subaerial and subaqueous depositional feature aggregated and shaped by waves, currents, and winds acting on various sediments; the color, composition, and texture of beach materials depend on the source of the materials and the wind, wave, tide, and current energy.

beach drifting Movement of beach materials in the longshore current and along the exposed beach face.

beach nourishment Application of sand to a beach to replenish that carried away by longshore transport and storm waves; also called beach replenishment.

bedding plane The approximately flat surface, or break, that separates one sedimentary rock layer from another.

Bernoulli theorem Principle that a constricted moving fluid gains momentum.

B-horizon Soil horizon below the A-horizon; known as the zone of accumulation or as the subsoil.

big bang theory Theory whereby the universe was created by an expansion of superhot plasma; new evidence suggests that the big bang may have occurred between 8 and 12 billion years ago.

bioclastic Describes sedimentary rock texture composed of broken, organically produced fragments, such as shells, coral rubble, or decayed plant materials.

biogenic Derived from organic activity.

bioluminescent Illuminated by chemical activity within an organism.

bioturbation Overturning of sediments by burrowing organisms, such as worms, clams, and crabs.

bird's-foot delta Delta formed by many distributaries that has reminded some of the shape of a bird's foot.

bitumen A tarlike substance that is rich in carbon; opaque, noncrystalline substance found in pore spaces and in fluid inclusions in sedimentary rocks.

bituminous coal Soft coal associated with much of the Appalachian region and the interior coalfields. May be considered as a type of sedimentary rock.

black hole Object from which light cannot escape; the densest object in the universe, formed from the complete collapse of a star 10 or more times the mass of our sun.

blowout Uncontrolled (and dangerous) release of oil and natural gas from a well bore; a deflation basin, or bowl-shaped depression in sediment caused by wind erosion.

body waves Earthquake waves (P-waves and S-waves) that travel through Earth rather than around its surface.

bora Katabatic winds at the boundary of southern Europe and the Adriatic Sea.

brackish Water that is slightly to moderately saline.

braided stream A stream whose channel consists of a number of migrating interconnected subchannels; this channel pattern commonly forms when a stream has a greater load of sediment than it is capable of transporting.

brass Copper-zinc alloy.

breakwater Constructed barrier designed to break up the energy of the incoming waves and to create a quiet, protected harbor.

brine Saline water contained in the spaces of sedimentary rocks; water containing halite and other mineral salts in solution.

bronze Copper-tin-zinc alloy.

caldera Wide, deep depression, much larger than a crater, that is the remains of a violently erupting volcanic cone; large depression representing the missing upper portion of a volcanic cone that has been destroyed by a combination of disintegration, collapse, and ejection during a violent volcanic eruption.

caliche Hard calcium carbonate; ground surface crust that is deposited when water evaporates in an arid region.

calving The breaking off of ice masses from glaciers that extend to or into a body of water.

cavern Interconnected, extensive, subsurface voids caused by dissolution of limestone.

cay Small Bahamian island or reef near or just above high-tide water level.

Celsius Temperature scale using 0° as the initial freezing point of water and 100° as the initial boiling point of water.

cement Binding material holding together mineral particles in sedimentary rocks; cements are usually carbonate (calcite), silica (quartz), and iron compounds; also, a product manufactured from limestone and shale that is used as the binding material in concrete.

centrifugal force Tendency for an object to move away from the axis of rotation or turning.

centripital force Tendency for an object to be pulled toward the axis of rotation.

chalcopyrite Most important copper ore.

channelization An attempt to modify a natural stream channel to accommodate more water by dredging, deepening, and/or straightening the channel.

channel pattern The appearance of a stream's channel when viewed from above; the most common patterns are straight, meandering, and braided.

chemical compound Combination of two or more atoms.

chemical weathering Chemical alteration of rock and mineral material in Earth's surface environment; synonymous with decomposition.

chemosynthesis The production of food from the assimilation of chemicals in the environment; the production of food by microorganisms, such as bacteria, that use elements available in hydrothermal springs on the ocean floor.

chinook wind Warm wind of late winter and early spring that increases evaporation and melts snow; from Native American word for "snow eater"; downslope wind.

chlorinity Total amount of chlorine in grams in a 1-kilogram sample of water.

C-horizon Soil transition zone between the weathered horizons above and the unweathered parent material below.

chromosphere Reddish rim of sun from which spicules, solar flares, or prominences appear to erupt; the "color" sphere.

cinder cone Volcanic cone, normally less than 450 meters (1,500 ft) high, consisting principally of pyroclastic debris and usually forming in clusters; each forms over a short span of time (10 to 20 years).

circumpolar water Cold surface water of high latitudes that averages 0.5° C (32.9° F) at the surface, with a salinity of 34.68‰.

cirque Semicircular depression gouged from rock by glacial ice and meltwater in mountainous regions; the starting point for an alpine glacier.

cirque glacier A small glacier confined to the cirque in which it first formed.

classification A grouping of objects and ideas based on similarities in structure, composition, process, or function.

clastic Textural term applied to sedimentary rocks that are formed by the accumulation and consolidation of rock and mineral fragments.

cleavage Splitting of a mineral along an internal plane of weakness in a crystal; in rocks, the ability to split along parallel surfaces.

climagraph A diagram of climate data that shows the mean monthly values for temperature and precipitation.

climate Condition of the atmosphere over a long period at a geographic locale.

climatology The science that seeks to determine and describe the various patterns of climate.

clinker End product in the process of making cement.

coal Combustible sedimentary rock formed from the accumulated and lithified remains of plants; combustible sedimentary rock whose energy is rated in BTUs per pound.

coarse texture *See* phaneritic texture.

coke Baked coal used in the manufacture of iron and steel; coal from which gases and liquids have been removed by heating.

cold current Ocean surface current that flows from high latitude to lower latitude, or longitudinally at high latitudes; slow, wide, and shallow current on eastern side of oceans.

cold dark matter A type of matter that is indirectly detected by its gravitational effects on galaxy rotation; suspected dominant form of matter of the universe.

cold occlusion A type of weather front that forms when trailing colder air undermines warm air.

column Depositional feature formed in a cavern by the merging of a stalactite and a stalagmite.

comet Wandering body of the Solar System composed of ice, dust, and rock material moving in a highly eccentric orbit.

compression Squeezing force; a type of stress caused by two opposing masses.

concordant Parallel to the surrounding rock beds; describes an igneous intrusive feature like a sill.

condensation Process that turns water vapor into liquid water.

conduction Transfer of heat energy between substances in contact.

cone of depression Localized, cone-shaped depression of the water table centered on a well and resulting from excessive pumping.

contact metamorphism Local alteration of rock that surrounds an igneous intrusion; alteration of rock localized in a halo or aureole surrounding the intrusion.

continental crust Thick unit of the lithosphere underlying the continental areas and composed primarily of rock with an average composition of granite.

continental glacier Large mass of ice, snow, and rock debris that can reach thicknesses in excess of 3 kilometers (2 mi) and cover hundreds of thousands of square kilometers.

continental margin Transition zone between a continent and deep ocean basin; includes the continental shelf, continental slope, and continental rise.

continental rise Sedimentary accumulation that is part of the continental margin and that is located between the continental slope and the abyssal plain.

continental shelf Part of the continent that is submerged beneath shallow marginal seas.

continental slope The portion of the continental margin between the shelf and the rise.

continental tropical (cT) air A dry, hot air mass that originates over areas like the American Southwest.

contraposed shoreline A shoreline of irregular shape developed from a straight, or regular, coastline.

convection Vertical heat transfer by a moving fluid.

convectional lifting Thermally induced rising of air.

convection cell Combined vertical and horizontal air movements that distribute fluids in a wheel-like cell.

convective zone An interior zone of the sun that lies between the radiative zone and the photosphere; a solar interior zone in which hotter gases rise through cooler gases.

convergence The collision of crustal plates; also a net horizontal inflow of air under certain atmospheric conditions.

coral reef Organic structure built by colonial organisms, principally corals, in warm, shallow, tropical water.

core The central portion of a celestial body; innermost layer of Earth, consisting of a solid inner core and a liquid outer core; the central portion of the sun, the solar furnace.

Coriolis force A deviation from a straight path on a rotating body; a tendency away from a straight trajectory observed in moving fluids on a rotating body; a tendency on Earth for moving fluids to veer to the right in the Northern Hemisphere and to the left in the Southern Hemisphere.

corona The outermost portion of the sun; the halo.

corpuscular radiation Charged atomic particles that make up the solar wind.

correlative rights The water rights doctrine that has evolved in California and that uses the groundwater aquifer or the surface watershed as the basic unit for determining water distribution.

country rock *In situ* rock that surrounds and is intruded by an igneous rock body.

crater The principal vent of a volcano; usually circular in form and located at the summit of the cone.

creep Slow, imperceptible movement of earth materials downslope at Earth's surface; a form of mass movement.

crest The high point, or peak, of a wave.

crevasse A fracture, or crack, in the ice surface of a glacier.

crossbed Generally small-scale, thin, sedimentary rock layers deposited at some angle to the horizontal by currents of water or air.

crust Thin, outermost portion of Earth; outermost rocky units of Earth usually divided into two types: a thinner, oceanic (basaltic) crust and a thicker, continental (granitic) crust.

crystal Outer, visible geometric form taken by a mineral as it grows and governed by its internal arrangement of ions.

crystal lattice Arrangement of ions in an orderly, repeated geometric pattern within a mineral.

crystalline Composed of interlocking crystals; synonymous with nonclastic.

crystallization Mineral growth from magma or water solutions; formation of crystals from molten mineral matter, molten metal, or water solutions.

cumuliform cloud A vertically developed, billowy cloud.

current Movement of a fluid (e.g., water) from one place to another through a standing body of that fluid.

cyclogenesis The process that develops, sustains, and intensifies a cyclone.

cyclone An inward and upward flow of air; a low-pressure system; a counterclockwise movement of air in the Northern Hemisphere; a stormlike movement.

declination Magnetic direction or alignment with relation to the magnetic lines of force at Earth's surface; the angular distance to an object on the celestial sphere.

decomposition *See* chemical weathering.

Deep-Sea Drilling Project Series of ocean-floor explorations that were carried out on the research vessel *Glomar Challenger.*

deep-water wave Wave in water in which the depth is greater than one-half the wavelength.

deflation Lifting and carrying away of sedimentary particles by the wind.

deflation basin (blowout) Shallow topographic depression caused by wind erosion.

degenerate gas Gas produced in white dwarfs by the separation of electrons from atomic nuclei.

delta At the mouth of a river, an alluvial deposit usually resembling a triangle or the Greek letter delta; delta shapes are influenced by river discharge, sediment deposition, tidal flow, wave energy, and ocean currents.

dendritic stream pattern Stream pattern, resembling the branching pattern of a tree, formed in a drainage basin by the random location and development of tributary streams.

density Mass per unit volume of a material.

deposition Settling under the influence of gravity of sedimentary particles in water, wind, or ice.

depositional center Area of sediment accumulation that occurs on the continental shelf near the mouth of a river.

desalinization The removal of dissolved salt ions from seawater to render it drinkable.

desert An arid region of sparse or no vegetation.

desertification The progressive conversion of marginally habitable areas to deserts by overpopulation and overfarming.

desert pavement A surface formed of adjacent pebbles and larger rock pieces in an arid region as intervening smaller particles are carried away by the wind.

detrital food Parts of decaying organisms and plant life that settle to the bottom of a water body.

deuterium Isotope of hydrogen with a proton and a neutron in its nucleus.

dew point Temperature at which an air mass becomes saturated with moisture.

diamond pipe Pipe-shaped, vertical, igneous intrusion consisting of the diamond-bearing rock kimberlite (after deposits around Kimberly, South Africa).

diastrophism Generic term for all crustal deformation, including mountain building and ocean basin formation.

diatom Algal life-form with siliceous hard part (test); the most important oxygen producer in the sea, with population densities exceeding 200,000 per liter (800,000 per gal) in the North Pacific.

diatomite (diatomaceous earth) Sedimentary rock formed from the siliceous remains of shell-secreting freshwater and marine diatoms.

dike Igneous intrusion that cuts across the orientation of existing rock; a tabular, discordant, igneous intrusive body.

dimension stone Stone that has been fashioned to the desired size and shape for the construction of dwellings and monuments.

dip The angle that any planar surface makes from the true horizontal; especially used to describe sedimentary rock layers whose original horizontal orientation has been altered by tectonic forces.

dipole Having two poles, such as the North and South Poles of Earth or of a bar magnet.

discharge Volume of water passing any point on a stream in a given time interval.

discordant Describes any igneous mass that intrudes across the orientation of surrounding rock beds.

disintegration *See* physical weathering.

disphotic The mesopelagic "twilight" zone in the ocean; the zone between depths of 200 and 1,000 meters (656 and 3,280 ft) in the open ocean.

dissolution The chemically erosive action that occurs whenever water comes in contact with soluble materials; that action that produces caverns in limestone.

dissolved salt Mineral material in solution.

distal turbidite Deposit of fine sediment at the end of a turbidity flow.

distillation The separation of water from dissolved ions by first evaporating and then condensing the water.

distributary Stream on a delta that distributes or channels the water from the main stream channel to the ocean.

divergence The separation of crustal plates accompanied by the formation of a rift valley; also, a net outflow of air under certain atmospheric conditions.

Doppler effect Measured changes in pitch as an object moves farther from or closer to a point of reference.

downwelling water Product of convergent currents driven by prevailing winds.

drainage basin (watershed) The land surface drained by a stream and its system of tributaries.

drainage divide An element of higher ground that separates adjacent drainage basins.

drift An archaic term used to refer to all sediment deposited by glaciers and meltwater streams; the term is derived from the concept that rock particles were incorporated in drifting icebergs and released as the ice melted.

dripstone A generic term to include all groundwater depositional features (stalagmites, stalactites, and columns) within a cave.

drumlin A stream-lined hill formed by the reshaping of glacial till as the ice readvanced across a till plain.

dry adiabatic rate Rate at which unsaturated air rising through the atmosphere cools until it reaches its dew point; temperature change equivalent to 10° C per 1,000 meters (5.5° F per 1,000 ft).

ductile Property that allows a metal to be drawn out into fine wire.

dune Accumulation of windblown sand that is moving or that has moved but can be temporarily stabilized by a protective covering of vegetation.

dune complex Site of moving and fixed sand dunes, with sand plains, ponds, and lakes.

earthflow The movement of unconsolidated earth material down slopes of moderate steepness under the pull of gravity; such movements are usually intimately associated with slumps and are found at the base (toe) of the displaced mass.

earthquake Trembling, shaking, or vibrating of the ground surface caused by faulting.

eddy Large, relatively homogeneous water body that turns clockwise or counterclockwise as it spins off a pinched meander of the Gulf Stream; any swirling fluid.

effluent stream A stream whose bed is below the water table and which is fed by water from the saturated zone.

Ekman Spiral A change in direction of currents with increasing depth in the ocean caused by friction and the Coriolis force.

electrical absorption hygrometer Instrument that measures humidity with a thin electrolytic film containing a water-absorbing salt.

electromagnetic radiation Energy in a wave form that originates from every vibrating body in the universe and that can traverse a vacuum at the speed of light; includes light and radio waves.

electromagnetic spectrum A graph of electromagnetic radiation based on an orderly progression of wavelengths.

electron Negatively charged particle that "orbits" an atomic nucleus.

element Matter with a specific chemical character; any one of 92 naturally occurring and 11 synthesized units of matter that serve as the building blocks of all substances.

El Niño A warming of the surface of the southeastern Pacific Ocean that usually occurs around Christmastime, which explains the name El Niño ("The Child"); an effect upon the world's weather that occurs because of warming of the southeastern Pacific Ocean's surface waters.

emery Natural mixture of corundum and magnetite used mostly on paper or cloth for polishing and finishing.

endogenous process A natural process that originates within Earth (e.g., metamorphism, volcanism, and earthquakes).

energy Ability to do work or produce motion.

enhanced recovery techniques Means, such as steam or waterflooding, by which additional oil beyond that produced by either natural flow or pumping can be recovered from a reservoir rock.

entrenched meander A meander confined between steep valley walls that was formed as an old-age meandering stream was given renewed powers of erosion as a result of regional uplift of the land or lowering of base level.

eolian Refers to any wind-related processes or wind-formed features.

ephemeral stream Stream that flows only during and immediately after periods of heavy rainfall.

epicenter Point on Earth's surface directly above the focus of an earthquake.

epicontinental sea Shallow sea that covers continental areas during a transgression, usually to depths of 50 meters (164 ft) or less.

epipelagic zone Upper 200 meters (656 ft) of the open ocean; also called the euphotic zone.

equatorial low Atmospheric low-pressure system centered near the equator.

equilibrium line The imaginary line across the surface of a valley glacier that separates the area of dominant ice accumulation (up-valley) from the area of dominant ice ablation (down-valley)—that is, where the net gain or loss of ice is zero.

erosion Wearing away of rock, soil, or sediment by moving fluids, ice, or gravity-driven mass wasting.

erratic A rock that is found in glacial till and that has been transported a considerable distance from its outcrop area.

escarpment Clifflike margin associated with a radical change in topography (such as a change from plain to plateau) or with earthquake fault lines.

esker An accumulation of sand and gravel that was deposited in the channel of a stream flowing within or under a glacier when the channel was blocked by shifting ice; the deposit of sediment remained as a sinuous ridge after the glacier melted away.

estuarine circulation   Special kind of water circulation that occurs when fresh water discharging from rivers mixes with seawater; a flow of fresh water and brackish water over salt water that is governed by density differences.

estuary   Bay, lagoon, delta, or river mouth in which salt water and fresh water meet.

euphotic zone   A well-lit, surface water layer in the ocean; *see* epipelagic zone.

eustatic change   A worldwide alteration in sea level.

evaporation   Process that turns a liquid into a gas; change from water to water vapor requiring the absorption of heat energy.

evaporite   Nonclastic sedimentary rock of either marine or nonmarine origin, formed by the precipitation of salts from a water solution.

evapotranspiration   Loss of water vapor through plant and soil surfaces.

exfoliation   Predominantly physical weathering process whereby rock layers are stripped away, similar to the peeling of an onion; layerlike peeling of rock along fractures formed by the reduction in pressure (stress) as overlying rocks are removed by erosion.

exfoliation dome   Rounded rock mass, commonly granite, formed by exfoliation.

exogenous process   A natural process that originates on or above Earth's surface (e.g., weathering and erosion).

exotic stream   A stream that has sufficient water from its source region to maintain its flow across a desert without receiving any tributaries.

Fahrenheit   Temperature scale using 32° as the initial freezing point of water and 212° as the initial boiling point of water.

fault   Break in a rock sequence or in Earth's crust or upper mantle along which displacement occurs.

faulting   Breaking and shifting of rocks in Earth's crust or upper mantle; immediate cause of most earthquakes.

fault scarp   Clifflike surface that results from faulting.

ferroalloy   Metal combined with iron to give it desirable properties, such as durability and corrosion resistance.

ferromagnesian mineral   Mineral rich in iron and magnesium, such as olivine, amphiboles, and pyroxenes.

fertilizer   Natural mineral supplements containing elements essential for plant growth.

fetch   Extent of open water across which the wind blows; an important factor in determining wave height.

filtration   The removal of dissolved ions from a solution by passing the fluid through a filter.

fine texture   *See* aphanitic texture.

fiord   A glacial trough that terminates in the sea and is flooded by seawater; these are usually narrow, deep, and steep-sided.

firn   New, granular ice that constantly forms across a zone of accumulation of a glacier when fallen snow changes by melting and refreezing.

fissure   Elongate opening in Earth's crust through which volcanic material is ejected or extruded.

flood   A condition of streamflow that involves excess water flowing out of the channel onto the surrounding floodplain.

floodplain   Flat area between the stream channel and the valley walls that is periodically subject to flooding.

flood stage   Level of a stream overflowing its banks; period when a stream spreads out of its channel onto its floodplain.

floodwall   An artifical barrier of steel or concrete used to protect a portion of the floodplain from flooding.

focus   Actual location, or zone, at or below Earth's surface where faulting has occurred; also known as the hypocenter.

foehn   Wind that occurs in the Alps, and is similar to the chinook.

fog   Ground cloud formed by condensation in the air close to Earth's surface.

fold   Structural feature that expresses itself in a wave-shaped rock unit; wavelike structural rock feature that results from compressive stresses; some folds are symmetrical; others, asymmetrical.

foliated   Metamorphic rock texture in which minerals present are aligned parallel to each other under pressure, giving the rock a layered appearance.

foliation   Any planar feature (e.g., slaty cleavage, layering, banding) occurring within a metamorphic rock; one of the principal features in the subdivision and classification of metamorphic rocks.

footwall   Block of crust along a fault plane on which you could walk if the fault plane were open; side of a fault opposite the hanging wall.

foreshock   One of a series of tremors or temblors, usually so weak as to be undetectable except by seismographs, that precedes an earthquake.

fossil   Traces or remains of organisms preserved from the geologic past; any evidence of past life.

fossil fuel   Combustible material, such as oil, gas, or coal, that was derived from organic materials.

fracture   Random, uneven breakage of minerals other than along planes of cleavage.

fracture zone   The upper portion of a glacier, where the ice tends to be brittle and subject to fracturing.

Frasch process   Method of sulfur production; process employing air and hot water pumped under pressure down a borehole drilled into sulfur-bearing formations.

freshwater lens   At a river mouth, a lens-shaped body of lighter water that slowly mixes with the seawater.

friction   Force that impedes the relative movement of objects in contact.

front   Leading edge of a moving air mass.

frontal fog   Ground cloud associated with weather fronts where warm air masses come in contact with colder air.

frontal lifting   Dynamically induced lifting or overrunning produced at the boundary between two air masses of differing temperature and density whenever the warmer and lighter air mass rises.

frost   Thin ice layers produced whenever the dew point is reached below the freezing point of water.

frost heaving   Process of alternate freezing and thawing of water in pore spaces and fractures, with the consequent downslope displacement of mineral grains, soil blocks, rocks, and constructed objects like sidewalks.

frost wedging   Type of physical weathering process; mechanical breakdown of rock due to the expansion of freezing water in cracks and crevasses.

fuller's earth   Variety of clay used as a soft polishing medium for metals.

fusion   Process by which atoms combine to make heavier elements; the process by which the sun produces its energy.

gabion   A large wire basket filled with rock and placed in a series along the base of a slope to stop or retard the downslope movement of earth material.

galaxy   System or aggregation of stars, dust clouds, and cold dark matter; aggregations of billions of stars.

gas injection   Enhanced recovery technique in which gas (natural or nitrogen) is forcibly injected into an oil-bearing rock formation to push and lower the viscosity of the oil so that it flows more freely to the well bore.

gem   Cut and polished gem mineral.

gemstone (gem mineral)   Natural substance that can be cut and polished into decorative minerals valued because they can be set in jewelry.

geologic agent   Any fluid substance that, when in motion, is capable of doing geologic work; any of several fluids, such as running water, groundwater, waves, currents, wind, and glaciers, that are capable of doing geologic work.

geologic structure   Rock feature that has been shaped by deforming forces.

geologic time scale   A time line of geologic and evolutionary events that is divided into eons, eras, periods, epochs, and ages.

geologic work   Erosion, transportation, and deposition of rock and mineral material by moving water, ice, or wind; the movement of earth material from one place to another.

geology   One of four earth science disciplines; the study of the solid Earth and its processes.

geostrophic flow   A continuously turning current of water influenced by Earth's rotation.

geostrophic wind   Constant horizontal ideal airflow parallel to isobars produced when the Coriolis force and the atmospheric pressure gradient balance each other.

glacial outwash   Sorted and stratified sediment deposited by glacial meltwater streams beyond the ice front.

glacial till   Sediment deposited by melting ice; heterogenous mixture of sediment deposited directly by melting glacial ice.

glacier   Thick mass (as a sheet or stream) of ice that moves when its weight responds to gravity and internal pressure.

glass   Unordered atoms in solid form.

globular cluster   Aggregation of millions of stars usually associated with galaxies.

gneissosity   Texture in metamorphic rocks that shows distinct banding of alternate dark and light minerals.

Gondwanaland   Southern supercontinent composed of Africa, South America, Australia, Antarctica, Madagascar, and India.

graben   Elongated, downdropped block of Earth's crust that is bordered by two faults.

gradient   Drop in elevation as a stream flows a certain distance; atmospheric pressure change.

gradient wind   Wind produced with balanced forces around high- and low-pressure systems that flows along either a curved clockwise or counterclockwise path.

granite   Coarse-grained, light-colored intrusive igneous rock consisting principally of the minerals microcline, quartz, plagioclase feldspar, muscovite mica, biotite mica, and hornblende.

granitic crust   That portion of Earth's crust dominated by light-colored and relatively low-density crystalline rocks typified by granite; synonymous with continental crust.

greenhouse effect   Atmospheric heating caused by the addition of heat-absorbing gases, such as carbon dioxide.

groin   Structure built perpendicular to the shoreline to absorb wave energy; artificial headland built to capture sand in its migration, to prevent beach erosion, and to protect a seawall.

ground moraine   Rock and soil debris left as a cover by a receding glacier.

groundwater   Water occupying pore spaces within the saturated zone of the subsurface soil, sediments, and rocks.

Gulf Stream   Largest and most intensified warm current in the Atlantic Ocean; fast western boundary current in the Atlantic that averages 5 kilometers (3 mi) per hour and carries more than 50 million cubic meters (1.75 billion cu. ft) of water per second.

guyot   Flat-topped, subsided oceanic volcano.

gyre   Large, clockwise and counterclockwise pelagic surface current patterns.

hadal zone   Deepest seafloor; water of the oceanic trenches.

hair hygrometer   Instrument that measures moisture in the air by means of a human hair that expands or lengthens upon absorbing moisture.

half-graben   Elongated, downdropped portion of Earth's crust bordered on one side by faults and associated with crustal rifting.

halocline   Water zone that shows a rapid change in salinity with depth.

hanging valley   Glacially eroded valley that lies above and tributary to another glacially eroded valley.

hanging wall   Block of crust along a fault plane that would be above your head if the fault plane were open and you could walk on it; block opposite the footwall.

hardness   Degree to which any mineral resists being scratched; comparative physical value of minerals on a scale devised by Friedrich Mohs on which the hardest mineral, diamond, ranks 10, and talc ranks 1.

hardpan   Concentrated zone of resistant soil components usually found in B-horizon.

headland   Most seaward extent of the land; a promontory.

heat   Quantifiable kinetic energy of particles of matter.

heat budget   Heat reception, storage, and transfer over Earth.

heavy water   Deuterium oxide; moderator in nuclear reactors.

helium flash   Process whereby a star turns helium into carbon; occurs during later stages of stellar life cycle when star collapses upon itself.

Hertzsprung-Russell diagram   Graph that astronomers use to categorize stars on the basis of size, color, luminosity, magnitude, and surface temperatures.

heterosphere   Outer, less dense, and unmixed layer of Earth's atmosphere.

highland climate   An undifferentiated mountain climate.

high tide   Largest water wave generated by the attractive gravitational forces of the moon and the sun and expressed as a high-water mark on shoreline features and structures.

holistic approach   A method of incorporating various disciplines to reveal the interrelationships among Earth processes and features.

homosphere   Lower, dense, mixed portion of Earth's atmosphere.

horizon   Each soil layer or zone.

horn   Glacial erosional remnant that forms a relatively sharp mountain peak at the juncture of adjacent cirques.

horst   Elongated, upthrown block of crust bounded by systems of faults on each side.

hot spot   Stationary magma chamber in the upper mantle linked to the surface by a fracture system up which magma moves to form volcanic features; source of magma for the Hawaiian Island chain.

humus   Dead plant material disaggregated by chemical processes and microorganisms in the soil, resulting in a concentration of dark, fine-grained organic material.

hurricane   Earth's biggest and longest-lasting atmospheric storm; tropical cyclonic storm system that is tracked and named; tropical storm with winds in excess of 120 kilometers (75 mi) per hour.

hydration   A wetting that occurs whenever water molecules bind to another element or compound; in hydration, the hydrogen end of water molecules bind to negative ions, whereas the oxygen end binds to the positive ions in another substance.

hydraulic gradient   The difference in elevation between any two points on the water table divided by the horizontal distance between them.

hydrocarbon compound   One of thousands of compounds, including methane and ethane, composed chiefly of hydrogen and carbon, that in various combinations form petroleum.

hydrogenous sediment   Sediment derived from precipitated compounds in the ocean.

hydrologic cycle   Recurrent process that moves moisture into and out of the atmosphere and through the life-forms, landforms, rocks, soils, and standing water bodies of Earth's surface.

hydrothermal deposit   Metallic salts that are precipitated from the hot fluids associated with magma chambers and volcanic, undersea vents called black or white smokers.

hydrothermal solution   Hot, watery fluids, rich in dissolved ions, that represent the final phase of the crystallization of a magma.

hygrometer   Instrument that uses water absorption or accumulation to register humidity.

hygroscopic (condensation) nuclei   Microscopic, airborne "dust" (pollen, organic debris, soil particles, volcanic ash, sea salts, etc.) that serves as condensation surfaces.

hypocenter   *See* focus.

hypothesis   An unproven conjecture used to explain certain observations.

hypsographic curve   A graph that shows the percentage of Earth's surface that lies above or below sea level; from the Greek *hypsos*, meaning "height," and *graphein*, meaning "to write."

iceberg   Calved block of glacial ice that floats in the ocean.

ice cap   A region of perpetual ice and snow.

ice-marginal lake   A lake formed along the ice front (margin) and contained in part by the ice front.

ice sheet   *See* continental glacier.

ice stream   *See* valley glacier.

igneous rock   Crystalline rock formed from molten mineral matter.

infiltration Soaking of water into and through the ground.

influent stream A stream whose bed is above the water table and which loses water to the saturated zone.

inner core Innermost zone of Earth occupying approximately one-fifth of its radius and thought to be formed of the solid, iron-nickel alloy kamacite.

insolation Acronym for incoming solar radiation.

intensity Measure of a storm or earthquake's strength in terms of structural damage and human perception; qualitative evaluation of an earthquake's strength that is, nevertheless, measured on a numerical scale, usually the Modified Mercalli scale.

intermittent stream Stream that flows during the wetter periods of the year, when its bed intersects the water table, and that dries up when the water table drops below the streambed.

Intertropical Convergence Zone (ITCZ) A shifting atmospheric zone or boundary between the Northeast Trades and the Southeast Trades.

inversion An atmospheric condition in which warmer air overlies cooler air; an atmospheric condition in which temperature rises with increasing altitude.

ion Atom with an electrical charge.

ionic substitution Process whereby ions of various elements of similar size and charge are able to substitute for one another at specific crystal lattice sites within a mineral.

island arc Group of volcanic islands oriented in an arc pattern, as seen in map view, and associated with a deep-sea trench.

isobar Weather mapping symbol used to connect points of equal pressure; a line on a map used to indicate a uniform atmospheric pressure along its extent.

isotherm Mapping symbol used to connect points of equal temperature; a line on a weather map that indicates a uniform atmospheric temperature along its extent.

isotope Atom of a particular weight controlled by its number of neutrons; variant of an element dependent on the number of neutrons in the nucleus.

jet stream High-altitude, high-velocity winds.

jetty Structure built on one or both sides of an inlet, channel, or river mouth to keep the passage open to navigation; jetties divert the flow of the longshore currents to deeper water, thereby causing deposition of sediment away from the channel or river mouth.

joint Break in rock along which no displacement has occurred.

Jovian planets The four, mostly gaseous, giant outer planets of the Solar System: Jupiter, Saturn, Uranus, and Neptune.

kamacite Mixture of iron and nickel in the inner 1,255 kilometers (780 mi) of Earth's radius (inner core).

karst topography Composite of surface and subsurface features formed by groundwater dissolution of soluble rock, usually limestone; topographic and subsurface expression of dissolution in a limestone region.

katabatic wind Downslope, mountain wind.

kettle Depression caused by the melting of a block of ice left by a retreating continental glacier.

kettle lake A small lake that occupies a depression in the ground surface (kettle) that formed when a detached block of stagnant glacial ice melted.

kimberlite Variety of peridotite usually associated with the diamonds of South Africa and elsewhere; both the fragmented nature of the kimberlite rock and the high-pressure origin of diamonds suggest that this rock was forced into the crust from some depth in the mantle.

kinetic energy The energy of motion; energy associated with and expended by moving bodies.

laccolith Concordant pluton made nontabular by a pronounced central thickening that "arches up" the overlying rock layers.

lag gravel An accumulation of rock particles of gravel size and larger formed when wind has removed the associated finer sediment; this may be a preliminary step in the formation of desert pavement.

lahar Rapidly moving volcanic mudflow.

laminar flow Flow in a body of liquid wherein the flow lines remain distinct and the flow directions remain unchanged with time; in nature, this occurs commonly in groundwater, but only in surface streams where fluid motion is slow and the bounding walls of the channel are smooth.

land breeze Nighttime seaward-flowing wind that develops as the land rapidly loses its heat, while the water maintains its accumulated heat; relatively cool land produces a local atmospheric high pressure, while the air over the water produces a local low pressure.

land bridge An area, now submerged below sea level, that was above sea level during major glaciations; such areas served as animal migration routes between landmasses.

landform Individual physiographic feature affected by geologic agents; includes mountains, plains, and plateaus.

lapse Decrease in temperature with increasing altitude.

latent heat of vaporization ´ Stored energy of evaporation, which can be returned to the environment through condensation.

lateral fault Type of fault characterized by predominantly horizontal displacement of rock units.

lateral moraine Rock debris eroded from a valley wall that forms an elongate mound along the side of a valley glacier.

laterite Thick, reddish, strongly leached soil formed by intense chemical weathering in the humid tropics and subtropics.

latitude Distance from the equator as measured in degrees; most significant control on the amount of heat available for the atmosphere.

lava Molten rock material (magma) that reaches Earth's surface; extrusive molten matter.

leaching Dissolution and removal of mineral material from the soil by downward percolating water.

lee side Side opposite the windward side of a mountain.

levee An artificial ridge of unconsolidated material emplaced to raise the top of a stream channel and thereby prevent water from leaving the channel. *See also* natural levee.

lifting Dominant mechanism for air-mass cooling and subsequent condensation.

light-year (lt-yr) Distance light travels in 1 year, or 9,467,280,000,000 kilometers (5,869,713,600,000 mi).

lignite Brownish-colored soft coal with relatively low heat value.

lineation The subparallel to parallel alignment of elongated mineral crystals in a metamorphic rock.

lithosphere Earth's rocky outer layer, which includes the continents and ocean basins as well as the uppermost mantle and which is broken into a number of moving segments (plates); the more rigid, rocky material above the asthenosphere.

littoral zone Seafloor between high and low tides.

loess An accumulation of silt-size particles transported and deposited by the wind; the angularity of the particles allows the sediment to stand in near-vertical slopes.

long (longitudinal) profile Cross-sectional (side) view or diagram of a stream from its headwaters to its mouth.

longshore current Narrow flow of water parallel to the shoreline; narrow shoreline current generated by breaking waves.

longshore transport Movement of sediment by the longshore current.

lopolith Plutonic, usually gabbroic, structure similar to a laccolith but with a distinctive downward bow that results from the sagging of underlying rock.

Love wave Type of earthquake surface wave that manifests itself in a side-to-side motion of the ground.

low tide A level of the ocean's surface between the crests of high tide.

lunar eclipse A shadow cast by Earth on the moon; an obscuration of the moon that occurs whenever all or part of the moon falls within Earth's shadow.

luster Peculiar reflective surface of a mineral; appearance of a mineral's surface as it reflects light.

M

maar A flat-floored volcanic crater; a volcanic vent crater.

magma Liquid rock material with dissolved gases that lies below ground; molten mineral matter that can extrude as lava or that can crystallize to form plutonic igneous rocks and rock features.

magnetic reversal A change in orientation of Earth's north and south magnetic poles; a flipping of the magnetosphere.

magnetosphere Lines of magnetic force that encompass Earth and that are shaped by the positions of the north and south magnetic poles and by the solar wind.

magnitude Quantification of earthquake strength determined from seismic records; earthquake strength measurement based on amount of energy released and quantified in the Richter scale; scale of stellar brightness based either on appearance in the night sky (relative) or on probable appearance if a stellar object were 10 parsecs from Earth.

malleable Capable of being hammered into a desired shape; characteristic of most metals.

mantle Spherical rocky layer of Earth that lies between the crust and the outer core.

marginal sea A sea adjacent and open to an ocean basin; either a eustatically or tectonically formed sea adjacent to an ocean.

maria Dark areas on the moon thought by Galileo to be seas; basaltic flows at the probable sites of large meteoritic impacts on the moon.

marine terrace A former portion of the seafloor that has been smoothed to a gently sloping surface by wave erosion and then exposed, either by elevation of the land or by lowering of sea level.

maritime polar (mP) air Cool, moist air mass that develops over high-latitude oceans.

mass number Approximate weight of an atom, defined as the sum of its protons and neutrons.

mass wasting Downslope movement of earth material under the direct influence of gravity; gravitationally generated downslope movement of earth material facilitated by water or ice.

matter Anything that occupies space and has mass.

meander Bend in a stream.

medial moraine Elongate aggregation of ice-eroded rock that divides two alpine glaciers; combination of two lateral moraines.

mercurial barometer An instrument that indicates atmospheric pressure by the length of a column of mercury contained in a glass tube.

mesopelagic zone Pelagic ocean water that lies at depths between 200 and 1,000 meters (656 and 3,280 ft); the "twilight" zone of pelagic water; also called the disphotic zone.

mesosphere A layer of Earth's atmosphere that lies above the stratopause and is defined by a lapse in temperature.

mesothermal climate A climate type found poleward of the tropical climates and distinguished by mild winters and hot summers.

metal Any element characterized by the physical properties of malleability, ductility, and conductivity and having the tendency to lose outer shell electrons to form positively charged ions.

metamorphic aureole Contact metamorphic rock in a "halo" surrounding an igneous intrusion; synonymous with metamorphic halo.

metamorphic rock Crystalline rock changed from its original state by heat, pressure, and the introduction of chemical fluids.

metamorphism Process involving heat, pressure, and chemical fluids that brings about solid-state changes in rocks and minerals.

meteor Light trail of a meteoroid burning in Earth's atmosphere.

meteoroid Material traversing the Solar System; meteoroids can be irons, stones, or stony-irons; some meteoroids contain carbon in dropletlike structures called chondrules (carbonaceous chondrites).

meteorologist Weather scientist; atmospheric physicist.

meteorology One of four earth science disciplines; predominantly observational and descriptive science of the atmosphere.

microthermal climate A climate type found on the equatorward margins of the polar regions and distinguished by long, cold winters and short summers.

Milky Way Galaxy Aggregation of stars in various stages of development, dust, gases, radiation, and possibly cold dark matter to which our Solar System belongs; our own spiral (or possibly barred-spiral) galaxy, which has an overall diameter of 100,000 light-years and a central thickness of 10,000 light-years.

mineral Naturally occurring, inorganic element or compound with a definite internal arrangement of ions and a chemical composition that is fixed or that varies within narrow limits; a natural compound with definite crystalline, physical, and chemical properties.

model Mathematical or graphic representation of natural processes.

Modified Mercalli scale An earthquake intensity scale that indicates the power of an earthquake by the level of destruction it causes.

Moho (Mohorovicic discontinuity, M-discontinuity) Seismic boundary that divides the crust from the mantle.

molecule Smallest individual unit of a compound formed by two or more atoms.

monadnock An area of higher relief that has temporarily escaped the erosion process and that stands above a peneplain; named for Mount Monadnock in New Hampshire.

monsoon A seasonal wind shift from land to sea in winter to sea-to-land in summer that is accompanied by abundant precipitation in summer.

moraine Landform produced by the accumulation of glacial till in varying shapes, thicknesses, and sizes; unsorted mass of rock and mineral material deposited by melting glacial ice. *See also* terminal moraine, ground moraine, recessional moraine, lateral moraine, and medial moraine.

mountain A landform that stands significantly above its surroundings and that possesses limited surface area at its summit.

mountain glacier *See* valley glacier.

mountain system System of mountains (such as the Rockies and Appalachians) whose dimensions are hundreds to thousands of kilometers long and tens to hundreds of kilometers wide and which are usually formed by plate collisions.

mud cracks Irregular fractures formed on the surface of fine-grained sediment when it dries and shrinks. These features may be destroyed when the sediment becomes wet once more, or they may be preserved in the resulting sedimentary rock.

mudflow Type of mass wasting especially characteristic of arid to semiarid regions in which viscous mixtures of sediment and water flow downslope, following stream channels.

multiple working hypotheses A scientific method that incorporates two or more approaches to a common problem.

N

native element Mineral formed from ions of a single uncombined element, such as gold (Au), graphite and diamond (C), sulfur (S), and copper (Cu).

natural gas Dominantly methane (CH_4); gaseous component of petroleum; explosive gas found in coal mines.

natural law An expression of the universality of specific natural processes.

natural leevee One of a pair of low, parallel ridges found on either side of a channel; a ridge along a stream channel formed when the stream leaves its banks during flooding and deposits its coarsest sediment immediately adjacent to the channel.

natural resource Anything taken from Earth to support life or a way of life.

neap tide Smallest tidal range that occurs approximately twice each month; a small tidal range caused by the alignment of the sun and the moon in a right angle to Earth that partially cancels their gravitational influence on the planet.

near-Earth object An asteroid or comet whose orbit crosses the orbit of Earth.

nebula Giant cloud of gas and dust that provides the material from which stars coalesce; giant cloud of gas produced by exploding star.

nebular hypothesis Account of the formation of the Solar System in which a large nebula condensed to form the sun and its attendant bodies.

neritic zone Shallow water zone that extends from the littoral zone to the edge of the continental shelf.

neutrino Very small, virtually massless, high-speed particle associated with stellar explosions and solar activity.

neutron   Uncharged particle in the atomic nucleus.

nodule   Oval or spherical sedimentary structure that is often rich in metals, such as iron and manganese, and the nonmetal phosphorous.

nonclastic   Without visible pieces (clasts); a type of sedimentary rock texture characterized by a lack of mineral or rock particles (clasts); the texture of chemical precipitates; formed by the precipitation of minerals from solutions.

nonfoliated   Exhibiting no planar features; metamorphic texture that has no layers.

nonrenewable resource   A substance that can be used by humans only once, such as coal or natural gas.

nontabular pluton   A pluton that lacks a tabular geometric shape.

normal fault   Fault in which the hanging wall drops relative to the footwall; a result of tension.

North Atlantic Deep Water (NADW) Norwegian Sea water that sinks lower than the Mediterranean intermediate water.

notch   An indentation carved by wave erosion in the base of a seacliff.

oceanic crust   The basaltic portion of Earth's crust; that portion of Earth's crust that is dominated by mafic minerals and dark igneous rocks; the crust that underlies the oceans.

oceanic ridge   One part of an extensive, linear volcanic submarine mountain system associated with seafloor spreading.

oceanography   One of four earth science disciplines; study of the oceans.

O-horizon   Uppermost few centimeters of the soil, composed of abundant decaying organic material mixed with some minerals.

oil   Liquid component of petroleum consisting of hundreds of individual hydrocarbon compounds.

oil shale   Shale permeated by a bituminous material known as kerogen.

ooze   A mud composed of a mixture of fine terrigenous sediment and biogenic sediment (hemipelagic ooze) or biogenic sediment (pelagic ooze).

ophiolite   Obducted, generally metaliferous ocean crust that can be identified by a suite of petrological characteristics, including pillow basalts.

orbit   The path of one celestial body around another.

ore mineral   Mineral that can be mined and refined at a profit.

orographic barrier   An upland landform over which air must pass; a topographic high over which rising air cools.

orographic lifting   Mechanically induced process that moves air to higher altitudes, where cooling takes place.

outer core   Mostly liquid iron sphere from the boundary with the inner core to the bottom of the mantle, approximately 3,975 kilometers (2,159 mi) out from Earth's center.

outlet glacier   A form of ice stream that flows out from a central ice sheet through a valley that crosses the confining mountains.

outwash   Transported sediment picked up by glacial meltwater streams and carried down a valley away from the ice front.

outwash plain   The regional surface composed of the merged outwash deposits laid down by a number of glacial meltwater streams.

overburden   Rock and soil overlying an economic mineral deposit.

overthrust fault   Low-angle reverse (thrust) fault along which older rocks are pushed over younger rocks.

overwash delta   Fanlike deposit that forms in a lagoon whenever storm waves breach barrier islands.

oxbow lake   Horseshoe-shaped, detached segment of a former stream channel, now filled with water.

ozone   Triatomic oxygen (O_3), a colorless, odorless gas naturally produced in Earth's atmosphere and found concentrated in the stratosphere, where it blocks much of the ultraviolet part of the spectrum; a surface pollutant.

paleomagnetism   Preservation in rock of the direction of Earth's magnetic field as it existed at the time the rock was formed; geomagnetism preserved whenever molten mineral matter cools below the Curie point and crystallizes to form igneous rock.

Pangaea   United landmass named by Alfred Wegener for the supercontinent that formed during the later Paleozoic from all the present-day continents ("all land").

paradigm   A significant model.

parallax   Apparent positional change of an object that results from a change of perspective.

parallel stream pattern   A stream pattern formed when a number of parallel to subparallel streams flow down a gently sloping regional surface, such as a coastal plain.

parent material   Bedrock, glacial till, or any other earth material from which a soil has developed.

parsec (pc)   Astronomical distance unit (3.26 lt-yr).

paternoster lake   One of a series of small lakes formed on flattened areas along a glacial trough and connected by streams and waterfalls.

patterned ground   Several related ground-surface features in which coarser rock debris is segregated from finer rock debris by the alternate freezing and thawing of water in the ground.

pause   Atmospheric boundary in which little or no change in temperature occurs with increasing altitude.

pearl   Hardened, spherical calcium carbonate secretions of oysters within their shells.

peat   Woodlike fossil fuel with approximately 60% carbon content; first stage in the conversion of plant material to coal.

pedalfer   Acidic soil with humus-rich A-horizon and clay-rich B-horizon that has been completely leached of calcite; characteristic soil of the humid eastern United States and Canada.

pedocal   Calcitic, alkaline soil found in dry climates, where leaching is minimal; characteristic soil of the arid and semiarid western United States.

pegmatitic texture   An igneous (plutonic) rock texture with very large crystals (grains).

pelagic water   The open ocean water; the water beyond the neritic zone.

peneplain   The flat to gently rolling surface that is envisioned as the landscape to which a region is reduced in the late (old-age) stage of the stream erosion cycle.

perched water table   A shallow water table formed on top of a local saturated zone above the regional water table and separated from the regional water table by an impervious zone.

perennial stream   Stream whose bed intersects the water table and whose flow is consequently maintained all year.

perigee   Position on an elliptical orbit where the orbiting body is closest to the object it orbits.

periglacial   A generic term that describes a large number of processes and surface features associated with the margin of a glacier.

perihelion   Orbital position of Earth when it is closest to the sun; Earth's orbital position in January.

permafrost   Ground material that remains frozen year-round; characteristic of high-altitude and high-latitude regions, where to a certain depth, the soil undergoes seasonal freeze and thaw, but below which, the soil remains permanently frozen.

permeability   Characteristic of a substance that allows the free passage of a fluid; ability to transmit water or other fluids; extent to which pore spaces are interconnected.

petroleum   Important fossil fuel formed exclusively in sedimentary rocks and consisting of a mixture of solid (bitumen or asphalt), liquid (oil), and gaseous (natural gas) hydrocarbon compounds.

phaneritic (coarse) texture   Igneous rock texture in which the individual mineral crystals are large enough to be visible to the naked eye; texture produced by slow cooling of magma; synonymous with coarse-grained.

photomultiplier   Instrument that measures the amount of light striking its surface.

photon   Particle or package of light energy.

photosphere   Visible portion of the sun with sun spots.

photosynthesis   Process by which plants convert carbon dioxide, water, and sunlight into carbohydrates, while releasing oxygen.

physical weathering   Reduction to smaller-size particles of rock and mineral material in Earth's surface environment; synonymous with mechanical weathering and disintegration.

piedmont glacier   An ice sheet formed by the merging of two or more ice streams at the foot of a mountain range.

piezometric (potentiometric) surface   The level to which water in an artesian system will rise.

pig iron   Molton iron produced from the blast furnace and usually poured into molds referred to as piglets.

placer deposit   Sedimentary accumulation of heavy mineral grains (e.g., gold, platinum, diamond, and tinstone) that were eroded from the primary vein deposits, transported some distance downstream or along a beach, and then deposited.

plains   Extensive continental or marine (abyssal) surfaces characterized by low elevations and low relief.

planetesimal   Term used to describe small bodies that accreted to form Earth and the other planets.

plasma   Superheated form of matter.

plastic   Tending to be slowly deformed without returning to original shape.

plastic zone   The lower portion of a glacier, where pressure is high and the ice tends to slowly deform plastically.

plate   Lithospheric unit; one of approximately 10 large and numerous small segments of Earth's outer shell (lithosphere) that are in motion relative to one another.

plateau   An extensive elevated continental surface underlain by essentially horizontal rock layers often bounded by escarpments; plateaus may have small to great relief, depending on the degree of uplifting and the extent of erosion.

plate tectonics   Theory that accounts for many observed geological phenomena that result from the movement of tectonic plates.

playa lake   An intermittent lake that occupies the flat area between mountains (playa) in an arid region during the wetter times of the year.

pluton   Mass of igneous rock that crystallized before reaching Earth's surface.

plutonic (intrusive)   Generic term that describes all intrusive igneous rock bodies.

pluvial   A term that refers to rain or to a period of higher than normal rainfall, as occurred in much of the western United States during the last period of widespread glaciation.

point bar   Sand deposit on inside of a stream meander, where stream velocity, and thus energy, is reduced.

polar glacier   A glacier whose temperature is below freezing to a great depth and in which, consequently, little or no melting takes place.

polar high   Atmospheric high-pressure system found above planetary poles.

porosity   Percentage of open space within soil, sediment, or rock.

porphyritic texture   Igneous rock texture characterized by two different crystal sizes, usually fine and coarse, that indicates a two-phase crystallization.

potential energy   Stored energy; energy that any body possesses by reason of its position or location.

pothole   A smooth, circular depression cut in the floor of a bedrock stream channel by the scouring action of pebbles and boulders as they are swirled around by the stream current.

precious gem   Gem mineral of especially high economic value; the four usually considered as precious are diamond, ruby, sapphire, and emerald.

pressure gradient   Difference in barometric pressure between two adjacent sites.

prior appropriation doctrine   The water rights doctrine that allocates the available water to the first landowner adjacent to the water body; this doctrine is most commonly applied in the arid western United States.

prodelta   Fine-grained deposit of sediments lying beyond the delta front.

prominences   Largest outward surface movements or jets of solar gas.

proper motion   The movement of an object across an observer's field of view; usually measured in degrees of arc.

proton   Positively charged particle that is part of the nucleus of an atom.

protoplanet   Second stage in the formation of a planet, created by planetesimals colliding and growing in size.

proximal turbidite   Coarse-grained sedimentary deposit that occurs near the origin of a turbidity flow.

psychrometer   Instrument that uses evaporation to measure humidity.

P-wave (primary wave)   Type of body wave that manifests itself in a push-pull (contraction-expansion) motion; first body wave to arrive after an earthquake; such a wave can be transmitted through solids, liquids, and gases.

pycnocline   Zone of rapid change in seawater density with depth.

pyroclastic debris   Generic term for all solid particles ejected from a volcano; any solid particle, ranging in size from fine dust to large blocks, that is ejected from a volcano.

quarrying   The dislodging and picking up of rock fragments by a moving glacier.

quick clay   A find-grained sediment, usually deposited under marine conditions and later leached by groundwater, that is subject to rapid collapse and movement by any sudden shock or vibration.

quicksand   A mass of sand-sized sediment that lacks the strength to support an object on its surface because water is moving constantly upward through it, causing the rock particles to separate.

radial motion   The movement of an object away from or toward an observer.

radial stream pattern   A stream pattern formed by a group of streams that emanate from a central point, such as the top of a volcanic cone, and flow downslope in all directions away from that point.

radial velocity   Speed with which an object moves away from an observer.

radiation   A mode of transfer for heat energy that involves the passage of electromagnetic waves through space; any transmission of electromagnetic waves or atomic and subatomic particles.

radiation fog   Ground cloud that occurs under clear skies whenever air is cooled because of loss of heat through radiation.

radiative zone   Sphere within the sun that extends from the core to approximately seven-tenths of the distance to the surface.

radiometric dating   General technique for determining absolute ages of both organic and inorganic materials by examining ratios of parent to daughter elements.

rainfall line   A line approximating 100°w that divides the United States into two nearly equal parts, with the area to the east of this line receiving, on average, more rainfall than that to the west.

rain forest   A tropical forest composed of a wide variety of broadleaf evergreens that form a high canopy of vegetation in areas with consistently abundant rainfall.

ramp   A subaerial sloped surface formed at the base of a retreating headland.

rarefaction   Expansion of the ground or a spring with the passage of a P-wave.

rare metal   A metal with an average crustal abundance of less than 0.01%.

Rayleigh wave   Type of earthquake surface wave that causes the ground particles to move in elliptical orbits.

recessional moraine   Ridge of till accumulated along the front of a retreating glacier; one of a series of linear ridges behind and subparallel to a terminal moraine, indicating either a pause in the glacier's retreat or a readvance of the ice.

recharge   The addition of water to the saturated zone either by natural water movement or artifically through wells.

recrystallization   The process whereby new (and generally larger) mineral crystals form in a rock, largely through solid state changes.

red giant   Type of star created when a main sequence star fuels itself by turning helium into carbon, resulting in an expansion of its outermost layers.

red shift   Electromagnetic shift toward the longer wavelengths derived from the radial motion of an object moving away from an observer.

refractory   Said of a material that can be used in applications that require high resistance to heat (such as the lining of a blast furnace); difficult to break down.

regional metamorphism A rock change that occurs over wide areas because of mountain building; especially indicative of great pressures generated deep in Earth's crust.

relative humidity Ratio (in percent) between the actual amount of water vapor present and the vapor-carrying capacity of the air mass.

relief Difference in elevation between high and low points of topography.

renewable resource Material that can be generated within a relatively short span of time (e.g., crops, timber) or that can be reused (e.g., air, water).

reserve Measured, evaluated, and currently exploitable portion of a resource.

reservoir rock Porous and permeable rock layer within which petroleum accumulates.

residence time Duration of the presence of a substance in some location (atmosphere, ocean, etc.).

respiration Process in which animals use oxygen and release carbon dioxide.

reverse (thrust) fault A fault caused by compressive forces in which the hanging wall moves upward relative to the footwall.

revolution Orbiting; the trip around another object.

Richter scale Open-ended logarithmic scale with increments that mark increasing releases of energy during an earthquake; a measure of earthquake magnitudes.

rill A very small channel through which surface water runoff initially moves.

riparian doctrine The water rights doctrine that allows the owner of the land adjacent to the water access to and use of the water, provided that the water is returned to the natural water body at the same level of quality as it was removed; this doctrine is commonly applied in the humid eastern United States.

rip current Backwash flow perpendicular to the shoreline and out to deep water.

ripple mark Small, wavelike form that develops on the surface of dunes and sandbars and that may be preserved in sandstone.

riprap A covering of rocks and boulders laid down to protect a shoreline or riverbank from erosion.

river A land-surface flow of water within a confining channel; a river is usually considered a "large" stream.

rock Aggregate or physical mixture of mineral grains or crystals.

rock creep The slow, downslope movement of surface rock masses and/or the overturning in a downslope direction of the exposed edges of thinly bedded rock layers due to the pull of gravity.

rock cycle Graphic method of portraying the interrelationships among the three basic rock types, as well as their modes of disintegration and formation.

rockfall The vertical free fall of rock material; a variety of mass movement.

rock glacier A type of slow mass movement in which a lobate mass of rock debris moves down a val-

ley much in the manner of a glacier; interstitial ice may facilitate the movement.

rockslide The movement of rock material down a steeply inclined slip surface, such as a fault plane or a sedimentary bedding plane; a variety of mass movement.

rotation Turning on an axis.

salinity Measurement of solid matter in grams contained in a kilogram (1,000 g, or 2.2 lb) of seawater after any carbonate has been converted to an oxide, any bromine and iodine have been replaced by chlorine, and any organic matter has been oxidized.

salinity profile A graph that plots ocean salinities through a water column.

saltation The bouncing movement of sand-size mineral grains by water or air currents.

salt dome Vertical column or pillar of salt that originated from a sedimentary salt layer at depth and that was squeezed upward plastically by the pressure of the overlying rocks.

salt marsh Low-lying, constantly wet area of silt, sand, and organic material at the boundary between land and sea; found mostly in temperate regions.

saturated (wet) adiabatic rate Variable rate at which a rising mass of air cools after its dew point has been reached.

saturated solution Solution with no additional capacity for hydrating salt ions.

savanna A tropical, open grassland of tall grasses and woody bushes.

schistosity Type of metamorphic foliation usually characterized by an abundance of subparallel mica crystals.

scientific method A series of intellectual processes that include identifying a problem and logically solving it through observation and experimentation.

sea arch Feature cut through a headland by the joining of opposing sea caves.

sea breeze Landward breeze developed when air pressure is low over land and high over the water, occurring primarily during the afternoon and early evening.

sea cave Cave cut in a headland or cliff by wave action.

seafloor spreading Mechanism that forms new seafloor material as new crustal material wells up from the mantle and pushes older material aside, constantly renewing the igneous rock at the axis by replacement.

sea level Position of the ocean surface relative to the geodesic sphere.

seamount Submarine volcanic pile that does not reach the ocean surface to form an island.

sea stack Islandlike remnant of an eroded headland.

seawall A metal or concrete wall designed to protect the land from flooding by the sea and from erosion.

seawater The salt water of the oceans, with an approximate average salinity of 34 ‰.

sediment Loose rock, mineral particles, or organic debris formed by weathering, salts precipitated from solution, or the fragmentation of the remains of organisms.

sedimentary rock Any rock that forms by accumulation and consolidation of loose rock and mineral material and/or by the accumulation of fossils and salts.

seismic sea wave (tsunami) Long-period, high-velocity, open-ocean surface wave created by earthquake, volcanic eruption, or landslide activity in or near the ocean; often mistakenly termed tidal wave.

seismic tomography Study of Earth's interior through seismic wave analysis by incorporating a number of seismic stations whose operators pool data to create a three-dimensional image.

seismogram Graphic or photographic record of the passage of earthquake waves.

seismograph Recording seismometer; an instrument that senses and records the passage of earthquake waves.

seismologist Earth scientist who specializes in the study of earthquakes and the study of seismic waves.

seismometer Instrument that is sensitive to the passage of earthquake waves.

semipermanent highs and lows A seasonal pressure of wide geographic extent occurring over either continents or oceans; one of a number of pressure systems that develop where air either ascends (low) or descends (high); the semipermanent highs and lows influence weather over large geographical areas—for example, the Bermuda High influences weather over the eastern United States and the western North Atlantic during summer.

semiprecious gem Any mineral used as a gem with the exception of the four precious gems (i.e., diamond, ruby, sapphire, and emerald).

shadow zone Area on Earth's surface that does not receive S-waves from an earthquake because they are damped out upon encountering Earth's liquid outer core (S-wave shadow zone); an area on Earth's surface that will not receive P-waves from an earthquake because of the refraction of the waves as they pass through the outer core (P-wave shadow zone).

shallow-water wave Wave in water that has a depth less than one-half the wave's length.

shelf break Edge of the continental shelf; boundary between shelf and slope; boundary between neritic and pelagic waters.

shield volcano Broad-based volcano with a low topographic profile, though it may reach to very high elevations; largest volcanic structure composed principally of basaltic lava flows.

shoaling Becoming shallower.

sial Term derived from the chemical symbols for silicon and aluminum; used synonymously with continental (granitic) crust.

side-looking sonar   Imaging system that bounces energy off the ocean floor at an oblique angle to produce detailed images.

sidereal month   Revolution of the moon considered against the stars as the reference point (27.32 solar days).

sigma-t (or T-S) diagram   Graph of the combined effects of salinity and temperature on water that enables scientists to establish density characteristics for particular water masses.

silicates   The largest of the mineral groups; includes most of the major rock-forming minerals, which, in turn, account for more than 90% of the volume of Earth's crust.

sill   Tabular, concordant pluton, usually basaltic (gabbroic) in composition.

sima   Term derived from the chemical symbol for silicon and the word *mafic* and used synonymously with oceanic (basaltic) crust.

sinkhole   Ground surface depression associated with the fall of a cavern roof.

slag   Waste material formed in a blast furnace as a result of limestone (added as a flux) combining with impurities released from the coke and the iron ore.

slaty cleavage   Variety of metamorphic rock foliation in which the parallel alignment of the minerals allows the rock to be easily split.

sling psychrometer   Psychrometer that speeds up evaporation process through the use of two thermometers that can be spun rapidly at the end of a chain or cord to measure humidity.

slump   Type of mass movement characterized by a rotational movement along a curved slip surface.

SOFAR channel   The low-density sound fixing and ranging channel or layer of water through which sound energy can travel great distances.

soil   Portion of Earth's loose surface material that is capable of supporting plants with root systems.

soil profile   Total vertical sequence of soil horizons.

solar eclipse   Blockage of our view of the sun by the moon.

solar flare   Very explosive, linear and usually arcing masses of gas ejected from the sun's surface in the vicinity of sunspots.

Solar System   All the attendant bodies of a sun; the nine planets, their various moons, asteroids, comets, meteoroids, and *Apollo* objects that are held in orbit around our sun.

solar wind   Charged particles that exit the sun at high speed; corpuscular radiation.

solifluction   A type of slow, downslope movement of the saturated upper soil layer due to freeze and thaw action.

sorting   Sedimentary process that concentrates particles of similar sizes and shapes.

source region   Point of origin for air mass weather or sediments.

source rock   Rock layer in which hydrocarbons formed.

Southern Oscillation   A seasonal latitudinal shift in the boundary between the trade winds and the prevailing westerlies.

spatter cone   A relatively small, often symmetrical, conical structure built up from eruptions of lava.

specific gravity   Density of a substance compared to the density of pure water at 4° C (39° F); the specific gravity of water is 1.0.

specific humidity   Ratio between the weight of the water vapor and the weight of the air parcel containing it.

spectrophotometer   Device used to separate light into different wavelengths to enable astronomers to study the spectrum of a star.

spicule   Smallest and most common outward movements of solar gas.

spit   Elongate subaerial deposit of unconsolidated sediments emplaced by the longshore current; an extension of the beach into the open and deeper water of a bay.

splash-and-spray zone   A nearshore zone in which waves break violently against sea stacks, isolated rocks, and cliffs.

splay   Fan-shaped deposit along river banks that forms when the water level breeches natural levees.

spring   Seepage of water that forms when the water table intersects the ground surface along steep slopes, a fracture system, or a sinkhole.

spring tide   Largest tidal range that occurs approximately twice each month, when Earth, the moon, and the sun are in a straight line so that their gravitational forces are enhanced.

squall line   Moving zone of intense precipitation and storm activity associated with a cold front.

stable air   An air parcel that has a tendency to return to its original position.

stable equilibrium   Point at which ambient air and air-mass temperatures are equal.

stainless steel   Alloy of iron that contains between 12% and 60% chromium.

stalactite   Icicle-like mineral deposit projecting down from the roof of a cavern and formed by precipitation from slowly dripping groundwater.

stalagmite   Moundlike or columnlike accumulation of mineral matter on the floor of a cavern that was deposited by slowly dripping groundwater.

steppe   A semiarid region of short grasses.

stock   Irregularly shaped, discordant pluton similar in composition to a batholith, but smaller (less than 100 sq. km, or 40 sq. mi, of surface exposure).

stone ring   A variety of patterned ground in which coarser rock material has been segregated by freeze and thaw action into polygonal acumulations surrounding masses of finer-grained material.

stone stripe   A variety of patterned ground in which coarser rock material has been segregated by freeze and thaw action into linear accumulations that display a downslope trend.

stratiform cloud   Layered cloud produced in stable air.

stratopause   Upper boundary of the stratosphere.

stratosphere   Earth's atmospheric zone above the zone of weather; the atmospheric zone that contains the ozone layer.

stratovolcano   Volcanic cone built up by a combination of andesitic (usually) lava flows and pyroclastic eruptions, often rising abruptly from the surrounding landscape to reach great elevations.

streak   Characteristic chalklike mark some minerals make when they are rubbed on an unglazed ceramic plate known as a streak plate; the color of a powdered specimen of a mineral.

stream   Water moving in a confining channel downslope across the surface of the land.

stream erosion cycle   The hypothetical cycle wherein a stream's characteristics, as well as the characteristics of the terrain across which it flows, change with time; recognized stages of development usually are considered to be youth, maturity, and old age.

stream gradient   The drop in elevation along a stream course; usually measured in meters per kilometer or feet per mile.

stream head   Point of origin (at higher elevations) of a stream.

stream mouth   Downslope end of a stream; end of a stream that empties into the base-level water body.

stream pattern   Any of several possible areal patterns formed within a drainage basin by large streams and their systems of tributaries; which pattern forms is governed primarily by topography and the structure of the underlying rocks.

striation   A groove or scratch in a bedrock surface caused by rocks incorporated in the base of a glacier that moves across the surface.

strike-slip fault   Type of lateral fault; a strike-slip fault derives its name from the dominant movement, which is along the line of strike (horizontal) rather than along the dip (vertical) of the fault system.

strip mining   Common method of mining by which shallow mineral deposits are removed by excavating all soil and overlying rock layers (overburden) to expose the deposits.

strong nuclear force   Atomic force that overcomes the natural repulsion of protons and binds the nucleus together.

strophic balance   An equilibrium of centrifugal and centripetal forces.

subaerial   Under air; above water.

subaqueous   Under water.

subbituminous coal   A brown coal; a coal with low heat value.

subduction   Underthrusting of one lithospheric plate by another.

sublimation   Phase change process by which a solid goes directly into the vapor state.

sublittoral   Seafloor immediately below the low-water (low-tide) mark; seafloor of continental shelf.

sublunar point   The point on Earth directly beneath the moon.

submarine canyon   A gorge cut into the continental slope by the erosive action of turbidity flows.

subpolar low   A low-pressure system that is established by ascending air between the polar and subtropic regions.

subsidence   Dropping or settling of the ground surface relative to the surrounding area; a type of mass movement.

subsoil   Another name for B-horizon; the zone of accumulation.

subtropical high   Seasonally fluctuating atmospheric high-pressure system of the subtropics that is bordered by the westerlies and the trade winds.

sunspot   Dark area in the photosphere of the sun with a temperature below 4,000 K.

supernova   An explosive stellar event during which most of the mass of a large star is expelled at high speed; a stellar explosion triggered by a rapid collapse of a massive star; the brilliant light given off by an exploding star.

supralittoral   Beach and dune area above the high-water mark.

surface wave   Wavelike motion of the ground that expands from an earthquake epicenter; Love and Rayleigh waves.

surf zone   Shallow water zone along the shoreline where the waves become unstable and break.

suspension   Continuous movement of sedimentary particles above the ground surface or streambed by moving air or water.

swash   Final expression of a breaking wave as the thin sheet of water that flows farthest up a beach face.

S-wave (secondary wave)   Type of earthquake body wave that moves with a vertical shaking motion and that arrives after P-waves; such a wave can only be transmitted through a solid (rigid) body.

syncline   Structural downfold in which rock layers on either side of the axis are "inclined" toward or "with" (*syn-*) one another; U-shaped structure.

synodic month   Revolution of the moon considered against the sun as the reference point (29.53 solar days).

tabular pluton   Igneous rock structure that resembles a tabletop—that is, relatively thin compared to its length and width.

taconite   Lake Superior-type iron ore of low grade consisting of alternating hematite-bearing and chert-bearing layers. *See* banded iron formation.

taiga   A region of cold, swampy, forested areas of the near-polar regions (high latitude).

talus   Loose rock particles, freed by weathering and moved downslope by gravity, that accumulate at the base of a steep slope.

talus cone   The cone-shaped form in which talus accumulates at the base of a steep slope.

talus slope   The landscape feature formed by the merging of individual talus cones at the base of a steep slope.

tangential velocity   Rate at which proper motion occurs, described in degrees and fractions of degrees of an arc.

tarn   A lake in a cirque.

tar sands   Sandstones impregnated with solid asphaltic hydrocarbons; nonliquid petroleum resources found in great abundance in Alberta, Canada.

temperate glacier   A glacier typical of temperate climatic zones, where temperatures during the ablation season are near the melting point of the ice.

temperature   Quantifiable mean kinetic energy of molecules.

temperature range   The daily or annual difference between high and low temperatures.

terminal moraine   Linear ridge of till formed at the end or terminus of a glacier.

terracette   One of a series of narrow, parallel, horizontal surfaces formed by the downward creep of surface materials under the pull of gravity; most commonly occurs on moderate to steep, grass-covered slopes in cool, humid regions.

terrane   Usually, an oceanic plateau or an island group, with a density between that of average continental and average oceanic crust, that may become sutured onto a continent.

terrestrial planets   The four Earth-like planets closest to the sun and similar in size and composition: Earth, Venus, Mars, and Mercury.

terrigenous   Derived from the continents or land.

Tethys   Ancient tropical sea that divided Gondwanaland from Laurasia.

texture   Size, shape, and arrangement of mineral grains or crystals in rock.

theory   Explanation for phenomena that is based on fact.

thermocline   Water zone of rapid temperature change with depth.

thermograph   Recording thermometer.

thermohaline circulation   Movement of ocean water driven by density differences that result from differences in temperature (thermo) and salinity (haline).

thermometer   Instrument used to measure temperatures.

thermosphere   A layer of Earth's atmosphere that lies above the mesopause (over 100 km altitude) and that is characterized by an inversion.

thrust fault   *See* reverse fault.

tidal bore   Low wall or wave of advancing seawater that moves upstream during the onset of high tide.

tidal channel   A channel in a salt marsh through which ebbing and flooding waters flow; an opening in a barrier bar through which the incoming and outgoing tides are funneled.

tidal range   The difference between the elevations of high and low tides.

tides   Largest of all shallow-water wave systems; bulges of water that encompass whole oceans, making their wavelengths much greater than water depth.

tombolo   Current-deposited, unconsolidated sedimentary structure that connects the mainland to an offshore island or sea stack.

topography   General configuration of the land surface; lie of the land.

topsoil   Nutrient-rich, dark surface layer of soil; synonymous with A-horizon.

tornado   A small-diameter rotary storm that is one of the most violent types of storms known; a small-diameter cyclonic storm with winds estimated as high as 300 kilometers per hour.

tractive force   A lateral force that moves the oceans toward the sublunar point, thus producing a tidal bulge, or crest.

transcurrent fault   Type of lateral fault along which there is no magmatic activity.

transform fault   Type of lateral fault along which there is some magmatic activity and crustal spreading perpendicular to the fault.

transgression   Progressive inundation of the land by a shallow sea.

transpiration   The evaporation of water from plant surfaces.

transportation   The movement of any earth materials on, above, or beneath Earth's surface.

trap   Location (e.g., anticlines, faults, salt domes) where migrating petroleum becomes trapped by surrounding impermeable rock units.

trellis stream pattern   A stream pattern formed when short tributaries flow down steep slopes to join larger streams at right angles; this pattern is most characteristic of terrain where linear ridges alternate with linear valleys.

trench   Elongate and deep, V-shaped, valleylike seafloor feature associated with subduction zones.

tributary   Stream that runs into another, larger stream.

tritium   Isotope of hydrogen with a proton and two neutrons in the nucleus.

tropical storm   Violent cyclonic movement with wind speeds reaching 119 kilometers (74 mi) per hour, cartographically expressed by several closed isobars.

tropopause   Uppermost fluctuating boundary of the troposphere.

troposphere   Zone of weather; lowermost sphere of Earth's atmosphere.

trough   The low point between successive wave crests; a stream valley that has been widened and deepened by glacial erosion; atmospheric low pressure.

tsunami   *See* seismic sea wave.

T Tauri   Second stage of a developing star, during which the star's energy production varies.

tundra   Polar climate with a very short period of plant growth.

turbidity flow Swiftly moving (up to 35 km/hr, or 22 mph), sediment-charged, bottom-flowing current in a lake, sea, or ocean responsible for cutting submarine canyons.

turbulent flow Irregular, eddying motion in a liquid; in natural water bodies, this commonly occurs at higher velocities and with increased roughness of the bounding walls of the channel.

ultimate base level Lowest level to which streams can erode their channels; usually taken as sea level because streams disperse upon flowing into the ocean.

ultraviolet (UV) radiation Electromagnetic radiation with a wavelength shorter than 0.4 micrometers; toxic radiation that causes sunburning and skin cancer; wavelength of radiation absorbed by the ozone layer.

uniformitarianism Principle that today's Earth processes are not different in kind from those processes that have operated throughout Earth history and that such history can be interpreted by studying the present.

unstable air Parcel of air that rises because it is warmer than its atmospheric environment.

upslope fog Ground clouds that occur at higher elevations with the adiabatic cooling of rising air.

upwelling Process in the oceans that brings cold, nutrient-rich water from depth up to the surface.

valley Linear depression in the land surface formed by stream erosion.

valley glacier An elongate mass of ice that flows downslope largely under the pull of gravity and that is confined to a former stream valley at high elevations; synonymous with ice stream, alpine glacier, and mountain glacier.

valley train A linear deposit of glacial outwash that extends down a single stream valley.

variable star Star that varies its magnitude over periods of 1 to 50 days.

varve A pair of sediment layers that, taken together, represent a single year of deposition in any lake subject to annual freezing; the lighter, coarser layer is formed by deposition during the summer, the darker, finer layer by deposition during the winter.

vein Small, irregularly-shaped mineral body formed in the final stages of magmatic crystallization and often containing concentrations of economically valuable minerals.

ventifact A rock mass that has been smoothed and shaped by the abrasion of wind-transported sand particles.

vesicular (porous) texture Igneous rock texture in which small pores or cavities (vesicles) are formed

by the crystallization of lava around escaping gas bubbles.

viscosity Measure of any fluid's resistance to flowing; the opposite of fluidity.

volcanic (extrusive) Term that describes igneous activity that occurs on Earth's surface.

volcano Cone-shaped topographic feature composed of an accumulation of lava and pyroclastic material that has been ejected from a fissure in Earth's surface; extrusive igneous feature often classified as active, dormant, or extinct, based on its history of eruption.

warm-core ring Gulf Stream loop that closes on the Sargasso Sea water from the south.

warm current Typically, a western boundary ocean-surface current traveling away from or along the equator; fast, narrow, and deep surface current.

warm occlusion An occlusion that occurs adjacent to the western coast of the United States, where the air to the rear of the front derives from the air over the oceans.

water Compound of hydrogen and oxygen that exists through the sharing of electrons.

water mass Large, three-dimensional body of water that has identifiable boundaries.

water purity A measure of the degree to which groundwater has been contaminated by the incorporation of microorganisms.

water quality A measure of the degree to which groundwater has been contaminated by the incorporation of dissolved mineral matter.

water table Boundary between aerated zone and saturated zone in the ground; upper limit of the saturated zone (groundwater).

wave Expression of energy in a medium; circular movement of water particles within a body of water in response to the passage of energy.

wave base Lowest level to which a standing body of water will be disturbed by the passage of a wave; a water depth approximately equal to one-half of the wavelength of a passing wave.

wave-cut platform Relatively flat shoreline area eroded by surf action.

wave diffraction The bending of a wave around an object, such as a jetty.

wave height The vertical distance from wave trough to wave crest.

wavelength The horizontal distance between successive wave crests or wave troughs.

wave of oscillation A wave in which water particle motion is essentially in circular orbits; characteristically, these are open-ocean, deep-water waves.

wave of translation A wave, characteristic of shallow water, in which a component of water movement is in a forward direction.

wave period The time between the passage of successive wave crests, as observed at a particular point.

wave refraction Bending of a wave front, a part of whose energy has been robbed by friction along a shoaling bottom.

wave train Successive series of wave crests and troughs.

weather Daily changes among gases of the atmosphere; temporary condition of the atmosphere at a given locality or region.

weather elements Quantifiable characteristics, such as temperature, humidity, pressure, precipitation, and wind, that define air masses.

weathering The chemical and physical alteration of rock and mineral material as a result of exposure to the gases of Earth's surface environment.

white dwarf Last shining stage of a star's development, where overall size is greatly reduced.

wind Advection; horizontal movement of air caused by pressure differences.

wind vane An instrument used to indicate wind direction.

xenolith A mass of country rock, of variable size, that has been surrounded by and incorporated into a mass of igneous rock; literally means "foreign rock."

zone of ablation Down-valley portion of a glacier, where loss of old ice exceeds gain of new ice; zone below the equilibrium line.

zone of accumulation Up-valley portion of a glacier, where aggregation of new ice exceeds loss of old ice; zone above the equilibrium line; in soil classification, is synonymous with B-horizon.

zone of aeration Uppermost ground layer that water traverses in its downward infiltration movement; soil zone in which the spaces between mineral grains are partly filled with air and partly occupied by the water.

zone of leaching *See* A-horizon.

zone of saturation Zone where the pore spaces in the soil, sediment, or rock are completely filled with water; the water occupying the pore spaces within the saturated zone is the groundwater.

zone of weather Dense, lowest 16 to 24 kilometers (10 to 15 mi) of the atmosphere where weather occurs; troposphere.

zooxanthellae Symbiotic algae that live with coral polyps in reef communities.

Line Art

CHAPTER 2

Figure 2.6: From Charles C. Plummer and David McGeary, *Physical Geology,* 7th ed. Copyright © 1996 Times Mirror Higher Education Group, Inc., Dubuque, Iowa. All Rights Reserved. Reprinted by permission. **Figure 2.9:** From Carla W. Montgomery, *Physical Geology,* 3d ed. Copyright © 1993 Times Mirror Higher Education Group, Inc., Dubuque, Iowa. All Rights Reserved. Reprinted by permission.

CHAPTER 3

Box Figure 3.A: From David Laing, *The Earth System.* Copyright © 1991 Times Mirror Higher Education Group, Inc., Dubuque, Iowa. All Rights Reserved. Reprinted by permission. **Box Figure 3.G:** Redrawn with permission from Lucy-Ann McFadden and Clark R. Chapman, "Interplanetary Fugitives" in *Astronomy* Aug. 1992, p. 31. © Kalmbach Publishing: *Astronomy* magazine.

CHAPTER 4

Figure 4.11: From Robert N. Wallen, *Introduction to Physical Geography.* Copyright © 1992 Times Mirror Higher Education Group, Inc., Dubuque, Iowa. All Rights Reserved. Reprinted by permission. **Figure 4.12d:** From Arthur Getis et al., *Introduction to Geography,* 5th ed. Copyright © 1996 Times Mirror Higher Education Group, Inc., Dubuque Iowa. All Rights Reserved. Reprinted by permission.

CHAPTER 5

Figure 5.1, Figure 5.9, Figure 5.13a,b, Figure 5.19: From Arthur Getis, et al., *Introduction to Geography,* 5th ed. Copyright © 1996 Times Mirror Higher Education Group, Inc., Dubuque, Iowa. All Rights Reserved. Reprinted by permission. **Figure 5.3, Figure 5.6, Figure 5.7, Figure 5.8, Figure 5.12, Figure 5.15, Figure 5.26:** From Robert N. Wallen, *Introduction to Physical Geography,* Copyright © 1992 Times Mirror Higher Education Group, Inc., Dubuque, Iowa. All Rights Reserved. Reprinted by permission. **Figure 5.13c:** From Arthur Getis, et al., *Introduction to Geography,* 3d ed. Copyright © 1991 Times Mirror Higher Education Group, Inc., Dubuque, Iowa. All Rights Reserved. Reprinted by permission.

CHAPTER 6

Figure 6.9, Figure 6.16, Figure 6.23, Figure 6.28, Figure 6.34: From Arthur Getis, et al., *Introduction to Geography,* 5th ed. Copyright © 1996 Times Mirror Higher Education Group, Inc., Dubuque, Iowa. All Rights Reserved. Reprinted by permission.

CHAPTER 7

Figure 7.1b, Figure 7.10: From Carla W. Montgomery, *Physical Geology,* 3d ed. Copyright © 1993 Times Mirror Higher Education Group, Inc., Dubuque, Iowa. All Rights Reserved. Reprinted by permission. **Figure 7.1a, Figure 7.9, Figure 7.19a,b:** From Charles C. Plummer and David McGeary, *Physical Geology,* 7th ed. Copyright © 1996 Times Mirror Higher Education Group, Inc., Dubuque, Iowa. All Rights Reserved. Reprinted by permission. **Figure 7.8:** From Carla W. Montgomery, *Physical Geology,* 2d ed. Copyright © 1990 Times Mirror Higher Education Group, Inc., Dubuque, Iowa. All Rights Reserved. Reprinted by permission. **Box Figure 7.A:** After Sylvia Bender-Lamb, "Magma Energy Exploratory Well Long Valley Caldera," *California Geology,* April 1991, p. 85. Used by permission of Mines and Geology, California Dept. of Conservation.

CHAPTER 8

Figure 8.3b, Figure 8.20, Figure 8.23: From Arthur Getis, et al., *Introduction to Geography,* 5th ed. Copyright © 1996 Times Mirror Higher Education Group, Inc., Dubuque, Iowa. All Rights Reserved. Reprinted by permission. **Figure 8.5, Figure 8.6, Figure 8.13:** From Carla W. Montgomery, *Physical Geology,* 3d ed. Copyright © 1993 Times Mirror Higher Education Group, Inc., Dubuque, Iowa. All Rights Reserved. Reprinted by permission. **Figures 8.7 and 8.8:** From Baranzangi and Dorman, *Bulletin of the Seismological Society of America,* El Cerrito, CA 95430. Used by permission. **Figure 8.9, Figure 8.12, Figure 8.14, Figure 8.15, Figure 8.17, Figure 8.26:** From Charles C. Plummer and David McGeary, *Physical Geology,* 7th ed. Copyright © 1996 Times Mirror Higher Education Group, Inc., Dubuque, Iowa. All Rights Reserved. Reprinted by permission. **Figure 8.11:** From David Laing, *The Earth System.* Copyright © 1991 Times Mirror Higher Education Group, Inc., Dubuque, Iowa. All Rights Reserved. Reprinted by permission.

CHAPTER 9

Figure 9.2a, Figure 9.13, Figures 9.16 and 9.17, Figure 9.27: From Charles C. Plummer and David McGeary, *Physical Geology,* 7th ed. Copyright © 1996 Times Mirror Higher Education Group, Inc., Dubuque, Iowa. All Rights Reserved. Reprinted by permission. **Figure 9.3:** From Alyn C. and Alison B. Duxbury, *An Introduction to the World's Oceans,* 4th ed. Copyright © 1994 Times Mirror Higher Education Group, Inc., Dubuque, Iowa. All Rights Reserved. Reprinted by permission. **Figure 9.4:** From A. Wegener, 1928, *The Origin of Continents and Oceans.* Reprinted copyrighted 1968, Dover Publications. Used by permission. **Figures 9.5b and 9.6b:** From David Laing, *The Earth System.* Copyright © 1991 Times Mirror Higher Education Group, Inc., Dubuque, Iowa. All Rights Reserved. Reprinted by permission. **Figure 9.15:** From David L. Clawson, *Latin America and the Caribbean: Lands and Peoples.* Copyright © 1996 Times Mirror Higher Education Group, Inc., Dubuque, Iowa. All Rights Reserved. Reprinted by permission. **Figure 9.24, Figure 9.25:** From Charles C. Plummer and David McGeary, *Physical Geology,* 5th ed. Copyright © 1991 Times Mirror Higher Education Group, Inc., Dubuque, Iowa. All Rights Reserved. Reprinted by permission. **Figure 9.B:** From Charles M. McCreery, et al., "Hydroacoustics Detect Submarine Volcanism," *Eos,* Feb. 23, 1993, pp. 85–86. Used by permission. **Figure 9.28:** Reproduced, with permission, from the *Annual Review of Earth and Planetary Science,* Volume 11, © 1983, by Annual Reviews Inc. **Figure 9.29:** Modified with permission from Tobisch, et al., "Nature and Timing of Deformation in the Foothills Terrane, Central Sierra Nevada, California," in *Geological Survey of America Bulletin,* vol. 101, no. 3, March 1989, pp. 401–402.

CHAPTER 10

Figure 10.14: From Carla W. Montgomery, *Physical Geology,* 3d ed. Copyright © 1993 Times Mirror Higher Education Group, Inc., Dubuque, Iowa. All Rights Reserved. Reprinted by permission. **Figure 10.23a,b:** From: *Geology, Resources, and Society* by Menard. Copyright © 1974 W.H. Freeman and Company. Used with permission.

CHAPTER 11

Figure 11.2, Figure 11.10, Figure 11.11, Figure 11.12, Figure 11.15: From Charles C. Plummer and David McGeary, *Physical Geology,* 7th ed. Copyright © 1996 Times Mirror Higher Education Group, Inc., Dubuque, Iowa. All Rights Reserved. Reprinted by permission. **Figure 11.21, Figure 11.22a,b:** From Carla W. Montgomery, *Physical Geology,* 3d ed. Copyright © 1993 Times Mirror Higher Education Group, Inc., Dubuque, Iowa. All Rights Reserved. Reprinted by permission.

CHAPTER 12

Figure 12.1a, Figure 12.3, Figure 12.10a, Figure 12.28a,b,e: From Charles C. Plummer and David McGeary, *Physical Geology,* 7th ed. Copyright

© 1996 Times Mirror Higher Education Group, Inc., Dubuque, Iowa. All Rights Reserved. Reprinted by permission. **Figure 12.5:** From Charles C. Plummer and David McGeary, *Physical Geology,* 5th ed. Copyright © 1991 Times Mirror Higher Education Group, Inc., Dubuque, Iowa. All Rights Reserved. Reprinted by permission. **Figure 12.16, Figure 12.21, Figure 12.27:** From Carla W. Montgomery, *Physical Geology,* 3d ed. Copyright © 1993 Times Mirror Higher Education Group, Inc., Dubuque, Iowa. All Rights Reserved. Reprinted by permission. **Figure 12.B:** After C.S. Denny, U.S. Geological Survey, *National Atlas of the United States.*

CHAPTER 13

Figure 13.1, Figure 13.3, Figure 13.5, Figure 13.11, Figure 13.16a,b: From Charles C. Plummer and David McGeary, *Physical Geology,* 7th ed. Copyright © 1996 Times Mirror Higher Education Group, Inc., Dubuque, Iowa. All Rights Reserved. Reprinted by permission. **Figure 13.2:** From Arthur Getis, et al., *Introduction to Geography,* 5th ed. Copyright © 1996 Times Mirror Higher Education Group, Inc., Dubuque, Iowa. All Rights Reserved. Reprinted by permission. **Figure 13.13:** From Alyn C. and Alison B. Duxbury, *An Introduction to the World's Oceans,* 4th ed. Copyright © 1994 Times Mirror Higher Education Group, Inc., Dubuque, Iowa. All Rights Reserved. Reprinted by permission. **Figure 13.14:** From Richard A. Davis, *Oceanography,* 2d ed. Copyright © 1991 Times Mirror Higher Education Group, Inc., Dubuque, Iowa. All Rights Reserved. Reprinted by permission.

CHAPTER 14

Figure 14.4, Figure 14.12, Figure 14.21, Figure 14.22, Figure 14.23, Figure 14.26, Figure 14.29, Figure 14.31: From Alyn C. and Alison B. Duxbury, *An Introduction to the World's Oceans,* 4th ed. Copyright © 1994 Times Mirror Higher Education Group, Inc., Dubuque, Iowa. All Rights Reserved. Reprinted by permission. **Figure 14.7:** Redrawn from G.L. Pickard and W.J. Emery, *Descriptive Physical Geography,* 4th ed., Copyright 1982, page 37, with kind permission from Pergamon Books Ltd., Oxford. **Figure 14.16:** Goode Homolosine projection courtesy of Committee on Geographic Studies, University of Chicago. **Figure 14.A:** Hsu, Kenneth J., *The Mediterranean Was A Desert.* Copyright © 1983 by PUP. Reproduced by permission of Princeton University Press. **Figure 14.17, 14.18:** From Richard A. Davis, Jr., *Oceanography,* 2d ed. Copyright © 1991 Times Mirror Higher Education Group, Inc., Dubuque, Iowa. All Rights Reserved. Reprinted by permission. **Figure 14.20:** From Arthur Getis, et al., *Introduction to Geography,* 5th ed. Copyright © 1996 Times Mirror Higher Education Group,

Inc., Dubuque, Iowa. All Rights Reserved. Reprinted by permission.

CHAPTER 15

Figure 15.10: From "Estuaries" by Nichols, et al., as appeared in *Coastal Sedimentary Environments* edited by R.A. Davis. Copyright © 1985 Springer-Verlag New York, Inc. Used by permission. **Figure 15.11, Figure 15.32, Figure 15.34:** From Alyn C. and Alison B. Duxbury, *An Introduction to the World's Oceans,* 4th ed. Copyright © 1994 Times Mirror Higher Education Group, Inc., Dubuque, Iowa. All Rights Reserved. Reprinted by permission. **Figure 15.14b:** From Richard A. Davis, Jr., *Oceanography,* 2d ed. Copyright © 1991 Times Mirror Higher Education Group, Inc., Dubuque, Iowa. All Rights Reserved. Reprinted by permission. **Figure 15.25:** From James L. Sumich, *Introduction to the Biology of Life,* 4th ed. Copyright © 1988 Times Mirror Higher Education Group, Inc., Dubuque, Iowa. All Rights Reserved. Reprinted by permission. **Figure 15.29:** From Carla W. Montgomery, *Physical Geology,* 3d ed. Copyright © 1993 Times Mirror Higher Education Group, Inc., Dubuque, Iowa. All Rights Reserved. Reprinted by permission.

CHAPTER 16

Figure 16.1, Figure 16.7, Figure 16.9: From Carla W. Montgomery, *Physical Geology,* 3d ed. Copyright © 1993 Times Mirror Higher Education Group, Inc., Dubuque, Iowa. All Rights Reserved. Reprinted by permission.

Photos

BOXED READING PHOTOS: © PHOTODISC

PART OPENERS

One: © PhotoDisc/U.S. Travel and Landmarks; **2,3:** © PhotoDisc/Science, Technology and Medicine; **4:** PhotoGear/Mountains; **5,6:** © PhotoDisc/U.S. Travel and Landmarks

CHAPTER 1

Opener: © Doug Sherman/Geofile; **1.1, 1.4:** NASA; **1.6:** Photo by N.H. Darton, U.S. Geological Survey; **1.7:** Courtesy of Otis Brown; **1.8:** © Steven Scher Collection/Black Star; **1.9:** © Paul X. Scott/Sygma; **1.10:** Photo by S.J. Williams, U.S. Geological Survey; **1.11:** © The Huntsville Times/Glen Baeske

CHAPTER 2

Opener: NASA; **2.1:** NASA; **Box 2.1 Figure 2A:** California Institute of Technology; **Box 2.1 Figure**

2.B: J. Trauger, JPL and NASA; **2.12, 2.13:** NASA; **2.14a,b:** National Optical Astronomy Observatory; **2.14c,d:** California Institute of California; **2.15:** NASA; **2.16:** Yerkes Observatory; **2.17:** C.R. O'Dell, Rice University and NASA; **2.18:** STScI/NASA; **2.20:** © The Anglo-Australian Telescope Board, photograph by David Malin; **2.24:** The Observatories of the Carnegie Institution of Washington; **2.25:** NOAA

CHAPTER 3

Opener: NASA; **3.2a:** Mark McCaughrean, Max-Planck Institute for Astronomy, and C. Robert O'Dell, Rice University, and NASA; **3.2b:** Courtesy of Cornell University; **3.3:** NASA; **3.4:** NASA, Jet Propulsion Lab; **3.5, 3.6, 3.7a, 3.7b:** Jet Propulsion Lab; **Box 3.1 Figure 3.E:** NASA; **3.8:** NASA; **3.9a:** NSSDC/Goddard Space Flight Center; **Box 3.2 Figure 3.F, 3.10, 3.11:** NASA; **Box 3.2 Figure 3.H:** Williams College-Hopkins Observatory, photo by Karen A. Gloria; **Box 3.2 Figure 3.I:** Space Telescope Science Institute; **3.12:** NASA; **3.13a:** Yerkes Observatory photo; **3.14:** NASA

CHAPTER 4

Opener: © Doug Sherman/Geofile; **4.1:** © Mark J. Terrill/AP/Wide World Photos; **4.2:** NOAA; **4.6:** Erwin Raisz © 1957, reprinted with permission of Geoplus, Danvers, MA; **4.7a, 4.7b, 4.9, 4.10:** NASA; **Box 4.2 Figure 4.D:** NASA, photo by Owen B. Toon

CHAPTER 5

Opener: © Howard Bluestein/Photo Researchers, Inc.; **5.14a:** Courtesy of Robert N. Wallen; **5.14b:** A.D. Copley/Visuals Unlimited; **Box 5.1 Figure 5A, 5B:** U.S. Dept. of Commerce/National Oceanic and Atmospheric Administration; **Box 5.1 Figure 5.F:** © Steve Starr/Saba

CHAPTER 6

Opener: © Doug Sherman/Geofile; **6.2:** © Kennan Ward; **6.17:** © Richard Thom/Tom Stack & Associates; **6.19, 6.21:** Courtesy of Dr. Charles Hogue, curator of Entomology, Los Angeles County Museum of Natural History; **6.24:** © Brian Parker/Tom Stack & Associates; **6.26:** Courtesy of Dr. Charles Hogue, Curator of Entomology, Los Angeles Museum of Natural History; **6.30:** Courtesy of Robert N. Wallen; **6.32:** © Terry Donnelly/Tom Stack & Associates; **6.35, 6.36:** © John Cunningham/Visuals Unlimited; **6.41:** © William Ferguson; **6.44:** Courtesy of Dr. H.H. Wallen, Jr.

CHAPTER 7

Opener: © Doug Sherman/Geofile; **7.2a, 7.2b, 7.4a:** © Doug Sherman/Geofile; **7.4b:** © Times Mirror Higher Education Group, Inc., Robert Rutford, and James Zumberge/James Carter, photographer; **7.5:** © Doug Sherman/Geofile; **7.7a:** © Times Mirror Higher Education Group, Inc., Robert Rutford, and James Zumberge/James Carter, photographer; **7.7b, 7.10a, 7.10b:** © Times Mirror Higher Education Group, Inc./Doug Sherman, photographer; **7.10c:** Courtesy of Carla Montgomery; **7.11a:** © Doug Sherman/Geofile; **7.11b:** © Times Mirror Higher Education Group, Inc., Robert Rutford, and James Zumberge/James Carter, photographer; **7.13a:** Jim Nieland, U.S. Forest Service; **7.13b:** Photo by Lyn Topinka, U.S.G.S. David A. Johnston, Cascade Volcano Observatory, Vancouver, WA; **7.16b:** © Doug Sherman/Geofile; **7.18a,b:** Photo by David McGeary; **7.19c:** The Rahm Collection, Western Washington University; **7.24a,b:** © Doug Sherman/Geofile; **7.25a:** © Times Mirror Higher Education Group, Inc./Doug Sherman, photographer; **7.29a,b:** © Times Mirror Higher Education Group, Inc., Robert Rutford, and James Zumberge/James Carter, photographer

CHAPTER 8

Opener: © Doug Sherman/Geofile; **8.1:** © Rory Lysaght/Gamma Liaison; **8.2:** AP/Wide World Photos; **8.3a:** National Geophysical Data Center; **8.4:** U.S. Geological Survey; **Box 8.3 Figure 8.A:** Maryland Geological Survey. Photo by John Thrasher

CHAPTER 9

Opener: © David Parker/Photo Researchers, Inc.; **9.5a, 9.6a:** Reprinted with permission of the Carnegie Museum of Natural History; **9.9:** Scripps Institution of Oceanography; **9.30:** Photo by W.R. Normark, U.S. Geological Survey

CHAPTER 10

Opener: © Doug Sherman/Geofile; **10.6:** © Doug Sherman/Geofile; **10.7:** Photo by Frank M. Hanna; **10.9:** © Doug Sherman/Geofile; **10.10:** Photo by J.R. Stacy, U.S. Geological Survey; **10.11:** © Robert Winslow; **10.12:** Photo by Ludwig, U.S.

Geological Survey; **10.13:** Photo by Servicio Aerofotografico de Peru, courtesy of the U.S. Geological Survey; **10.14b:** Photo by J.T. McGill, U.S. Geological Survey; **10.15:** © Richard B. Levine; **10.16:** U.S. Geological Survey; **10.17:** © Hulton Deutsh; **10.20b:** © Timothy O'Keefe/Tom Stack & Associates; **10.21:** © Robert W. Ginn/Unicorn Stock Photos; **10.24:** U.S. Army photo; **10.26:** courtesy of Carla Montgomery; **10.27, 10.28:** The Rahm Collection, Western Washington University; **Box 10.1 Figure 10.B:** Courtesy of Carla Montgomery

CHAPTER 11

Opener: © Doug Sherman/Geofile; **11.5:** © S. Liles/Unicorn Stock Photos; **Box 11.1 Figure 11.A:** Quad City Times photo by Greg Boll; **11.9B:** Photo by David McGeary; **Box 11.1 Figure 11.B(left):** Jonas N. Jordan USACE © 1995 CNES Provided by SPOT Image Corporation; **Box 11.1 Figure 11.B(right):** Jonas N. Jordan USACE Landsat data by the Earth Observation Satellite Company, Lanham, Maryland; **Box 11.2 Figure 11.C:** NASA; **11.13B:** Photo by Frank M. Hanna; **11.14, 11.16:** NASA; **11.17, Box 11.3 Figure 11.E, 11.24b:** © Doug Sherman/Geofile

CHAPTER 12

Opener: © Doug Sherman/Geofile; **12.2:** © Wolfgang Kaehler; **12.4:** Courtesy of C.C. Plummer; **12.6:** © Ed Cooper; **12.7, 12.8:** © Doug Sherman/Geofile; **12.9:** The Rahm Collection, Western Washington University; **12.10b:** Courtesy of C.C. Plummer; **12.10c:** The Rahm Collection, Western Washington University; **12.11, 12.12:** © Doug Sherman/Geofile; **12.13:** The Rahm Collection, Western Washington University **12.17:** NASA; **12.19:** Photo by Brian Atwater, U.S. Geological Survey; **Box 12.3 Figure 12.C:** © 1995 Discover Magazine; **12.22:** Photo by David McGeary; **12.24:** © Scott Berner/Visuals Unlimited; **12.25:** NASA image provided by The Lunar and Planetary Institute; **12.26a, 12.26b:** © Doug Sherman/Geofile; **12.30:** Courtesy of Kenneth Hamblin

CHAPTER 13

Opener: © Doug Sherman/Geofile; **13.4, 13.6, 13.7, 13.8, 13.9:** © Doug Sherman/Geofile; **13.10:** NASA; **13.12:** © George J. Wilder/Visuals Unlimited; **13.15:** The Rahm Collection, Western Washington University; **13.16c,d:** Photo by S. Jeffress Williams; **13.17:** Photo by Lee, U.S. Geological Survey; **Box 13.1 Figure 13.A:** © Kelsey-Kennard Photographers, Inc.

CHAPTER 14

Opener: © Tammy Peluso/Tom Stack & Associates; **14.11A:** Courtesy of Kathy Newell, School of Oceanography, University of Washington; **14.11b:** © Joyce Photographics/Photo Researchers, Inc.; **14.24:** Courtesy of Otis Brown and R. Evans; **14.25:** Courtesy of Alyn and Alison Duxbury

CHAPTER 15

Opener: © David Muench; **15.4:** From D.J. Fornari, D.G. Gallo, M.H. Edwards, J.A. Madsen, M.R. Perfit, and A.N. Shor, "Structure and Topography of the Siqueiros Transform Fault System: Evidence for the Development of Intra-Transform Spreading Centers," *Marine Geophysical Researchers,* 11: 263–299, 1989. © Kluwer Academic Publishers; **15.5:** © Alex S. Maclean/Landslides; **15.8:** © Jeff Greenberg/Photo Researchers, Inc.; **15.9:** NASA; **15.15:** Courtesy Stephen P. Leatherman; **15.16B:** U.S. Geological Survey; **15.21:** NASA; **15.22:** Courtesy Richard Davis; **15.26:** © Manfred Gottschalk/Tom Stack & Associates; **15.30:** © WHOI/Visuals Unlimited; **15.31b:** Courtesy of Ken Adkins, School of Oceanography, University of Washington; **15.33:** © Paolo Curto/The Image Bank

CHAPTER 16

Opener: © Byron Augustine/Tom Stack & Associates; **16.8:** Courtesy of Kennecott Corporation

Index